Also by the Editors at America's Test Kitchen

The Complete Mediterranean Cookbook

Cook's Science

Bread Illustrated

Master of the Grill

Kitchen Hacks

100 Recipes: The Absolute Best Ways to Make the True Essentials

The Best of America's Test Kitchen (2007–2017 Editions)

The Complete America's Test Kitchen TV Show Cookbook 2001–2017

The New Family Cookbook

The Complete Vegetarian Cookbook

The Complete Cooking for Two Cookbook

The America's Test Kitchen Cooking School Cookbook

The Cook's Illustrated Meat Book

The Cook's Illustrated Baking Book

The Cook's Illustrated Cookbook

The Science of Good Cooking

The New Best Recipe

Soups, Stews, and Chilis

The America's Test Kitchen Quick Family Cookbook

The America's Test Kitchen Healthy Family Cookbook

The America's Test Kitchen Family Baking Book

THE COOK'S ILLUSTRATED ALL-TIME BEST SERIES

All-Time Best Appetizers

All-Time Best Soups

THE AMERICA'S TEST KITCHEN LIBRARY SERIES

Naturally Sweet

Foolproof Preserving

Paleo Perfected

The How Can It Be Gluten-Free Cookbook: Volume 2

The How Can It Be Gluten-Free Cookbook

The Best Mexican Recipes

The Make-Ahead Cook

Healthy Slow Cooker Revolution

Slow Cooker Revolution Volume 2: The Easy-Prep Edition

Slow Cooker Revolution

The Six-Ingredient Solution

Pressure Cooker Perfection

The America's Test Kitchen D.I.Y. Cookbook

Pasta Revolution

THE COOK'S COUNTRY SERIES

Cook It in Cast Iron

Cook's Country Eats Local

The Complete Cook's Country TV Show Cookbook

FOR A FULL LISTING OF ALL OUR BOOKS

CooksIllustrated.com

AmericasTestKitchen.com

Praise for Other America's Test Kitchen Titles

"A terrifically accessible and useful guide to grilling in all its forms that sets a new bar for its competitors on the bookshelf. . . . The book is packed with practical advice, simple tips, and approachable recipes."
PUBLISHERS WEEKLY (STARRED REVIEW) ON *MASTER OF THE GRILL*

"From thick-cut steaks to skillet chocolate chip cookies, this manual from the masters at America's Test Kitchen will help you make the most of that hefty cast-iron pan."
ENTERTAINMENT WEEKLY ON *COOK IT IN CAST IRON*

"An exceptional resource for novice canners, though preserving veterans will find plenty here to love as well."
LIBRARY JOURNAL (STARRED REVIEW) ON *FOOLPROOF PRESERVING*

"True to its name, this smart and endlessly enlightening cookbook is about as definitive as it's possible to get in the modern vegetarian realm."
MEN'S JOURNAL ON *THE COMPLETE VEGETARIAN COOKBOOK*

"The sum total of exhaustive experimentation . . . anyone interested in gluten-free cookery simply shouldn't be without it."
NIGELLA LAWSON ON *THE HOW CAN IT BE GLUTEN-FREE COOKBOOK*

"The 21st-century *Fannie Farmer Cookbook* or *The Joy of Cooking*. If you had to have one cookbook and that's all you could have, this one would do it."
CBS SAN FRANCISCO ON *THE NEW FAMILY COOKBOOK*

"This book upgrades slow cooking for discriminating, 21st-century palates—that is indeed revolutionary."
THE DALLAS MORNING NEWS ON *SLOW COOKER REVOLUTION*

"The go-to gift book for newlyweds, small families, or empty nesters."
ORLANDO SENTINEL ON *THE COMPLETE COOKING FOR TWO COOKBOOK*

"Some 2,500 photos walk readers through 600 painstakingly tested recipes, leaving little room for error."
ASSOCIATED PRESS ON *THE AMERICA'S TEST KITCHEN COOKING SCHOOL COOKBOOK*

"A one-volume kitchen seminar, addressing in one smart chapter after another the sometimes surprising whys behind a cook's best practices. . . . You get the myth, the theory, the science, and the proof, all rigorously interrogated as only America's Test Kitchen can do."
NPR ON *THE SCIENCE OF GOOD COOKING*

"Carnivores with an obsession for perfection will likely have found their new bible in this comprehensive collection."
PUBLISHERS WEEKLY (STARRED REVIEW) ON *THE COOK'S ILLUSTRATED MEAT BOOK*

"This encyclopedia of meat cookery would feel completely overwhelming if it weren't so meticulously organized and artfully designed. This is *Cook's Illustrated* at its finest."
THE KITCHN ON *THE COOK'S ILLUSTRATED MEAT BOOK*

"This book is a comprehensive, no-nonsense guide . . . a well-thought-out, clearly explained primer for every aspect of home baking."
THE WALL STREET JOURNAL ON *THE COOK'S ILLUSTRATED BAKING BOOK*

"Buy this gem for the foodie in your family, and spend the extra money to get yourself a copy too."
THE MISSOURIAN ON *THE BEST OF AMERICA'S TEST KITCHEN 2015*

"The perfect kitchen home companion. . . . The practical side of things is very much on display . . . cook-friendly and kitchen-oriented, illuminating the process of preparing food instead of mystifying it."
THE WALL STREET JOURNAL ON *THE COOK'S ILLUSTRATED COOKBOOK*

"There are pasta books . . . and then there's this pasta book. Flip your carbohydrate dreams upside down and strain them through this sieve of revolutionary, creative, and also traditional recipes."
SAN FRANCISCO BOOK REVIEW ON *PASTA REVOLUTION*

"Further proof that practice makes perfect, if not transcendent. . . . If an intermediate cook follows the directions exactly, the results will be better than takeout or Mom's."
THE NEW YORK TIMES ON *THE NEW BEST RECIPE*

what good cooks know

**20 YEARS OF TEST KITCHEN EXPERTISE
IN ONE ESSENTIAL HANDBOOK**

BY THE EDITORS AT AMERICA'S TEST KITCHEN

Library of Congress Cataloging-in-Publication Data

Names: America's Test Kitchen (Firm)
Title: What good cooks know : 20 years of Test Kitchen
    expertise in one essential handbook / by the editors at
    America's Test Kitchen.
Description: Brookline, MA : America's Test Kitchen, [2016]
    | Includes index.
Identifiers: LCCN 2016016477 | ISBN 9781940352664
Subjects: LCSH: Kitchen utensils. | Cooking--Equipment
    and supplies. | Cooking. | LCGFT: Cookbooks.
Classification: LCC TX656 .U48 2016 | DDC 643/.3--dc23
LC record available at https://lccn.loc.gov/2016016477

AMERICA'S TEST KITCHEN

17 Station Street, Brookline, MA 02445

Manufactured in Canada

10 9 8 7 6 5 4 3 2 1

Distributed by Penguin Random House Publisher Services
Tel: 800.733.3000

CHIEF CREATIVE OFFICER: Jack Bishop

EDITORIAL DIRECTOR, BOOKS: Elizabeth Carduff

EXECUTIVE EDITOR: Julia Collin Davison

ASSOCIATE EDITOR: Rachel Greenhaus

EDITORIAL ASSISTANT: Alyssa Langer

TASTING AND TESTING TEAM:

    EXECUTIVE EDITOR: Lisa McManus

    DEPUTY EDITOR: Hannah Crowley

    MANAGING EDITOR: Scott Kathan

    ASSOCIATE EDITORS: Lauren Savoie and Kate Shannon

    ASSISTANT EDITORS: Jason Alvarez and Miye Bromberg

    EDITORIAL ASSISTANT: Carolyn Grillo

DESIGN DIRECTOR: Greg Galvan

ART DIRECTOR: Carole Goodman

ASSOCIATE ART DIRECTORS: Allison Boales and Jen Kanavos Hoffman

PRODUCTION DESIGNER: Reinaldo Cruz

GRAPHIC DESIGNER: Aleko Giatrakis

PHOTOGRAPHY DIRECTOR: Julie Bozzo Cote

ASSISTANT PHOTOGRAPHY PRODUCER: Mary Ball

SENIOR STAFF PHOTOGRAPHER: Daniel J. van Ackere

STAFF PHOTOGRAPHER: Steve Klise

PHOTOGRAPHY: Keller + Keller and Carl Tremblay

FOOD STYLING: Catrine Kelty, Marie Piraino, and Sally Staub

PHOTOSHOOT KITCHEN TEAM:

    SENIOR EDITOR: Chris O'Connor

    ASSOCIATE EDITOR: Daniel Cellucci

    TEST COOK: Matthew Fairman

    ASSISTANT TEST COOK: Allison Berkey

PRODUCTION DIRECTOR: Guy Rochford

SENIOR PRODUCTION MANAGER: Jessica Lindheimer Quirk

PRODUCTION MANAGER: Christine Walsh

IMAGING MANAGER: Lauren Robbins

PRODUCTION AND IMAGING SPECIALISTS: Heather Dube, Sean MacDonald, Dennis Noble, and Jessica Voas

COPY EDITOR: Cheryl Redmond

PROOFREADER: Elizabeth Wray Emery

INDEXER: Elizabeth Parson

TABLE OF CONTENTS

WELCOME TO AMERICA'S TEST KITCHEN

This book has been tested, written, and edited by the folks at America's Test Kitchen, a very real 2,500-square-foot kitchen located just outside of Boston. It is the home of *Cook's Illustrated* magazine and *Cook's Country* magazine and is the Monday-through-Friday destination for more than 60 test cooks, editors, and cookware specialists. Our mission is to test recipes over and over again until we understand how and why they work and until we arrive at the "best" version.

We start the process of testing a recipe with a complete lack of preconceptions, which means that we accept no claim, no technique, and no recipe at face value. We simply assemble as many variations as possible, test a half-dozen of the most promising, and taste the results blind. We then construct our own recipe and continue to test it, varying ingredients, techniques, and cooking times until we reach a consensus. As we like to say in the test kitchen, "We make the mistakes so you don't have to." The result, we hope, is the best version of a particular recipe, but we realize that only you can be the final judge of our success (or failure). We use the same rigorous approach when we test equipment and taste ingredients.

All of this would not be possible without a belief that good cooking, much like good music, is based on a foundation of objective technique. Some people like spicy foods and others don't, but there is a right way to sauté, there is a best way to cook a pot roast, and there are measurable scientific principles involved in producing perfectly beaten, stable egg whites. Our ultimate goal is to investigate the fundamental principles of cooking to give you the techniques, tools, and ingredients you need to become a better cook. It is as simple as that.

To see what goes on behind the scenes at America's Test Kitchen, check out our social media channels for kitchen snapshots, exclusive content, video tips, and much more. You can watch us work (in our actual test kitchen) by tuning in to *America's Test Kitchen* or *Cook's Country from America's Test Kitchen* on public television or on our websites. Listen in to *America's Test Kitchen Radio* (ATKradio.com) on public radio to hear insights that illuminate the truth about real home cooking. Want to hone your cooking skills or finally learn how to bake—with an America's Test Kitchen test cook? Enroll in one of our online cooking classes. If the big questions about the hows and whys of food science are your passion, join our Cook's Science experts for a deep dive. However you choose to visit us, we welcome you into our kitchen, where you can stand by our side as we test our way to the best recipes in America.

facebook.com/AmericasTestKitchen
twitter.com/TestKitchen
youtube.com/AmericasTestKitchen
instagram.com/TestKitchen
pinterest.com/TestKitchen
google.com/+AmericasTestKitchen

AmericasTestKitchen.com
CooksIllustrated.com
CooksCountry.com
CooksScience.com
OnlineCookingSchool.com

INTRODUCTION

This book is for all the cooks who have ever wished that their kitchens came with an instruction manual. From the tiniest details, like how to chop fresh herbs and which grade of eggs to choose, to major kitchen decisions like whether to shell out for a high-end stand mixer or how to cook a pricey prime rib to perfection, cooking presents challenges and requires thoughtful decision-making at every turn. The experts at America's Test Kitchen are here to guide you through all the trickiest parts of your culinary life. Never before have we pulled together our most valuable (and interesting) reference information into one book, from our equipment and product reviews to the key kitchen techniques we've developed that make cooking easier, plus the most useful lessons from our extensive investigations into practical kitchen science and step-by-step tutorials for our foolproof recipes.

Today there are thousands upon thousands of places you can go to get answers to your food and cooking questions. Looking up which brand of cheddar cheese is best or how to make scrambled eggs is as easy as typing keywords into a search engine—but finding a reliable answer is not so simple. Behind every piece of information in this book—every equipment recommendation, every storage tip, every step-by-step technique—are the inquisitive, exhaustive protocols that have been developed over the years in the test kitchen. You can read more about these in the Behind the Scenes essays throughout this book. These protocols are the reasons why you can trust us when we tell you to buy a colander with a raised base or to add half-and-half and extra yolks to your scrambled eggs. Here in the test kitchen, we take nothing for granted, so in these pages you'll find improvements on classic techniques as well as completely new, innovative approaches to age-old problems: Who else would have figured out that adding vodka helps make a more tender pie dough? And who else can you trust to cut through all the marketing hype and sponsored content to tell you that a $40 chef's knife really is better than other options costing 10 times as much?

Here at America's Test Kitchen, after more than 20 years of teaching people how to master their home kitchens, giving them the information they need to choose the best equipment, and helping them stock their pantries and refrigerators with the top ingredients on the market, we've amassed an enormous wealth of information related to food and cooking. This book is the first time that the cumulative wisdom of the test kitchen has been collected and organized to create a go-to kitchen handbook for home cooks. This is your new one-stop reference, whether you're a brand-new cook just starting out and need a guide to basic knife skills or an experienced cook who wants a refresher on how to butterfly a chicken. This book is the definitive field guide to the wild and wonderful world of your kitchen.

OUTFITTING YOUR KITCHEN

HOW WE TEST EQUIPMENT

With a well-stocked kitchen, you'll be able to take on any recipe. But when there's so much equipment out there on the market, how do you figure out what's what? Price often correlates with design, not performance, making it even harder to judge at a glance which tools are going to be the best. Over the years, the experts on the test kitchen's tasting and testing team have evaluated more than 4,000 products and our ratings have become some of the most highly valued and widely trusted in the business; the test kitchen's approval is one of the best recommendations a brand can earn. And because we accept no advertising or free products from manufacturers, you can trust our ratings. Here's an inside look at the months of hard work and research that go into each and every product review that we publish.

Journalists, Cooks, and Mad Scientists

Although most of the tests we perform require a serious amount of cooking, Executive Tasting and Testing Editor Lisa McManus says the day-to-day tasks involved make the job more like a journalist's than an average cook's. Like journalists, we do in-depth research into our subjects to find out everything we can about how products are manufactured and which parts of the manufacturing process make the biggest differences in the way the equipment performs. Since much of this information ends up being proprietary to the companies that invented the products, we interview researchers and academics around the country who have specialized information on topics such as what chemicals are used to make a pan nonstick or how soap actually works. We then translate the information we get from these experts for our readers. And this research process goes far beyond phone calls, books, and the Internet: When we tested fire extinguishers, for instance, we went out to the Worcester Fire Department Training Center in central Massachusetts to get professional assistance setting and dousing kitchen fires, while a test of carbon-steel chef's knives inspired a trip to the MIT blacksmithing forge for lessons on the properties of metal from an instructor in materials science.

We rely on experts outside the test kitchen to help us answer the questions that come up during our equipment tests.

When it comes to the kitchen tests, we move from being journalists to working like scientists: We design and perform structured, controlled experiments to examine the key elements of each piece of equipment that is featured in our magazines, books, television shows, and web articles. Because the results of these tests are so highly valued by the fans of America's Test Kitchen, accuracy and reliability are essential. Every test must consider all variables, a process that requires months of planning. Every piece of equipment must stand up to harsh durability tests that simulate years of use as well as tests designed to measure how well the products will perform when pressed into service in everyday cooking tasks by a home cook.

Our equipment tests are designed to support the recipe development in the test kitchen. Our test cooks work to create foolproof recipes that will really work for the home cook. In the same way, the tasting and testing team works to find equipment that will help home cooks be successful in the kitchen, every time. The tools you use can have a huge effect on how your recipes turn out; a well-designed skillet will make it much easier to achieve good, even browning without scorching or hot spots when you tackle our latest pan-seared steak recipe.

Our tests are designed to assess how each piece of equipment performs in a variety of common tasks as well as to mimic the wear a tool might experience over years of kitchen use.

As part of our testing, we also enlist employees from outside the tasting and testing department to come and test equipment under observation in the test kitchen. This ensures that we get a good mix of different users for each test—tall people, short people, left-handed and right-handed people, and a variety of skill levels and arm strengths. That way we can make sure that the gear will work for everyone. Sometimes the team even sends equipment home with coworkers to get an idea of how the tools perform out in the real world. For a recent test of reusable water bottles, staffers took the bottles around with them for two weeks, through hikes, gym visits, car rides, and train commutes.

This excerpt illustrates the kinds of tests that we develop to put equipment through its paces.

Surveying the Field

Of course, before any of the research and experimenting can start, there's the initial question of what kind of equipment the team should be testing in the first place. While some items—wooden spoons, mixing bowls, blenders—might seem pretty obvious, we also keep up with the latest (although not always greatest) innovations in kitchenware. Every year, we visit the International Home + Housewares Show to review what's on the market and generate ideas for testing. We also look to our own lives and take suggestions from test cooks and readers about what to test next. When trends recently turned toward healthier home cooking, for instance, the team tested vegetable spiralizers, smoothie blenders, and salad gadgets.

While we're always open to the next exciting tool, we have also performed tests where the winning basic models from years ago continue to outperform cutting-edge inventions. For example, innovative collapsible colanders, which many brands started marketing a few years ago, might seem like a great new design alteration, but our tests quickly revealed that in addition to collapsing for easy storage, these supposedly convenient gadgets frequently collapsed mid-draining, dumping pasta all over the sink. Our evidence-based testing processes are designed to make sure that we're always recommending the products that actually work best, regardless of "cool factor" or price. We pride ourselves on being thorough but also practical. We don't recommend anything we don't believe a home cook really needs, nor do we ask readers to spend more than is necessary.

Once the editors have picked a topic, the next step is to decide which brands to include. We survey the retail market for the top-selling brands and any popular or interesting special features or design differences that we should include. The size of the lineup depends on the type of equipment being tested and how many options are available—for a recent testing of liquid measuring cups we started with 27 different models. We only test products that are currently, widely available—no prototypes, special editions, or soon-to-be-discontinued models. And we purchase the items that will be tested ourselves, buying directly from online and brick-and-mortar retailers to ensure that we are evaluating the exact same products a home cook would buy.

Testing, Testing, Testing

When the lineup of equipment models has been finalized, the next step in the process is to figure out what kind of tests to put the tools through. The team determines the most common uses for each product and the recipes that will best test those uses. To test slow cookers, we used a range of recipes from the most forgiving to the most finicky, testing both 10-hour caramelized onions and quick-cooking bone-less, skinless chicken breasts to see whether one model was impressive enough to handle every challenge. Choosing the specific trials leads to the creation of the testing protocols, which include the experiments and recipes that have been chosen as well as the rating criteria—what kind of results will be considered good, fair, or poor for each test. The testing protocol is like a recipe for an equipment test, outlining every step and the desired results. For instance, the protocol for serrated knives (shown at left) includes tests to evaluate out-of-the-box sharpness as well slicing ability in a variety of applications.

Once the protocols are established, the testing begins. Of course, the protocols can change and develop as we find out more about the equipment we're testing and the kind of information we want to collect. For instance, partway through the slow-cooker testing, we realized that the way one machine performed on "low" and "high" might actually be very different from how another machine functions on the same settings, so we devised a test that could give us a better idea of each model's heating cycle by heating a set amount of water in each one for a set amount of time and then taking the temperature of the water.

While the specific testing criteria vary for individual tests, the team is always very careful to make sure that our tests are as consistent and scientifically rigorous as possible. We keep the conditions the same for each test, controlling for all possible variables. Each editor runs his or her own tests to ensure that there won't be any variation in style or execution. Everything is extensively fact-checked before, during, and after testing to ensure that we publish the most accurate information possible. The editors also often take photographs during the testing to keep a visual record of the results for their own reference. The photos some-times run alongside the articles that the editors write for publication.

We never rely on a single test to evaluate a piece of equipment. In fact, depending on the equipment in question, we might run more than a dozen different tests before we're finished. Here's a list of all the trials we used during a recent testing of food processors. These powerhouse tools claim to be able to tackle a huge variety of jobs (and have a price tag to match), so we made sure to put the models we tested through a whole battery of tasks.

- chopping onion, carrot, and celery
- grinding whole almonds
- mincing parsley
- grinding beef
- slicing plum tomatoes
- slicing russet potatoes
- shredding carrots
- shredding cheese
- mixing pie dough
- mixing pizza dough
- making mayonnaise
- blending food coloring into yogurt (for a uniform mixture)
- pureeing whole tomatoes
- filling to max level to check for leaks

Not Afraid to Get Messy

Equipment testing isn't all careful calculations and number crunching; we know that cooking is an unpredictable, hands-on pursuit, and our tests are designed to reflect the realities of the kitchen—both good and bad. To test the durability of plastic food storage bags, the team filled bags with tomato sauce and knocked them off the counter to see which bags broke and splattered sauce everywhere. The test re-created an unfortunate—yet not unimaginable—situation that a home cook might face and yielded a very valuable data set. While some of the bags survived the drop, others revealed serious flaws that made a big difference in the results of the test and our final recommendations. The giant mess that this all made in the test kitchen was totally worthwhile if it saves even one home cook from experiencing a similar situation at home. (We make the messes so you don't have to.) Similarly, for a test of glass mixing bowls, we dropped all the models onto our hard kitchen floors to test durability. Believe it our not, a few samples actually survived this extreme testing, and we definitely took that into account for our final ratings.

Our testing includes anticipating all the things that could go wrong in your home kitchen and evaluating how your equipment will fare in the event of a worst-case scenario.

Testing for the Ages

Another big part of the tasting and testing team's job is checking back in on products we've reviewed in the past to see how the equipment has held up or whether new options have appeared that might give old winners a run for their money. The shelves of the test kitchen are kept stocked with our winning equipment, so the test cooks use our top-rated products every day. This means that the equipment testing actually continues long after the editors on the tasting and testing team publish our initial verdicts. When the test cooks are unhappy with the equipment, the team is sure to hear about it; conversely, if a tool works well for professionals who cook all day, it's likely that it will satisfy the typical home cook, too. This also helps our recipe development, since our test cooks are using equipment that's available to the home cook, rather than specialized restaurant tools. (Our recipes are developed in small batches like a home cook would make, not mass-produced on the scale of restaurant food; see more about our recipe development and testing processes on page 168–173.)

Once we choose a winning product, we stock that model and use it in all of our recipe development in the test kitchen.

While our experiments are designed to approximate the kind of use the equipment would be subjected to in a home kitchen over a long period, there are some things that can only be discovered by actually using a particular tool on a regular basis over many months or even years. After our initial rating of blenders, for example, we followed up by making over 500 kale-and-frozen-fruit smoothies in our winning blender over the next 18 months. Metal tools may start to rust, plastic vessels may warp after many cycles in the dishwasher, appliances may lose their oomph; and when we notice these developments, we let you know. We regularly publish updates, especially for the workhorse tools we use the most.

This chapter presents the results of dozens of tests done over the years to evaluate the equipment we think is most useful and necessary for stocking an everyday cook's kitchen. In the **Inside the Testing** sections we've also included longer examples that provide much more detail about the tests that the team did while working with a particularly interesting piece of equipment and give you a glimpse of the form all that work takes when it is pulled together for publication in one of our books, magazines, or web features.

THE EQUIPMENT GUIDE

It can be paralyzing to walk into a kitchenware store or browse online for the perfect knife, the right saucepan, or a food processor, given all the choices. This guide will help you sort out what you need (and what you don't) as well as which brands we think are best. You don't need a lot of fancy equipment to be a good cook, but the right tools definitely help. Here are our suggestions for what we consider to be the basics—the thermometers, knives, utensils, pots, and pans that are not only going to get the job done well, but that will also be in it for the long haul. In the following pages, we provide the key details about what we've learned in our years of equipment testing plus in-depth sections (called **Inside the Testing**) that reveal the details behind some of our most interesting reviews.

For at-a-glance information on these products plus other items that have more specialized uses, see **The America's Test Kitchen Shopping Guide** on pages 357–386. Check out AmericasTestKitchen.com for updates to these testings.

THERMOMETERS AND TIMERS

Instant-Read Thermometer

A fast, accurate thermometer is the best way to know when your food is done, which does wonders to improve the safety and quality of your food. **See page 10 for Inside the Testing.**

What to Look For
Look for a model with a wide temperature range (at least 0 to 400 degrees). We prefer digital models because they are faster and easier to read. A long stem is necessary to reach the center of whole birds and large roasts. Water-resistant models are easier to clean and an automatic shut-off will help with battery life.

Test Kitchen Top Pick
ThermoWorks
Thermapen Mk4, $99.00
Best Buy
ThermoWorks ThermoPop, $29.00

Oven Thermometer

Fact: Ovens are inaccurate. Since all ovens cycle on and off to maintain temperature, even the best models periodically deviate from the desired heat by at least a few degrees. And we've found they can be off by as much as 50 degrees unless they're recalibrated regularly. A good oven thermometer can literally save your bacon.

What to Look For
Oven thermometers come in two styles: bulb and dial-face. We prefer dial-face models, as we've found that the tinted alcohol used in bulb thermometers can get stuck, compromising accuracy. In addition to giving accurate temperature readings, an oven thermometer should be easy to read and easy to mount securely and safely out of the way. It should also be durable.

Test Kitchen Top Pick
CDN Pro Accurate Oven Thermometer, $8.70

Meat Probe/Candy/Deep-Fry Thermometer

Accuracy is paramount when cooking, especially for delicate tasks like frying or candy-making. A few degrees in the wrong direction can result in scorched sugar or soggy fried chicken. In the test kitchen, we use hands-free clip-on digital thermometers to monitor temperatures when deep-frying food, making candy, and—with some models—checking food in the oven without needing to open the oven door.

What to Look For
You want a simple and straightforward clip-on mechanism with a large, easy-to-use control panel. Clear high- and low-temperature alarms are ideal. Look for a model that can be recalibrated so that it stays accurate over the long term.

Test Kitchen Top Pick
Thermoworks ChefAlarm, $59.00
Best Buy
Polder Classic Digital Thermometer/Timer, $24.99

Remote Thermometer

Remote thermometers allow you to monitor, from a distance, the temperature of food cooking on the grill, on the stovetop, or in the oven. One or more temperature probes inserted into the food connect to a battery-powered base that communicates wirelessly with a receiver: either a pager or (via Bluetooth) your smartphone or tablet.

What to Look For
Make sure that the model has a probe long enough to reach into thick cuts of meat and thin connector cables that don't obstruct grill lids or oven doors. We prefer Bluetooth devices, which pair effortlessly with a smartphone and are far easier to operate than pager models. Be aware that none of the models we tested met their advertised distance range, though each company noted that ranges will vary depending on building materials and interference. But if the shorter distance isn't a problem, our winner connects quickly and delivers accurate, clear temperature readouts.

Test Kitchen Top Pick
iDevices Kitchen Thermometer, $78.00

Refrigerator/Freezer Thermometer

Maintaining the proper refrigerator and freezer temperature is essential to keep food as safe as possible and avoid ruined food.

What to Look For
While even an inexpensive model will give you an accurate reading across a wide temperature range, spending a little more will buy you a thermometer that attaches to the wall of your refrigerator or freezer for space-saving convenience. We prefer digital readouts for exact readings and ultraclear displays. Some models also offer alerts when temperatures rise into danger zones (above 40 degrees for the refrigerator; above 0 degrees for the freezer), and others can even display simultaneous fridge and freezer readings.

Test Kitchen Top Pick
Maverick Cold-Chek Digital Refrigerator/ Freezer Thermometer, $19.99

Kitchen Timer

A kitchen timer is one of those pieces of equipment that most home cooks don't give much thought to, but we've found that a good timer is an essential tool for perfect recipes. In the kitchen, timing is everything.

What to Look For
Look for a timer with a range of at least 10 hours (for longer braises, brines, and barbecues) that can count up after the alarm and time at least three separate processes simultaneously. Ideal design includes compact size and an easy-to-read display. Make sure that the timer is easy and intuitive to use.

Test Kitchen Top Pick
OXO Good Grips Triple Timer, $19.99

The Testing Lineup

Recommended
THERMOWORKS
ThermoPop
Top Pick $29.00

POLDER
Stable-Read
Instant Read
Thermometer
$18.42

LE CREUSET
Digital
Instant-Read
Thermometer
$34.95

Recommended with Reservations
ACURITE
Digital Instant
Read Meat
Thermometer
$12.70

CDN
ProAccurate
Thermometer
$17.90

Not Recommended
WEBER
Original
Instant-Read
Thermometer
$9.99

TAYLOR
Pro LED Digital
Thermometer
$13.79

FARBERWARE
Protek
Instant Read
Thermometer
$13.92

The axiom "knowledge is power" holds especially true in the kitchen—the more you know about what's going on inside your food as it cooks, the more you can control the result. That's why we're so gung ho about using an instant-read thermometer in the kitchen, as more control means less stress and better results.

In fact, the test kitchen might be described as fanatical when it comes to thermometers. Over the years we've learned that it pays to monitor the temperature not only of meat but also of pies, cakes, breads, poaching water, butter, tea, coffee, caramel, custards, and even baked potatoes. And if you're going to use a thermometer, it should be a digital instant-read model (old dial thermometers are slow and inaccurate in comparison). Our go-to is the Thermapen from ThermoWorks, which is unquestionably the best digital kitchen thermometer on the market.

But at $79 for the basic Thermapen model and $99 for the deluxe, it is an investment. In search of a cheaper alternative, we set out to test inexpensive digital thermometers and find out which model reigns supreme. In selecting our lineup, we capped the price at $35. But as we were narrowing our testing field, we found many thermometers that only read up to about 300 degrees—fine for meat but not much else. So we added another qualifier to our selection process: Each thermometer had to read up to 400 degrees so that it could be used when making candy, caramel, and other foods requiring high temperatures.

We ran the thermometers through a battery of tests, including taking the temperature of ice water, boiling water, roasted chicken thighs, and bubbling caramel. Through each test we evaluated every model's accuracy, speed, usability, visibility, comfort, and durability with a mix of lefties, righties, small- and large-handed testers, professional chefs, and lay cooks.

A good digital thermometer needs to be accurate—otherwise, what's the point? Aside from a few buggy models, most thermometers in our lineup were indeed accurate. We next

METHODOLOGY

We tested eight instant-read thermometers in common kitchen tasks and evaluated them according to the following criteria. Items appear in The Testing Lineup in order of preference.

Price
We capped the price at $35 for our testing of inexpensive options.

Readability
Thermometers were rated on how clearly we could see and read the numbers.

Response Time
The faster, the better. When tested in boiling water, times of 10 to 20 seconds to achieve a readout of 212 degrees were rated excellent, 20 to 30 seconds were rated fair, and times above 30 seconds were rated poor.

Accuracy
Thermometers should register exactly 212 degrees in boiling water and exactly 32 degrees in a slurry of crushed ice and water. If these readings were off, the thermometer was downgraded.

Design/Features
This category encompasses disparate factors that can make the thermometer a breeze or a pain to use, such as length of the stem; ease of cleaning screens or dials; on/off switches or automatic shutoff; battery availability; and accurate readings in shallow liquids.

Temperature Range
More often than not, instant-read thermometers are used within the relatively narrow temperature range necessary to monitor the internal temperature of meat, poultry, or bread. Occasionally, though, you may wish to know the temperature of a freezing sorbet or ice cream, or double-check the temperature of hot oil prior to frying in it. Therefore, thermometers capable of taking very low (0 degrees and below) through very high (400 degrees and above) readings were upgraded.

turned to speed and were pleased to find that three-quarters of the thermometers gave accurate readings in under 10 seconds, with the fastest clocking in at just over 6 seconds.

Most of the thermometers were accurate and reasonably fast, but that doesn't mean they were always easy to use. Our testers found three major factors that impacted how user-friendly the thermometers were: length, grip, and visibility. Regarding length, the eight thermometers ranged from 5.75 to 8.7 inches long, and we found that longer was better—otherwise, our hands were too close to the heat, and we had to fumble with bulky potholders.

Next up was grip. All of the thermometers have two basic parts, a long metal probe and a head with a digital screen, but only some felt ergonomic and secure in our hands. A few only allowed for dainty two-fingered grips, like a damsel waving a hanky, which simply won't do when you're spearing a chicken thigh that's spitting hot fat.

Lastly, visibility. Larger and clearer displays were best. Testers also preferred screens situated on the side of the thermometer's head as opposed to on top, because they were easier to read from different angles. The best thermometer was lollipop-shaped and had a display that was visible at any angle for both lefties and righties. Said model was also fast, accurate, and easy to use. Manufactured by the same company as the Thermapen, the Thermo Works ThermoPop ($29) is our top pick for the budget-conscious cook.

AN INVESTMENT IN PERFECT RESULTS

While we fully endorse the winner of our inexpensive instant-read thermometer testing, our everyday go-to in the test kitchen is the high-end Thermapen Mk4 from ThermoWorks. At $99, it's an investment, but we think it's well worth the money. It has longer battery life, better water resistance, and sensors that make the display incredibly easy to use.

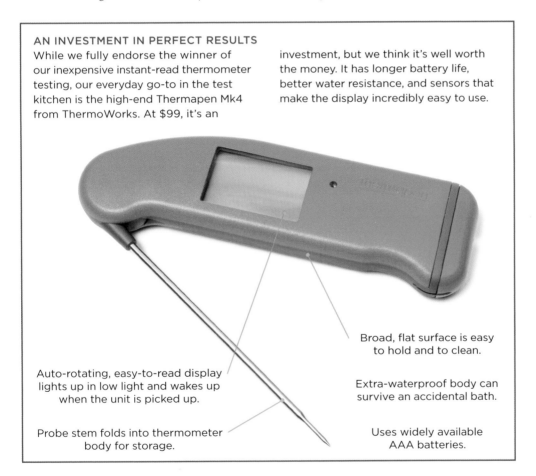

Auto-rotating, easy-to-read display lights up in low light and wakes up when the unit is picked up.

Probe stem folds into thermometer body for storage.

Broad, flat surface is easy to hold and to clean.

Extra-waterproof body can survive an accidental bath.

Uses widely available AAA batteries.

MEASURING TOOLS

Dry Measuring Cups

Dry ingredients must be measured in cups specifically designed for dry measures, not liquid measuring cups. It is impossible to accurately gauge dry ingredients in a cup designed to measure liquids.

What to Look For

Dry measuring cups vary tremendously in material, shape, weight, and price. We like long handles that extend straight out; angled or raised handles obstruct your ability to draw a straight edge across the rim to level off the ingredient. Look for a set with durable markings that can be read clearly even when the cup is full (i.e. not on the bottoms of the cups).

Test Kitchen Top Pick
OXO Good Grips Stainless Steel Measuring Cups, $19.99

Liquid Measuring Cup

While liquid ingredients can be measured fairly accurately in cups designed for dry ingredients, wet measures are generally much easier to work with since they don't need to be filled to the brim, making it much less likely that you'll spill the liquid in the process of carrying it to the bowl or pot.

What to Look For

Make sure your cup is durable, heatproof, and sturdy enough not to tip when filled with liquid. Handles are also a must for protecting hands from hot ingredients. You want a cup with clear, accurate markings that can easily be read even when the cup is full.

Test Kitchen Top Pick
Pyrex 2-Cup Measuring Cup, $5.99

Measuring Spoons

Even cooks who can't be bothered to pull out a measuring spoon for stovetop recipes know that such imprecision won't cut it for baking. In the test kitchen, we have found that the most accurate way to measure dry ingredients is a method we call "dip and sweep." You scoop up a heaping spoonful of the ingredient and then sweep across the rim of the measuring spoon with a flat blade to level the contents. Finding spoons that are easy to use and accurate every time can be quite a challenge.

What to Look For

Design flaws can have a significant impact on accuracy and usability. Make sure your spoons allow for the dip-and-sweep technique, with no bumps or dips in the handles. Longer, slimmer handles are easier to use as long as they are lightweight. We prefer spoon sets that come on a ring but are easy to pull off (and return) to the ring or that have a design that makes it simple to use the spoons while they're on the ring.

Test Kitchen Top Pick
Cuisipro Stainless Steel Measuring Spoons Set, $11.95

Digital Scale

Handy as they are, measuring cups will never measure up to the accuracy of a digital scale. We've found that when measuring dry ingredients using a dip-and-sweep method, different cooks can be off by as much as 20 percent—a variance that, in baking, can mean the difference between a dense cake and a perfectly fluffy, tender crumb. **See page 13 for Inside the Testing.**

What to Look For

The design of the scale should be clean, simple, and intuitive to use. A clear display with backlighting is ideal. The buttons should be sensitive, accessible, and easy to read. Make sure the scale is large enough: The platform should be at least 6 inches and the capacity should be at least 7 pounds for everyday cooking.

Test Kitchen Top Pick
OXO Good Grips 11 lb. Food Scale with Pull Out Display, $49.95
Best Buy
Ozeri Pronto Digital Multifunction Kitchen and Food Scale, $11.79

If you don't own a digital scale, you might not realize what a game changer it can be in the kitchen. First and foremost, a scale is critical for baking recipes, where measuring dry ingredients by weight is the only way to guarantee accuracy. We've proven this in tests where we've repeatedly measured a cup of flour by volume, using a "dip and sweep" method, and found that there can be up to a 20 percent difference in the weight—a variance that can mean the difference between a cake that's squat and dense and one that's fluffy and tender. But scales have many applications in cooking as well as baking. Using one to portion burgers, for example, means no more guessing if the patties are the same size and will thus cook at the same rate.

We bought 10 scales, priced from $11.79 to $67.27, with maximum capacities between 9 and 15 pounds. We tested them for accuracy and also assessed their design, countertop stability, and how easy they were to clean and store. All of the scales were acceptably accurate. When we weighed calibrated lab weights on multiple copies of each model, most gave the exact same reading every time. Only two of them consistently displayed fluctuating readings, and even those were just a few grams off the mark. (Note that we tested only consumer-grade scales, which are not certified by the National Conference on Weights and Measures. More-expensive commercial-grade scales are too pricey for the home cook.)

The bad news was that half the scales were either so unintuitive to operate or so hard to read that we can't recommend them. The first flaw became obvious when we timed testers as they weighed 5 ounces of flour on each model and watched them fumble around for a switch or button to change the unit of measurement from grams to ounces. On one of the losing models, this turned out to be a tiny toggle on the underside of the scale underneath the battery cover, which we only found once we referred to the owner's manual. On another, you must gently press the "on/off" button as the scale powers up—and if you miss that brief window, you have to turn it off and start all over. Start to finish, it took roughly twice as long to complete the task on these models as it did on our top-rated scales.

Legibility was problematic on models with tiny, hard-to-read, or obscurely labeled buttons but was even more of an issue on scales where the control panel was flush with the platform rather than set into a separate part of the scale body. No matter how big and crisp the display was on these scales, larger bowls cast a shadow

Inside the Testing continued on next page

The Testing Lineup

Highly Recommended
OXO
Good Grips 11-lb Food Scale with Pull Out Display
Top Pick $49.95

POLDER
Easy Read Digital Kitchen Scale
$27.98

OZERI
Pronto Digital Multifunction Kitchen and Food Scale
Best Buy $11.79

Recommended
SALTER
Aquatronic Glass Electronic Kitchen Scale
$36.23

Recommended with Reservations
ESCALI
Alimento Digital Scale
$67.27

Continued on next page

METHODOLOGY
We tested 10 digital kitchen scales and rated them according to the criteria listed below. Items appear in The Testing Lineup in order of preference.

Accuracy
We tested three units of each model, weighing 30-, 200-, and 500-gram lab-calibrated weights 10 times on each unit, at the beginning and end of testing. Models that routinely varied by more than 2 grams lost points.

Cleanup
We stained the platforms with a measured amount of yellow mustard, tomato paste, and canola oil; after 36 hours, we washed them by hand. The best models had removable platforms that we could wipe off or scrub. Scales that trapped water and food residue lost points.

Legibility
We preferred digital displays with sharp color contrast or a backlight option, big digits, and large screens. Scales lost points if a 5-quart mixing bowl blocked or obscured the screen.

Durability
We dropped each model onto the counter from a height of 2 inches, checking for damage or lost parts.

Ease Of Use
We timed turning on the scales, switching from grams to ounces, and measuring 5 ounces of flour. Test cooks also subjected top-performing models to a week of daily use. The best models had intuitive controls that were easy to access.

over, or completely blocked, the screen, forcing us to bend down to peer underneath or nudge the bowl backward until it threatened to fall off the back end of the platform. Only one from OXO, which had been our winner in a past test of digital scales, truly excelled in this test: Its display bar can be pulled out 4 inches from the platform, ensuring that the screen is visible under even the biggest, bulkiest items.

When it came to countertop stability, lighter-weight (under 1 pound) scales with feet frequently teetered back and forth or slid around on the counter. In general, squat scales with smooth bottoms stayed put more reliably; plus, they were easier to store. Cleanup was a finicky job for a few models, which trapped flour—or, worse, water that could seep in and damage the internal hardware—in their crevices. We preferred two models that featured removable platforms, which allowed us to scrub them without risking water damage.

By the end of testing, we'd found three scales that impressed us with accuracy; intuitive design; responsive, clearly labeled buttons positioned on an easily visible control panel; and slim frames that were easy to slip into a drawer or cabinet. The best of t hese, our previous champ from OXO, also boasted great stability, a bright backlight, and a removable platform that made cleanup a snap. But if its nearly $50 price tag is too steep, consider our best buy from Ozeri ($11.79). Though it feels a bit lightweight and lacks the winner's removable platform, its performance was otherwise stellar.

ON A TARE

When measuring multiple ingredients that will be combined, such as the dry mix for baked goods, using a digital scale's tare button is more accurate than the "dip and sweep" method and reduces the number of dirty dishes. Set one bowl on the scale for measuring each ingredient and a larger one next to the scale for compiling the measured ingredients, then press the tare button to reset the scale to zero. Add the ingredient to the bowl on the scale until it registers the correct amount and then transfer the measured item to the larger bowl. Repeat with the empty bowl and another item.

WHAT ABOUT MECHANICAL SCALES?

Digital scales can be expensive, but there are some important reasons why we recommend digital over mechanical. First and foremost, a scale must be accurate. The tightly spaced lines on most mechanical scales make it quite difficult to distinguish between 4 ounces and 4½ ounces. Digital scales can indicate much smaller increments. For this feature alone, digital scales are the better choice.

There are several more good reasons to spend the extra money on a digital scale. Weight is expressed in numbers on a digital display whereas with a mechanical scale, the user must judge where the needle falls, which is not always easy when the ruler is small and it measures both grams and ounces. It is also much easier to use the tare function (that is, to reset the scale to zero with something on it) on a digital scale. This allows you to measure the weight of the ingredients in a bowl without having to account for the weight of the bowl. On a mechanical scale, this is achieved by physically resetting the scale to zero by turning the base or using the knob to bring the needle back, which is much more cumbersome.

In addition, digital scales are much more compact than mechanical scales and can be stored in a drawer. You may be tempted to choose a mechanical scale because they are inexpensive and seem straightforward, but we think a good digital scale is more than worth the extra money for the increased accuracy, convenience, and ease of use.

KNIVES AND BOARDS

Chef's Knife

Ask a group of chefs to name the most essential piece of kitchen equipment and most will reply "a good knife." The right knife will make prep a breeze, while a bad one will not only slow you down but actually make you less safe. But you don't have to shell out big bucks for a great knife. **See page 17 for Inside the Testing.**

What to Look For

An 8-inch knife is the most all-purpose size. Choose a knife with a thinly sharpened blade—our top choices all have blades sharpened to a 15-degree (or narrower) point. We like a slightly curved blade that rocks nicely. You also want to pay attention to the handle. We prefer a simple design with no ergonomic grooves or bumps. A plainer handle allows you to grasp the knife in whichever way is most comfortable for your hand.

Test Kitchen Top Pick
Victorinox Swiss Army Fibrox Pro
8-Inch Chef's Knife,
$39.95

Carbon-Steel Knife

Carbon steel is considered superior to stainless steel by many chefs and knife enthusiasts because it is believed to be stronger and able to retain a keener edge. But it is also a high-maintenance metal that rusts if not kept dry. Still, if you are willing to pay a premium and do a little extra work, a carbon-steel blade is a real showstopper.

What to Look For

Narrow, razor-sharp blades cut quickly and evenly. Our favorites are sharpened to between 10 and 15 degrees on either side of the blade. Knives with smooth, nonangular handles of medium width and length are the easiest to use. We prefer blades with rounded top spines that don't dig into fingers.

Test Kitchen Top Pick
Bob Kramer 8" Carbon Steel
Chef's Knife by Zwilling
J.A. Henckels,
$299.95
Best Buy
Togiharu Virgin Carbon Steel Gyutou, 8.2", $98.50

Paring Knife

For detail work like hulling strawberries, coring fruit, scraping out vanilla beans, or trimming away a tough patch of silverskin on a roast, smaller, more maneuverable paring knives are far better tools than large chef's knives.

What to Look For

We prefer the versatility of the classic style, with its slightly curved blade and pointed tip resembling a mini chef's knife. You want a blade that's no longer than 3½ inches for maximum precision and agility. Look for an even balance between blade and handle—heavier handles will make handheld tasks more awkward. For optimum sharpness, pick a knife with a cutting edge angle around 15 to 17 degrees. We also prefer all-purpose paring knives to specialty blades like the "bird's beak" and "sheep's foot" styles with curved or rounded tips.

Test Kitchen Top Pick
Wüsthof Classic with
PEtec, 3½-Inch,
$39.95
Best Buy
Victorinox Swiss Army Fibrox Pro 3¼-Inch
Paring Knife, $4.95

Serrated Knife

A serrated knife relies on a slicing motion in which the blade is dragged across the food's surface as it moves down through it. Serrated knives are ideal tools for cutting bread, slicing tomatoes, splitting cake layers, and cutting through sticky doughs.

What to Look For

Look for a knife with fewer broader, deeper, pointed serrations so it will cut your food without shredding it. The ideal length is about 10 inches; long enough to handle cake layers and big loaves of bread without getting unwieldy. A comfortable, grippy handle and medium weight make the knife easier to maneuver.

Test Kitchen Top Pick
Mercer Culinary Millennia
10" Wide Bread
Knife,
$22.10

Slicing Knife

Unlike shorter chef's knives and pointed, flexible carving knives, slicing knives are long and straight for smooth, even slicing. They also have rounded tips so as to be less threatening for tableside serving.

What to Look For

Comfortable, grippy handles are imperative, as is the right degree of flexibility: Bendy blades bail out midcut, leaving behind ragged slices. Stiff blades go where they want, not where we ask. Subtle but present flexibility allows for control and strength. You also want a taller, longer, narrower blade that will make it easy to get full, clean slices. We prefer blades with a Granton edge, which refers to scallops or indentations along the side of the knife blade. These break up the resistance on the blade, and the reduced friction makes it easier to cut even slices, thick or thin.

Test Kitchen Top Pick

Victorinox Swiss Army Fibrox Pro 12-Inch Granton Edge Slicing/Carving Knife, $54.65

Knife Sharpener

American chef's knives are increasingly emulating the Japanese style, which are sharpened to about 15 degrees. Maintaining the edge on these razor-sharp blades requires a specially designed tool.

What to Look For

For routine sharpening, manual and electric knife sharpeners perform comparably. Diamond-abrasive sharpeners are the most effective and long-lasting. The sharpening chamber should have guides to keep the knife from wobbling. Manual sharpeners are smaller, cheaper, and easier to store, but to repair extensive blade damage, you'll need an electric model, which puts the abrasive in contact with the blade at much higher speeds.

Test Kitchen Top Picks

Chef'sChoice Trizor XV Knife Sharpener Model #15, $149.99 (Electric)
Chef'sChoice Pronto Manual Diamond Hone Asian Knife Sharpener Model #463, $49.99 (Manual)
Best Buy
Chef'sChoice Diamond Sharpener for Asian Knives, Model #316, $79.99 (Electric)

Carving Board

A carving board may seem like a luxury you pull out only a few times a year, but anyone who's tried carving a roast on a flat cutting board knows what a disaster that can be. Carving boards have trenches around their perimeters that keep juices from dribbling onto the counter and avoid mess.

What to Look For

The ideal proportions for a carving board are 20 by 14 or 15 inches. A board around 1 inch tall has enough heft to sit securely on the counter but is still easy to lift. Make sure that the trenches are wide and deep enough to hold at least ½ cup of liquid. A basic board will be easier to use and clean than one with fancy innovations like pour spouts and cutting grooves. Our winning board has a reversible design with a flat side suited to slicing roasts and an indented side with a poultry-shaped well to hold food snugly in place.

Test Kitchen Top Pick

J.K. Adams Maple Reversible Carving Board, $69.95

Cutting Board

Cutting boards are one of the most used tools in your kitchen. Ideally a cutting board will last for decades, but there's always the danger that it will eventually suffer deep gouges, dull the edge of your knife, or even warp or split. A good cutting board is an investment.

What to Look For

The board should be at least 20 by 15 inches. Any smaller and it will feel cramped. You'll also want some heft to keep the board from slipping and sliding around the counter. Finally, durability is crucial. We expect shallow scratches, since a blade should stick to the surface just a little; it makes for safer, steadier knife work. Deep gashes, however, are a deal breaker. Wood and bamboo boards are best. Look for an edge-grain board, which is less likely to warp than an end-grain board.

Test Kitchen Top Picks

Proteak Edge Grain Teak Cutting Board, $84.99 (Wooden)
OXO Good Grips Carving & Cutting Board, $21.99 (Plastic)

What exactly separates a good chef's knife from an inferior one? Over the years, we've tested dozens of models labeled as "hybrid," "innovative," and even "for kids," at prices that rose well above $100 for a single blade. But the most important chef's knife is the most basic one—the knife you can use for almost any cutting or chopping task in the kitchen and rely upon day in and day out. Is an expensive, handcrafted knife always better than one made by a machine? To answer these questions, we sought out 8-inch chef's knives (the most all-purpose size) and capped our budget at $50. We enlisted six testers, male and female and with varying hand sizes and kitchen abilities, and got each of them to spend weeks hacking, dicing, and chopping their way through 10 whole chickens, 10 butternut squashes, 10 onions, and 10 bunches of parsley. We were looking for a strong yet agile blade that felt comfortable and secure in our hands.

By the time we wrapped up testing, we'd found one standout favorite and a couple of other knives that passed muster, but the rest of the models lagged behind, many of them by a considerable margin. While the top performers capably broke down whole birds and slid through dense squash, the bulk of the lot struggled—and at the end of testing, we had piles of ragged onion pieces and bruised parsley leaves to prove it.

The obvious question: What was it about our lone winner that made it a stellar performer? Its design wasn't radically different from that of other knives, and it was one of the least expensive knives in an already low-cost lineup. We decided to get to the bottom of what made this one knife so much better than all the others.

The top priority for a good knife is razor sharpness. Right out of the box, some knives were sharper than others. Still others started out fairly sharp and quickly lost their edge. A dull knife turns a small pile of potatoes into a mountain and makes for sloppy food. ("I can hear the cells bursting," said one tester as a dull blade sprayed onion juice across the cutting board. "Chicken, I feel sorry for you," said a second frustrated tester, vainly hacking away with another comparatively blunt edge.) But a razor-thin cutting edge isn't everything: If the metal is too soft, it will easily develop microscopic chips, dings, and dents, and the edge will wear down quickly. We found that knives made from certain steel alloys that contained more carbon, as well as vanadium, an element that acts as a hardening agent, were sharper and

Inside the Testing continued on next page

METHODOLOGY
Six test kitchen staffers subjected ten 8-inch chef's knives, priced at $50 or less, to a range of kitchen tasks and also assessed comfort and edge retention. Items appear in The Testing Lineup in order of preference.

Blade Design
We preferred slightly curved blades that rocked nicely and spines that didn't dig into our hands.

Edge Retention
We evaluated each blade fresh out of the box, during testing, and at the end of testing by slicing through sheets of copier paper— our standard sharpness test.

Kitchen Tasks
We butchered whole chickens, chopped unwieldy butternut squash, diced onions, and minced parsley, carrying out each task 60 times. We averaged scores from each test to get the overall rating.

Handle
Handles that felt comfortable and secure for a range of tasks and a variety of grips rated highest.

more resilient. How the metal is heated and cooled also matters. Just as baking time and temperature affect the crumb of a cake, the "cooking" process determines the grain of a metal. For a harder product, small, close-knit grains are the goal. All manufacturers start the knife-making process the same way: by slowly cooling the molten metal. Next comes the proprietary part: a multistep tempering process of reheating and cooling the metal to help shrink the grains and/or encourage new, smaller ones to form. Variations in tempering can lead to differences in grain size and pattern. We're betting that the specific way it was tempered helped give our front-runner superior hardness.

As for the other half of the knife—the handle—we figured that preferences would be a dividing point among testers. After all, the comfort of a grip is largely subjective and depends on a variety of factors: the size of your hand; how you hold the blade; your knife skills; whether you prefer a brawnier or more svelte handle; and whether the handle is crafted from metal, nylon, or wood. Surprisingly, though, all six testers unanimously preferred one handle: that of our winner. This handle boasted no ergonomic grooves or bumps; compared with other models that we tested, it actually lacked design features. How could one grip feel like a "natural extension" of so many different hands?

We showed the knives to Jack Dennerlein, professor of ergonomics and safety at Northeastern and Harvard Universities, who offered a one-word explanation: "affordance." This term, he explained, is what ergonomists

THE BLADE: WHAT MAKES IT SHARP AND KEEPS IT THAT WAY
Creating the sharpest, most durable knives is a bit like baking a cake: Start with the right ingredients and then treat the metal just so.

THE RIGHT MIX OF METALS
Because steel is an alloy, it can come in countless forms, depending on what metals it contains and in what proportion.

PRECISE TEMPERING
How the steel is heated and cooled helps determine the hardness of the metal.

THIN CUTTING EDGE
The narrower the angle of the cutting edge, the sharper the blade will be. We like knives sharpened to 15 degrees.

use to describe the versatility that we ask of tools like chef's knives. Cutting is a complex task, and a well-designed handle affords multiple grips for the range of angles and forces required. Dennerlein said that when knife makers add grooves and curves to a handle, like those on some of the less comfortable handles in our lineup, they are telling us how to hold the knife instead of allowing us to choose what's most comfortable.

After nearly two months of testing, we tallied our results—and we can't say that we were shocked to learn the winner. Our favorite effortlessly ascended to the top spot for its exceptional cutting ability and a grip that all testers found particularly comfortable. Don't be misled by its unprepossessing design: This model has a number of subtle features that helped propel it to the top of our rankings. For one, there's its plain-Jane handle. Made from a grippy nylon material called polyamide, it has enough traction to stay put in your hand, and its basic design boasts the so-called affordance that makes it well suited for any kind of grip. Second, its blade is made of hard steel—an alloy that is likely put through a very fine-tuned heating and cooling process to develop the optimal hardness. Third, the blade is sharpened to a thin 15 degrees. Traditionally, Western knives have been sharpened to 20 to 22 degrees on each side of the blade while Asian knives are thinner—just 15 degrees on each side, but those style markers appear to be blurring: our top three favorite knives all sported 15-degree (or narrower) blades.

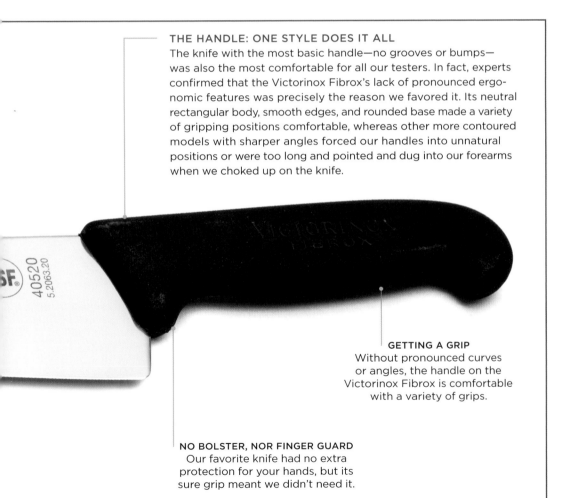

THE HANDLE: ONE STYLE DOES IT ALL
The knife with the most basic handle—no grooves or bumps—was also the most comfortable for all our testers. In fact, experts confirmed that the Victorinox Fibrox's lack of pronounced ergonomic features was precisely the reason we favored it. Its neutral rectangular body, smooth edges, and rounded base made a variety of gripping positions comfortable, whereas other more contoured models with sharper angles forced our handles into unnatural positions or were too long and pointed and dug into our forearms when we choked up on the knife.

GETTING A GRIP
Without pronounced curves or angles, the handle on the Victorinox Fibrox is comfortable with a variety of grips.

NO BOLSTER, NOR FINGER GUARD
Our favorite knife had no extra protection for your hands, but its sure grip meant we didn't need it.

POTS AND PANS

Saucepan

Every kitchen should have two saucepans: one with a capacity of 3 to 4 quarts, and one 2-quart nonstick saucepan. A larger saucepan is great for sauces and vegetables, while a smaller nonstick saucepan can be used for cooking foods that stick easily and for reheating leftovers.

What to Look For

A comfortable, stay-cool handle is a must and it should be long enough for two-handed carrying when the pan is full. Make sure the pans also have tight-fitting lids.

Test Kitchen Top Picks
All-Clad Stainless 4-Quart Saucepan with Lid and Loop, $224.95 (Large)
Calphalon Contemporary Nonstick 2½-Quart Shallow Saucepan with Cover, $39.95 (Small)
Best Buy
Cuisinart MultiClad Unlimited 4-Quart Saucepan, $69.99 (Large)

Stockpot

Most home kitchens only have room for a single stockpot, so it must handle a variety of big jobs—from steaming lobsters to canning and making huge batches of chili or homemade stock.

What to Look For

A 12-quart stockpot is the most useful size. We prefer wide stockpots to tall and narrow ones; they allow you to see and manipulate food better. Lighter-weight pots are fine for cooking corn and pasta, but for cooking applications where sticking and scorching are risks, you need a heavier pot with a thick bottom. Look for flat or round handles that extend from the pot at least 1¾ inches.

Test Kitchen Top Pick
All-Clad Stainless 12-Quart Stock Pot, $389.95
Best Buy
Cuisinart Chef's Classic Stainless 12-Quart Stock Pot, $69.99

Traditional Skillet

This multiuse pan is key when we want to pan-sear meat or pan-roast chicken parts. The finish (which is not nonstick) helps develop fond—the crusty browned bits that are used to make pan sauces. The flared, shallow sides encourage rapid evaporation of moisture, so foods sear and brown, rather than steam, and pan sauces reduce quickly.

What to Look For

A 12-inch pan is a must. Although there are times when you might need a smaller skillet, the 12-inch diameter is the best all-around choice. For the best conduction of heat, the pan should be clad, meaning the entire pan is made of three or more metal layers and does not have a disk bottom (an attached disk of metal). A heavy clad base will distribute heat evenly. Look for a comfortable, ovensafe handle that will help you lift and hold on to the pan with no worries when sliding it into the oven or under the broiler.

Test Kitchen Top Pick
All-Clad 12-Inch Stainless Fry Pan, $154.95

Nonstick Skillet

We use this pan to cook or sauté delicate items that tend to stick or break apart during cooking, like fish, stir-fries, pancakes, and egg dishes. Flared sides allow for the quick redistribution of food (think omelet) by jerking and sliding the pan. Plus, cleanup is a snap.

What to Look For

A 12-inch nonstick skillet is the most versatile choice to handle fish fillets or a stir-fry serving four. Smaller nonstick skillets (8-inch or 10-inch) can be a good choice if you frequently cook fewer or smaller servings. The handle should feel comfortable and sturdy, and stay cool during cooking. Look for a handle that can go into the oven since many recipes start on the stovetop and finish in the oven.

Test Kitchen Top Pick
OXO Good Grips Non-Stick 12-inch Open Frypan, $39.99

Cast-Iron Skillet

Cast iron heats to high temperatures and stays hot, and, if well seasoned, releases food just as well as a nonstick surface. Newer enameled cast-iron pans also offer all these advantages without the need to season the metal.
See page 23 for Inside the Testing.

What to Look For

Look for a heavy pan with a large cooking surface. An 11- or 12-inch pan is best. We prefer factory-preseasoned pans, which perform better than unseasoned pans and require less effort to use and maintain. Both preseasoned and unseasoned cast-iron skillets should be oiled to help keep them in good working order and prevent rust.

Test Kitchen Top Picks
Lodge Classic 12-Inch Cast Iron Skillet, $33.31 (Traditional)
Le Creuset Signature 11¾" Iron Handle Skillet, $179.95 (Enameled)
Best Buy
Mario Batali by Dansk 12" Open Sauté Pan, $59.95 (Enameled)

Grill Pan

When you can't fire up the grill, it's handy to have a stovetop grill pan. Though it can't replicate the flavor of the open flame, a ridged grill pan does make tasty char-grill marks on food. Some even come with presses for grilled sandwiches.

What to Look For

Grill pans with ridges ranging from 4 millimeters to 5.5 millimeters high make the best grill marks. The taller ridges ensure intact grill marks on both sides by keeping food perched above any rendered fat. Nonstick aluminum pans can't have ridges as high as cast-iron pans because the material will tear and deform, so we prefer cast iron. If you're a fan of grilled sandwiches, look for a pan with a matching panini press.

Test Kitchen Top Pick
Staub 12-Inch American Square Grill Pan and Press, $219.95
Best Buy
Lodge Square Grill Pan, $18.97, and Lodge Ribbed Panini Press, $14.98

Cookware is made from a variety of metals, each with its own pros and cons.

Cast Iron

Cast iron heats up slowly but retains heat well. Cast-iron cookware is also inexpensive and lasts a lifetime, but it is heavy, reactive, and must be seasoned before use unless you buy preseasoned cast iron (which we recommend).
The Bottom Line Traditional cast iron is great for skillets. We like enameled cast iron for Dutch ovens since the enamel coating prevents the iron from rusting and from reacting with foods.

Aluminum

Aluminum is second only to copper (which we don't think is worth the expense) in conductivity, plus it's light and inexpensive and retains heat well; however, the soft metal dents and scratches easily. Anodized aluminum has a harder and less reactive outer surface, but its dark color makes it tricky to monitor the development of fond.
The Bottom Line Unless anodized, aluminum is best used in combination with other metals.

Stainless Steel

Stainless steel is a poor heat conductor. Inexpensive cookware made entirely of thin-gauge stainless steel is prone to hot spots and warping. Stainless steel is, however, nonreactive, durable, and attractive, making it an excellent choice for coating, or "cladding," aluminum or copper.
The Bottom Line Don't buy cookware made from stainless steel alone—it should be combined with other metals.

Clad Cookware

Clad cookware, sometimes called tri-ply, is what we recommend most of the time. Clad cookware is made from layers of metal that have been bonded under intense pressure and heat. These layers often form a sandwich, with the "filling" made of aluminum and the other layers made of stainless steel. This gives you the best characteristics of both metals for more even heating.
The Bottom Line Clad cookware heats evenly and quickly, and is easy to care for. We rely on it.

Sauté Pan

Despite their name, these wide, flat-bottomed pans with high, L-shaped sides are not the best choice for searing. For that, we prefer skillets with low, sloping walls. That said, sauté pans are ideal for braising recipes that require browning before adding liquid. The walls prevent spills as you stir, pour off oil, or transfer the pan from stove to oven.

What to Look For

The pan should be thick and heavy enough to modulate heat but not so bulky that it retains too much of it. Ideally, the handle should have some kind of traction or edge and be made of a stay-cool material. A "helper" loop opposite the main handle makes it easier to lift the pan when full. Lids should be weighty, ovensafe, and create a tight seal on the pan.

Test Kitchen Top Pick

All-Clad Stainless 3-Quart Tri-Ply Sauté Pan, $224.95

Best Buy

Cuisinart MultiClad Pro Stainless 3½-Quart Sauté Pan with Helper and Cover, $78.13

Dutch Oven

The best choice for soups and stews, a Dutch oven is also ideal for frying, braising, steaming, and boiling. Built for both oven and stovetop use, a Dutch oven is generally wider, shallower, and heavier than a conventional stockpot. That heft translates into plenty of heat retention.

What to Look For

Buy big and wide. We find the most useful size to be 6 to 8 quarts. Our favorite pots measure more than 9 inches across. Look for wide, looping handles. They should be extremely sturdy and wide enough to grab with thick oven mitts. Lids should be tight-fitting and heavy enough not to clatter when the pot contents are simmering.

Test Kitchen Top Picks

All-Clad Stainless 8-Quart Stockpot, $279.95 (Lighter) Le Creuset 7¼-Quart Round French Oven, $349.95 (Heavier)

Best Buy

Lodge Color Enamel 6-Quart Dutch Oven, $76.82

Rimmed Baking Sheet

We use rimmed aluminum baking sheets for everything from roasting vegetables to baking cookies and the occasional sheet cake. Fitted with the right-size wire cooling rack, this pan is also good for broiling or roasting and for prep work such as holding breaded food before frying.

What to Look For

A light-colored surface will heat and brown evenly, making for perfectly cooked meat, vegetables, or cookies. Make sure the pan is sturdy so it won't buckle but lightweight enough to be lifted easily even when it's full of food. Buy at least two baking sheets. They have so many different uses that having more than one available is a good plan. We prefer pans that are 18 by 13 inches with a 1-inch rim all around, often called half sheet pans. If you buy one with different dimensions, parchment paper and standard cooling racks won't fit.

Test Kitchen Top Pick

Nordic Ware Bakers Half Sheet, $14.97

Roasting Pan

Besides roasting our Thanksgiving turkey, this pan shows up whenever we want to tackle large cuts of meat. Its low sides and open design provide roasts with maximum exposure for even browning.

What to Look For

Bigger is better, but be sure to measure your oven before shopping; the pan should fit with about 2 inches of clearance on all sides. Handles should be sturdy, upright, and large enough to accommodate thick oven mitts. Make sure the pan is flameproof, since it may end up on the stovetop when you're making gravy. Some pans come with a V-shaped rack for holding meat; if yours doesn't, buy one separately.

Test Kitchen Top Pick

Calphalon Contemporary Stainless Roasting Pan with Rack, $99.99

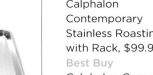

Best Buy

Calphalon Commercial Hard-Anodized Roasting Pan with Nonstick Rack, $59.99

Few pieces of kitchen gear improve after years of heavy use. In fact, we can think of only one: a cast-iron pan. As you cook in it, cast iron gradually takes on a natural, slick patina that releases food easily. A well-seasoned cast-iron pan can rival, and certainly outlast, a nonstick pan. Cast-iron pans are virtually indestructible and easily restored if mistreated. Their special talent is heat retention, making them ideal for browning, searing, and shallow frying.

A recent cast iron renaissance means that manufacturers have launched new versions of traditional cast-iron pans with innovative design tweaks to their handles and overall shapes in an attempt to rival the bare-bones traditional pans. Perhaps more notably, there's been a boom in the number of enameled cast-iron skillets. These pans cloak the rough surface of the cast iron inside and out with the same kind of porcelain coating found on Dutch ovens. Enameling promises a cast-iron pan with advantages: The glossy coating prevents the metal from rusting or reacting with acidic foods, both of which are concerns with traditional cast iron. It also lets you thoroughly scrub dirty pans with soap—generally taboo with traditional pans since using too much soap will damage the patina. While a handful of expensive enameled skillets have been around for years, new models are now appearing at lower prices. We had to wonder: Should we be trading out our traditional pan for an enameled one?

We bought 10 cast-iron skillets, six enameled and four traditional, each about 12 inches in diameter. We set about scrambling eggs, searing steaks, making a tomato-caper pan sauce (to check if its acidity reacted with the pan surface), skillet-roasting thick fish fillets that went from stove to oven, baking cornbread, and shallow-frying chicken cutlets. At the end of testing, we scrambled more eggs to see whether the pans' surfaces had evolved. To simulate years of kitchen use, we plunged hot pans into ice water, banged a metal spoon on their rims, cut in them with a chef's knife, and scraped them with a metal spatula.

Despite their coatings, some of the cooking surfaces in the enameled pans were nearly as rough as sandpaper. But surprisingly, the finish didn't always relate directly to how much the food stuck—the top enameled pan was quite smooth, but its closest competitor was rough. In recipes that required plenty of fat, such as steaks or fried chicken cutlets, the enameled pans all released foods well and delivered good browning. But with foods that often stick—fish, eggs, and cornbread—the differences between the enameled and traditional pans finally emerged. While in the main the enameled pans performed reasonably well, they tended to grab on to the food a little more. All the traditional skillets instantly turned

Inside the Testing continued on next page

METHODOLOGY
We purchased ten 12-inch cast-iron skillets (six enameled and four traditional) and performed a variety of tests to assess the following criteria. Items appear in The Testing Lineup in order of preference.

Browning
We seared steaks and made an acidic sauce, looking for good crust and flavor without off-notes. We rated browning with skillet-roasted fish fillets, shallow-fried breaded chicken cutlets, and cornbread.

Sticking
We cooked thick fish fillets and baked cornbread; we scrambled eggs as first and last tests to evaluate changes in the pans' surfaces.

Ease of Use
We considered features that helped make the pans easy to use and clean.

Durability
We heated pans to 400 degrees and then plunged them into ice water, made five cuts inside with a chef's knife, scraped with a metal spatula 10 times, and whacked a metal spoon five times on the rims and sides of pans.

out crisp-crusted cornbread loaves when we flipped them, but four of six enameled models tore out a chunk of bottom crust. Most telling, traditional pans became slicker each time we used them, but enamel coatings remained the same, and a few even released slightly less well by the end of testing.

Next we looked more generally at how the pans handled and functioned. One of cast iron's selling points is that it holds heat well, producing excellent browning. But, for the same reason, it's slow to heat up and can have hot spots. You must preheat it thoroughly to give the heat time to spread. The enamel coatings didn't dramatically affect how quickly the pans heated or cooled down. Rather, the pan's ability to retain heat, whether traditional or enameled, is related mainly to the thickness and overall mass of the cast iron. Two of the thickest pans,

both enameled (plus another pan that was thinner but had an unusually large cooking surface), were more sluggish to heat, hung on to hot spots for longer, and finally became too hot, making it a challenge to brown food evenly.

Another note about heating: While traditional cast iron has no upper temperature limits, this is not true of enamel because high temperatures can cause the coating to develop numerous small cracks (called "crazing"). This restriction makes them less versatile; one pan's maximum was just 400 degrees. Our favorite enameled pan fell in line with the traditional pans; with no recommended upper limit by the manufacturer, it's even broiler-safe. It also proved itself above the rest on the abuse front. It was the only enameled pan to emerge perfectly unmarked.

NONSTICK SURFACE COMES WITH TIME
We found that all traditional cast-iron pans will become more nonstick with time. While you might think this will take years, we found a significant difference after just a few weeks in the test kitchen.

STICKY MESS
Scrambled eggs stick to the surface of a new preseasoned cast-iron skillet just out of the box.

SEASONED PRO
After a few weeks, the same pan became more seasoned and released all but a few wisps of egg.

CAST-IRON HISTORY
Cast-iron cookware is formed by pouring molten iron into a mold made of sand, which is used only once, making each pan unique. The process originated in China in the 6th century B.C. and has been mostly unchanged for centuries, with the exception that machines now pour the hot metal into the molds. Cast iron was the material of choice for cookware in America until the early 20th century, when aluminum became affordable. At one time, there were dozens of American companies making cast-iron cookware. Today, there is just one major producer, Lodge. Most of the pans we tested are made in China.

OLDER, NOT BETTER
We purchased a 100-year-old Wagner pan from a collector for $110. This pan had a nice patina and aced the scrambled egg test, but it is lighter than the modern cast-iron pans in our lineup and didn't perform as well in the searing and frying tests.

Enameled or not, weight, handle length, and breadth made a big difference in how easy the pans were to use. Our pans ranged from 6½ pounds to nearly 9 pounds. Longer handles gave better leverage, though shorter ones worked if the pan had a good helper handle. Low, flaring, curved sides are usually ideal in a skillet to encourage evaporation and help food brown. But a thoroughly preheated cast-iron skillet radiates heat so intensely that browning was easy even in pans with higher, straighter sides, as long as they had a broad enough cooking surface. Our top pans were at least 10 inches across the cooking surface, which provided enough room for even the biggest steaks to brown without crowding and steaming.

In the final analysis, neither enameled nor traditional cast iron was "best." Both offer great heat retention and superior browning, but beyond that it's a matter of comparing pros and cons and determining what's best for your own needs. If you find seasoning traditional cast iron intimidating, paying more up front for an enameled pan is probably worth it. But keep in mind, while a good enameled pan may be more "nonstick" than a traditional stainless-steel pan, it isn't ever going to match a well-seasoned traditional cast-iron pan (in fairness, enameled pans aren't marketed as nonstick). On the flip side, if you don't want to pamper your pan to prevent chipping and scratching and are OK with maintaining the seasoning, traditional cast iron is for you. What's more, if you want to use metal utensils and high heat, if you want a pan that over time will release food more easily, and if you want to save some money, choose traditional cast iron.

The Testing Lineup, CONTINUED

Enameled

Highly Recommended
LE CREUSET
Signature
11¾" Iron
Handle Skillet
Top Pick $179.95

Recommended
MARIO BATALI
BY DANSK
12" Open
Sauté Pan
Best Buy $59.95

LODGE
Enamel Coated
Cast Iron Skillet
$48.90

Recommended with Reservations
RACHAEL RAY
Cast Iron 12-Inch
Open Skillet with
Helper Handle
$79.95

STAUB
Cast Iron
12" Fry Pan
$174.99

TRAMONTINA
GOURMET
Enameled Cast
Iron 12 in Skillet
with Lid
$69.60

WHICH CAST IRON IS RIGHT FOR YOU?

Buy a Traditional Cast-Iron Pan If:

- You're never going to baby your cookware. You want to use it at any temperature, under the broiler or on the grill, with metal utensils, and bang it around with no fear of damage.
- You don't want to spend a lot. Our favorite 12-inch traditional skillet will cost around $30 and last a lifetime.
- You don't mind simple maintenance. Wash, dry thoroughly, and lightly oil to prevent rust.
- You are OK with using little to no soap (hot water and a scrub brush suffice).
- You don't plan to make long-simmered acidic sauces like marinara in it.
- You won't leave it soaking.

Buy an Enameled Cast-Iron Pan If:

- You never want to think about seasoning the pan.
- You don't mind spending more. Our recommended 12-inch skillets range from $50 to $180.
- You're prepared to protect the glass-like enamel. You won't use it under the broiler (unless you're prepared to buy our durable, and expensive, winner); you'll avoid metal utensils and banging or scraping the pan; and you'll stack with care.
- You dislike the idea of not using soap.
- You plan to use it for long-simmered acidic sauces.
- You don't mind that it will not become more nonstick. An enameled pan will never be as nonstick as a well-seasoned traditional pan.

TOOLS AND UTENSILS

Kitchen Shears

Kitchen shears are the best all-around tool on the counter, useful for butterflying chicken, trimming pie dough, shaping parchment to line cake pans, snipping herbs, or cutting lengths of kitchen twine.

What to Look For

Comfortable handles are key. Pull-apart handles make for easy cleaning, but make sure to look for a pair that separates at a wide angle and won't spontaneously come apart. Of course, supersharp blades are crucial, and our favorite shears have microserrations to help grip objects while cutting. We also prefer shears with adjustable tension settings. If you or someone you cook with is left-handed, be sure to look for shears with symmetrical handles.

Test Kitchen Top Pick
Kershaw Taskmaster Shears/
Shun Multi-Purpose
Shears, $49.95
Best Buy
J.A. Henckels International Kitchen Shears—
Take Apart, $14.95

Tongs

In the test kitchen and our home kitchens alike, we use tongs to lift, flip, turn, rotate, and otherwise move every conceivable type of food while it cooks, from ramekins of custard in a water bath to small shrimp sautéing in a pan to gargantuan prime rib roasts emerging from the oven.

What to Look For

During testing, we found that nonstick versus regular materials made less difference than the shape of the pincers. We prefer slightly concave pincers with wide, shallow scallops around the edges. Soft cushioning on the handles makes gripping easier and keeps them from overheating. We prefer a length of 12 inches, which keeps our hands far from the heat but is still easily maneuverable. Tongs should open and close easily and fit comfortably in your hand.

Test Kitchen
Top Pick
OXO Good Grips
12-Inch Locking Tongs, $12.09

Wooden Spoon

A wooden spoon is one of the most basic cooking tools—an enterprising caveman probably fashioned the first one, snapping a twig from a nearby sapling to prod a hunk of meat over an open fire. Simple yet indispensable, wooden spoons stir, scrape, and scoop.

What to Look For

A comfortable handle is essential; we prefer squared-off sides, which leave your hand less clenched than a traditional round handle, and give your thumb a place to rest securely on top for leverage. Height and width of the head was also important: Wide, squat designs were like stirring with a ping-pong paddle, with too much surface area to push through the soup and not enough handle to leverage against the weight.

Test Kitchen Top Pick
SCI Bamboo Wood
Cooking Spoon, $2.40

Ladle

Serving soup seems straightforward—until you try to do it with a poorly designed ladle.

What to Look For

The critical element of a ladle is the angle of its offset handle. A deeply bent handle offers a better grip and maximum control. A long ladle also makes it easier to scoop soup out of a tall stockpot. A shallow bowl is helpful for scraping the bottom of a pot.

Test Kitchen Top Pick
Rösle Hook Ladle with
Pouring Rim, $34.00
Best Buy
OXO Good Grips Brushed Stainless Steel Ladle, $9.99

All-Around Spatula

Because spatulas are fairly cheap, most people own a drawer full of assorted styles and brands. But wouldn't it be better to own the perfect spatula that feels natural and makes cooking easier? We all need a plastic spatula to protect nonstick pans and a metal spatula for traditional pans, where thick, blunt plastic ones just won't do.

What to Look For
A good spatula must have a slim front edge that can slip under any food. The head should be about 3 inches wide and 5½ inches long. The handle should measure roughly 6 inches, for a total length of about 11 inches, tip to handle. Avoid steeply angled handles and look for a spatula with long vertical slots: They make it easier to slide the spatula under food.

Test Kitchen Top Picks
Wüsthof Gourmet Turner/Fish Spatula, $44.95 (Metal)
Matfer Bourgeat Pelton Spatula, $8.23 (Plastic)
Best Buy
OXO Good Grips Flexible Turner — Steel (Metal), $7.99

Rubber/Silicone Spatula

A rubber spatula is invaluable for scraping bowls clean, stirring batters, and folding egg whites.

What to Look For
As a general rule, we prefer larger-bladed spatulas. Large heads minimize the amount of folding necessary, keeping batters light and fully aerated. Thin, flexible edges aid in agility and scraping ability, making it easy to get the last traces of batter from a bowl or honey from a measuring cup. We've found that both silicone and rubber are reasonably heat-resistant, despite the claimed superiority of silicone. A spatula's blade is the most important element, but we also recommend stiff, relatively long handles with round edges for comfort and efficiency.

Test Kitchen Top Pick
Rubbermaid Professional 13½-Inch High-Heat Scraper, $18.99
Best Buy
Tovolo Silicone Spatula, $8.99

All-Purpose Whisk

Most people have a whole collection of whisks, from fat to skinny, tapered to short, with wires that twist at odd angles or sport a colorful silicone coating. We wanted to find one all-purpose whisk that could tackle everything from whipping cream to blending a silky pan sauce.

What to Look For
A skinny balloon-style whisk is your best bet for an all-purpose whisk. The more wires a whisk has, the more streams of air it pulls through the ingredients, creating foam. Our top performers had at least 10 wires. The best whisks also had wire loops that were thin and flexible. Moderately thin wires (1.3 to 1.4 millimeters) were best able to address both ends of the whisking spectrum, from thick cookie dough to delicate egg whites. Look for a whisk with a total length of 10 to 11 inches and a handle that's ergonomic but not too slender.

Test Kitchen Top Pick
OXO Good Grips 11" Balloon Whisk, $9.99

Pepper Mill

Adding freshly ground pepper to your food is one of the simplest ways to improve it. For our money, a pepper mill has one purpose: to swiftly crank out the desired size and amount of fresh ground pepper, without any guesswork in grind selection or extra strain on our wrists. Simple criteria, and yet many models fail to measure up.
See page 30 for Inside the Testing.

What to Look For
Go for a manually operated model rather than one run on batteries. This will allow you to have more control over the output. An efficient, comfortable grinding mechanism is key, as are easy-to-adjust, clearly marked grind settings. Mills with steel grinding mechanisms were the most effective and durable in our tests. We also appreciate mills with a generous capacity that are made of clear materials that allow you to track when they need a refill.

Test Kitchen Top Pick
Cole & Mason Derwent Gourmet Precision Pepper Mill, $40.00

Can Opener

Ezra J. Warner patented the first U.S. can opener in Connecticut in 1858, made from a bayonet and a sickle lashed together. At the time, most cans were about ³⁄₁₆ inch thick and were typically opened with a hammer and chisel. Luckily for modern cooks, technology has improved.

What to Look For
A safety-style opener that cuts into the side of the can rather than the top leaves dull edges and saves fingers. Openers with blades on the side rather than underneath the head of the opener make it easier to align with the can. Straight, oval, textured handles are the simplest and smoothest to operate. The rotating handle is similarly easiest to use when it's longer for better leverage and easier turning, with ergonomic grooves that securely brace the user's thumbs. Look for a model that incorporates a lid disposal device, such as blades and gears that automatically clamp onto the lid and remove it when it is completely severed.

Fissler Magic Smooth-Edge Can Opener, $29.00

Manual Citrus Juicer

While you can juice citrus without a tool (or with something you already have around the house, like a fork), it's more efficient and effective to use a juicer. Unless you're juicing dozens of oranges every day, you probably only need a manual juicer, not an electric model.

What to Look For
A good juicer should extract maximum juice from a piece of citrus with minimum mess. It shouldn't hurt your hands—or your budget. We prefer a squeeze-style juice presser. Look for one with curved handles and a well-shaped plunger that will extract as much juice as possible. Make sure that the drainage holes are small enough to keep seeds from leaking out with the juice.

Chef'n FreshForce Citrus Juicer, $23.04

Garlic Press

Over the years, we've learned that for the average home cook, using a garlic press is faster and easier than trying to get a fine, even mince with a chef's knife. Even our test cooks, trained to mince with a knife, generally grab a garlic press when cooking. And here's the best part: With a good garlic press, you don't even have to stop and peel the cloves.

What to Look For
The most important attribute of a garlic press is the ability to produce a fine and uniform garlic consistency. It should be solidly built, with no contest between the press and the garlic about which is going to break first. It should be able to hold more than one clove and should crush the garlic completely through the sieve, leaving little behind in the hopper. It should handle unpeeled cloves with ease. Finally, it should be simple to clean, by hand or dishwasher, and not require a toothpick to get the last pieces of garlic out.

Kuhn Rikon Stainless Steel Epicurean Garlic Press, $39.95

Vegetable Peeler

A good peeler should be fast and smooth, shaving off just enough of the skin to avoid the need for repeat trips over the same section but not so much that the blade digs deeply into the flesh and wastes food. Whatever the task, the peeler should handle bumps and curves with ease and without clogging or losing its edge. And when the work is done, your hand shouldn't feel worse for the wear.

What to Look For
Stainless or carbon steel blades are better than ceramic blades. Both "straight" and "Y" peelers can be highly effective. Ideally, the gap between the blade and handle should measure about an inch at its highest point; any narrower and the peels get stuck in the opening. Look for a peeler with a raised ridge along its front "guide" blade, which helps the peeling blade glide smoothly.

Kuhn Rikon Original Swiss Peeler, $3.50

Colander

A colander is simply a perforated bowl designed to allow liquid to drain through the holes, but for all that simplicity, there are actually lots of ways one can fail, ruining a perfectly good pasta dinner.

What to Look For
Avoid collapsible colanders. The tendency of these "innovative" models to come unclipped or tip over cancels out their flat storage appeal. Pick a colander with small all-over perforations that are evenly distributed around the bowl. Make sure your colander has feet or a base that give it at least 1 inch of clearance above the sink floor to avoid any backwash of drained liquid (and whatever grunge may have escaped your last sink scrubbing). But make sure that the base won't interfere with the colander's ability to rest over a bowl. Look for a colander that's dishwasher safe to make cleaning easier.

Test Kitchen Top Pick
RSVP International Endurance Precision Pierced 5 Qt. Colander, $25.99

Salad Spinner

All salad spinners share a basic design: a perforated basket that balances on a point in the center of a larger bowl. The lid houses a mechanism that grabs the basket and makes it spin. Centrifugal force created by the spinning basket propels the contents of the spinner away from the center; greens are trapped while water passes through the perforations and collects in the outer bowl.

What to Look For
Choose a spinner with a large round basket. The round design is sturdier than a conical shape and less likely to wobble during use. We prefer spinners with a pump mechanism for simplicity and ease of use. A white or clear basket makes it easier to spot trapped greens when washing up the spinner. Flat lids that come apart also make cleanup a lot easier.

Test Kitchen Top Pick
OXO Good Grips Salad Spinner, $29.99

Rasp Grater

The razor-sharp teeth of a handheld rasp grater can finely grate ingredients like Parmesan, shallots, garlic, ginger, nutmeg, chocolate, and citrus zest in a flash.

What to Look For
Sharp teeth are the most important element— a good rasp grater should require little to no effort or pressure when grating. Pick a rasp grater that also has a solid, comfortable handle.

Test Kitchen Top Pick
Microplane Classic Zester Grater, $12.35

Grater

A grater is the go-to tool for shredding cheese and vegetables by hand.

What to Look For
Unless you know that you'll use all the different functions on a traditional box grater, we think that a paddle grater with just one set of holes in the most common size (extra-large, for a coarse grate) is a more useful tool. Shredded food is less likely to get caught in these simple designs. A sturdy, inflexible grater with bent, rubber-bottomed legs stays put at any angle and securely hooks around the edges of bowls for sturdier, neater shredding.

Test Kitchen Top Pick
Rösle Coarse Grater, $35.95

To find a pepper mill that could swiftly crank out the desired size and amount of fresh ground pepper, without any guesswork in grind selection or extra strain on our wrists, we rounded up both manual and battery-powered options, priced from $27 to nearly $100, and got grinding. To get a handle on grind speed and ease of operation, we first tested each mill by fine-grinding peppercorns over a digital scale and timing how long it took for each model to produce the equivalent of 2 tablespoons, or 15.3 grams. Speeds ranged from just longer than 1½ minutes to a whopping 14 minutes. The surprise here was that the bigger mills, with the capacity to grind more peppercorns at one time, were not always the fastest. We realized that part of the success of smaller models was due to their handles. Instead of twisting at the top, these mills use crank handles that rotate in a wide arc, grinding continuously as well as offering greater leverage with each turn for faster grinding.

Crank handles may be the most efficient, but comfort is important, too. Heavy, awkward models slowed testers down; models that took extra work to grasp, like one "key-top" design mill, had testers constantly repositioning their hands. Mills with smooth, padded handles or rounded tops that fit users' hands aided, rather than hampered, grinding. And while battery-driven mills sound enticing, they turned out to be nonstarters. One, which cost an astounding $99.95, had us prying apart a complicated mechanism at the base to insert six AAA batteries. The other was the mill that took a painful 14 minutes to grind 2 tablespoons of pepper.

If quick output were everything, it would be easy to sort winners from losers. But we often want a different-size grind of pepper depending on the dish, and changing the grind size on many of the mills caused trouble. Some relied on a small adjustable screw at the bottom of the grinder that frequently had us resorting to pliers to loosen it. Mills with a finial at the top controlling adjustment meant that every time we filled the hopper with peppercorns we had to recalibrate the grind size as well. Our favorite mills removed the trial and error of grind selection with clear markings that shifted neatly into place. The final consideration for a pepper mill is grind quality. Getting a mix of fine powder and coarse chunks doesn't help in recipes when you want one or the other. Only two of the models in our lineup consistently produced just the right grind size in every setting, while the rest spat out a mix of dust and cracked

METHODOLOGY

We tested 10 pepper mills with steel or ceramic grind mechanisms, both manual and battery-driven, and evaluated them on the criteria below. Items appear in The Testing Lineup in order of preference.

Grind Quality
We ground 1 tablespoon of fine pepper with each mill and shook it through a fine-mesh sieve for 30 seconds; we then weighed what was too coarse to pass through the sieve. For coarse-grind consistency, we ground 1 tablespoon of coarse pepper with each mill, shook it through a fine-mesh sieve for 30 seconds, and weighed what was too fine to remain in the sieve. For the grinds in between, we visually assessed the ground pepper, comparing it with both coarse and fine.

Ease of Use
We rated each mill on how easy it was to fill with peppercorns, adjust to different grind settings, and hold and operate for right- and left-handed users with different hand sizes.

Fine-Grind Speed
We timed how long it took for each mill to grind 15.3 grams (2 tablespoons) of fine pepper.

peppercorns. When we took the mills apart, we began to understand why.

All pepper mills work more or less the same way: A grooved and serrated rotating nut, which is attached to a metal shaft, fits into a stationary, serrated ring. As the nut rotates, its grooved channels lead peppercorns toward the serrations on both the ring and the nut, first cracking and then slicing the peppercorns between them. When you turn the adjustment knob, a spring at the center presses the nut and the ring together to change the grind size: tighter for fine, looser for coarse. But in some mills, the spring lacked the ability to fully compress its ring and nut, impeding their ability to deliver a truly fine grind. In other models, the ring and nut were set so far apart in the coarse grind setting that they frequently spat out whole, uncracked peppercorns. The successful models had well-proportioned springs that allowed the ring and nut to be cranked to just the right distance apart. Looking inside also provided a

clue as to why two mills in particular lagged far behind the others in speed: the material of their nuts and rings. While the most efficient models in our lineup used steel mechanisms, the nuts and rings of these poky models were made of ceramic. Because ceramic is more brittle than steel—and more prone to breaking—their grooves and serrations weren't as deep or sharp. As a result, these mills took far longer to grind.

The carbon-steel grind mechanism in our winning model features seven large grooves on the nut (most have only five) that taper into finer grooves at the base. These allow it to swiftly channel peppercorns toward the deep, sharp serrations on its ring, for fast, efficient grinding. Its spring provides just the right tension to bring the nut and the ring the appropriate distance together (or apart) to create a uniform grind in each of its six fixed, clearly marked grind sizes. We also appreciated its clear acrylic body, which allows you to track when you need a refill.

A GREAT SET OF GEARS

All pepper mills operate the same way: A nut revolves inside a stationary ring, crushing peppercorns between them. But fine differences in the design of our winning mill, the Derwent from Cole & Mason, made a big difference in its performance.

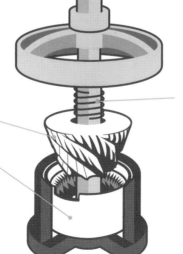

Carbon steel construction allows for deep, sharp serrations in both the nut and the ring that swiftly slice and shear the peppercorns.

Lots of grooves in the **nut** quickly guide peppercorns toward the **ring**.

A well-proportioned spring brings the nut and the ring just the right distance apart to create the target grind size.

BAKEWARE

Glass Baking Dish

While a metal baking pan is ideal for many recipes, glass dishes are a must for certain jobs; glass won't react with acidic foods such as tomatoes and is safe for use with sharp knives and metal utensils. Its transparency also lets you track browning on the bottom and sides of dishes as they bake to avoid burning.

What to Look For

Sturdy tempered Pyrex is our first choice. Pick a dish that's dishwasher-safe, has wide, solid handles, and is scratch-resistant. Rounded corners make it easy to scoop out soupy desserts and casseroles.

Test Kitchen Top Pick
Pyrex Bakeware
9 x 13-Inch
Baking Dish,
$9.09

Metal Baking Pan

We can't think of a piece of bakeware that's more basic than the 13 by 9-inch metal baking pan, but we also can't think of one that's more essential. We pull ours out for everything from sheet cakes and sticky buns to cornbread and bar cookies.

What to Look For

Pick a pan with sharp, 90-degree corners (rather than sloped or curved). You want a pan with a surface color that falls somewhere in between dark and light for perfect browning. A nonstick coating is key for any recipe for which you might need to invert the pan to release the food once baked, such as an upside-down cake or sticky buns. Nonstick pans are also easier to clean.

Test Kitchen Top Pick
Williams-Sonoma
Goldtouch
Nonstick
Rectangular Cake
Pan, 9" x 13", $32.95

Square Baking Pan

A 13 by 9-inch pan is the best all-around option for a variety of recipes, but 8-inch and 9-inch square pans are good to have on hand for smaller batches.

What to Look For

Pick a pan with sharp, 90-degree corners (rather than sloped or curved). Straight sides also make it easier to cut symmetrical pieces and split cakes and breads into two even layers. We prefer a pan with a surface color that falls somewhere in between dark and light. Pans with a nonstick coating are easier to remove sticky foods from and simpler to clean.

Test Kitchen Top Pick
Williams-Sonoma
Goldtouch Nonstick
Square Cake Pan, 8",
$21.00

Round Cake Pan

We use our cake pans to bake not only cakes, but deep-dish pizza, too. And we've also encountered a few hidden uses, like using them as a shallow dish when rolling cookies in sugar, or for small baking tasks like toasting a few nuts in the oven.

What to Look For

It's best to have two sets of cake pans, preferably two 8-inch pans and two 9-inch pans. Look for pans with high, straight sides. In general, we prefer aluminum or tinned-steel pans, ideally with a nonstick coating. Light-colored pans are better for cakes; for deeper browning, choose a darker finish.

Test Kitchen Top Picks
Nordic Ware Naturals
Nonstick 9-Inch Round
Cake Pan, $14.32
(Best All-Around)
Chicago Metallic Non-Stick
9" Round Cake Pan, $10.97
(Best for Browning)

Pie Plate

The angled sides, wide rim, and shallow bowl of a pie plate are necessary for perfect pies and quiches.

What to Look For

We have found that neither ceramic nor metal pie plates turn out evenly browned crusts as reliably as trusty, inexpensive Pyrex. Clear glass is also useful for monitoring the progress of a crust as it browns, and because glass is nonreactive, you can store a pie filled with acidic fruit in a Pyrex dish and not worry about the dish giving the fruit an off-flavor. Pyrex pie plates are also scratch-resistant so you can cut and serve right from the dish. A wide lip is essential; it makes the plate easier to move in and out of the oven, and pretty pies with a decorated or fluted edge need a roomy lip around the pie plate for support. Also, when the crust edge rests on the pie plate lip, it helps prevent it from slipping down during baking.

Test Kitchen Top Pick
Pyrex Bakeware 9 Inch Pie Plate, $8.16

Loaf Pan

A good loaf pan will evenly brown quick breads, such as banana bread, as well as yeast breads.

What to Look For

Light-colored aluminum finishes yield pale, anemic-looking baked goods. On the other hand, dark surfaces actually brown bread and pound cake a shade too much. We prefer a pan with a finish somewhere between dark and light. A nonstick coating also makes the release of baked breads especially easy. We prefer pans that are 8½ by 4½ inches for loaves with tall, round tops. Many recipes yield two loaves, so it's good to have at least two pans.

Test Kitchen Top Pick
Williams-Sonoma Goldtouch Nonstick Loaf Pan, $21.00

Muffin Tin

Bad muffin tins are a nuisance. They can warp, rust, or cause sticking, tearing your baked goods to shreds. If there is nowhere for your oven mitt to hold on to, it will get gummed up with batter or dent your fresh-baked cupcakes. And have fun scrubbing out each one of those little cups afterward.

What to Look For

The two must-have features in a muffin tin are a nonstick coating and handles—or at least extended rims—for easy gripping. Darker coated metals, which absorb heat, do the best job of browning, producing muffins and cupcakes that not only come out the perfect shade of golden brown but also rise higher and sport more nicely domed tops.

Test Kitchen Top Pick
Anolon Advanced Bakeware 12-Cup Muffin Pan, $24.99

Bundt Pan

This pan, modeled on a classic German pan called the *kugelhopf*, ushered in a revolution in home baking. This decorative pan produces a cake that looks impressive; all it needs is a dusting of confectioners' sugar or drizzle with a simple glaze and the cake is ready to serve.

What to Look For

Make sure that your Bundt pan is heavy and nonstick. The nooks and crannies mean that sticking is a threat with this pan, even more so if it is lightweight. Look for defined ridges. A pan that has clearly defined ridges will deliver a cake that not only has neat lines but is also less likely to stick. Handles are helpful, given the pan's weight and somewhat awkward shape. A 12- or 15-cup capacity is fine.

Test Kitchen Top Pick
Nordic Ware Platinum Collection Anniversary Bundt Pan, $26.95

Rolling Pin

A good rolling pin should spread finicky, delicate dough easily and smoothly, without sticking or tearing, as well as be up to tackling sticky cookie doughs and springy pizza dough.

What to Look For

We prefer the classic French-style handle-free wood rolling pins; they easily turn and pivot and allow you to feel the thickness of the dough and apply pressure as needed—plus, they're economical to boot. Look for a pin that measures about 20 inches long, a suitable length for any task. A slightly rough texture to the wood of the pin will help move dough without slipping or sticking.

Test Kitchen Top Pick
J.K. Adams Plain Maple
Rolling Dowel,
$13.95

Mixing Bowls

We reach for our mixing bowls any time we mix up pancake batter or vinaigrette, or when simply melting butter.
See page 35 for Inside the Testing.

What to Look For

You want to have a variety of sizes—at the very least, small (1- to 1½-quart), medium (2½- to 3-quart), and large (4- to 6-quart). You should have two sets: stainless steel and glass. Lighter metal bowls are convenient most of the time, but glass is necessary for use in the microwave. We don't recommend plastic or ceramic bowls. Gently curving sides make it easier to reach into the bowls to stir. A rim on the bowls will also make them easier to hold. Make sure that the bowls are heat-safe so they can be used as part of a double boiler.

Test Kitchen Top Picks
Vollrath Economy
Stainless Steel
Mixing Bowls, $2.90
(1½ qt), $4.50 (3 qt),
$6.90 (5 qt) (Metal)
Pyrex Smart Essentials Mixing Bowl Set with Colored Lids, $27.98 for a 4-bowl set (Glass)

Oven Mitt

Above all, a good oven mitt must be functional, offering protection from burns (obviously), but also letting the cook easily maneuver everything from a baking sheet to a heavy casserole dish to the handle of a hot skillet.

What to Look For

While it may seem like a thicker mitt would be the best way to protect your hand, oversize, overpadded mitts end up making it hard to get a good grip, which quickly becomes unsafe when you're trying to position hot, heavy dishes. Thinner, more form-fitting styles are easier to maneuver. Look for mitts made of especially heat-resistant materials such as silicone or specialty fabrics. Make sure your mitt is machine-washable.

Test Kitchen Top Pick
Kool-Tek 15-Inch Oven
Mitt by KatchAll, $44.95

Cooling Rack

You can cool cookies, cakes, and bread on a wire rack, but we also set these racks inside a rimmed baking sheet for roasting meats and poultry.

What to Look For

A woven grid is best to support both delicate and heavy foods. Don't buy a rack with bars that run in just one direction. Bigger is also better—buy racks that fit snugly inside a standard 18 by 13-inch rimmed baking sheet. Dishwasher-safe is a plus, since cleaning the crannies of a wire rack is a pain.

Test Kitchen
Top Pick
CIA Bakeware
12-Inch x 17-Inch
Cooling Rack, $15.95

They may not be as sexy as chef's knives or as cutting-edge as sous vide circulators, but when it comes to basic cooking tasks, plain old mixing bowls can't be beat. A good bowl should be so steady, durable, and comfortable to handle that it goes almost unnoticed while you work. For those reasons, we shop carefully when outfitting the test kitchen with mixing bowls. Our criteria start with size: At the very least, we need small, medium, and large bowls—by which we mean 1- to 1½-quart; 2½- to 3-quart; and 4- to 6-quart bowls, respectively. We also find it useful to have a set in both stainless steel and glass: The lightness of metal makes it easy to use, but only glass can go in the microwave. Plastic and ceramic bowls just aren't practical: The former's porous surface scratches and retains oils, while the latter is so heavy that it's a detriment.

To single out a set of each, we scooped up three stainless-steel sets and four sets made of tempered glass (glass that has undergone a mechanical strengthening process to increase its impact and thermal resistance), all priced from $14.30 to $59.99. We bought nesting sets when possible and cobbled together a custom set if the sizes we wanted were available only as open stock. We then subjected the bowls to the core tasks that we think any mixing bowl should be able to handle. In each of the small bowls, we whisked oil into vinegar to make dressing. In the medium and large bowls we mixed up muffin and pancake batters. We also used the large bowls to mix bread dough and the medium bowls to melt chocolate in a makeshift double boiler, with the bowl set over a saucepan of simmering water.

Not all of the bowls excelled at these basic functions. Some models even made easy work annoyingly difficult, thanks to a variety of design defects. Take bowl height. A vessel's walls should neatly contain the food but be shallow enough that users—particularly shorter folks—can still easily access the food. A side-by-side comparison of the 5-quart bowls from two different makers illustrated this point: Standing nearly 5 inches tall, one model forced some testers to reach farther up and over its rim than felt comfortable, while the other, which was shorter by almost an inch, allowed easy access to the bowl's contents.

Not only did some makers get the height right, they also got the shape of the walls right. In relation to their bases, these bowls' sides curved gently, which made it comfortable for testers to not only reach into the bowls to stir but also to hold the bowls aloft to pour and scrape ingredients out of them. Conversely, testers had to tilt bowls with steeper walls more dramatically if they wanted to scrape out every last bit of food, and once a bowl was nearly upside-down, it was awkward to maneuver a spatula around the inside. That's why some shorter testers found the relatively tall and narrow bowl set by one manufacturer challenging to access, although, since those bowls

Inside the Testing continued on next page

The Testing Lineup

Stainless Steel

Highly Recommended
VOLLRATH
Economy Stainless Steel Mixing Bowls
Top Pick
$2.90 (1½ qt),
$4.50 (3 qt),
$6.90 (5 qt)

Recommended
CUISINART
Set of 3 Stainless Steel Mixing Bowls with Lids
$29.99

Not Recommended
OXO
Good Grips Stainless Steel Mixing Bowl Set
$59.99

Continued on next page

METHODOLOGY
We tested seven sets of mixing bowls, available in existing sets or from open stock; we singled out sizes closest to 1 to 1½ quarts, 2½ to 3 quarts, and 4 to 6 quarts. All the bowls we tested are dishwasher-safe and all glass bowls are microwave-safe. Items appear in The Testing Lineup in order of preference.

Performance
We used the bowls to prepare vinaigrette, muffin and pancake batters, and bread dough and also in jury-rigged double boilers. Bowls rated highly if they were sturdy and minimized splashes and spills.

Ease of Use
We rated each set of bowls on how easy and comfortable they were to handle, averaging the impressions of testers of varying heights, strengths, and skills.

Durability
We ran all sets through the dishwasher 15 times before inspecting them for clouding, chipping, and dents. We also bumped the bowls against Dutch ovens, dropped them from 18 inches onto the counter, and pushed them off the counter onto the floor, noting any cracks or breaks. We docked points from models that weren't safe for double boilers.

were made of lightweight stainless steel, their shape was still manageable. The same couldn't be said for one set of glass bowls, a brutally heavy fleet with L-shaped walls and sharp corners that were hard to scrape clean. Testers observed that they looked more like storage containers than mixing bowls.

Whether a bowl had a rim also affected how comfortable—or not—it was to hold. The rimmed models, which included all the stainless-steel bowls as well as a glass set, offered roughly ¼ to ½ inch of grippable material. The alternative, the thickened collar that ringed the other glass bowls, was better than nothing, but not much. Grasping the 4-quart bowl by one maker, which weighed more than 3½ pounds empty, by its collar took some serious muscle. Its only perk: Its collar sloped smoothly down the inside of the bowl, whereas those on two other bowls stuck out, trapping food in the crevices.

As for countertop stability, we used the vinaigrette test to determine how far each bowl moved as we vigorously whisked oil into the dressing. To our surprise, there were no clear advantages or disadvantages to using heavier glass or lighter-weight metal, nor to using bowls with broader or narrower base diameters. In fact, the bowl that traveled the farthest was the heaviest and the broadest at its base. The only model that flat-out flunked the stability test was, ironically, from a maker touting stability as its supposed selling point. Its rubber-coated base was its downfall: Instead of keeping the bowl stable, the coating clung to the counter and caused the bowl to twirl to the point of tipping over. (The final blow to that set: The manufacturer of these bowls cautioned against using its bowl as part of a double boiler, since its exterior plastic coating could overheat.) In durability tests, one glass bowl cracked and another shattered, but all stainless bowls emerged unscathed.

Fortunately, the best models in both categories were also reasonably priced. Our winning three-bowl, stainless-steel set will set you back just $14.30, and our winning set of four glass bowls (and lids) is as functional as it is affordable.

A CASE FOR BOTH METAL AND GLASS

Our winning metal and glass bowls, from Vollrath and Pyrex, respectively, share traits that make them sturdy and easy to handle, but each material also offers benefits of its own.

STAINLESS STEEL
Because lightweight stainless steel is so easy to handle and won't break, it's a default choice for most mixing tasks—particularly those for which a large bowl is needed, since metal will never get very heavy. Metal also conducts heat faster than glass, making it the better choice for a jury-rigged double boiler.

GLASS
Tempered glass is a must for the microwave. Its transparency also lets you check for pockets of unmixed ingredients. Good glass bowls can be surprisingly durable; our winners from Pyrex resisted chipping when knocked against a Dutch oven and even survived an 18-inch drop onto the counter.

APPLIANCES

Food Processor

A food processor is great for prepping everything you probably don't like to do by hand: chopping messy things such as canned tomatoes, grinding delicate foods like fresh bread, slicing vegetables, and shredding cheese without straining a muscle.

What to Look For

Less-expensive food processors (under $150 or so) just aren't worth the money; they can't perform even basic tasks very well. The better pricier models have motors with more weight, run quieter, and don't slow down under a heavy load. Blades should be sharp and sturdy. If the blades aren't sharp, they will mangle the food rather than cut it. The feed tube should be large enough to fit potatoes, hunks of cheese, and other big foods, but not so big that unnecessary safety features are required.

Test Kitchen Top Pick
Cuisinart Custom 14-Cup Food Processor, $199.99

Stand Mixer

If you are a serious cook or baker, a stand mixer is simply something you need. If you bake only occasionally, a handheld mixer is fine. **See page 38 for Inside the Testing.**

What to Look For

Look for a mixer with a stationary bowl and a single mixing arm that uses planetary action. A slightly squat bowl that holds at least 4½ quarts is ideal. If the bowl is too large, small batches of batter won't get mixed properly. Operation should be intuitive and construction should be solid.

Test Kitchen Top Picks
KitchenAid Pro Line Series 7-Qt Bowl Lift Stand Mixer, $549.95
Best Buy
KitchenAid Classic Plus Series 4.5-Quart Tilt-Head Stand Mixer, $199.99

Handheld Mixer

The handheld mixer's light weight and ease of use make it an essential tool for anyone who wants to bake, even if only occasionally. It's great for most baking tasks, like whipping cream or egg whites, creaming butter and sugar, or making a cake batter; the only thing it can't handle is kneading dough, especially wet or heavy bread doughs. It's also easy to store (compared with a stand mixer).

What to Look For

Look for a lightweight mixer. You want one that is comfortable to hold and easy to maneuver around a work bowl. Also, an angled handle helps because it allows you to relax your elbow at your side when mixing. We prefer simple, slim beaters to traditional beaters with flat metal strips around a center post, since the post tends to be a good spot for batter to collect.

Test Kitchen Top Pick
KitchenAid 5-Speed Ultra Power Hand Mixer, $69.99
Best Buy
Cuisinart PowerSelect 3-Speed Hand Mixer, $26.77

Blender

A blender is the only tool that can blend all manner of liquid-y foods (whether hot or cold) to a smooth texture. Blenders are great for making smoothies, milkshakes, and frozen drinks as well as for pureeing soups and sauces.

What to Look For

A tapered jar funnels the liquid down around the spinning blades for the smoothest possible texture. (And don't be impressed with any advertised "extra" blades, especially if the jar isn't tapered.) Heavy plastic or glass beats thin plastic. Cheap plastic jars are prone to scratching and retaining color and odor over years of use. Wattage doesn't matter, but pulse does. High speed, at which nearly all blending takes place, is essentially the same in all blenders. The pulse feature, however, is useful; it gets food moving and breaks it down.

Test Kitchen Top Pick
Vitamix 5200, $449.00
Best Buy
Breville The Hemisphere Control, $199.99

Kneading wet, heavy bread dough by hand is hard work. So is mixing together thick cookie dough. Thus, when KitchenAid debuted the first stand mixer designed for home cooks in 1919, it caused a big stir. For households that invested in one of these machines—and at $189 a pop, the equivalent of about $2,551 today, they were an investment—one of the most tasking elements of making breads and baked goods was gone with the flip of a switch.

As their relative cost has dropped considerably over the years, the appeal of stand mixers has only grown, and these days the appliance is a fixture in many kitchens. But deciding which one to buy has never been more complicated. KitchenAid still makes the majority of stand mixers, but other manufacturers now offer small commercial-grade machines that promise to knead, whip, and mix with even more ease and efficiency. Improvements range from bigger bowl capacities and more horse-power to timers with automatic shutoff and easy-to-use splash guards.

Given the dizzying range of features and still-considerable cost of stand mixers, we shop carefully—and test exhaustively—before we commit. We ordered nine models, priced from nearly $200 to a jaw-dropping $849, to find out.

All but one of the stand mixers came with three standard attachments: a whisk for whipping cream and egg whites, a paddle for creaming and incorporating cake and cookie ingredients, and a dough hook for kneading bread and pizza dough. Every manufacturer designed its parts a little differently, but as we put each model through a battery of tests, we noticed that the relationship between the attachment and the bowl usually mattered more than the design of the attachment itself.

Consider whipping a pair of egg whites. This test, which involves only a small quantity of liquid, made it obvious which bowls and attachments had been carefully designed together for maximum contact between the whisk and the food and which hadn't. The best combination came from one manufacturer: Its 7-quart model features a wide, shallow bowl that raised the whites relatively close to the attachment and a 22-tine whisk, the outer layer of which featured elbow-bent tines that almost grazed the walls when the whisk circled the bowl. Conversely, whipping was a struggle for other machines because their bowls and whisks didn't align closely enough for the whisk to engage all the whites. As a result, these

METHODOLOGY

We tested nine stand mixers from leading brands, focusing on the key tasks of whipping, creaming, and kneading and also rating them on design and ease of use. Items appear in The Testing Lineup in order of preference.

Whipping
We whipped average and very small amounts of ingredients, including two egg whites, four egg whites plus hot sugar syrup for meringue, and 1 and 2 cups of heavy cream. High marks went to machines that quickly and easily handled all quantities and tasks.

Kneading
We preferred mixers that could handle both single and double batches of glossy, elastic pizza dough and also knead stiff, heavy bagel dough into a smooth, cohesive mass without jamming or struggling. Mixers that failed at these jobs were downgraded significantly.

Ease of Use
The best mixers were intuitive to set up, use, and clean.

Design
We evaluated the weight, shape, controls, and operation of each mixer and its parts, including the whisk, mixing paddle, dough hook, and splash guard (when included). We also assessed the usable capacity of each model by measuring how much water we needed to pour into the bowl to reach the top of each mixing attachment, and we compared those results with the stated capacity.

Creaming
The best mixers quickly and thoroughly creamed butter and sugar for sugar cookie dough and reverse-creamed yellow cake batter, and required minimal scraping of the bowl or paddle.

machines took longer to whip small quantities and in some cases left an untouched pool of liquid beneath the cloud of silky peaks.

The same principle of bowl-to-attachment proximity applied when we used the paddles to cream together butter and sugar. In most cases, the lateral reach of these flat beaters wasn't enough to grab food that had clung to the sides of the bowl, forcing us to regularly scrape down the unincorporated portions of the batter and remix. Only one mixer came with a beater that specifically addressed this problem: an extra "scraper" paddle with silicone extensions that continually swiped the sides of the bowl. As a result, it reduced the need to scrape, shaving minutes off mixing times

Attachment issues followed a couple of the 7-quart mixers into kneading tests, too. Their dough hooks made limited or no contact at all with the ingredients when we added enough for a single batch of pizza dough but capably mixed the ingredients when we added twice as much flour and water for double batches. However, the shape of the bowl and the dough hook were secondary factors when it came to kneading; heavyweight tasks like kneading are more affected by the machinery itself than by the attachments.

During kneading, dough develops more gluten and becomes stiffer; the stiffer it gets the more it pushes back against the machine and increases the "load" on the motor. If a machine has enough power, it can keep moving and mixing at its set speed despite that load; if it doesn't, the mixer will slow, which causes the motor to heat up and potentially burn out.

So what makes a stand mixer powerful? Initially, we thought it boiled down to horsepower—that is, the force that the mixer exerts. But that wasn't the whole story: Several

Inside the Testing continued on next page

The Testing Lineup, CONTINUED

Not Recommended
VOLLRATH
7-Quart Countertop Commercial Mixer
$849.00

CUISINART
7.0 Quart 12-Speed Stand Mixer
$449.90

BOSCH
Universal Plus Mixer
$399.99

BREVILLE
Scraper Mixer Pro
$280.95

A STAND(OUT) MIXER

Here's why we think the pricey **KitchenAid Pro Line Series 7-Qt Bowl Lift Stand Mixer** ($549.95) is worth shelling out for.

Powerful Engine
Plenty of torque made this the only mixer that kneaded double batches of pizza dough and bagel dough without flinching.

Heavyweight Build
At 27 pounds, this mixer's die-cast frame stays anchored to the counter.

Perfect Paddle
Open Y-shaped branches mixed ingredients without trapping them in tight crevices.

Wide-Armed Whip
The bent tines making up the outer layer of this whisk enable them to reach food near the bowl's sides and bottom.

Crank It Up
Bowl lift models allow you to access the bowl by cranking it up and down rather than tilting the mixer's entire head up and down—a perk if your mixer lives under low cabinets.

Broad Bowl, Big Handle
A wide, shallow bowl keeps contents within easy reach of attachments. Its long vertical handle provides plenty of leverage and control for pouring.

Splash On, Splash Off
Unlike most splash guards, this C-shaped one slides on just as easily as it slips off for instant access to the bowl.

machines with relatively high horsepower performed either inconsistently or markedly worse than mixers with less than half as much oomph. We later learned that a mixer's power depends on a combination of factors—horsepower, yes, but also the machine's torque, or rotational force, which provides leverage: The more torque a machine has the more effectively it will not only push on dough but also rotate it in the bowl. "Abundant torque availability allows [the mixer's] speed to be held constant over a wide load range, while the beater of an underpowered mixer will lose speed as ingredients are added or dough stiffens, resulting in inconsistent mixing batch to batch," explained Michael Borgen, lead mechanical engineer at Metis Design Corporation in Boston, Massachusetts.

We were surprised by the performance of a seemingly low-powered machine, KitchenAid's smallest and cheapest model, the Classic Plus. This mixer outperformed almost every challenger, producing billowy egg whites as capably as it did a double batch of pizza dough.

In fact, its only real competition was its sibling, the KitchenAid Pro Line, a machine with more than three times as much horsepower, nearly twice the capacity, and a much heftier price tag. The only time the inexpensive model faltered was in an abuse test: a KitchenAid versus KitchenAid showdown to see which could mix 10 batches of bagel dough and 10 batches of pizza dough (with 30-minute rests between batches) without flinching. After finishing the pizza dough, it was only on the sixth batch of bagels that the latch locking down the tilt head on the Classic Plus stopped working—a result that indicated more about the potential disadvantage of tilt-head mixers than it did about this machine's motor, which, by the way, carried on just fine if we held the mixer's head in place.

Besides a bowl-lift rather than a tilt-head design, we had a few wish list items for the Classic Plus machine: a bowl handle, preferably a vertical one to help us control the weight of the vessel and keep our other hand free for scraping, and a splash guard that could slip on and off easily. An easy-to-set timer with automatic shutoff is also nice. (Notably, a larger bowl capacity is not something we missed, as evidenced by its strong performance with a double batch of pizza dough. What's more, we measured each mixer bowl's usable capacity— the volume of the space between the top of the attachment and the bottom of the bowl—and discovered that no model actually made use of its bowl's total volume; some used barely more than half. Bottom line: A stand mixer's stated capacity may not only be misleading but it also may not be a good indication of the machine's ability to handle large loads.)

Thanks to its power, heft (at 21.5 pounds, it's one of the heaviest mixers we tested), compact size, simple operation, and relatively wallet-friendly price, the Classic Plus earned our Best Buy status. But if you do a lot of heavy-duty baking, you'll want to save up for the Pro Line, a stand mixer whose range of ability and durability make it truly worthy of the investment.

DON'T JUDGE A MIXER BY THE SIZE OF ITS BOWL

Just because a stand mixer comes with a 7-quart bowl doesn't mean that all 7 quarts are available to use. When we measured how much water we needed to pour into each mixer bowl to reach the top of each mixer's attachment and compared that figure—the usable capacity—with the bowl's stated volume, we discovered that there were dramatic discrepancies. In fact, no mixer used its bowl's full volume, and some, like the Cuisinart 5.5 Quart Stand Mixer, used barely more than half.

More important, most larger-volume stand mixers didn't perform better than "smaller-capacity" models. The KitchenAid Classic Plus, the mixer with the smallest stated capacity that we tested (4½ quarts), handled double batches of pizza dough at least as well as mixers with larger stated capacities.

SPEAKS VOLUMES
The usable capacity of the Cuisinart 5.5 Quart Stand Mixer is only 3 quarts.

GRILLING EQUIPMENT

Charcoal Grill

In summer, there's nothing better than cooking outdoors. Grilling and barbecue enthusiasts insist that charcoal grills are the gold standard for outdoor cooking.

What to Look For

Look for a grill that can accommodate a full 6-quart chimney starter's worth of charcoal, that maintains heat levels, and that has well-placed vents that allow you to control the temperature. Side trays, wheels, and ease of storage are also pluses.

Test Kitchen Top Pick
Weber Performer Deluxe Charcoal Grill, $399.00

Best Buy
Weber Original Kettle Premium Charcoal Grill, 22-Inch, $149.00

Gas Grill

Gas grills deliver what 21st-century Americans prize most: ease. Turn on the gas, hit the ignition switch, and voilà—an instant fire of whatever intensity you need for tonight's recipe. **See page 43 for Inside the Testing.**

What To Look For

High BTUs (British Thermal Units—a measure of heat output per hour) are not indicative of a better grill. The real measure of a grill is how well it retains heat (and smoke) and spreads it across the grates. Look for a wide main grate with diffusers between the burners to help it heat evenly, minimal vents to keep heat in, and a cookbox made of thick, heat-retaining materials like cast aluminum and enameled steel. You also want a lid that opens wide to direct smoke away from your face.

Test Kitchen Top Pick
Weber Spirit E-310 Gas Grill, $499.00

Chimney Starter

We wouldn't dream of starting a charcoal fire without a chimney starter, a cylindrical canister that quickly ignites quarts of briquettes without lighter fluid (which can leave residual flavor on grilled food). You place briquettes in the large top chamber of the chimney, which is shaped like a giant metal coffee mug. Then you crumple a sheet of newspaper, place it in the smaller chamber under the coals, and light it. In about 20 minutes, the coals are covered in a fine, gray ash and ready to be poured into the grill.

What to Look For

Look for a chimney that holds 6 quarts, enough for most kettle grills. Make sure that your chimney has small holes in the sides for good air circulation. Sturdy, heat-resistant handles are also important so you can lift and maneuver the chimney safely when it's time to pour out the red-hot coals.

Test Kitchen Top Pick
Weber Rapidfire Chimney Starter, $14.99

Grill Tongs

To the uninitiated, all grill tongs look the same. But small design nuances have a huge impact on how well tongs turn an awkward, floppy rack of ribs on the grill. Tongs are extensions of your hands, and a great pair should work nearly as naturally.

What to Look For

The main difference between kitchen and grill tongs is length: Grill tongs must keep you a comfortable distance from the fire. We found that about 16 inches is best. Any longer, and we had to work to lever heavy foods or contort our arms to stand close enough to work over the grill; shorter, and we risked getting scorched. As with kitchen tongs, look for a pair with slightly concave pincers and wide, shallow scallops around the edges. Soft cushioning on the handles makes gripping easier and keeps them from overheating. Our favorite grill tongs are simply a longer version of our favorite kitchen tongs.

Test Kitchen Top Pick
OXO Good Grips 16-Inch Locking Tongs, $14.99

Grill Brush

Anyone who has ever grilled sticky barbecued ribs has had to deal with removing the sugary, burnt-on mess that gets left behind. The ideal time to do this is soon after your food comes off the grill, but, if you're like most of us, you close the lid and save the mess for next time. A good brush should make cleaning a gunked-up grate more efficient.

What to Look For

The less complicated the brush the better. Brushes fitted with multiple scrubbing mechanisms usually meant that one was in the way when we tried to employ the other. Our tested method is to preheat the grill to loosen residue before scrubbing, and brushes with short handles got us too close to the heat. However, excessively long handles subtracted scrubbing leverage and often flexed under pressure. We prefer brushes with scrub pads rather than bristles; bristles are more likely to come loose during scrubbing and present a health hazard.

Test Kitchen Top Pick
Grill Wizard 18-Inch China Grill Brush, $31.50

Grill Spatula

Grill spatulas are long-handled turners designed to keep your hands away from the flames while grilling.

What to Look For

Don't just use your normal kitchen spatula on the grill—you really do need a longer handle and larger head to work on the grill. Ideally, the spatula head will be wide enough to support pizzas and broad swordfish steaks but not too large to maneuver between crowded burgers. Spatulas with heads of medium width, roughly 4 inches, offer the best compromise of support and dexterity. Rounded grips without any edges are universally comfortable, and we prefer plastic and wood over metal grips, which get hot if left right next to the body of the grill. An offset handle provides extra clearance between the griller's hand and the grill.

Test Kitchen Top Pick
Weber Original Stainless Steel Spatula, $14.99

Smoker

Though plenty of rib and brisket enthusiasts convert their grills into makeshift smokers, proper lower-temperature smoking is best achieved with a designated appliance. Other than introducing wood to the fire, smoking is all about holding the heat at a low, steady temperature for a long time—a full day, in some cases—a process that bathes the meat in smoke flavor and helps tenderize tough connective tissue.

What to Look For

Find a model with a large fuel capacity (for a longer-burning fire), a water reservoir (to produce moister results), and plenty of vents (to control the air flow and temperature within a smaller, more precise range). Make sure the grate is large enough to fit at least a whole turkey or several racks of ribs. Handles make it easy to transport the smoker.

Test Kitchen Top Pick
Weber Smokey Mountain Cooker Smoker 18", $298.95

Barbecue Basting Brush

When you're trying to brush sauce on chicken or meat that's on a ripping-hot grill, you want to keep your fingers safe. A good barbecue basting brush allows you to both neatly and safely baste your food, even over the highest grilling heat.

What to Look For

Look for a basting brush with a long handle made from a heat-resistant material that is dishwasher-safe. An angled brush head facilitates basting. We prefer silicone brush bristles, which won't melt or singe, to nylon or boar bristles.

Test Kitchen Top Pick
Elizabeth Karmel's Super Silicone Angled Barbecue Brush, $9.16

It's easy to drop several hundred dollars on a gas grill and not get what you need. We've cooked on models that never got hot enough or were too small to cook more than a couple of burgers at once and models that rusted, wobbled, and warped or couldn't handle anything beyond the simplest jobs—never mind roasting a holiday turkey or smoking tender ribs. The bottom line: For the best results, you need a well-designed, responsive, durable grill. We focused on six major brands. The grills in our lineup were outfitted with three to five burners, as well as two wing-like side tables. Half were equipped with a side burner set into one of the wings. All were fitted with warming racks and all featured thermometers built into the lid. You can buy a gas grill fully assembled (usually for a price) or opt to put it together yourself. After trying both, we would strongly encourage you to order your grill assembled. Some stores even do it for free.

Most people choose a gas grill because it's convenient: Turn a knob and you can start cooking in minutes. But whether that grill performs as it should is another matter. For simple grilling, the most important requirement is strong heat that spreads evenly across the grates. To determine which grills met the mark,

we preheated each grill on high heat for 15 minutes (our standard method) and mapped the heat by covering the entire grill surface with white sandwich bread. Top grills gave us evenly browned toast. The worst made an uneven patchwork of black, brown, and white toast. Wrecked toast is no big deal, but when we grilled a quartet of pricey, thick New York strip steaks, the same thing happened. Spreading 4-inch burger patties across the hot grills, we saw those heat patterns a third time.

So what made the difference in how well food cooked? While manufacturers may try to dazzle customers with their burners' high BTUs (British Thermal Units, a measure of heat output per hour), in our tests this number turned out to be less relevant than the grill's construction and heat distribution. All gas grills share a similar construction: At the bottom, perforated metal tubes (the burners) produce a row of flames when the gas is ignited. Above them are metal bars shaped like inverted V's. As we used the grills, we realized that these tent-like bars are very important. First, they shield burners to keep fallen food from clogging holes. Second, when dripping fat hits them,

Inside the Testing continued on next page

METHODOLOGY

We tested six gas grills priced under $500, assessing them on the following criteria. Items appear in The Testing Lineup in order of preference.

Burners
Grills are described by their number of burners, though we found that this did not correlate with performance or capacity.

Grates
Material of the cooking grates.

Size of Main Cooking Grate & Heat Output
Manufacturers typically list the combined total square inches. Heat output is measured in BTUs (British Thermal Units).

Features
Side burners or other extras.

Grilling
We grilled hamburgers and steaks over direct heat and mapped the heat pattern of each grill by covering its preheated surface with bread slices and examining the toast.

Indirect Cooking
We prepared pulled pork, keeping the grill at 300 degrees for more than 4 hours. Thermocouples confirmed whether lid thermometers were accurate.

Design
Grills received higher marks if their designs made it easier to set them up and cook on them.

Durability
Models that were hard to roll; lost parts; or showed greater wear received lower scores.

Cleanup
We rated whether grates were easy to clean and whether grills had secure, large grease trays and catch pans that were easy to reach.

The Testing Line-Up

Highly Recommended
WEBER
Spirit E-310
Gas Grill
Top Pick $499.00

Recommended
CHAR-BROIL
Commercial Series
4-Burner Gas Grill
$499.99

Not Recommended
DYNA-GLO
5-Burner Propane
Gas Grill with
Side Burner and
Rotisserie Burner
$483.65

NEXGRILL
4 Burner Liquid
Propane Gas Grill
$269.00

BROIL KING
Baron 440
$499.00

KITCHENAID
3 Burner Gas
Grill & Side Burner
$469.00

the fat turns into smoke that makes food taste grilled. Third, they help spread heat horizontally across the grill. The flames' heat wants to rise straight up, and without these bars to deflect it there would be distinct hot spots directly over each burner and cooler zones everywhere else.

All of the grills we tested had bars right over each burner, but our top-performing grills had further design tweaks to help spread out the rising heat for more even distribution and much-improved cooking results. One achieved this with extra bars between the burners, while the other featured a full layer of perforated stainless-steel plates beneath the grates, which, like the flavor bars, worked to diffuse heat.

While powerful, even heat is critical in a good grill, so are a few other factors. First up: capacity. While the grills in our lineup featured different numbers of burners, more burners didn't always correspond to more cooking space. The "smallest" grill—the only one with just three burners—held 19 burgers, while one of the four-burner models fit just 15 burgers. As it turned out, the four-burner grill was only 2 inches wider than the three-burner model (they were the same depth), a negligible advantage that was negated by the fact that the four-burner grill's wide warming rack blocked access to the back of its cooking grates.

Grate material also mattered: Our two highest-ranking grills had cast-iron grates, while most of the lower-ranked ones used stainless steel. Cast iron did a better job of transferring heat for crisp, flavorful grill marks. Finally, the angle of the open lid also mattered. Curved, low-angled lids directed smoke right into our faces, even when fully open. Our favorite grills had lids that opened wide to let smoke flow straight up.

Direct cooking is important, but a good gas grill must also excel at cooking with indirect heat. To do this, after preheating the grill, you leave one burner on, turn off the rest, and set the meat over the unlit burners. For our test, we put wood chip packets over each lit burner and set pork butts (each cut into three pieces) over pans of water on the cooler side of each grill, maintaining a temperature of 300 degrees by watching the grills' lid thermometers. All of the roasts should have reached an internal temperature of 200 degrees in 4 hours, yet even after a whopping 7½ hours, some roasts still weren't done. Others yielded tender meat but no smoke flavor. Only one grill rendered the meat both tender and smoky.

We realized that the problem causing this almost-uniformly poor performance lies in the grills' construction and is, in fact, endemic to gas grills. For indirect grill-roasting or barbecuing on charcoal, you push all of the coals to one side of the grill, put the meat on the other side, and then adjust vents to customize heat level and airflow. But all of this control is out of your hands with gas grills. The clamshell-shaped "cookbox" on a gas grill has nonadjustable vents, and all of those vents are in one place: across the back of the box. That means hot air and smoke flow in one direction when the lid is closed: straight out the back of the grill. This didn't cause a problem with our previous winning grill (which has been discontinued). Its burners ran from side to side, so we could send the smoke and heat over the meat by turning on the burner in the front of the grill, putting the wood chips on this burner, and putting the meat directly behind. But the burners in all of the grills for our current testing run from front to back. We're not sure why manufacturers have all gone this route, but it means that the lit burner with the chip packet is always to the side of the meat, and so heat and smoke travel straight back to the vent—bypassing the meat.

Because of this, the integrity of the cookbox—specifically the box material and the number and position of the vents—became essential to success. Lower-performing grills had row after row of vents that perforated the back of their cookboxes (some even lacked full back panels). The boxes themselves were thin, with lids that closed loosely over the grates. This translated to an inability to retain heat. By contrast, our top grill—the only one that gave us smoky, tender meat—has a thick cast-aluminum cookbox and a heavy, double-layered steel lid. The lid seals tightly, and the box has just one narrow vent across the back. This fortified construction and minimal venting forced most of the smoke and heat to stay in the box with the food.

In the end, this grill's competence and versatility, its sturdiness, and its easy cleanup (including the largest, most stable grease tray, which can be lined with a disposable pan) earned it the top spot. The Weber Spirit E-310 ($499.95) is an updated three-burner version of our former winner. This grill is fairly basic, with no side burner (available on model E-320 for about $50 more), but it does the job. For the same price, you may buy a bigger grill with more frills, but you won't get a better one.

KITCHEN STAPLES

Fire Extinguisher

Most home fires start in the kitchen. Keeping a reliable, easy-to-use fire extinguisher on hand is one of the key elements of kitchen and home safety. **See page 47 for Inside the Testing.**

What to Look For
We prefer small, traditional canister models in the smallest size (2½ pounds), which are easiest to handle. Choose an ABC or "multipurpose" device (for combustible material, flammable liquid, and electrical fires) or BC extinguisher (for flammable liquid and electrical fires) that has been tested by Underwriters Laboratory, the respected independent organization that confirms manufacturer performance claims.

Test Kitchen Top Pick
Kidde Kitchen Fire Extinguisher, $18.97

Liquid Dish Soap

As much as we love our dishwashers, when washing delicate china, wooden cutting boards, sharp knives, and pots and pans, we still rely on soap and a sponge, so we need a good dish soap to help us out.

What to Look For
A good dish soap should work well no matter how you wash your dishes. Natural products can be just as effective as petroleum-based soaps; the origin of the surfactants (tadpole-shaped chemicals with water-loving heads and oil-loving tails that encourage water and fat to mix and therefore allow fat to wash away) doesn't determine the strength of the soap. We prefer lightly scented, naturally derived products.

Test Kitchen Top Pick
Mrs. Meyer's Clean Day Liquid Dish Soap, Lavender, $3.99 for 16 ounces

All-Purpose Spray Cleaner

When it's time to clean grease, grime, and food splatters from your kitchen, a spray cleaner is a great solution. We wanted a spray that first and foremost works fast, cleaning thoroughly without leaving a sticky residue or damaging surfaces.

What to Look For
We prefer a natural, green product—these may not contain chemical antibacterials but they can still get your kitchen clean and there's no danger of exposing yourself or your household to toxic ingredients. We also like a product with a light, natural scent.

Test Kitchen Top Pick
Method All-Purpose Natural Surface Cleaner, French Lavender, $3.79 for 28 ounces

Food Storage Bags

Crummy plastic food storage bags leak, rip, and are tricky to seal. We want a strong, leakproof bag that closes securely without a fuss and keeps food fresher longer.

What to Look For
We like gallon-size freezer bags, which are big enough to store all manner of foods and are made of thicker plastic. Thicker plastic can keep food fresh longer than the thinner plastic of regular storage bags, even if the food isn't actually going into the freezer. The zipper should be simple and sturdy, and the plastic should be leakproof. Strong seals are the most important element—if the seal isn't secure, your food is exposed to air and is also in danger of spilling out.

Test Kitchen Top Pick
Ziploc Brand Double Zipper Gallon Freezer Bags with the Smart Zip Seal, $3.99 for 30 bags

Plastic Wrap

Plastic wrap is essential for storing, freezing, and keeping food fresh, but design flaws in the material and packaging can make it a pain to use.

What to Look For

The wrap should be strong, with great cling. It should also be seriously impermeable to air and moisture. Look for wrap made of low-density polyethylene (LDPE) rather than polyvinyl chloride (PVC); while PVC is more clingy, it is not impermeable. We prefer packaging with metal teeth on the top edge, inside the cover, rather than versions with teeth on the exposed bottom of the box. Look for a box that also has a sticky pad on the front to hold the sheet, keeping it from rolling back on itself and getting tangled and crumpled.

Test Kitchen Top Pick
Glad Cling Wrap Clear Plastic, $1.20 per 100 square feet

Heavy-Duty Handled Scrub Brush

It takes a serious cleaning tool to tackle seriously dirty pots and pans. For a tool that puts a premium on comfort, we recommend a handled scrub brush.

What to Look For

Natural bristles have more friction than synthetic bristles, which makes them more effective cleaners. The handle of the brush should be long enough to keep hands well out of hot water but compact enough to give you good leverage for hard scrubbing and comfortable enough to get a good grip on. Ideally the brush should be dishwasher-safe.

Test Kitchen Top Pick
Caldrea Dishwashing Brush, $5.00

Laundry Stain Remover

Bacon sizzles and spits and your favorite shirt gets a grease spot. Frosting a cake, you find chocolate smeared on a sleeve. Food stains are all too commonplace in the kitchen, so you need a reliable laundry stain remover on your side as a weapon against permanent stains.

What to Look For

Look for a product that uses sodium percarbonate, a combination of sodium carbonate and hydrogen peroxide. Activated when dissolved in water, the sodium percarbonate releases oxygen, which bubbles up and helps lift the stain from the fabric, while the hydrogen peroxide, a color-safe bleaching agent, decolorizes the stains. These ingredients are most effective on stains from natural substances, e.g., food-based stains.

Test Kitchen Top Pick
OxiClean Versatile Stain Remover, $8.59 for 3-pound tub

Kitchen Twine

Kitchen twine is indispensable for trussing whole chickens, tying roasts and rolled stuffed meats, and making bundles of herbs for flavoring stews.

What to Look For

Never cook with twines that aren't specifically labeled "kitchen" or "food-safe." We tested cotton and linen kitchen twine as well as two brands of silicone food ties, using them on stuffed 11-inch-long flank steaks for braciole and to truss chickens. When all was said and done, nothing beat cotton twine. It never frayed, singed, split, or broke, and it stayed put when we tied knots. It's inexpensive and efficient.

Test Kitchen Top Pick
Librett Cotton Butcher's Twine, $8.29 for 370 ft

According to the National Fire Protection Association, cooking mishaps are the number-one cause of home fires and home fire injuries. Like most of us, you probably have an extinguisher—somewhere. The trouble is, once a fire starts, you have less than 2 minutes to find it and figure out how to operate it before the smoke turns deadly and your kitchen is at risk for flashover, the point at which surrounding surfaces and objects erupt into flames. Even if you locate your extinguisher in time, do you know how to use it?

The biggest issue with fire extinguishers is that you can't take them out for a practice run. Once you've squeezed the trigger and released the pressurized contents, the device can't be reused. What you need is a fire extinguisher that is not only absolutely reliable and effective at combating common kitchen fires, but so utterly transparent to operate that a fire drill isn't necessary.

To find the fire extinguisher that best met those requirements, we packed up a van with extinguishers, a stack of frying pans, a half-dozen electric hot plates, and piles of cotton dish towels and headed west out of Boston. Our destination: the Worcester Fire Department Training Center and its "burn building." The center serves as a command post during statewide emergencies and a training facility for firefighters throughout central Massachusetts. Under the supervision of Fire Chief Gerard Dio and Captain Kevin Maloney, we planned to start fires and put them out using the residential fire extinguishers we'd brought along. Six of the brands were traditional "ABC" extinguishers that fight the three most common types of fires that can break out in the home: combustible material (A), flammable liquid (B), and electrical (C). We also brought four nontraditional devices: a fire blanket designed to smother flames, two extinguishers in small aerosol cans, and a "designer" canister engineered to look so good you wouldn't need to keep it hidden. All the traditional models were the smallest size, just 2½ pounds. Though canisters go up to 20 pounds, our feeling was that a small, light model would be easiest to handle. (Plus, as Captain Maloney pointed out, a fire big enough to require a super-size extinguisher is best left to the professionals. "There's a very small window of time when a fire is small and contained enough that you have a chance to put it out yourself," he emphasized. "After that, get out of the house and call the fire department.")

Inside the Testing continued on next page

METHODOLOGY

We tested nine fire extinguishers plus one flame-retardant blanket on burning vegetable oil and cotton dish towels, rating them on speed, ease of use, and effectiveness. Firefighters supervised our safety during testing, but all opinions and observations are our own. Items appear in The Testing Lineup in order of preference.

UL Rating
In products that bear the UL mark, ratings have been tested and confirmed by Underwriters Laboratories, an independent product safety and compliance certification firm. "A": for combustible materials such as paper, wood, cardboard, cloth, and most plastics; "B": for flammable liquids such as grease, oil, gasoline, and kerosene; "C": for electrical fires.

Extinguishing Agent
Principal type of dry chemical or other agent used.

Firefighting Ability
We averaged scores for speed, effectiveness, and control with both grease and cloth fires.

Ease of Use
Because fire extinguishers are used in moments of stress, we gave high ratings to intuitive, simple-to-operate devices.

Lack of Side Effects
We preferred devices that did not create noxious fumes, leave lots of residue, or cause eye or skin irritations, but this was given less weight than firefighting ability.

Potential Damage to Kitchen Surfaces
Dry chemical extinguishers containing monoammonium phosphate can bond to appliance surfaces and cause damage.

The Testing Lineup

Highly Recommended
KIDDE
Kitchen Fire Extinguisher
Top Pick $18.97

KIDDE
ABC Dry Chemical Fire Extinguisher
$19.99

Recommended
FIRST ALERT
Kitchen Fire Extinguisher
$22.34

FIRST ALERT
Multipurpose Fire Extinguisher
$21.99

Recommended with Reservations
FIRST ALERT
Tundra Fire Extinguishing Spray
$14.97

BUCKEYE
Multipurpose Dry Chemical Fire Extinguisher
$29.90

AMEREX
2½-lb Multipurpose Fire Extinguisher
$34.66

Continued on next page

The Testing Lineup, CONTINUED

Not Recommended

FIREADE 2000
Fire Extinguisher Spray
$18.95

HOMEHERO
Fire Extinguisher
$29.97

FIRE BLANKET CORPORATION'S
Fire Blanket
$35.00

We jury-rigged a grease fire, setting a frying pan on one of the electric burners, pouring in some oil, and switching the heat to high. The instant that flames began flickering, we clicked on a stopwatch and snatched up the first extinguisher in the lineup. After quickly scanning the brief instructions highlighted on the side of the small, aerosol-style can, we found ourselves immediately thwarted by step one: removal of a tab from the black plastic top. Crucial seconds ticked by before we managed to find the tab, rip it off, point the can, and spray. Primed for a big spray, we were unprepared when a thin string of watery foam spewed out and only a few ineffectual-looking dribbles reached the pan. Then, to our shock, a tower of flames suddenly shot into the air. We kept spraying, and just as suddenly, the fire was out. The whole thing took 11 seconds. Later we read the fine print on the can: "When the agent comes in contact with fire, the fire will flare and appear to grow larger. This is a normal, temporary reaction." Really? We weren't about to trust an extinguisher that might have done the job but scared the pants off us in the process.

Overall, the performance on grease fires was mixed. In our inexperienced hands, the 10 devices put out the grease fire in times ranging from a mere 6 seconds to more than a minute and a half. Average time: just under 20 seconds. A few extinguishers didn't seem up to the job, clogging or dripping instead of emitting a strong, directed stream. Others were far too powerful and blasted with so much force we feared the burning oil would splatter out of the pan and spread the fire. Finally, it must be said that walking toward a tower of flaming oil armed only with a blanket extinguisher was an experience we'd rather not repeat. Plus, this device failed to put the fire out quickly.

After putting out grease fires, we moved on to dish towels. There was a frightening tendency for the spray from the more powerful canisters to blow the flaming towels off the counter, still burning. All of the extinguishers took longer to put out the towel than the grease fire, an average of 31 seconds. When the towel was still smoldering under the fire blanket after 2 minutes, we gave up. If it couldn't fully douse a fire in less time than that, it wasn't a contender. We took this device out of our lineup.

Fire needs three things to keep burning: fuel, oxygen, and a source of heat. Fire extinguishers work by breaking the chemical reaction between one or more of these elements.

The ABC, or "multipurpose," devices are filled with monoammonium phosphate, which forms a barrier between the fuel and oxygen. The BC extinguishers contain sodium bicarbonate, which coats the fuel to similarly cut off its supply of oxygen. The nontraditional models used proprietary formulas that manufacturers wouldn't reveal; all we could learn was that their contents were water-based.

Ultimately, we found we felt safer with the power, reliability, and effectiveness of the better traditional extinguishers, all of which have been tested by Underwriters Laboratory, the respected independent organization that confirms manufacturer performance claims. Yes, these extinguishers do spew powder everywhere—and the monoammonium phosphate in the ABC models can permanently scar the surface of appliances. But which would you rather replace, your stove or your house? The winner's virtues were undeniable. It stood out among the traditional models for being especially simple to operate and for its powerful, extremely controlled spray with spot-on aim that was remarkably efficient. It took just 7 seconds to put out the grease fire and 21 seconds to completely snuff out the burning dish towel (and it's not even rated for combustible material). When the smoke cleared, this extinguisher was our top choice for safety in the kitchen.

TAKING A PASS

The firefighting industry uses the acronym **PASS** to help you remember the best way to use a fire extinguisher:

P = Pull the pin (if there is one).

A = Aim at the base of the fire (for a grease fire, aim just above the pan and let the spray drip down).

S = Squeeze the handle.

S = Sweep the extinguisher from side to side as you spray.

TO LEARN MORE
The National Fire Protection Association, an international nonprofit organization founded in 1896, based in Quincy, Mass., is an excellent resource on fire safety.
See www.nfpa.org.

HOW TO CLEAN AND CARE FOR EQUIPMENT

We've created our share of messes in the test kitchen and have had a few cooking snafus that required tons of cleanup. We've also long debated the merits of various cleaning methods and cleansers. We decided to end the debate by applying the same exhaustive methods we use when testing equipment and developing recipes to figuring out the best, most efficient ways to clean up in the kitchen. Along the way, we learned a few tricks to get those dirty, greasy pans shining like new again. In the pages that follow, you will find our best advice for cleaning a variety of cookware and tools, including our instructions for those that require special treatment, such as cast-iron pans and copper pots. After weeks of work, our testers' hands were rough and chapped, but we did find some winners and losers among the wide variety of cleaning techniques. And by the end of this marathon cleaning session, the cookware in the test kitchen was certainly looking much brighter.

Stainless-Steel/Clad Cookware

For cleaning everyday messes, you can soak the pan overnight in sudsy water, but if you don't want to be greeted with greasy dishwater in the morning, try boiling water in the pan. And you don't need to add either vinegar or baking soda to the water, as some sources recommend; we tried these formulas and they were no more effective than plain water.

- Fill the pan halfway with tap water and put it on the stovetop, uncovered.

- Bring the water to a boil and continue to boil briskly for about three minutes, then turn off the burner.

- Using a wooden spatula, scrape the pan and pour off the water.

- Let the pan sit for a few minutes; the residue will flake off as the pan dries.

- Wash the pan with hot water and dishwashing liquid, and dry.

Over time, stainless-steel cookware can develop brown stains that appear to be cooked onto their interiors and exteriors. For these tough stains, we recommend Bar Keeper's Friend cleanser and polish, available nationwide in large grocery or hardware stores.

- Start by moistening the pan with water, then shake a film of cleanser over it.

- Using a copper scrubber for stainless steel or a nylon scrubber for nonstick or anodized aluminum, scrub using circular motions.

- Finish by washing the pan with hot water and dishwashing liquid, and drying.

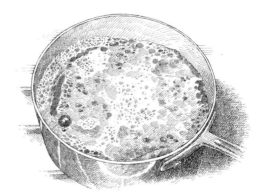

Cast-Iron Cookware

Properly maintaining a cast-iron pan begins with properly cleaning it.

- While the pan is still warm, wipe it clean with paper towels.

- Rinse the pan under hot running water, scrubbing with a brush or nonabrasive scrub pad. Use a small amount of soap if you like, but make sure to rinse it all off.

- Dry the pan thoroughly (do not let it drip-dry) and put it back on the burner over medium-low heat until all traces of moisture disappear.

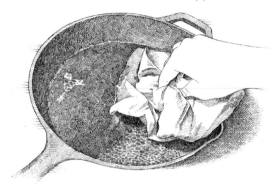

- Add ½ teaspoon of vegetable oil to the warm, dry pan and wipe with a wad of paper towels until it is lightly covered with oil. Continue to rub, until the metal looks dark and shiny. Turn off the heat and allow the pan to cool completely before putting it away.

If your cast-iron cookware gets really dirty, try this approach:

- Start by rubbing the pan with fine steel wool (we normally don't use steel wool on cast iron, but it's necessary when dealing with serious grime).

- Wipe out the loose dirt, pour in vegetable oil to a depth of ¼ inch, and then heat the pan over medium-low heat for 5 minutes.

- Remove the pan from the heat and add ¼ cup of kosher salt. Using a potholder to grip the handle, scrub the pan with a thick cushion of paper towels (hold the paper towels with tongs to protect yourself). The warm oil will loosen bits of food and salt will clean the pan without posing any danger to its seasoning.

- Rinse the pan under hot running water, dry well, and repeat, if necessary.

Copper Cookware

Salt. A salted lemon half. Worcestershire sauce. Tomato sauce. Ketchup. Vinegar. Vinegar and salt. Vinegar and salt and flour. Cream of tartar and water. Yogurt. Boiling milk. Each of these are among the scores of methods recommended to remove tarnish from copper—not counting commercial copper polishes. But as enterprising and interesting as they are, these home remedies were not as effective as the traditional commercial polishes we tried, which not only removed tarnish but also added shine. Among the home remedies, only the ketchup could be said to effectively remove tarnish, but it didn't add shine. When you're desperate to clean up a tarnished copper pan and have no commercial polish on hand, ketchup does a decent job.

Among widely available polishes, Weiman Metal Polish did the best job of removing tarnish and adding shine to copper pots and pans.

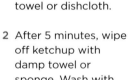

1 Spread even layer of ketchup over surface of pan with paper towel or dishcloth.

2 After 5 minutes, wipe off ketchup with damp towel or sponge. Wash with warm water and dishwashing liquid, and dry.

Nonstick Pans

Nearly all nonstick pans rely on a top coat of polytetrafluoroethylene (PTFE) that keeps the surface slick and prevents food from sticking. Cooking over high heat, using abrasive pads, or washing the pan in the dishwasher will all cause this polymer to wear away. To prolong the nonstick coating's life, wash nonstick pans gently with a nonabrasive pad, and once they are dry, store them using a barrier between the nonstick surface and anything that will be stacked on top of it. We recommend putting a double sheet of paper towels, bubble wrap, or a cheap paper plate between nonstick pans as you stack them. Alternatively, before stacking smaller nonstick pans, slide them into large zipper-lock bags (2-gallon size for 10-inch pans and 1-gallon size for 8-inch pans). The plastic will protect the nonstick surface.

Enameled Cookware

We are very fond of enameled cast-iron Dutch ovens; the 12 or so we have in the test kitchen get a lot of use. The downside to these workhorses is that their light-colored enamel interiors become discolored and stained with use. This is not at all unsafe or unsanitary, but it can be a bit unsightly, so we set out to find an easy cleaning method.

We took a couple of stained pots from the kitchen and filled them with Le Creuset's recommended stain-removal solution of 1 teaspoon of bleach per 1 pint of water. The pots were slightly improved but still far from their original hue. We then tried a much stronger solution (which was OK'd by the manufacturer) of 1 part bleach to 3 parts water. After standing overnight, a lightly stained pot was just as good as new, but a heavily stained one required an additional night of soaking before it, too, was looking natty.

Wooden Pizza Peels

In the test kitchen, we prefer metal peels because of their durability. Wooden peels require more care, but if you start with a clean, dry peel, there will be less to clean later (moisture invites substances to stick). Keep wet dough from sticking to the peel by generously dusting it with cornmeal or flour and try to keep oil, sauce, and toppings on the pizza and off the peel.

- To clean a wooden peel after use, first dust off any loose debris and then gently loosen any stuck-on dough with a plastic bench or bowl scraper; be careful not to mar the surface of wooden peels, since scratches can cause dough to stick.

- Next, wash the peel in warm soapy water, rinse it, and dry it thoroughly. Hang wooden peels so that air can flow around them, which promotes even drying, prevents warping, and discourages mold.

Garlic Presses

Although our winning model of garlic press flips out for easy cleaning, not every brand is that easy to deal with, and dirty garlic presses are notoriously challenging to clean. An old toothbrush, kept handy at the sink, makes it much easier to clean the garlic press (as well as tight or hard-to-reach spots on other dirty kitchen utensils).

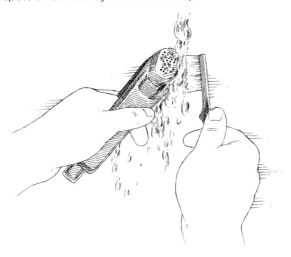

Spice Grinders

The oils in dried chiles can cling to a spice grinder, even after you've wiped it with a brush or cloth. Since most grinders can't be immersed in water, we developed a method to "dry-clean" ours: Add several tablespoons of raw white rice to the grinder and pulverize to a fine powder. The powder will absorb residue and oils. Discard the ground rice—and your grinder will be clean.

Wooden Salad Bowls

Years of exposure to oily salad dressings can leave wooden salad bowls with a gummy residue that all the soap and hot water in the world can't wash off. To find a better solution, we decided to get tough.

• Using medium-grit sandpaper (80 to 120 grit), gently rub the bowl's surface until it turns matte and pale.

• Thoroughly wash and dry the bowl.

• Give it a new coat of food-grade mineral oil (don't use vegetable oil or lard, which quickly turn rancid and sticky). With a paper towel, liberally apply the oil to all surfaces of the bowl, let it soak in for 15 minutes, and then wipe it with a fresh paper towel. Reapply oil whenever the bowl becomes dry or dull.

It's fine to use mild dish soap and warm water to clean well-seasoned wooden bowls; doing this will help maintain the seasoning and prevent oil buildup. Dry the bowl thoroughly after cleaning and never put it in the dishwasher or let it soak in water; otherwise, it can warp and crack.

Wooden Utensils

We love wooden spoons, but because of their tendency to retain odors and transfer flavors, a hint of yesterday's French onion soup can end up in today's coffee cake. Since it isn't advisable to put wooden utensils in the dishwasher, what's the best way to remove odors?

To find out, we stood six brand-new wooden spoons in a container of freshly chopped raw onions for 30 minutes, rinsed them with water, then cleaned them with the following substances: dish soap and water, vinegar and water, bleach and water, a lemon dipped in salt, a tablespoon of baking soda mixed with a teaspoon of water, and just plain water as a control.

The only spoon that our panel of sniffers deemed odor-free was the one scrubbed with baking soda. Here's why: Odors left behind in the porous surface of a wooden spoon are often caused by weak organic acids. Baking soda neutralizes such acids, eliminating their odor. Furthermore, since baking soda is water-soluble, it is drawn into the wood along with the moisture in the paste, thus working its magic as far as the water is able to penetrate.

Cutting Boards

Routine cleaning is essential for cutting boards; scrub your board thoroughly in hot, soapy water (or put it through the dishwasher if it's dishwasher-safe) to kill harmful bacteria and then rinse it well and dry it completely. For stubborn odors, scrub the cutting board with a paste of 1 tablespoon of baking soda and 1 tablespoon of water and then wash with hot, soapy water.

To remove stubborn stains from plastic boards, mix a solution of 1 tablespoon of bleach per quart of water in the sink and immerse the board, dirty side up. When the board rises to the surface, drape a kitchen towel or two over its surface and sprinkle the towel with about ¼ cup bleach solution. Let it sit overnight and then wash it with hot, soapy water.

If you're using a wood or bamboo board, maintain it by applying a food-grade mineral oil every few weeks when the board is new, and a few times a year thereafter. The oil soaks into the fibers, creating a barrier to excess moisture. (Don't use lard or vegetable oil, which can become rancid.) Avoid leaving wood or bamboo boards resting in water, or they will eventually split.

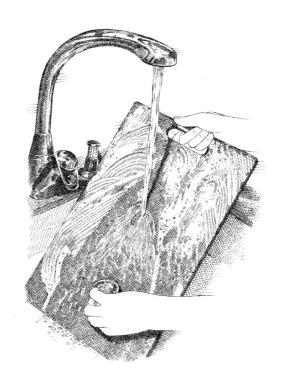

Silicone Spatulas

When silicone spatulas pick up stains from tomato sauce, turmeric, or pesto, often even an aggressive soapy scrubbing won't get them completely clean. So we set out to find a better cleaner.

After staining one set of white silicone spatulas bright yellow with a turmeric-and-water paste and another set red with tomato sauce, we soaked each one in potential stain fighters: white vinegar; a slurry of dish soap and baking soda; 3 percent hydrogen peroxide; a bleach solution (made by diluting 2½ tablespoons of bleach in 2 cups of water); and a control mixture of soapy water. After 24 hours of soaking, only the spatulas soaked in hydrogen peroxide or the bleach solution were back to their original white.

Our science editor explained that soap can help break up and wash away oil, but to remove intensely colored stains the compounds that provide the color need to be broken down into colorless molecules. Hydrogen peroxide and bleach are both oxidants, a type of compound that excels at this task. Just remember to wash your stain-free spatulas in warm, soapy water before use.

Basting Brushes

It can be very difficult to get a basting brush that has been dipped in oil or sauce thoroughly clean, and, as a result, the bristles often remain sticky and sometimes even get smelly as the brush sits in a drawer. Here's a better way to care for them:

- Wash the dirty bristles thoroughly with dish soap and very hot water, rinse well, and shake dry.

- Place the brush, bristles pointing down, into a cup and fill the cup with coarse salt until the bristles are covered. The salt draws the moisture out of the bristles and keeps them dry and fresh between uses.

- Next time you need the brush, simply shake off the salt and you're ready to go.

Pizza Stones

Much like cast iron, pizza stones are porous and become seasoned with use; unfinished stoneware is very absorbent. So grease and oily ingredients that soak into the stone during baking actually minimize the chance of dough sticking to the stone later on. Because of this natural absorbency, stones should never be cleaned with soap of any kind (or put in the dishwasher) or the food subsequently cooked on the stone will taste and smell soapy. Don't clean your pizza stone using the self-clean cycle of the oven, either; it could crack.

To test cleaning methods, we baked a mess of tomato sauce, shredded mozzarella, and powdered sugar onto a stone and let the stone cool completely. We easily loosened the bulk of the burned-on material with a hard plastic spatula, and then scrubbed off the remaining bits with a clean, nonsoapy nylon sponge and hot water. After this treatment, the pizza stone was free of stuck-on material, but it was stained. We tried soaking the stone overnight in water; scrubbing it with a paste made from baking soda and water; and scrubbing it with a paste of baking soda, salt, and water. None of these methods removed the stains, but really, so what? The dry stone worked perfectly the next time we baked a pizza. Elbow grease, hot water, and a nonscratching scrubber will keep your stone clean, but they won't remove stains. A stained stone, however, works just fine.

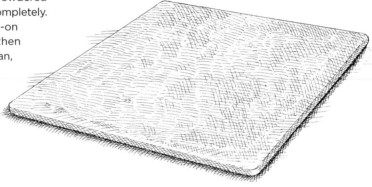

Blenders

Even blenders that are deemed dishwasher-safe may not be immune to shrinking or warping after enough trips through the dishwasher, especially vulnerable rubber gaskets, which can cause leaking when they become damaged. To extend the life of your blender, we recommend hand-washing whenever possible. To make the job easier, especially when cleaning sticky or pasty ingredients such as peanut butter and hummus, fill the bottom third of the jar with hot tap water and a drop or two of dishwashing liquid and give it a 20-second whir to loosen any material trapped underneath the blades. Repeat once or twice with hot water only. To finish the job, unscrew the bottom of the jar and hand-wash each piece using a soapy sponge. For one-piece jar models, use a long, plastic-handled wand-style sponge to reach food stuck on the bottom or sides.

Immersion blenders can be treated in a similar way. Scrubbing the blade of an immersion blender with a thick sponge can be a frustrating and dangerous task. For a better approach, keep your fingers out of it:

- Fill a bowl with hot, soapy water and place it in the sink.

- Place the dirty blender blade in the water.

- Turn the blender on to whirl away the stuck-on food and then rinse it clean with hot water.

Microwave Ovens

In busy households where the microwave sees a lot of use, people sometimes forget to cover a dish when reheating food. This results in splatters inside the oven. Since scrubbing is tedious and has the potential to damage the interior surface, we prefer a simpler cleaning method. Place a microwave-safe bowl full of water in the oven and heat it on high for 10 minutes; the steam loosens dried food particles so they can be wiped off with ease.

Grill Lids

We're fanatics about making sure that we thoroughly clean our grill grates before grilling, but we often forget to give the same attention to the grill lid. Over time, grease and smoke oxidize and turn into carbon that builds up under the lid and eventually becomes patchy flakes that look like peeling paint. To see if this carbon buildup imparts any ashy off-flavors to food, we took the filthiest lid we could find in the test kitchen and used it to grill-roast turkey and fish, comparing the results after following the same recipes on a new grill with a shiny clean lid. Most of us didn't detect any off-flavors, but we do recommend cleaning the inside of the grill lid on a regular basis to prevent the strips from flaking off and landing on your food. The peeling carbon comes off easily with light scrubbing with steel wool and water. (Don't waste your time trying to clean off any buildup that isn't already flaking. When we attempted to remove every speck of the shiny carbon layer, none of the methods we tried—lemon juice and salt; vinegar and baking soda; S.O.S pads; or even spraying the surface with Easy-Off, sealing the lid in a plastic garbage bag, and letting it sit in the sun for several hours—made much of a dent.)

Grill Grates

Food that is being grilled is much less likely to stick to a clean grate. We recommend cleaning the hot grate with a wire brush designed for that purpose specifically, followed by rubbing the grate with a large wad of paper towels dipped in vegetable oil (grab the wad with tongs to protect your hands).

Not only will the oil lubricate the grate and prevent sticking, it also removes any remaining residue on the grate, which might mar the flavor of other foods. If you don't have a grill brush, you can improvise with a pair of tongs and a crumpled wad of aluminum foil.

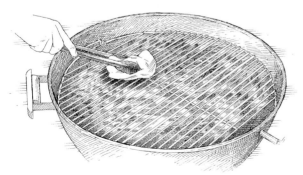

EQUIPMENT AND GADGETS TO AVOID

The equipment testing team spends thousands of hours separating the good from the bad. Most of the time, after all the research and testing, the team comes up with a clear favorite that they can recommend, although of course we will always note the places where even the top-rated equipment has minor flaws or falls short on some aspects of the testing. But once in a while, after testing an entire category of equipment, we decide that your best bet is to avoid it altogether. Other times, we come across specific gadgets that perform so poorly, they deserve special mention to inform readers why they should be avoided. These situations are unusual, but over the years we have collected a bit of a hall of shame.

Item	Notes
Quesadilla Maker 	If we're going to shell out money for a gadget devoted to just one dish, it better be awfully good. An electric quesadilla maker neatly sequesters the cheesy fillings into sections and eliminates the need to flip the quesadilla. The problem is that the recipes that came with the device we tried advised a paltry ¼ cup cheese for two 10-inch flour tortillas—not nearly enough, in our opinion. When we ignored these stingy instructions and added more cheese, the cheese flooded into the moat surrounding the heating plates. So for our quesadilla needs—which include healthy amounts of *queso*—we'll stick with a skillet.
Shrimp Butler 	The Shrimp Butler is a plastic contraption with a small, razor-sharp blade affixed to the inside. Shrimp are fed into a slot at the top of the machine and conveyed past the blade and out the bottom of the machine by means of a ridged wheel. You place a shrimp on the wheel, pull the lever, watch the shrimp come flying out of a chute, and then push the lever back up so you can start the whole process again. Each shrimp pops out with its back sliced neatly open, clearly revealing the vein, if any, that runs just under the back of the shell. This certainly facilitates the task of deveining (by revealing the vein) and shelling (by giving you a good place to start from when peeling), but is this assistance worth $39.99? The Shrimp Butler must also be taken apart and washed thoroughly, a process that takes several minutes. Washing a paring knife and your hands is much quicker.
Thermometer Fork 	Put away your thermo fork and grab a pair of tongs and an instant-read thermometer instead (see our recommendations on page 10). Thermometer forks are designed to enable the user to move the food being cooked on the grill and take its temperature at the same time. We found this gadget awkward to use, especially when trying to flip or turn meat for even browning.

Item	Notes

Food Chopper

Chopping a pile of vegetables can be wearisome work even for cooks with sharp knife skills, so the idea of a helper tool sounded appealing. We hacked through assorted vegetables, herbs, and nuts with five manual choppers ranging in price from $20 to $45. The results were miserable. All models failed at chopping carrots and celery into even dice, producing anything from rough chunks to fine bits. Even worse, the hard and fibrous textures of these veggies, respectively, got caught in the blades, bringing chopping to a halt. Delicate herbs fared no better. Onions, furthermore, wound up flattened and crushed. Most models managed to chop almonds into reasonably uniform bits—but mainly because their containers kept the nuts from jumping all over the counter. We'll stick with our chef's knife.

Burger Press

We wondered if a burger press could make the job of shaping patties easier and the results more consistent. We tried out five models, priced from $6.90 to $22.17. Those designed like a waffle iron or tortilla press—load ground meat and press down the top to produce the patty—squished the meat, splattering it across the counter or onto our clothes, and the resulting patties had to be peeled from the press with a spatula and then reshaped by hand. It was no surprise that the resulting burgers were tough. One model, made by the same manufacturer as our favorite adjustable measuring cup, fared better. Its clear plastic barrel and plunger design works much the same way as the measuring cup: Twist and lock the plunger to produce a ¼-, ⅓-, or ½-pound burger; loosely pack meat into the barrel; and then push to eject the patty. Though it produced tender burgers, the plunger required significant force, and meat clung to the crevices. Worse, ink markings on the plunger rubbed off onto the patties. We'll pass on the press and just use our hands.

Electric Knife

Often overlooked since their heyday in the 1960s, electric knives remain on the market and claim to be able to cut every course of a holiday meal, from appetizers right on through to dessert. We selected four models under $20 and tested them slicing roast beef, turkey breast, angel food cake, and apple pie. The results were clear: Contrary to manufacturer claims, electric knives are not adept at slicing meat neatly and thinly—all four models shredded the beef roasts. While they may offer minor advantages in very specific tasks, such as cutting through delicate baked goods, we're not convinced that's reason enough to add them to your knife set. Plus, they're aggravatingly loud; we prefer to carve with our favorite slicing knife (see our recommendation on page 16).

Item	Notes

Lightweight Cast-Iron Skillet

We were intrigued by the idea of taking a heavy, solid traditional cast-iron skillet and making it lighter and easier to handle. After all, our favorite cast-iron skillet checks in at more than 7 pounds. But could a lighter pan, made with considerably less cast iron, really have the same ability to retain heat that produces perfectly seared steak and golden-brown fried foods? Unlike traditional cast-iron pans (which are made by pouring molten metal into a sand mold, so the pan emerges in one piece, handle included), lightweight cast-iron pans are made in a metal mold, which allows them to be made thinner. They are also machined or milled to thin them further, and their handles are attached separately with rivets. We tried three lightweight cast-iron skillets, comparing them with our favorite traditional cast-iron skillet in several tests. All of the pans we tried were indeed lighter than a traditional cast-iron skillet—but that was pretty much their only advantage. While they were easier to lift and handle, they were also far more reactive to heat changes, which caused them to cook much less evenly, with a distinct tendency to scorch along the outer edges. Overall, lightweight cast-iron skillets proved a disappointment, so we do not recommend them.

Banana Hanger

Supermarkets often suspend unripe bananas from tall poles covered with small hooks. Banana hangers miniaturize this idea for the home kitchen. Sounds good, but we found no difference in ripening when we hung underripe bananas from this plastic gadget and put others from the same bunch in a bowl. After monitoring the fruit for a week, both bunches ripened and then turned spotty brown at the same rate. Our conclusion? Just stick with the bowl.

Grill Flare-Spray

Grill flare-ups, caused by dripping fat, can ruin food. Our usual remedy is to move the food away from the flames. Recently, we found another possible solution: FlareDown, a food-safe liquid containing water, potassium salts, and grease-cutting surfactants in a 21.5-ounce spray bottle. We spritzed FlareDown onto flames when grilling fatty pork and found that the product fared worse than the methods already in our arsenal, such as moving the food away from the flames and keeping a spray bottle filled with water handy. In fact, the FlareDown kicked up ashes onto the meat and only tamed the flames for a few seconds. Worse, we could taste its bitter, salty residue on the food.

Item	Notes

Bread Machine

When bread machines debuted in the late 1980s, their appeal was obvious: Consumers who wanted fresh bread but didn't have time to make it could simply add the ingredients in order (liquids first, followed by dry ingredients, and then yeast), push a button, and come back a few hours later to the finished product. But there were considerable drawbacks, too—namely their space-hogging footprints and sky-high prices (some approached $400)—that eventually caused bread machines to fall out of favor. Recently, however, manufacturers have answered back with a new generation of smaller, somewhat cheaper bread machines. Persuaded that the category deserved a second look, we rounded up five models across a range of sizes and price points. But the news wasn't good. While a few machines produced loaves with a uniform crumb, all the breads emerged overbrowned and stiff on the sides, with pallid, squishy tops. The bottom of each loaf was punctured by at least one large hole where the mixing paddle(s) remained during baking (the only way to avoid this is to remove the paddles after the mixing cycle). The nonstick coating on the paddle of one model actually rubbed off into the dough, creating inedible black spots. Some models suffered mechanical flaws, too: The large body of one machine shook noisily on its unsteady feet as it mixed. Given those defects, we can't fully recommend any of the models we tested.

Collapsible Colander

A good colander is a must-have for draining, rinsing, and soaking, but new, supposedly innovative collapsible models have an annoying tendency to come unclipped or tip over and dump pasta all over the sink that cancels out their flat storage appeal. They also tend to have small or nonexistent bases, which means they have very little elevation from the bottom of the sink, causing backwash from draining liquid to flow back into the colander bowl. While we liked using a miniature version of this product to wash small quantities of fruit and vegetables, we found that the larger versions caused far more problems than they solved and made very poor replacements for our go-to favorite metal colander (see our recommendation on page 29).

Bagel Slicer

Unless you're really worried about bagel-related injuries, avoid these gadgets and just go with a serrated bread knife, which is a superior tool for consistency and control and works on more than just bagels, too. If you feel like you just can't cut a bagel without an assist, we recommend a straightforward guillotine-style slicer as opposed to any of the other various models we tested, which included a plastic bagel-shaped "pod" that held the bagel while you supposedly sliced it with an internal blade mechanism—not only did we struggle to get the blade to cut at all, but when it did slice into the bagels, it made uneven, torn halves. A guillotine-style model will cause some squashing and distortion of the bagels but at least you can have peace of mind that your fingers are safe.

STOCKING YOUR FRIDGE AND PANTRY

HOW WE TASTE INGREDIENTS

Fans of America's Test Kitchen have come to rely on and look forward to our in-depth ingredient taste tests. That's no surprise when you stop to consider how much money (and time) we all spend at the grocery store making choices. Which brand of jarred pasta sauce should you reach for? Which Greek yogurt among the many available today has the best texture and just the right tanginess? What about olive oil: Do you need to use an imported version or is there a California producer whose oil tastes just as rich and fruity? Our tasting and testing team knows that even the best cook in the world is only as good as the ingredients he or she has to use. The can of whole tomatoes you use for your homemade sauce can make or break even a simple pasta dinner, and when it comes to the big choices, like a turkey for the holiday table, a pricey heritage bird can take dinner from acceptable to amazing. Our company slogan, "Recipes That Work," forms the mission for our taste tests. We want to help home cooks succeed in the kitchen by making it easier to buy the ingredients to make great food at home every day. We investigate and plan dozens of tests a year to figure out which ingredients will deliver the best results possible every time, no matter what you're cooking. For us, the best ingredients aren't necessarily the priciest, most exciting, fanciest, or most exotic options; our definition of best is about how the ingredients perform in the recipes you make every day.

Grocery Store Sleuths

So exactly how do we decide what to taste? We find inspiration everywhere: in the supermarket, in conversations with our friends and coworkers, while watching commercials on television, when we go out to eat at restaurants, and by keeping a close watch on food industry trends. We also listen to our readers when you give us recommendations and we send out surveys to ask what you are interested in seeing us taste. Since we can only fit a limited number of taste tests into our magazines every year, we want to make sure the products we pick are going to be as useful as possible. This means that in addition to testing ingredients, we also test convenience products, like boxed macaroni and cheese and bottled salad dressing—if you're using it, we'll test it. To stay on the cutting edge of what home cooks are likely to see in the supermarket in the near future, the tasting and testing team makes an annual pilgrimage to the Summer Fancy Food Show in New York City, where thousands of exhibitors present new and interesting food and beverage products for sampling. Changing food trends definitely influence our tests. For instance, when blue corn tortilla chips started showing up more and more alongside white and yellow options on supermarket shelves, we ran a test to see how the colorful newcomers stacked up against traditional chips. Despite the popularity of blue tortilla chips, we found that they tended to be under-salted and that the very same natural chemicals that make them blue (anthocyanins) also make them taste bitter and sour. The novelty of these colored chips might have been part of their appeal to consumers, but our scientific tests revealed the downsides of simply buying based on trends.

In addition to testing new foods and ingredients, the team is continually investigating the ever-evolving field of kitchen staples. Take chicken broth for example: Broth is a very common ingredient in our recipes and we know that making it from scratch at home is not always an option. Because of this, we try to keep on top of the products available to the consumer, which means we've tested and retested chicken broth about half a dozen different times over the years as new versions appeared that catered to consumers' desires for low-sodium broths, broth concentrates, and new types of packaging. We are always on the lookout for new products, new formulations, and new brands of the ingredients we use most frequently so we can provide you with the most accurate and useful information about what you should be cooking with when you make our recipes—or any recipes.

A big tasting can include over a dozen brands.

Creating an All-Star Lineup

Once we have decided on a topic to tackle, we put together a lineup of brands to taste. Since a major part of our goal is to provide information that's useful to as many people as possible, we focus on top-selling, nationally available brands that almost everyone can access at their nearest supermarket. We use national sales data from a top market-research firm to help determine the most widely available products, and follow up with our own product research. Generic and store brands are never tested because not everyone in America has access to the same stores, although we do occasionally include mail-order products. Sometimes, before we can choose brands to test, we have to figure out how to actually define the category—for instance, there are almost no real rules about what can be called "dark chocolate." The percentages of cacao, cocoa butter, and sugar vary wildly. For our dark chocolate tasting, we decided to evaluate supermarket options that had at least 35 percent cacao, which is the only thing the U.S. Food and Drug Administration (FDA) requires for a product to call itself "bittersweet" or "semisweet" chocolate (it doesn't differentiate between the two terms). It turned out that both of our favorite brands had 60 percent cacao, and that most of what's labeled as "dark chocolate" in the supermarket is actually pretty bad.

For an individual taste test, the final lineup will have anywhere from four items (for a tasting of a specialty item like fish sauce) to 12 items (for an extensive tasting of a very common or popular product like supermarket olive oil). We buy the ingredients that we test the same way that home cooks buy ingredients—in the supermarket.

Putting It to the Test

After the lineup is set, we develop a protocol for tasting the chosen ingredient. All tastings are blind, meaning tasters do not know what brands they are tasting, and we always taste products multiple ways: First, as simply as possible, then, in recipes that represent common uses of the ingredient. To earn the "highly recommended" designation, a brand has to earn top results in all the different types of tastings. This means that tasters get to weigh in on dark chocolate eaten plain, baked into brownies, and in chocolate pots de crème, but it also means that sometimes tasters have to drink plain vinegar before they can try it mixed with oil on salad greens. In addition, the tasting and testing editors sometimes have to get creative when designing tests for plain ingredients like spices. Instead of giving volunteers the gag-inducing task of trying to taste several samples of dry five-spice powder, for example, the team mixed the spice into warm, sweetened milk. Similarly, black pepper was tasted on plain white rice, with the added step of having the tasters sniff ground coffee after each sample to clear their senses. These carefully designed tests make it easier for the tasters to pay attention to flavor nuances in each ingredient.

Next come the tests where the ingredient is incorporated in a recipe. There are always several of these to highlight a variety of common applications of the ingredient. The tastings and testings team meticulously prepares all of the versions of the recipes exactly the same; the only variable is which brand of the ingredient is being used so that any variations can be confidently attributed to that specific product.

The team enlists at least 21 tasters for every test, and anyone in the office can participate, which means that while some of the tasters might be professionally trained cooks, many of the participants are pulled from the rest of the employees of America's Test Kitchen, including departments as varied as book production, accounting, and web design. Some are avid home cooks with strong culinary backgrounds, but others will readily tell you that they have no cooking skills at all. The primary concern is always how the product tastes, so everyone's opinion is equally valid (although tasters are not allowed to discuss the tasting in progress). The tasting sheets are submitted anonymously.

The tasting process is serious business. While being a taste tester might sound like an enviable job, it's actually hard work and demands a taster's full attention and focus. Some tastings, like those for bacon or frozen yogurt, quickly fill up, but it might take a little more convincing to fill the chairs for

NO ONE-HIT WONDERS HERE

You use most of the ingredients in your pantry for a wide variety of recipes, so we design our tests to evaluate how they fare in a set of key applications. Here are some examples that show the range of tests used for a few important ingredients.

Extra-Virgin Olive Oil	Ground Cinnamon	Coconut Milk
• plain	• mixed into applesauce	• in coconut pudding
• with bread for dipping	• in rice pudding	• in coconut rice
• over tomatoes and mozzarella	• in cinnamon swirl cookies	• in Thai chicken soup
• in vinaigrette	• in cinnamon buns	• in green chicken curry

a sampling of plain Worcestershire sauce. Regardless, the team always makes certain to serve the samples at an appropriate temperature, especially since flavors can change in a melty ice cream or lukewarm soup. The tasters never see any packaging, labels, or other information about the brands while they are tasting. All the samples are made to look as similar as possible; we'll even scrape the logos off pieces of chocolate. As they taste, the volunteers answer very specific, neutral, non-leading questions that have been designed to get at key characteristics of the ingredient in question. In addition to numerical scores, tasters are also required to leave comments about the foods they're tasting. Sometimes those comments get a little colorful—"I hate you for making me taste this" is one that has stuck with our executive tasting and testing editor over the years—but they aren't always so snarky (and are usually much more detailed and descriptive). Often the comments provide key insights: During a distilled white vinegar tasting, several tasters complained that the samples smelled "like nail-polish remover." This led us to investigate further and we soon discovered that processes used in manufacturing the vinegar led to the creation of ethyl acetate compounds—the same ones that give nail-polish remover its characteristic smell. Lab tests revealed that the vinegars with the highest concentrations of ethyl acetate were the least popular with tasters. (However, in cooked applications, the results were almost the reverse—the ethyl acetate and its associated off-flavors boiled off and left a clean, bright flavor behind, which illustrates the importance of our holistic approach to testing ingredients.)

The Test Kitchen Taster's Kit

1. Water

2. Numbered samples

3. Pen

4. Unsalted crackers

5. Evaluation sheets

Accounting for Taste

After the tasting, the number crunching begins. Ideally most tasters will agree about the best and worst entries in the lineup, or at least they will agree about the qualities—such as sweetness or saltiness or crunchiness—even if they don't agree on whether those qualities are positive or negative. After all, taste and preference are very personal. Of course, the results of the first tests may not be sufficient, so often further testing is in order—sometimes ad nauseum. In our latest tasting of pure maple syrup, multiple rounds of testing with both plain samples and syrup baked into a maple syrup pie failed to reveal an obvious winner. The team even tried putting the plain syrup into dark-colored sample cups (rather than the usual clear cups) to make sure that tasters weren't letting the color of the syrup affect their opinions on the taste. In the end, the tasters simply liked all the samples about the same, so in our final evaluation, all eight samples were recommended equally in our ratings. (The reasons for this became clearer as we learned more about maple syrup manufacturing—see pages 162–163.)

Tasters are encouraged to taste each sample more than once and to leave detailed comments.

After the taste tests are done, the next step is to dig deeper into what the tasters liked best and why. This includes detailed research into the ways ingredients are made and what happens to them when they are incorporated into dishes. We contact the manufacturers to find out about the techniques that go into making their versions of the ingredient. If those formulations turn out to be trade secrets, we turn to outside experts from academia and industry to help analyze the results—we'll also typically send products to an independent laboratory for a more detailed scientific breakdown. Our editors may also consult scholarly sources like scientific journal articles—one break-through in a boneless, skinless chicken breast tasting came from a high-level industry paper that discussed how long the chicken stayed on the bone before being processed. The investigations prompted by this reading material led us to connect longer "aging" on the bone to improved tenderness in the processed chicken breasts. Most home cooks probably aren't reading scientific papers on poultry processing, but they can benefit from our team's willingness to do just that, along with a host of other inventive investigative tasks.

While the number one thing our tasting and testing team is looking for is a product that tastes great and works in a variety of applications, we also consider price when making our final recommendations to our readers and thus we'll try to present a Best Buy option for a category where the winning option is relatively expensive. This means that while we found that high-end, $60-per-ounce balsamic vinegar is an amazing treat, we also recommend a supermarket brand that is less than 50 cents per ounce. More expensive brands of some ingredients may offer taste advantages, but presenting a variety of options makes our recommendations more useful to a broad span of home cooks. In the end, we also try to give the reader some practical takeaways from each test to use when making decisions on the fly at the supermarket—even if you can't remember which specific brands we liked, you might recall that we vastly preferred multigrain gluten-free sandwich bread to white gluten-free sandwich bread,

Our tasting sheets are organized so not everyone tastes the samples in the same order to avoid "tasting fatigue" and ensure each sample gets full and fair consideration.

which automatically makes your choice that much easier. Our goal is to make you a smarter shopper and more informed consumer even if you don't always (or ever) buy our winning products.

The Tasting Never Stops

Once the tasting and testing team crowns a winner for a particular ingredient test, we stock that brand in our test kitchen pantry for all the test cooks to use in their recipe development. This means that if you use our recommended brands, you'll be cooking with the exact same ingredients that we use in the test kitchen. It also means that we're constantly putting our winning ingredients through more and more tests as we work on new recipes (for more details about our recipe development process, see pages 168–173). If over time a particular ingredient proves to be less reliable than we thought it would be, or if an interesting new option presents itself, we will run new tests and update our stories and product recommendations.

At the end of the day, our scientific, unbiased approach helps strip away the hype of trends and advertising as well as the deeply entrenched biases that most people have about brands—to us, Skippy, Jif, and Peter Pan are just samples 1, 2, and 3. In this chapter, you'll find the results of dozens of ingredient taste tests we've done over the years as well as buying and storage information for fresh items like meat, dairy, and produce. We've also included longer articles, called **Inside the Tasting**, that provide much more detail about the team's work with particularly interesting products or ingredients.

THE INGREDIENT GUIDE

The ingredients on the following pages are used over and over again in countless recipes. Here's what you need to know about buying, storing, and using these key components. This information will not only save you time and money but also protect you from potential kitchen disasters; the right ingredients can make all the difference in recipes of all kinds. We've spent years tasting and evaluating to bring you specific brand recommendations for the products you use the most and here we reveal those details (plus in-depth notes on our process in **Inside the Tasting**).

For at-a-glance information on the specific brands mentioned in this chapter plus other supermarket staples, see **The America's Test Kitchen Shopping Guide** on pages 387–409. Check out AmericasTestKitchen.com for updates to our tastings.

FRUITS AND VEGETABLES A–Z

Apples

The fact that an apple tastes great out of hand does not mean that it will be good in a recipe. Choosing the right apple varieties for different applications is critical. Apart from flavor differences, some turn mushy in the oven while others hold their shape. In general, more tart apples—Cortland, Empire, Granny Smith—hold their shape. Meanwhile, Golden Delicious, Braeburn, and Jonagold varieties are all sweeter and will break down in the oven. (There are exceptions: McIntosh apples, although tart, fall apart and become very watery when baked.) We often use a mixture of sweet and tart apples in a recipe for balanced flavor and texture. Underripe apples will continue to ripen on the counter and can then be refrigerated to keep them fresh once they are completely ripe. Apples can be stored anywhere in the fridge, provided the temperature doesn't freeze them.

Golden Delicious   Braeburn   Jonagold

MORE SWEET

Cortland   Empire   Granny Smith

MORE TART

Artichokes

Buy small or medium artichokes; larger ones can be tough and fibrous. Look for artichokes that are compact, unblemished, and bright green. Avoid those with shriveled brown stems or leaves. If you tug at a leaf, it should snap off cleanly. It is important to submerge artichokes in acidulated water (water with a small amount of vinegar, or lemon or lime juice) as soon as they are cut to prevent browning. Steam medium artichokes and serve with a lemony vinaigrette. Small or baby artichokes are best roasted. Artichokes will keep for up to five days if sprinkled lightly with water and stored in a zipper-lock bag in the fridge.

Asparagus

Thicker stalks are better for broiling, roasting, and grilling. Quick-cooking thinner spears are good candidates for steaming and stir-frying. Medium-thick asparagus (about ⅝ inch) works in most recipes. White asparagus's delicate flavor doesn't survive long-distance shipping, so buy it only if it's very fresh. To preserve asparagus's bright color and crisp texture, trim the bottom ½ inch off of the stalks and stand the spears upright in a glass. Add enough water to cover the bottom of the stalks by 1 inch, cover with plastic wrap, and place the glass in the refrigerator. Asparagus stored this way will remain fresh for about four days; you may need to add more water every couple days. Re-trim the very bottom of the stalks before using. This method can also perk up limp asparagus.

Avocados

Buy the small, rough-skinned Hass variety of avocado rather than the larger, smooth-skinned Fuerte; Hass avocados are creamier and less watery. For a perfectly ripe Hass avocado, look for one that is purple-black (not green) and yields slightly when gently squeezed. Avoid avocados that are overly mushy or bruised or flat in spots or whose skin seems loose—these are well past their prime. When in doubt, try to remove the small stem; it should flick off easily and reveal green underneath. Florida avocados, also called "skinny" avocados, have less fat and more sugar than Hass avocados. They're fine in salads or other dishes where a fresh, mild fruit flavor is desired. If you can't find perfectly ripe avocados, buy the fruit while it's still hard and be patient. Underripe avocados will ripen in about two days on the counter, but they will do so unevenly; it's better to ripen them in the refrigerator, though this will take about four days. Ripe avocados last two days on average at room temperature, or five days in the refrigerator. Halved and pitted avocados can be stored cut side down on a plate drizzled with olive oil. Leftover avocados should not be frozen unless you plan to use the defrosted avocados for a pureed application such as a dressing—they will lose their creamy texture in the freezing and defrosting process.

Bananas

Bananas continue to ripen after you buy them, so if you are not going to use them for a few days it is fine to buy green bananas and store them at room temperature. Do not store them in a plastic produce bag because the moisture that collects in the bag could cause them to rot. Bananas that have developed a smattering of black speckles on the skin are the sweetest (more than three times sweeter than unspeckled) but will soon turn overripe, so use them soon. If you need to ripen bananas in a hurry, enclose them in a paper bag for a couple of days. The bag will trap the ethylene gas produced by the fruit and hasten ripening. Store ripe bananas in the refrigerator to decelerate the ripening process. The skins may turn black, but the fruit inside will keep for almost two weeks before it becomes overripe. To save extra bananas in the freezer for later use in baking or smoothies, peel them and freeze in a zipper-lock freezer bag.

Not all frozen vegetables are created equal. Vegetables with a lower moisture content generally freeze well, while their high-moisture counterparts turn mushy when frozen. Here are the frozen vegetables we like best, as well as the ones we don't recommend.

Recommended

Peas We prefer frozen peas to fresh—they are more convenient (you don't have to shell them) and reliably sweeter. Peas that are to be frozen are blanched almost immediately after picking, which halts the conversion of sugar into starch, keeping frozen peas sweet.

Corn During the summer months, freshly picked corn is clearly superior, but for the rest of the year, we prefer frozen corn kernels because they are consistently sweet.

Pearl Onions Because pearl onions are generally used in long-cooked recipes, such as beef stew, the compromised texture of the frozen variety doesn't much matter. Frozen pearl onions also come peeled and therefore require none of the laborious preparation of fresh.

Lima Beans We rarely use fresh lima beans, which are hard to find, and we never use the canned variety, which are too mushy. Frozen lima beans have good texture and flavor, and they hold up well in a variety of dishes.

Spinach While frozen spinach is clearly not suitable for a salad, it is a good option for cooked dishes. Make sure to thaw and thoroughly dry frozen spinach before cooking.

Acceptable

Frozen broccoli, cauliflower, carrots, and green beans are acceptable options for soups, stews, and long-cooked dishes, where their less-than-crisp texture isn't a factor. But we always prefer fresh when these vegetables are the main component of a dish.

Don't Bother

High-moisture vegetables like bell peppers, snow peas, snap peas, asparagus, and mushrooms do not freeze well, and you should avoid them both on their own and in frozen vegetable medleys.

Beets

Healthy leaves are an easy-to-recognize sign of freshness when buying beets with stems and leaves attached. If buying roots only, make sure they are firm and the skin is smooth. Beets are best steamed or roasted (wrapped in foil). Beets with greens attached can be stored in the refrigerator in a loosely sealed zipper-lock bag for several days. If you remove the greens, beets will keep for one week.

Berries

Fresh berries of any kind require special handling to preserve their delicate texture and flavor. Don't wash berries until you are going to use them. To store berries, it is best to take them out of the containers in which they were purchased. Place the berries in a zipper-lock bag or other container between layers of paper towels. Store in the front of the fridge. Buy fresh berries when they're in season (especially those with a short season like wild blueberries and fresh cranberries) and then freeze them for later use. Most berries freeze very well. Never wash berries before freezing, as berries easily absorb excess water when rinsed; the water expands when frozen, causing the berry skins to rupture. Instead, spread them on a baking sheet or plate and freeze. After they are frozen solid, transfer the berries to a zipper-lock bag and freeze them for up to two months. A quick rinse helps jump-start the defrosting process. But don't expect frozen berries to have the same texture as fresh. We use frozen berries in recipes that call for cooking the berries or as a topping for hot cereals.

VOLUME AND WEIGHT FOR BERRIES	
Volume	Weight
1 cup fresh blueberries, raspberries, strawberries, or blackberries	5 ounces
1 cup frozen blueberries, raspberries, or blackberries	5 ounces
1 cup frozen strawberries	4½ ounces
1 cup cranberries	4 ounces

Bok Choy

Also called Chinese white cabbage, bok choy looks like a wide-stalked version of Swiss chard. Its tender, spinachy leaves and crisp stalks are common ingredients in stir-fries. Buy bok choy with leaves that are bright green and crisp; wilted leaves are a sign of age. Stalks should be bright white and should not have any visible brown spots. Bok choy is best stir-fried or braised. Bok choy comes in various sizes, from diminutive baby bok choy that weigh just a few ounces to mammoth heads that weigh more than 2 pounds. Any variety of bok choy (with either white or green stems) picked at an early age can be called baby bok choy. Most heads weigh just 3 or 4 ounces and will fit in your hand. Because of their small size, the stalks are fairly tender, so there's no need to cook them separately from the leaves. Baby bok choy is best halved and seared. Store bok choy in the refrigerator in a loosely sealed zipper-lock bag for up to three days. Don't wash bok choy until you are ready to cook it.

Broccoli

Buy whole broccoli, not just the crowns or florets. The stalks are quite flavorful. Avoid broccoli stalks that have dry cracks or that bend easily, and avoid florets that are yellow or brown. The cut ends of the stalks should look fresh, not dry or brown. Broccoli is best steamed, stir-fried, or roasted. Store broccoli unrinsed in an open zipper-lock bag in the crisper drawer. It will keep for about one week. To revive limp broccoli, trim the stalk, stand it in 1 inch of water, and refrigerate it overnight.

Broccolini

Broccolini is a hybrid of Chinese kale and broccoli. It is typically sold in bunches like asparagus, and it can be prepared similarly. It is sometimes called baby broccoli. Unlike regular broccoli, the stalks are quite tender. The flavor of broccolini is slightly mineral and sweet, like a cross between spinach and asparagus. Buy broccolini that is bright green with firm stems. Discard the bottom inch of the stems and steam, boil, sauté, or drizzle with olive oil and grill. Store broccolini unrinsed in an open zipper-lock bag in the crisper drawer, where it will keep for several days.

Broccoli Rabe

Broccoli rabe (also called rapini) is more pungent and bitter than broccoli. Look for broccoli rabe with fresh leaves and an abundance of small green florets. Store broccoli rabe in an open zipper-lock bag in the crisper drawer, where it will keep for several days.

Brussels Sprouts

For the best flavor, buy Brussels sprouts with small, tight heads, no more than 1½ inches in diameter. Look for sprouts that are bright green with no black spots or yellowing. The best ways to cook Brussels sprouts are to braise or roast them. Store Brussels sprouts in a vented container in the refrigerator for up to five days. Don't wash them until you are ready to cook them. If you have bought them on the stem, remove the stem for storage.

Cabbage

When buying red or green cabbage, look for smaller, looser heads covered with thin outer leaves. Red and green cabbage are best braised or salted and used to make coleslaw. Napa cabbage is perfect for stir-frying and salads. Store cabbage loosely wrapped in plastic in the refrigerator for about four days. Remove the tough outer leaves before using.

WHERE TO STORE PRODUCE: AT A GLANCE

In the Pantry
The following produce should be kept at cool room temperature away from light to prolong shelf life:

Garlic, Onions, Potatoes, Shallots, Sweet Potatoes, Winter Squash

In the Front of the Fridge
These items are sensitive to chilling injury and should be placed in the front of the fridge, where the temperatures tend to be higher:

Berries, Corn on the Cob, Oranges, Melons, Peas

Anywhere in the Fridge
These items are not prone to chilling injury and can be stored anywhere in the fridge (including its coldest zones), provided the temperature doesn't freeze them:

Apples, Cherries, Grapes

In the Crisper Drawer
These items do best in the humid environment of the crisper:

Artichokes, Beets, Broccoli, Cabbages, Carrots, Cauliflower, Celery, Chiles, Cucumbers, Fresh Herbs, Green Beans, Leafy Greens, Leeks, Lemons, Lettuce, Limes, Mushrooms, Peppers, Radishes, Scallions, Summer Squash, Turnips, Zucchini

On the Counter
These items are very sensitive to chilling injury and are subject to dehydration, internal browning, and/or pitting if stored in the refrigerator:

Apricots, Avocados*, Bananas*, Eggplant, Kiwis*, Mangos, Nectarines, Papayas, Peaches, Pears, Pineapples, Plums, Tomatoes

* Once they've reached their peak ripeness, these fruits can be stored in the refrigerator to prevent overripening, but some discoloration may occur.

Carrots

Buy fresh carrots with the greens attached for the best flavor. If buying bagged carrots, check that they are evenly sized and firm (they shouldn't bend). Don't buy extra-large carrots, which are often woody and bitter. Different colors do have different flavors; mix in purple, white, or yellow carrots with the usual orange variety for some variation. The most flavorful ways to cook carrots are roasting and braising. To prevent shrivelling, store carrots in the crisper drawer in a partially open zipper-lock bag or in their original plastic bag. Before storing green-topped carrots, remove and discard the greens or the carrots will become limp. Both bagged and fresh carrots will keep for several weeks.

Cassava

Also called yuca or manioc, cassava is a tropical root vegetable with a dry, super-starchy texture and a flavor vaguely reminiscent of popcorn. Although raw cassava can be poisonous, thorough cooking eliminates any danger. Cassava works as a potato replacement. Peel and then steam, boil, or fry. Fresh cassava is quite perishable and will only keep for a few days. Store in a cool, dry place.

Cauliflower

Buy heads of cauliflower with tight, firm florets without any discoloration. The orange variety has about 25 times more vitamin A than regular cauliflower and tastes like winter squash. Purple cauliflower is high in antioxidants with a slightly bitter flavor. Both can be substituted for regular cauliflower in any application. The chalky texture and bland flavor of raw cauliflower are improved with cooking. Steam, boil, or roast florets to bring out their subtle, earthy sweetness and firm, crunchy texture. Overcooked cauliflower may develop an unpleasant sulfurous smell. Cauliflower wrapped in plastic can be stored in the refrigerator for several days.

Celery

Buy loose celery heads, not bagged celery heads (with clipped leaves) or bagged celery hearts. Loose celery heads tend to be fuller and fresher. Look for glossy green stalks without brown edges or yellowing leaves. Try adding the leaves next time you're using chopped celery in a recipe: They have lots of flavor. The best way to store celery is to wrap it in foil and store it in the refrigerator. It will keep for several weeks. Revive limp celery stalks by cutting off about 1 inch from both ends and submerging the stalks in a bowl of ice water for 30 minutes.

Celery Root

Also known as celeriac, this gnarled bulb is a variety of celery grown specifically for the root. The flavor is a cross between celery and parsley, with a lemony tinge and soft but slightly fibrous texture. Buy celery root that feels heavy for its size and has a hard and firm exterior. Peel, finely chop, and eat raw or steam, boil, or roast. Celery root is also good mashed or in soups or stews. Store celery root in the refrigerator wrapped tightly in plastic wrap for up to two weeks. If you buy celery root with stalks and leaves attached, remove these before storing.

Cherries

Buy cherries with firm, plump, unwrinkled, and unblemished flesh. Darker color corresponds to greater ripeness in many sweet cherry varietals (Rainier cherries are an exception). While fresh sweet cherries are great for eating out of hand, we find that fresh sour cherries are the best option for baking. However, because these are only available for a few weeks during the summer, and regionally at that, we recommend jarred sour cherries in sugar syrup for use in out-of-season baking. If you need sweet cherries for a recipe out of season, your best bet is the freezer section; pick a brand that is individually quick frozen, or IQF. Our favorite is **Cascadian Farms Premium Organic Sweet Cherries**. Store fresh cherries in the refrigerator in a zipper-lock bag, and do not wash them until you are ready to use them.

Chile Peppers

Chiles, both fresh and dried, have a variety of unique flavors that range from mild and fresh to acidic and spicy to rich and deeply toasty. Fresh chiles often have vegetal or grassy flavors, with clean, punchy heat. Dried chiles tend to have deeper, fruitier flavors, with nutty or even smoky undertones. There is no way to gauge heat in fresh chiles—the white lines that sometimes appear on the skin do not indicate heat. Chiles get their heat from a compound called capsaicin, which is concentrated mostly in the inner whitish pith (called ribs), with progressively smaller amounts in the seeds and flesh. If you like a lot of heat, you can use the entire chile while cooking. If you prefer a milder dish, remove the ribs and seeds. Keep in mind, though, that even among chiles of the same variety, heat levels can vary. When shopping for fresh chiles, look for those with bright color and tight, unblemished skin. When shopping for dried chiles, look for those that are pliable and smell slightly fruity. Store fresh chiles in the crisper drawer. Do not freeze fresh chiles; they will turn mushy and lose their heat and flavor.

RIPENING FRUIT

Fruits fall into two categories: "climacteric" fruits, which can ripen off the parent plant, and "nonclimacteric" fruits, which cannot. The difference lies in their responses to a gas called ethylene, which occurs naturally in plants but can also be introduced in an industrial setting. Climacteric fruits respond to ethylene by producing their own ethylene. This in turn triggers accelerated use of oxygen and release of carbon dioxide and enzymatic actions that lead to softening and, in many such fruits, the conversion of starches into sugar—in other words, ripening. Storing unripe climacteric fruits in a paper bag with a ripe fruit (which is giving off ethylene) can help speed ripening because the bag traps some ethylene, concentrating it in the air around the fruit. Nonclimacteric fruits produce very little ethylene after they are harvested, and they usually don't convert their starches to sugars. This means that once they are severed from the parent plant, they don't get any sweeter.

Will Ripen on the Counter
Apples, Apricots, Avocados, Bananas, Cantaloupe, Kiwis, Mangos, Peaches, Pears, Plums, Tomatoes

No More Ripening
Bell Peppers, Cherries, Grapes, Lemons, Oranges, Pineapples, Strawberries

SHOPPING FOR FRESH CHILES

Chile	Appearance and Flavor	Heat	Swaps
Poblano	Large, triangular, green to red-brown; crisp, vegetal	🌶	Bell Pepper, Anaheim
Anaheim	Large, long, skinny, yellow-green to red; mildly tangy, vegetal	🌶🌶	Poblano
Jalapeño	Small, smooth, shiny, green or red; bright, grassy	🌶🌶½	Serrano
Serrano	Small, dark green; bright, citrusy	🌶🌶🌶	Jalapeño
Habanero	Bulbous, bright orange to red; deeply floral, fruity	🌶🌶🌶🌶	Thai

Orange Juice

We found that juices that are pasteurized at lower temperatures have better flavor, so look for a brand that is "gently pasteurized." We also prefer fresher juices—our winner, **Natalie's 100% Florida Orange Juice, Gourmet Pasteurized**, squeezes its oranges to order and ships its juice within 24 hours. This eliminates the need for elaborate processing and additives. For a more convenient and economical option, try a frozen concentrate like **Minute Maid Original Frozen Concentrated Orange Juice,** which is made from evaporated fresh orange juice and pulp enhanced with oils extracted from peels for a flavor and texture that come surprisingly close to fresh juice. **See page 86 for Inside the Tasting.**

Lemonade

For a supermarket lemonade with real lemon flavor, look for one with an ingredient list that sticks closely to the traditional recipe of water, lemon juice, and sugar, and that has a high percentage of juice. Our winner, **Natalie's Natural Lemonade**, has a whopping 20 percent juice and all our favorites had more than 10 percent. The sugar content should also be high, to balance out the tartness of the acidic lemon, but make sure it comes from sucrose, not corn syrup. If you need a longer-lasting option, try **Minute Maid Premium Frozen Lemonade Concentrate**. We do not recommend unrefrigerated shelf-stable lemonades.

Grapefruit Juice

Our favorite brand of grapefruit juice, **Natalie's 100% Florida Grapefruit Juice**, uses a mix of citrusy pink grapefruits and sweet ruby reds for a juice that is sweet but not cloyingly so, and bitter but not astringent. Look for a brand with between 20 and 25 grams of sugar per 8-ounce serving. Juices outside that range will be either too bitter or too sweet.

Persian Limes versus Key Limes

Key lime aficionados herald the fruit's "distinctive" flavor and fragrance compared with conventional Persian limes, but we found the distinction pretty minor—when we made Key lime bars with both varieties, the Persian-lime version tasted a bit more tart, though tasters were split over which variety made the better bar. The deciding factor may be the amount of work involved: To get the half cup of lime juice called for in our bar recipe, we had to squeeze three Persian limes. With the Key limes, it took almost 20.

White Grapefruit versus Ruby Red Grapefruit

These large tropical fruits are grown primarily in the southern U.S. and are so named because they grow in tight clusters, much like grapes. The white variety is bracingly sharp and sour, while the ruby red variety is slightly sour with hints of honey and a pleasantly bitter finish.

Common Lemons versus Meyer Lemons

The common lemon is a variety called Eureka. Its juice has a mouth-puckering tartness. The Meyer's skin is smooth and yellowish-orange, and its juice is sweeter than other types of lemon.

Tangerines versus Clementines

Both of these small citrus fruits are sweet and easy to peel, but tangerines are full of seeds while clementines are seedless.

Citrus

Citrus fruits are at their best in the winter months, although most varieties are available year-round. Look for fruit that feels heavy, with brightly colored skin that is free of blemishes. The fruit should not be overly firm and should yield when the skin is pressed (this indicates which fruit has the most juice). With the exception of lemons and limes, citrus fruits are sensitive to chill-injury and should be placed in the front of the fridge, where the temperatures tend to be higher. Lemons and limes are best stored in a sealed zipper-lock bag in the crisper. Citrus zest can be frozen in a zipper-lock bag for up to three weeks. It will lose its color but will work fine for baking. We do not recommend buying shelf-stable lemon or lime juice unless it's specifically called for in a recipe. We find bottled juice to be bitter at best and rancid in some cases. (And since you will most likely also need zest in a recipe that calls for juice, you are better off buying fresh fruit.)

Corn

Corn loses its sweetness soon after it is harvested, so buy the freshest corn you can find. Look for plump ears with green husks and golden silk extending from the tops (the more silk the better since it is an indicator of the number of kernels). Peel back the husk to check for brown spots and to make sure the kernels are firm. If you must store corn, wrap it, husk and all, in a wet paper bag and then in a zipper-lock bag and place it in the refrigerator for up to 24 hours.

Eggplants

Four of the most common varieties of eggplant found in the supermarket are large globe, small Italian, slender Chinese, and apple-shaped Thai. Buy globe eggplants unless a recipe specifies another type of eggplant. Look for one that is firm, deep purple, glossy, and without blemishes. A ripe eggplant will feel heavy in your hand. Larger eggplants tend to be more bitter and have more seeds. In most applications, the eggplant must be salted first to draw out excess water. Store eggplants at room temperature away from direct sunlight.

Cucumbers

Buy regular American cucumbers that are dark green, firm, and without shriveled ends. Seedless English cucumbers have a weak cellular structure that turns them mushy when cut and salted (which we do for salads), and they have less flavor. Cucumbers can be stored in the crisper drawer as is; the waxed coating most wholesalers apply will keep cucumbers fresh for at least one week. Unwaxed cucumbers can be stored in a loosely sealed zipper-lock bag for up to one week.

Dates

Fresh dates should look plump and juicy; skip over any that look withered or dry. While the variety of dates available to you may vary, we most like Medjools, which are particularly sweet and densely textured. Store fresh dates in a zipper-lock bag in the refrigerator.

Edamame

Like peanuts, edamame, which are fresh soybeans, taste nutty. Our tasters also noted their firm, dense texture. Sold fresh or frozen, edamame should be boiled in their pods, then salted and eaten out of hand, in salads, or mixed into stir-fries or rice dishes. (But don't eat the fibrous, fuzzy pod.) Store edamame in the refrigerator in a partially open zipper-lock bag.

Globe

Italian

Chinese

Thai

Fennel

Buy fennel bulbs that are creamy white and firm with little or no discoloration. The stems should be crisp and the feathery fronds bright green. Fennel bulbs are great sautéed, grilled, or roasted, all of which concentrate their anise flavor. Braising is another good cooking method. Store fennel in the refrigerator in a zipper-lock bag for up to three days.

Fiddleheads

The young, unfurled shoots of several types of ferns are a much-prized early spring vegetable. Their high price reflects the fact that they're wild, delicate, and highly perishable, and their season is short. Fiddleheads have a grassy, nutty flavor similar to that of asparagus and green beans. Clean them carefully before blanching them in boiling water, shocking them in an ice bath, and briefly sautéing them in butter. Store fresh fiddleheads in the refrigerator in a partially open zipper-lock bag for up to two weeks.

Figs

Most varieties of fresh fig are brown or purple when fully ripe and should be slightly soft to the touch. Do not substitute dried figs for fresh. Store fresh figs in a zipper-lock bag in the refrigerator.

Fresh   Dried

Garlic

Most of the garlic at the supermarket is soft-neck garlic, which stores well and is heat tolerant. You may also find hard-neck garlic, which has a stiff center staff. Hard-neck garlic has a more intense, complex flavor, but it's easily damaged and doesn't store as well as soft-neck garlic. Wait to buy hard-neck garlic at the farmers' market and use it soon after purchase. Another variety you may see at the supermarket is elephant garlic, which has huge individual cloves and is actually a member of the leek family. We find it far milder than regular garlic and don't recommend it for recipes. Buy heads of garlic with firm, tightly bound cloves. Do not buy garlic with green sprouts emerging from the cloves (the sprouts taste bitter). Squeeze the heads to make sure they are not rubbery, have no soft spots, and aren't missing cloves. The garlic shouldn't have much of a scent; if it does, you're risking spoilage. Store garlic at room temperature in an open basket. Do not remove the papery outer skin until you are ready to use the cloves. Garlic scapes are the flower stalk of the garlic bulb. Each bright green shoot loops in a circle and ends in a mini clove called a bulbil. A darling of foodies, garlic scapes show up at farmers' markets in the late spring or early summer. Snipping them promotes growth underground, meaning plump garlic cloves; plus, it gives farmers two products to sell. The scapes taste like very mild garlic. Sauté them in olive oil or puree into a white bean dip or pesto.

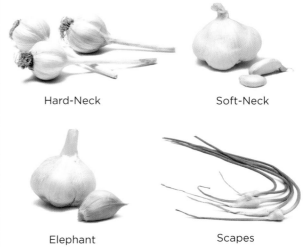

Hard-Neck   Soft-Neck

Elephant   Scapes

Ginger

If possible, buy small pieces of ginger and use it while it's fresh. As ginger ages, it loses its signature pungency. Older, wizened ginger is fine to use, but it will have a more mild, flat flavor. If you're polishing off an older piece, be prepared to use more than the recipe calls for and add it as close as possible to the end of cooking. Store fresh, unpeeled ginger in the refrigerator unwrapped for up to two weeks (wrapping the ginger will cause it to develop mold).

Grapes

Buy stem-on grapes and don't remove them from their stems until you're ready to serve them. Hold off on rinsing until just before serving, too. Unrinsed grapes still on the stem should keep in the refrigerator for up to a month.

Green Beans

Buy green beans that are brightly colored and fresh-looking. Thinner beans are generally sweeter and more tender. The best ways to cook green beans are boiling, braising, and roasting. Store green beans in the refrigerator in a loosely sealed zipper-lock bag.

Hearty (Winter) Greens

Buy kale, Swiss chard, and collard greens with leaves that are dark green and crisp with no signs of wilting or yellowing. We recommend cleaning these greens in a sink full of water, where there is ample room to swish the leaves. These assertive greens are best blanched and then sautéed or braised. They also work well in soups and stews. You can store greens in the refrigerator in an open zipper-lock bag for several days. Blot any excess moisture from the leaves before storing them. Do not clean the greens until you are ready to cook them.

Kale   Swiss Chard

Collard Greens

Greens

Prewashed bags of arugula and mesclun mix offer great convenience, but be sure to turn over the bags and inspect the greens as closely as you can; the sell-by date alone doesn't ensure quality, so if you see moisture in the bag or hints of blackened leaf edges, move on. Don't buy bags of already cut lettuce that you can otherwise buy as whole heads, like romaine or Bibb or red leaf; the leaves begin to spoil once they are cut (bagged hearts of romaine are fine). Endive and radicchio are always sold in heads. Crisp heads such as iceberg and romaine should be cored, wrapped in moist paper towels, and refrigerated in a plastic produce bag or zipper-lock bag left slightly open. Leafy greens such as arugula and mesclun should be stored in their original container or bag if you buy them prewashed. If not prewashed, store the washed and dried greens in paper towels in a zipper-lock bag left slightly open. If the lettuce for tender heads, such as Boston and Bibb, comes with the root attached, store the entire head in the original plastic container or bag, or a zipper-lock bag left slightly open. If the lettuce is without its root, wrap the leaves in moist paper towels and refrigerate in a plastic produce bag or zipper-lock bag left slightly open.

Romaine   Bibb

Endive   Radicchio

Jícama

Jícama's thin skin is easily peeled to reveal cream-colored, crisp-textured flesh that tastes like a mix of apple, potato, and watermelon. It is often cut into matchsticks for salads, but it can also be steamed, boiled, fried, or even pickled. Jícama will keep for about one week in the crisper drawer.

Lemon Grass

Lemon grass is ubiquitous in curries, soups, and salads across Southeast Asian cuisines. Many supermarkets carry it in the produce section. Lemon grass has a delicate, citrusy, slightly peppery flavor. Wrap lemon grass in plastic wrap and store in the refrigerator. It will keep for several weeks.

Kohlrabi

This vegetable is sometimes referred to as a cabbage turnip. Look for firm kohlrabi bulbs that are no wider than 3 inches. Though kohlrabi is most often sold without leaves, the greens have an earthy, mineral quality when quickly sautéed, while the bulbs are slightly bitter and have a garlicky kick. The bulb should be peeled and sliced prior to being steamed, boiled, or stir-fried. Store kohlrabi in the refrigerator in a loosely sealed plastic bag. It will keep for several days.

Melons

Melons of many kinds are widely available in the late spring and summer. Because they have hard rinds, it can be difficult to judge ripeness; there is nothing worse that bringing home a melon, cutting into it, and seeing a green ring around the edge of tough, unripe fruit. In general, look for a melon that is heavy and firm and that has no indentations or soft spots. Smell the stem end—a ripe melon will have a slightly sweet fragrance. Cantaloupe should have corky veins that are visible over the rind, but the rind should not be green. It will continue to ripen at room temperature; once it's ripe, the rind will be golden yellow. Honeydew should be creamy white with a smooth surface. Once harvested, it will not ripen further. A ripe watermelon will sound hollow when tapped. Look for a watermelon that is firm and symmetrical. Melons can be stored at room temperature but will last a few weeks if refrigerated.

Leeks

Buy leeks that have not been trimmed (some markets remove the tops when leeks start to wilt) and that appear to have most of their green leaves intact. Look for leeks that are firm with crisp, dark green leaves. Leeks are best braised or steamed. Store leeks in the crisper drawer wrapped tightly in plastic; they will stay fresh for up to one week.

Mushrooms

There are many varieties of fresh mushrooms available at the supermarket now: the humble white button mushroom, as well as cremini, shiitake, oyster, and portobello mushrooms, for starters. We find cremini mushrooms to be firmer and more flavorful than white mushrooms; the two are interchangeable in any recipe. Buy mushrooms loose if possible so that you can inspect their quality. When buying white or cremini mushrooms, look for mushrooms with whole, intact caps; avoid those with discoloration or dry, shriveled patches. Pick mushrooms with large caps and minimal stems. You can store loose mushrooms in the crisper drawer in a partially open zipper-lock bag for several days. Store packaged mushrooms in their original containers, as these are designed to "breathe," maximizing the life of the mushrooms.

Green Olives

Often labeled "Spanish" olives, green olives are picked before they fully ripen, and their mild flavor adds a bright, acidic dimension to food. Manzanillas, produced in Spain and California, are the pimento-stuffed olives best known for garnishing martinis. Add green olives at the end of cooking to avoid bitterness.

Brine-Cured versus Salt-Cured

Jarred olives come in three basic types at the supermarket: brine-cured green, brine-cured black, and salt-cured black (often labeled "oil-cured"). Brine-cured olives are soaked in a salt solution for periods of up to a year to remove bitterness and develop flavor. Salt-cured olives are packed in salt until nearly all their liquid has been extracted and then covered in oil to be replumped. Generally we find that brine-cured black and green olives can be used interchangeably in any recipe. Among our test cooks, only a few olive aficionados favored the concentrated, bitter taste of salt-cured olives. We don't recommend cooking with them unless a recipe specifically calls for them. Avoid canned olives entirely; they are almost tasteless, with an odd, slippery texture.

Black Olives

Picked when mature, black olives have a robust, fruity taste. The most common types are kalamata olives, which have an earthy flavor and creamy flesh, and niçoise olives, which boast an assertive, somewhat bitter flavor. We prefer the fresher kalamatas from the refrigerator section of the supermarket; the jarred shelf-stable ones are bland and mushy in comparison. If you can't find kalamatas in the refrigerator section of your market, look for them at the salad bar.

Pitted versus Unpitted

Pitted olives are certainly convenient, but they lack the complex, fruity flavors of unpitted olives and often have a mushier texture. After being brined for up to a year, the pitted olives are returned to the brine for packing, which can penetrate the inside of the olive and turn it mushy and pasty, and can also increase the absorption of salt. That saltier taste can mask subtler flavors. If you have the time, we recommend that you buy unpitted olives and pit them yourself.

Onions

Choose onions with dry, papery skins. They should be rock-hard, with no soft spots or powdery mold on the skin. Avoid onions with green sprouts. Our first choice for cooking is yellow onions, which have the richest flavor, but milder, sweeter red onions are great grilled or minced raw for a salad or salsa. White onions are similar to yellow onions but lack some of their complexity. Sweet onions such as Vidalias, Mauis, and Walla Wallas are best used raw, since they can become stringy when cooked. Pearl onions are generally used in soups, stews, and side dishes. Peeling them is a chore, so we recommend buying frozen pearl onions that are already peeled. Scallions have an earthy flavor and delicate crunch that work well in dishes that involve little or no cooking, like stir-fries. Chives, the smallest member of the onion family, have a very mild flavor and are sold near the herbs in supermarket produce sections. Store onions in a cool, well-ventilated spot away from light. Do not store onions in the refrigerator, where their odors can permeate other foods. The exceptions are scallions and chives, which should be stored in the crisper drawer.

Pearl Onions

Scallions

Chives

Parsnips

This relative of the carrot has a sweeter, more floral taste. Look for parsnips that are on the smaller side (about 4 ounces) because they are sweeter. Large parsnips (8 ounces and larger) have a core that must be cut out. Look for hard parsnips without any soft spots. Parsnips can be prepared and cooked in the same way as carrots and are particularly well suited to braising and roasting. You can store parsnips in the refrigerator in a partially open zipper-lock bag for at least one week.

Pears

Although you may see as many as a half dozen pear varieties at some supermarkets, the three most common are Bartlett, Bosc, and Anjou. Bartlett pears remain firm when baked. Bosc are a bit grainy when baked and are better poached. Anjou pears are very juicy and too soft in baking applications, but they are great for roasting. Since pears will continue to ripen after they have been harvested, choose pears that are ripe but firm—the flesh at the base of the stem should give slightly when gently pressed with a finger—and store them at room temperature for a few days to ensure the best quality. Ripening can be accelerated by putting them in a paper bag with a banana, but check them frequently; they go from just right to mush in a matter of hours.

| Bartlett | Bosc | Anjou |

Peas

When buying snow peas or sugar snap peas, look for crisp, bright green pods without obvious blemishes or dry spots. If buying shelling peas, look for pods that are filled out. (Note that shelling peas are hard to find and require a lot of work, so we use frozen peas in many applications. They are frozen right after being shucked and are often sweeter and fresher-tasting than shelling peas.) Snow peas are best stir-fried. Sugar snap peas should be blanched and then sautéed or stir-fried. Shelling peas are best boiled and buttered or braised, or used in soups and stews. Store peas in the refrigerator in a partially open zipper-lock bag. Fresh shelling peas are very perishable and should be used right away. Snow and sugar snap peas will keep for several days.

| Snow Peas | Sugar Snap Peas |

Pineapples

We prefer Costa Rican–grown pineapples, also labeled "extra-sweet" or "gold." They are consistently honey-sweet in comparison with the acidic Hawaiian pineapples, which have greenish (not yellow) skin. Pineapples will not ripen further once picked, so purchase golden, fragrant fruit that gives slightly when pressed. You can also tell if a pineapple is ripe by tugging at a leaf in the center of the fruit: If the leaf releases with little effort, the pineapple is ripe. Avoid pineapples with dried-out leaves and a fermented aroma, as these indicate that the fruit is overripe. Peeled strips of pineapple sold at supermarkets make a fine stand-in for buying and peeling a whole pineapple yourself, especially if you don't need a lot. We do not recommend buying pre-cubed pineapple. Store unpeeled pineapples at room temperature.

Almost any fruit can be dried. The drying process concentrates flavor and sugar. But should you buy dried fruit sugared or unsweetened? Unsulfured or not? Not all dried fruit is created equal.

Raisins start life as green Thompson (or Sultana) grapes. They are largely still dried the old-fashioned way—in the sun for two to four weeks. Golden raisins come from the same grape as ordinary black raisins, but are dried mechanically and treated with sulfur dioxide to preserve their color. They can be used interchangeably with ordinary raisins.

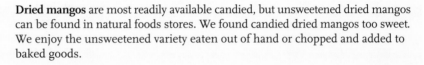

Fresh, naturally tart cranberries are infused with sweetened cranberry juice in the process of being dried. **Dried cranberries**, which are sometimes sold as "Craisins," make a good addition to salads and pilafs.

Dried mangos are most readily available candied, but unsweetened dried mangos can be found in natural foods stores. We found candied dried mangos too sweet. We enjoy the unsweetened variety eaten out of hand or chopped and added to baked goods.

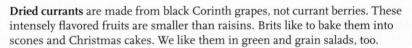

Dried currants are made from black Corinth grapes, not currant berries. These intensely flavored fruits are smaller than raisins. Brits like to bake them into scones and Christmas cakes. We like them in green and grain salads, too.

Ninety percent of **dried cherries** are made from sour cherries, because their tart flavor stands up to the drying process. We use dried cherries in both sweet and savory recipes.

Dried pineapples come as either dehydrated, brown slices or fruit juice–soaked or sugared bright-yellow slices. We didn't like either. The former were chalky and chewy while the sweet variety lacked all pineapple tang and had the taste and texture of gumdrops.

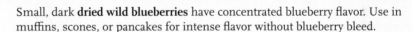

Small, dark **dried wild blueberries** have concentrated blueberry flavor. Use in muffins, scones, or pancakes for intense flavor without blueberry bleed.

In the U.S., **prunes** are best known for their, ahem, health benefits (although old cookbooks offer a plethora of prune whips, stewed prunes, and cakes). In recent years, prune promoters have renamed them "dried plums" and infused them with cherry and orange. Eat in sweet or savory dishes or as a snack.

The **Calimyrna fig** is the California version of the Turkish Smyrna fig. The dried version is seedy and chewy with caramel notes. Add dried figs raw to salads, serve with cheese, or cook in sauces or stuffings for chicken or pork.

Most supermarket **dried apricots** are treated with sulfur dioxide to preserve their sunny color and extend shelf life. Eaten out of hand, these plump sulfured apricots have citrus and honey flavors. Unsulfured apricots are drier and chewier, but reveal bright, true apricot flavor when baked.

Mass-market **dried apples** have little or no real apple flavor, but organic varieties are tart and sweet with a fresh, just-picked flavor. Both are sponge-like and rubbery, which is why we like them for baking, not snacking. Add finely chopped dried apples to fruit pies to soak up moisture and keep crusts crisp.

Baking Potatoes

This group contains more total starch (20 to 22 percent) than other categories, giving these varieties a dry, mealy texture. These are the best choice when baking and frying, and in our opinion, they are the best potatoes for mashing because they can drink up butter and cream. They are also good for when you want to thicken a stew or soup, but not when you want distinct chunks of potatoes.

Common Varieties Russet, Russet Burbank, Idaho

Boiling Potatoes

These contain a relatively low amount of total starch (16 to 18 percent), which means they have a firm, smooth, and waxy texture. Often they are called "new" potatoes because they are less mature and harvested in the late spring and summer. They are less starchy than "old" potatoes because they haven't had time to convert their sugars to starch (they also have thinner skins). Firm, waxy potatoes are perfect when you want the potatoes to hold their shape, as with potato salad. They are also a good choice when roasting or boiling.

Common Varieties Red Bliss, French Fingerling, Red Creamer, White Rose

All-Purpose Potatoes

These potatoes contain less total starch (18 to 20 percent) than dry, floury baking potatoes but more than firm, waxy boiling potatoes. Although they are considered "in between" potatoes, their texture is actually mealier than that of waxy potatoes, putting them closer to baking potatoes. These "in between" potatoes can be mashed or baked but won't be as fluffy as baking potatoes. They can also be used in salads and soups but won't be quite as firm as boiling potatoes.

Common Varieties Yukon Gold, Yellow Finn, Purple Peruvian, Kennebec, Katahdin

Pomegranates

The hundreds of small, sparkling crimson kernels inside a pomegranate are tart, slightly crunchy, and completely edible. Use the seeds in green or fruit salads or to top a pudding or a custard pie. Whole pomegranates can be stored at room temperature for several days or refrigerated for up to three months in a zipper-lock bag.

Potatoes

Since potatoes have varying textures (determined by starch level), you can't just reach for any potato and expect great results. Potatoes fall into three main categories (baking, boiling, or all-purpose) depending on texture. Buy potatoes that show no signs of sprouting. Potatoes with a greenish tinge beneath the skin have had too much exposure to light and should also be avoided. Try to buy loose potatoes since plastic bags can hasten sprouting and deterioration. Store potatoes in a paper bag in a cool, dry place and away from onions, which give off gases that hasten sprouting. New potatoes should be used within one month, but other potato varieties will hold for several months.

Quince

Quince is a fragrant winter fruit. Although hard, dry, and astringent when raw, quinces are delicious cooked. Peel and poach for tarts or compotes; roast to serve alongside meats; or add a few slices to your next apple pie. Thanks to loads of pectin (a natural thickener), quinces are also ideal for jams, jellies, and preserves. Quinces can be stored at room temperature for up to one month.

Radishes

Try to buy radishes with their greens attached; if the greens are healthy and crisp, it is a good sign that the radishes are fresh. If the radishes are sold without their greens, make sure they are firm and the skin is smooth and not cracked. Avoid very large radishes, which can be woody. Radishes can be braised, roasted, or eaten raw in salads. You can store radishes in a partially open zipper-lock bag for up to one week. If you buy radishes with greens attached, remove the greens before storing them.

Rhubarb

Because it's usually paired with strawberries and made into pie, rhubarb is often mistaken for a fruit. Actually, it's a vegetable, and though very tart and astringent, sugar transforms it into dessert. Buy it red or green: The color doesn't indicate ripeness or affect the taste. Look for rhubarb that is crisp, with shiny, firm skin. Slice rhubarb thin across the grain to reduce stringiness. Don't eat the leaves; they are poisonous. Rhubarb should be stored loosely wrapped in plastic in the crisper drawer.

Rutabagas

A close relative of the turnip, this large root has thin skin and sweet, golden flesh. Its flavor is reminiscent of broccoli and mustard, with a horseradish aftertaste and dense, crunchy texture. Most rutabagas are quite large (1 to 2 pounds) and usually waxed to prolong their shelf life. Buy small, unwaxed rutabagas if you can. Avoid those that have cracks or look shriveled. Rutabagas are best when mashed or roasted. Store rutabagas in the crisper drawer; they will stay fresh for several weeks.

Shallots

Shallots have a complex, subtly sweet flavor. When shopping, avoid shallots packaged in cardboard and cellophane boxes, which prevent you from checking out each shallot. Instead, go for loose shallots or the ones packed in plastic netting. They should feel firm and heavy and have no soft spots. Shallots are perfect in sauces. Store shallots in a cool, dark place.

Spinach

Flat-leaf spinach is available in bunches; baby spinach is sold either loose or in bags; and curly-leaf spinach is bagged. Look for spinach that is a deep green in color (never yellow), with smooth leaves and crisp stems. Curly-leaf and baby spinach (if bought bagged) should be stored in their original packaging, which is designed to keep the spinach fresh. Flat-leaf spinach should be stored in a dry, open zipper-lock bag.

Stone Fruits

Stone fruits such as apricots, peaches, nectarines, and plums will continue to ripen after they are picked. Peaches are generally classified as clingstone, freestone, or semifreestone, all of which refer to how firmly the pit attaches to the flesh of the peach. In most supermarkets, you will find freestone peaches, which are obviously easier to deal with. The usual choices among varieties are yellow or white, distinguished by the hue of the skin and the flavor and color of the flesh. Yellow peaches are more acidic but they tend to mellow as they soften, while white peaches are prized for their very sweet taste. Nectarines resemble peaches but are smoother skinned and taste sweeter. Nectarines have dense flesh that is either white or yellow. You can use nectarines in any recipe that calls for peaches. Store stone fruits on the counter at room temperature, not in the refrigerator.

Sweet Peppers

Choose sweeter red, yellow, and orange bell peppers over green peppers, which taste bitter. Look for brightly colored peppers that are glossy and firm to the touch. If you are making stuffed peppers, choose those with a well-rounded shape and even bottoms. Other common sweet peppers include Cubanelles, also called "Italian frying peppers"; banana peppers, which are fruity with a gentle heat; and pimento peppers, the key ingredient in pimento cheese. You can store peppers in a loosely sealed zipper-lock bag in the refrigerator for up to one week.

Banana

Pimento

Sweet Potatoes

Sweet potatoes, which are often mislabeled as yams in U.S. grocery stores, can have light-yellow to deep-orange flesh; as a rule, the orange-fleshed tubers are sweeter and more tender. Choose firm sweet potatoes with skins that are taut, not wrinkled. Many varieties are available, and they can range quite a bit in color, texture, and flavor. Beauregard (usually sold as a conventional sweet potato) and Jewel are sweet and moist and have the familiar sweet-potato flavor. Red Garnet is more savory and has a looser texture. Nontraditional varieties that are lighter in color, like the Japanese White, White Sweet, and Batata, tend to be starchier and drier. Store sweet potatoes in a dark, well-ventilated spot (do not store them in a zipper-lock bag); they will keep for about one week.

Tomatoes

Choose locally grown tomatoes if at all possible, as this is the best way to ensure a flavorful tomato. Heirloom tomatoes are some of the best local tomatoes you can find. Choose tomatoes that smell fruity and feel heavy. If supermarket tomatoes are your only option, look for tomatoes sold on the vine. They are better than regular supermarket tomatoes, which are picked when still green and blasted with ethylene gas to develop texture and color. For cherry tomatoes, our favorite varieties are Red Cherry, Sun Gold, Green Grape, Sweet Gold, and Black Cherry. For cooking, try the Juliet variety of cherry tomatoes. Never refrigerate tomatoes; the cold damages enzymes that produce flavor compounds, and it ruins their texture. Even cut tomatoes should be kept at room temperature (wrap them tightly in plastic wrap). If the vine is still attached, leave it on and store the tomatoes stem end up. Store stemmed tomatoes stem side down at room temperature. This prevents moisture from escaping and bacteria from entering, and thus prolongs shelf life. To quickly ripen hard, unripened tomatoes, store them in a paper bag with a banana or an apple, both of which emit ethylene gas, which hastens ripening. For our recommendations on canned tomato products, see pages 138–139.

Turnips

Turnips are recognizable by their off-white skin capped with a purple halo. When young, turnips are tender and sweet, but as they age they become increasingly sulphurous, with a tough, woody texture and bitter aftertaste. Peeled turnips can be steamed, boiled, or roasted. Store turnips in the crisper drawer of the refrigerator.

Winter Squash

Whether acorn, butternut, delicata, or another variety, squash should feel hard; soft spots are an indication that the squash has been mishandled. Squash should also feel heavy for its size, a sign that the flesh is moist and soft. Whole squash you peel yourself has the best flavor and texture, but if you are looking to save a few minutes of prep, we have found that peeled and halved squash is fine. We don't like the butternut squash sold in chunks; while it's a timesaver, the flavor is wan and the texture stringy. You can store winter squash in a cool, well-ventilated spot for several weeks.

Acorn   Butternut

Delicata

Yams

Despite persistent mislabeling, yams and sweet potatoes are actually two completely unrelated vegetables. True yams are tropical tubers with light-colored flesh and woolly skin. They are bland, with an ultrastarchy texture. Steaming or boiling is the best way to prepare them. Store yams at room temperature. They will keep for about one month.

Yellow Summer Squash and Zucchini

Choose zucchini and yellow summer squash that are firm and without soft spots. Smaller squash are more flavorful and less watery than larger specimens; they also have fewer seeds. Look for zucchini and summer squash no heavier than 8 ounces, and preferably just 6 ounces. You can store the squash in the refrigerator in a partially open zipper-lock bag for several days.

EXOTIC FRUITS

Coconuts

The flesh of a coconut is dense and earthy, with a vanilla-like finish. When choosing coconuts, give them a shake: They should be heavy and full of liquid. Store at room temperature for up to six months.

Guavas

The pebbly skin of this Brazilian fruit can be green or purple, and its soft flesh ranges from stark white to bright pink. Guava's complex flavor is honey-sweet and funky. Fresh guavas are riddled with rock-hard seeds and are highly susceptible to fruit fly infestation: We recommend sticking with prepared guava juices or purees. Whole guavas can be stored in the crisper drawer for up to four days.

Kiwis

Beneath this fruit's furry skin lies brilliant green or gold flesh studded with tiny, crunchy black seeds. Its flavor is sweet-tart and it has a firm but juicy texture. Kiwis will ripen at room temperature and can be refrigerated for up to three weeks.

Mangos

Native to Southeast Asia, mangos have sweet, floral, and silky-smooth flesh that clings to a large, flat pit. Mangos are very fragrant when ripe and should yield to gentle pressure. Store mangos on the counter; they will ripen at room temperature.

Papayas

Papayas come in a wide range of shapes, colors, and sizes (they can weigh up to 20 pounds!). Their juicy, custard-smooth flesh holds hundreds of edible, peppery seeds. Ripe papayas are best eaten raw, but unripe papayas can be shredded and used in salads or cooked like a vegetable. Ripe papayas will yield to gentle pressure. Store papaya on the counter at room temperature.

Passion Fruit

A passion fruit is roughly the size of a lime and has a tough, leathery skin that wrinkles slightly when ripe. The interior is filled with a seedy, mustard-yellow, gelatinous pulp that is intensely aromatic, with hints of peach and raspberry. Passion fruit pulp is often strained to extract the juice. Passion fruit can be refrigerated for up to a week or frozen for up to a month.

Plantains

This large, starchy variety of banana is popular in Latin American, African, and Asian cuisines. Plantains mature from green to yellow to black. Store on the counter until ripe, then refrigerate. Though fully ripe plantains can be eaten out of hand, most plantains are cooked when they are still underripe. Their flavor is reminiscent of squash and potato, and they have a dense, spongy texture. Peel and fry, sauté, or boil.

The Tasting Lineup

Recommended

NATALIE'S
100% Florida Orange Juice, Gourmet Pasteurized
Top Pick $5.99 for 64 oz ($0.09 per oz)

SIMPLY ORANGE
Not from Concentrate 100% Pure Squeezed Pasteurized Orange Juice, Medium Pulp
$3.99 for 59 oz ($0.07 per oz)

MINUTE MAID
Pure Squeezed Never from Concentrate Pasteurized 100% Orange Juice, Some Pulp
$3.79 for 59 oz ($0.06 per oz)

MINUTE MAID
Original Frozen Concentrated Orange Juice
$2.99 for 64 oz ($0.05 per oz)

Orange juice is America's most popular juice, a breakfast staple with a sunny, wholesome image. Package labels tempt us with phrases like "fresh squeezed" and "grove to glass" and with images of oranges speared with straws. Even brand names like Simply Orange and Florida's Natural suggest that these juices are just a notch away from freshly picked fruit squeezed into a glass. But the truth is, commercial orange juice can't be that simple an enterprise because of the complex challenge that manufacturers face. What's at stake: how to produce (and profit from) a juice that has fresh and consistent flavor 365 days a year and a shelf life long enough to withstand transport to and storage in supermarkets. Mind you, this is all from a seasonal fruit crop with natural variation in flavor and that is susceptible to the whims of disease, bugs, and volatile weather patterns.

We built a tasting lineup around five nationally available refrigerated orange juices. (We selected medium pulp when available, as it's the style most akin to fresh squeezed and often the most popular.) We also included two frozen concentrates, because in previous tastings they had rated surprisingly high. And we threw in two lower-calorie juices—an increasingly popular subcategory made by cutting juice with water and sweetening it with stevia. All nine juices were served lightly chilled and evaluated for freshness, flavor, texture, and overall appeal.

Tasters panned the two lower-calorie juices for tasting "ridiculously sweet"—evidence that these producers may have overdone it with the stevia, which is up to 300 times sweeter than granulated sugar. As for the other juices, three self-described "gourmet" or "pure" products

earned the highest marks, with tasters touting their "nice balance of acidity and sweetness" and "fresh," "honest" flavors. However, the buzzwords on the labels didn't help explain why some juices performed better, as none of those terms are industry-regulated. Also not helpful were the nutrition labels, which indicated that all seven full-calorie samples had the same single ingredient—orange juice—and nearly identical nutritional makeups. That left us looking to processing methods for clues—an investigation that showed us just how far from fresh squeezed most commercial orange juice really is.

We figured that pasteurization would be an obvious place to start, particularly because a couple of the top-ranking products advertised that their juices were "gently pasteurized." But in most cases we were thwarted in our efforts to tie better flavor to juice being subjected to lower heat. It turns out that the FDA doesn't recognize the term "gently pasteurized," and most producers won't elaborate on what they mean by it either. Only one juice, a top performer, shared a pasteurization detail with us that indicated that the company is being gentler with its juice. The manufacturer heats it to around 160 degrees, which is the minimum pasteurization temperature recommended by the FDA to ensure safety and shelf-life stability. It's a temperature that industry experts say is, in fact, lower than what most juice makers use.

Still in search of other reasons for the flavor differences we perceived, we moved on to examine the next stage of orange juice processing: storage. Because different varieties of oranges are in season at different times, most

METHODOLOGY

We tasted nine nationally available supermarket orange juices, including two frozen concentrates; we rated them on freshness, sweetness, acidity, and overall appeal. An independent lab assessed levels of ethyl butyrate, a compound that occurs naturally in oranges and is added back to most commercial juice to make its flavor seem fresher, as well as the Brix (sugar content) and acidity. Products are listed in The Tasting Lineup in order of preference.

manufacturers squeeze the juice immediately and store it for months to maintain a year-round supply of particular varieties. To keep the juice from turning rancid, they must prevent it from oxidizing. These days, the answer for most companies is deaeration, a process in which they strip away the juice's oxygen and store the juice, sometimes for as long as a year, in million-gallon tanks—so-called tank farms—topped with a layer of nitrogen to prevent further deterioration.

The downside is that stripping the oxygen out of juice also strips out the juice's flavor-providing compounds. That's where blend technicians, who correct for flavor deficiencies, come in. Their job isn't simply a matter of blending multiple batches of juice to balance sweetness and acidity (though this is part of their process, and experts told us that blending likely contributed to some of the flavor differences that we detected). The technicians also restore taste to the juice through the addition of "flavor packs." These highly engineered additives are made from essential orange flavor volatiles that have been harvested from the fruit and its skin and then chemically reassembled by scientists at leading fragrance companies. By reorganizing these compounds, scientists are able to compensate for the flavor-destroying effects of pasteurization and deaeration, and to tailor the flavor of the juice to each juice company's exact specifications. Juice blending is an industry-wide practice, and most of the juices that we tasted were enhanced by flavor packs. What we learned is that the makers of our top-ranking juices did a better job of figuring out and executing the exact flavor profile that consumers wanted.

Consumer preferences vary across different cultures when it comes to orange juice flavor; what North Americans want their juice to taste like differs from what consumers in South America prefer, so juice companies often tweak their flavor pack formulas to vary the levels of perceived sweetness, freshness, and acidity. In the United States, fresh flavor is paramount, so juice makers include a compound called ethyl butyrate in the flavor packs. This compound isn't an artificial flavor: It occurs naturally in fresh-squeezed orange juice as an aroma, but because it's volatile, much of it is driven off during pasteurization and deaeration. Adding more ethyl butyrate to the juice after these processes actually restores the impression of freshness. We sent samples of all nine juices to an independent laboratory to get them analyzed for the compound. The results were convincing: Three of the juices that ranked highest for fresh flavor contained relatively high levels of ethyl butyrate (as high as 4.92 milligrams per liter), indicating that their respective companies were adding plenty of it to their flavor packs.

Notably, one juice that ranked high for freshness contained a much lower amount of ethyl butyrate (1.01 milligrams per liter) compared with other "fresh-tasting" juices. But as it turns out, fresh-squeezed orange juice naturally contains about 1.19 milligrams of ethyl butyrate per liter, so the amount in that juice isn't far off from what occurs naturally in the fruit. That statistic made even more sense when we learned the juice by that manufacturer is, in fact, a genuinely much fresher product than other orange juices. Rather than create an illusion of freshness by treating juice that's been deaerated with flavor packs, the manu-facturer squeezes oranges to order and ships its juice within 24 hours. Short storage times also allow the company to forgo deaeration.

Because the company squeezes oranges year-round, the flavor of its juice shifts as different varieties come into season; tasters reported that the batch we sampled was "superfresh" and pleasantly "tropical," with hints of mango, guava, and pineapple. It also has a much shorter shelf life than most commercial orange juices—26 days compared with about a year for juice that's been deaerated. That kind of flavor variability might not be what consumers expect from their orange juice, but it doesn't bother us. In fact, we named this juice our favorite because we think a juice that actually is fresher, not just engineered to taste that way, is worth seeking out—and paying a bit more for (it costs about 38 percent more than other high-ranking orange juices do). But if you're in the market for a juice that's consistent from bottle to bottle and costs a bit less, our runner-up tastes "very fresh" and does a nice job of balancing sweetness and acidity.

The
Tasting
Lineup,
CONTINUED

Recommended, continued
FLORIDA'S NATURAL
100% Pure Florida Orange Juice, with Pulp
$3.79 for 59 oz
($0.06 per oz)

TROPICANA
100% Frozen Concentrated Orange Juice
$1.89 for 48 oz
($0.04 per oz)

Recommended with Reservations
TROPICANA
Pure Premium Orange Juice, Homestyle
$3.99 for 59 oz
($0.07 per oz)

Not Recommended
MINUTE MAID
Pure Squeezed Light Orange Juice Beverage
$3.39 for 59 oz
($0.06 per oz)

TROPICANA
Trop50 Orange Juice Beverage
$3.99 for 59 oz
($0.07 per oz)

HERBS AND SPICES

HERBS

Basil

Sometimes labeled Genoa basil, this slightly acidic herb balances licorice and citrus notes. Avoid the basil sold in plastic clamshell boxes: It is of inconsistent quality and is usually overpriced. A bunch of basil sold with its roots attached is a far better option. Not only will the leaves of this basil be more flavorful, but the basil will also last longer if you store it upright in a glass at room temperature, with the roots submerged in an inch or two of water (change the water every day). Don't use dried basil in place of fresh.

Bay Leaf

Bay leaves are a standard addition to soups, stews, and bean dishes. We prefer dried bay leaves to fresh; they work just as well in long-cooked recipes, are cheaper, and will keep for months in the freezer. We prefer Turkish bay leaves to those from California. The California bay leaf has a medicinal and potent flavor. Turkish bay leaves have a mild, green, and slightly clove-like flavor.

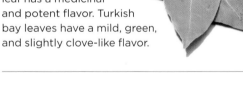

Cilantro

Cilantro, the fresh leaves and stems of the coriander plant, is also called Chinese parsley. This love-it-or-loathe-it herb is frequently used in Southeast Asian and Latin cuisines. Store it with its stems in water, or wrap it in damp paper towels and store it in a zipper-lock bag in the crisper drawer. Don't use dried cilantro in place of fresh.

Dill

Dill's feathery fronds are slightly bitter, with a refreshing, lemony quality and aroma akin to caraway seeds. Dill matches perfectly with cucumbers (both pickled and raw); its summery freshness also works well for seafood, potatoes, and eggs. It's best used as a finishing herb. Store fresh dill in the refrigerator with its stems in water. Avoid dried dill weed, which is tasteless, but for dishes that require an assertive dill flavor beyond the power of fresh dill, try dill seeds from the spice aisle.

Marjoram

A member of the mint family, fresh marjoram is often mistaken for oregano. Its flavor is sweet, with a delicate, fleeting spiciness. Marjoram is often paired with poultry, lamb, or vegetables, and is best used as a finishing herb. To store fresh marjoram, wrap in damp paper towels and place in a zipper-lock bag in the crisper drawer. Dried marjoram is widely available and acceptable in cooked applications.

Mint

Although there are more than 2,000 varieties of mint, spearmint is the most common. The flavor of mint can be described as smooth and bright, with a eucalyptus quality. Store fresh mint in the refrigerator with its stems in water. Don't use dried mint in place of fresh.

Oregano

This hardy perennial shrub has fuzzy, spade-shaped leaves and tough woody stems. Another member of the mint family, it has a potent flavor that can be described as earthy and musty, with a spicy-hot bite. Oregano is great in tomato sauces, chili, and Mexican and Latin dishes, and sprinkled on pizzas. To store fresh oregano, wrap it in damp paper towels and place in a zipper-lock bag in the crisper drawer. Dried oregano does not have the same sharp bite as fresh, but it does have a distinct and recognizable floral element.

Parsley

In the test kitchen, we prefer flat-leaf (or Italian) parsley, which is more assertive than curly-leaf parsley. Store parsley either with its stems in water or wrapped in damp paper towels and refrigerated in the crisper in a zipper-lock bag. Parsley freezes well (with some discoloration that doesn't affect flavor) in an airtight container for up to four months.

Tarragon

Tarragon is very assertive, with a mouth-numbing, anesthetic quality and a sweet orange-anise aroma. Tarragon can be used in fish, egg, and chicken dishes. Store fresh tarragon in the refrigerator with its stems in water.

Rosemary

This evergreen-like herb has an obvious pine aroma. When it's used in moderation its taste is clean, sweet, and floral, but if overused it can be like Vicks VapoRub. Rosemary works well in long-cooked dishes (especially those with Italian flavors) like soups, stews, and braises. Too much dried rosemary can turn a dish bitter, so use sparingly. For a gentle hint of rosemary in a soup, stew, or sauce, try adding a sprig of fresh rosemary during cooking and then remove it before serving. To store, wrap in damp paper towels and place in a zipper-lock bag in the crisper drawer.

Thyme

Thyme is good in long-cooked soups and stews and with roasted meats and poultry; it pairs well with mustard and lemon flavors. Its flavor mellows with cooking, so we often add extra at the end of a recipe. Wrap thyme in damp paper towels and store in a zipper-lock bag in the crisper.

GENERAL RULES FOR SUBSTITUTING DRIED HERBS

- Use only about one-third as much dried herbs as you would fresh.
- Add dried herbs at the same time you would add fresh.
- Avoid dried forms of delicate, leafy herbs such as basil, parsley, chives, mint, and cilantro.
- Heartier herbs, such as oregano, sage, and thyme, dry well and are good substitutes for fresh in most recipe—especially those in which the herbs will cook in liquid (such as sauces and stews).

Sage

Perhaps best known as the main herb in poultry seasoning, sage flavors a range of foods, from breakfast sausage to Thanksgiving stuffing. The flavor of sage is earthy and floral, with a musky bite. To store, wrap fresh sage in damp paper towels and place in a zipper-lock bag in the crisper drawer. Because of its cottony texture when raw, sage should be cooked. In its dried form, we prefer rubbed (or finely crumbled) sage to the ground and chopped kinds.

SPICES

Allspice

Allspice is a pea-size berry from the evergreen pimento tree that grows in tropical climates, such as Jamaica's. While allspice is often included in savory Caribbean seasonings, such as jerk, it's better known in the United States as a baking spice. Allspice tastes like a combination of cinnamon, cloves, and nutmeg, hence its name. However, we have found that it's impossible to capture the unique flavors of allspice by simply mixing other spices.

Anise

Anise seeds flavor sweets (think biscotti) and such liqueurs as Pernod, pastis, sambuca, and ouzo. They are a close cousin to fennel seeds, which are larger and more savory. Both contain the essential oil anethol, which gives them their licorice flavor. In the test kitchen, we've found that one can usually be substituted for the other, although we prefer to bake with the sweeter anise seeds.

Caraway

The Greeks used caraway as a cure for an upset stomach, and it's no coincidence that the seeds are still often paired with notoriously hard-to-digest foods like cabbage, cream sauces, and cheese. They are pungent and herbaceous, with a slightly bitter finish, making them a natural fit with fatty meats and in rye bread.

Cardamom

Fragrant cardamom comes in pods, either green or black, and in ground form. The seeds of the more common green form are used in many Scandinavian baked goods, in Indian sweets, and in chai tea. Most of the aromatic flavors live in the seeds and the flavor doesn't stick around, so buy whole pods and then remove and grind the seeds as needed.

Chili Powder

Chili powder is a seasoning blend made from ground dried chiles and an assortment of other ingredients. As with curry powder, there is no single recipe, but cumin, garlic, and oregano are traditional additions. Chili powder is not to be confused with the lesser-known chile powder (also often spelled chili powder), made solely from ground chiles without additional seasonings. We use the blend to season batches of chili and in spice rubs and marinades. A great chili powder is more than just heat. Our top product, **Morton & Bassett Chili Powder**, uses a combination of peppers to achieve complexity. This layering of multiple peppers creates depth that tasters preferred to the "flat" single-pepper powders. Supporting spices like cumin, oregano, garlic, and black pepper also play a role. These round out flavor, complementing the peppers without dominating or distracting from them. Look for a product with no added salt.

Cinnamon

Most cinnamon sold in the U.S. is actually cassia, not true Ceylon cinnamon (also known as canela). Both are the dried bark of tropical evergreen trees, but the bolder, spicier cassia is cheaper to process. Dried cinnamon is best for baking applications for an ideal fine, powdery consistency. While most brands will work fine as long as they're fresh, investing a little extra in a really good product like our winner, **Penzeys Extra Fancy Vietnamese Cassia Cinnamon**, will give you the best flavor for your baked goods. Stick cinnamon is best for mulling cider and wine, poaching fruit, and in some pan sauces and marinades.

Cloves

Pungent, peppery cloves are the dried, unopened buds of an Indonesian tree. Ground cloves are potent, so the test kitchen uses them sparingly. Add whole cloves to the poaching liquid for fruit or, on the savory side, employ them to flavor stock and to stud holiday hams.

Coriander

These light-brown spherical seeds are the dried fruit of the herb cilantro, a member of the parsley family. Coriander possesses a sweet, almost fruity flavor with just a hint of the soapy-metallic character of mature cilantro.

Cumin

Like coriander, these tiny, elongated seeds belong to a plant in the parsley family. Their flavor is earthy and warm, but it's their pungent, almost musty aroma that sets them apart from other warm spices. We often use ground cumin in chili, barbecue sauces, and rubs. Cumin seeds can also add toastiness, crunch, and a distinctive woodsy aroma to vegetables like sautéed snap peas or roasted beets.

Curry Powder

Though blends can vary dramatically, curry powders come in two basic styles—mild (or sweet), and a hotter version called Madras. We tend to use the former, which is more widely adaptable to a variety of recipes. Mild curry powder combines as many as 20 different ground spices, herbs, and seeds, the staples being turmeric (which accounts for the traditional ocher color), coriander, cumin, black and red pepper, cinnamon, cloves, fennel seeds, cardamom, ginger, and fenugreek. Our favorite is a mail-order brand, **Penzeys Sweet Curry Powder**, that strikes the perfect balance between sweetness and heat.

Fennel Seeds

Fennel seeds come from a bulbless variety of the fennel plant. They have a heavy anise flavor and an earthy, butterscotch-like aroma. Fennel seeds are frequently found in sausages and spice rubs.

Five-Spice Powder

Chinese five-spice powder adds a kick that offsets richness in both sweet and savory recipes. In traditional Chinese cooking, the five elements of the cosmos—earth, fire, metal, water, and wood—are represented by the elements of five-spice powder. Most blends include cinnamon, star anise, cloves, fennel, and pepper. Star anise, with its licorice notes and tangy heat is a key player in the flavor profile of this spice blend, so we prefer brands that foreground it, like our favorite, **Frontier Natural Products Co-op Five Spice Powder**. Some "five-spice" blends actually include more than five ingredients, which can help round out the flavors.

KEEPING SPICES AND DRIED HERBS FRESHER LONGER

- Buy spices whole, not ground, whenever possible and grind them just before using, either with a small coffee grinder reserved for this purpose or with a mortar and pestle. Grinding releases the volatile compounds that give a spice its flavor and aroma.

- Clean out your pantry regularly. The longer spices or herbs are stored, the less potent their flavor will be. We recommend using stick-on dots to label each jar with a purchase date and then regularly purging your pantry of jars that are more than 12 months old.

- Don't buy dried herbs or spices in the bulk section.

- Heat, light, and moisture shorten the shelf life of spices and herbs, so keep them in a cool, dark place to prolong their freshness.

- Check dried herbs for freshness by crumbling a small amount between your fingers and taking a whiff. If they release a lively aroma, they're still good to go. If the aroma and the color of the herb have faded, it's time to restock.

Garam Masala

Though there are countless variations of garam masala, the warm flavors (garam means "warm" or "hot" and masala means "spice blend") dominating this Indian spice mix are consistent: black pepper, dried chiles, cinnamon, cardamom, and coriander are staples, while cloves, cumin, fennel, mace, and nutmeg frequently turn up as supporting players. Usually we recommend grinding whole spices (such as black pepper and nutmeg), but concocting this complex spice blend at home can add a great deal of time to your cooking—not to mention crowding your pantry with jar after jar of seldom-used ingredients and running up a hefty shopping tab. Look for a supermarket version that includes most of the traditional spices listed above and no unusual additions, such as autolyzed yeast extract or dehydrated onion. Our favorite brand, **McCormick Gourmet Collection Garam Masala**, sticks with core ingredients for a mellow, well-balanced flavor profile.

Garlic Powder

Garlic powder is handy when mixing spice rubs, letting you add subtle garlic flavor without garlic texture. Made from dehydrated, ground garlic cloves, it's easy to keep on hand as a pantry staple. Make sure you buy a brand that lists "garlic" as its only ingredient. In the few applications where you don't want the moisture of fresh garlic or where the garlic could easily burn (like on a hot grill) we found that just about any garlic powder will do, especially when mixed with other spices in a rub. Our top pick is **Spice Islands Garlic Powder**, which came closest to actual garlic cloves with its strong, pungent flavor.

Ginger

Yes, ground ginger comes from the dried fresh root, but don't substitute one for the other. They taste quite different, as fresh is more floral while dried is spicier. They also work differently in baking; fresh ginger is moister and less potent. We do, however, sometimes reinforce ground ginger with grated fresh ginger in the test kitchen (to make gingerbread, for instance). A staple in bakers' pantries, ground ginger adds a warm, spicy flavor and aroma to baked goods and many Asian and Indian dishes. We prefer a brand like **Spice Islands Ground Ginger**, which has a full ginger flavor and moderate heat.

Mustard

These acrid seeds are typically yellow, brown, or black. Mustard seeds have almost no aroma, but their flavor is earthy and sharp, with a strong peppery kick. We often use them for pickling and canning. Ground mustard powder is good for spice rubs and adds a kick to sauces.

Nutmeg

Heady and powerful, nutmeg is a hard brown seed from a tropical tree. It's often used in dairy-based savory dishes, like quiche and creamed spinach, or for sweets such as spice cake. We compared fresh with preground and found that in dishes in which nutmeg is the sole spice, grinding it yourself (we like to use a rasp-style grater) is important. But in foods with lots of spices, preground nutmeg is fine.

Paprika

"Paprika" is a generic term for a spice made from ground dried red peppers. Sweet paprika (sometimes called "Hungarian paprika" or simply "paprika") is the most common. Our hands-down favorite, **The Spice House Hungarian Sweet Paprika**, boasts a "fruity," "earthy" balance. Smoked paprika, a Spanish favorite, is produced by drying peppers (either sweet or hot) over smoldering oak embers. Since smoked paprika has a deep, musky flavor all its own, we do not recommend using it for all applications; it is best used to add a smoky aroma to boldly flavored dishes. Our favorite brand is **Simply Organic Smoked Paprika**. Hot paprika, most often used in chilis, curries, or stews, can be made from any number of hot peppers. It can range from slightly spicy to punishingly assertive, and it shouldn't be substituted for sweet paprika in cooking. On the other hand, sweet paprika can be substituted for hot by simply adding cayenne pepper to boost the burn.

Peppercorns

Preground pepper is not worth buying. Replacing your pepper shaker with a good pepper mill is one of the simplest ways to enhance your cooking. For supermarket brands, we like peppercorns that have spice and moderate heat. Our favorite supermarket brand is **Morton & Bassett Organic Whole Black Peppercorns**. You can get even more flavor nuance from a premium mail-order brand like **Kalustyan's Indian Tellicherry Black Peppercorns**, but it's only worth it for a recipe that really highlights the pepper, like a steak au poivre. In applications that call for a small dose, any pepper will be fine as long as it is freshly ground. If a recipe calls for white pepper, don't substitute black pepper—not only will it affect the look of the dish, but you'll miss the floral, earthy flavors of the white pepper.

See page 94 for Inside the Tasting.

Saffron

Sometimes known as "red gold," saffron is the world's most expensive spice. It's made from the dried stigmas of Crocus sativus flowers; the stigmas are so delicate they must be harvested by hand in a painstaking process. Luckily, a little saffron goes a long way, adding a distinct reddish-gold color, notes of honey and grass, and a slight hint of bitterness to dishes like bouillabaisse, paella, and risotto. You can find it as powder or threads. The major producers are Iran and Spain; the saffron you find in the supermarket is usually Spanish. Look for bottles that contain dark red threads—saffron is graded, and the richly hued, high-grade threads from the top of the stigma yield more flavor than the lighter, lesser-grade threads from the base. Unless saffron is the main flavoring in your recipe, you'll likely be fine with any brand.

SALT SUBSTITUTES

Salt substitutes typically replace some or all of the sodium chloride (table salt) with potassium chloride, a salty-tasting mineral. Potassium chloride is naturally bitter, so look for a salt substitute that compensates for this bitterness with the addition of varying amounts of real table salt. Those containing at least some sodium chloride will taste a whole lot better than those that have none at all.

Salt

Salt is one of the most integral ingredients in cooking. The three types we use most often are table salt, kosher salt, and sea salt. Table salt, also known as common salt, consists of tiny, uniformly shaped crystals which dissolve easily, making it our go-to for most applications. Avoid iodized salt, which can impart a subtle chemical flavor. Kosher salt has larger, coarser grains than table salt and is our top choice for seasoning meat. The large grains distribute easily and cling well to the meat's surfaces. The two major brands of kosher salt—Morton and Diamond Crystal—work equally well; however, their crystal sizes differ considerably and this makes a difference when measuring by volume. Sea salt is the product of seawater evaporation—a time-consuming, expensive process that yields irregularly shaped, mineral-rich flakes. Don't bother cooking with pricey sea salt; mixed into food, it doesn't taste any different than table salt. Instead, use it as a "finishing salt," where its delicate crunch stands out. Look for brands boasting large, flaky crystals such as our favorite, **Maldon Sea Salt**. You can substitute kosher or sea salt for table salt, but you'll need more of them, since the small size of table salt grains makes it "saltier" (more crystals fit in a measuring spoon). Kosher salt and coarse sea salt do not dissolve as readily as table salt; for this reason, we do not recommend using them in baking recipes. The two most popular brands of kosher salt are made differently and therefore measure differently. Our recipes are formulated using Diamond Crystal Kosher Salt.

1 teaspoon table salt =
1½ teaspoons Morton Kosher Salt =
2 teaspoons Diamond Crystal Kosher Salt

Star Anise

As the name suggests, these pods are star-shaped and they taste like anise. The warm, licorice-like flavor of star anise works well in both sweet and savory foods (such as custards or Asian marinades). It's an essential element of five-spice powder. Try flavoring sugar syrup with whole pods and drizzling the syrup over citrus fruits.

Beyond its heat and sharp bite, black pepper enhances our ability to taste food, stimulating our salivary glands so we experience flavors more fully. But this effect only comes from freshly ground pepper. Once the hard, black shell of the peppercorn is cracked open, its aroma immediately starts to fade, and most of its flavor and scent disappear within a half hour. Not surprisingly, we have never found axpreground pepper worth buying. In fact, replacing your pepper shaker with a good pepper mill is one of the simplest ways to enhance your cooking. But can choosing a better variety of peppercorn improve it even more?

Until recently, spice brands sold in supermarkets never specified the origin or variety of their peppercorns, as they simply bought the cheapest they could get. But specialty spice retailers offering multiple varieties bearing exotic names such as Sarawak, Lampong, Malabar, and Tellicherry have raised consumer awareness, and now even some of the largest supermarket brands have added "gourmet" Tellicherry peppercorns to their lines. Though Tellicherry is generally considered to be the world's finest pepper, all true peppercorns—black, green, and white—actually come from the same plant, *Piper nigrum*. Native to India, this flowering vine is now grown in many other tropical areas close to the equator, including Vietnam, Ecuador, Brazil, and Madagascar. It sprouts clusters of berries that are dried and treated to become peppercorns. Like grapes, coffee beans, and cacao beans, the flavor of peppercorns depends on where they are cultivated, when the berries are picked, and how they are processed. But all peppercorns are defined by the heat-bearing compound piperine, which perks up our taste buds. Their complex flavor and aroma also come from volatile oils called terpenes, which contribute notes of turpentine, clove, and citrus; and pyrazines, which provide earthy, roasty, green vegetable aromas. While most peppercorns are picked as soon as the immature green berries appear on the vine, Tellicherry berries (named after a port town in the state of Kerala on India's Malabar Coast) are left to ripen the longest. This allows the pepper's flavor to fully develop, becoming deeper and more complex, even a little fruity—not just sharp, hot, and bright like peppercorns made from younger berries. But given that we generally use just a few grinds of pepper on our food, would we be able to detect such differences?

To find out, we sampled Tellicherry peppercorns from the two largest supermarket brands against six of the other most popular supermarket brands. Priced from about $1.35 to $2.22 per ounce, most of these brands did not specify variety. As we tasted each black pepper freshly ground with optional white rice, it was immediately clear that there were big differences among brands. Some were searingly hot, others mild; some one-dimensional, others complex. Only two peppers impressed our tasters enough to be recommended without reservation. The most widely available peppercorns in the country were not recommended at all, finishing dead last.

If fancier supermarket peppercorns were good, would peppercorns from specialty merchants taste better? We ordered some online to find out. We focused on Tellicherry peppercorns for their stellar reputation, choosing six mail-order brands to pit against our two supermarket winners.

Though tasters detected a range of flavor nuances from brand to brand, final rankings were close. We gave top marks to highly aromatic peppercorns with complex flavor, and preferred moderate rather than strong heat, which tended to overpower any other taste. Peppercorns also lost points for having an alluring aroma with no flavor to back it up. Our favorite peppercorn was the fresh, earthy,

METHODOLOGY

We tasted eight samples of freshly ground whole black peppercorns plain (with optional white rice). The samples included six mail-order Tellicherry peppercorns and two supermarket brands. The supermarket peppercorns were singled out as favorites in an earlier tasting of the eight top-selling brands. We rated the peppercorns on aroma, heat, complexity, and overall taste. Products are listed in The Tasting Lineup in order of preference.

and moderately hot Tellicherry sold online by a Manhattan emporium. Coming in as a close second, however, was one of the supermarket winners. As with the winning brand, tasters praised this pepper for being spicy but not too hot, as well as fresh, fragrant, and floral. Sampled against this steep competition, our other supermarket Tellicherry brand was deemed "unremarkable."

So what would account for differences in the flavor and heat levels of the Tellicherry peppercorns, when they all come from the same region? The most important factor probably has to do with differences in cultivars, or varieties, of the plant itself, which grows on plantations in the state of Kerala, an area about the size of the Netherlands. Though none of the spice companies we spoke to would share details of the processing methods used by their suppliers, these approaches can also influence taste—peppercorns can be picked by hand or by machine, dried in the sunlight or a kiln, or even boiled. Storage also has an impact on flavor. Peppercorns that are subjected to too much heat or moisture grow musty-smelling mold and bacteria, all the while losing flavor. In fact, some peppercorns, including our winner, get a special cleaning in the United States before they go on sale, restoring freshness after months at sea.

Now that we had our winners, an important question remained: Would a better pepper's complexity be evident if we just added the usual pinch or two in cooking? We chose polar opposites—our winner and the bottom-ranked peppercorns from our supermarket tasting—and sampled them stirred into scrambled eggs and tomato soup. Interestingly, with pepper as a mere accent, the distinctions between these two very differently rated brands became difficult to detect: Votes were split as to which brand tasted better.

But what if peppercorns are one of the main attractions, as in steak au poivre, which is thickly crusted with crushed peppercorns and pan-seared? We compared steaks made with three different brands. This time, the nuances of the peppercorns came through, with tasters echoing their original assessments. Our winner impressed tasters most for its "fruity, pungent, really complex berry-like flavors," while our second place finisher came in right behind it with a "very bold, full flavor." The other brand ranked a few steps down from those top two—just as it had in the plain tasting.

The verdict? In applications that call for a small dose, any pepper will be fine as long as it is freshly ground. But if you're cooking a peppery specialty, or you like to grind fresh pepper over your food before eating, choosing a superior peppercorn can make a difference.

SICHUAN PEPPERCORNS

Despite their name, the small, reddish brown husks called Sichuan peppercorns aren't peppercorns at all. They're the dried fruit rinds from a small Chinese citrus tree called the prickly ash. Though typically ground and added to spicy dishes, they don't contribute heat. Instead, they contribute a unique tingling or buzzing sensation much like carbonation, which is due to a pungent compound called *sanshool* that acts on receptors that usually respond to touch. According to research conducted by the Institute of Cognitive Neuroscience, University College London, the peppercorns send signals to the brain that we interpret as a vibration; some also mistakenly perceive these signals as heat. We tried five samples cracked over white rice (which left our brave tasters' tongues buzzing for minutes) and ground in our recipe for Crispy Salt and Pepper Shrimp. We were pleased to find that each product smelled fresh and potent; a too-mild aroma can be a sign of a low-quality product. We detected everything from deep, earthy notes of pine and black tea to the more floral, herbal fragrance of citrus and mint, which translated to the same complex spectrum of flavors. Whether sprinkled over rice or cooked with other flavorings in the shrimp, the peppercorns had a unique taste and aroma that stood out. When we evaluated the trademark tingle, our tasters preferred those with the most pronounced effect. Our favorite, **Dean & DeLuca Szechuan Peppercorns**, combined "earthy, piney flavor" and a "sharp," "zippy" tingle.

The Tasting Lineup

Recommended
KALUSTYAN'S
Indian Tellicherry Black Peppercorns
Top Pick $6.99 for 2.5 oz

MORTON & BASSETT
Organic Whole Black Peppercorns
Best Buy $5.39 for 2 oz

ZINGERMAN'S
Tellicherry Peppercorns
$8 for 2.53 oz

Recommended with Reservations
VANNS SPICES
Tellicherry Peppercorns
$3.77 for 2.25 oz

MCCORMICK GOURMET COLLECTION
Tellicherry Black Peppercorns
$4.99 for 1.87 oz

PENZEYS
India Tellicherry Peppercorns
$3.49 for 2.2 oz

THE SPICE HOUSE
Tellicherry Black Peppercorns
$2.98 for 2.5 oz

DEAN & DELUCA
Tellicherry Peppercorns
$5.75 for 2 oz

EGGS AND DAIRY

EGGS

Grading

The U.S. Department of Agriculture (USDA) labels eggs AA, A, or B according to their shell appearance and the quality of the egg inside. A misshapen or thin shell typically merits the lowest B grade, and such eggs are usually used commercially. To distinguish AA from A, graders use a method called candling: Each egg is held up to a bright light in a dark room to check the interior quality. Grade AA eggs have whites that are so thick that the yolk is hard to see; these are rare and expensive in supermarkets. Grade A eggs have slightly looser whites and softer yolks and account for most of the eggs sold in supermarkets. Both are acceptable in any application.

Color

The shell's hue depends on the breed of the chicken. The run-of-the-mill leghorn chicken produces the typical white egg. Brown-feathered birds, such as Rhode Island Reds, produce ecru- to coffee-colored eggs. Despite marketing hype extolling the virtues of nonwhite eggs, our tests proved that shell color has no effect on flavor.

Farm-Fresh and Organic

In our taste tests, farm-fresh eggs were standouts. The large yolks were shockingly orange and sat very high above the comparatively small whites, and the flavor of these eggs was exceptionally rich and complex. The organic eggs followed in second place, with eggs from hens raised on a vegetarian diet in third, and the standard supermarket eggs last. Differences were easily detected in egg-based dishes like an omelet or a frittata but not in cakes or cookies.

Pasteurization

In rare cases, eating raw egg (in cookie dough, homemade mayonnaise, etc.) can result in the bacterial infection salmonella, but pasteurized eggs promise a safer alternative. Whole, in-the-shell eggs are pasteurized by going through a succession of heated water baths (warm enough to kill bacteria, but not so warm as to cook the eggs) before being chilled and waxed so that the porous shells cannot be recontaminated. Pasteurized eggs are a suitable substitute for regular eggs in any application, but pasteurized egg whites will take more than twice as long to whip, as they are much looser and more watery than their unpasteurized counterparts.

Size

Depending on the chicken's size, eggs can vary from about 1 to 3 ounces. In the test kitchen, we typically use large eggs, but other sizes can be substituted according to weight.

Egg Weights

Size	Weight (in oz)
Medium	1.75
Large	2.00
Extra-Large	2.25
Jumbo	2.50

Egg Size Equivalents

Large		Jumbo	Extra-Large	Medium
1	=	1	1	1
2	=	1½	2	2
3	=	2½	2½	3½
4	=	3	3½	4½
5	=	4	4	6
6	=	5	5	7

For half an egg, whisk the yolk and white together and use half of the liquid.

Storage

According to the USDA, all eggs sold in U.S. supermarkets must be washed and sanitized before being transported and stored at temperatures no higher than 45 degrees Fahrenheit. They must remain refrigerated (the USDA recommends storing eggs at 40 degrees) for two main reasons: to keep existing bacteria from multiplying rapidly and to stop additional bacteria from entering through the shell, made porous because washing removes a protective outer layer. Thus eggs purchased from a grocery store in the United States should always be refrigerated, not kept on the counter. Eggs should also be kept off the refrigerator door and in their original carton (rather than a built-in refrigerator egg tray) for several reasons. Most important, the door is probably the warmest spot in your refrigerator. We placed thermometers in the doors of six test-kitchen refrigerators and found that the temperature averaged 45 degrees. The temperature on the shelves is between 35 and 40 degrees, an ideal temperature for prolonging the shelf life of eggs. Even if your refrigerator door is cold enough, we suggest keeping eggs in the carton. Believe it or not, eggs can dry out, and the carton offers them some protection against this. Eggs can also readily absorb flavors from pungent foods, such as onions, and the carton helps to keep these odors at bay.

Freshness

Egg cartons are marked with both a sell-by date and a pack date. The pack date is the day the eggs were graded and packed, which is generally a week within being laid but, legally, it only needs to be within 30 days. The pack date is printed on egg cartons as a three-digit code near the sell-by date, and it runs consecutively from 001 (January 1) to 365 (December 31). The sell-by date is within 30 days of the pack date. In short, a carton of eggs may be up to two months old by the end of the sell-by date. Even so, according to the USDA, eggs are still fit for consumption for an additional three to five weeks past the sell-by date. We tasted two- and three-month-old eggs and found them perfectly palatable. At four months, the white was very loose and the yolk tasted faintly of the refrigerator, though it was still edible. Our advice is to use your discretion. If the eggs smell odd or display discoloration, pitch them. Older eggs also lack the structure-lending properties of fresh eggs, so beware when baking.

Eggs and Omega-3

Several companies are marketing eggs with a high level of omega-3 fatty acids, the healthful unsaturated fats also found in some fish. We set up a blind tasting of eggs containing various levels of omega-3. Our finding: More omega-3s translates into a richer egg flavor and a deeper yolk color. Why? Commercially raised chickens usually peck on corn and soy, while chickens on an omega-3-enriched diet have supplements of greens, flaxseeds, and algae, which add flavor, complexity, and color to their eggs. When shopping for a good egg, buyer beware: Brands may claim a high level of omega-3s, but the fine print sometimes reveals that the number refers to the level present in two eggs, not one. Look for brands that guarantee at least 200 milligrams per egg.

Liquid Egg Whites

To avoid tossing egg yolks down the drain when making recipes that call for egg whites only, you may want to try liquid egg whites. We tested three brands of liquid egg whites alongside hand-separated whites in our recipes for egg white omelets, meringue cookies, and angel food cake. They all made acceptable substitutes in omelets; in baked goods, however, they came up a bit short—literally. The USDA requires that liquid egg whites be pasteurized, which compromises the whites' structure. They can't achieve the same volume when whipped as fresh whites. Our top-ranked brand, **Eggology 100% Egg Whites**, makes a good substitute for fresh whites in omelets, scrambles, and frittatas, and is satisfactory in baked goods.

BUTTER

Salted Butter

Avoid buying salted butter for use in recipes. The amount of salt varies from brand to brand (although ⅜ teaspoon per stick is the average). In some recipes, that level of salt will ruin the dish. We do use salted butter as a condiment for foods like corn on the cob or toast when we want extra-salty, savory flavor. On those occasions, it's worth investing in a premium option. Look for brands that come wrapped in foil instead of wax parchment, which will help protect the butter from off-flavors. Our favorite, **Lurpak Slightly Salted Butter**, is also cultured, which results in a complex, rich product.

Unsalted Butter

We use regular unsalted butter when cooking or baking. We don't think premium, high-fat butters are worth the extra money, at least for cooking. The USDA requires that all butter must consist of at least 80 percent milk fat. Because fat costs money, regular supermarket butter rarely contains more than 80 percent. Premium butters, many of which are imported from Europe, have a slightly higher fat level, up to 86 percent. Our tasting of leading butters, both regular and premium, indicated that fat level doesn't really make much difference. Our favorite butter for everyday use and baking is **Land O' Lakes Unsalted Sweet Butter**. For a premium unsalted option, we like **Plugrá European-Style Unsalted Butter**.

Cultured Butter

Culturing, or fermenting cream before churning it into butter, is standard practice in Europe and builds tangy, complex flavors. Our tasters found it fairly easy to detect cultured butter's nuances when spread on toast, though in baking and cooking the differences are quite slight. Cultured butter also tends to be more expensive, and as such, we recommend buying it for use as a spread rather than for cooking or baking.

Storage

Placed in the back of the fridge where it's coldest (not in the small door compartment), butter will keep for 2½ weeks. Butter can pick up off-flavors and turn rancid when kept in the refrigerator for longer than a month. If you don't need to use it much, store butter in the freezer for up to four months in a zipper-lock storage bag and thaw sticks as needed.

Format

Whipped butter, made by beating air into butter, makes a creamy spread but isn't always a good alternative to stick butter for cooking. It won't make a big difference in baking, but in uncooked applications such as frosting, whipped butter can give foods a plastic-like taste. If you want to use whipped butter, base your substitution on weight, not volume. (Adding air increases the volume, not the weight.) A standard tub of whipped butter weighs 8 ounces, equal to two sticks of butter.

MILK, CREAM, AND OTHER DAIRY PRODUCTS

Milk

Whole milk contains 3.5 percent milk fat. In general, we use whole milk in the test kitchen. As implied by their labels, 2 percent and 1 percent milk contain 2 percent fat and 1 percent fat, respectively. Skim milk must contain less than 0.5 percent fat. It's usually okay to substitute low-fat milk for whole milk in baking, but skim milk can cause serious texture and flavor problems, since fat adds moisture and carries flavor.

Heavy Cream

Heavy cream must contain at least 36 percent fat. We prefer pasteurized heavy cream with a fat content of 40 percent (6 grams per tablespoon); it's the best all-purpose cream to have on hand for whipping, baking, and cooking. The next best choice is an ultrapasteurized heavy cream with a high fat content. Try to avoid cream that contains additives like emulsifiers or stabilizing agents.

Whipping Cream

Whipping cream must have at least 30 percent fat but no more than 36 percent (less than heavy cream). We find that heavy cream actually whips better than whipping cream and keeps its whipped consistency for longer. We don't recommend whipping cream.

Half-and-Half

As the name suggests, half-and-half is a mixture of milk and cream. According to the USDA, half-and-half must contain 10.5 to 18 percent fat, which is much more than whole milk, but we find that in most baked goods that call for half-and-half you can get away with using whole milk. In dishes where you're looking for creaminess (not just fat and flavor), the differences will be notable although generally not unacceptable. You can also make a closer approximation of half-and-half by mixing regular milk and heavy cream.

1 cup half-and-half =
⅓ cup heavy cream + ⅔ cup skim milk

1 cup half-and-half =
¼ cup heavy cream + ¾ cup whole milk

Buttermilk

Buttermilk was traditionally the liquid left over from churning butter. Most modern buttermilk, however, is cultured milk. You can use non-fat and low-fat buttermilk interchangeably in most recipes. However, if you're making a custard-style dessert, stick with the low-fat type. Buttermilk keeps for several weeks in the refrigerator. You can also freeze it for up to a month, but the emulsion will break, so blend it after thawing to re-emulsify it for salad dressings or dips. (Thawed buttermilk is fine as is in recipes for baked goods.) If you don't have buttermilk, homemade clabbered milk is a good substitute: Add 1 tablespoon of lemon juice to 1 cup of milk. Powdered buttermilk (found in the baking section of the supermarket) is a good, easy replacement for liquid buttermilk in baking (the powder is added to the recipe along with the dry ingredients, and water is added when the liquid buttermilk is called for).

Shelf-Stable Milk Products

Both sweetened condensed milk and evaporated milk consist of milk from which 60 percent of the water has been removed. The only difference is that sweetened condensed milk, as its name suggests, is highly sweetened. Our favorite brands of sweetened condensed milk are **Borden Eagle Brand Sweetened Condensed Milk** and **Nestlé Carnation Sweetened Condensed Milk**. Evaporated milk can be substituted for regular milk by adding an equal amount of water (1 cup evaporated milk plus 1 cup water equals 2 cups whole milk). Because of its high sugar content, sweetened condensed milk cannot be substituted for evaporated or regular milk. Instant milk (dried milk powder that can be reconstituted with water) can be used as a substitute for regular whole milk with minor compromises in flavor and texture.

Sour Cream

Sour cream is an American product made from light cream (approximately 18 to 20 percent fat). It is pasteurized and then treated with lactic-acid producing bacteria. The bacterial action thickens the cream to a semisolid and gives it its recognizably piquant flavor. Sour cream has a markedly wet texture—the whey often floats atop—and a light, fleeting flavor.

Crème Fraîche

Crème fraîche is often considered the French equivalent of sour cream, but it is quite different. It is made from 30 to 40 percent butterfat cream that has been left out to mature and naturally sour without the addition of bacteria starters (which are generally added to sour cream). The final product is not sour or acidic, as is sour cream, but has a nutty flavor and is mildly tangy. The texture is smooth, rich, and spoonable.

ALTERNATIVE MILKS

There are a number of dairy-free milks on the market today, including those made from soy, rice, hemp, oats, quinoa, almonds, hazelnuts, cashews, and coconut. We have found that almond milk and soy milk generally make the best replacements for regular milk in recipes. See below for more notes on milk substitutes.

Almond Milk

Unflavored almond milk is a decent milk substitute in baked goods, but think twice before using it in custards, pudding, or sauces—almond lovers may be satisfied with the results, but you won't be fooling anyone.

Soy Milk

Most brands of soy milk come in sweetened and unsweetened versions. Both will work as substitutes for regular milk in desserts and unsweetened soy milk will work in savory dishes, as long as there is enough richness in the recipe to make up for its leanness.

Coconut Milk

Coconut milk is made by steeping equal parts shredded coconut meat and either warm milk or water. A brand with low sugar content, like **Chaokoh Coconut Milk**, can be used in some applications, but the flavor of coconut milk is too specific to make it a basic milk substitute.

Lactose-Free Milk

Lactose-free milk can be used interchangeably with regular milk in baking applications, but it will add off-flavors to savory applications.

Nonrefrigerated Boxed Milk

This product, which has a flavor profile akin to that of cooked milk, can be used as an acceptable substitute for fresh milk in most sweet and savory applications. Boxed milk can be kept for up to six months unopened and unrefrigerated.

Yogurt

When we use plain yogurt in a recipe, we usually prefer a whole-milk version. Whole-milk yogurt has three times as much fat as low-fat yogurt and far more flavor. In fact, we prefer brands that have the most fat, like **Brown Cow Cream Top Plain Yogurt**, which has a rich flavor profile and creamy, smooth texture. We don't recommend cooking with nonfat yogurt. Excess yogurt can be frozen and then thawed and used in baking applications (don't use it for sauces or eating plain, as it will tend to separate and curdle).

Greek Yogurt

Greek-style yogurt is made by allowing the watery whey to drain from yogurt, giving it a smooth, thick texture. Because of this, even low-fat and nonfat versions taste remarkably decadent. In the test kitchen we prefer it to thinner, runnier American yogurt in creamy dips and sauces. Look for Greek yogurt with low carbohydrate levels and minimal additives to ensure you're choosing a brand that actually strains its product rather than uses thickeners to mimic the texture of a strained yogurt. **Fage Total** makes our favorite nonfat, low-fat (2%), and whole-milk plain Greek yogurts. All of their products have a mild tang and rich texture. To substitute Greek-style yogurt for American-style yogurt in baked goods, use only two-thirds of the amount of yogurt called for in the recipe and make up the difference with water.

Ice Cream

The best ice creams add richness with egg yolks (mass-market brands use emulsifiers), and by lowering overrun (the amount of air churned into ice cream). Less overrun means denser, creamier ice cream. **Ben & Jerry's** makes both our favorite chocolate and vanilla varieties. **See page 106 for Inside the Tasting.**

CHEESE

Storing Cheeses

For long-term storage in the refrigerator, we find that cheeses are best wrapped in parchment paper and then in aluminum foil. The paper allows the cheese to breathe a bit, while the foil keeps out off-flavors from the refrigerator and prevents the cheese from drying out. Simply placing the cheese in a zipper-lock bag, pressing out all the air, and then sealing the bag tightly is our second choice. Pressing plastic wrap directly against the surface of most cheeses will cause a slight sour flavor to develop over time, so we do not recommend this storage method.

American Cheese

American cheese can range dramatically in color, flavor, and texture. Look for a brand like our top pick, **Boar's Head American Cheese**, which lists just five ingredients on its packaging—cheese, water, cream, sodium phosphates, and salt. It won top marks for its nutty, creamy taste. Avoid products that use cheaper dairy ingredients like milk, whey, or milk protein concentrate instead of cheese. Higher fat and protein contents are good ways to judge which American cheese will have the most flavor and best texture for melting. Look for brands labeled as "process cheese" rather than "cheese product" or "cheese food." In order to be called "process cheese," a product must meet strict FDA specifications.

Asiago

This cow's-milk cheese is sold at various ages. Fresh Asiago is firm like cheddar or Havarti, with a fairly mild flavor. Aged Asiago is drier, almost like Parmesan, and has a much sharper, saltier flavor. Our winning brand of Asiago is **BelGioioso**.

Blue Cheese

Named for its streaks (called veins) of bluish-green mold, blue cheese may be made from goat's, sheep's, or cow's milk, or a combination thereof. At one extreme are pricey imports like Roquefort, a soft, pungent sheep's milk cheese, and Stilton, a crumbly, nutty English cow's milk cheese. At the milder end of the spectrum is the firm, tangy Danish Blue. Another popular variety is Gorgonzola, which can be aged and crumbly or young and creamy. Our favorite basic blue cheese is **Stella Blue**.

Brie

Brie is a popular soft cow's-milk cheese from France that is creamy with a slight mushroom flavor, subtle nuttiness, and a white, edible rind. It is a classic choice for a cheese tray. With the rind removed, it's a good melting cheese. Our winning brand of supermarket brie is **Fromager D'Affinois**, an ultracreamy French import.
See page 104 for Inside the Tasting.

Camembert

Camembert is a soft cow's-milk cheese from France with an edible rind. Camembert is more pungent than Brie, with a stronger flavor.

Cheddar

This cow's-milk cheese is made predominantly in Great Britain and the United States. The American versions are usually softer in texture, with a tangy sharpness, whereas British cheddars are drier and nuttier. Older farmhouse cheddar is best eaten by itself. Young cheddar is the quintessential melting cheese. We like Cabot cheddar for both extra-sharp (**Cabot Private Stock**) and sharp options (**Cabot Vermont Sharp**). Our favorite premium cheddar is **Milton Creamery Prairie Breeze**. Cheddar can also be found smoked. It is made in both white and orange forms (the color comes from the addition of annatto), but we've found the flavor difference between the two is nearly imperceptible.

Colby

Colby is a semisoft cow's-milk cheese from the United States that is very mild in flavor. One of only a few cheeses that have true American roots, Colby is a wonderful melting cheese. Colby Jack is a mixture of Colby and Monterey Jack cheeses.

Cottage Cheese

Cottage cheese is a fresh cow's milk cheese that is curdled and drained, but not pressed, and then washed to mellow any excess acidity or sour flavors for a very soft consistency and a slightly sweet fresh-cream flavor. Textures range from wet to dry. "California-style" refers to a drier cottage cheese, while "country-style" refers to a creamier, wetter mixture. We prefer whole-milk cottage cheese, usually advertised as 4%. Our favorite brand is **Hood Country Style Cottage Cheese**. Avoid nonfat cottage cheese for cooking applications—it will compromise texture and flavor.

Cream Cheese

Although we like the easy spreadability of whipped cream cheese, classic **Philadelphia Brand Cream Cheese** is our favorite for both baking and eating plain on bagels. Cream cheese can be frozen but once thawed it will be crumbly and grainy, so it can only be used in applications where this texture won't stand out, such as biscuits or pound cake. Neufchatel, which is often found side-by-side with cream cheese, is a similarly dense, tangy, spreadable cheese made from milk and cream that contains one-third less fat than traditional cream cheese. (Neufchâtel is the name of a soft French cow's milk cheese with a bloomy rind similar to Brie or Camembert.)

Feta

A fresh cheese made from cow's, goat's, or sheep's milk (or a combination thereof), feta is a staple in many Mediterranean countries. It can be made in a variety of styles, from dry and crumbly to soft and creamy; flavors range from mild to tangy and salty. It is often crumbled over salads and eaten with fresh vegetables. We like **Mt. Vikos Traditional Feta** for its pleasing creamy, crumbly texture and tangy flavor.

Fontina

True fontina is a semisoft cow's-milk cheese from Italy with an earthy and delicately herbaceous flavor. We like **Fontina Val d'Aosta** for cheese plates and snacking. The domestic variety (with its bright red coating) is buttery and melts well but lacks the complex flavor of the Italian original. For cooking, we like **Italian Fontina**.

Goat Cheese

Produced in many countries in numerous forms, goat cheeses range from creamy fresh cheeses with a mild tanginess to aged cheeses that are firm, dry, and pungent. French goat cheeses (called *chèvres*) are typically more complex in flavor than most of their American counterparts. Our favorite brand is **Laura Chenel's Chèvre**. Its high salt content helps enhance flavor and also contributes to keeping the cheese creamy when heated.

Gouda

Gouda is a semifirm to firm cow's-milk cheese from Denmark. Young gouda is mild and slightly sweet, whereas aged gouda is dry and crumbly, with deep caramel flavors and a sharp zing.

Gruyère

Gruyère is a semifirm cow's-milk cheese from France and Switzerland that is strong, fruity, and earthy in flavor, with a hint of honey-flavored sweetness. Look for a true import that's been aged 10 or more months to develop stronger flavor. We like **Gruyère Reserve Wheel**.

Mascarpone

Mascarpone is a fresh temperature- and acid-treated Italian cheese made from cream with a fat content of 30 to 46 percent. Its texture is compact, but it is also supple and spreadable. Its flavor is unique—mildly sweet and refreshing. Usually distributed in small containers, mascarpone has a very short shelf life.

Monterey Jack

Monterey Jack is semisoft, tangy cow's milk cheese from California that's great for melting. Add hot pickled peppers to Monterey Jack and you've got pepper Jack, which has the same creamy melting properties plus a spicy bite. We prefer to buy pepper Jack in blocks instead of preshredded. Our favorite brand, **Boar's Head Monterey Jack Cheese with Jalapeño**, has a pleasant cheddar-like tang and an assertive kick of peppers.

Mozzarella

Originally, all mozzarella was made from the milk of water buffaloes; today, most is made from cow's milk. Shrink-wrapped mozzarella is fine for pizzas. The test kitchen's top-rated supermarket mozzarella is block-style **Sorrento Galbani Whole Milk Mozzarella**. However, in simple salads, we prefer fresh mozzarella packed in water. We generally prefer the richer flavor of whole-milk mozzarella, although part-skim mozzarella can be used successfully in most recipes. The best storage method for supermarket mozzarella is to first wrap the cheese in waxed or parchment paper, and then loosely wrap the paper in aluminum foil. Fresh mozzarella does not store well and is best eaten within a day or two. You may also see burrata displayed near the mozzarella at your supermarket. Burrata is a deluxe version of fresh mozzarella in which the supple cheese is bound around a filling of cream and bits of cheese. It is richer than traditional mozzarella.

Parmesan

Parmesan is a hard, grainy cheese made from cow's milk. When it comes to buying Parmesan, there is a wide range of options, from the whitish powder in green-topped containers to imported wedges. We recommend buying an authentic Italian import like **Boar's Head Parmigiano-Reggiano**, which has a depth and complexity of flavor and a smooth, melting texture that others can't match. Most other Parmesan-type cheeses are too salty and one-dimensional; we suggest spending the money on the real deal. When shopping, make sure that "Parmigiano-Reggiano" is stenciled on the golden rind.

Pecorino Romano

Like Parmesan, Pecorino Romano is designed for grating, but it has a much saltier and more pungent flavor. It is traditionally made entirely from sheep's milk, although some manufacturers add cow's milk. Look for the aged imported cheese clearly labeled Pecorino Romano and avoid the bland domestic version called simply "Romano."

Provolone

Provolone, a cow's-milk cheese from Italy, is made in two styles. The semifirm mild version is widely available and is usually sold sliced. There is also a firm, aged style that is salty, nutty, and spicy, with a light caramel sweetness. The latter makes a nice addition to any cheese platter, and for this purpose we recommend **Provolone Vernengo**.

Ricotta

Good ricotta is creamy and thick, not watery and curdish like so many supermarket brands. In the United States, fresh ricotta with a dry, firm consistency that's similar to goat cheese is available in and near urban centers with large Italian-American populations. If you can't find that, we recommend **Calabro Part Skim Ricotta Cheese** from the supermarket. Ricotta salata is made by pressing and salting fresh ricotta into a firm block that is similar to feta but with milder flavor.

Swiss

Emmentaler is the real name for the cheese Americans call Swiss. It is a semifirm cow's-milk cheese from Switzerland and France. It has a fruity flavor with a sweet, buttery nuttiness. Our favorite brand for cheese plates, **Edelweiss Creamery Emmentaler Switzerland Swiss Cheese**, is actually made in Wisconsin, using traditional Swiss methods. If you just want a Swiss cheese for cooking, we recommend **Boar's Head Gold Label Switzerland Swiss Cheese** for its great meltability. For a one-cheese-fits-all option, try **Emmi Emmentaler Cheese AOC**. Jarlsberg is the name for the Norwegian version of Swiss-style cheese.

A few decades ago, Brie was the pinnacle of sophistication on American cheese plates. Its longtime French reputation as the "cheese of kings," coupled with its lush, buttery, not-too-pungent profile and velvety edible rind, made it at once fashionable and approachable. But Brie sold in America has changed over the years. The original name-protected French versions have been banned by the FDA for using raw milk, and these days most products found in supermarkets are produced domestically. You're also increasingly likely to find specimens that are bland, rubbery, and encased in rinds as stiff as cardboard. Still, if there was a creamy, satiny, richly flavorful Brie available in the average grocery store, we wanted to know about it. So we gathered 10 nationally available brands that ranged broadly in price, purposely selecting cheeses that spanned a variety of traits that we thought might affect flavor and texture—in particular, fat content (we included standard-fat, double, and triple crème cheeses), nationality (American or French), and format (some are sold as small wheels, others as wedges cut from larger wheels). We sampled the Bries plain at room temperature (the ideal serving temperature) and also baked into phyllo cups with dollops of red currant jelly to see how the cheeses behaved when heated.

We could tell just by handling the cheeses that their textures varied considerably: Wheels and wedges alike ranged from soft and pliable to almost rigid. When we tasted the cheeses, we found that their flavors varied just as much—some were "boring," with "almost no flavor," while others tasted "mushroomy" and "nutty-rich." Heating the cheeses only underscored these differences: Fuller flavors intensified and creamier textures became even plusher, while bland cheeses tasted the same and barely melted at all. When we tallied

the scores, we were pleased to find that we could recommend without reservation four out of the 10 cheeses—in particular, a standout wedge that embodied everything we want in Brie: a lush, buttery, full-flavored interior encased in a pillowy rind.

But surprisingly, factors like origin, price, and format had no bearing on our preferences. Though our favorite was a wedge from France, our runner-up was an 8-ounce wheel made in California. And a bargain wedge from Michigan outranked French Bries costing two or three times as much.

We also assumed that Bries labeled triple and double crème would taste richer and creamier than standard-fat cheeses—but that wasn't always the case. Though cream is generally added to the milk when making both double and triple crèmes, the amount can vary substantially within each category. (Triple crèmes contain upwards of 75 percent butterfat while double crèmes range from 60 to 75 percent.)

It wasn't until we dug deeper into the Brie-making process that we uncovered the key factor explaining what gave a cheese the lush texture and earthy flavor we liked best: the culturing process. Cultures in the milk and on the exterior of the Brie react with the milk proteins as the cheese ages—a process called proteolysis—and cause the proteins to break down. This results in a rind forming on the wheel and its interior softening and developing flavor from the outside in, a process known as surface-ripening.

According to Dean Sommer and Mark Johnson at the University of Wisconsin-Madison's Center for Dairy Research, the nature of that ripening—and the flavor and texture of Brie—largely depends on the type of cultures a cheesemaker uses. French *appellation*

METHODOLOGY

We tasted 10 nationally available Brie-style cheeses served plain at room temperature (the ideal serving temperature) and then baked with red currant jelly in phyllo cups, rating each sample on flavor, texture, and overall appeal. We obtained information about the age, butterfat content, and style of cheese (either traditional or stabilized, dependent on the type of cultures used) from manufacturers. Products are listed in The Tasting Lineup in order of preference.

d'origine contrôlée (AOC) Bries are made exclusively with raw milk, which can contain enough natural bacteria to culture the cheese. But Bries made with pasteurized milk need added cultures. These fall into two main strains: mesophilic or thermophilic. Mesophilic cultures are more reactive with milk proteins and lead to so-called traditional Brie that more closely mimics the AOC raw-milk cheese with fuller flavor, gooier texture, and a thinner, spottier rind. Thermophilic cultures are less reactive and create milder, firmer cheese with a thicker, more uniform rind. Such cheeses are referred to as "stabilized" in the industry.

Since labels don't indicate whether a Brie is traditional or stabilized, we asked each manufacturer directly—and among those that answered, we saw a pattern. Most of our top-ranking cheeses were traditional, which correlated with our tasters' preferences for Brie with creamier body and somewhat fuller flavor, while stabilized cheeses dominated the middle and bottom of the pack. What's more, the makers of our top two Bries add Geotrichum, a yeast-like fungus that is naturally present in raw milk, which contributes to a gooey, silky texture, more delicate rind, and rich, earthy flavor with less bitterness.

So why would a manufacturer make a stabilized Brie? For one thing, there's a market demand for blander cheese both here and in France (where stabilized Brie is often fed to schoolchildren). Another more compelling reason is quality control: As long as a wheel of traditional Brie is left uncut, it will continue to soften and develop flavor, so makers must rely on supermarket staff to handle and rotate the stock appropriately. Stabilized Brie, on the other hand, will remain consistently firm and mild as it sits at the store.

The makers of our winner wouldn't confirm that their cheese is made with mesophilic cultures but its silky body, buttery-rich flavor, and downy-soft rind are the qualities that we associate with traditional Brie. It's a double crème that we'll happily seek out for our cheese plates.

IS THAT WHITE STUFF EDIBLE?

The soft, pillowy rind of Brie and other bloomed-rind cheeses, such as Camembert, is not only edible, it's the most flavorful part. The ripening process of Brie begins with the application of *Penicillium candidum*, a harmless white mold, on the surface of the immature cheese. Over the next several weeks the mold grows (or "blooms") into a tender white crust around the cheese that provides both textural contrast and concentrated flavor. The mold is also at work internally; as the cheese ages, the mold grows roots that make their way to the center of the Brie, breaking down the protein and softening the cheese as they go. You can tell that the roots have reached the middle and that the Brie is fully ripe when the center feels soft and tender to the touch. If you have an aversion to the rind, it can certainly be trimmed off, but watch where you cut. Brie ripens from the outside in, so you might be slicing off the creamiest part of the cheese with the rind.

REAL BRIE? NOT IN THE STATES

Most Americans have never tasted authentic French Brie, which is a regional product made according to strict criteria governed by the *appellation d'origine contrôlée* (AOC). That's because AOC Brie is made with raw milk and is aged for only a few weeks, and the FDA bans raw-milk cheeses unless they've been aged at least 60 days.

The Tasting Lineup

Highly Recommended
FROMAGER D'AFFINOIS
Top Pick $17.99 per lb

Recommended
MARIN
Triple Crème Brie
$19.98 per lb

FROMAGE DE MEAUX
$17.99 per lb

RENY PICOT
Brie
$5.92 per lb

Recommended with Reservations
ALOUETTE
Double Crème Brie
$12.98 per lb

BRIE D'ISIGNY
$11.99 per lb

PRÉSIDENT
BRIE
$15.38 per lb

JOAN OF ARC
Double Crème Brie
$13.99 per lb

Not Recommended
ILE DE FRANCE
Brie
$12.99 per lb

BRIE DE NANGIS
$17.99 per lb

You think vanilla is plain? Take a good look at the freezer section of your supermarket—the sheer number of choices in vanilla ice cream could make your head spin. With nearly 40 brands on the market nationwide and each one offering a slew of different styles (vanilla bean, natural vanilla, French vanilla, homemade vanilla, and extra-creamy vanilla, to name but a few), who knows which to pick?

For help winnowing down the options, we asked manufacturers of the eight top-selling brands which of their many styles of vanilla ice cream was the most popular and put these selections before our tasting panel.

A quick scan of the samples showed they looked nothing alike: Some were practically yellow, others were pure white, a few looked grayish, and many were flecked with tiny black bits of vanilla bean. After digging in, we found their textures were just as varied, ranging from thin and milky to creamy and rich. Despite being frozen at the same temperature and served under identical conditions, some had the softness of Marshmallow Fluff, while others were as hard and dense as snowballs. When it came down to the final results, however, texture and consistency took a back seat. What mattered most to our tasters boiled down to one thing: vanilla taste.

Like everything else, vanilla flavoring was all over the map in these ice creams, ranging from barely detectable in some to overpowering in others. We looked on the back of the cartons and noticed that each brand seemed to list vanilla in a different way, from the wordy and virtuous "fair-traded certified vanilla extract" to "natural vanilla flavor" to simply "vanilla." Dairy expert Scott Rankin, a professor of food science at the University of Wisconsin-Madison, explained that the different wordings on the labels amount to an industry shorthand for specific kinds of natural or artificial flavorings. As he helped us break the code, we looked at our favorite (and not-so-favorite) ice creams according to the type of vanilla.

First, a little background: The flavor in vanilla beans is predominantly due to the presence of a compound known as vanillin. Vanillin is produced three ways: from vanilla beans, from wood, and from resins. The first two types are considered natural, while the vanillin from resins is synthetic. Not surprisingly, our three top-ranked brands all contained the real deal—"vanilla extract"—natural vanillin extracted from vanilla beans, just like the real vanilla extract in your pantry. Less favored brands were made with vanillin extracted from wood ("natural vanilla flavor"), which is chemically identical to the synthetic vanillin found in artificial vanilla extract. Simple "vanilla" turned out to be code for a combination of synthetic and natural vanillin, while "natural flavors" (with no mention of vanilla at all) indicates just a trace of natural vanillin (there's no required level) and other flavorings such as nutmeg that merely trigger an association. Our tasters strongly preferred brands containing real vanilla extract.

Half our lineup (including our winner) listed vanilla beans or seeds in their ingredient lists, but our tasters found no correlation between vanilla flecks and good vanilla flavor. Skip Rosskam, an expert in vanilla and ice cream and president of flavor manufacturer David Michael & Co. in Philadelphia, Pennsylvania, confirmed our suspicion that the use of ground beans is all for show: It does little to boost vanilla taste, since such beans are leftovers from the extraction process and have already had their vanillin removed.

As ice cream travels from factory to store to your freezer, thawing and refreezing can wreak

METHODOLOGY

We tasted eight top-selling brands of supermarket vanilla ice creams. The lineup included both French-style brands (made with egg yolks) and regular products (made without egg yolks). Overrun was estimated by comparing the weight of 1 gallon of each ice cream to 9 pounds, the approximate weight of 1 gallon of commercial ice cream mix before processing. Vanillin content was determined by an independent laboratory; fat and sugar content (per ½-cup serving) were taken from the labeling information. Products are listed in The Tasting Lineup in order of preference.

havoc on texture. Melting separates fat from liquid, while refreezing creates ice crystals that destroy creaminess. Enter stabilizers such as carob gum, guar gum, tara gum, and carrageenan. Since the 1950s, when ice cream switched from being a treat enjoyed primarily at the soda fountain to a commodity served at home, manufacturers have used these additives to keep ice cream viscous and creamy as it is inevitably subjected to thawing and refreezing. Our tasters found that an excess of such additives can turn an ice cream gummy and pasty—more akin to "Play-Doh" than dessert. They can also make ice cream overly resilient. One brand in our lineup was so chockablock with stabilizers, it barely melted even after sitting out for 20 minutes. But here's the surprising news about stabilizers: a small amount isn't a bad thing: Our winning brand contains both guar gum and carrageenan and trumped the three brands in the lineup without these additives.

While stabilizers might be fine in ice cream, other additives were not. Another texture trick manufacturers have used for decades is to incorporate mono- and diglycerides into ice cream, emulsifiers that keep the milk fat from separating and lead to a creamier, smoother product. These cheap, extremely shelf-stable chemicals mimic the role once played exclusively by egg yolks in ice cream. But our tasters found these additives couldn't mimic egg yolks' complex, fatty flavor. Our three top-ranked ice creams not only boast egg yolks as a main ingredient, but also have the highest fat content of the brands in the lineup.

Though it's not listed on the label, another important component of modern-day ice cream is air. Manufacturers aerate their ice creams to produce a lighter texture—but also, more important from a cost perspective, to increase the overall volume. "Overrun" refers to the percentage increase in volume from aeration, which by law can go as high as 100 percent. Our top two brands have the lowest overrun of the lineup, while the brand with the highest (a whopping 97 percent) came in dead last. But if the markedly more airy texture of a high overrun product doesn't put you off, paying for all that air should: When we weighed an equal volume of the ice cream with the lowest and the highest overrun, respectively, the super-pumped-up brand weighed a full pound less.

How did our brands rank in sweetness? Per serving, they contain anywhere from 11 to 21 grams of sugar. But what mattered wasn't the amount of sugar—it was the type. Brands that use corn syrup sank to the bottom of the list, deemed by our tasters "unnaturally sweet" regardless of their sugar levels. Our preferred brands use the ordinary sugar found in old-fashioned homemade ice cream. Our winner contains liquid sugar, which is granulated white sugar dissolved in water.

Ice cream containing much beyond the old-fashioned starting points of cream, milk, sugar, eggs, and vanilla extract also fell to the bottom of the pack. We preferred ice creams with real vanilla extract that wasn't hidden behind artificial or other natural flavors, and creamy texture achieved without a raft of high-tech emulsifiers and stabilizers. Our favorite vanilla ice cream was buttery-tasting and rich, full of "indulgent" vanilla flavor, sweetened with real sugar, and enriched with egg yolks. While it does contain two gums, it wasn't overloaded, so the texture was as ultracreamy and silky as that of its closest competitor, the only ice cream in the pack without such additives. In the end, our winner's complex yet balanced vanilla flavor was what gave it an edge over the runner-up, which, despite its dense creaminess and unadulterated flavor, featured a "raw" vanilla taste that some found too strong. In our book, if an ice cream is going to call itself vanilla, that flavoring better be perfect.

FULL OF (COLD) AIR

Manufacturers aerate their ice creams to produce a lighter texture and increase overall volume. The more air in the ice cream (referred to as "overrun"), the less ice cream you're actually buying. We weighed an equal volume (1½ quarts) of ice creams with the highest and lowest overrun, minus their cartons. Our winner, Ben & Jerry's, with 24 percent overrun, weighed about 2.7 pounds. Edy's, with 97 percent overrun, weighed 1.7 pounds—a full pound less. This accounts for the dramatic package size and cost-per-pint differences between our top pick and our least favorite brand. Though it may seem like Edy's is a much better deal than Ben & Jerry's, you're actually paying for a lot of air (not to mention an inferior product).

The
Tasting
Lineup

Highly Recommended
BEN & JERRY'S
Vanilla
Top Pick $4.39
for 1 pint

Recommended
HÄAGEN-DAZS
Vanilla
$3.50 for 14 oz
($4.00 per pint)

WELLS BLUE BUNNY
All Natural Vanilla
$3.10 for 1.75 qt
($0.89 per pint)

BREYERS
Natural Vanilla
$5.49 for 1.5 qt
($1.83 per pint)

Recommended with Reservations
FRIENDLY'S
Vanilla
$5.49 for 1.5 qt
($1.83 per pint)

BLUE BELL
Homemade Vanilla
$6.65 for 2 qt
($1.66 per pint)

TURKEY HILL
Vanilla Bean
$5.29 for 1.5 qt
($1.77 per pint)

Not Recommended
EDY'S
Grand Vanilla
$5.59 for 1.5 qt
($1.86 per pint)

MEAT, POULTRY, AND FISH

HOW TO BUY MEAT

There are dozens of beef cuts and just as many pork cuts, and the naming conventions vary from market to market (and region to region). Some markets sell multiple grades of meat, and then there's the issue of provenance (whether to pick organic meat, grass-fed beef, or imported lamb). Which should you buy? Let's start with some broad strategies for successful meat shopping.

Steaks, Chops, and Roasts

The terms "steak" and "chop" refer to any thin cut, with or without a bone. Most steaks and chops are tender and need only a quick sear in a hot pan or a brief sizzle on the grill. (Exceptions to this rule include fattier chops, such as lamb shoulder chops or pork blade chops, which can be braised.) Most steaks and chops are sold in individual portions. In contrast, a roast is suitable for longer cooking. Tender roasts, generally from the loin section of the animal, are best roasted or grilled to desired doneness (we think medium-rare is best for most beef and lamb roasts, and medium-well is best for most pork roasts). This category includes everything from beef tenderloin and pork loin to rack of lamb and butterflied leg of lamb.

Bone-In or Boneless?

Sure, if you're making a stew you want boneless meat. And flank steak will always be boneless. But many cuts are sold with and without the bone. Prime rib, a roast cut from the cow's rib section, contains a large muscle and several bones. If this roast is cut between the bones into individual steaks, you have rib steaks, which have a single bone running along one side. If the meat is removed from the bone, you have rib-eye steaks. All three cuts are from the same part of the cow. When it makes sense for the dish, we often prefer bone-in cuts because bones help retain moisture and add flavor.

Serving Sizes

If you're serving a cut that should be served whole (chops or small steaks), buy meat by the piece: four chops for four people. If you plan to slice the meat before serving (roasts), buy between 6 and 8 ounces of meat per person, which will yield a slightly smaller serving once the meat is cooked. If you're buying a bone-in or fatty cut, you will want to compensate and buy a bit more per person.

Cooking Methods

It's imperative to match the cut with the cooking method. Tough cuts, which generally come from heavily exercised parts of the animal, such as the shoulder or rump, respond best to slow-cooking methods, such as pot roasting, stewing, or barbecuing. The primary goal of slow cooking is to melt collagen in the connective tissue, thereby transforming a tough piece of meat into a tender one. These cuts are always served well done. Tender cuts with little connective tissue generally come from parts of the animal that receive little exercise (like the loin, the area along the back of the cow or pig). These cuts respond best to quicker, dry-heat cooking methods, such as grilling or roasting. These cuts are cooked to a specific doneness.

Fat Is Flavor

Marbling of fat throughout meat, especially beef, adds flavor. Don't confuse marbling with gristle, which is often translucent rather than white. Note that some exterior fat is desirable, especially when selecting roasts. In the oven or on the grill, this fat will melt and flavor the meat. However, excess exterior fat will need to be trimmed. More than ½ inch of exterior fat is generally less than ideal.

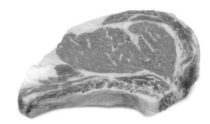

Looks Matter

Meat should look moist but not sodden. An excessive amount of juices inside a meat package can be an indication that the meat has been on the shelf too long. As for color, meat that has turned brown all the way through is on its way to spoiling. Avoid meat that has green spots—this is another indication of spoilage and bacteria. The meat should have a tight, even grain. A broken grain can indicate poor handling. Note that packaged parts, whether pork chops, chicken breasts, or steaks, may be of varying sizes and thicknesses. If possible, buy parts individually so you can make sure they're of similar size.

Pay Attention to Temperature

Looks tell you a lot, but temperature is important, too. Is the packaging cool to the touch? Even at the farmers' market, meat should be stored under 40 degrees. On especially hot days, take advantage of your market's insulated shopping bags (or pack an insulated cooler bag—the type used to keep lunches cool). Of course, you can also keep a cooler in the trunk of your car. If you have a lot of items on your grocery list, make the meat counter one of your last stops, so the meat stays cooler until you can get it home.

Use Your Nose

You know how fresh fish shouldn't smell overtly fishy? The same goes for meat. Truly fresh meat should have little aroma. Any strong off-odors or sour odors indicate spoilage.

Pasture-Raised

The term "pasture-raised" is not regulated by the USDA and is not clearly defined in the industry. As with the term "free-range" (used for poultry and eggs), the animals' access to a pasture may be extremely limited. Geography may also affect the duration of pasture-raising; animals in colder climates might spend less time in the pasture than those in more temperate areas. A "pasture-raised" label can be an indication of quality, but to be sure, you should find out how the producer defines the term.

No Hormones and No Antibiotics

While beef may be labeled "no hormones administered" if the producer can provide documentation proving that the animal wasn't raised with hormones, the USDA prohibits the use of hormones (and steroids) in the production of both poultry and pork. The agency requires that if a "no hormones" label is used, it must be followed by the statement, "Federal regulations prohibit the use of hormones." In short, the label is an empty reassurance since the practice is prohibited for pork and poultry. Like the "no hormones" label, the term "no antibiotics" can be applied if the producer provides documentation that the animal was not raised with antibiotics.

Natural

"Natural" has no official definition, but usually means that the meat was minimally processed and contains no artificial ingredients. The USDA defines minimally processed meat as meat "processed in a manner that does not fundamentally alter the product." Our advice is to stick to buying your meat fresh if possible and skip the frozen food aisle, where there's probably not much natural about frozen sliced sandwich "steak," chicken nuggets and patties, and bags of frozen meatballs.

Organic

In contrast to "natural," the USDA's definition of "organic" is a bit more involved: Organic food is produced by farmers who emphasize the use of renewable resources and the conservation of soil and water to enhance environmental quality for future generations. Organic meat, poultry, eggs, and dairy products come from animals that are given no antibiotics or growth hormones. Organic food is produced without using most conventional pesticides; fertilizers made with synthetic ingredients or sewage sludge; bioengineering; or ionizing radiation. Before a product can be labeled "organic," a government-approved certifier inspects the farm where the food is grown to make sure the farmer is following all the rules necessary to meet USDA organic standards. A farm must use organic processes for three years before it can become accredited.

MEAT STORAGE

Meat should be refrigerated promptly after purchase. Check the temperature of your refrigerator regularly to ensure that it is between 35 and 40 degrees; your freezer should be below zero degrees. Make sure that raw meat is stored well wrapped and never on shelves that are above other food, especially when thawing. In general, meat tastes best when it hasn't been frozen. Freezing causes large ice crystals to form which rupture the cell walls of the meat, permitting the release of juices during cooking. That said, if you're going to freeze meat, the best method for small cuts is to remove them from their packaging, vacuum-seal them or simply wrap them well in plastic, and then place the wrapped meat in a zipper-lock bag and squeeze out excess air. Freeze large cuts and whole birds in their original packaging.

Quick Chilling Meat

When freezing cuts like steaks, pork chops, chicken parts, or small roasts like tenderloins for long-term storage, we like to quick-chill the meat before it goes into the freezer. Faster freezing translates into less cellular damage and less loss of juices during cooking. We quick-chill through an ice bath with added salt. Adding salt to an ice bath lowers the freezing point of water and turns the bath into a superfast freezer. In the test kitchen we were able to achieve slushy ice baths with temperatures as low as 17 degrees. To make an ice bath for quick chilling, combine 1 pound ice, ⅓ cup salt, and ⅓ cup water, which is enough to quick chill four steaks, chops, or chicken parts. Wrap the meat in plastic wrap, place the pieces in a zipper-lock bag, and submerge the bag in the ice, salt, and water. Once the meat is frozen solid (thick cuts will take longer than thin ones), remove the bag from the ice bath, dry it off, and transfer it to the freezer.

Thawing Large Cuts or Whole Birds

Large roasts or whole birds are best defrosted in the refrigerator. Allow one day for every 4 pounds. A 12-pound turkey requires three days to thaw in the refrigerator. If you need to thaw a large frozen roast or whole bird quickly, leave it wrapped in the original packaging, place it in a large bucket of cold water, and set it in the refrigerator. Plan on 30 minutes of defrosting for every 1 pound; a 12-pound turkey will take about 6 hours.

Thawing Small Cuts

We defrost thicker (1 inch or greater) cuts in the refrigerator and place thinner cuts on a cast-iron or steel pan at room temperature; the metal's rapid heat transfer safely thaws the meat in about an hour. For an even faster thaw, simply seal chicken breasts, steaks, or chops in a zipper-lock bag and submerge the packages in very hot (140-degree) water. Chicken will take less than 8 minutes and the other cuts roughly 12 minutes, both fast enough that the rate of bacterial growth falls into the "safe" category. (This technique is not suitable for large roasts or whole birds.)

Refrigerating And Freezing Meat And Poultry

	Refrigerator Storage Time	Freezer Storage Time
Beef, Pork, Lamb, Veal	Fresh cuts and roasts: 3-5 days	About 1 month
	Smoked ham and bacon: 2 weeks once opened	
	Ground meat: 2 days	
	Defrosted cuts: 2-3 days	
	Cooked meat: 2–3 days	
Chicken, Turkey	Fresh whole birds or parts: 2 days	About 1 month
	Ground chicken and turkey: 2 days	
	Defrosted: 2 days	
	Cooked chicken and turkey: 2–3 days	

HOW TO BUY BEEF

Buying a steak or a roast or even a package of beef isn't as easy as it used to be. First, there are many cuts of beef in the market, many of which are sold under a variety of alternate names. Beef labels can also be confusing. Here, we explain more about labels specific to beef and help you understand shopping for beef, cut by cut.

Grain-Fed versus Grass-Fed

Most U.S. beef is raised on grain, but grass-fed beef is becoming increasingly popular. Grain-fed beef is generally considered to be richer and fattier, while grass-fed is leaner, chewier, and gamier—or at least that's the conventional wisdom. In our taste tests, we pitted grain-fed and grass-fed rib-eye steaks and strip steaks against each other. We found differences between the strip steaks to be small. Grain-fed rib-eyes had a milder flavor compared with the nutty, complex flavor of the grass-fed rib-eyes, but our tasters' preferences were evenly split. The texture of all samples was similar.

Organic versus Natural

The government regulates the use of the term "organic" on beef labels, but producers set their own guidelines when it comes to the term "natural." If you want to ensure that you're buying meat raised without antibiotics or hormones and fed an organic diet (and no mammalian or aviary products), then look for the USDA organic seal.

Ground Beef

Supermarkets label ground beef either by fat content (for example, "90 percent lean" or "80 percent lean") or by cut (for example, "ground chuck"). Ideally, we like to buy meat that is labeled both ways, but you may not always have that option. Ground chuck generally has quite a lot of fat, which translates to rich flavor and tender texture—it's the best choice for burgers. Ground sirloin has good flavor but is a bit less tender (because it's leaner). Ground sirloin is great in meatloaf and Bolognese sauce but can be a bit dry in burgers. Ground round is often gristly and lacking in beef flavor; we don't recommend it. For burgers, we recommend buying beef labeled 80 percent lean (or 85 percent lean). Ideally, the label will indicate that the meat is from the chuck, but round can have a similar content. For recipes with additional sources of fat and moisture (such as meatloaf), 85 percent lean or even 90 percent lean ground beef is best. Ground sirloin usually is 90 percent to 93 percent lean and is a good choice here.

Beef Grades: Prime, Choice, and Select

Most meat available to consumers is confined to three of the quality grades assigned by the USDA: prime, choice, and select. Grading is voluntary on the part of the meat packer. If meat is graded, it should bear a USDA stamp indicating the grade, though it may not be visible. To grade meat, inspectors evaluate color, grain, surface texture, and fat content and distribution. Prime meat is heavily marbled with intramuscular fat, which makes for a tender, flavorful steak. About 2 percent of graded beef is considered prime and it's most often served in restaurants or sold in high-end butcher shops. The majority of graded beef found in supermarkets is choice, which is generally moderately marbled. Select beef has little marbling. Our advice: When you're willing to splurge, prime meat is worth the extra money, but choice meat is a fine, affordable option. Stay clear of select-grade steak.

PRIME
Heavily marbled, tender, and flavorful

CHOICE
Moderately marbled, good flavor and value

SELECT
Lightly marbled, tough, poor flavor

PRIMAL CUTS OF BEEF

Because the flavor and texture of steaks and roasts can vary widely depending on what part of the cow they come from, it's helpful to understand the primal cuts from which retails cuts are butchered. At the wholesale level, a cow is divided into eight different primal cuts. From these, butchers make the retail cuts that are available in the supermarket. How you choose to cook a particular piece of beef depends on where the meat comes from on the cow and how it was butchered.

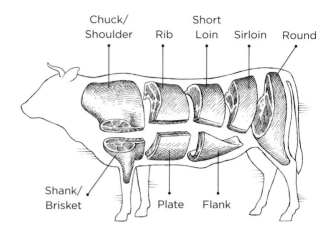

Chuck/Shoulder

The chuck (or shoulder) runs from the neck down to the fifth rib. There are four major muscles in this region. Meat from the chuck tends to be flavorful and fairly fatty, which is why ground chuck makes the best hamburgers. Chuck also contains a fair amount of connective tissue, so when the meat is not ground it generally requires a long cooking time.

Rib

The rib section extends along the back of the animal from the sixth to the 12th rib. Prime rib and rib-eye steaks come from this area. Rib cuts have great beefy flavor and are tender.

Short Loin

The short loin (also called the loin) extends from the last rib back through the midsection of the animal to the hip area. It contains two major muscles: the tenderloin and the shell. The tenderloin is extremely tender (it is positioned right under the spine) and has a quite mild flavor. The shell is a much larger muscle and has a more robust beef flavor as well as more fat.

Sirloin

The sirloin contains relatively inexpensive cuts that are sold as both steaks and roasts. We find that sirloin cuts are fairly lean and tough. In general, we prefer other parts of the animal, although top sirloin makes a decent roast.

Round

Roasts and steaks cut from the back of the cow, called the round, are usually sold boneless; they are quite lean and can be tough. Again, we generally prefer cuts from other parts of the cow, although we have found that top round can be roasted with some success.

Shank/Brisket, Plate, and Flank

Moderately thick boneless cuts are removed from the three primal cuts that run along the underside of the animal. The brisket (also called shank) is rather tough and contains a lot of connective tissue. The plate is rarely sold at the retail level (it is used to make pastrami). The flank is a leaner cut that makes an excellent steak when grilled.

With the wide variety of steaks at the supermarket these days, it's tough to know which cut of meat to buy. And the cut you choose has everything to do with the flavor of the steak. Here are 12 of the test kitchen's favorite beef steaks. We've rated each steak on a scale from one to four stars for both tenderness and flavor and have indicated the best cooking method(s) for each. We've also listed the primal cut from which the steak is cut. See Primal Cuts of Beef for more information.

Type	Tenderness	Flavor
Top Blade Steak (Chuck/Shoulder) Top blade (or simply blade) steak is a small shoulder cut. It is an all-purpose steak. While it is very tender and richly flavored, a line of gristle that runs through the center of the meat makes it a poor option for serving whole. Remove the gristle before slicing or cubing the steak for a recipe.	★★★	★★★
Shoulder Steak (Chuck/Shoulder) Sometimes labeled as London broil or chuck steak, this 1½- to 2-pound boneless steak is a great value. Although cut from the shoulder, it is relatively lean, with a moderately beefy flavor. Since this steak can be a bit tough, it should be sliced thin on the bias after cooking. Grill or pan-roast.	★★	★★
Rib-Eye Steak (Rib) Cut from the rib area just behind the shoulder, a rib-eye steak is essentially a boneless piece of prime rib. This pricey, fat-streaked steak is tender and juicy. In the West, rib eyes are sometimes labeled Spencer steaks; in the East, they may be called Delmonico steaks. Grill, pan-sear, or broil.	★★★	★★★★
Strip Steak (Short Loin) Available both boneless and bone-in, this moderately expensive steak is also called top loin, shell, sirloin strip, Kansas city strip, or New York strip. Cut from the shell muscle that runs along the middle of the steer's back, strip steaks are well marbled, with a tight grain, pleasantly chewy texture, and big, beefy flavor. Grill, pan-sear, or broil.	★★★	★★★★
Tenderloin Steak (Short Loin) Cut from the center of the back, the tenderloin is the most tender (and most expensive) cut of the cow. Depending on their thickness, tenderloin steaks may be labeled (from thickest to thinnest) Châteaubriand, filet mignon, or tournedos. Tenderloin steaks are buttery smooth and very tender, but they have little flavor. Grill, pan-sear, or broil.	★★★★	★
T-Bone Steak (Short Loin) This cut is named for the T-shaped bone that separates two muscles, the flavorful strip (or shell) and the buttery tenderloin. Because the tenderloin is small and will cook more quickly than the strip, this side should be positioned over the cooler side of the fire when grilling. Grill.	★★★	★★★★
Porterhouse Steak (Short Loin) The porterhouse is really just a huge T-bone steak with a larger tenderloin section. It is cut farther back on the animal than the T-bone. Like the T-bone steak, the porterhouse steak has well-balanced flavor and texture. Most porterhouse steaks are big enough to serve two. Grill.	★★★	★★★★

	Type	Tenderness	Flavor
	Top Sirloin Steak (Sirloin) Cut from the hip, this steak (along with its bone-in version, round-bone steak) is also called New York sirloin steak or sirloin butt. Do not confuse it with the superior strip steak. Slice thin against the grain after cooking. Grill or pan-sear.	★★	★★
	Flap Meat Sirloin Steak (Sirloin) Cut from the area just before the hip, this large steak is most often sold in strips or cubes. To ensure that you are buying the real thing, buy the whole steak and cut it yourself. Though not particularly tender, flap meat has a robust beefiness. Slice thin against the grain after cooking. Grill, pan-roast (whole), or pan-sear (strips).	★★	★★★
	Flank Steak (Flank) Flank steak, aka jiffy steak, is a large, flat cut from the underside of the cow, with a distinct longitudinal grain. Thin flank steak cooks quickly, making it ideal for the grill. Although very flavorful, flank is slightly chewy. It should not be cooked past medium and should always be sliced thin across the grain. Grill, pan-sear, or slice thin and stir-fry.	★★	★★★
	Skirt Steak (Plate) This long, thin steak is cut from the underside (or "plate") of the cow. Also known as fajita or Philadelphia steak, it has a distinct grain and an especially beefy taste. Sliced skirt is a good option for fajitas, but it can also be cooked as a whole steak. Grill, pan-sear, or slice thin and stir-fry.	★★	★★★
	Top Round Steak (Round) This inexpensive steak is cut from the round. Also known as London broil, it has good beefy flavor, but a tough texture. To diminish chewiness, slice this steak ultrathin. Grill or broil.	★	★★★

Mail-Order Steaks

To guarantee quality, more and more people are looking beyond the confines of their local supermarket butcher case and buying their steaks through mail-order sources. If you're going to drop the dough on mail-order strip steaks, we highly suggest going for Wagyu beef, which is extremely well-marbled, tender, and rich. We love **Lobel's Wagyu (Kobe-Style) Boneless Strip Steak**. Our winner for mail-order porterhouse steaks, **Brandt Beef USDA Dry-Aged Prime Porterhouse Steak**, comes from Holstein cows fed on a hormone- and antibiotic-free diet of corn, alfalfa, and grass. Once aged, the meat ships fresh, not frozen, to help preserve its rich, buttery-smooth texture and fresh, complex beef flavor.

Hot Dogs

Our favorite all-beef hot dog, **Nathan's Famous Skinless Beef Franks**, has rich, beefy flavor and a good mixture of seasonings. Make sure you pick a brand that has 0 grams of sugar and minimal additives and preservatives, whenever possible.

These beef roasts are the test kitchen's top picks. We've rated each on a scale from one to four stars for flavor. Since even the toughest cut can make a great roast if cooked properly, we don't rate these cuts for tenderness. We've also listed the primal cut from which each roast is cut. See page 112 for more on primal cuts.

	Type	Flavor
	Chuck-Eye Roast (Chuck/Shoulder) This boneless roast is cut from the center of the first five ribs (the term "eye" refers to any center-cut piece of meat). It is very tender and juicy but also contains an excessive amount of fat. This cut should be trussed using kitchen twine. It is also called boneless chuck roll and boneless chuck fillet. We like the chuck-eye roast for its compact, uniform shape, deep flavor, and tenderness in pot roast. This is our top choice for stewing and braising.	★ ★ ★
	Top Blade Roast (Chuck/Shoulder) This broad, flat cut is quite flavorful, and because it is boneless it's the best substitute for a chuck-eye roast. Even after cooking, this cut retains a distinctive strip of connective tissue, which is not unpleasant to eat. This roast is sometimes labeled as blade roast or top chuck roast.	★ ★ ★
	Rib Roast, First Cut (Rib) Butchers tend to cut a rib roast, which consists of ribs 6 through 12, into two distinct cuts. The more desirable cut consists of ribs 10 through 12, sometimes called the "loin end," "small end" or "first cut." Whatever it is called, it is more desirable because it contains the large, single rib-eye muscle and is less fatty. The less desirable second cut (ribs 6 through 9) is fattier and more irregularly shaped but still an excellent roast.	★ ★ ★ ★
	Tenderloin Roast (Short Loin) The tenderloin (also called the whole filet) is the most tender piece of beef you can buy. Its flavor is mild, almost nonbeefy. Unpeeled tenderloins come with a thick layer of exterior fat still attached, which should be removed. This roast can be cut into individual steaks to make filets mignons.	★
	Top Sirloin Roast (Sirloin) This cut from the hip area tastes incredibly meaty and has plenty of marbling, which makes for a succulent roast. Aside from the vein of gristle that runs through it, and that we find slightly unpleasant to eat, the roast is tender and juicy, with big, beefy flavor. Other parts of the sirloin are lean and tough, but top sirloin roast is one of our favorite inexpensive roasts.	★ ★ ★
	Eye-Round Roast (Round) This inexpensive boneless roast is not nearly as flavorful as the top cuts, but it does have a nice shape that slices neatly. In order to make this lean cut as tender as possible, roast it at a very low temperature.	★ ★
	Top Round Roast (Round) Round roast is a bargain cut from the cow's rump. It has good flavor, is relatively juicy, and, when sliced thin, isn't too chewy. Most deli roast beef is from the top round. This roast has an odd shape, which makes even cooking (and carving) a challenge. Salt, sear, and then roast at a very low temperature.	★ ★ ★
	Brisket (Shank/Brisket) This large cut weights 13 pounds, so it is often divided into subcuts. The flat cut is leaner, thinner, and more widely available. Look for flat cut with a decent fat cap. The point cut is well marbled and thicker. You can use it in place of flat-cut brisket in most recipes; however, the cooking time might need to be extended slightly. Barbecue or braise.	★ ★ ★

HOW TO BUY PORK

Before you shop for pork, it's helpful to understand some basic information about buying and cooking it. Here we address labels specific to pork and how to shop for pork, cut by cut.

Enhanced or Not?

Modern pork is very lean and therefore somewhat bland and prone to dryness if overcooked, so many producers inject their pork with a sodium solution. So-called enhanced pork is now the only option at many supermarkets, especially when buying lean cuts like tenderloin. (To be sure, read the label; if the pork has been enhanced it will have an ingredient label.) While enhanced pork does cook up juicier, we find the texture almost spongy, and the flavor is often unpleasantly salty. We prefer the genuine pork flavor of natural pork and we brine lean cuts to keep them juicy (see page 351 for information on brining). Note that enhanced pork loses six times more moisture when frozen and thawed compared to natural pork—yet another reason to avoid it.

Nitrites and Nitrates

Cured pork products, such as bacon, often contain nitrites and/or nitrates. Nitrites have been shown to form carcinogenic compounds when heated in the presence of proteins. While nitrites and nitrates are virtually identical, only nitrites form these compounds. So should you buy "nitrite-free" bacon? The problem is that while technically these products have no added nitrites, some of the ingredients used to brine them actually form the same problematic compounds during production. In fact, regular bacon contains lower levels of nitrites than some brands labeled "no nitrites or nitrates added." All the bacons we tested fell well within federal standards, but if you want to avoid nitrites and nitrates you need to avoid bacon and other processed pork products altogether.

PRIMAL CUTS OF PORK

Five different cuts of pork are sold at the wholesale level. From this first series of cuts, known in the trade as primal cuts, a butcher will make the retail cuts that you bring home from the market.

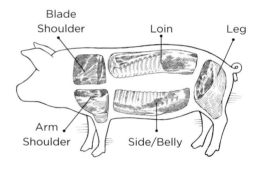

Blade Shoulder

Cuts from the upper shoulder are well marbled with fat and contain a lot of connective tissue, making them ideal for slow-cooking methods.

Arm Shoulder

Cuts from the arm shoulder are more economical than blade cuts but otherwise similar.

Loin

Between the shoulder and back legs is the leanest, most tender part of the animal. These cuts will be dry if overcooked.

Leg

The rear legs are often referred to as "ham." This cut is sold as large roasts available fresh or cured.

Side/Belly

The underside is the fattiest part of the animal and is the source of bacon and spareribs.

The pork cuts listed here are the test kitchen's top picks. We've rated each cut on a scale from one to four stars for flavor. Since even the toughest cut can be great if cooked properly, we haven't rated these cuts for tenderness.

	Type	Flavor
	Pork Butt (Blade Shoulder) This large, flavorful cut (often labeled Boston butt or pork shoulder) can weigh as much as 8 pounds when sold bone-in. Many markets take out the bone and sell the meat in smaller chunks, often wrapped in netting. This cut is ideal for slow roasting, barbecuing, stewing, or braising.	★ ★ ★ ★
	Pork Shoulder (Arm Shoulder) This affordable cut (often labeled "picnic roast") can be sold bone-in or boneless. It is rich in fat and connective tissue. Use it like pork butt for barbecuing, braising, or other slow-cooking methods.	★ ★ ★ ★
	Boneless Blade-End Roast (Loin) This is our favorite boneless roast for roasting. It is cut from the shoulder end of the loin and has more fat (and flavor) than the boneless center-cut loin roast. Unfortunately, this cut (and the bone-in version) can be hard to find.	★ ★ ★ ★
	Center-Cut Loin Roast (Loin) This boneless roast is widely available and a good choice for roasting. We prefer the more flavorful boneless blade-end roast, but the two cuts can be used interchangeably. Make sure to buy a roast with a decent fat cap on top.	★ ★
	Center Rib Roast (Loin) Referred to as the pork equivalent of prime rib, this mild, lean roast consists of a single muscle with a protective fat cap. It may be cut with anywhere from five to eight ribs. Because the bones (and nearby fat) are still attached, we like this roast better than the center-cut loin roast for most applications.	★ ★ ★
	Tenderloin Roast (Loin) This small, lean, boneless roast cooks quickly. Since there is little marbling, this roast (which is equivalent to beef tenderloin) cannot be overcooked without ruining its texture. Tenderloins are often sold two to a package. Look for a tenderloin that has no ingredients other than pork on the label.	★
	Blade Chop (Loin) Cut from the shoulder end of the loin, these chops can be difficult to find at the market. They are fatty and tough, despite good flavor and juiciness. These chops are best suited to low-and-slow cooking methods that break down their connective tissue, such as braising or barbecuing.	★ ★ ★
	Rib Chop (Loin) Cut from the rib section of the loin, these chops have a relatively high fat content, rendering them flavorful and unlikely to dry out during cooking. They are a favorite in the test kitchen. These chops are easily identified by the bone that runs along one side and the one large eye of loin muscle. These tender chops are a good choice for grilling and pan searing.	★ ★ ★
	Center-Cut Chop (Loin) These chops can be identified by the bone that divides the loin meat from the tenderloin muscle. The lean tenderloin section cooks more quickly than the loin section, making these chops a challenge. They have good flavor, but since they contain less fat than rib chops, they are not as moist. Because the loin and tenderloin muscles are bisected by bone or cartilage, these chops don't lie flat, making them a poor choice for pan searing. Save them for the grill; position the tenderloin away from the fire to keep it from drying out.	★ ★

	Type	Flavor
	**Baby Back Ribs (Loin)** Baby back ribs (also referred to as loin back ribs) are from the section of the rib cage closest to the backbone. Loin center-cut roasts and chops come from the same part of the pig, which explains why baby back ribs can be expensive. This location also explains why they are much leaner than spareribs and need special attention to keep from drying out on the grill.	★ ★ ★
	**St. Louis Spareribs (Side/Belly)** Regular spareribs are cut close to the belly of the pig. Whole spareribs contain the brisket bone and surrounding meat, so each rack can weigh upward of 5 pounds. We prefer this more manageable cut because the brisket bone and surrounding meat are trimmed off to produce a narrower, rectangular rack that usually weighs in at a relatively svelte 3 pounds.	★ ★ ★ ★
	**Country-Style Ribs (Loin)** These tender, boneless ribs are cut from the upper side of the rib cage from the fatty blade end of the loin. Butchers usually cut them into individual ribs and package several ribs together. These ribs can be braised and shredded for pasta sauce, or pounded flat and grilled or pan-seared as cutlets.	★ ★ ★
	**Fresh Ham, Shank End (Leg)** The leg is divided into two cuts—the tapered shank end and the more rounded sirloin end. The sirloin end has a lot of bones that make carving tricky. We prefer the shank end. The thick layer of fat and skin should be scored before roasting. This cut benefits from brining.	★ ★ ★

Supermarket Bacon

Good bacon is balanced between meaty, smoky, salty, and sweet flavors. We prefer cured and dry-smoked versions (make sure the label says "naturally smoked" or "old-fashioned smoked"). Look for a thick-sliced brand with a high protein-to-fat ratio. We had two co-winners in our supermarket bacon test: **Farmland Thick Sliced Bacon** and **Plumrose Premium Thick Sliced Bacon**.

Sausages

Sausage can be made from almost any type of meat (or combination of meats), although many of the world's most popular sausages are made from pork, including hot and sweet Italian sausage, Spanish and Mexican chorizo, andouille, linguiça, and traditional kielbasa. Some sausages, such as kielbasa, Spanish chorizo, and andouille are generally sold fully cooked, while other types are sold raw. Although all made with pork, these sausages include a wide variety of spices and seasoning and are generally not interchangeable.

Prosciutto

Not too long ago, the only way to buy prosciutto was to find an Italian market and wait while someone sliced imported prosciutto by hand. But since domestic producers have gotten into the game, many supermarkets now carry this cured pork product in grab 'n' go packages. Look for a brand that's aged for at least 12 months for complex flavor. The ingredients list should be just pork and salt. Go for paper-thin slices to avoid chewiness. Our favorite is the tender, buttery **Volpi Traditional Prosciutto**.

Pepperoni

Pepperoni is made from cured and fermented pork with just a little beef and seasoned with black pepper, sugar, anise, cayenne, paprika (the source of its orange color), and salt. Look for an option with a high sodium percentage and thinly cut slices like our favorite, **Margherita Italian Style Pepperoni**.

HOW TO BUY LAMB

Lamb, which has traditionally been less popular than beef and pork, has been staging somewhat of a comeback—and for good reason. Lamb can be relatively inexpensive; it takes well to a variety of cooking methods, such as roasting, stewing, and grilling; and its rich flavor can't be beat. While almost all the beef and pork sold in American markets is raised domestically, you can purchase imported as well as domestic lamb. Domestic lamb is distinguished by its larger size and milder flavor, while lamb imported from Australia or New Zealand features a far gamier taste. Imported lamb is pasture-fed on mixed grasses, while lamb raised in the United States begins on a diet of grass but finishes with grain. The switch to grain has a direct impact on the composition of the animal's fat, reducing the concentration of the medium-length branched fatty-acid chains that give lamb its characteristic "lamby" flavor—and ultimately leading to sweeter-tasting meat. Note that most markets contain just a few cuts, and you may need to special-order lamb. Generally, younger lamb has a milder flavor that most people prefer. The only indication of slaughter age at the supermarket is size. A whole leg of lamb weighing 9 pounds is likely to have come from an older animal than a whole leg weighing just 6 pounds.

PRIMAL CUTS OF LAMB

These are the five cuts of lamb sold at the wholesale level, from which all retail cuts are made.

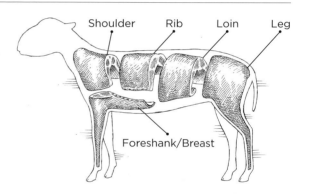

Shoulder
This area extends from the neck through the fourth rib. Meat from this area is flavorful, although it contains a fair amount of connective tissue and can be tough. Chops, roasts, and boneless stew meat all come from the shoulder.

Rib
The rib area is directly behind the shoulder and extends from the fifth to the 12th rib. The rack (all eight ribs from this section) is cut from the rib. When cut into individual chops, the meat is called rib chops. Meat from this area has a fine, tender grain and a mild flavor.

Loin
The loin extends from the last rib down to the hip area. The loin chop is the most familiar cut from this part of the lamb. Like the rib chop, it is tender and has a mild, sweet flavor.

Leg
The leg may be sold whole or broken into smaller roasts and shanks. These roasts may be sold bone-in, or they may be butterflied and sold boneless.

Foreshank/Breast
The final primal cut is from the underside of the animal and is called the foreshank and breast. This area includes the two front legs as well as the breast, which is rarely sold in supermarkets.

HOW TO BUY VEAL

Veal can be controversial. Many people are opposed to milk-fed veal because the calves are confined to small stalls before being butchered. "Natural" is the term used to inform the consumer that the calves are allowed to move freely, without the confines of the stalls. Natural veal is also generally raised on grass (the calves can forage) and without hormones or antibiotics. Moral issues aside, the differences in how the calves are raised create differences in texture and flavor. Natural veal is darker, meatier, and more like beef. Milk-fed veal is paler in color, more tender, and milder in flavor. The choice is really a personal one. Milk-fed veal is sold in most grocery stores, while natural veal is available at butcher shops, specialty markets, and natural foods stores. When shopping, read labels and check the color of the meat. If the meat is red (rather than pale pink), it most likely came from an animal raised on grass rather than milk.

PRIMAL CUTS OF VEAL

Veal is sold in five different primal or major cuts at the wholesale level and then processed into retail cuts by a butcher.

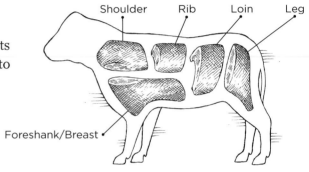

Shoulder

This area includes the front of the animal and runs from the neck through the fifth rib. Cuts from the shoulder are moderately tough and better suited to stewing than grilling. Many markets sell cutlets cut from the shoulder but they will buckle in the pan and are not recommended.

Rib

Our favorite chops come from this prime area of the calf, which includes ribs 6 through 12 along the top half of the animal. Expensive rib chops are ideal candidates for grilling.

Loin

Farther back from the rib, the loin section runs along the top half of the animal from the 13th rib to the hip bone. Meat from this area is tender and lean. It is also expensive and best suited to grilling.

Leg

This section includes both the sirloin (the hip) and the actual leg. Cuts from this section often contain multiple muscles and connective tissue. Veal cutlets, known as scaloppini, come from this portion of the animal.

Foreshank/Breast

The underside of the animal yields various cuts, most of which require prolonged cooking to become tender. Veal shanks, also known as osso buco, come from this area, which is also home to the breast roast.

HOW TO BUY POULTRY

Owing in large part to its relatively low cost and fat content, poultry has become America's favorite type of meat. But problems with shopping for, preparing, and cooking chicken and turkey at home abound—mostly because there are so many conflicting theories about how to handle it and cook it. Here's what you need to know.

Chicken Labels

A lot of labeling doesn't (necessarily) mean much. Companies can exploit loopholes to qualify for "Natural/All-Natural," "Hormone-Free," and "Vegetarian Diet/Fed" labeling. "USDA Organic," however, isn't all hype: The chickens must eat all organic feed without animal byproducts, be raised without antibiotics, and have access to the outdoors. Processing is the major player in chicken's texture and flavor. Brands labeled "water-chilled" (soaked in a water bath in which they absorb up to 14 percent of their weight in water) or "enhanced" (injected with broth and flavoring) are unnaturally spongy and best avoided. Law requires water gain to be shown on the product label, so these should be easily identifiable. When buying whole chickens or chicken parts, look for those that are labeled "air-chilled." These brands are less spongy in texture (but still plenty juicy) and have more flavor.

Boneless, Skinless Chicken Breasts and Cutlets

Boneless, skinless chicken breasts are the most popular cut of chicken sold in American grocery stores. Flavor differences in various brands of chicken breasts are minimal, but texture differences can be quite noticeable. Our favorite brand, **Bell & Evans Air Chilled Boneless, Skinless Chicken Breasts**, is "aged" for 12 hours after being broken down into parts but before being boned, which helps with tenderness. Try to pick a package with breasts of similar size, and pound them to an even thickness. Store-bought cutlets are usually ragged and of various sizes; it's better to cut your own cutlets from breasts (see page 215).

Bone-In Chicken Parts

You can buy chicken parts at the supermarket, but they aren't always properly butchered. Consider buying a whole chicken and butchering it yourself (see page 214).

Whole Chickens

Whole chickens come in various sizes. Broilers and fryers are younger chickens that weigh 2½ to 4½ pounds. A roaster (or "oven-stuffer roaster") is an older chicken and usually clocks in between 5 and 7 pounds. Stewing chickens, which are older laying hens, are best used for stews since the meat is tougher and more stringy. A 3½- to 4-pound bird will feed 3 to 4 people. Look for a bird that is air-chilled (not water-chilled) like our winner, **Mary's Free Range Air Chilled Chicken**. A high percentage of fat also contributes to great flavor and moist meat.
See page 127 for Inside the Tasting.

Ground Poultry

Prepackaged ground chicken is made from either dark or white meat. Higher-end markets and specialty markets grind their chicken to order, and therefore the choice of meat is yours. When it comes to flavor, however, dark meat is far more flavorful and juicy due to its higher fat content. The guidelines for buying ground turkey are the same as those for buying ground chicken: Dark meat has more flavor than white, so make sure you buy ground turkey that is a mix of the two. Do not buy ground turkey breast (also labeled 99 percent fat free).

Poultry Storage

Keep poultry refrigerated until just before cooking. Bacteria thrive at temperatures between 40 and 140 degrees. Leftover cooked poultry should be promptly refrigerated and consumed within three days. Poultry can be frozen in its original packaging or after repackaging. If you are freezing it for longer than two months, rewrap (or wrap over packaging) with foil or plastic wrap, or place it inside a zipper-lock bag. You can keep poultry frozen for several months, but after two months the texture and flavor will suffer.

Whole Turkeys

Whole turkeys can be fresh, frozen, organic, kosher, or even heritage. We recommend buying a fresh or frozen untreated turkey and brining it yourself. You can also use a self-basting turkey (such as a frozen Butterball) or kosher turkey (which has been salted and rinsed according to Jewish dietary laws), in which case brining is not necessary, although we have found that the saline solution used to brine self-basting turkeys can mask the meat's natural flavor. For kosher turkeys, we like **Empire Kosher Turkey**.

Heritage Turkeys

Heritage turkeys forage for food and live twice as long as modern birds. They can also cost 10 times as much. Our top pick, **Mary's Free-Range Heritage Turkey**, is from a large family-owned farm in California that also produces our winning brand of chicken. It has everything we're looking for in turkey, with rich, full flavor and naturally moist meat. Look for the Standard Bronze breed. **See page 130 for Inside the Tasting.**

WHAT'S IN THAT BAG?

The turkey neck and the "giblets," or internal organs, are mechanically separated, washed, and then repackaged for the purpose of making gravy.

Neck
The neck is the large muscle with a bone through the center. It contains some very flavorful meat. Cut it into several pieces for easy browning and then simmer it in the broth. Discard after straining the broth.

Heart, Gizzard, and Liver
The heart is the small, dark-colored organ. Brown it along with the neck and gizzard, then simmer it in the broth. Reserve it after straining the broth, and then dice it and return it to the gravy before serving. The gizzard is the grinding organ from the bird's digestive tract, recognizable by a butterfly-shaped strip of connective tissue. Cut the gizzard in half, brown it along with the heart and neck, and reserve it after straining the broth. Dice the gizzard and return it to the gravy along with the heart. The liver is the brownish, flat organ. We don't recommend using it to make gravy.

Turkey Breasts

Most supermarkets regularly offer two different styles of whole bone-in turkey breast: regular, or "true cut" and hotel, or country-style, turkey breast. Regular turkey breast includes the whole bone-in breast with ribs, a portion of the wing meat, and a portion of the back and neck skin. The hotel-cut turkey breast is essentially the same cut, though it comes with its wings, neck, and giblets, all important material if you intend to make gravy or stock. These tend to cost a little more and are almost always sold fresh, not frozen. Whichever style you find and purchase, avoid turkey breasts that have been injected with saline solution, often called "self-basters," as the solution masks the natural flavor of the turkey. (If you can only find a "self-baster," omit the brining step as the meat will already be quite salty.) If your turkey comes with a pop-up timer, leave it in but ignore it and gauge doneness according to an instant-read thermometer; the meat will be long overcooked before the popper pops. Don't remove the timer before the meat is done or juices will leak out of the hole it leaves behind.

Duck

The duck breasts and whole ducks sold in supermarkets are usually Pekin, or Long Island, ducks. Once raised on Long Island, these birds are grown on farms around the country. Most duck breasts are sold whole, with the skin on but without the bones. Other duck species are available if you are willing to order by mail or can shop at a specialty butcher. The Muscovy is a South American bird that is less fatty than the Pekin and has a stronger game flavor. The Moulard is the sterile offspring of a Muscovy and a Pekin duck and is popular in France. Because these birds are so much leaner, they require different cooking methods than Pekin ducks.

Cornish Game Hens

Cornish game hens typically weigh less than 2 pounds, so they cook faster than larger chickens and look nice on a plate—traits that make them popular with consumers. The fatty underside bastes the meat as it cooks, which might explain why we found both their white and dark portions more juicy and flavorful than those of chickens. We prefer **Bell & Evans Cornish Game Hens**.

HOW TO BUY SEAFOOD

Buying top-quality fish and seafood is just as important as employing the proper cooking technique. Here, we explain how to select the right fish for every application and how to pick the best specimens at the market. Shellfish presents its own challenges, so we also give the low-down on buying shrimp, mussels, clams, scallops, crabmeat, and lobsters.

Fresh Fish

The most important factor when buying fish is freshness. Always buy from a trusted source. The store, and the fish in it, should smell like the sea, not fishy or sour. The fish should be on ice or properly refrigerated. Fillets and steaks should look bright and firm and whole fish should have moist, taut skin, clear eyes, and bright red gills. It is always better to get steaks and fillets sliced to order rather than buying precut pieces. Don't be afraid to be picky at the seafood counter; a ragged piece of cod or a tail end of salmon will be difficult to cook properly. If you have a long ride home, ask for a bag of ice. Because fish is so perishable, it's best to buy it the day it will be cooked. If that's not possible, it's important to store it properly. Unwrap the fish, pat it dry, put it in a zipper-lock bag, press out the air, and seal the bag. Set the fish on a bed of ice in a bowl and place it in the back of the fridge. If the ice melts before you use the fish, replenish it. The fish should keep for one day.

Frozen Fish

Thin fish fillets like flounder and sole are the best choice if you have to buy your fish frozen, because thin fillets freeze quickly, minimizing moisture loss. Firm fillets like halibut, snapper, tilapia, and salmon are acceptable to buy frozen if cooked beyond medium-rare, but at lower degrees of doneness they will have a dry, stringy texture. When buying frozen fish, make sure it is frozen solid, with no signs of freezer burn around the edges and no blood in the packaging. The ingredients should include only the name of the fish you are buying.

Anchovies

All preserved anchovies—small silver-skinned fish usually caught in warm Mediterranean waters—have been cured in salt, but they come to the market in two forms: packed in olive oil in small, flat tins or packed in salt. The salt-packed variety is the least processed, having only their heads and some entrails removed, leaving the filleting and rinsing to the home cook. We prefer oil-packed anchovies that have been filleted at the factory and are ready to use. Our favorite brand is **King Oscar Anchovies — Flat Fillets in Olive Oil**. Another option for recipes that call for small quantities of chopped anchovies is to use anchovy paste. A tube of anchovy paste is easier to keep on hand and lasts longer than an open jar.

Salmon

In season, we prefer the more pronounced flavor of wild-caught salmon to farmed Atlantic salmon. Our preference is to buy thick, center-cut fillets. Buy a piece that is the total amount you need and cut the individual fillets yourself. Stay away from thin, tail-end fillets, which will always cook unevenly. For smoked salmon (also called nova lox), we prefer fish cured with just salt, no additional sweeteners or spices. We also prefer thinly sliced fish rather than thicker slabs. Look for a product like our winner, **Spence & Co. Traditional Scottish Style Smoked Salmon**, that follows the Scottish tradition of trimming off the pellicle, the smokier, drier surface that forms as salmon is cured and smoked. This creates a uniformly buttery texture and a subtly smoky flavor.

Canned Tuna

Look for hand-packed tuna; it will have better flavor and texture than machine-packed brands, which must go through a double-cooking process that cheapens the quality of the fish. We like **Wild Planet Wild Albacore Tuna**. For a premium option, try **Nardin Bonito Del Norte Ventresca Fillets**, which is cut from the fatty belly and packed in olive oil for a buttery flavor and tender texture.

Buying fish can be confusing and markets don't always stock the type of fish or cut that you need. This chart will help you sort out your options and explain what you'll generally find at the market. We've also listed what we think are the best cooking methods for each type of fish.

Type of Fish	What You'll Find at the Market	Texture	Flavor	Best Cooking Methods
Bluefish	Whole fish and fillets	Medium firm, dark-fleshed fish	Pronounced, well suited to robust sauces and flavors	Stuffing and roasting or grilling (whole fish); steaming, braising, broiling, baking (fillets)
Catfish	Whole fish and fillets	Medium firm, flaky white fish	Mild to slightly earthy	Pan searing, sautéing, baking, pan frying, deep frying
Cod	Whole and portioned fillets (both with and without skin)	Medium firm, meaty white fish	Clean, mild flavor; suited to most any preparation and flavor combination	Steaming, braising, baking, oven frying, deep frying, grilling; also great for soups and stews
Flounder	Whole fish and very thin fillets, interchangeable with sole	Delicate and flaky white fish	Sweet and mild, identical to sole	Stuffing and baking (whole fish); steaming, sautéing, pan frying (fillets)
Haddock	Fillets, usually with skin on; ask fishmonger to remove skin	Medium firm white fish; similar in texture to cod, but slightly thinner	Very mild, well suited to robust flavors	Steaming, poaching, braising, sautéing, baking, oven frying, pan frying
Halibut	Whole steaks, belly steaks, fillets	Very firm, lean white fish; steaks similar to swordfish	Mild but rich, well suited to robust flavors	Steaming, pan-searing, roasting, grilling (steaks); steaming, pan searing, sautéing, baking, roasting, deep frying, grilling (fillets)
Mahi-Mahi	Steaks, fillets, whole fish; usually without skin	Medium firm, off-white flaky fish	Sweet and mild; well suited to robust flavors	Baking (fillets), braising, pan frying, grilling (small whole fish, fillets with skin), soups and stews

Type of Fish	What You'll Find at the Market	Texture	Flavor	Best Cooking Methods
Red Snapper 	Whole fish (with colorful skin and many bones), fillets, occasionally steaks	Medium firm, flaky white fish	Mild to moderate, stands up well to bold flavors	Baking, deep frying, grilling, stuffing and roasting (whole fish); steaming, poaching, braising, pan searing, sautéing, broiling, baking, pan frying, grilling (fillets)
Salmon 	Available wild and farm raised; whole fish, whole sides, bone-in and boneless steaks, fillets	Medium firm, deep pink to orange in color; wild salmon is larger and leaner; farm-raised salmon is smaller and fattier	Mild (farm raised), moderate to pronounced (wild)	Poaching, roasting (whole fish and sides); steaming, poaching, pan searing, broiling, baking, roasting, grilling (steaks and fillets)
Sole 	Filets, interchangeable with flounder	Very delicate, flaky white fish	Sweet and mild, best suited to simple preparations	Steaming, sautéing, stuffing and baking
Spanish Mackerel 	Steaks, fillets, whole fish; best for practicing filleting, as bones are easily removed	Medium firm, off-white, flaky, oily fish	Full, rich, pronounced flavor	Braising, poaching, pan frying (small whole fish, fillets, steaks), pan searing, broiling, grilling, smoking
Swordfish 	Steaks	Very firm and meaty	Mild to moderate, well suited to robust flavors	Pan searing, broiling, grilling
Tilapia 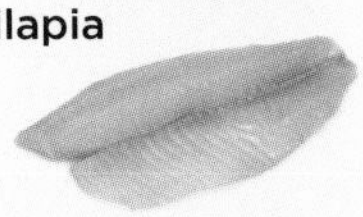	Mostly fillets (with and without skin)	Medium firm, pale-pink flesh	Moderate	Braising, sautéing, baking, oven frying, pan frying
Trout 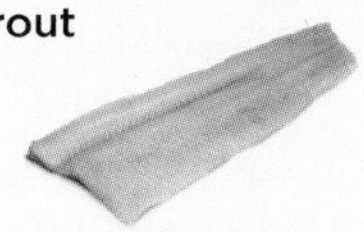	Whole fish and fillets	Delicate and flaky, ranges in color from pale golden to pink	Rich and flavorful	Pan frying, grilling, stuffing and roasting (whole fish); sautéing, pan frying (fillets)
Tuna 	Steaks	Very firm, meaty fish that ranges in color from pink to deep ruby red	Mild to moderate	Braising, pan searing, grilling; best cooked rare to medium, not beyond

Scallops

Scallops are shucked at sea, so before cooking, simply remove the crescent-shaped muscle that attaches the scallop to the shell. The scallops at the supermarket are one of two types: dry or wet. Wet scallops are dipped in preservatives to extend their shelf life, which affects their flavor and texture. Unprocessed, or dry, scallops have much more flavor and a creamy texture. Dry scallops look ivory or pinkish; wet scallops are bright white. If all you can find is wet scallops, soak them in 1 quart of cold water, ¼ cup of lemon juice, and 2 tablespoons of salt for 30 minutes to mask any chemical flavors.

Shrimp

Virtually all of the shrimp sold in supermarkets have been previously frozen, either in large blocks of ice or by a method called "individually quick-frozen," or IQF. We recommend purchasing bags of still-frozen shrimp and defrosting them as needed at home. IQF shrimp have a better flavor and texture than shrimp frozen in blocks, and it's easy to defrost just the amount you need. Shrimp should be the only ingredient listed on the bag; some packagers add preservatives, which creates an unpleasant, rubbery texture. Shrimp are sold both with and without their shells, but we find shell-on shrimp to be firmer and sweeter. See page 218 for more information on peeling and deveining shrimp.

Sorting Out Shrimp Sizes

Shrimp are sold both by size and by the number needed to make 1 pound, usually given in a range. Here's how the two systems compare:

Shrimp Size	1 Pound
Small	51 to 60 per pound
Medium	41 to 50 per pound
Medium-Large	31 to 40 per pound
Large	26 to 30 per pound
Extra-Large	21 to 25 per pound
Jumbo	16 to 20 per pound

Lobster

In late June and into July or August, depending on the location, lobsters start to molt, meaning that the lobsters available during the later summer weeks and into the early fall are generally soft-shell lobsters, which have less-meaty claws and are more perishable than hard-shell lobsters. That said, the meat from soft-shell lobsters is just as flavorful. They should, however, be cooked slightly less than hard-shell lobsters. If serving whole soft-shell lobsters, you may consider buying larger ones or, if the price is good, buying two small ones per person. Markets don't usually advertise which type of lobster they are selling but it is easy to tell which type of lobster you have: Soft-shell lobsters will yield to pressure when squeezed while hard-shell lobsters will be brittle and tightly packed.

Mussels and Clams

For the best flavor and texture, mussels and clams should be as fresh as possible. They should smell clean, not sour or sulfurous, and the shells should look moist. Look for intact, tightly closed shells. Some shells may gape slightly, but should close when they are tapped. Discard any that won't close; they may be dead and should not be eaten. Most mussels and clams today are farmed and free of grit. Soft-shell clams, however, almost always contain a lot of sand and should be submerged in a large bowl of cold water and drained several times before cooking. Both clams and mussels need to be cleaned before cooking. Some mussels may also need to be debearded (see page 218). The best way to store mussels and clams is in the refrigerator in a colander of ice set over a bowl; discard any water that accumulates so that the shellfish are never submerged.

Crabs and Crabmeat

Fresh crabs are a truly local product. On the West Coast you are likely to find Dungeness crabs, while blue crabs are the most common offering at markets on the East Coast. Whatever type you're buying, make sure to buy live crabs. Check the fish counter for containers of fresh or pasteurized crabmeat. We like **Phillips Premium Crab Jumbo**. Always use fresh crabmeat for crab cakes where the texture and flavor of crab is center stage. Pasteurized crabmeat is fine for dips and casseroles. Jumbo lump is the highest-quality option.

We've seen some pretty staggering statistics about meat consumption in this country, but this one really takes the cake: The U.S. poultry industry, the largest in the world, processes upwards of 8 billion chickens each year. Today, Americans consume about 84 pounds of chicken per person annually. These birds, once such a symbol of prosperity that a 1928 presidential campaign ad promised "a chicken for every pot," have become a cheap supermarket staple.

But the ability to pick up a chicken at any local market doesn't make shopping easy. On the contrary, there's a multitude of brands and a wide range of prices—not to mention alarming news reports that raise concerns about health, conscience, and politics. Beyond that, you need a degree in agribusiness to decode most of the packaging lingo: What's the difference between "all natural," "free range," and "organic"? What does "vegetarian fed" mean—and if other birds are not being fed vegetarian meal, just what are they eating? And most important, what tastes best when you strip away the sales pitches?

Those were the questions we started with as we rounded up eight national and large regional brands of whole fresh supermarket chicken, which we seasoned minimally, roasted, and carved into piles of white and dark meat for tasting. What we were looking for: meat that was rich, clean-tasting, tender, and moist. What we got: an astonishing range of flavors and textures. Some birds boasted "chicken-y" meat that was pleasantly moist; others tasted utterly bland or, worse, faintly metallic, bitter, or liver-y. Chalky, dry meat was a common, predictable complaint, but surprisingly, so was too much moisture.

Puzzled by the dramatic differences among the brands, we compared product labels and processing claims; talked to experts; and sent the chickens to an independent laboratory for analysis of their protein, fat, sodium, moisture, and other characteristics to help us figure out what might have shaped our preferences.

One characteristic we could rule out immediately: breed. Almost all supermarket chickens are white-feathered Cornish Crosses, a variety that has been bred to grow to full weight in a mere five to eight weeks, on the smallest possible amount of chicken feed, as well as to feature large breasts and stumpy legs to yield more white meat. "They're breast-meat machines," said Doug Smith, associate professor of poultry science at North Carolina State University. Most of the big poultry companies are vertically integrated, meaning they control everything from breeding and feeding the birds to medical care to slaughter and processing to transportation to sales and marketing. This keeps costs down and production up—hence the 8 billion served.

Along the way, intensive farming has led to trade-offs. Typically, birds get doses of antibiotics from their earliest days not only to help prevent and treat diseases rampant in their crowded conditions but also to help them grow faster. Some producers even inject antibiotics into eggs, and most routinely add them to the chicken's feed, a soy and corn mix often bulked up with feather meal (ground-up chicken feathers) and other animal byproducts left over from slaughter, as well as scraps like commercial bakery leftovers. (This may sound bad enough, but it gets worse. In a recent study analyzing feather meal, Johns Hopkins researchers found residue of arsenic; they also found traces of caffeine and the active ingredients in Benadryl, Tylenol, and Prozac, which had been fed to chickens to alter their moods.) Raised indoors, the birds move little

Inside the Tasting continued on next page

METHODOLOGY

We sampled eight brands of whole chickens (seasoned lightly and roasted, in our preferred size of 4 pounds). In blind tastings, tasters evaluated the light and dark meat on flavor, texture, moistness, and overall appeal. Sodium per serving was taken from product labels; fat percentages of the whole birds were determined by an independent laboratory. Information about antibiotics, feed, and chilling method were obtained from packaging labels and/or directly from manufacturers. Products are listed in The Tasting Lineup in order of preference.

The Tasting Lineup

Highly Recommended

MARY'S
Free Range Air Chilled Chicken (also sold as Pitman's)
Top Pick $1.99 per lb

BELL & EVANS
Air Chilled Premium Fresh Chicken
$3.29 per lb

Recommended

SPRINGER MOUNTAIN FARMS
Fresh Chicken
$1.89 per lb

COLEMAN
Organic Whole Chicken (also sold as Rosie Organic Whole Chicken)
$2.29 per lb

EMPIRE
Kosher Broiler Chicken
$3.89 per lb

and feed constantly until they're rounded up for the processing plant. Once there, the chickens are hung by their feet and dipped headfirst into an electrically charged bath that stuns them. Next, a machine cuts their throats, and they are bled, plunged into hot water and plucked, eviscerated by machines, and then chilled together in a cold bath (where bacterial contamination can spread).

It is in this water chilling system that chickens plump up, absorbing up to 14 percent of their body weight in water, which is chlorinated to help kill bacteria. (Since chicken is priced by the pound, of course you're paying for that water.) Labeling law says that this water gain must be shown on the product label, and in fact, six of the eight chickens in our lineup were processed this way. Of those six, one was also "enhanced" (read: injected) with a solution of chicken broth, salt, and flavorings, further plumping up its weight. This water chilling process (and/or enhancing) helped explain why tasters found the meat in several of these birds to be unnaturally spongy, with washed-out flavor.

That left just two birds that weren't water-chilled. Instead, they were air-chilled, a method in which each bird is hung from a conveyor belt that circulates them along the ceiling of a cold room. According to Theo Weening, the global meat buyer for Whole Foods Markets, this popular European chilling method is just catching on in the United States, and it produces a superior bird. Why?

"First, you don't add water, so you don't dilute the flavor," Weening said. He also noted that "air chilling breaks down the muscle tissue and gives a better texture." Our tasters concurred and these two chickens took top marks for flavor and texture. They were juicy without being soggy. What's more, the lab tests showed that these two air-chilled birds also contained more fat, giving them an inherent flavor advantage. (A higher percentage of fat in these birds makes sense, since water accounts for a smaller percentage of their total composition.)

Flavor and texture aside, there's another major factor to consider: your conscience. Consumer concern about poultry factory processing methods has motivated some companies to do a little better by us—and by the birds. This includes limiting or eliminating antibiotic use because of concerns about bacteria becoming drug-resistant and affecting human health; allowing chickens some (usually limited) access to the outdoors, the only legal definition of "free range"; and using "vegetarian" (free of animal byproducts) feed and swearing off "junk" food like low-quality bakery leftovers and other scraps used to fatten birds. Some brands seek organic certification. Translation: The birds are not given antibiotics; eat organic, vegetarian feed that's free of pesticides and animal byproducts; and have some access to the outdoors (although how much is not regulated—and may, in fact, be extremely limited). (Our top two brands have organic

NO MORE CHICKEN LITTLE
Today's commercial chickens grow to twice the size in about half the time as chickens raised 60 years ago. These days, most producers use the Cornish Cross, a breed genetically engineered to have more breast meat.

1950
Typical broiler live weight at 10 weeks: 3 pounds.

1980
Typical broiler live weight at 7 weeks: 4 pounds.

2016
Typical broiler live weight at 6 weeks: 6 pounds.

lines, but we chose to taste their more widely available conventional birds.) A few even adopt more "humane" killing processes, including a new method of administering anesthesia developed by animal rights activist and scientist Temple Grandin.

After we tallied the results, we were glad to learn that both of our winning brands follow these more responsible production methods (including use of anesthesia), though neither yet indicates it on the label. (Labeling claims on poultry, however, come with lots of caveats. See "Decoding Chicken Labels.") Other than air chilling, these alternative growing and processing methods may not directly affect the flavor of the chickens, but they may keep the birds, and us, healthier down the road, which makes us feel better about buying them.

DECODING CHICKEN LABELS

Many claims cited on poultry packaging have no government regulation, while those that do are often poorly enforced. Here's how to evaluate which claims are meaningful—and which are full of loopholes or empty hype.

Not Just Hype

Air-Chilled means that chickens were not water-chilled en masse in a chlorinated bath and the meat did not absorb any water during processing. (Water-chilled birds can retain up to 14 percent water—which must be printed on the label—diluting flavor and inflating cost.) Instead, individual chickens hang from a conveyor belt and circulate around a cold room.

USDA Organic is considered the gold standard seal for organic labeling. Poultry must eat organic feed that doesn't contain animal byproducts, be raised without antibiotics, and have access to the outdoors (how much, however, isn't regulated).

Buyer Beware

Raised Without Antibiotics and other claims regarding antibiotic use are important; too bad they're not strictly enforced. (The only rigorous enforcement is when the claim is subject to the USDA Organic seal.) Loopholes seem rife, like injecting the eggs—not the chickens—with antibiotics or feeding them feather meal laced with residual antibiotics from treated birds.

Natural and All Natural are ubiquitous on food labels. In actuality, the USDA has defined the term just for fresh meat, stipulating only that no synthetic substances have been added to the cut. Producers may thus raise their chickens under the most unnatural circumstances on the most unnatural diets, inject birds with broth during processing, and still put the claim on their packaging.

Hormone-Free is empty reassurance, since the USDA does not allow the use of hormones or steroids in poultry production.

Vegetarian Fed and Vegetarian Diet sound healthy, but are they? Since such terms aren't regulated by the government, you're relying on the producer's notion of the claim, which may mean feeding chickens cheap "vegetarian" bakery leftovers. The winners of our whole chicken tasting assured us that their definitions mean a diet consisting of corn and soy.

Recommended with Reservations

PERDUE
Fresh Whole Chicken
$1.99 per lb

GOLD KIST FARMS
Young 'n Tender All Natural Chicken (also sold as Pilgrim's)
$1.99 per lb

TYSON
Young Chicken
$1.69 per lb

Eating turkey on Thanksgiving is an American tradition, but today's supermarket turkeys barely resemble those enjoyed by early settlers. Starting in the 1950s, turkey breeders, catering to consumer preferences for white meat, started breeding turkeys to have big breasts and small legs. These birds grew to full size on less feed and in half the time as the old-breed turkeys could, making turkey cheaper than ever before. Farmers also started raising the birds indoors and introduced artificial insemination, which made turkey dinner a year-round option (in nature, turkeys hatch in the spring and reach "eating size" by late fall—not coincidentally, around Thanksgiving).

While supermarket turkey can taste great if it's carefully cooked, something has been lost. Near extinction not so long ago—and still on the "priority" list of the Livestock Conservancy— old-breed heritage turkeys have had a renaissance in the past decade, with a handful of farmers putting in the extra time, expense, and effort to raise these birds that, unlike modern commercial turkeys, can fly, roam freely, and breed on their own. Could turning back the clock bring back the flavor that's disappeared from modern turkeys?

To find out, we bought heritage turkeys from six farms across the United States. Breeds included Standard Bronze, American Bronze, and Bourbon Red, as well as a bird whose label read "parent stock includes five different heritage breeds" and even an Eastern wild turkey raised in semicaptivity. All were pastured, meaning they were free to range outdoors and forage to supplement their feed.

The turkeys we unpacked were a far cry from the usual pale, plump supermarket turkey. All featured startlingly long legs and wings, a more angular breast, almost bluish-purple dark meat (a sign of well-exercised birds), and traces of dark pinfeathers in the skin around the tail. When we cooked one set according to a standard method, we also found their flavor worlds apart from ordinary turkey—far more rich and flavorful. We then roasted all six types of birds again according to an America's Test Kitchen recipe customized to their unusual anatomy, and their flavor was even more extraordinary.

Tasters raved about the "buttery," "nutty-sweet," "incredibly satisfying, rich flavor" of the meat. The biggest revelation was the white meat. Tasters found their favorite samples "amazing," "unctuous and silky," with "sweet, succulent flavor," and a texture that was "perfectly tender" and "really moist." So what was it about these birds that made them, as one taster put it, "the turkey of my dreams"?

During carving, we'd noticed a distinct layer of fat under the skin on the breast—more than what we've seen on a supermarket turkey. Fat not only adds flavor but also helps keep meat moist during cooking. But, as Scott Beyer, extension poultry specialist at Kansas State University, explained, the fat under turkey skin is especially important. "If you peel off the skin, you strip most of the fat right off with it," he explained, noting that turkey meat doesn't become marbled with fat like beef. Our science editor also pointed out that the moistness and lubrication from fat reduces friction as you bite through the meat, making it more tender.

But how much of a difference was it, really? To find out, we sent samples from each heritage turkey to a lab to analyze the fat in both skin-on dark and skin-on white meat (uncooked). We also sent the lab a Broad Breasted White from Butterball, the largest producer of turkey products in the United States.

The results were convincing. The Butterball turkey had just 1.24 percent fat in its breast meat and skin, while breast-meat fat levels for the heritage birds ranged from a 4.56 percent in the wild turkey to 10.63 percent in a Standard Bronze. (In the dark meat, heritage birds' legs and thighs were actually slightly leaner than supermarket turkeys'. This was not surprising since they are more physically active,

METHODOLOGY

We tasted six heritage turkeys prepared using our recipe for Roast Heritage Turkey. An independent laboratory measured fat and protein in light and dark meat (including skin). Prices are what we paid to mail-order a turkey (shipping was extra). (Note: To avoid shipping costs for our winning turkey, check the manufacturer's website for stores that carry fresh birds during the holiday months.) Products are listed in The Tasting Lineup in order of preference.

but overall the heritage birds still had far more fat.) No wonder tasters found the heritage turkeys so moist and tender.

So why would heritage turkey contain more fat? "Age," said turkey breeder Frank Reese Jr. of Good Shepherd Poultry Ranch in Lindsborg, Kansas, who has been raising heritage turkeys since the 1950s and sells breeding stock to other farms. According to Reese, commercial growers can raise a 20-pound turkey in 12 weeks, whereas "it would take six months with a heritage bird. And if a turkey lives to be six to seven months old, it has lived long enough to start putting on that fat."

Older birds also have much thicker skin, which helps shield the meat and trap moisture, "like putting it in a Baggie," Beyer said. Meanwhile, most young, lean supermarket turkeys contain added liquid. Our Butterball's label said it "contains up to 8% of a solution of water, salt, spices, and natural flavor."

Finally, turkey breed may have played a part in our preferences. In first and third place were Standard Bronze turkeys (both from Frank Reese's breeding stock). The bird with a "mixed" parentage was unremarkable, according to our tasters, and while flavorful, the wild turkey meat was somewhat tough.

There's no denying that price is a big factor when considering heritage turkeys. Supermarket turkeys averaged $1.72 per pound nationwide last Thanksgiving, and promotional prices often dip well below $1 per pound. Heritage turkeys can cost upwards of $10 per pound; plus, the required overnight or two-day shipping can nearly double the price. Also, farms aren't charging a per-pound price but rather a flat price for a range of weights, such as 6 to 9 pounds or 7 to 14 pounds (similarly, you may be looking for a particular weight but sometimes smaller or larger birds are the only choices available). While we have a quibble with this pricing structure, farmers aren't getting rich; their rare, slow-growing, odd-size birds are far more expensive to raise and process.

A heritage bird is a centerpiece for a special occasion, like beef tenderloin or prime rib (which can cost $75 to $100). Our top pick was from a large family-owned farm in California that also produces our winning brand of chicken. It has everything we're looking for in turkey, with rich, full flavor and naturally moist meat. We'll be happy to splurge on our recommended heritage birds for the holidays—not just to save them from extinction, but for the great taste they bring to the table.

The Tasting Lineup

Highly Recommended
MARY'S
Free-Range
Heritage Turkey
Top Pick $166.72
for 7- to 14-lb bird

Recommended
ELMWOOD STOCK FARM
Organic Heritage
Turkey
$149 for 9- to
10.9-lb bird

GOOD SHEPHERD POULTRY RANCH
Heritage Turkey
$119 for 12- to
14-lb bird

HERITAGE TURKEY FARM
Heritage Turkey
Best Buy $85 for
10- to 13-lb bird

Recommended with Reservations
EBERLY
Heritage Turkey
$84 for 8- to
9-lb bird

BN RANCH
Heritage Turkey
$138.98 for 10- to
12-lb bird

HERITAGE TURKEY DEFINED

Heritage turkey is not just a matter of colorful feathers or romantic breed names like Narragansett or Bourbon Red; the Livestock Conservancy and the American Poultry Association agree that a heritage turkey is defined by these three criteria:

1 Heritage turkeys must have a long productive lifespan—five to seven years for breeding hens, three to five years for breeding toms—and have a genetic ability to withstand the environmental rigors of outdoor production systems.

2 Heritage turkey must have a slow to moderate rate of growth, reaching marketable weight in about 28 weeks, giving the birds time to develop a strong skeletal structure and healthy organs before building muscle mass. Commercial turkeys grow to full size in only 12 to 14 weeks.

3 Unlike commercial turkeys that must be artificially inseminated, heritage birds are the result of naturally mating pairs of both grandparent and parent stock.

PASTA, RICE, AND GRAINS

Dried Pasta

To make dried pasta, semolina (coarsely ground durum wheat) is mixed with water, kneaded into a dough, and pressed through a die to make specific shapes. Then the pasta is dried and the finished product is shelf-stable for years. The dried pasta we typically buy at the supermarket is made from semolina that has been refined during processing to remove the bran and germ. In addition to refined durum wheat flour, classic dried pasta contains just water and salt. With a few exceptions, in our taste tests of various shapes and brands we have found minimal differences. Yes, some brands have stronger wheaty, buttery, or nutty notes. But once the sauce is added, those flavor differences are relatively hard to detect. Some brands do cook up firmer, but the differences are quite small. We have found both Italian and American brands that we like. So while we include our specific brand recommendations in this section and in our Shopping Guide on page 400-401, most supermarket options are likely to be passable.

Spaghetti

Since most brands of spaghetti list simply durum semolina and maybe added vitamins as their ingredients, you might think any brand will do. However, our tests have found appreciable differences between brands when it comes to texture. For best results, choose a product that includes only semolina and not the more finely ground durum flour, like our winner, **De Cecco Spaghetti No. 12**. For a healthier option, our favorite brand of whole-wheat spaghetti, **Bionaturae Organic 100% Whole Wheat Spaghetti**, boasts superior flavor and texture with no white flour or other grains mixed in. For gluten-free pasta, we recommend picking a brand with a relatively high combined total of fiber and protein that has brown rice flour as its main ingredient, such as **Jovial Organic Gluten Free Brown Rice Spaghetti**.
See page 136 for Inside the Tasting.

Tortellini

Store-bought tortellini makes a great alternative to homemade. Our favorite is a dried brand, **Barilla Three Cheese Tortellini**, that has a creamy, tangy blend of ricotta, Emmentaler, and Grana Padano cheeses and tender texture.

Lasagna Noodles

No-boil, oven-ready lasagna noodles are a great option for cutting out one of the many steps in making this layered dish. We also prefer no-boil noodles because we find their thinner, more delicate texture closer to that of fresh pasta. Look for noodles in a traditional rectangle shape measuring about 7 by 3½ inches. Straight-edged and rippled noodles both work well. We like **Barilla No Boil Lasagne**. We also recommend **Bionaturae Organic 100% Whole Wheat Lasagne** for recipes where their complex nutty flavor would be an asset (these are traditional noodles and must be cooked before layering into the casserole).

Ravioli

For an easy alternative to homemade ravioli, look for a frozen supermarket brand with plenty of cheese flavor from Parmesan or Pecorino Romano in addition to the usual ricotta. We also prefer brands that use a light hand with spices, herbs, and additional fillers, but are generous with salt. Our favorite is **Rosetto Cheese Ravioli**. If you have a recipe where the pasta cooks in the sauce and you need fresh ravioli, try **Buitoni Four Cheese Ravioli**.

Fresh Pasta

Fresh pasta has a rough, porous surface that is perfect for absorbing sauce. Homemade pasta is the best (and cheapest) option, but making it can be time-consuming. When homemade isn't an option but dried pasta just won't cut it, look for the freshest option you can find—check the dates on the packaging. Our favorite brand of fresh pasta from the supermarket is **Contadina Buitoni Fettuccine**, which has good chew and a mild, pleasant egg flavor.

Fresh Chinese Noodles

Fresh Chinese noodles are more starchy and chewy than dried noodles. Their flavor is less wheaty than Italian pasta, so they are a great match for potent, highly seasoned sauces.

Rice Noodles

Rice noodles are used in a variety of dishes in Southeast Asia and southern China. These noodles should be steeped in hot water to soften them; they overcook quickly, so boiling tends to make them mushy. Rice noodles come in flat and round versions and a variety of widths.

Ramen Noodles

Ramen noodles are traditionally made from wheat flour and eggs, but we often rely on the easier-to-find instant variety, which doesn't contain eggs—just be sure to discard the dusty seasoning packet found in the package in favor of fresh sauce or broth.

Soba Noodles

Soba noodles possess a rich, nutty flavor and delicate texture. They get their unusual flavor from buckwheat flour, which contains no gluten so a binder, usually wheat, is added to give the noodles structure. The higher the percentage of buckwheat flour, the higher the price. Soba noodles are traditionally served chilled with a dipping sauce.

Somen Noodles

Somen noodles are made from high-gluten wheat flour, and the dough is stretched rather than cut. They are sold only in their dry form, and many believe that their flavor improves after aging over one to two years. Somen are eaten in much the same way as soba noodles, accompanied by a dipping sauce.

Udon Noodles

Udon noodles are made with all-purpose flour, water, and salt. The result is a highly elastic dough that yields thick, chewy noodles. Udon noodles can be purchased both fresh and dried. We think their chewy, hearty texture works especially well in ultrarich, savory dishes.

There's one basic rule for pairing pasta shapes and sauces: Thick, chunky sauces go with short pastas, and thin, smooth, or light sauces go with strand pastas. Feel free to substitute shapes as long as you're following that advice.

Short Pastas

Farfalle, Orecchiette, Fusilli, Penne, Macaroni, Ziti, Conchiglie, Gemelli, Rigatoni, Rotelle, Campanelle

Sauces with very large chunks are best with rigatoni or other large tubes. Sauces with small chunks pair better with fusilli or penne.

Strand Pastas

Vermicelli, Spaghettini, Linguine, Fettuccine, Spaghetti, Pappardelle, Bucatini

Long strands are best with smooth sauces or sauces with very small chunks. In general, wider noodles can support slightly chunkier sauces.

Arborio Rice

The stubby, starchy grains of Arborio are the traditional choice for risotto. The desirable "bite" in risotto is due to a defect in Arborio rice: During maturation, the starch structures at the grain's core deform, making for a firm, toothy center when cooked. Our winning brand is **RiceSelect Arborio Rice** and we highly recommend making the effort to get Arborio for a risotto recipe. However, if you're in a pinch and can't find it, look for medium- or short-grain rice for an acceptable—but not perfect—substitute.

Basmati Rice

For a truly great version of this nutty, aromatic rice that's eaten worldwide in pilafs and with curries, choose an imported brand from India that has been aged. Aging dehydrates the rice, which translates to grains that, once cooked, expand greatly. Our favorite, **Tilda Pure Basmati Rice**, also had the longest grains of any brand we tried.

Brown Rice

We prefer long-grain brown rice for its fluffy and discrete kernels. Most brands will be good if prepared correctly, but don't always trust package directions; many advise adding too much water. The most successful ratio that we've found for stovetop cooking is 1 cup of rice to 1¾ cups of water, as advertised on the package of our winning brand, **Lundberg Organic Brown Long Grain Rice**. If you'd rather use a convenience product, **Minute Ready to Serve Brown Rice** consistently turned out decent rice in 60 seconds, although there were definitely some sacrifices in taste and texture.

Jasmine Rice

This variety of long-grain white rice has a delicate floral and buttery scent and cooks up relatively soft and sticky. Pick a brand imported from Thailand like **Dynasty Jasmine Rice**, which has a distinct fragrance and tender, discrete grains.

Long-Grain White Rice

Plain long-grain rice cooks up light and fluffy with firm, distinct grains, making it good for pilafs and salads. This is also what makes it different from medium- or short-grain rice (the kinds used in risotto or sushi, respectively). Higher-quality white rice, like our favorite brand, **Lundberg Organic Long Grain White Rice**, offers a pleasingly chewy texture and a slightly buttery natural flavor. All rice starts out brown; to become white, it is milled, a process that removes the husk, bran, and germ, which contain flavor compounds as well as nutrients. The longer the rice is milled, the whiter it becomes—and the more flavor is removed. (Many brands of rice are then enriched to replace lost nutrients.) If you're looking for a convenience product, pick one that doesn't include glucono delta lactone (GDL), an additive that causes a sour, metallic taste. Our favorite is **Minute Ready to Serve White Rice**.

Avoid converted rice, which is parboiled during processing—its grains cook up too separate, and the flavor is a bit off.

Wild Rice

Wild rice is not in the same family as other rices; it's actually an aquatic grass. We prefer brands that parboil the grains during processing to create a shelf-stable product without destroying the grains. Our favorite, **Goose Valley Wild Rice**, has grains that are crunchy on the exterior and tender inside.

Couscous

Couscous is made from durum semolina, the wheat flour that is also used to make Italian pasta. The boxed couscous found in most supermarkets is a precooked version that needs only a few minutes of steeping in hot liquid to be fully cooked. Israeli couscous, also known as pearl couscous, is larger than traditional couscous and is not precooked. It has a unique, nutty flavor. When picking a brand of Israeli couscous, we recommend one with a higher protein-to-carbohydrate ratio and larger grains like our winner, **Roland Israeli Couscous**.

Your can find more than a dozen types of grain at the average supermarket. The following are our favorites. For information on our recommended cooking techniques and timing for each, see the chart on page 348.

Amaranth

Amaranth, a staple of the Incas and Aztecs, is second only to quinoa for protein content among grains. It is also high in vitamins and minerals. Amaranth has a complex flavor that's very nutty and earthy. It is often dry-toasted before being cooked and can be prepared like porridge or rice.

Barley

Best known in the United States as a staple used in soups, high-fiber barley's nutty, subtly sweet flavor makes it an ideal accompaniment to meat, chicken, and fish. We prefer quicker-cooking pearl barley, which has been stripped of its tough outer covering and polished to remove the bran layer, rather than hulled barley.

Buckwheat and Kasha

Buckwheat has an assertive flavor and can be found in several forms. Hulled, crushed buckwheat seeds are known as buckwheat groats, and because of their high carbohydrate content, they are generally eaten as a staple like rice or baked into puddings and porridges. Kasha is buckwheat groats that have been roasted. Kasha is often served pilaf-style or as a hot cereal.

Bulgur

Bulgur is made from parboiled or steamed wheat kernels/berries that are then dried, partially stripped of their outer bran layer, and coarsely ground. Coarse-grind bulgur is our top choice for making pilaf. Medium-grind bulgur can work in most applications if you make adjustments to soaking or cooking times. Cracked wheat, on the other hand, often sold alongside bulgur, is not precooked and cannot be substituted for bulgur.

Farro

A favorite ingredient in Tuscan cuisine, these hulled whole-wheat kernels boast a sweet, nutty flavor and chewy bite. In Italy, farro is available in three sizes—*farro piccolo*, *farro medio*, and *farro grande*— but the midsize type is most common in the United States.

Millet

Believed to be the first domesticated cereal grain, this tiny cereal grass seed has a long history and is still a staple in a large part of the world, particularly in Asia and Africa. The seeds can be ground into flour or used whole. Millet has a mellow corn flavor that works well in both savory and sweet applications. It can be cooked pilaf-style, or it can be turned into a creamy breakfast porridge or polenta-like dish by slightly overcooking the seeds, which causes them to burst and release starch. To add texture to baked goods, try incorporating a small amount of millet into the batter.

Oat Berries

Labeled either oat berries or oat groats, this whole grain is simply whole oats that have been hulled and cleaned. Because they have hardly been processed, they retain a high nutritional value. They have an appealing chewy texture and a mildly nutty flavor. Oat berries make a great savory side dish cooked pilaf-style.

Quinoa

Though actually a seed, quinoa is often referred to as a "supergrain" because it's a nutritionally complete protein. We love the pinhead-size seeds (which can be white, red, black, or purple) for their faint crunch and mineral taste. Unless labeled "prewashed," quinoa should always be rinsed before cooking to remove its protective layer (called saponin), which is unpleasantly bitter.

Wheat Berries

Wheat berries, often erroneously referred to as "whole wheat," are whole, unprocessed kernels of wheat. Since none of the grain has been removed, wheat berries are an excellent source of nutrition. Compared to more refined forms of wheat, wheat berries require a relatively long cooking time. We like to toast the dry wheat berries until they are fragrant and then simmer them for about an hour until they are tender but still retain a good bite.

The Tasting Lineup

Recommended

JOVIAL
Organic Gluten Free Brown Rice Spaghetti
Top Pick $3.49 for 12 oz

BARILLA
Gluten Free Spaghetti
$2.69 for 12 oz

Recommended with Reservations

DELALLO
Gluten Free Whole Grain Rice Spaghetti
$5.19 for 12 oz

Not Recommended

ANDEAN DREAM
Gluten/Corn Free Quinoa Pasta, Spaghetti
$4.49 for 8 oz

LUNDBERG
Organic Brown Rice Spaghetti Pasta
$3.99 for 10 oz

RONZONI
Gluten Free Spaghetti
$2.40 for 12 oz

DEBOLES
Gluten Free Multigrain Spaghetti Style Pasta
$3.30 for 8 oz

Gluten is the protein matrix that gives wheat noodles their structure and pleasant chew. For people who are avoiding gluten in their diets, finding good wheat-free pasta that achieves a similar structure and chew is a challenge, and one which has been met in a variety of ways by pasta manufacturers. We first evaluated gluten-free pasta several years ago and the results were grim. We tasted products made variously with rice, corn, and quinoa. Unfortunately, most samples absolutely failed to meet our standards for spaghetti. Most were gritty and grainy or dissolved into a mushy, gummy mess. We hoped that, given the number of new companies jumping on the gluten-free band-wagon recently, we might have better luck this time around. To find out, we pitted our top two scorers from the old tasting against five new products, tasting them cooked in salted water and tossed with canola oil, and a second time served with our favorite tomato sauce.

To our dismay, the majority of the brands again failed to meet our expectations. Even when we closely monitored their cooking time and strained them promptly, some of them practically disintegrated. But our old runner-up fell into the other end of the texture spectrum. Last time, we'd noticed a slight rubbery quality that we were willing to overlook due to its neutral flavor. But now our standards are higher. This time around, our tasters deemed it unacceptably chewy and firm.

Looking to the product labels for an explanation, we made a few discoveries. The better gluten-free pastas were made from brown rice flour. Thanks to its bran content, the brown rice flour pasta contained a relatively high combined total of fiber and protein, which helps keep the noodles intact during cooking. The flavor of brown rice pasta also came closest to that of the wheat-based kind.

Our top brown rice product was also dried at a low temperature, which helps preserve flavor and ensures that the proteins coagulate and provide structure for the starch. The combination of those factors helped account for its tasting "pretty close to the real deal" and made it our favorite by a long shot. Plus, at 33 cents per ounce, it was among the cheaper gluten-free options we tasted (all of which were much more expensive than wheat pasta).

A newcomer, made with a combination of corn and rice flours, joined our brown rice favorite at the top. The proteins in corn are more water-soluble than those in rice and therefore more likely to escape the pasta, resulting in soggy and sticky noodles. We'd nixed corn flour pastas in our first testing because they had been especially clumpy and gummy, but this new pasta remained intact and had an al dente texture. A closer look revealed that this pasta also contained stabilizers to help hold the starches together and keep the pasta tender.

For all types of pasta, protein is the most important factor in determining texture. However, gluten-free pastas don't behave in exactly the same ways as pastas made with white or whole-wheat flour. Most get their strength from rice flour, which is much lower in protein than either white or whole-wheat flour. Although particles of fiber can interfere with the protein bonds in wheat pasta and cause it to weaken during cooking, rice fiber actually plays a helpful role in gluten-free pasta—to a point. The ideal combination for pasta that cooks up tender and intact turns out to be a relatively high amount of protein (at least 4 grams) and a fiber content that's less than half that amount.

Many products are still disappointing, but it is possible to find good-quality gluten-free spaghetti made entirely from brown rice flour or with a combination of corn and rice flour. In both, a relatively high amount of protein and proportionate amount of fiber is the key to pasta that doesn't disintegrate during cooking.

METHODOLOGY

Seven pastas were boiled in abundant salted water until al dente and then promptly drained. Our tasting panel tasted each sample twice—once tossed with canola oil and once with a basic tomato sauce. The scores from the two tastings were averaged to determine overall rankings. Products are listed in The Tasting Lineup in order of preference.

PANTRY STAPLES

Canned Baked Beans

We prefer brands that are made with molasses, a classic baked beans seasoning that adds complexity and depth. Beans with higher sugar contents also have better texture and flavor. Steer clear of any brand made with tomato products, which can make the beans taste ketchup-y. Our favorite brand is **B&M Vegetarian Baked Beans**.

Canned Black Beans

Higher sodium levels make for much more well-seasoned beans—look for a product with at least 400 milligrams of sodium per half-cup serving, like our winner, **Bush's Best Black Beans**. Salt also helps with texture, as does the addition of calcium chloride, which strengthens the pectin in the cell walls of the beans.

Canned White Beans

Our favorite type of white beans are cannellini beans like **Goya Cannellini**. Some additives are okay—look for a brand with calcium chloride, which maintains firmness and prevents splitting, and calcium disodium EDTA, a preservative that binds iron in the water and prevents white beans from turning brown. Higher sodium levels will also help with flavor, tenderness, and creaminess.

Canned Chickpeas

Look for a product with at least 250 milligrams of sodium per half-cup serving; anything less than this will be bland at best and bitter or even metallic-tasting at worst. We like **Pastene Chick Peas** for their clean, salty flavor and firm yet tender texture.

Refried Beans

Traditional *frijoles refritos* start with dried pinto beans that are cooked, "fried well" in lard, and then mashed. It's time-consuming, so many cooks opt for a store-bought version. Despite the traditional preparation, we found that brands that used lard had no advantage over those that used vegetable oil. The real key is texture. Our favorite brand, **Taco Bell Home Originals Refried Beans** is super-smooth and well seasoned. Avoid dehydrated, instant refried beans; these are stale and unappealing.

Dried Beans

Dried beans come in a range of colors, shapes, and sizes, with flavors from earthy to nutty. Cooking times vary depending on the type of bean and its age. Buy them at a store with good turnover; very old beans can refuse to soften. Beans can have trouble softening in mineral-rich tap water (hard water). If you are in a hard-water area, cook them in bottled water. For substitutions, 1 cup of dried beans equals 3 cups of canned beans.

Lentils

Lentils come in dozens of sizes and colors. We find that brining them in warm salt water for an hour improves their texture. French green lentils, or *lentilles du Puy*, are our preferred choice for most recipes, but supermarket brown lentils are fine for salads and soups. Red and yellow lentils disintegrate completely when cooked and are best used in Indian recipes, such as dal.

Tofu

Tofu is created by pressing coagulated soy-milk curds in a mold to extract the liquid whey. Depending on how long the tofu is pressed, and how much coagulant is used, the resulting tofu can have a range of textures from soft to firm. We prefer extra-firm or firm tofu for stir-fries and for marinating. Medium and soft tofu have a creamy texture that's good for pan-frying or scrambling like eggs. Ultracreamy silken tofu is often used as a base for dips or desserts, or as an egg replacement in baked goods. Tofu is highly perishable and has the best flavor and texture when it is fresh, so look for a package with the latest expiration date possible. To store an opened package, cover the tofu with water and store, refrigerated, in a covered container, changing the water daily. Any hint of sourness means the tofu is past its prime.

Canned Whole Tomatoes

Whole tomatoes are peeled tomatoes packed in their own juice or puree. They are best used in recipes where fresh tomato flavor is a must. Whole tomatoes are quite soft and break down quickly when cooked. The best canned whole tomatoes have a fruity sweetness balanced by bright, tangy acidity. Balance is also a key element in the fruits' texture: too firm and they'll feel rubbery, but too soft and mushiness becomes a problem. Additives like calcium chloride help maintain firmness in canned whole tomatoes. We like an American brand, **Muir Glen Organic Whole Peeled Tomatoes**, for its acidity, high sugar content, and firm bite. **See page 140 for Inside the Tasting.**

Canned Diced Tomatoes

Diced tomatoes are peeled whole tomatoes that have been machine-diced and packed in their own juice or puree. Unlike most kinds of canned produce, a great can of diced tomatoes offers flavor almost every bit as intense as ripe, in-season fruit. Diced tomatoes are best for rustic tomato sauces with a chunky texture and in long-cooked stews and soups where you want the tomatoes to hold their shape. We favor diced tomatoes packed in juice because they have a fresher flavor. While we found that color and size were not good indicators of quality, we did notice that our favorite samples had a good amount of sodium in them, which brought out the fresh tomato flavor. Our winner, **Hunt's Diced Tomatoes**, is fresh and bright, with a sweet-tart flavor and juicy chunks that cook up beautifully in a sauce.

Canned Fire-Roasted Tomatoes

To compete with the sweet, smoky depth of fresh tomatoes charred over an open fire, canned versions need to offer smokiness without sacrificing basic tomato flavor and texture. The best brands include some natural additives, such as onion and garlic powders and yeast extract (which boosts umami). While fire-roasted tomatoes won't add much to recipes that already have complex flavor, they are an easy way to add subtly caramelized, smoky flavor to simple dishes like salsa. Our winning brand is **DeLallo Fire-Roasted Diced Tomatoes in Juice with Seasonings**.

Canned Crushed Tomatoes

Crushed tomatoes are whole tomatoes ground very fine and enriched with tomato puree. They work well in smoother sauces, and their thicker consistency makes them ideal when you want to make a sauce quickly. Texture varies dramatically among brands, from watery and thin to so thick you could stand a spoon in it. You might get peels or no peels; plentiful seeds or none; big, rough-cut chunks of tomato or a smooth consistency with no chunks at all. The ideal can of crushed tomatoes contains actual tomato pieces and a fair amount of liquid—our favorites are a little more than 50 percent tomatoes. Typically, you'll have better-tasting tomatoes if they are processed at a lower temperature and if they contain a moderate amount of additives, particularly salt and citric acid, which corrects the acidity of the tomatoes. Finally, look for a can that has tomatoes as its first ingredient, rather than tomato puree. Manufacturers often disguise less-than-perfect tomatoes with puree, which imparts a deeper red color to the contents of the can. Our winning brand is **Tuttorosso Crushed Tomatoes in Thick Puree with Basil**. Tasters liked its chunky texture and fresh flavors. If you can't find an acceptable brand, crush your own using canned diced tomatoes and a food processor.

Canned Pureed Tomatoes

While whole and diced tomatoes offer a passable substitute for fresh tomatoes (they are simply skinned and processed), tomato puree is cooked and strained, removing all seeds and all illusions of freshness. Thus it is more suited to long-cooked dishes where the thick, even texture of puree is important and fresh tomato flavor is not. Although we found it easy to sort out the winners and losers in the straight puree tasting (we preferred **Muir Glen Organic Tomato Puree** for its thick texture and good flavor), the differences were not so clear once the puree had simmered for 2 hours with a half-dozen spices in a chili recipe. Given that most recipes calling for tomato puree involve long cooking times and lots of ingredients, it's safe to say that one brand is not going to make much of a difference over another in the final dish.

Tomato Paste

Tomato paste is the backbone of many of our recipes at America's Test Kitchen, providing deep, rich tomato flavor. Because it's naturally full of glutamates, which stimulate tastebuds just like salt and sugar, it brings out subtle depth and savory notes. To make tomato paste, ripe tomatoes are heated and ruptured, a process called "break." The seeds, pulp, and skin are filtered out, and the juice is evaporated into a thick paste. Tomato paste lends a deeper, rounded tomato flavor and color to many slow-simmered pasta sauces as well as to Italian soups and stews. Our winner, **Goya Tomato Paste**, has low sodium and high levels of natural sugars. However, while better tomato pastes will improve the taste of a marinara, no brand will ruin the dish. Any tomato paste will supply reasonably good concentrated tomato flavor.

Beef Broth

Historically, we've found beef broth to be light on flavor, but sometimes it adds a much-needed kick in a recipe. Most of the beefiness in commercial broths comes from a lab rather than from a cow, but the right additives can actually do a lot for flavor. Our winner, **Better Than Bouillon Beef Base**, includes both yeast extract and hydrolized soy protein, which give it full, rounded flavor despite its low protein level. The paste is also economical and stores easily. When choosing beef broth, be sure to pick a brand with at least 450 milligrams of sodium per serving—anything less than that will taste underseasoned.

Chicken Broth

There are a lot of options out there for chicken broth. To narrow it down, we recommend choosing a product with between 400 and 700 milligrams of sodium. We've found this to be the best range for results that are flavorful but not too salty. Note that high protein levels are not necessarily indicative of good meaty flavor; although our winner, **Swanson Chicken Stock**, is high in protein, we also liked **Better Than Bouillon Chicken Base**, a concentrate that is cost-effective and long-lasting, but which has a much lower protein content. Savory depth can come from glutamates and nucleotides (naturally occurring compounds that enhance flavor) as well as from actual meat content.
See page 142 for Inside the Tasting.

Vegetarian Broth

Vegetable broth is the natural choice for vegetarian dishes as well as for lighter soups or vegetable dishes that might be overwhelmed by the flavor of chicken broth. Often we use a mix of chicken and vegetable broths since vegetable broth can be too sweet when used alone. Choose a vegetable broth with less than 750 milligrams of sodium. Counterintuitively, the best vegetable broths are not those made mostly of vegetables, since it's very hard to create a concentrate of vibrant flavor from real vegetables without getting bitter or sour aftertastes. Instead, our winner, **Orrington Farms Vegan Chicken Flavored Broth Base & Seasoning** uses additives like yeast extract to develop flavor. The same is true of our low-sodium vegetable broth winner, **Edward & Sons Low Sodium Not-Chick'n Natural Bouillon Cubes**.

HOMEMADE STOCK

When Homemade Stock Is a Must
Homemade stock makes a big difference in brothy soups with simple flavorings, such as chicken noodle soup, matzo ball soup, or egg drop soup. The stock is the main element in all of these soups, so you can really appreciate the flavor and gelatinous consistency of the stock. We wouldn't make them with packaged broths.

When Homemade Stock Is Optional
Soups with bold flavors, such as Mexican tortilla soup or Thai coconut chicken soup, can be made with either homemade stock or packaged broth. The flavor of the broth is important, but it's really in the background. These soups will definitely taste better with homemade stock, but supermarket broth makes a fine substitute—just use a light hand with added salt since packaged broths already contain so much sodium.

When Homemade Stock Won't Make a Big Difference
It's a waste to use homemade stock in dairy-rich pureed soups. Also, it will be hard to appreciate homemade stock in a soup thick with beans or a soup with lots of canned tomatoes. Packaged broth will also work just fine in all stews.

If you believe all the hype from Italian chefs and cookbooks, then San Marzano tomatoes are the best tomatoes in the world. Promoters of the prized crop claim that the climate and fertile soil in the eponymous southern region of Italy where they grow are behind the fruit's meaty texture, juiciness, and exceptional flavor. Only tomatoes grown in that region from seeds dating back to the original cultivar and according to strict standards may receive the elite *Denominazione di Origine Protetta* (DOP) label. In the past, San Marzanos were hard to come by in the United States, but that never deterred loyalists, who sought out cans from gourmet markets and online retailers. In recent years, however, San Marzano tomatoes have become easier to find, showing up in regular supermarkets and under different brand names. That's partly because not all brands labeled "San Marzano" are DOP-certified. These days, some of the tomatoes are even grown in the United States from San Marzano seeds.

The wider availability of San Marzanos renewed our general interest in canned whole tomatoes—a product that we frequently prefer to diced or crushed. (Oftentimes, the latter two are selected from fruit that's been damaged during harvesting and have been more thoroughly treated with firming agents to prevent them from breaking down.) We decided to hold a taste-off: San Marzanos versus everything else. After collecting 10 different brands—three labeled San Marzano, the other seven a mix of Italian, Canadian, and American products—we sampled them straight out of the can as well as simmered in both quick- and long-cooked tomato sauces.

Our questions: Are San Marzanos really the ultimate canned whole tomatoes—that is, bright, sweet, and tangy, with meat that's plush and soft enough to melt into a sauce but without completely dissolving? More important, would they taste noticeably better than regular tomatoes once they'd been cooked down in a sauce with aromatics and wine?

Surprisingly, the answer to both questions was a definitive "no." Though each of the three San Marzano samples elicited a few lukewarm compliments here and there, none of them delivered the bold, deeply fruity taste that we were expecting, nor did they hold their shape well. In fact, these tomatoes scored well below several of the domestic samples, the best of which were deemed "bright," "complex," "meaty," and—as one taster noted in amazement—like "real" tomatoes. Whether or not the tomato was a true San Marzano didn't matter. The DOP-certified brand was actually our least favorite of the three, which debunked the hype over the San Marzano pedigree once and for all. But now we had a more challenging question to answer: What made the other samples taste good?

For starters, sweetness. Scientists gauge this particular quality in tomatoes according to the Brix scale—a measurement of the sugar (per 100 grams) in liquid. Generally, the higher the Brix of tomatoes, the greater the perception of good, ripe tomato flavor. When we had an independent lab measure the Brix of each brand's tomato solids, the results were conclusive: Our three least favorite brands (including the DOP-certified San Marzanos) were the least sweet, with tasters panning their "weak," "washed out" flavor, whether cooked or eaten straight from the can. Conversely, tasters praised the "fruity," "real summer" sweetness of our two favorite tomatoes, whose sweetness levels were relatively high. However, the sweetest samples of all—which happened to be the other two San Marzanos—landed in the middle of the pack, proving that when it comes to optimal tomato flavor, sweetness is not the only dynamic in play.

METHODOLOGY

We sampled 10 nationally available brands of supermarket canned whole tomatoes in three blind tastings—plain and simmered in quick- and long-cooked tomato sauces—rating the samples on tomato flavor, texture, and overall appeal. An independent laboratory also measured the Brix (sugar levels) and pH (acidity) of all the samples; a higher Brix means more sweetness, while a lower pH corresponds to greater acidity. Products are listed in The Tasting Lineup in order of preference.

The other half of good tomato flavor is acidity—and lots of it. Bright tanginess balances out the sweetness and enhances other pleasing flavors by masking bitterness. Sure enough, when we had the lab measure the pH of all the samples, we discovered that the tomatoes with the lowest pH (i.e., the most acidic tomatoes) almost invariably scored the highest, earning tasters' approval for their "fresh," "fruity" flavors, while the least acidic tomatoes tanked. The lone exception was our bottom-ranked brand, which boasted a good level of acidity but not much sweetness—a combination that gave it an "unbalanced" flavor that tasters assailed for being "nothing like a summer tomato."

Salt played only a relatively minor role in our overall preferences. The American samples contained a lot more sodium than did imported brands (at least 20 times more, in some cases), and in the plain tasting some tasters preferred them for it. But sodium levels didn't influence our preferences in either of the cooked applications, and since canned tomatoes are rarely eaten uncooked, we didn't factor salt content into our rankings.

Good balance was the key to optimal tomato flavor, and it was a quality that tasters looked for in the fruits' texture, too. Overly firm specimens lost points for their "rubbery" bite, while tomatoes that broke down completely were docked for "mushiness." Our three top-ranking brands boasted a firm but tender bite, even after a lengthy simmer. But what accounted for the differences in texture?

For one thing, calcium chloride. All five American products were treated with this salt, which manufacturers add to maintain the tomatoes' firmness, whereas the imported brands were not. We figured that for better or for worse, the widespread use of this additive in domestic canned tomatoes couldn't help but drive our American tasters' preference for tomatoes that retain a little structure.

While we liked the tomatoes to be somewhat firm, we didn't like their flesh to be overly thick. In the 1960s, mechanical harvesting replaced handpicking in this country, speeding up the process. Growers then had to breed a tomato sturdy enough to withstand the rigors of machine harvesting, which meant they needed a fruit with thicker walls (known as pericarp). The trade-off was less flavor. The reason? Tomato flesh isn't where most of the flavor is; it's in the "jelly" that surrounds the seeds. When the flesh got thicker, those cavities got smaller, leaving less room for the jelly.

To see if this trend lined up with our results, we took a sample from each can, measured the thickness of its pericarp with a caliper, and scooped out and weighed its jelly. Indeed, our least favorite tomatoes had the thickest pericarp, with tasters describing them as "tough," "chewy," and "bland." The tomatoes we liked best had thinner, tender-firm walls, and their cavities were the largest and most full of flavorful jelly.

As it turned out, the San Marzano hype was all for naught. We didn't even prefer Italian-grown tomatoes. Rather, we most enjoyed the bold acidity, high sugar content, and firm bite of our favorite all-American brand. Another American brand finished a close second, with tasters particularly admiring their firm texture and pleasing acidity. We'll be stocking up on both.

ENGINEERING THE IDEAL CANNED TOMATO

Farmed for Flavor
The best tomatoes are cultivated to be both highly acidic and very sweet. The walls of their flesh shouldn't be too thick, allowing for an abundance of jelly and seeds—the most flavorful part of the tomato.

Processed for Firmness
Italian cooks might feel just the opposite, but our American tasters preferred brands that included calcium chloride, which helps ensure that the tomatoes won't turn mushy during cooking—an issue with the additive-free imports.

The Tasting Lineup, CONTINUED

Recommended with Reservations, continued
SAN MARZANO
Whole Peeled Tomatoes
$3.99 for 28 oz

RIENZI
Selected Italian Plum Tomatoes
$1.95 for 28 oz

EDEN ORGANIC
Whole Roma Tomatoes
$3.79 for 28 oz

PASTENE
San Marzano Tomatoes of Sarnese Nocerino Area D.O.P.
$4.53 for 28 oz

Not Recommended
TUTTOROSSO
Peeled Plum Shaped Tomatoes
$1.79 for 28 oz

The Tasting Lineup

Recommended

SWANSON
Chicken Stock
Top Pick $3.19
for 3 cups
($1.06 per cup)

BETTER THAN BOUILLON
Chicken Base
Best Buy $5.99
for 8-oz jar that
makes 38 cups
($0.16 per cup)

Recommended with Reservations

KNORR
Homestyle Stock
Reduced Sodium
Chicken
$3.99 for 4 tubs
that make 3.5 cups
each, 14 cups total
($0.29 per cup)

SWANSON
Natural Goodness
Chicken Broth
$2.99 for 4 cups
($0.75 per cup)

PROGRESSO
Reduced Sodium
Chicken Broth
$2.79 for 4 cups
($0.70 per cup)

Chicken broth isn't sexy like black truffles or trendy like pork belly, but in the test kitchen we rarely go a day without using it. As the backbone of much of our savory cooking, it appears in hundreds of our recipes. We use it as a base for soups and stews; for simmering pilafs and risottos; and to moisten braises, pan sauces, and gravies. Of course, we use homemade stock when possible, but truth be told, it's not that often. Most of the time, we rely on commercial alternatives. When we surveyed supermarket shelves, we found them teeming with options, including many alternatives to canned or boxed liquid broths. Between the granulated powders, cubes, concentrates, and liquids—not to mention a headache-inducing array of sodium levels—we found more than 50 different chicken broth products.

To pare down this unwieldy number, we looked at salt levels. Our first move was to eliminate any broths with more than 700 milligrams of sodium per serving, since in previous taste tests we've found that broths containing more than this amount become too salty when reduced in a sauce or a gravy. We also avoided anything with less than 400 milligrams, since a judicious amount of salt is required to bring out chicken taste. We also learned in a previous tasting that broths with less salt than this are entirely bland.

That left us with 10 broths: eight liquids (including our previous favorite) and two concentrates that are reconstituted with water. We set about tasting the finalists warmed plain, in a simple risotto, and reduced in an all-purpose gravy. Our goal: to find the richest, most chicken-y stand-in for homemade stock.

Several of the samples tasted awful. In fact, five flunked every test. Some of these had chicken flavor so wan that it was practically nonexistent; others were "beefy" or "vegetal" or had bizarre off-flavors. Most of the remaining samples tasted promising out of the box but exhibited flaws when cooked. A couple turned candy-sweet when reduced in gravy; the flavor of others disappeared entirely in the starchy risotto rice. Out of the 10 samples, there were only two that stood apart: One was a traditional boxed liquid, and the other was a concentrate. While tasters praised the boxed stock's meaty flavor, they were even more impressed by the clean, savory taste of the concentrate.

We have to admit that we weren't expecting a concentrate to perform so well. However, we did a little digging and it turns out that nearly all supermarket chicken broths actually start out as concentrates; not only that, but most of them are made by the same company. According to Roger Dake, director of research and development for International Dehydrated Foods (IDF), most of the liquid broths in our lineup were made to order by IDF, which prepares them according to a brand's specifications. The broths are left concentrated because this makes them lighter and thus cheaper to ship. At the food production sites, the concentrates are reconstituted to their final liquid form, flavored with the other ingredients shown on the label, packaged, and shipped out for sale.

Given this, our awarding highest marks to a concentrate wasn't all that remarkable. But there was something we weren't expecting: the difference in protein between our two favorites. While the boxed liquid had a relatively high

METHODOLOGY

After choosing from a list of top sellers and narrowing our results by sodium levels, we tasted 10 widely available chicken broths in three blind tastings: plain, in a simple risotto, and in gravy. The broths were rated on flavor, saltiness, and off-flavors, as well as on overall appeal. Nutrition information was taken from product labels. Products are listed in The Tasting Lineup in order of preference.

4 grams of protein per cup, the concentrate had just 1 gram. It turns out that the USDA has no minimum required protein content for chicken broth or "stock." What's more, higher protein content wasn't actually a guarantee of bigger chicken flavor: The broth with the highest amount of protein per cup (5 grams) was panned for its "sour," "vegetal" flavor. What we couldn't figure out, though, was how our favorite concentrate obtained its rich, chicken-y flavor with such a measly amount of protein.

Savoriness is often associated with glutamates, forms of an amino acid that enhance a food's meaty, umami flavor. Glutamates are already found in chicken, but many companies add extra, so we made glutamates our next point of investigation. We packed up the broths and shipped them to an independent laboratory to be analyzed. The data helped confirm why our winner tasted good—it had the highest level of glutamates in the lineup. But it didn't shed any light on why we liked the concentrate, which ranked among the lowest by far.

Then we noticed that the concentrate adds nucleotides called disodium inosinate and disodium guanylate to its product. Like glutamates, these compounds are flavor enhancers that occur naturally in certain foods including meat, seafood, and dried mushrooms. Now things started to make sense. A while back, we learned that when nucleotides and glutamates are combined, they can dramatically increase savory flavors. By including both types of compounds, the concentrate was able to create the savory qualities we associate with good chicken flavor—even without much protein.

We were intrigued by the concentrate and decided to stretch its legs in the kitchen by incorporating it into more recipes. Then we hit a snag: Some dishes—particularly those that called for more than a quart of chicken broth, like soups, or those that were considerably reduced, like pan sauces—occasionally turned overly salty with the concentrate in the mix.

That saltiness was in part explained by the fact that the concentrate added more sodium than any of the other brands we sampled (680 milligrams per serving), just pushing at our upper acceptable limit. But we couldn't understand why the concentrate tasted nicely seasoned in some tests but too salty in others, until we took into account that the nutrition numbers for any product are allowed to vary by as much as 20 percent on either side of the stated value. We rounded up 10 jars from 10 different batches (as determined by batch numbers on the labels) and sent them to the lab to analyze their sodium contents. Sure enough, the numbers were all over the map—from 380 to 770 milligrams per cup—which explained why our taste test results were, too.

Our favorite concentrate's tendency toward saltiness made us hesitate about stocking it in the test kitchen, but it did have other merits. It was the cheapest by far—more than seven times cheaper than the priciest liquid broth—since you aren't paying to transport all the water. Most cartons of liquid broth weigh 2 pounds and yield 4 cups, but an 8-ounce jar of concentrate yields 38 cups. That much liquid broth would weigh nearly 20 pounds.

Another plus: Once opened, the concentrate will last for two years stored in the refrigerator. Liquid broths keep for no more than two weeks once opened. Even better, you can reconstitute only as much as you need—several cups for making soup or stew or just a few tablespoons for making a pan sauce. Having thrown away plenty of partially used cartons of broth, we really appreciate that option. Reconstituting also allowed us to adjust the concentration of the broth. The package label prescribes 1 teaspoon of concentrate per cup of water. Scaling back to ¾ teaspoon per cup brought the saltiness in check without noticeably diluting the broth's flavor.

Those perks made the concentrate an appealing option, but we ultimately felt that we couldn't award it the top spot if it meant we had to ignore the package instructions. Instead, our boxed, liquid winning broth will be our stand-in for homemade, although we'd still like to see more actual meat in factory-made chicken broth. However, the concentrate is certainly proof positive that smart food science can go a long way toward engineering a better commercial broth.

The Tasting Lineup, CONTINUED

Not Recommended

IMAGINE
Chicken Cooking Stock
$4.29 for 4 cups
($1.07 per cup)

COLLEGE INN
Light & Fat Free Chicken Broth, 50% Less Sodium
$2.59 for 4 cups
($0.65 per cup)

KITCHEN BASICS
Original Chicken Cooking Stock
$3.29 for 4 cups
($0.82 per cup)

SWANSON
Certified Organic Free Range Chicken Broth
$3.29 for 4 cups
($0.82 per cup)

PACIFIC
Organic Free Range Chicken Broth
$4.59 for 4 cups
($1.15 per cup)

OILS, VINEGARS, AND CONDIMENTS

Vegetable Oil

Vegetable oil is a workhorse of the kitchen partly because of its neutral taste: Fat conveys flavor, and with no strong taste of its own, vegetable oil highlights other ingredients. That unobtrusive flavor profile makes it ideal not only for frying and sautéing, but also for baked goods that need more moisture than butter alone can offer, and salad dressings where the stronger presence of olive oil is not preferred. The average grocery store stocks more than a dozen vegetable oils, from canola to corn to soybean, plus blends of two or more oils. For a one-size-fits-all oil—one that can function seamlessly in everything from rich, creamy mayonnaise or vinaigrette to moist, sweet cake and crisp, golden fried food without off-flavors— we recommend a blend. We like **Crisco Blends**, which incorporates canola, soybean, and sunflower oils. Canola oil on its own should not be used for deep frying (it can give food an off-flavor when the oil is heated for a long time).

Extra-Virgin Olive Oil

Olive oil is simply juice pressed from olives. The highest grade of olive oil is called extra-virgin and has flavors that range from peppery to buttery depending on the variety of olives and how ripe they are when harvested. We use extra-virgin olive oil as a condiment on grilled meat, fish, vegetables, and pastas; a source of richness in soups and sauces; and a star player in vinaigrette. Look for extra-virgin olive oil that is sourced from a single region and processed and bottled soon after the olives are picked, like our winning brand, **California Olive Ranch Everyday Extra Virgin Olive Oil**. The best indication of freshness is the harvest date (not the "best by" date). Look for the most recent date, and note that in Europe and the United States, olives are harvested in the fall and winter, so most bottles will list the previous year. Avoid clear glass or plastic bottles; dark glass shields the oil from damaging light. Avoid refrigerating olive oil. An opened bottle of extra-virgin olive oil should last at least three months if stored properly.
See page 149 for Inside the Tasting.

Toasted Sesame Oil

The potent flavor of toasted sesame oil (sometimes labeled Asian sesame oil) fades quickly when exposed to heat, so we add this oil in the final moments of cooking. We use toasted sesame oil in Asian-inspired dishes, dressings, sauces, and marinades. It is highly perishable, so store it in the refrigerator.

Peanut Oil

Refined peanut oil is our first choice for deep frying. It has a neutral flavor and high smoke point, and it doesn't break down and impart off-flavors, even with prolonged exposure to heat (a problem we've had with other oils). Unrefined peanut oil, which has a nutty flavor that we like in stir-fries, is sold in small bottles for a hefty price.

KEEPING OILS FRESHER LONGER

- Check the harvest date printed on the label of high-end oils to ensure the freshest bottle possible. (Some labels cite an expiration date, which is typically 18 months from harvesting. We think unopened olive oil can go rancid as soon as one year after the harvest date, so be sure to test oil from older bottles before using it.)

- Don't store oils on the countertop or windowsill; move them to a dark pantry or cupboard (or the refrigerator, if they need to be kept chilled). Strong sunlight will oxidize the oils, producing stale, harsh flavors.

- Don't buy olive oil in bulk. Once opened, it has a very short shelf life.

- To check oil for freshness, test it by heating a few tablespoons in a skillet. If vegetable oil smells anything other than neutral—and if olive oil smells musty rather than fruity—discard it.

Here's a quick guide to storing open bottles of oil in your kitchen. Properly stored, vegetable oil should last six months once opened and extra-virgin olive oil should last at least three months.

Store in Pantry
Canola, Corn, Olive, Peanut, Vegetable

Store in Fridge
Sesame, Walnut

Distilled White Vinegar

Made from grain alcohol, white vinegar has no added flavor and is therefore the harshest—and yet most pure—vinegar. We use it in pickling and, diluted with water, as a cleaning agent for kitchen surfaces and hard-skinned fruits and vegetables.

Apple Cider Vinegar

This vinegar has a tangy bite and a fruity sweetness that work perfectly in bread-and-butter pickles, barbecue sauce, and coleslaw. For a versatile option with moderate acidity and clear apple notes, look for **Heinz Filtered Apple Cider Vinegar**.

Balsamic Vinegar

We use this vinegar in vinaigrettes and glazes and to finish soups and sauces. For basic, everyday use, choose a supermarket brand labeled "balsamic vinegar of Modena." It should also bear an *Indicazione Geografica Protetta* (IGP) seal on its label. Our top pick is **Bertolli Balsamic Vinegar of Modena**. For a special condiment to drizzle over berries or a piece of grilled fish, pick up a bottle of the small-batch, long-aged *aceto balsamico tradizionale*. Our winning product, **Cavalli Gold Seal Extra Vecchio Aceto Balsamico Tradizionale de Reggio Emilia**, is aged for 25 years and costs $60 per ounce, but it has flavor and texture that are truly worth it. **See page 152 for Inside the Tasting.**

Red Wine Vinegar

Use this slightly sweet, sharp vinegar for bold vinaigrettes and rich sauces. Our favorite, **Laurent du Clos Red Wine Vinegar**, is a French import made from a blend of different types of grapes, which gives it a complex and pleasing taste. However, it can be hard to find; if you're unable to locate it, we recommend our second-place finisher, **Pompeian Gourmet Red Wine Vinegar**.

Rice Vinegar

Also referred to as rice wine vinegar, this vinegar is made from steamed rice. Since rice vinegar has lower acidity than other vinegars, we use it to add gentle balance to Asian-influenced recipes.

White Wine Vinegar

White wine vinegar is key to punching up pickle brine, brightening sauces, and providing an unobtrusive, untinted foundation for delicate dressings. For uncooked applications like vinaigrettes, we prefer the fermented richness of **Spectrum Naturals Organic White Wine Vinegar**. In cooked applications, the smooth sweetness of **Colavita Aged White Wine Vinegar** is better.

WINE FOR COOKING

Over the years, the test kitchen has developed hundreds of recipes with wine. We've learned that you should not cook with anything you would not drink. This includes the super-salty "cooking wines" sold in many supermarkets. That said, there's no need to spend a fortune on wine destined for sauces or stews. We've tested good $10 bottles versus better-tasting $30 wines and while we can tell the difference in the glass, it's not appreciable in a cooked application.

Red Wine

The best red wines for cooking are medium-bodied, unoaked varieties that aren't terribly tannic. Go with blended (nonvarietal) American or Australian wines, or a French Côtes du Rhône. Avoid heavy Cabernets.

White Wine

Medium-bodied, unoaked varieties that aren't terribly sweet are the best white wines for cooking. We prefer clean, dry Sauvignon Blancs to Rieslings or heavily oaked Chardonnays, which can dominate subtle flavors.

Vermouth

Vermouth, which has a shelf life of several months, makes a good substitute for wine in many recipes. Replace white wine with an equal amount of white vermouth and red wine with red vermouth.

Nonalcoholic Substitutes for Wine

Broth can work as an equal replacement in sauces and stews that call for small amounts of wine. The dish won't taste exactly the same, but at least the recipe will work. For every ½ cup broth used, you should also stir in ½ teaspoon red or white wine vinegar or lemon juice before serving, which will mimic some of the acidity otherwise provided by the wine.

Beer is the nectar created when malt (a grain that has germinated and then been dried and/or roasted) is mixed with water, strained, and the resulting liquid is fermented. Fermentation converts the sugar in the malt into acid, gas, and/or alcohol. Many beers are flavored with hops, the seed cones of a climbing vine, which add flowery, bitter, and piney flavors to the mix. We use beer's flavor and fizz in dozens of recipes.

Session

Session beers were invented as a response to ever-increasing alcohol percentages in craft beers such as India Pale Ales. The addition of more hops doesn't just increase a craft beer's flavor, it also sends its alcohol content by volume (ABV) sky-high (between 8 and 12 percent). Session beers are brewed with the same care for flavor as craft beers, but with an ABV usually between 4 and 5 percent.

Lager

Unlike ales, which ferment at high temperatures, lagers ferment at cool temperatures before aging to develop more subtle, crisp flavors. Lagers tend to be light- to medium-bodied, which makes them ideal for use in cooking.

Pilsner

This light, gold- to straw-colored beer gets its name from its birthplace in Pilsen, Bohemia (now Czech Republic). Though it's brewed like lager, it's lighter in color and body and has a floral, slightly spicy finish. True pilsners often have a high level of carbonation due to months of aging.

Saison

Saisons are funky, yeasty, hoppy European ales made from mixed grains and noble hops. Saisons pair well with food, especially cheese. American beers brewed in the same style are often labeled "farmhouse" ales.

India Pale Ale

The extra hops in this style of beer were originally added as a preservative to help it survive long journeys in the late 18th century. European hops lend vegetal, grassy flavors to some IPAs, while hops from North America add flavors of citrus and pine. Beware: the hoppier the beer, the higher the ABV.

Porter

Relatively low-alcohol porters are known for their chocolate, toffee, and toasty flavors, which come from the malts used to make them—these dark malts are also what make porter so dark. The roasted malt flavors make porter a great match for grilled meats.

Stout

This dark brew uses toasted malts, giving it roasted, sometimes bitter coffee-like notes. Since sugars are cooked off during roasting, the resulting stouts are usually lower in alcohol than you'd expect. The deep flavor and full body of stout makes it a natural pairing with roasted meats.

Wheat Beer

Wheat beers have a hazy, unfiltered look and taste of clove, banana, and citrus. Brewers rely on warm fermentation and a particular strain of yeast to produce the yeasty, spicy flavor of what they call *Weissbier*, *Weizenbier*, or *Hefeweizen* (*hefe* is yeast, *weizen* is wheat).

Lambic

Lambics are dry, sour, and tart Belgian wheat beers that are often infused with fruit. Before brewing, lambic wort (a mix of crushed grain and water) is fermented in the open air, where it develops flavor from wild yeasts. Kreik and framboise are lambics fermented with cherries and raspberries, respectively. The high acidity of lambics makes them pair well with shellfish or oily fish like salmon.

Sour Beer

Sour beer starts with sweet malt that undergoes warm fermentation. The fermented beer is then placed in old wooden barrels full of wild yeasts and other yeast strains for a second or third fermentation. Bacteria in the barrels eat the sugars in the beer, which produces a beer that is tart and sour. Like lambic, sour beers are excellent paired with rich or fatty foods.

Cider

Hard cider is an alcoholic beverage made from fermented apple juice. Ciders are available in a variety of styles and flavors from sweet to dry. We recommend ciders with a high sugar content, which contributes to stronger apple flavor, especially when used in recipes.

Ketchup

In the past, almost all ketchup was made with high-fructose corn syrup, but recent developments in the market mean that there are now many alternatives. We like boldly seasoned brands with all the flavor elements—salt, sweet, tang, and tomato—that are assertive yet harmonious. Whether high-fructose corn syrup is really as bad as some say is a matter for debate, but our blind tastings showed that we prefer ketchups made with sugar, which has a cleaner, purer sweetness that doesn't lead to off-flavors. Our winning brand, **Heinz Organic Tomato Ketchup**, is made with sugar and has a relatively high salt content for perfect tangy flavor.

Yellow Mustard

Smooth and mild, yellow mustard is a North American thing. In other parts of the world, mustards are hotter, darker, and grainier. But what yellow mustard may lack in worldliness and guts, it makes up for in versatility. Yellow mustard is as much at home on a ballpark hot dog as it is on cold cuts or in potato salad, barbecue sauce, salad dressing, or marinades for chicken or pork. Yellow mustard is made from white (also called yellow) mustard seeds, which are flavorful but don't cause any of the nasal burn of brown or black mustard seeds; these last two are used in Dijon, Chinese, and other spicy mustards. But this doesn't mean it shouldn't have flavor—our favorite brand, **Annie's Naturals Organic Yellow Mustard**, lists mustard seed second in its ingredients. It also has a low sodium level, which keeps the saltiness from throwing the flavors out of balance.

Brown Mustard

Brown mustard is made from small, hot brown mustard seeds, along with some of their bran, which gives the mustard its speckled look. We use brown mustard to pack a punch when we're eating rich foods like pastrami, ham, or eggy breads. Mustards with both a high percentage of mustard oil and a moderate amount of vinegar taste complex and multidimensional. Brands that were gritty, chunky, or runny got lower scores. In the end, our winner, **Gulden's Spicy Brown Mustard**, took the top spot thanks to its bold heat, gentle tang, and smooth texture.

Dijon Mustard

Good Dijon mustard is creamy, with more body than conventional yellow mustard, and it packs a wallop of clean, nose-tingling heat. We eat it on sandwiches, hot dogs, and sausages, and add it to everything from salad dressings and dips to pan sauces and glazes for roasted meats, fish, and vegetables. Our favorite, **Trois Petits Cochons Moutarde de Dijon**, brought together all the traits we were looking for. Its pH was the highest of all the mustards in the lineup, and it contained a small amount of fat. It was also the only dijon mustard we tasted to list mustard seeds as the first ingredient.

Coarse-Grain Mustard

Mustard aficionados argue that the coarse-grained condiment improves any ham sandwich or grilled sausage—unless you pick the wrong jar. Tasters appreciated spiciness, tanginess, and the pleasant pop of seeds. They disliked mustards with superfluous ingredients such as xanthan gum, artificial flavors, and garlic and onion powders. But the more noteworthy factor turned out to be salt. Mustards with a meager quantity ranked low, while the winners contained roughly twice as much of this flavor amplifier. Our co-winners, **Grey Poupon Harvest Coarse Ground Mustard** and **Grey Poupon Country Dijon Mustard**, make good pantry staples.

Mayonnaise

You can make mayonnaise yourself, but doing so requires careful technique, and the shelf life of homemade mayo is short. Luckily, a good supermarket product can rival homemade. The best-tasting brands have the fewest ingredients. Tasters downgraded dressed-up variations that used cider vinegar instead of more neutral distilled vinegar, or honey instead of sugar. We didn't like add-ins such as dried garlic or onion either. Our top-rated brand didn't even include lemon juice or mustard. Surprisingly, fat levels in the mayonnaises didn't affect our rankings. As is often the case at our tastings, what did matter was salt; the top-ranked portion of the lineup had more than the bottom portion. Our winner, **Blue Plate Real Mayonnaise**, also uses just egg yolks (no whites) for a richer, deeper flavor. For a lighter option, we prefer **Hellmann's Light Mayonnaise**.

Soy Sauce

Soy sauce is a dark, salty fermented liquid made from soybeans and wheat. It is used throughout Asian cuisines to enhance flavor and contribute complexity to food. Soybeans contribute a strong, pungent taste, while wheat lends sweetness. Tamari is a type of soy sauce traditionally made with all soybeans and no wheat—though, confusingly, many tamaris do contain a little wheat. As a result, tamari has a more pungent flavor than soy sauce. Similarly, stronger, earthier Chinese soy sauce tends to be made with a lower proportion of wheat than the sweeter, lighter Japanese soy sauce. Pasteurized soy sauce can be stored at room temperature, but unpasteurized soy sauce should be refrigerated. While you can't go wrong as long as you buy a soy sauce that's labeled "fermented" or "brewed," we like **Kikkoman Soy Sauce** for its good salty-sweet balance and simple ingredient list; unlike other sauces, it contains just wheat, soybeans, water, and salt, with no added sugar or flavor enhancers.

Oyster Sauce

Bottled oyster-flavored sauce is a rich, concentrated mixture of oyster extractives, soy sauce, brine and assorted seasonings. The brown sauce is thick, salty, and strong. Very salty and fishy-tasting, oyster sauce is too strong to be used as a condiment. Rather, it is used sparingly to enhance the flavor of many dishes and stir-fries that have a long list of additional wet and aromatic ingredients, and it is the base for many Asian dipping sauces. Our winner, **Lee Kum Kee's Premium Oyster Flavored Sauce**, is the real deal, intense and fishy. This sauce will keep indefinitely when refrigerated.

Hot Sauce

A stroll down the condiment aisle reveals a dizzying array of options for hot sauce, and that's before you consider online sources and specialty stores. Even cooks who don't crave spicy food are likely to keep a bottle handy to give recipes a little kick. On any given day in the test kitchen, you'll find us adding a few drops to everything from eggs and pasta to soups, sandwiches, and sauces. Our winner, **Huy Fong Sriracha Hot Chili Sauce**, is made with red jalapeño, a milder, fruitier-tasting chile than cayenne. It was the only hot sauce we sampled that contains sugar, giving it a noticeably sweeter quality that tasters enjoyed. They also liked its thick texture and bright flavor, both of which come from the fact that this condiment is made with freshly ground peppers that go into the sauce unstrained, and its flavor balance, which featured just the right combination of punchy heat, saltiness, sweetness, and garlic.

Jellies, Jams, Preserves, and Marmalade

Commercial jellies, jams, and preserves are all made in the same basic manner: by cooking fruit down with sugar and an acid. What differentiates the trio, according to the standards of identity regulated by the FDA, are the size and structure of the fruit products used. Which one you pick will depend on what you plan to use it for. Jellies are made with fruit juices and cook up into thick, clear, homogeneous mixtures. Jams contain fruit pieces (crushed, chopped, sliced, or pureed) and have a slightly chunky, slightly firm texture. Preserves are made with large chunks or even whole fruits and are usually described as fruit suspended in thick syrup. Preserves tend to be less sweet than jams and jellies. Marmalade almost always contains pieces of rind, which gives it a unique texture and also a faint bitterness. We use jam as a filling for pastries and other desserts, and jelly can be melted and used as a glaze. Preserves and marmalade are usually reserved for spreading on toast, muffins, or other baked goods.

Olive oil, which is simply juice pressed from olives, tastes great when it's fresh. The highest grade, called extra-virgin, is lively, bright, and full-bodied at its best, with flavors that range from peppery to buttery depending on the variety of olives used and how ripe they are when harvested. (In general, an earlier harvest yields greener, more peppery oil; a later harvest results in a mellower, more golden oil.) But like any other fresh fruit, olives are highly perishable, and their pristine, complex flavor degrades quickly, which makes producing—and handling—a top-notch oil time-sensitive, labor-intensive, and expensive. But the results couldn't be more worth it. We use extra-virgin olive oil as a condiment on grilled meat, fish, vegetables, and pastas; a source of richness and body in soups and sauces; and a star player in vinaigrette.

Unfortunately, the supermarket extra-virgin olive oils we have tasted in the past were wan facsimiles of the good stuff. Most were either as bland as vegetable oil or, worse, funky, overpowering, and stale. We learned that Americans were literally getting the bottom of the barrel, and a number of more recent articles and books have pointed out a big reason why: With no meaningful U.S. standards for olive oil, lower-quality oils found a ready market here. In fact, one widely reported 2010 University of California, Davis Olive Center study revealed that a whopping 69 percent of tested supermarket olive oils sold as "extra-virgin" actually weren't according to the standards set by the International Olive Council (IOC), the industry's worldwide governing body. They were in fact lesser grades being passed off at premium prices.

Since then, the U.S. olive oil industry has taken steps to be more stringent. California,

where olive oil production has grown tenfold over the past decade, passed its own standards in 2008 and tightened them last year. And in 2010, after the UC Davis Olive Center study and at the urging of domestic producers, the USDA adopted chemical and sensory standards for olive oil grades similar to those established by the IOC. Among the chemical standards: An oil must not exceed certain levels of free fatty acids and peroxides, which would indicate olive deterioration, poor processing, and oxidation. To meet sensory criteria, an oil must taste not just flawless—or have what experts call "zero defects"—but also possess good fruity flavor.

To see if these new standards have led to better-quality oils in supermarkets, we decided to take a fresh look. We sampled 10 top-selling nationally available supermarket extra-virgin olive oils in a series of blind tastings: plain, with bread, over tomatoes and mozzarella, and in a vinaigrette served over salad greens. We also sent each of the oils to an independent laboratory for chemical evaluation and to 10 trained olive oil tasters to get a second opinion on their flavor quality.

Every stage of the process affects the quality of the oil. Producers must start with good fruit—that is, ripe olives that have been harvested carefully and aren't bruised or fermented—and get it to the mill as quickly as possible, before spoilage sets in. Extra-virgin olive oil (sometimes abbreviated EVOO) must also be pressed—or, in modern terms, spun out by a centrifuge to separate the water from the oil—with clean equipment that won't add impurities and without using high heat or chemicals. While heat and chemicals extract

Inside the Tasting continued on next page

METHODOLOGY

We tasted 10 top-selling extra-virgin olive oils plain, with bread, over tomatoes and mozzarella, and in vinaigrette, rating the oils on their fruity, fresh, bitter, and peppery flavors and overall appeal. Information about source, olive varieties, and bottling location were obtained from manufacturers. We also had the oils tested at an independent laboratory for quality and freshness. (An independent group of trained olive oil tasters conducted a separate double-blind tasting of the oils, but we didn't factor their assessment into our rankings.) Products are listed in The Tasting Lineup in order of preference.

more oil from the olives, it's at the cost of preserving important aromatics and antioxidants that help keep the oil fresh-tasting. That said, producing high-quality oil is only half the challenge. Because olive oil begins to degrade as soon as it's exposed to air, heat, and light, producers must transport and store it carefully to preserve its freshness.

Any of these factors might account for the fact that, while all the oils in our tasting did just pass the lab tests we commissioned (a limited spectrum of some of the same freshness and quality tests required by the IOC and USDA), only one passed all the tests with solid scores. The rest showed spotty results that weren't indicative of a truly fresh, high-quality oil. As for our sensory evaluations, these were even more discouraging. Both panels agreed that only two out of the 10 oils had good fruity flavor without off-notes. Our in-house panel found the remaining oils merely lackluster, but the experts were harsher in their criticism. Oils that we deemed simply flat or dull they decried as borderline rancid or "fusty," an industry term for a fermented taste.

When we spoke about these results with Alexandra Kicenik Devarenne, an independent California-based olive oil consultant and educator, judge in international olive oil competitions, and author of *Olive Oil: A Field Guide* (2014), she confirmed what we suspected: "If this had been an official panel tasting, the problems in these oils would make them a lower grade. They would be virgin, as opposed to extra-virgin."

But how could so many subpar oils labeled "extra-virgin" still appear in supermarkets, given the standards the USDA has put in place? The answer is simple: The standards aren't enforced. In fact, they're not enforced anywhere in the olive oil industry. A 2013 U.S. International Trade Commission report noted that even in Europe, the IOC standards are "widely unenforced," allowing "a wide range of oil qualities to be marketed as extra-virgin." (In the United States, a different reason might eventually force more compliance: Manufacturers of two of the oils in our lineup, Bertolli and Filippo Berio, are the targets of class-action suits for misleading labeling. Both have denied the claims.)

Standard bottling practices and "best by" dates also might be part of the problem. Devarenne explained that the oils in our lineup may have had the necessary flavor profile to qualify as extra-virgin when they were first pressed, but the fact that oils are commonly stored in stainless-steel tanks for multiple years and given a "best by" date from the time of bottling rather than harvest may have meant that they weren't especially fresh by the time we tasted them.

For Devarenne, the issue with most of the oils we tasted is not that they don't have a place in the kitchen—she thinks most would be acceptable as cooking oils rather than condiment oils, and we agree. Instead, it's what she calls "the 'truth in labeling' thing." "If, overnight, all of the olive oil in the supermarket magically relabeled itself to accurately reflect what was inside the bottle, we would have a vigorous trade in virgin grade olive oil in this country," she said. Instead, mislabeling cheapens the consumer's impression of what a real extra-virgin oil should be.

So what about those better-quality oils in our lineup? Our runner-up was from Lucini, a supermarket brand of extra-virgin we've liked in the past. Our top-ranking sample was from California Olive Ranch, the winner of our earlier tasting of California extra-virgin olive oil. The latter stood out for its "fragrant," "complex," and "fruity" flavors. Not surprisingly, it also was the oil that bested the others in our chemical tests. So what does California Olive Ranch do differently that makes their product better than the others? Mostly, it boils down to the company's control over every stage of the production process, which preserves the freshness of the oil as much as possible.

It starts with the source. Six of the 10 brands we tasted are sourced from multiple regions—and from one to as many as 11 different countries—which increases the likelihood that the oils were collected from a price-driven global bulk market that prioritizes cheap, not high-quality, oil. Conversely, California Olive Ranch, the lone domestic oil in our tasting, is made from olives that are grown within 150 miles of the pressing and bottling facility. The company knows exactly what types of olives go into its oils and is willing to share the information, whereas the bottlers of some lower-ranking brands wouldn't reveal the varieties used in their products, making us wonder if they even tracked such information (one brand admitted that it didn't).

Second, the company uses a relatively new growing and harvesting process called super-high-density planting, in which the trees are planted together much more tightly than they would be in traditional groves. As a result, the olives can be harvested by machines more efficiently than they would be if they were picked by hand or shaken into nets on the ground. (Speed is of the essence, since olives begin to change flavor from the moment they are separated from the tree and must be pressed as quickly as possible to ensure they retain the desired flavor profile.) Then, by bottling very close to the source, the company cuts out the risk that the oil will oxidize and spoil during transport to another facility. And unlike some producers that sell their oil in clear glass or even plastic bottles, which expose the oil to more damaging light, California Olive Ranch uses dark-green glass bottles that help shield the oil. The upshot of all these factors: fresher olive oil, and our winning product.

INDICATIONS OF A FRESHER OIL
These three things can help you assess the quality of an extra-virgin olive oil before you buy it.

Harvest Date
Since a "best by" date might be 24 to 32 months after the oil was bottled and one to two years after it was pressed, a harvest date is a more precise indication of freshness. Look for the most recent date, and note that in Europe and the United States, olives are harvested in the fall and winter, so most bottles will list the previous year.

Dark Glass
Avoid clear glass; dark glass shields the oil from damaging light. Avoid clear plastic, too; it's not a good barrier to light or air.

Oil Origin
Bottlers often print where their oil has been sourced from on the label; look for oil that has been sourced from a single country.

HOW OIL GETS ROBBED OF ITS EXTRA-VIRGINITY
In the multibillion dollar olive oil industry, there can be many detours on the way to true extra-virgin status.

BAD FRUIT
Bruised or fermented olives can lead to off-notes in oil.

IMPROPER PROCESSING
Use of high heat and chemicals extracts more oil but damages flavor.

ADULTERATION
To mask defects, some makers cut oil with tasteless, odorless refined olive oil.

SHODDY STORAGE
Heat, air, and light will all make an oil degrade faster.

OLD AGE
Even under ideal conditions, all olive oils will oxidize and become rancid over time.

The Tasting Lineup, CONTINUED

Recommended with Reservations, continued

FILIPPO BERIO
Extra Virgin Olive Oil
$5.99 for 16.9 oz
($0.35 per oz)

OLIVARI
Extra-Virgin Olive Oil
$6.99 for 17 oz
($0.41 per oz)

STAR
Extra Virgin Olive Oil
$9.99 for 500 ml
($0.59 per oz)

POMPEIAN
Extra Virgin Olive Oil
$12.99 for 32 oz
($0.41 per oz)

BERTOLLI
Extra Virgin Olive Oil
$8.99 for 25 oz
($0.36 per oz)

The Tasting Lineup

Recommended

BERTOLLI
Balsamic Vinegar
of Modena
Top Pick $3.49
for 8.5 fl oz
($0.41 per fl oz)

**MONARI
FEDERZONI**
Balsamic Vinegar
of Modena
$2.50 for 16.9 fl oz
($0.15 per fl oz)

COLAVITA
Balsamic Vinegar
of Modena
$2.99 for 17 fl oz
($0.18 per fl oz)

ORTALLI
Balsamic Vinegar
of Modena
$6.69 for 16.9 fl oz
($0.40 per fl oz)

BELLINO
Balsamic Vinegar
of Modena
$5.49 for 16.9 fl oz
($0.32 per fl oz)

LUCINI
Aged Balsamic
Vinegar of
Modena
$13.99 for 8.5 fl oz
($1.65 per fl oz)

The first thing to understand when you set out to buy balsamic vinegar at the grocery store is that it has little to do with the traditionally made, name-protected Italian artisanal product called *aceto balsamico tradizionale*. It's not even made for the same purpose. The traditional stuff is a small-batch, long-aged product that bears a *Denominazione di Origine Protetta* (DOP) seal indicating use of locally grown ingredients and adherence to strict guidelines. Costing as much as $250 for a tiny 3.4-ounce bottle, it's meant to be drizzled sparingly over steak or strawberries—or even sipped. Masking its flavors in vinaigrette or burning them off in a cooked application would be a tragic mistake. That's where the supermarket stuff comes in. This inexpensive mass-produced product is designed for salad dressing or to make a sweet-tart reduction to drizzle over vegetables or grilled meats. While its flavor isn't anywhere near as complex as traditional balsamic, it can still have a pleasing fruity bite, which makes it a staple in most American kitchens.

Since we last tasted supermarket balsamic vinegar, a new certification process for this product has been put in place. Vinegars that are produced in either Reggio Emilia or Modena (the only two provinces where traditional balsamic can be made) and follow certain other guidelines can call themselves "balsamic vinegar of Modena" and bear an *Indicazione Geografica Protetta*, or IGP, seal on their labels. Curious if this certification process would raise the standards and give us a better supermarket option at the same affordable price, we rounded up nine widely available balsamic vinegars of Modena with an IGP seal (including our

former winner), all sold for no more than $15 a bottle, and conducted a series of blind taste tests. We sampled them plain, whisked into vinaigrette, and reduced to make a quick glaze that we served over asparagus.

Straight from the bottles, the vinegars ranged from nearly as thick as traditional balsamic to as watery as distilled white vinegar. The plain tasting revealed a similarly wide array of flavors. The best versions tasted of caramelized sugar or roasted fruit and had a smooth, pleasant tang; others had a fake, candy-like sweetness or, at the opposite end of the spectrum, tasted harshly acidic. We were puzzled. How could all these products qualify under the exact same standards?

We did a little investigating and discovered that the guidelines governing the use of the seal are pretty loose. IGP laws do outline a list of approved ingredients—namely, the must (the skin, seeds, and juice) from select native Italian grape varietals. But they require that only 20 percent of the finished product consist of grape must (compared with the 100 percent required for traditional balsamic). So what makes up the remaining 80 percent? Regular wine vinegar made anywhere. Second, although some aging is mandatory, 60 days are all that's required—a far cry from traditional vinegar's 12-year minimum. And finally, while production must take place within Reggio Emilia or Modena and certain varieties of grapes are required, the grapes can be grown anywhere in the world.

But here's the kicker: Unlike batches of traditional balsamic vinegar, which are subjected to a final taste test so rigorous that roughly 20 percent of submissions fail it, nearly every vat

METHODOLOGY

We sampled nine top-selling balsamic vinegars of Modena with Indicazione Geografica Protetta, or IGP, certification. We tasted our lineup plain, in vinaigrette, and as a glaze over asparagus to assess flavor, consistency, and overall appeal. Ingredients are based on label information. Products are listed in The Tasting Lineup in order of preference.

of vinegar that follows the loose IGP rules for production becomes certified, explaining the wide range we'd observed in our tastings.

We now knew why vinegars bearing the IGP seal could taste so different. And yet we couldn't find a trend in our plain tasting results that connected our preferences to any particular manufacturing methods. Some products use more of the native grape must than others and/or cook the must in open vats as do traditional balsamic makers (cooking in vats allows for caramelization and, thus, more complex flavor development than what is produced by mechanical processing)—but neither of these variables was necessarily linked to the vinegars we preferred. Seven of the nine manufacturers confirmed that they age their balsamics for the minimum time. Of the two remaining, one cited the vague range of "60 days to two years," and the other, our former winner, qualified as what is known as *invecchiato*, meaning that it is aged for more than three years. Our front-runner ages for the minimum time.

But we still had the reduction and vinaigrette tastings to go, and interestingly, after these two tastings the playing field leveled off just a bit. Six of the products we tried were perfectly acceptable once incorporated into a vinaigrette or reduced and drizzled over asparagus. The additional ingredients in the dressing softened any sharp acidity, while reducing these vinegars added body to thinner products but didn't adversely affect the thickest. Our objections to the other three vinegars in the lineup only mellowed enough to recommend them with reservations. Though they'd do in a pinch, they retained the artificial sweetness or harshness tasters had objected to in the plain tasting.

While each of our top six balanced fruity sweetness with bright acidity, one came out on top. Our winner has a "lush," "syrupy" texture in vinaigrette and an "almost drinkable" flavor with notes of apple, molasses, and dried fruit. Best of all, it's affordable enough to use every day.

The Tasting Lineup, CONTINUED

Recommended with Reservations
STAR
Balsamic Vinegar of Modena
$2.99 for 8.5 fl oz
($0.35 per fl oz)

CENTO
Balsamic Vinegar of Modena
$3.49 for 16.9 fl oz
($0.21 per fl oz)

DE NIGRIS
Balsamic Vinegar of Modena, White Eagle
$5.49 for 16.9 fl oz
($0.32 per fl oz)

LEVELING UP YOUR BALSAMIC

Inexpensive supermarket balsamic is best for everyday use, but sometimes you need something a little fancier to drizzle over berries, steaks, or a good cheese. We conducted a special tasting of truly high-end balsamics. Our winner, **Cavalli Gold Seal Extra Vecchio Aceto Balsamico Tradizionale de Reggio Emilia** (priced at $180 for 3 ounces), topped nearly everyone's list, with tasters waxing poetic about its "pomegranate," "caramel," "smoky" flavor that "coats the tongue" and tastes "amazing." In such rich company, our supermarket winner couldn't compete. However, there's another category of balsamic vinegar, sold in specialty shops and some supermarkets, that falls between the two. Many of these vinegars hold themselves to a higher standard than most supermarket balsamics, including adding less wine vinegar and aging longer. Straight out of the bottle, these vinegars have a syrupy consistency closer to that of traditional vinegar, and when we drizzled them over berries, our tasters actually deemed their consistency, honeyed sweetness, and fruity complexity a surprisingly close approximation of 25-year-aged tradizionale, though the nuances of each vinegar varied a bit. But also like a traditional balsamic, these midrange vinegars were ill-suited to vinaigrette—the dressings made with them were all sticky and gloppy, more like a tart caramel sauce than a salad dressing. This is because like the traditional balsamics, these vinegars have more of what are known as polymeric pigments, which form gel-like droplets with oil, than supermarket vinegars. Our recommendation? For use as an everyday ingredient in dressings and cooking, opt for balsamic vinegar of Modena from the supermarket. But if you want a vinegar that can affordably do the job of the pricey traditional vinegar, these midprice balsamics are a great option. Because the flavor and consistency can vary from brand to brand, ask for recommendations at your local gourmet shop.

BAKING

All-Purpose Flour

This type of flour is a workhorse because its protein content (between 9 and 12 percent) is high enough to provide structure to sandwich breads yet low enough to produce a tender crumb in many cakes. We prefer unbleached flour: We've found that some bleached flours carry off-flavors. In the test kitchen, we develop recipes with widely available **Pillsbury Unbleached Enriched All-Purpose Flour**. We also like **King Arthur Unbleached Enriched All-Purpose Flour**, which has a slightly higher protein content.

Whole-Wheat Flour

Whole-wheat flour has a distinctive flavor and texture because it contains the entire wheat kernel, including the germ, which means that it's higher in fiber, fat, and protein than all-purpose flour. White whole-wheat flour also contains the whole grain but is milled from a different type of wheat and has a milder taste than traditional whole wheat. Whole-wheat flour behaves very differently than white flour in recipes. That said, you can often replace up to one-third of the all-purpose or bread flour in a recipe with an equal amount of whole-wheat flour and still obtain good results. Look for a finely milled whole wheat flour with a texture that resembles regular all-purpose flour, with no graininess. Our favorite is **King Arthur Premium 100% Whole Wheat Flour**.

Cake Flour

This lower-protein flour (6 to 8 percent) creates a finer, more delicate crumb than all-purpose flour. Not all cakes require cake flour, and we call for it only in a few recipes, like angel food cake, where we feel it delivers decidedly better results than all-purpose flour. If you don't have cake flour, you can make a substitute from all-purpose flour and cornstarch.

1 cup cake flour =
⅞ cup all-purpose flour +
2 tablespoons cornstarch

Pastry Flour

Primarily used by professional bakers, pastry flour is a soft wheat flour with a protein content between that of all-purpose flour and that of cake flour. It produces a fine crumb in baked goods. We've found that in most recipes, all-purpose or cake flour (used singularly or in combination) can approximate pastry flour's effect.

Bread Flour

With a protein content of 12 to 14 percent, bread flour is the highest-protein flour available. It's aces at developing gluten, which in turn gives great structure and chew to breads. Not all breads and pizzas require bread flour, so be sure to check the recipe before shopping.

Self-Rising Flour

Self-rising flour has leavener and salt already added. It has a protein content similar to that of cake flour and is often used in biscuits and quick breads. Don't substitute self-rising flour for other flours in recipes. However, in recipes that call for self-rising flour, you can substitute cake flour and add your own leavener and salt.

1 cup self-rising flour =
1 cup cake flour +
1½ teaspoons baking powder +
½ teaspoon salt

Instant Flour

Instant flour (Wondra is the most common brand) is finely ground, low-protein flour that is able to dissolve instantly (with very few lumps) in hot or cold liquids like sauces, gravies, and soups. Instant flour is also sometimes used as a coating for fried chicken or fish, as the tiny particles distribute evenly into thin crusts.

Flour Storage

The shelf life of flour is about one year. All-purpose flour can be stored in the pantry in an airtight container (transfer it out of its paper bag to protect it from humidity). Whole-wheat flour should be enclosed in a zipper-lock bag and stored in the freezer. It contains natural oils that will go rancid in as little as three months otherwise. (All-purpose flour can also be stored in the freezer, although it doesn't need to be.) Flour stored in the freezer should be brought to room temperature before use; cold flour will inhibit rise in baked goods and yield denser, chewier results.

Baking Soda

Baking soda is a leavener that provides lift to cakes, muffins, biscuits, and other baked goods. When baking soda, which is alkaline, encounters an acidic ingredient (such as buttermilk, sour cream, or brown sugar), carbon and oxygen combine to form carbon dioxide. The tiny bubbles of carbon dioxide then lift up the dough. Baking soda also promotes browning. Baking soda has a shelf life of about six months.

Baking Powder

Like baking soda, baking powder also creates carbon dioxide to provide lift to baked goods. The active ingredients in baking powder are baking soda and an acidic element, such as cream of tartar. Use baking powder rather than baking soda when there is no natural acidity in the batter. We recommend using double-acting baking powder, which helps baked goods rise higher by adding one or more extra acids that provide extra rise once the dish is put in the oven. Our favorite brand is **Argo Double Acting Baking Powder**. Aluminum-free baking powders work just as well as brands with aluminum compounds, but if you are highly sensitive to metallic flavors or wish to limit your ingestion of aluminum, choose an aluminum-free powder. Baking powder has a shelf life of about six months.

Cream of Tartar

Cream of tartar, also known as potassium bitartrate, is a powdered byproduct of the winemaking process and, along with baking soda, is one of the two main ingredients in baking powder. Cream of tartar is often added to egg whites before they are whipped; its acidic nature lowers the pH of the egg whites, which encourages the eggs' proteins to unfold, thus creating more volume, greater stability, and a glossier appearance.

Yeast

Yeast is a living organism that is grown in liquid, where it feeds on sugar and starch until it reaches the desired volume and maturity. The two most common types of yeast you will find at the supermarket are active dry yeast and instant (rapid-rise) yeast. Active dry yeast sold in packets or jars is probably called for the most in bread recipes. In order to use active dry yeast, you must first proof the granules, or dissolve them in warm liquid, with some sugar to speed up the process, which renders the yeast active. Instant, or rapid-rise, yeast is much like active dry yeast, but it does not require proofing and can be added directly to the dry ingredients when making bread—hence the name "instant." We prefer instant yeast because it's easier to use. Active dry yeast and rapid-rise (or instant) yeast have been dehydrated and can last up to two years unopened. Technically, these types do not require refrigeration. However, we found that both rapid-rise and active dry yeast benefit from being stored in a cool, dry place; a pantry, refrigerator, or, best of all, the freezer. Because yeast is a living organism, the expiration date on the package should be observed. A packet of active dry or instant yeast contains about 2¼ teaspoons (0.25 ounce) of yeast. To substitute instant yeast for active dry yeast, reduce the amount of yeast used by 25 percent. You don't need to proof the yeast; just add it to the dry ingredients. We do not recommend cake yeast, aka fresh yeast or compressed yeast; it is very perishable and no more reliable than other, longer-lasting forms of yeast. We also don't recommend yeast specially formulated for pizza crust; it contains a cocktail of chemicals and enzymes designed to relax the dough that negatively impact the texture and flavor of the finished product.

1 teaspoon active dry yeast =
¾ teaspoon instant yeast

Oats

Whole hulled oats are also known as groats. After being heated to inhibit rancidity, they are further processed, according to a particular style. Some of the types you may see at the supermarket include steel-cut oats, stone-ground oats, old-fashioned or rolled oats, quick oats, and instant oats. Steel-cut and stone-ground oats are groats that, as their names suggest, have been sliced by steel blades or coarsely stone ground. These are mostly used for hot cereal or porridge. Old-fashioned, quick, and instant oats are all groats that have been flattened between rollers into the familiar oval shape, which helps speed cooking. For even faster cooking, both instant and quick oats are steamed, toasted, and cut into smaller pieces (instant are smaller than quick) before packaging. Old-fashioned oats and quick oats can be freely substituted for each other in baking, but do not use instant oats, as they will turn out gummy and raw in cooked applications. We don't even like instant oats as cereal—they tend to be mushy. Old-fashioned rolled oats have the best texture in plain cooked oatmeal and take only a few minutes longer to cook. Our favorite brand for both breakfast and baking is **Bob's Red Mill Organic Extra Thick Rolled Oats**.

Steel-Cut Oats

Stone-Ground Oats

Old-Fashioned Rolled Oats

Cornmeal

Make sure you read the recipe—and the package—carefully, as the type of cornmeal you use can make a big difference. In most cases, we recommend choosing stone-ground over commercially produced cornmeal for its better flavor and texture. For a basic baking cornmeal, look for more finely ground whole grain cornmeal like **Arrowhead Mills Organic Yellow Cornmeal**. White and yellow cornmeal can be used interchangeably, since the flavor differences are minor.

Bread Crumbs

We definitely prefer homemade bread crumbs, but if you're going to opt for store-bought options, we recommend the Japanese-style bread crumbs called panko. Don't buy "Italian" bread crumbs or other varieties with additional seasonings and flavorings. A shorter ingredient list is better. Our favorite brand, **Ian's Panko Breadcrumbs, Original Style**, strikes a balance between the large, crispy flakes of traditional panko and the small, dense ones of regular bread crumbs for great coating and crunch.

RECIPE CONVENTIONS

Unless a recipe in one of our books or magazines specifically states otherwise, you should assume the following ingredient rules are being observed.

Ingredient	Test Kitchen Default
Flour	Unbleached, all-purpose
Sugar	Granulated
Salt	Table
Kosher Salt	Diamond Crystal (see page 93 if using Morton)
Pepper	Freshly ground black
Spices	Ground
Herbs	Fresh
Broths	Low-sodium
Butter	Unsalted
Eggs	Large
Dairy	Whole milk, or full-fat (although low-fat will generally work, skim won't)

White Sugar

This common "table" sugar is (like all sugar) refined from sugar cane or beets; in taste tests, cane and beet sugars were indistinguishable from each other. The relatively fine crystals and neutral flavor make this sugar the most versatile sweetening agent.

Brown Sugar

Brown sugar, whether light or dark, is simply white sugar with molasses added. Dark brown sugar has more molasses and thus a stronger flavor than light brown. Store brown sugar in an airtight container; if it is exposed to air, moisture in the molasses can evaporate, causing the brown sugar to dry out. To approximate 1 cup of light brown sugar, pulse 1 cup of granulated sugar with 1 tablespoon of mild molasses in a food processor until blended. Use 2 tablespoons of molasses for dark brown sugar.

Turbinado and Demerara Sugars

These are also referred to as "raw" sugar. The large crystals of these sugars do not readily dissolve. Instead, they can be sprinkled on top of muffins to create a crunchy top or used to form the caramel crust on crème brûlée.

Molasses and Cane Syrup

Molasses is a dark, thick syrup that is the byproduct of sugar cane refining. Molasses comes in three types: light and mild; dark and robust; and blackstrap. We prefer either light or dark molasses in baking and generally avoid using bitter blackstrap molasses. Our favorite brand is **Brer Rabbit All Natural Unsulphured Molasses Mild Flavor**, which is both strong and balanced in its sweet-spicy flavors. Store molasses in the pantry. Cane syrup is a caramelized, concentrated version of pure cane juice. Its texture is thinner than molasses and it has a boozy, burnt caramel flavor.

Confectioners' Sugar

Confectioners' sugar, also called powdered sugar or icing sugar, is finely milled sugar that has been mixed with cornstarch to prevent clumping. Confectioners' sugar is used for dusting cakes and cookies and in making quick glazes and icings. You can also approximate confectioners' sugar with this method: For 1 cup confectioners' sugar, process 1 cup of granulated sugar with 1 tablespoon of cornstarch in a blender (not a food processor) until fine, 30 to 40 seconds.

Superfine Sugar

Also called caster sugar, superfine sugar is finely processed and has extra-small crystals that dissolve quickly. It promotes a melt-in-the-mouth texture in delicate cookies such as shortbread and butter cookies. (And because it dissolves easily in liquid, it's a must for iced tea, iced coffee, and other cold beverages.) To make your own superfine sugar, simply process granulated sugar in a food processor for about 30 seconds. Superfine sugar can often be found in the baking or cocktail mixer aisle of the supermarket.

Honey

Traditional honey is usually heated to thin it to the point where it can pass under high pressure through fine strainers to remove pollen and give the honey a clear appearance, which many consumers prefer. Raw honey, by contrast, is usually only heated high enough (about 120 degrees) to prevent it from crystallizing on store shelves. The honey is then lightly strained to remove debris and leftover wax, but it's not filtered under high pressure and retains most of its pollen. We prefer raw honey for its complexity and balanced sweetness. When shopping, look for the word "raw" on the label and choose a product that comes from bees with a varied diet (rather than solely clover). Our favorite brand is **Nature Nate's 100% Pure Raw and Unfiltered Honey**. Store honey in the pantry. Honey never spoils and can be stored indefinitely. If it crystallizes, put the opened jar in a saucepan filled with 1 inch of water, and heat the honey until it reaches 160 degrees (make sure the container is heatproof).

Sucanat

Sucanat is an abbreviation for *sucre de canne naturel*, meaning "natural sugar cane." This unrefined cane sugar is made by beating cane juice with paddles to form golden-brown granules. It has a deep, molasses flavor, and a small amount goes a long way in developing flavor. Sucanat is one of our favorite alternative sweeteners.

Coconut Sugar

Coconut sugar is an unrefined, granular (not crystallized) sweetener made from coconut palm flower sap that is heated, then poured into molds or beaten with paddles to form granules. While its flavor is more neutral than Sucanat's it still contributes a robust and almost nutty flavor in baked goods.

Date Sugar

Date sugar is simply dried dates that have been pulverized into a powder. Because it is essentially dried fruit, date sugar retains a lot more nutrients than other sweeteners (relatively speaking). This also means it won't behave like other sweeteners in recipes; it absorbs a large amount of liquid and won't melt or dissolve like other dry sugars, so be sure to take that into account in your recipe.

Stevia

Stevia is a natural, calorie-free sweetener extracted from the leaves of the stevia plant (a cousin of the sunflower). We don't recommend stevia as a sugar substitute. Recipes made with this sweetener have an unacceptable bitter aftertaste.

Agave Nectar

Agave nectar is a liquid sweetener made from the sap of agave plants, succulent desert dwellers native to North America that are also the raw material for tequila. Agave nectar has been on natural foods store shelves for decades, but now industry giant Domino is selling it in the sugar aisle of ordinary supermarkets. It comes in both light and amber varieties. You can use light agave nectar in place of honey in baking, but don't expect honey flavor. We don't recommend amber agave nectar as a honey substitute.

Brown Rice Syrup

Like corn syrup, brown rice syrup is made by treating the cooked grain with enzymes that convert starches into sugar; the resulting liquid is reduced until thick. It can be used as a stand-in for corn syrup, although it is more expensive.

Maple Syrup

Pure maple syrup is simply sap from sugar maple trees that is collected and boiled to concentrate its sugar. Commercial maple syrup comes in various grades, although there is no universal system for grading. While color is used to grade syrup, we have found that color differences do not correlate with flavor differences. During a recent tasting of eight different brands of pure maple syrups, we found that they all tasted very similar, so our advice is to buy the cheapest all-maple product you can find. International grading uses color and flavor combinations to label syrup; if you're looking for a syrup to use in baking or cooking applications, look for labels that say "dark." Because of its high moisture level and lack of preservatives, maple syrup is susceptible to the growth of yeasts, molds, and bacteria. For this reason, we recommend refrigerating it. Once opened, maple syrup will keep six months to a year in the refrigerator. For long-term storage, maple syrup can be kept in the freezer. It will never freeze solid because of the high sugar concentration. At most, the syrup will become thick, viscous, or crystallized during freezing, but a quick zap in the microwave will restore it. We do not recommend so-called pancake syrup, which is artificially flavored corn syrup that often contains no real maple syrup at all.

See page 162 for Inside the Tasting.

Corn Syrup

Corn syrup is made by adding enzymes to a mixture of cornstarch and water to break the long starch strands into glucose molecules. It's valuable in candy making because it discourages crystallization; it also helps baked goods retain moisture. And because it is less sweet than granulated sugar, corn syrup makes an excellent addition to savory glazes, contributing body and sticking power. It is not the same thing as high-fructose corn syrup, which is made by putting regular corn syrup through an additional enzymatic process that converts a portion of the glucose molecules into fructose, boosting its sweetness to a level even higher than that of cane sugar. Because high-fructose corn syrup is considerably less expensive than cane sugar, it is widely used in processed foods, but it is not sold directly to consumers.

Chocolate Storage

All chocolate begins as cacao beans, which are seeds found in large pods that grow on cacao trees in regions around the equator. These beans are fermented, dried, and roasted and then the inner meat (or nib) of the bean is removed from the shell and ground into a paste. This paste is called chocolate liquor (although it contains no alcohol) and consists of cocoa solids and cocoa butter. Chocolate liquor is then further processed and mixed with sugar and flavorings to make the various types of chocolate. Using the right type and brand of chocolate in baking can make a big difference. Never store chocolate in the refrigerator or freezer, as cocoa butter can easily pick up off-flavors from other foods. To extend the shelf life of chocolate, wrap it tightly in plastic wrap and store it in a cool, dry place. If chocolate is exposed to rapid changes in humidity or temperature, sugar or fat may dissolve and migrate, discoloring the surface. This condition, known as bloom, is cosmetic and not harmful—bloomed chocolate is safe to eat and cook with.

Dark Chocolate

Semisweet and bittersweet chocolates, also called dark chocolate, must contain at least 35 percent chocolate liquor, although most contain more than 55 percent and some go as high as 99 percent. (Chocolates containing 70 percent or more cacao usually require recipe adjustments to get good results.) We have found that 60 percent cacao is close to ideal in terms of a balance between chocolate flavor and good texture in cooking applications. Our favorite is **Ghirardelli 60% Cacao Bittersweet Chocolate Premium Baking Bar**. Its high milk fat content also makes it supremely easy to work with when it's melted. You can replace 1 ounce of bittersweet or semisweet chocolate with ⅔ ounce of unsweetened chocolate and 2 teaspoons of granulated sugar in a pinch, but the unsweetened chocolate will not provide the same smooth, creamy texture as bittersweet or semisweet chocolate. Dark chocolate keeps for several years.

Milk Chocolate

Milk chocolate must contain at least 10 percent chocolate liquor and 12 percent milk solids, with sweeteners and flavorings making up the balance. The result is a mellow, smooth flavor. Yet because of its relatively weak chocolate flavor (milk chocolate is usually more than 50 percent sugar), we reserve milk chocolate for frostings and eating out of hand. We prefer smoother chocolates that are higher in fat like our favorite, **Dove Silky Smooth Milk Chocolate**. Milk chocolate should last six months to a year.

Unsweetened Chocolate

Unsweetened chocolate is the traditional choice for recipes in which a bold hit of chocolate flavor is more important than a smooth or delicate texture. Our favorite brand, **Hershey's Unsweetened Baking Bar**, has more cocoa solids and less cocoa butter (as evidenced by its lower fat content), as well as added cocoa, which gives it rich chocolate flavor. If you don't have unsweetened chocolate, you can replace 1 ounce of unsweetened chocolate with 3 tablespoons of cocoa powder and 1 tablespoon of butter or oil. This substitution is best for small quantities.

White Chocolate

White chocolate is technically not chocolate since it contains no cocoa solids. Authentic white chocolate contains at least 20 percent cocoa butter. If a product is called "white chips" or "white confection," it is made with little or no cocoa butter. That said, since both styles derive their flavor from milk and sugar, not the fat, we find this distinction makes little difference in recipes. In fact, real white chocolate produces oily, grainy desserts when melted. Because of this, our favorite brand is actually an artificial white chip: **Guittard Choc-Au-Lait White Chips**. The imitation white chocolate also lasts longer, since it's not as susceptible to rancidity as white chocolate made from cocoa butter. White chocolate should last six months to a year.

Cocoa Powder

Cocoa powder is chocolate liquor that is processed to remove all but 10 to 24 percent of the cocoa butter. Cocoa powder comes in natural and Dutched versions. Dutching raises the powder's pH, which neutralizes its acids and astringent notes and rounds out its flavor. (It also darkens the color.) Both natural and Dutched cocoa will work in recipes; Dutch-processed cocoa will produce baked goods with a darker color and a moister texture. Our winning brand, **Hershey's Cocoa Natural Unsweetened**, is a natural product with a very fine texture and assertive chocolate flavor.

Chocolate Chips

Chocolate chips contain less cocoa butter than bar chocolate. The lower fat content means that chips don't melt as readily, which is a good thing—they hold their shape better when baked—but it also means that you shouldn't substitute chips for bar chocolate. For both milk and dark chocolate chips, we prefer brands with bold chocolate flavor, higher fat content, and lower sugar content. Our favorites are **Hershey's Milk Chocolate Chips** and **Ghirardelli 60% Cacao Bittersweet Chocolate Chips**.

Almonds

Almonds are sold in a dizzying array of varieties: raw, roasted, blanched, slivered, sliced, and Marcona, to name a few. When it comes to decorating cookies, we usually prefer the clean presentation of whole skinless blanched almonds. For cakes, other baked goods, leafy salads, and light side dishes, we find that thinly sliced raw almonds (with or without their skins) deliver a nice, light flavor and texture. On the other hand, we love the substantial crunch of thick-cut slivered almonds in stir-fries and rice pilafs. Roasted almonds are best for eating out of hand. As for Marcona almonds, this sweet, pricey Spanish variety is good as an accent in salads, cheese plates, and desserts. Like all nuts, almonds are highly perishable (the oils in the nuts go rancid quickly) and are best stored in the freezer to prevent spoilage.

Vanilla Extract and Vanilla Beans

Pure vanilla extract is made by soaking vanilla beans in a solution of water and alcohol and then aging the mixture in holding tanks prior to bottling. This lengthy process contributes to the high cost of pure vanilla extract. The less-expensive imitation extract, on the other hand, relies primarily on the synthetic compound vanillin to mimic the smell and taste of real vanilla. Through extensive testing, we've found that both extracts are acceptable in a variety of applications; the choice comes down to cost and personal philosophy about using imitation products. If you plan to use the vanilla for a wider variety of recipes beyond baking, including for cold and creamy desserts, we recommend **McCormick Pure Vanilla Extract**. If you need whole vanilla beans, we like **McCormick Madagascar Vanilla Beans**. Vanilla beans dry out in storage unless well wrapped. We recommend cutting the beans in half and standing them cut side down in ½ inch of vodka (which is flavorless) or rum (which has flavors that complement that of vanilla) in a jar that is then sealed and stored in the fridge. After about two weeks, the alcohol will have traveled up the inside of the bean, turning the seeds into a paste that is easily removed by pinching the bean between two fingers and squeezing.

PACKAGED CHOPPED NUTS VERSUS FRESHLY CHOPPED NUTS

We prepared batches of banana bread (in which the nuts are mixed into the batter) and brownies (the nuts are sprinkled on top) using both whole nuts we chopped in the test kitchen and packaged chopped nuts. The results were mixed, with tasters showing only a slight preference for the fresh-chopped nuts. So go ahead and use the packaged chopped nuts—you won't be able to taste the difference.

STORING NUTS

All nuts are high in oil and will become rancid rather quickly. In the test kitchen, we store all nuts in the freezer in sealed freezer-safe zipper-lock bags. Frozen nuts will keep for months and there's no need to defrost them before toasting or chopping.

Peanut Butter

Our favorite creamy peanut butter is regular creamy **Skippy Peanut Butter**. We find that texture is the most important factor in peanut butter, both for eating in a sandwich and for cooked applications. The hydrogenated fats in conventional peanut butter are the key ingredient for a perfectly smooth, creamy product. While many people do not consider foods with hydrogenated oils to be the "best" in any sense, all of our tests concluded that they really do produce the most successful results. Don't be taken in by the word "natural" on the label of a peanut butter; the FDA does not regulate the term "natural," so manufacturers can literally put almost anything in the jar and still use that label, including abundant sweeteners, salt, and saturated fats. For crunchy peanut butter, however, we actually prefer a product labeled "natural"— **Jif Natural Crunchy Peanut Butter Spread**—which has to be called a "spread" because it contains less than 90 percent peanuts and more than 55 percent fat, which makes it wonderfully rich. **See page 164 for Inside the Tasting.**

See page 164 for Inside the Tasting.

PEANUT BUTTER ALTERNATIVES

Cashew Butter
Cashew butter has a very similar texture to peanut butter because of its similar fat content, but its flavor is very subtle, so keep that in mind if you want to make the swap.

Almond Butter
It's hard to substitute almond butter for peanut butter in recipes because it has slightly more fat and a much higher proportion of unsaturated fat, which changes the melting point. If you want to bake with almond butter, we recommend finding a recipe specially formulated for this ingredient rather than just substituting it for peanut butter.

Soy Butter
We don't recommend using soy butter as a substitute for peanut butter. Its strong soy flavor and chalky, gritty texture will ruin a recipe.

Sunflower Seed Butter
Sunflower seed butter is our favorite replacement for peanut butter. It has a mild, pleasant nutty flavor and though runny, its texture is still perfectly acceptable. Like peanut butter, it even comes in both smooth and crunchy varieties.

SEEDS

Chia Seeds
Mild, nutty chia seeds are a popular health food due to their high fiber content. The seeds can be eaten dry, ground and used as a powder, or combined with water to create a gel.

Flaxseeds
Flaxseeds can be toasted, sprouted, or ground; they're most easily digested when eaten ground. Flaxseeds have a wheaty, earthy flavor, making them a nice addition to whole-grain breads. Store them in the refrigerator or freezer.

Nigella Seeds
Nigella seeds (also called *charnushka*) are common in the cuisines of India and the Middle East. The seeds have an oniony bite and a slightly astringent, piney taste. They are often mislabeled as black cumin or black caraway.

Poppy Seeds
Poppy seeds are used for their peppery, smoky-sweet flavor. Try them in baked goods, coleslaw, egg noodles, and salad dressing.

Pumpkin Seeds
Whole white pumpkin seeds are sold for snacking and have a pleasant vegetal taste. The green hulled versions (pepitas) are popular in Mexico and are used in mole sauces.

Sesame Seeds
Sesame seeds can be grayish ivory, brown, red, or black and are used in both savory and sweet recipes. Their nutty, subtle honey quality suits candies, granola, bread, and sweets.

Sunflower Seeds
Sunflower seeds are mildly sweet and creamy. Remove the black-and-white shells and eat the seeds out of hand or in salads or slaws.

It's early March, and a team of our editors is driving along a winding dirt road in Vermont to visit a sugar shack tucked against a mountain covered with thousands of maples. At first glance, the passing forest scape is a canvas of barren trees and snowy fields, but a closer look brings into focus a web of silver taps and clear plastic tubing weaving among the trees— the sign that it's sugaring season.

We've timed our trip carefully because sugaring season is both short and temperamental. Not only is the majority of the world's maple syrup produced on relatively small-scale farms, like this one, throughout Canada and the northern United States over a period of just two months each year, but the sap production is entirely weather-dependent: Syrup makers must wait for freezing nights that are followed by warm days, a pattern that causes higher pressure within the tree to push sap out of the tree. Couple that with the fact that it takes 40 gallons of sap to produce just 1 gallon of maple syrup and it's not surprising that this product can fetch more than $1.50 per ounce.

Anyone who's tasted real maple syrup on pancakes, in desserts, or even in savory glazes or dressings knows that there is no cheap substitute. We confirmed as much a few years ago when we compared a few maple syrups with pancake syrups; the latter, corn syrup–based products that are a fifth of maple syrup's price, tasted cloying and candy-like. This time, we decided to home in on pure maple syrup and gathered eight products, all Grade A Dark Amber since it's the most widely available grade, tasting them plain and baked into maple syrup pie.

Pure maple syrup is simply sap from sugar maple trees that has been boiled to concentrate its sugar. To harvest it, taps connected to plastic tubing are drilled into the trees; the sap flows through the tubing into large storage containers where it's held for no more than 24 hours (unprocessed sap is only about 2 to 3 percent sugar, so it spoils quickly). When it's time to boil, the sap is transferred to an evaporator pan set over a large fire and reduced until it reaches 66 percent sugar density. (If it's boiled much longer, the syrup will start to crystallize; any less and it will eventually spoil.)

After the sap has been boiled and filtered, it's graded according to color, which also helps categorize the strength of its flavor. David Lutz, a forest ecologist at Dartmouth College, explained that syrup color and flavor are primarily determined by changes in the chemical composition of the sap throughout the sugaring season. At the start of the season, the syrup is very light-colored because the sap is infused with stored sucrose from the winter and generally free from compounds that impart strong flavors or a dark color. (The earliest, clearest sap was historically graded "A, extra fancy" because it was the best representation of a neutral-tasting sugar substitute.) As the season progresses, the environment becomes more biologically active, the tree prepares to bloom, and hundreds of phenolic compounds— the same types of chemicals found in tea and wine—start flowing through the sap, darkening its color and deepening its flavor.

Although Vermont and some other states have their own grading systems, there are no universal grading standards in the syrup industry. But there are five main grades that range from Grade A Light Amber to Commercial—the latter a syrup so strong-tasting that it's reserved for industrial use. To assess color and assign a grade, some syrup producers use a spectrometer, a tool that measures the amount of light transmitted through the syrup, but more often grading is low-tech and subjective:

METHODOLOGY

We sampled eight nationally available supermarket brands of Grade A Dark Amber maple syrup in two blind tastings—plain and in maple syrup pie—and rated them on flavor, sweetness, and strength of maple flavor. We obtained information about processing methods from manufacturers and industry experts. Because we found all the syrups to be very similar and recommend them all, we don't have a favorite; instead, they appear in The Tasting Lineup in order of price per fluid ounce.

Syrup makers simply compare their finished syrup to color charts or small vials of dyed glycerin. If the syrup falls between two hues, producers often choose the darker grade because syrup may darken with time due to oxidation. (Note: The USDA and a handful of syrup-producing states will be issuing new grading conventions with labels based on color and flavor combinations effective in 2017.) Perhaps because grading is such an imprecise process, we noticed some differences among the syrups in our testing, even though they were all labeled Grade A Dark Amber. Some were dark like molasses, while others were only faintly golden—but surprisingly these color differences did not correlate to the syrups' flavors. Most of the lighter-colored products tasted just as robust as darker ones. In fact, we were hard-pressed to find any distinct differences among the syrups other than color. Ultimately, we recommend them all.

Still, we were curious about the discrepancy between syrup color and flavor and turned to Michael Farrell, director of Cornell's Sugar Maple Research & Extension Field Station, Uihlein Forest, for an explanation. He noted that unless you're comparing the very lightest grade with the darkest one, the differences in flavor can be pretty subtle. More significantly, he added, the distinct flavors in maple syrup have been literally blended out of most supermarket brands. Because each maple tree averages only ¼ gallon of maple syrup over the entire season, it's impossible for most producers to acquire the land or resources necessary to yield enough volume for national distribution. Instead, most producers sell their syrup to large packagers, which pool hundreds of different products and bottle the blends under a brand name. Farrell and other experts told us that to get the color and flavor profile that falls within the Grade A Dark Amber spectrum, the most marketable grade of syrup, they blend different grades. "If their Dark Amber is looking a little too dark, they might mix in medium to lighten it up," Farrell said. The goal is "to try to make a consistent product."

Some packagers might even doctor the syrups with cheaper sweeteners to maximize their yield, but Farrell doesn't feel that it's a major issue in the industry. His bigger concern is pancake syrups masquerading as pure maple syrup, either from packaging that makes pancake syrup look like the real thing or from the inclusion of a small amount of pure maple syrup. "It changes people's opinions of real maple syrup," he said.

To us, there's a distinct advantage to blending: It means that all Grade A Dark Amber syrups sold in supermarkets are going to taste very similar, so our advice is to buy the cheapest all-maple product you can find.

The Tasting Lineup, CONTINUED

Recommended, continued

MAPLE GROVE FARMS
Pure Maple Syrup, Grade A Dark Amber
$6.99 for 8.5 fl oz
($0.82 per fl oz)

MAPLE GOLD
Pure Maple Syrup, Grade A Dark Amber
$16.50 for 12 fl oz
($1.38 per fl oz)

SPRING TREE
Pure Maple Syrup, Grade A Dark Amber
$18.49 for 12.5 fl oz
($1.48 per fl oz)

CAMP
Pure Maple Syrup, Grade A Dark Amber
$19.95 for 12.7 fl oz
($1.57 per fl oz)

HOW NATURE COLORS SYRUP

The color of maple syrup ranges dramatically over the course of the two-month sugaring season due to natural chemical changes in the sap. As the tree becomes more biologically active, phenolic compounds develop that infuse the sap, imparting color (and flavor). First-of-the-season sap is almost clear because it contains few of these compounds. As the season progresses and the tree prepares to bloom, more compounds deepen the color of the sap.

EARLY SEASON, PALE SYRUP
Few phenolic compounds

LATE SEASON, DARK SYRUP
Many phenolic compounds

The Tasting Lineup

Recommended

SKIPPY
Peanut Butter
Top Pick $2.39
for 16.3 oz
($0.15 per oz)

JIF
Natural Peanut
Butter Spread
$2.29 for 18 oz
($0.13 per oz)

REESE'S
Peanut Butter
$2.59 for 18 oz
($0.14 per oz)

JIF
Peanut Butter
$2.29 for 18 oz
($0.13 per oz)

SKIPPY
Natural Peanut
Butter Spread
$2.39 for 15 oz
($0.16 per oz)

Selecting a jar of peanut butter never used to be complicated. Once you aligned yourself with either creamy or crunchy, you had two basic choices: conventional peanut butters made with hydrogenated oil and other additives, or the barely processed versions containing just nuts and maybe a pinch of salt. In the past, we've been firm believers in the conventional kind. Although we like the idea of a healthier spread, these generally offer the texture of Spackle and a taste sorely in need of added salt and sweeteners—and yes, hydrogenated fat. (Let's be clear: Hydrogenated fat is not the same as partially hydrogenated fat, a trans fat that we all want to avoid.)

But these days it seems as though manufacturers have literally gone nuts, cramming supermarket shelves with every option they can think of. You'll find organic varieties; reduced-fat specimens; sea-salt, no-salt, and low-salt versions; and omega 3–enriched spreads—not to mention "honey-roasted," "no-stir," and "whipped" styles. One of the most intriguing developments has been the proliferation of peanut butters now declaring themselves "natural." Would these spreads offer a taste and texture good enough to lure us away from the "unnatural" conventional butters made with hydrogenated oil?

To answer that question, we went to the supermarket and came home with a staggering number of peanut butters—15 creamy spreads. We whittled the field down to a more manageable number in preliminary tastings. The final lineup had four representatives from the conventional category, five brands with "natural" in their names, and one organic style.

Before dipping in, we spun the jars around to examine their contents. We were immediately disabused of any notion that "natural" on the label meant bare-bones peanuts. Only one jar contained just peanuts (and less than 1 percent salt). The other four included some of the same additives found in conventional butters, including sweeteners and salt, as well as molasses and even flaxseed oil. But instead of hydrogenated fat, they contained palm oil.

The prevalence of palm oil in the so-called natural butters made us curious, so we did a little research. It turns out that because the FDA doesn't regulate the term "natural," manufacturers can put almost anything in the jar and still use that label. It also turns out that in terms of saturated fat, palm oil is as much of a culprit as hydrogenated oil. Most of the "natural" peanut butters made with this oil contained at least 3 grams of saturated fat per serving—the same amount as conventional spreads made with hydrogenated oil.

But the real question was how these palm-oil products would taste—and spread—compared with other brands. We sampled the peanut butters straight up, in peanut butter cookies, and in a spicy satay sauce. While some tasters were staunchly in favor of a particular flavor profile, the bottom line was all about texture. The creamiest, most spreadable peanut butters—even those with less-than-robust peanut flavor—jumped to the top of the chart. To our surprise, these included not only the conventional butters but a couple of the "natural" styles as well. At the same time, samples that were gritty and sludgy, dribbly and goopy, or too sticky were panned, no matter how nutty or well rounded they tasted.

Texture was also the number-one factor in recipes: Dry, gritty peanut butters made for predictably dry, gritty cookies. And the sauces they made? Unpalatably "stiff" and "pasty." Meanwhile, creamier samples, particularly the two top-ranking "natural" brands from the plain tasting, turned out cookies with "nice softness"

METHODOLOGY

We did three blind tastings of 10 creamy peanut butters. In the first tasting the peanut butters were pure, plain peanut butter. The peanut butters were tasted as they are sold, and the oil on natural peanut butters was mixed in before it was tasted. Our tasters were asked to rate the samples in terms of peanut flavor, sweetness, saltiness, texture, and overall preference. The panel later completed two more tastings: peanut butter cookies and a spicy satay sauce. Products are listed in The Tasting Lineup in order of preference.

and "satisfying chew," along with sauces with such good consistency that tasters were happy to "eat them by the spoonful."

That said, one brand, whose "runny," "mouth-coating" texture stranded it near the bottom rungs in the plain tasting, actually took bronze in the cookie round, where its more fluid composition lent moisture to the dough and turned out "sturdy" yet "pleasantly soft" cookies. Furthermore, the satay sauce brought out a flaw in the winner of our plain tasting—namely that its somewhat "muted" peanut flavor became even more faded in the presence of spicy ingredients and tart lime juice.

When we tallied our final results, nobody was especially surprised by the overall champ. A regular old hydrogenated oil–based spread took top honors for a supremely "smooth," "creamy" texture that even made up for what a few tasters deemed a "slightly weak" nutty flavor. Nor were we particularly stunned when the only truly additive-free peanut butter in the bunch (not counting its tiny bit of salt) fell to the bottom of the rankings due to a texture that

tasters deemed "inedible" and, when baked into cookies, as intractable as a "hockey puck."

What did surprise us, however, was that a very close runner-up was one of two palm oil–based peanut butters. Like our winner, it garnered praise for a "wonderfully" smooth texture. Tasters also praised its "dark roast-y" flavor, which we attribute in part to the inclusion of molasses, an ingredient common to three out of our five favorite peanut butters (and absent in four of the five lower-ranking contenders). Like the other favored palm-oil brand, it's not actually a peanut butter but a "spread." By FDA regulations, if a product has less than 90 percent peanuts and more than 55 percent fat, it must be labeled a "spread." Nomenclature aside, the extra fat in this brand may have contributed to its creaminess.

Maybe someday manufacturers will figure out a way to make an übercreamy, full-flavored peanut butter with just the nuts. In the meantime, we'll be making our PB&Js with our longtime favorite.

The Tasting Lineup, CONTINUED

Recommended with Reservations

PEANUT BUTTER & CO.
No-Stir Natural
Smooth Operator
$4.49 for 18 oz
($0.25 per oz)

MARANATHA
Organic No Stir
Peanut Butter
$5.69 for 16 oz
($0.36 per oz)

PETER PAN
Peanut Butter
$2.49 for 18 oz
($0.14 per oz)

Not Recommended

SMART BALANCE
All Natural Rich
Roast Peanut
Butter
$3.59 for 16 oz
($0.22 per oz)

SMUCKER'S
Natural Peanut
Butter
$2.69 for 16 oz
($0.17 per oz)

KEEPING PEANUT BUTTER CREAMY

In 1922, a chemist named Joseph L. Rosefield solved the problem of separating oil and rancidity in peanut butter by removing some of the natural peanut oil, which is liquid at room temperature, and replacing it with hydrogenated oil, an animal or vegetable fat chemically altered to include more saturated fatty acids to make it solid at room temperature. The result: a shelf-stable, semisolid spread. These days, an increasing number of peanut butter manufacturers are replacing hydrogenated fat with palm oil, a naturally highly saturated fat that works much the same way. However, we found palm oil to be less effective in keeping a peanut butter smooth and creamy.

SUPER CREAMY
The hydrogenated fat in our winner, Skippy Peanut Butter, makes for a supremely creamy texture.

LESS CREAMY
The palm oil in this "natural" butter from Peanut Butter & Co. wasn't fully effective in keeping the spread emulsified.

OIL SLICK
Smucker's Natural is made from nothing but ground peanuts and a little salt—and it's got a thick film of oil to prove it.

IN THE KITCHEN AND AT THE STOVE

WHAT IT TAKES TO BE A TEST COOK

America's Test Kitchen's reputation is built upon recipes that work . . . the first time and every time. And to make good on this promise day after day, our staff includes more than 60 professional cooks (we call them test cooks), who develop the recipes that appear in print in *Cook's Illustrated* and *Cook's Country* magazines and in the books we publish every year. The test cooks also man the back kitchen during the filming of our television shows to make sure the recipes you see on TV look (and taste) like they should.

Our recipes are the product of a team of cooks, editors, and many others working together.

Our test cooks come from a wide variety of backgrounds and experiences. Many of them have followed a traditional path from culinary school to restaurant work and then to our door. Others honed their skills solely through working in restaurants—many have cooked in fine kitchens around the world and they bring that deep knowledge of other cuisines and their finely developed palates to their work in the test kitchen. Restaurant work can be exciting but the repetition and the demanding hours often get tiresome—the cooks that join the test kitchen team are looking for new and different challenges outside the world of restaurant cooking. Sometimes, our test cooks are career-changers who discover their true passion for cooking after working in finance or academia or industry for years and invest in culinary training much later in life. There is no single path to a job at America's Test Kitchen. We are open to candidates with many kinds of culinary backgrounds, in part because we value having a team with deep but diverse skills. Also, our hiring process has several parts and is not simply a matter of a good résumé and a good interview. We really need to know that a candidate can cook (and write, too!). Above all, test cooks need to be curious and passionate about food and excited to work as part of our team to create foolproof recipes using the test kitchen's unique approach.

A Job Interview with Knives

It's hard to tell from just reading a résumé whether a candidate knows enough about food or has the hands-on skills to be successful on one of our kitchen teams. Recipe development is far different from cooking in a restaurant, cooking at home, or running a catering business. That is why every serious candidate for a test cook position has to take what is called a bench test where they make a few of our recipes under the watchful eye of senior members of the kitchen team. Observing a prospective candidate in action reveals a lot about how comfortable they are in the kitchen, how exacting they are, whether they have good knife skills, and if they can follow a recipe in every last detail. Many incredibly talented cooks who come from restaurant backgrounds are used to cooking from the hip instead of carefully following a recipe. The bench test helps us figure out which cooks are a good match for the kind of cooking that the test cooks must do and also helps give candidates a feel for the test kitchen and what working in it would be like.

After a successful bench test, the potential test cook is asked for an on-the-spot writing sample. If we like what we see, we ask the interviewee to write an essay and develop a recipe in the style of our publications. This allows the candidate to take a little more time to show off his or her writing skills and grasp of our rigorous and scientific approach to cooking. Candidates who are successful in completing all these different challenges become part of one of our kitchen teams. And although there are differences in how test cooks operate depending upon whether they are on a book or magazine team, there is one constant: We test our way to rock-solid recipes by following well-established procedures with many steps along the way.

Starting from Scratch

Our magazines only publish a limited number of recipes in each issue, so each and every one gets serious, focused attention from a test cook. When they start work on a new recipe, the test cooks on the magazines always begin without any preconceived ideas about what the "right" way to make it is. Thus the first step with any recipe is research. The test cooks have many different resources at their disposal for this research, including the test kitchen's cookbook library (which houses thousands of books, some dating back to the 1800s), the Internet, our on-call culinary historian and food scientist, and of course their test kitchen coworkers. One of the main focuses of *Cook's Country* magazine is American regional recipes, so the research for those projects might also include going on the road to investigate a local dish in its natural habitat—pierogi in Pittsburgh, butter burgers in Wisconsin, shrimp and grits in South Carolina, or puffy tacos in Texas. This research is used to draft a proposal for the story the test cook will write for publication, including a summary of the history of the recipe, key variables in different versions of the recipe, notes on the anticipated challenges associated with the recipe, and questions that the test cook wants to answer about the recipe.

The America's Test Kitchen in-house library includes thousands of culinary tomes.

Once the proposal is accepted by the test cook's editors, most of the magazine recipes begin with what's called a five-recipe test (although there may actually be anywhere from four to six recipes involved), in which the test cook prepares a set of diverse versions of the recipe that came up in the course of all that research. These may range from very old, traditional versions of a dish to cutting-edge takes on the same recipe. The test cook serves these to the other test cooks and editors on the team and together they critique the various recipes. This helps determine the most (and least) popular characteristics of each sample, which the test cook will then work to include (or avoid) in the final version of the dish. In the weeks that follow, the test cook will pursue his or her own take on the recipe, experimenting broadly with techniques, ingredients, and approaches before moving on to more controlled, scientific testing, tweaking individual variables one at a time. The cook might change ingredient quantities or qualities, oven temperature or rack position, baking time, or any other aspect of the recipe, including elements that most of us would never think to question or change. The other test cooks and editors on the team will taste all the different versions and give feedback at each step in the process. This means that our recipes are always the product of many different palates and tastes working together, so it's not just one person's idea of spicy or salty or crispy that shapes the final product.

This teamwork aspect is even more central for the test cooks who work on our cookbooks. They also complete multiple rounds of testing for every recipe, but instead of working on just one or two recipes for months at a time, they work in

Gluten-Free Blueberry Muffin Recipe Development

Ingredients	V1	V2	V3	V4	V5	V6	V7	V8
Sugar	7 oz	7 oz	4 5/8 oz	4 5/8 oz	4 5/8 oz	4 5/8 oz	4 5/8 oz	4 5/8 oz
Baking Powder	1 T	1 T	2 tsp	2 tsp	1 T	1 T	1 T	1 T
Baking Soda	1/2 tsp	1/2 tsp						
Table Salt	1/2 tsp	1/2 tsp	1/2 tsp	1/2 tsp	1/2 tsp	1/2 tsp	1/2 tsp	1/2 tsp
Butter	8 T	8 T	4 oz. creamed	4 oz. creamed	4 oz. creamed	4 oz. creamed	4 oz. creamed	4 oz. creamed
Vanilla Extract	X	X	1 tsp	1 tsp	1 tsp	1 tsp	1 tsp	1 tsp
Nutmeg/ Cinnamon	X	X	N 1/4 tsp	N 1/4 tsp	N 1/4 tsp	N 1/4 tsp	N 1/4 tsp	N 1/4 tsp
Eggs	2	2	2	2	2	2	2	2
Liquid	Yogurt: 1 1/2 cup	Yogurt: 1 1/2 cup	Milk: 4 oz	Milk: 4 oz	Milk: 4 oz	Milk: 4 oz	Buttermilk: 4 oz	Yogurt: 4 oz
Flour	15 3/4 oz	AP Standard	10 5/8 oz	10 5/8 oz	10 5/8 oz	10 5/8 oz	10 5/8 oz	10 5/8 oz
Xanthum Gum	1/4 tsp	x	1 tsp	1/2 tsp	1 tsp	1/2 tsp	1/2 tsp	1/2 tsp
Guar Gum	X	X						
Mix-In	X	X	X	1 c Frozen Blueberries	1 c Frozen Blueberries	1 c Frozen Blueberries	1 c Frozen Blueberries	1 c Frozen Blueberries
Method	1 hour soak w/o butter	per recipe	creaming	creaming	creaming	creaming	creaming	creaming
Time	25 mins	16-20	16-20	16-20	16-20	16-20	16-20	16-20
Oven Temp	375	375	375	375	375	375	375	375
Notes	Good but a little tough on the outside and gummy on the inside. Very sweet!	KA standard recipe	Gritty. Good flavor & ok texture, esp w/ mix-ins. Without mix-ins outside is resistent.	10 min in-pan sit	10 min in-pan sit	Good milk flavor, slightly gritty, moist and crumbly resembling an AP muffin 10 min in-pan sit	Acidic, dry taste, very gritty and take out the nutmeg and substitute cinnamon for future-10 min in-pan sit	Good texture, slightly gritty, nice mosture possibly more yogurt? Test sit time of 30 minutes in muffin tins. 10 min in-pan sit

Our test cooks take extensive notes throughout the development process to track how even the slightest changes and tweaks affect the way a recipe behaves.

small groups on a specific book, and they work chapter by chapter. So over the course of a few weeks, a cook on the book team will test and develop a set of recipes that work together as a coherent chapter and that work in tandem with the other chapters of the book, which are being developed by his or her teammates. For instance, one of our recent book projects featured our first foray into gluten-free baking. Initial development for this book included engineering our ideal gluten-free flour blend, which each cook then applied to the projects in his or her individual chapters, including breads, pastries, breakfast dishes, comfort foods, and desserts. Discoveries that were made by one cook while working on over 200 batches of blueberry muffins—changing the ingredients used and the way those ingredients were mixed, and determining what visual cues would mean the muffins were done—could then be applied to improve a recipe for cupcakes that another cook was developing.

The experimentation stage is where the real discoveries occur. For instance, in lieu of adding ground veal to our meatloaf recipe (it's a traditional component of meatloaf mix, but can be hard to find), we found that using unflavored gelatin gave us the same tender, moist texture and was much cheaper and easier to find at the supermarket. Or take our recipe called Weeknight Roast Chicken: We solved the problem of getting the light and dark meat to finish cooking at the same time by placing the chicken breast side up in a preheated pan in a very hot oven to give the thighs a jump start on cooking—then we actually turned the oven off and let the chicken finish cooking gently for moist, tender meat. These kinds of creative solutions can only come out of the innovative, curious minds of our test cooks.

Recipe development often starts with trying several different versions of the same recipe.

Cooking: A Science and an Art

Many of the most interesting innovations in our recipes happen when the test cooks dig deeper into the science of the recipes they're working on. We have a food science expert, Guy Crosby, who's always on call to help with the tricky issues that come up during recipe development. When we can't explain why a cast-iron skillet heats up the way it does or how to make fermented recipes safe and reliable for home cooks, we call on Guy or our in-house science editor, Dan Souza. As with our tasting and testing team, the test cooks pursue their projects much like scientists tackling a complex problem. Cooking and eating may seem like highly visceral, subjective pursuits but our test cooks take an analytical, problem-solving approach to making the most foolproof, delicious recipes possible.

Our kitchen tools go beyond pans and spatulas to scientific equipment like this texture analyzer.

In addition to the regular testing process that all our recipes undergo, some recipes also require additional research. The test cooks design experiments that the average home cook might never think of and almost certainly wouldn't have the resources to undertake. We've used a texture analyzer to assess optimum tenderness in meat. We've put an infrared thermometer gun to work determining where the hot spots are in a pan. We've worked with outside labs to analyze relative levels of chemical compounds in ingredients in support of hypotheses about what exactly makes them taste the way they do. And then we put all of this investigation to practical use in the recipes that really work for home cooks, who can read about the research and see the results as they cook the food for themselves. While you may not fully grasp every detail behind the way mustard affects the chemical makeup of an emulsification, you'll certainly appreciate what it does when you make our foolproof vinaigrette recipe.

Never Too Many Cooks

Once the editors and the test cooks are satisfied with the working recipe, it's tested even further; our team of in-house test kitchen interns cook every recipe, with no special instructions, to make sure that the way it's written makes sense. From there, the recipes are updated and clarified with any necessary changes and then many of them are also sent to our outside team of volunteer home cooks who prepare them in their own kitchens and provide feedback about how the recipe turned out and whether they liked it. Each recipe that goes out to survey will move on to the next stage of development if and only if at least 80 percent of the home cooks report that they would make the recipe again; otherwise, it goes back for further testing and improvements.

The last part of recipe development is what we call "abuse testing." We know that not every home cook is going to use exactly the same equipment and ingredients that we use, and some might not even follow the directions that closely. So the test cooks try to anticipate the common issues that might arise in our readers' home kitchens. Working with the interns, they prepare the recipe using less-than-optimal equipment, common ingredient substitutions, and imprecise techniques. The test cooks use the results of these tests when they write the informational notes and step-by-step diagrams that accompany their recipes. If there's one ingredient that you simply cannot skip or swap out if you want the recipe to work, we'll make sure to call that out as clearly as possible, and if there's a particular step that needs to be done exactly as written, we'll usually include some extra instructions to make sure the technique is as clear as possible.

As soon as one project is finished and sent off for publication, the test cook who worked on it will pick up something completely different and dive into a whole new project with challenges all its own. While every test cook has their personal specialty—pastry making, Southern food, barbecuing—they all work on a wide variety of recipes. A test cook on our cookbook team might move from several months working with her team on our new gluten-free cookbook to a team tackling a book that's all about baking breads from around the world. Also, because of our publishing schedules, you will find our dedicated test cooks outside behind our offices grilling in the middle of winter in their parkas and snow boots in order to get those recipes ready to be published in time for summer cookout season. (Naturally, we bake our holiday cookies in May.)

Not even Massachusetts winters will stop our test cooks from pursuing perfection.

Culinary Storytelling

Creating the actual recipe is only one part of the recipe development process. Once the ingredients and techniques have been finalized, the test cook turns to writing the story that will accompany the recipes when they're published. For a recipe in one of our cookbooks, this might be just one paragraph, while for a full-length magazine piece it could be several pages long. Either way, the copy will explain what happened during the process of recipe development and why the recipe works. We also surround each recipe with photos that illustrate the key processes and notes on fundamental kitchen tips that our test cooks think are most important for a home cook to know. In this chapter and the next one, you'll find examples of all this work, as well as 50 of our favorite and most indispensable recipes, each with a set of detailed photos and notes outlining the key steps that make the recipe work.

RECIPE DEVELOPMENT BY THE NUMBERS	
Books in the America's Test Kitchen Office Cookbook Library	4,564
Average Number of Recipes Developed Per Year	1,000
Average Number of Tests Per Recipe	30
Average Number of People Who Taste Each Recipe Test	8
Volunteer Home Cooks Who Participate in Our Recipe Testing Program Per Year	20,000
America's Test Kitchen Yearly Grocery Bill	$600,000

FOOD SAFETY

Safety first. Depending on factors such as moisture, temperature, and surface porosity, microbes can live as long as 60 hours. But you don't need anything special to clean your kitchen—for the most part, we rely on old-fashioned soap and hot water or a bleach solution. There are a couple of other simple things you can do to ensure better hygiene around the kitchen. Following basic sanitation practices can dramatically reduce the risk of food-borne illness.

KEEPING A CLEAN KITCHEN

Wash Your Hands

Washing your hands is one of the best ways to stop the spread of food-borne pathogens. Wash before and during cooking, especially after touching raw meat and poultry. The U.S. Food and Drug Administration (FDA) recommends at least 20 seconds in warm, soapy water. How long is that? Try singing "Happy Birthday."

Sanitize Your Sink

Studies have found that the kitchen sink is crawling with even more bacteria than the garbage bin. The faucet handle, which can reintroduce bacteria to your hands after you've washed them, is a close second. Though we've found that hot, soapy water is amazingly effective at eliminating bacteria, for added insurance, clean these areas frequently with a solution of 1 tablespoon bleach per quart of water.

Clean Your Cutting Boards

While bamboo boards do have natural antimicrobial properties that help kill off bacteria, we have found that cutting boards of all materials will come perfectly clean when scrubbed thoroughly with hot, soapy water. Some boards are dishwasher-safe, but wooden boards should never go through the dishwasher. See page 53 for tips on removing odors and stains from your cutting boards.

Clean Your Sponges

A wet sponge is an ideal host for bacteria; whenever possible, use a paper towel or dishcloth instead. If you do use a sponge, disinfect it. We tested myriad methods, including microwaving, freezing, bleaching, and boiling, and lab results showed that microwaving and boiling were most effective. Since sponges have been known to catch fire in high-powered microwaves, we prefer to boil them for 5 minutes.

KEEPING YOUR FRIDGE COOL

A refrigerator thermometer will tell you if your fridge and freezer are working properly. Check the temperature of your refrigerator regularly to ensure that it is between 35 and 40 degrees; your freezer should be below zero degrees. Listed here are the recommended storage temperatures for specific foods. Keep in mind that the back of a refrigerator is the coldest area while the door is the least cold (for more information about using your refrigerator effectively, see pages 177–178). Make sure that raw meat is stored well wrapped and never on shelves that are above other food.

Recommended Storage Temperature	
Fish and Shellfish	30 to 34 degrees
Meat and Poultry	32 to 36 degrees
Dairy Products	36 to 40 degrees
Eggs	38 to 40 degrees
Produce	40 to 45 degrees

HANDLING FOODS CAREFULLY

Raw meat, poultry, and eggs may carry harmful bacteria like salmonella, listeria, or E. coli. Cooking kills off these bacteria—ensuring the food is perfectly safe to eat—but it's critical to be careful about how you handle raw foods in the kitchen in order to avoid cross-contamination.

Separate Raw and Cooked Foods

Keep raw and cooked foods separate to prevent the spread of bacteria. Never place cooked food on a plate or cutting board that has come into contact with raw food (meat or not), and wash any utensil (including a thermometer) that comes in contact with raw food before reusing it.

Put Up Barriers

Items that come in contact with both raw and cooked food, like scales and platters, should be covered with aluminum foil or plastic wrap to create a protective barrier. Once the item has been used, the protective layer should be discarded—taking any bacteria with it. Similarly, wrapping your cutting board with plastic wrap before pounding meat and poultry on it will limit the spread of bacteria.

Season Safely

Though most bacteria can't live for more than a few minutes in direct contact with salt, it can live on the edges of a box or shaker. To avoid contamination, we grind pepper into a clean small bowl and then mix it with salt (in a ratio of 1 part pepper to 4 parts kosher salt or 2 parts table salt).

You can reach into the bowl for seasoning without washing your hands every time. Any leftover seasoning is discarded, and then the bowl goes in the dishwasher.

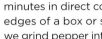

Don't Rinse Raw Meat and Poultry

Avoid rinsing raw meat and poultry. Contrary to what some cookbooks (or your grandmother) might advise, rinsing is more likely to spread contaminants around your sink than send them down the drain. Cooking food to a safe internal temperature will kill surface bacteria more effectively than rinsing.

Don't Recycle Used Marinades

It may seem economical to reuse marinades, but used marinade is contaminated with raw meat juice and is therefore unsafe to consume. If you want a sauce to serve with cooked meat, make a little extra marinade and set it aside before adding the rest to the raw meat.

STORING FOODS SAFELY

Avoid the "danger zone"—in the temperature range from 40 to 140 degrees, bacteria double about every 20 minutes. As a general rule, food shouldn't stay in this zone for more than 2 hours (1 hour if the room temperature is over 90 degrees).

Defrost in the Fridge

Always defrost in the refrigerator. On the counter the temperature is higher and bacteria multiply rapidly. Place food on a plate or in a bowl to collect any liquid it releases. Most food will take 24 hours to thaw. (Larger items, like whole turkeys, can take far longer, about 6 hours per pound.)

Reheat Rapidly

When food is reheated, it should be brought through the danger zone as rapidly as possible—don't let it come slowly to a simmer. Bring leftover sauces, soups, and gravies to a boil and make sure casseroles reach at least 165 degrees.

Cool on the Counter, Not in the Fridge

Don't put hot foods in the fridge right after cooking. This will cause the temperature in the refrigerator to rise, potentially making it hospitable to the spread of bacteria. The FDA recommends cooling foods to 70 degrees within the first 2 hours after cooking, and to 40 degrees within another 4 hours. We cool food on the counter for about an hour and then put it in the fridge.

Wrap It Right

You may have heard that it's not safe to place plastic wrap directly on the surface of still-warm foods, especially fatty foods. This is because in the past, plastic wraps were made with polyvinyl chloride (PVC) or polyvinylidene chloride (PVDC) as well as compounds known as "plasticizers" that enhanced clinginess and stretchiness. These materials were more likely to migrate into warm, fatty foods since many plastic additives are more soluble in fats and oils than in water. However, health concerns associated with these plastics as well as many plasticizers have led most manufacturers to switch to polyethylene, which requires no plasticizers (at the expense of some clinginess). While there is no evidence to suggest that the newer, reformulated plastic wraps leach harmful compounds into food, keeping the wrap at least 1 inch from food surfaces will eliminate any potential risk. Another solution is to use parchment paper for direct surface contact, as we do in the test kitchen for fatty puddings and custards.

GETTING TO KNOW YOUR REFRIGERATOR

Although we don't often think about it, every refrigerator has warmer, cooler, and more humid spots. Together they create a complex food storage matrix. You can make the different temperature zones in your refrigerator work to your advantage by learning a few facts about storing different kinds of foods. Of course, conditions inside individual refrigerators do vary somewhat, but experts agree on certain general trends in terms of which areas are warmer or cooler. We spent some time verifying what the refrigeration experts told us, and when we were finished we had a much better idea of how best to use a refrigerator. Follow the tips and guidelines shown here to keep your meat, dairy, and produce fresh and flavorful.

Refrigerator Temperature Basics

To verify the information we gathered from refrigeration experts, we hooked up a test kitchen refrigerator to a piece of equipment called a chart scan data recorder. The recorder was connected to a laptop computer as well as several temperature monitors placed in strategic locations on the shelves and drawers inside the refrigerator. The refrigerator was then closed and left undisturbed for 24 hours while the interior temperatures were monitored.

Keeping in mind that a refrigerator goes through many cooling cycles throughout a 24-hour period (that is, at times the temperature may be well above or below 34 degrees Fahrenheit, the optimal temperature for a home refrigerator), our results provided some interesting information. For example, the butter compartment was not the warmest spot in the fridge, as we had expected. Instead, the middle shelf on the door and the front portion of the bottom cabinet shelf registered the highest readings—all the way up to 43 degrees. Not a place where you would want to store your milk or eggs, each of which should be kept at 40 degrees or below. The meat compartment remained the coolest area of the refrigerator (on average, 33 degrees), making it perfect for storing what it is supposed to store: meat.

If you'd like to find the warmer and cooler spots in your home refrigerator, you can purchase a couple of inexpensive refrigerator thermometers and place them on the top, middle, and bottom shelves of your refrigerator, recording the temperature every couple of hours. Generally, though, you can expect your readings to follow the trends shown in the diagram on page 178.

A Rain Forest in Your Crisper

A crisper or humidity compartment allows more or less cold air in through small vents located by the slide control. (If your crisper doesn't have a slide control, it is always at the highest humidity level of which it is capable.) The more cold air that is let in, the less humid the environment. A humid environment provides vegetables with water, without which they shrivel and rot. But if the humidity is too high, water can build up on the surface of the food and condense; this gives fungi and bacteria a chance to grow and compromises the quality and safety of your food. Some produce, such as prewashed, bagged salad greens, is sold in containers that are designed to allow carbon dioxide to escape while still regulating moisture.

REFRIGERATOR STORAGE TIPS

Storing Meat
Storing meat on a rimmed baking sheet helps keep refrigerator shelves sanitary and allows other food items, such as fruits and vegetables, to be stored on the same shelf without risk of cross-contamination.

Storing Cheese
Wrap cheese first in parchment paper and then in aluminum foil. Store the wrapped cheese in the crisper or in an airtight plastic bag or container.

Storing Greens
To prevent bacterial growth, greens must be completely dried before being stored. Store washed and dried greens in paper towels in a zipper-lock bag left slightly open.

ANATOMY OF A WELL-ORGANIZED REFRIGERATOR

Top Shelf, Front
Temperature Moderate
Eggs in the Carton

Meat Compartment
Temperature Cool
Ground Meat
Chops
Cutlets
Steaks
Chicken Parts

Middle Shelf, Front
Temperature Moderate
Chill-Sensitive Fruits and
Vegetables

Door, Middle Compartment
Temperature Warm
Beverages
Condiments

Bottom Shelf, Front
Temperature Warm
Chill-Sensitive Fruits and
Vegetables

Door, Bottom Compartment
Temperature Cool
Milk (gallon-size containers
may be stored on the back
portion of the top shelf)
Sour Cream
Yogurt

*For detailed storage information
for many more specific foods, see
Stocking Your Fridge and Pantry,
pages 60–165.*

Top Shelf, Back
Temperature Cool
Butter (stored in a
butter dish)
Refrigerator-Safe Fruits
Lunch Meats

Middle Shelf, Back
Temperature Cool
Prepared Foods and
Leftovers

Bottom Shelf, Back
Temperature Cool
Whole Birds, Roasts
Fish and Shellfish (placed
on top of zipper-lock bags
of ice inside a deep plastic
container)

Crisper(s)
Temperature Moderate to
Cool
Leafy Greens
Celery
Broccoli
Carrots
Cucumbers
Fresh Herbs
Lemons and Limes
Mushrooms
Peppers
Cheese (wrapped in parch-
ment paper and then foil)

HOW LONG WILL IT KEEP?

Beef		Poultry	
Steaks, Roasts	3–5 days	Fresh, Whole	2 days
Ground	2 days	Fresh, pieces	2 days
Defrosted	2–3 days	Defrosted	2 days
Cooked	2–3 days	Cooked	2–3 days
Lunchmeats		**Fish and Seafood**	
Sliced to Order	3–5 days	Fresh	1–2 days
Prepackaged	1 week	Cooked	3–4 days
Pork		Bisques, Chowders	1–2 days
Fresh Chops, Roasts	3 days	Fresh Crab, in Shell	2 days
Smoked Ham, Bacon	2 weeks once opened	Other Fresh Shellfish	1 day

BASIC KITCHEN SKILLS

Once you have the right pans and the best ingredients, there are a few basic skills that you should practice in order to ensure success in the kitchen. Foundational elements like proper measuring, knife work, and seasoning know-how will help you in every single recipe you tackle.

TIPS THAT WILL MAKE YOU A BETTER COOK

Cooking is a skill that can take a lifetime to perfect, and even the best cooks sometimes produce disappointing results. However, there are some basic rules you can follow that will help you use recipes successfully in your kitchen.

Read the Recipe Carefully

Almost everyone has embarked upon preparing a recipe only to realize midway through that the dish needs hours of chilling before it can be finished and served. By reading the recipe completely through before you start to cook, you will avoid any surprises along the way.

Follow Directions (at Least the First Time)

Cooking is a science, but it is also an art. Our advice is simple: Make the recipe as directed the first time. Once you understand the recipe, you can improvise and make it your own.

Be Prepared

Set out and organize all of the equipment you will need for a recipe and prep all of the ingredients for it before you start to cook. In culinary school, this is referred to as creating a *mise en place*.

Start with Good Ingredients

Don't expect to turn old eggs into a nicely risen soufflé. Likewise, low-quality meat will yield low-quality results. Freshness matters. When it comes to pantry items, try to use our recommended products (pages 387–409) if possible. The right can of tomatoes can make or break your sauce.

Prepare Ingredients as Directed

Be sure to prepare food as instructed in the ingredient list. Food that is uniformly and properly cut will not only cook at the same rate but will also be more visually appealing.

Keep Substitutions to a Minimum

In general, it is best if you use the ingredients called for in the recipe; this is especially true in baking, where even the slightest change can spell disaster. See page 356 for the list of emergency substitutions we've found to work in a pinch.

Use Appropriately Sized Equipment

Make sure to use the cookware and bakeware sizes noted in the recipe. If you try to cook four chicken cutlets in a 10-inch skillet, rather than in the 12-inch skillet called for in the recipe, the chicken will steam in the overcrowded pan rather than giving you the good sear you're looking for.

Preheat Your Oven

Most ovens need at least 15 minutes to preheat fully. If you don't preheat your oven sufficiently, your food will spend more time in the oven and will suffer the consequences. Also, position the oven racks as directed.

Monitor the Dish as It Cooks

The cooking times in our recipes are meant as guidelines only. Because ingredients and equipment inevitably vary, it is important to follow the visual cues provided in the recipe. It is good practice to start checking for doneness 5 to 10 minutes before the designated time.

Taste the Dish Before Serving

Most recipes end by instructing the cook to adjust the seasonings. You must taste the food in order to do this successfully. We generally season food lightly throughout the cooking process and then add more salt as needed. Foods that will be served chilled should be tasted again before serving, as cold mutes the effects of seasoning.

Learn from Your Mistakes

Even our test cooks sometimes turn out less-than-perfect food. A good cook is able to analyze failure, pinpoint the cause, and then avoid that pitfall the next time. Repetition is the key to any learning process, and cooking is no different. Make a dish at least once or twice a month until you master it. Practice really does make perfect.

HOW TO USE AND CALIBRATE THERMOMETERS

Thermometers take the guesswork out of knowing when foods are done. They are vital for ensuring success in the kitchen. A well-stocked kitchen will contain an instant-read thermometer; a clip-on probe thermometer for meat, deep frying, and candy making; and an oven thermometer. In addition to these three, a refrigerator/freezer thermometer is also a good idea. See our recommendations for choosing the right models on pages 8–11.

Checking Your Thermometer's Accuracy

You should check that your thermometer takes accurate readings when you first buy it and then again periodically over time. Here's how.

Put a mixture of ice and cold tap water in a glass or bowl; allow this mixture to sit for several minutes to let the temperature stabilize. Put the probe in the slush, being careful not to touch the sides or bottom of the glass or bowl. On a digital thermometer, press the "calibrate" button to 32 degrees; on a dial-face thermometer, turn the dial to 32 degrees (the method differs from model to model; you may need pliers to turn a small knob on the back).

Knowing When Foods Are Done

Whether cooking a burger or roasting a beef tenderloin, you should always take the temperature of the area of the meat that will be the last to finish cooking, which is the thickest part or, in some cases, the center. Bones conduct heat, so if the meat you are cooking contains bone, make sure that the thermometer does not touch it. For especially large roasts, take more than one reading to confirm you're at the right point of doneness. Also see the doneness temperatures in the chart on page 352, which represent the test kitchen's best assessment of palatability weighed against safety. In most cases, those concerns align. Rare chicken isn't very tasty, or very safe. There are a few notable exceptions, especially in regards to ground meat. If safety is your primary concern, you don't want to eat rare burgers. The U.S. Department of Agriculture (USDA) has issued a complex set of rules regarding the cooking of meat and poultry. Here are the basics of their rules: Cook whole cuts of meat, including pork, to an internal temperature of at least 145 degrees and let rest at least 3 minutes. Cook all ground meats to an internal temperature of at least 160 degrees. Cook all poultry, including ground poultry, to an internal temperature of at least 165 degrees.

Burgers

Leave the burger in the pan (or on the grill), slide the tip of the thermometer into the burger at the top edge, and push it toward the center, making sure to avoid hitting the pan (or grill) with the probe. This technique keeps the burger in the pan (rather than requiring you pick it up with tongs) and prevents it from falling apart.

Steaks, Chops, and Small Roasts

When taking the temperature of thin steaks or pork chops, it's easy to insert the thermometer too far or not far enough. To avoid this, use tongs to hold the meat, then insert the thermometer sideways into the center, taking care not to hit any bones. You can also use this technique for pork tenderloin or rack of lamb; just lift the meat with a pair of tongs and insert the thermometer into the end, parallel to the meat.

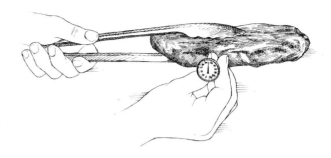

Poultry

Because breast meat cooks faster than thigh meat, you should take the temperature of both when cooking poultry. When doing so, try to avoid hitting bones, cavities, or the surface of the pan, as this will result in an inaccurate reading. When temping a whole bird, use the following methods:

For Thigh Meat

Insert the thermometer at an angle into the area between the drumstick and the breast, taking care not to hit the bone. It should register 175 degrees.

For Breast Meat

Insert the thermometer from the neck end, holding the thermometer parallel to the bird. It should register 160 degrees.

If cooking chicken or turkey pieces, use the same technique described above, while lifting the piece with tongs and inserting the thermometer sideways into the thickest part of the meat, taking care to avoid bones.

Bread

A thermometer is useful when baking bread. First, you can use it to check the temperature of the liquid, which is crucial in many recipes. And you can use it to be sure your bread is done. Rustic breads are generally done at 195 to 210 degrees, while rich, buttery yeast breads are done when they reach 190 to 200 degrees.

For Free-Form Loaves

Insert the probe through the top, side, or bottom of the loaf, making sure the probe reaches the center.

For Loaves Baked in a Pan

To avoid a hole in the top crust, insert the thermometer from the side, just above the edge of the pan, directing it downward toward the center of the loaf.

HOW TO MEASURE

Accurate measuring is often the difference between success and failure in the kitchen. Even though weight is a more accurate way to measure than volume, we know that most cooks rely on measuring cups and spoons, not scales, so here are some ways to increase your accuracy when using volume measures. Don't use liquid and dry measuring cups interchangeably—if you do, your ingredient amounts may be significantly off. See our recommendations for all the tools you need to measure correctly on pages 12–14. Also see Conversions and Equivalents on page 354.

Measuring Dry Ingredients

For absolute reliability, always weigh flour and sugar when baking. Otherwise, for dry ingredients we recommend the "dip and sweep" method, which reliably yields a 5-ounce cup of unbleached all-purpose flour and a 7-ounce cup of granulated sugar. Dip the measuring cup into the container and scoop up the ingredient in a heaping mound. Use a straight edge, like the back of a knife, to sweep the excess back into the container.

Measuring Liquid Ingredients

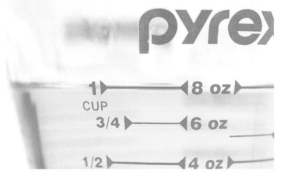

For liquid ingredients, use a liquid measuring cup set on the counter and lean down to read the measurement at eye level. When emptying the cup, use a rubber spatula to scrape it clean.

Measuring Brown Sugar

Brown sugar is clumpy, so it must be packed into a measuring cup to get an accurate reading. To do this, use your fingers or the bottom of a smaller cup to press the sugar into the measuring cup.

Measuring In-Between Ingredients

For sticky and/or semisolid ingredients like mayonnaise, peanut butter, sour cream, and honey, we prefer an adjustable measuring cup. An adjustable measuring cup has a clear cylinder with volume markings and a plunger insert. You withdraw the plunger to the desired measurement and then fill the cylinder, level it off, and plunge to empty it. This design makes it easy to push out every last bit of the ingredient. If you don't own an adjustable measuring cup, a dry measuring cup is the next most consistent tool.

When to Measure

It addition to how you measure, it matters when you measure an ingredient. For instance, "1 cup walnuts, chopped" is not the same thing as "1 cup chopped walnuts." In the first example, "1 cup walnuts, chopped," the cook should measure and then chop the walnuts. In the second example, "1 cup chopped walnuts," the cook should chop and then measure. One cup of unchopped walnuts weighs 4 ounces, while one cup of chopped walnuts weighs 4.8 ounces—that's 20 percent more nuts. Apply this principle to other ingredients (such as "sifted flour" versus "flour, sifted") and you can see how this makes a significant difference in the final outcome of a recipe.

KNIFE SKILLS

Knives are the most important tools in your kitchen; using them properly is essential. Your knife skills will improve with time and practice. Here are some key tips for safe, efficient use.

Holding a Knife

Much as how someone holds a baseball bat, how you hold a knife makes a difference in terms of control and force. And don't forget about the other hand—the one that holds the food securely in place while you cut. How you hold the food steady makes a big difference in terms of fingertip safety.

Control Grip

For more control, choke up on the handle and actually grip the blade of the knife between your thumb and forefinger.

Force Grip

Holding the knife on the handle allows you to use more force and is helpful when cutting through hard foods or bone.

Protect Your Fingertips

Use the "bear claw" grip to hold food in place and minimize danger. Tuck your fingertips in, away from the knife, and rest your knuckles against the blade. During the upward motion of slicing, reposition your guiding hand for the next cut.

Setting Up Your Cutting Station

In our test kitchen, "setting up your board" means arranging your cooking station before you begin to prep and cook. Setting up your board at home is key for organization and efficiency.

Anchor Your Board

A cutting board that slides all over the counter is not only annoying, it is unsafe. If your cutting board doesn't have nonslip grips on the bottom, place a square of wet paper towel, a dish towel, or a small piece of shelf liner between the counter and the cutting board.

Keep It Tidy

Don't push vegetable trimmings to one side of the cutting board; this reduces the usable work area on your board. Designate a small bowl or plastic grocery bag for trimmings.

Organize Your Prep

Organizing your prepped ingredients into little bowls isn't just for TV chefs—it's a great idea for home cooks too. This setup makes it easy to grab an ingredient and add it to a hot pan at just the right moment.

Basic Cutting Motions

Depending on the food being prepared, you will use different parts of the knife blade and different motions. Here are four basic motions.

Small Items: Keep Tip Down

To cut small items, such as celery, push the blade forward and down, using the blade's curve to guide the middle of the knife through smooth strokes. The tip of the blade should touch the board at all times when cutting small food.

Large Items: Lift Blade Up

To cut large items, such as eggplant, lift the entire blade off the board to help make smooth strokes.

Mincing: Use Both Hands

To mince herbs and garlic, grip the handle with one hand and rest the fingers of the other hand lightly on the knife tip. This grip facilitates the up-and-down rocking motion needed for mincing. To make sure the food is evenly minced, pivot the knife through the pile of food as you work.

Tough Items: Use the Heel

To cut tough foods like winter squash or bone-in chicken parts, use the heel of the knife. Use one hand to grip the handle, and place the flat palm of your other hand on top of the blade. Cut straight down into the item, pushing the blade gently. Be careful and make sure your hand and the knife are dry to prevent slippage.

Caring for Your Knives

A sharp knife is a fast knife, and a dull knife is an accident waiting to happen. Dull knives are dangerous because a dull blade requires more force to do the job and so has a higher chance of slipping and missing the mark. Even the best knives will dull over time with regular use.

Is It Sharp?

To determine if your knife needs sharpening, try the paper test. Hold a single piece of printer/copy paper firmly at the top with one hand. Draw the blade down through the paper, heel to tip, with the other hand. If the knife fails to slice cleanly, try steeling it. If it still fails, it needs sharpening.

When to Use a Sharpening Steel

A so-called sharpening steel, the metal rod sold with most knife sets, doesn't really sharpen a knife. Rather, sweeping the blade along the steel corrects and realigns the edge of a slightly dulled knife by pulling off burrs and smoothing the edge. Throughout this motion, make sure to maintain a 15-degree angle between the blade and the steel.

When to Use a Knife Sharpener

If your knife is quite dull, you'll need to reshape its edge. This requires removing a fair amount of metal—more than you could ever remove with a steel. To restore a very dull knife, you have three choices: You can send it out; you can use a whetstone (tricky for anyone but a professional); or—the most convenient option—you can use an electric or manual sharpener.

How to Use a Sharpening Steel

1 To safely use a steel, hold it vertically with the tip firmly planted on the counter. Place the heel of the blade against the top of the steel and point the knife tip slightly upward. Hold the blade at a 15-degree angle away from the steel.

2 Maintaining light pressure and a 15-degree angle between the blade and the steel, slide the blade down the length of the steel in a sweeping motion, pulling the knife toward your body so that the middle of the blade is in contact with the middle of the steel.

3 Finish the motion by passing the tip of the blade over the bottom of the steel. Repeat this motion on the other side of the blade. Four or five strokes on each side of the blade (a total of eight to 10 alternating passes) should realign the edge.

More Than Just Finger Safety

While protecting yourself from nicks and cuts is definitely a key part of learning knife skills, there are other reasons to practice your technique as well.

Good Technique = Less Risk

If you use proper techniques, you are less likely to injure yourself. It is crucial to keep knives sharp so that they cut through food with less slippage. It is also important to grip the knife correctly and know how to position your noncutting hand.

Good Technique = Faster Results

If you use proper techniques, you will be able to prepare food faster. It may not seem like a big difference, but in a recipe with a lot of vegetable or protein prep, all those extra minutes can really add up.

Good Technique = Better Results

If you use proper techniques, you will produce food that is evenly cut and therefore will cook at an even rate. Poorly cut food will not cook properly. For instance, those large hunks of garlic will burn and impart a harsh flavor to your food.

HOW TO MAKE FOOD TASTE BETTER

Sometimes it's the small touches that make the biggest difference. These simple tricks for prepping, cooking, and seasoning are designed to boost flavor in everyday cooking.

Don't Prepare Garlic and Onions in Advance

Chopping garlic and onions releases sharp odors and strong flavors that become overpowering with time, so it's best to cut them at the last minute.

Trim Green Shoots from Garlic

Those little green shoots are quite bitter. Always trim and discard them before preparing garlic.

Don't Seed Tomatoes

The seeds and surrounding "jelly" contain most of the flavor, so don't seed tomatoes unless called for in a recipe where excess moisture will ruin a dish.

Score Meat Before Marinating It

Prick meat all over with a fork to help marinades penetrate quickly. And forget about acidic marinades—salty ones work better.

Flip or Stir Meat While Marinating

Place meat in a zipper-lock bag or use a large baking dish covered with plastic wrap. Flip the bag or stir the meat halfway through the soaking time to ensure that all of the meat gets equal exposure to the marinade.

Trim Beef Stew Meat; Leave Fat on Pork

Remove all hard fat and connective tissue from the exterior of beef stew meat before cooking; its intramuscular marbling will keep it moist and tender during cooking. But a thick layer of fat left on pork will baste and flavor the leaner meat.

Strike Only When the Pan Is Hot

The temperature of the cooking surface will drop the minute food is added, so don't rush the preheating step at the start of most sautés. Wait for the oil to shimmer when cooking vegetables. When cooking proteins, wait until you see the first wisps of smoke rise from the oil.

Season with Sugar, Too

Browned food tastes better, and the best way to accelerate this process is with a pinch of sugar sprinkled on lean proteins or vegetables.

Never Discard the Fond

Those caramelized browned bits that stick to the bottom of the pan after cooking are packed with savory flavor. Deglaze the hot pan with liquid and scrape the bits free with a wooden spoon to incorporate the fond into sauces, soups, or stews.

Save Those Meat Juices

As meat rests, it releases flavorful juices that can be added back to the skillet when making a pan sauce. If the juices are plentiful enough to thin the sauce, allow it to simmer an additional minute or two to restore its proper consistency.

Always Toast Nuts

Toasting nuts brings out their aromatic oils, contributing to a stronger, more complex flavor and aroma. See page 227 for more information.

Bloom Spices and Dried Herbs in Fat

To intensify the flavor of ground spices and dried herbs, cook them for a minute or two in a little butter or oil before adding liquid to the pan. If the recipe calls for sautéing aromatics (like onions), add the spices to the fat in the pan when the vegetables are nearly cooked.

Brown Breads, Pies, and Pastries

Browning equals flavor, so don't take breads, pies, or even cakes out of the oven until the exterior is deep golden brown.

Underbake Chocolate Desserts

The flavor compounds in chocolate are extremely volatile, so the longer you cook brownies or cookies the more flavor is lost. Err on the side of underbaking and remember that residual heat will continue to cook baked goods as they cool.

HOW TO SEASON FOOD

Add Acid Before Serving

We usually focus on seasoning with salt and pepper before serving, but just as important, many soups, stews, and sauces benefit from a last-minute addition of lemon juice or vinegar. As little as ⅛ teaspoon will brighten other flavors in the dish.

Use Kosher Salt for Seasoning Before Cooking

The large grains of kosher salt distribute more evenly than fine table salt, making kosher salt the best choice for seasoning proteins before cooking.

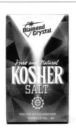

When Seasonings Go Awry

If you've added too much salt, sugar, or spice to a dish, the damage is usually done. In mild cases, however, it can sometimes be masked by the addition of another seasoning from the opposite end of the flavor spectrum. Remember to account for the reduction of liquids when seasoning a dish. Note: Despite popular lore, a few slices of potato cannot fix an overseasoned soup or stew. Yes, the potatoes might absorb some of the salty liquid, but the remaining liquid will still be too salty.

If Your Food Is	Add	Such As
Too Salty	an acid or sweetener	vinegar, citrus juice, or canned, unsalted tomatoes; sugar, honey, or maple syrup
Too Sweet	an acid or seasonings	vinegar or citrus juice; chopped fresh herbs, cayenne, or, for sweet dishes, a bit of liqueur or espresso powder
Too Spicy or Acidic	a fat or sweetener	butter, cream, sour cream, cheese, or olive oil; sugar, honey, or maple syrup

Pep Up—or Tone Down—Your Pepper

When exactly you apply black pepper to meat—before or after searing—will affect the strength of its bite. If you want assertive pepper flavor, season meat after searing since keeping the pepper away from the heat will preserve its volatile compounds. Alternatively, seasoning before cooking will tame pepper's punch.

Season Cold Food Aggressively

Chilling foods dulls flavors and aromas, so it's important to compensate by seasoning cold dishes generously— but judiciously. To keep from overdoing it, season with a normal amount of salt before chilling and then taste and add more salt (as well as fresh herbs and acidic ingredients like vinegar) just before serving.

Incorporate Fresh Herbs at the Right Time

Add hardy herbs like thyme, rosemary, oregano, sage, and marjoram to dishes early in the cooking process; this way, they release maximum flavor while ensuring that their texture will be less intrusive. Save delicate herbs like parsley, cilantro, chives, and basil for the last minute.

Add a Little Umami or Savoriness

Soy sauce and anchovies contain high levels of glutamates, which give dishes a savory, meaty boost. Add a teaspoon or two of soy sauce to chili, or cook a few minced anchovies along with the vegetables in a soup or stew.

HOW TO FIX COMMON MISTAKES

Even the best cooks sometimes make mistakes. These tips and guidelines are the next-best thing to a 24-hour food emergency hotline. Here's what to do if . . .

The Food Won't Simmer Slowly

If it's hard to get your stovetop burners to maintain a very low flame (necessary when trying to cook soups or stews at a bare simmer) and you don't have a flame tamer, improvise one out of a thick ring of aluminum foil. Set the foil ring on the burner and place the pot on top.

The Pan Gets Too Dark

Searing meat in a pan produces fond, which can add great flavor to soups, stews, and sauces. But when those brown bits turn black, that's a problem. Areas between pieces of meat are often the first to blacken. To guard against this, position the meat over the darker spots. The juices released will help to deglaze the pan.

The Pan Is on Fire

The fat in the pan splatters, catches the edge of the flame, and suddenly your whole pan is on fire. The solution is to act fast and put a metal lid or baking sheet over the pan and then turn off all the burners. Salt or baking soda will also help to put out the fire, if handy. If the fire grows quickly, however, don't hesitate to get everyone out of the house and call the fire department. Also, be sure to stock your kitchen with a portable fire extinguisher (see page 47–48 for more information).

You Have a Big, Greasy Spill

A greasy spill is both tedious to clean up and dangerous if not carefully taken care of. Rather than trying to wipe up the mess with paper towels, which will spread the grease around and make a bigger mess, sprinkle a thick layer of flour over the grease spill and let it absorb for a few minutes. The greasy flour can easily be swept up and the floor cleaned quickly with window cleaner.

The Food Sticks to the Pan

Food that initially sticks to the pan usually releases on its own after a crust begins to form. As long as the food is not burning, wait a minute or two and then try again. For stubbornly stuck-on pieces of meat or fish, dip a thin, flexible spatula into cold water and slide the inverted spatula blade underneath the food.

The Meat Is Undercooked

The meat has rested and been sliced, but it's still underdone in the center. Simply putting the slices in the oven to finish cooking is not a good idea—they will dry out and quickly turn gray. Try this: Place the sliced meat on a wire rack set in a rimmed baking sheet, then cover the meat with lettuce leaves and put it under the broiler. The meat will gently steam under the lettuce.

Your Soup or Sauce Is Too Thin

To fix thin, watery soups or sauces, you have several options. Simmering the dish further on the stovetop will work, but it can also overcook vegetables and intensify unwanted flavors. Adding an actual thickener is often a better solution. Try whisking in cold pieces of butter before serving to add both richness and body. A cornstarch slurry (cornstarch mixed with cold water) can be whisked into any sauce, soup, or stew and then brought to a quick simmer to activate the cornstarch and thicken the dish. You can also soak a piece of crustless bread in some of the soup liquid until soggy and puree it in a blender, adding more of the liquid as needed, until smooth. Add the puree to the soup as needed to thicken.

SCIENCE LESSONS THAT WILL MAKE YOU A BETTER COOK

Understanding the science that leads to success or failure in the kitchen is much simpler than you think. The following pages present a set of concepts that we think every good cook should know.

The Science of Time and Temperature

Time is a useful measure when cooking, but many cooks make the mistake of giving it too much weight. All of our recipes include times as well as sensory cues to tell you when a step in a recipe is complete. The times are guidelines meant to help you plan meals (will the roast take 1 hour or 2 hours?) rather than precise measures. Always rely on your five senses to determine if a step or recipe is completed. Does the food look like the description given? If a recipe says cook "until firm," then touch the food. Likewise, if a recipe says cook "until fragrant," then rely on that cue, rather than time, to determine when this step is complete.

So why is time such an unreliable measure? Variations in equipment and variations in ingredients. Heat output in grills and cooktops varies greatly. In addition, the weight and diameter of your cookware will affect cooking time.

Even your oven isn't as reliable as you think. But while variations in equipment will affect cooking time, they are hard to track. How can you know if your skillet heats up faster than the ones we use in the test kitchen? Luckily, the other big variable in cooking time is easier to track. The initial temperature of ingredients is a key factor in many recipes. Cold food cooks more slowly than room-temperature food. So when a recipe calls for a "chilled" or "room-temperature" ingredient, pay heed to these instructions. In addition to affecting cooking time, the temperature of an ingredient will affect the quality of the finished recipe. If your butter is not well chilled, pie dough will turn out tough rather than tender and flaky. Eggs are much easier to separate when cold because the white is thicker and the yolks are taut. Here are some general assumptions and rules you should follow regarding the temperature of ingredients.

Common Temperature Terms	
Room Temperature	Generally considered to be about 70 degrees.
Chilled	As in refrigerated; generally considered to be 35 to 40 degrees. If the temperature inside your refrigerator is higher than 40 degrees, food is spoiling. If the temperature is 32 degrees or lower, food is freezing.
Frozen	Generally considered to be 0 to 10 degrees. The temperature inside your freezer should be 0 degrees.

Ingredient Temperature Rules	
Eggs	Eggs are assumed to be chilled unless otherwise noted. To bring eggs quickly to room temperature, place them (still in their shells) in a bowl of warm water for 5 minutes.
Butter	Butter is chilled unless otherwise noted. Softened butter should be between 60 and 68 degrees. Butter that has been melted and cooled should be still fluid and just warm to the touch, ideally 85 to 90 degrees.
Meat, Chicken, and Fish	These are chilled unless otherwise noted. Note that at temperatures above 40 degrees, bacteria will start to grow in all perishable foods, especially meat, chicken, and fish.
Flours and Grains	These are assumed to be at room temperature. If you store whole-grain flours and cornmeal in the freezer to prevent rancidity, bring them to room temperature before baking with them. Cold flour will inhibit rise and yield dense baked goods.

The Science of the Senses

Taste is the most obvious sense involved in cooking. In grade school we learned that we experience four primary taste sensations: salty, sweet, bitter, and sour. In recent years, scientists have agreed that there is a fifth taste called umami, which is best described as "meaty" or "savory."

The cells in our mouth that respond to taste are located in clusters called tastebuds or taste papillae. Buds for the various tastes are evenly distributed all over the tongue as well as the rest of the mouth. Due to genetic variations, different individuals taste things differently. One person can have up to 10 times as many tastebuds as another. Things seem sweeter, spicier, and more bitter to these "super-tasters" than to other people.

In addition to balancing the five tastes, good cooks will focus on smell. The aroma that wafts up to your nose from a piping-hot bowl of soup affects your perception of the flavor. The other three senses are also important; food that looks attractive will seem to taste better. We really do eat with our eyes. Texture might be even more important than appearance. A dry, chewy steak isn't nearly as enjoyable as a juicy, tender steak. And don't neglect sound—vegetables should sizzle when added to a hot pan, and if you don't hear this sound, you know the pan is too cold.

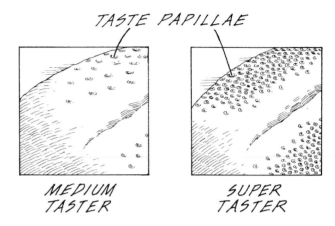

The Science of Spices

Spices are generally berries, plant seeds, roots, or bark. When dried, their flavor intensifies, and they can be sold in "whole" form or as ground powders. But why do spices have so much flavor? The flavor of spices comes mainly from their aroma, which we detect from the volatile molecules they release into the air. Spices have a high proportion of these flavor molecules, which is why they are incredibly potent—in fact, spices in their naked form are almost impossible to ingest alone. Most spices glean their flavors from a host of different flavor compounds, the mixture giving them character and complexity.

What really makes a difference in the flavor (and intensity of flavor) of spices is the way we use heat. We can directly apply heat to spices, as when we toast spices or when the spice rub applied to the outside of a cut of meat hits the grill. Toasting a spice whole brings its aromatic oils to the surface, contributing to a stronger, more complex aroma. We find it's best to toast spices before grinding them, as grinding releases moisture and aromatic oils into the air, subsequently leaving the spice with less to give when toasted. We can also cook spices in fat, a process called blooming. This works for spices that are fat-soluble and intensifies the flavors of both ground and whole spices. When we bloom spices, the fat-soluble flavor molecules are released from a solid state into solution form, where they mix and interact, thereby producing an even more complex flavor.

Spices and herbs bloomed in oil can have 10 times more flavor than those simply simmered in water.

The Science of Heat and Flavor

High heat not only cooks a cut of meat but changes the flavor, too. (Think steak tartare versus a grilled steak.) Much of this change is related to the complex chemical interactions known as the Maillard reaction, named for the French scientist Louis-Camille Maillard, who first described the process in the early 1900s. Simply put, in many foods, heat causes the creation of new, distinct flavor compounds.

The Maillard reaction describes interactions that occur between sugars, proteins, and heat. (This process is separate from caramelization, which occurs when any sugar is heated to the point that its molecules begin to break apart and generate hundreds of new flavor, color, and aroma compounds, as in crème brûlée or roasted onions.) In general, the Maillard reaction occurs when the surface temperature of the food exceeds 300 degrees. Thus, significant heat is required to jump-start the chemical reaction that causes food to brown and to develop flavor. In the absence of other variables (such as other flavorful ingredients in the dish), well-browned food always has a richer flavor profile than poorly browned food.

THE MAILLARD REACTION IN ACTION

COOKED OVER MEDIUM-LOW
The surface temperature of the chicken never exceeded 300 degrees and thus little browning occurred. The sauce made from the pan drippings was bland and pale.

COOKED OVER HIGH
The surface temperature of the chicken reached 440 degrees and thus a lot of browning occurred. The sauce made from the pan drippings was rich and brown.

The Science of Cold

A wide variety of changes occur when food is exposed to cold temperatures. Many naturally occurring processes stop in the cold, which can be beneficial for food storage. At temperatures below 40 degrees the activity of naturally occurring bacteria is suppressed, which prevents food from spoiling or developing food-borne illnesses.

The moisture in food begins to freeze and form ice crystals at temperatures below 32 degrees. These crystals rupture cell walls in fresh foods, like fruits or vegetables, which releases enzymes. When thawed, these enzymes cause produce to develop off-flavors and turn brown and soggy. Ice crystals also damage the cell structure in meat and, as a result, frozen meat loses more moisture when cooked than meat that was never frozen.
You can change the way food behaves in cold temperatures by changing its freezing point. Think about an ice cream recipe; when you freeze water, it turns into a hard, impenetrable block of ice, but when you freeze the base for an ice cream recipe, it

remains soft and smooth enough to scoop. This is because the sugar in the mixture makes it harder for the water molecules to form ice crystals and thus lowers the freezing temperature of the mixture. As the temperature of the ice cream mixture drops below 32 degrees, some water starts to freeze into solid ice crystals, but the remaining water and sugar remain unfrozen in syrup form. Sugar also reduces the size of the ice crystals that do form, creating a smoother texture.

NO SUGAR ADDED
Hard and icy

2 CUPS SUGAR ADDED
Smooth and creamy

The Science of Glutamates

In grade school, we learned that we experience four primary taste sensations: salty, sweet, bitter, and sour. But what gives food a savory, meaty flavor? Japanese physical chemistry professor Kikunae Ikeda answered this question in 1909 when he extracted a white compound from kombu, a giant sea kelp used to give Japanese broths a savory and meaty flavor, even in the absence of meat. Ikeda identified the substance as glutamate and named the taste effect it produced *umami*, which translates as "delicious" or "savory." Like foods that contain the other four basic tastes—salty, sweet, bitter, and sour—foods containing umami have been found to stimulate different receptor proteins in the mouth. A wide variety of foods contain glutamates.

Pure glutamates produce a relatively weak umami taste, but in combination with naturally occurring substances called nucleotides, the sensation of umami is greatly magnified. The nucleotides affect the tongue, altering the glutamate receptors and allowing them to send stronger signals to the brain. Combining ingredients rich in glutamates with ingredients rich in nucleotides can heighten the savory, umami taste in countless dishes.

Glutamates (milligrams per 100 grams)

Kombu	2240
Parmigiano-Reggiano	1680
Soy Sauce	1100
Tomato Paste	556
Cured Ham	340
Tomatoes	246
Garlic	112
Onions	102
Red Wine	122

Nucleotides (milligrams per 100 grams)

Anchovies	300 (+4300 mg glutamates)
Chicken	288
Pork	262
Sardines	193 (+300 mg glutamates)
Tuna	188
Beef	94 (+100 mg glutamates)
Shrimp	92 (+45 mg glutamates)

The Science of Residual Cooking

Judging when meat hits the desired doneness is tricky, in part because a big piece of meat doesn't have a single temperature; the exterior of the meat gets much hotter than the interior. But what many cooks may not know is that because of how heat is transferred, food can continue to cook even after it has been removed from the heat source. This effect is called carryover cooking and is an important factor in determining when meat is ready to come out of the oven or off the grill.

During cooking, conduction causes heat to move from a hotter to a cooler region within a food. After removing meat from the oven or taking it off the grill, this transfer will slow, and eventually stop, as internal and external temperatures approach each other and equal out. But this heat transfer can result in a significant 5- to 10-degree increase in the internal temperature of a large roast, bringing it from a perfect pink to a disappointing gray. This is why we advise you to remove meat from the heat when it reaches a point about 10 degrees away from your desired temperature and then let it rest until it reaches the perfect doneness (see page 352 for more information).

CHARTING THE TEMPERATURE OF MEAT
Just before our pork roast left the oven, its exterior registered 270 degrees while its interior had just reached 140 degrees. With time, the internal temperature continued to rise as the surface heat rapidly decreased. After 15 minutes, the internal temperature reached 150 degrees, surpassing the 130 degrees of the exterior.

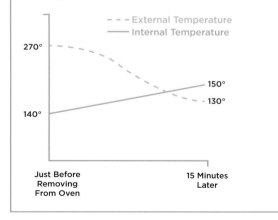

The Science of Resting Meat

Meat is mostly water (the rest is protein and fat). Most of this water is referred to as "bound water" because the proteins in the meat trap the water molecules inside. As a result, a piece of raw beef will not shed liquid when you cut it up. However, if you slice into a just-cooked steak, suddenly a flood of juices will cover the cutting board. What's happening?

When meat is heated, the protein molecules inside it begin to chemically bond with each other, causing them to compress and contract. A single muscle fiber can shrink to as little as half of its original volume during the cooking process. When these proteins contract, they squeeze out part of the liquid trapped within their structures, which then moves into the spaces created between them. But the contraction process is at least partly reversible: When you allow cooked meat to rest, the proteins relax and some of the expelled moisture moves back in. As a result, rested meat holds on to more of its natural juices, making the meat seem less dry and more tender.

JUICES LOST WHEN ROASTS ARE SLICED AFTER COOKING

Sliced Immediately   Rested 10 Minutes   Rested 20 Minutes   Rested 30 Minutes   Rested 40 Minutes

The Science of Frying

Many cooks shy away from frying, thinking that the technique adds loads of fat to their food. We put this notion to the test. We heated 3 cups of fat to 350 degrees in a 12-inch skillet, pan-fried a whole chicken, and poured back almost exactly 3 cups of fat after frying. We conducted the test a number of times to confirm the findings, and each time found ourselves with nearly the same amount of fat before and after.

The explanation is simple: If the water in the food you are frying is kept above the boiling point (212 degrees), the outward pressure of the escaping water vapor keeps oil from soaking into the food. If the frying oil is not hot enough, on the other hand, it will seep into the food, making it greasy. The key is to get the oil hot enough at the start (350 degrees works well) to maintain a temperature (between 250 and 300 degrees) during cooking that will keep the moisture in the food, in essence, boiling.

For fearless frying, choose a good-quality oil with a high smoke point, like our top choice, refined peanut oil. Frying oil can transfer flavors from food to food, so remember what you've cooked in the oil. As a rule, we discard oil in which fish is fried; multiple batches of chicken or potatoes may be cooked in the same oil, but oil used for doughnuts should only be used for doughnuts. The oil should also be kept clean when frying: skim away any detritus and keep salt and/or water out of the oil. And, lastly, pay keen attention to oil temperature: If it gets too hot, the oil will quickly deteriorate.

The right frying temperature prevents greasiness.

The Science of Gluten

Gluten—an elastic protein that has the ability to trap air, much like a balloon—is formed when two important proteins in wheat flour, glutenin and gliadin, bond together in the presence of water. We designed a simple experiment to demonstrate the inner workings of gluten.

We made two basic doughs by mixing flour and water in a food processor until a smooth ball formed. For one dough we used cake flour, which contains between 6 and 8 percent protein, and for the other one we used bread flour, which usually runs from 12 to 14 percent protein. After making the doughs, we placed each in a mesh strainer and massaged them under running water to wash away all the starch. Once the water ran clear (a sign that the starch was gone), we were essentially left with two piles of pure gluten.

Low-protein cake flour formed a very small amount of sticky, weak gluten. This characteristic is a boon to cakes and muffins, in which too much gluten can turn the crumb unappealingly tough. High-protein bread flour formed a large ball of highly resilient, rubbery gluten that could be stretched very thin

without tearing. We use high-protein bread flour for breads because it develops a lot of very flexible gluten, which acts like a balloon, trapping air and creating higher-rising loaves. All-purpose flour, as its name suggests, is good for a lot of foods that fall in between these extremes—such as pie dough, heartier muffins, and cookies.

A CLOSER LOOK AT GLUTEN

BREAD FLOUR VERSUS CAKE FLOUR
When you rinse away all the starch from bread flour, there's a lot of gluten left behind. Remove the starch from low-protein cake flour and there's not much of anything left.

The Science of Fat

Essentially, fat means flavor. Fat is not only an efficient carrier of flavor, it also dissolves flavor components, carrying them into sauce and other surrounding ingredients. Some meat scientists claim that if you removed all of the fat from meat you could not tell the difference between, say, pork and beef because so many of the flavor components reside in the fat. Fat also gives flavors roundness and, by coating your mouth, lets you savor them. This is why adding a fat (such as butter, sour cream, cheese, or oil) to an overly spicy dish can help counteract the offending ingredient and balance out the flavors.

This also explains why animal fats taste so good. In refined oils such as pure olive oil, many of the volatile fatty acids and aroma compounds have been stripped away to make a neutral-tasting oil that will work in a variety of applications. Meanwhile, unrefined oils like extra-virgin olive oil have plenty of flavor, but because some of their volatile fatty acids and aroma compounds evaporate when

exposed to heat, they lose most of it after a few minutes of cooking. But when the fatty acids in an unrefined animal fat are exposed to heat, they oxidize to form new flavor compounds that actually improve flavor and make it taste more complex.

While fat is flavorful, recent studies have shown that it also activates parts of the brain that influence how flavors are perceived. In particular, it has a dulling effect on taste. This means that you need more stimulus from other tastes in order to perceive them when there is more fat present. This explains why fattier meat needs more salt in order to taste properly seasoned. Fat doesn't reduce your ability to perceive odor (which is most of flavor), nor your ability to perceive the taste of the fat itself, but it does dull your perception of other tastes, including saltiness. So when you season meat, remember to use a heavier hand on fatty burgers than you would on moderately fatty meats like strip steak. Use a lighter hand on lean meats like turkey breast and pork loin.

The Science of Sugar

Sugar can be a single molecule made up of carbon, hydrogen, and oxygen—like glucose and fructose. Other sugars, like sucrose, are made of two or more molecules, like one glucose and one fructose, tied together with chemical bonds. Table sugar, for example, consists of virtually pure sucrose. Sucrose is abundant in many plants, especially fruits.

Sugar is key in baking because of its effect on moisture. Sucrose is hygroscopic, which means it has an affinity for water molecules. When water and sugar are combined, they link together and form hydrogen bonds. As a result, table sugar will hold on to moisture in food. Because of this tendency, sugar can slow the evaporation of moisture from cookies and cakes as they bake, which makes a tremendous difference when it comes to producing moist, tender baked goods.

In addition, when sucrose is heated along with some acid, it breaks back down into two simple sugars, glucose and fructose. When this happens, the result is called an invert sugar. Because fructose does not easily crystallize in the presence of glucose, invert sugars are always viscous liquids.

A benefit of invert sugar comes into play when making, for example, chewy cookies. Invert sugar is especially hygroscopic, pulling water from wherever it can be found, the best source being the air. Because brown sugar has more invert sugar than granulated sugar does, it is our sugar of choice when baking chewy cookies—especially because invert sugar keeps on drawing in moisture even after cookies have been baked, thus helping them to stay chewy as they cool

THE EFFECT OF SUGAR ON TEXTURE

BROWN SUGAR VERSUS WHITE SUGAR
The cookie made with brown sugar (left) baked up chewy and easily bent around a rolling pin. The cookie made with white sugar (right) emerged from the oven crisp and dry, and snapped immediately when bent.

The Science of Yeast

Yeast is a plant-like living organism. Its function in baked goods is to consume sugars and starches in the flour and convert them into carbon dioxide and alcohol, which creates lift and flavor. This process is known as fermentation. Flavor compounds and alcohol—byproducts of fermentation—give yeasted bread its characteristic aroma and flavor. A small amount of honey or sugar is sometimes added to dough to enhance the fermentation process, as yeast grows faster and better when it has enough food (sugar) to feed on. Warm water (about 110 degrees) is also necessary to activate dry yeast; very hot or cold water may impair its functioning.

Heat is generated during fermentation and rising, and punching the dough down during kneading mixes the warmer dough (in the center) with the cooler dough (on the outside edges), thus normalizing the overall temperature. Punching down also releases any excess carbon dioxide, breaks apart yeast particles that are clinging together, and redistributes the sugars, giving the yeast a refreshed food source. After punching down, the dough is often given a second rise,

which is accomplished more quickly because there is more yeast at work.

During the first few minutes of baking, the alcohol (formed earlier during fermentation) evaporates, gases expand, and bubbles enlarge, fostering more rise. This is referred to as oven spring. The yeast cells are killed off during the first few minutes in the oven.

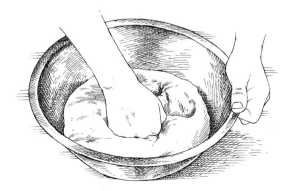

Punching down helps yeast do its job.

The Science of Leaveners

Quick breads, muffins, and biscuits as well as cookies and most cakes get their rise from chemical leaveners—baking soda and baking powder—rather than yeast. Chemical leaveners react with acids to produce carbon dioxide, the gas that causes these baked goods to rise.

To do its work, baking soda, which is alkaline, relies on acid in the recipe, provided by ingredients such as buttermilk, sour cream, yogurt, or molasses. When baking soda and an acid interact, they immediately begin to produce carbon dioxide, forming bubbles within the batter or dough.

Baking powder, on the other hand, is nothing more than baking soda (about one-quarter to one-third of the total makeup) mixed with a dry acid, such as cream of tartar, and double-dried cornstarch. The cornstarch absorbs moisture and keeps the baking soda and dry acid apart during storage, preventing premature production of the gas. When baking powder becomes wet, the dry acid comes into contact with the baking soda, producing carbon dioxide. Cooks use baking powder rather than baking soda when there is no natural acidity in the batter.

There are two kinds of baking powder. A single-acting baking powder has only one acid combined with the baking soda—a quick-acting acid that begins to work when liquid is added to the batter. A double-acting baking powder (virtually all supermarket brands) has two or more acids added to the baking soda. One of the acids (often sodium aluminum sulfate, also known as alum) begins to work only after the dish is put in the oven, when its temperature has climbed above 120 degrees. We recommend using double-acting baking powder in all recipes. Baked goods made with double-acting baking powder rise higher since most of the rise with baking powder occurs at oven temperatures. Also, we have found that single-acting baking powder doesn't provide sufficient leavening for doughs with little liquid.

In many of our recipes, we use both baking soda and baking powder because the combination gives better control over how fast gas is released as well as the alkalinity of the dough.

TWO LEAVENERS ARE BETTER THAN ONE

BAKING POWDER ALONE
Drop biscuits made with only one leavener emerged from the oven smooth and light-colored, with a decidedly bland flavor.

BAKING SODA AND BAKING POWDER
The drop biscuits made with both leaveners finished craggy and browned, and had better flavor.

The Science of Alcohol

We are frequently asked how much alcohol is cooked off from wine, beer, and spirits used to flavor dishes. The common belief is that the alcohol (ethanol) completely burns off with time or direct heat, but it's not that simple. When alcohol and water mix, they form a solution called an azeotrope—a mixture of two different liquids that behaves as if it were a single compound. Even though alcohol evaporates at a lower temperature than water, the vapors coming off of an alcohol-water azeotrope will contain both alcohol and water—they become inextricably mixed.

The amount of alcohol that evaporates from a dish will depend on cooking time and technique. A dish that is cooked covered will retain more alcohol than one cooked without a lid. If the surface of the liquid is not ventilated, alcohol vapor will accumulate, reducing further evaporation. As long as a liquid starts with an alcohol content higher than 5 percent, the final alcohol content will remain at about 5 percent. One way to quickly reduce the amount of alcohol in a liquid is to ignite the vapors that lie above the pan, a technique known as flambéing (see page 222 for more information). In the case of a flambé, the addition of heat (not just the flame from a match) can make a significant difference in the strength of the finished sauce. We found that brandy ignited over high heat retains 29 percent of its original alcohol concentration, while brandy flamed in a cold pan held 57 percent. Though it is possible to remove the majority of alcohol in food through cooking, traces will almost always remain.

A wide, uncovered pan facilitates the process by which alcohol cooks off.

The Science of Salt

Salt may well be the most important ingredient in cooking. It is one of our five basic tastes, and a nutrient our body cannot live without. It adds an essential depth of flavor to food, and we add it to almost every single dish. Salt has the ability to change the molecular makeup of food and is used to preserve and to add moisture to meat. Salt's two basic ions—sodium and chloride—are small, nimble ions with positive and negative charges, respectively, that can easily penetrate food.

Whether mined from underground salt deposits or obtained by evaporating seawater, salt in its most basic form is the same: sodium chloride. What distinguishes one salt from another is texture, size, and mineral content. These qualities can affect how a salt tastes and how it interacts with foods.

Table salt consists of tiny, uniformly shaped crystals created during rapid vacuum evaporation. Because of its fine grains, table salt dissolves easily. Coarse-grain kosher salt is raked during the evaporation process to yield flaky crystals originally used for koshering meat. The large grains distribute easily and cling well. Sea salt is the product of seawater evaporation—a time-consuming, expensive process that yields irregularly shaped, mineral-rich flakes that vary in color but only slightly in flavor.

Table Salt

Kosher Salt

Sea Salt

MASTERING BASIC PREP AND KEY TECHNIQUES

Small variables can have a significant effect on your finished recipe. The best tools and ingredients won't save you if you don't employ strong fundamental technique at every step of the process. Here are our guidelines for everything from washing greens to frosting a layer cake to help you turn out perfect food each and every time.

HOW TO PREPARE VEGETABLES A–Z

Whether you are simply steaming a vegetable or using it as one component of a more involved recipe, usually some basic prep is required. True, you might cook a vegetable any number of ways—for example, a potato could be fried, boiled, mashed, or roasted—but generally there are some standard prep steps you need to do first. After years of peeling, seeding, and chopping vegetables in the test kitchen, we've found the following methods are the easiest and most efficient ways to prepare a number of vegetables for myriad uses.

Artichokes Preparing

1 Grasp artichoke by stem and hold horizontal to counter. Use kitchen shears to trim pin-sharp thorns from tips of leaves, skipping top 2 rows.

2 Rest artichoke on cutting board. Holding base in your hand, cut off top 2 rows of leaf tips with chef's knife.

3 Cut stem flush with base of bulb. To prevent browning, drop trimmed artichoke into bowl of water mixed with juice of 1 lemon until ready to steam.

Asparagus Trimming

1 Remove 1 stalk of asparagus from bunch and bend it at thicker end until it snaps.

2 With broken asparagus as guide, trim tough ends from remaining asparagus bunch using chef's knife.

Avocados Cutting Up

 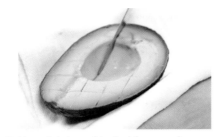 

1 After slicing avocado in half around pit with chef's knife, lodge edge of knife blade into pit and twist to remove. Use large wooden spoon to pry pit safely off knife.

2 Use dish towel to hold avocado steady. Make ½-inch crosshatch incisions in flesh of each avocado half with knife, cutting down to, but not through, skin.

3 Insert soupspoon between skin and flesh and gently scoop out avocado cubes.

Bell Peppers Cutting Up

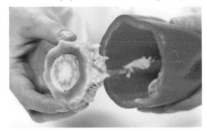  

1 Slice off top and bottom of pepper and remove seeds and stem.

2 Slice down through side of pepper.

3 Lay pepper flat, trim away remaining ribs and seeds, then cut into pieces or strips as desired.

Bok Choy Preparing

1 Trim bottom 1 inch from head of bok choy. Wash and pat leaves and stalks dry. Cut leafy green portion away from either side of white stalk.

2 Cut each white stalk in half lengthwise, then crosswise into thin strips.

3 Stack leafy greens and slice crosswise into thin strips. Keep sliced stalks and leaves separate.

Broccoli Cutting Up

1 Place head of broccoli upside down on cutting board and use chef's knife to trim off florets very close to heads.

2 Slice larger florets into bite-size pieces by slicing through stem.

3 Cut away tough outer peel and square off stalks using chef's knife, then slice stalks into pieces.

Broccolini Trimming

For any stems ½ inch or thicker, use paring knife to trim bottom 2 inches from stems.

Broccoli Rabe Trimming

Trim off and discard thick stalk ends (usually bottom 2 inches of each stalk).

Brussels Sprouts Preparing

Peel off any loose or discolored leaves and use paring knife to slice off bottom of stem end, leaving leaves attached.

Cabbage Shredding

1 Cut cabbage into quarters, then trim and discard hard core.

2 Separate cabbage into small stacks of leaves that flatten when pressed.

3 Use chef's knife to cut each stack of leaves into thin shreds (you can also use slicing disk of food processor to do this).

Carrots Cutting on Bias and into Matchsticks

1 Slice peeled carrot on bias into 2-inch-long oval-shaped pieces.

2 For matchsticks, lay ovals flat on cutting board, then slice into 2-inch-long matchsticks, about ¼ inch thick.

Cauliflower Cutting Up

1 Pull off any leaves, then cut out core of cauliflower using paring knife.

2 Separate florets from inner stem using tip of paring knife.

3 Cut larger florets into smaller pieces by slicing through stem.

Celery Chopping Quickly

Using chef's knife, trim leaves from top of celery. Chop across bunch until you have desired amount.

Celery Root Peeling

1 Using chef's knife, cut ½ inch from both root end and opposite end.

2 To peel, cut from top to bottom, rotating celery root while removing wide strips of skin.

Corn Cutting Kernels

After removing husk and silk, stand ear upright in bowl and use paring knife to slice kernels off of cob.

Corn Preparing for Grilling

1 Remove all but innermost layer of husk from each ear of corn.

2 Use scissors to snip off tassel.

Cucumbers Seeding

Halve peeled cucumber lengthwise. Run spoon inside each half to scoop out seeds and surrounding liquid.

Endives Preparing for Braising

1 Trim off discolored end of endive (cut thinnest slice possible so leaves remain intact).

2 Cut endive in half lengthwise through core end.

Fennel Preparing

1 Cut off stems and feathery fronds. Trim thin slice from base and remove any tough or blemished outer layers from bulb.

2A For braising or grilling, slice bulb vertically through base into ½-inch-thick slices, making sure to leave core intact.

2B For sautéing, roasting, or salads, cut bulb in half through base, then use paring knife to remove core. Slice each half into thin strips, cutting from base to stem end.

Fresh Herbs Preparing

A To mince, place your hand on knife handle and rest fingers of your other hand on top of blade. Use rocking motion, pivoting knife as you chop.

B For rosemary or thyme with thin stems, chop stems with leaves. For thick stems, run your thumb and forefinger along stem to release leaves.

C To shred (or chiffonade) basil, stack several leaves on top of one another. Roll them up, then slice roll crosswise into shreds.

Garlic Mincing

Garlic Mincing to a Paste

1 Trim root end, then crush clove between side of chef's knife and cutting board to loosen papery skin.

2 Using 2-handed chopping motion, run knife over garlic repeatedly to mince it.

Sprinkle minced garlic with salt, then scrape blade of knife back and forth until garlic forms sticky paste.

Green Beans Trimming

Greens Washing

Line beans up on cutting board and trim ends with 1 slice.

Fill salad spinner with cool water, add greens, and swish around. Lift greens out. Drain water. Repeat until greens are completely clean.

Ginger Preparing

1 To quickly peel knob of ginger, hold it firmly against cutting board and use edge of dinner spoon to scrape away thin brown skin.

2 To grate ginger, peel small section then grate peeled portion using rasp-style grater, using unpeeled ginger as handle.

3 For smashed coins of ginger, slice peeled ginger crosswise into coins, then use corner of heavy pan or mallet to gently smash ginger.

Hearty (Winter) Greens Preparing Swiss Chard, Kale, or Collard Greens

1 Cut away leafy portion from stalk or stem using chef's knife.

2 Stack several leaves and either slice crosswise or chop into pieces according to recipe.

3 If using chard stems in recipe, cut into pieces as directed after separating from leafy portion. (Discard collard and kale stems.)

Leeks Preparing

1 Trim and discard root and dark green leaves.

2 Cut trimmed leek in half lengthwise, then slice crosswise into ½-inch-thick pieces.

3 Rinse cut leeks thoroughly to remove dirt and sand using salad spinner or bowl of water.

Mushrooms Preparing

1 Rinse mushrooms under cold water just before cooking. If eating raw, simply brush dirt away with cloth.

2 Stems on white mushrooms or cremini can be trimmed and cooked with caps. Stems on shiitakes and portobellos should be removed.

Mushrooms Removing Gills

When cooking portobello mushrooms in soups and stews, use soupspoon to scrape gills off underside of mushroom cap.

Onions Chopping

1 Halve onion through root end, then peel onion and trim top. Make several horizontal cuts from 1 end of onion to other but don't cut through root end.

2 Make several vertical cuts. Be sure to cut up to but not through root end.

3 Rotate onion so root end is in back; slice onion thin across previous cuts. As you slice, onion will fall apart into chopped pieces.

Potatoes Cutting into Evenly Sized Pieces

1 Cut thin sliver from 1 side of potato. Set potato on cut side and slice crosswise into even planks.

2 Stack several planks and cut crosswise, then rotate 90 degrees and cut crosswise again to create evenly sized pieces.

Shallots Mincing

1 Make closely spaced horizontal cuts through shallot, leaving root intact.

2 Next, make several vertical cuts through shallot.

3 Finally, slice shallot thin crosswise, creating fine mince.

Snow & Snap Peas Trimming

Use paring knife and thumb to snip off tip of pod and pull along flat side to remove string at same time.

Tomatoes Seeding

1 Halve tomato through equator.

2 Use your finger to pull out seeds and surrounding gel.

Tomatoes Peeling

1 Score X at each tomato's base using paring knife. Using slotted spoon, lower tomatoes into pot of boiling water. Boil for 30 to 60 seconds, just until skin at X begins to loosen.

2 Using slotted spoon, quickly transfer tomatoes to prepared ice bath and let cool for 1 minute.

3 Starting at X, use paring knife to remove loosened peel in strips.

Tomatoes Coring and Dicing

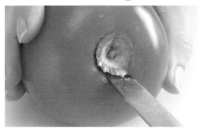

1 Remove core of tomato using paring knife.

2 Slice tomato crosswise.

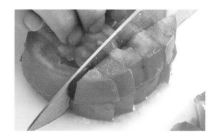

3 Stack several slices of tomato, then slice both crosswise and widthwise into pieces as desired.

Winter Squash Cutting Up Butternut Squash

1 After peeling squash, use chef's knife to trim off top and bottom and then cut squash in half where narrow neck and wide curved bottom meet.

2 Cut neck of squash into evenly sized planks according to recipe.

3 Cut planks into evenly sized pieces according to recipe.

4 Cut base in half lengthwise. Scoop out and discard seeds and fibers. Slice each base half into evenly sized lengths according to recipe.

5 Cut lengths into evenly sized pieces according to recipe.

Winter Squash Seeding Safely

1 Set squash on damp dish towel. Position cleaver on skin of squash. Strike back of cleaver with mallet. Continue to hit cleaver until it cuts completely through squash.

2 Using soupspoon, scoop out and discard seeds.

Zucchini Seeding

Halve zucchini lengthwise. Run small spoon inside each zucchini half to scoop out seeds.

HOW TO MAKE A VINAIGRETTE

In addition to dressing greens, vinaigrettes can be used to sauce chicken, fish, or vegetables. Our vinaigrette is especially well suited to mild, tender greens. Master this technique and you can vary the vinegar, the oil, and the seasonings to create dozens of dressings. Our vinaigrette can be refrigerated for up to two weeks. If you plan to store vinaigrette, keep it in a nonreactive container (such as glass).

Combine 1 tablespoon red, white, or champagne vinegar, 1½ teaspoons minced shallot, ½ teaspoon mayonnaise, ½ teaspoon Dijon mustard, ⅛ teaspoon salt, and pepper to taste in small bowl. Whisk until mixture is milky in appearance and no lumps of mayonnaise remain. Place 3 tablespoons extra-virgin olive oil in small measuring cup. Whisking constantly, very slowly drizzle oil into vinegar mixture. If pools of oil gather on surface as you whisk, stop addition of oil and whisk mixture well to combine, then resume drizzling oil in slow stream while continuing to whisk steadily. Vinaigrette should be glossy and lightly thickened.

1 Combine Vinegar and Mayonnaise

2 Whisk Well

3 Put Oil in Measuring Cup

4 Drizzle in Oil

HOW TO DRESS A SALAD

Once you make your vinaigrette, the route to a properly dressed salad requires a few simple steps. To avoid overdressing, drizzling and tossing a couple of times is the best way to go. For the freshest salad, make sure to dress your greens just before serving. Also, for just a hint of garlic flavor, you can rub the inside of the salad bowl with half a clove of peeled garlic before adding the lettuce.

Tear leaves into bite-size pieces just before serving and place in wide, shallow salad bowl. You will need 2 cups of greens per person. Rewhisk dressing and drizzle small amount over greens. Using tongs, toss greens carefully until dressing is incorporated. Taste greens and, if necessary, add more dressing until greens are lightly coated.

1 Tear Greens into Pieces

2 Drizzle Dressing

3 Toss Greens

4 Taste and Add More Dressing

HOW TO CRACK AND SEPARATE EGGS

We strongly recommend that you separate eggs when they are cold. Yolks are more taut and less apt to break into the whites when cold. If a recipe calls for separated eggs at room temperature, separate the eggs while cold, cover both bowls with plastic wrap (make sure the wrap touches the surface of the eggs to keep them from drying out), and let them sit on the counter.

Crack side of egg against flat surface of counter or cutting board for clean break. To separate with shell, hold shell halves over bowl and gently transfer egg yolk back and forth between them, letting egg white fall between shells and into bowl. To separate with your hands, cup your hand over bowl, then open cracked egg into your palm. Slowly unclench your fingers to allow white to slide through and into bowl, leaving yolk intact in your palm. Use 3 bowls: Separate each egg over first bowl and let white fall in. Pour yolk into second bowl and then move white to third bowl before separating next egg.

1 Crack on Counter

2A Separate with Shell

2B Separate by Hand

3 Use Three Bowls

HOW TO WHIP EGG WHITES

Perfectly whipped egg whites begin with a scrupulously clean bowl—fat inhibits egg whites from whipping properly. Choosing the right bowl is essential too. The two best choices are stainless steel and, for those who have it, copper. Wash the bowl in soapy, hot-as-you-can-stand-it water, rinse with more hot water, and dry with paper towels before whipping.

Whip egg whites and pinch cream of tartar (with whisk attachment if using stand mixer) on medium-low speed until foamy, about 1 minute. Increase mixer speed to medium-high, adding sugar if called for. Continue to whip whites until soft and billowy. Turn off mixer and lift tip of whisk from whites. Soft peaks will droop slightly downward while stiff peaks will stand tall. Overbeaten whites will look curdled and separated. If you overbeat, you must start over with fresh whites.

1 Start Low

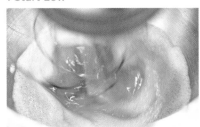

2 Increase Speed (and Add Sugar)

3 Slow Down and Assess

4 Avoid Overbeating

HOW TO HARD-COOK EGGS

Boiled eggs that start in cold water are hard to peel because the proteins in the white fuse to the membrane. We place cold eggs directly into hot steam, which helps the egg white proteins pull away from the membrane. The shell slips off easily to reveal smooth, unblemished hard-cooked eggs. Be sure to use large eggs that have no cracks and are cold from the refrigerator. If you don't have a steamer basket, use a spoon or tongs to gently place the eggs in the water. For a recipe that uses hard-cooked eggs, see our Classic Deviled Eggs (page 240) or All-American Potato Salad (page 242).

1 Boil Small Amount of Water

Bring 1 inch water to rolling boil in medium saucepan over high heat.

2 Add Eggs in Steamer Basket

Place eggs in steamer basket. Transfer basket to saucepan.

3 Cover and Cook

Cover, reduce heat to medium-low, and cook eggs for 13 minutes.

4 Make Ice Bath

When eggs are almost finished cooking, combine 2 cups ice cubes and 2 cups cold water in medium bowl.

5 Transfer Eggs to Ice Bath

Using tongs or spoon, transfer eggs to ice bath; let sit for 15 minutes.

6 Peel

Starting at wider end of each egg, peel away shell. If necessary, dunk egg back into ice bath to remove any remaining bits of shell.

HOW TO FRY EGGS

The key first step to perfect fried eggs is to use a nonstick skillet and preheat it on low heat for a full 5 minutes. Make sure you also cover the skillet as soon as the eggs are added. Since burners vary, it may take cooking an egg or two to determine the ideal heat setting for your stovetop. Follow visual cues and increase or lower the heat if necessary. The exact amounts for each ingredient and the skillet size depend on the number of servings; see the chart on page 349.

1 Preheat Skillet

Heat oil in nonstick skillet for 5 minutes. This ensures that it is evenly heated but not searing hot.

2 Crack Eggs into Bowls

While skillet heats, crack egg(s) into small bowls or teacups and season with salt and pepper, 2 eggs per bowl. Bowls make it possible to add eggs simultaneously.

3 Swirl Butter in Hot Skillet

Add unsalted butter to skillet. Quickly swirl to coat pan. Using butter in addition to oil adds richness.

4 Add Eggs

Working quickly, pour 1 bowl of eggs in 1 side of pan and second bowl of eggs in other side.

5 Cover It Up

Cover skillet immediately and cook for 1 minute. If you don't get lid on quickly, timing will be off.

6 Finish Off Heat

Remove skillet from heat and let stand, covered, 15 to 45 seconds for runny yolks, 45 to 60 seconds for soft but set yolks, and 2 minutes for medium-set yolks.

HOW TO SCRAMBLE EGGS

If you can crack an egg and stir, you can make scrambled eggs—at least in theory. But good scrambled eggs do require some finesse. Heat is what puffs up the eggs into large, moist curds, but heat will also make eggs rubbery and tough. Our technique focuses on the key steps to perfect scrambled eggs, such as using half-and-half to add extra fat and keep the eggs soft. The exact amounts for each ingredient and the skillet size depend on the number of servings; see the chart on page 349.

1 Add Extra Yolk(s)

Crack eggs into bowl and add extra yolk(s). Extra yolks give finished dish rich flavor and better texture.

2 Season Before Cooking

Add salt and pepper to bowl with eggs. Adding salt to raw (rather than cooked) eggs will make scrambled eggs more tender.

3 Add Dairy and Beat Lightly

Beat eggs, half-and-half, salt, and pepper in bowl with fork just until eggs are thoroughly combined, bubbles have formed, and color is pure yellow.

4 Heat Butter in Nonstick Skillet

Heat unsalted butter in nonstick skillet over medium-high heat until foaming subsides, swirling to coat skillet (butter should not brown).

5 Cook and Scrape

Add egg mixture and, using rubber spatula, firmly scrape bottom and sides of skillet until spatula leaves trail on bottom of skillet, 30 seconds to 2½ minutes.

6 Lower Heat

Reduce heat to low. Gently but constantly fold eggs until clumped and slightly wet, 30 to 60 seconds. Transfer eggs to warmed plates and season with salt to taste.

HOW TO POACH EGGS

The challenge when poaching eggs is to keep the white from fraying and to make sure that the yolk flows when the diner cuts into it. Our method takes the guesswork out of poaching eggs. This technique can be used to poach two eggs or 12 eggs, although timing will change based on the number of eggs added to the pan. The times in the chart on page 349 will yield set whites and slightly runny yolks. For firmer yolks, cook for an additional 30 to 60 seconds. All times are for large eggs.

1 Add Salt and Vinegar to Water

Fill 12-inch nonstick skillet with water. Add 1 teaspoon salt and 2 tablespoons distilled white vinegar. Vinegar helps proteins in whites set and reduces fraying.

2 Heat Water

Bring to boil over high heat. Eggs will be poached using residual heat; if water is merely simmering, there won't be sufficient heat to cook eggs properly.

3 Crack Eggs into Teacups

Crack 2 eggs into teacup. Repeat with more eggs and up to 3 more teacups, as desired. For dozen eggs, crack 3 eggs into each teacup. Teacups allow you to add eggs all at once.

4 Add Eggs

Simultaneously lower lips of cups into water and tip eggs into water. If using more than 1 teacup, hold cups in each hand and lower eggs into pan from opposite sides.

5 Cook Covered off Heat

Cover skillet, slide off heat, and cook until whites are cooked but yolks are still runny in center, 3½ to 6 minutes. Lid traps heat and ensures that eggs will cook properly.

6 Remove Eggs

Using slotted spoon, quickly and carefully remove eggs, one at a time and transfer to paper towel–lined plate. Season with salt and pepper to taste, and serve immediately.

HOW TO MAKE RICE PILAF

Rice pilaf should be fragrant, fluffy, and tender. We found that most recipes use too much water to avoid scorching, and the resulting pilaf is sticky and soft. Our recipe uses far less water and relies on very low heat and a nonstick saucepan to avoid scorching. The recipe here will serve six people; you can double it to serve 10 or 12; use 4½ cups water and 3 cups rice, and switch to a Dutch oven.

1 Rinse Rice

Place 1½ cups long-grain white, basmati, jasmine, or Texmati rice in fine-mesh strainer. Rinse under cold water until water runs clear, occasionally stirring. Drain.

2 Cook Onion

Cook 1 small finely chopped onion and ¼ teaspoon salt in 1 tablespoon olive oil or butter over medium heat until softened, about 5 minutes.

3 Toast Rice

Stir in rice and cook, stirring often, until edges of grains begin to turn translucent, about 3 minutes.

4 Use Less Water

Stir in 2¼ cups water and bring to simmer. Reduce heat to low, cover, and continue to simmer until rice is tender and water is absorbed, 16 to 18 minutes.

5 Steam Off Heat

Remove pot from heat. Lay folded dish towel under lid. Let sit for 10 minutes.

6 Fluff and Serve

Fluff rice with fork, season with salt and pepper to taste, and serve.

HOW TO COOK DRIED PASTA

Pasta is easy to cook, but hard to cook just right. You must pay attention to everything from the water-to-pasta ratio to the time between draining and saucing. Use plenty of water and a large pot—4 quarts of water in a 6-quart pot for 1 pound of pasta. We also recommend saucing the pasta in the pot to ensure evenly coated, hot pasta. Plan on 3 to 4 cups of sauce per pound of pasta. For recipes that use dried pasta, see our Pasta with Classic Bolognese Sauce (page 286) and Meatballs and Marinara (page 288).

1 Use Plenty of Water

To cook 1 pound pasta, bring 4 quarts water to rolling boil in Dutch oven or large pot.

2 Salt Water, Don't Oil It

Add 1 tablespoon salt to boiling water to add flavor. Don't add oil; it prevents sauce from adhering to pasta.

3 Add Pasta and Stir

Add pasta to boiling salted water and stir constantly for 1 to 2 minutes to prevent sticking.

4 Check Often for Doneness

Several minutes before pasta should be done, begin tasting it. When pasta is almost al dente, remove pot from heat.

5 Reserve Cooking Water, Then Drain

Reserve ½ cup cooking water (amount can vary based on recipe), then drain pasta in colander. Shake drained pasta once or twice to remove excess liquid.

6 Sauce in Pot

Return drained pasta to now-empty pot, add sauce, and toss using tongs or pasta fork. Add pasta cooking water as needed until sauce reaches proper consistency.

HOW TO CUT UP A WHOLE CHICKEN

Cutting up a whole chicken may seem like an intimidating process, but it's a handy technique to learn. For one thing, cutting up a chicken yourself is economical since you aren't paying for the labor to have someone cut up the chicken for you. If a recipe calls for four split breasts, you can simply butcher two whole chickens and save the thighs, wings, and drumsticks for another recipe. Second, butchering your own chicken ensures the parts are the right size and properly butchered—not always the case with the prepackaged pieces you buy at the supermarket.

1 Remove Each Leg Quarter

Discard chicken giblets. Using chef's knife, cut off legs. Start cutting where leg attaches to breast, then pop leg joint out of socket and cut through to detach leg.

2 Halve Each Leg Quarter

Cut each leg into 2 pieces—drumstick and thigh—by slicing through joint, marked by thin line of fat. (Skip if recipe calls for whole leg quarters.)

3 Remove Wings

Flip chicken over and remove wings by slicing through each wing joint. Then cut through cartilage around wingtip to remove and discard.

4 Remove Backbone

Turn chicken on its side and, using kitchen shears, remove backbone.

5 Split Breast

Flip breast skin side down and, using chef's knife, cut in half through breast plate, which is marked by thin white line of cartilage.

6 Cut Breast into Quarters

Flip each breast piece over and cut in half crosswise. Cutting each split breast in half crosswise speeds up cooking time.

HOW TO BUTTERFLY A WHOLE CHICKEN

Butterflying a chicken ensures that the thighs cook at the same rate as the more delicate white breast meat. If you are grilling or roasting, it's wise to brine the chicken prior to butterflying it to help protect the meat from drying out (see the brining chart on page 350). You can use this same method to butterfly a turkey. See our Crisp Roast Butterflied Chicken with Rosemary and Garlic (page 256).

Place chicken on cutting board breast side down and use kitchen shears to cut along each side of backbone to remove it. Flip chicken breast side up, tuck thin, small wingtips behind back of chicken to prevent burning, and then use heel of your hand to flatten chicken. Some recipes may also call for pounding chicken with mallet or meat pounder once you've flattened it by hand to ensure even thickness. Slip your fingers between skin and breast, loosening membrane. You can spread compound butter or spice rub under skin, or simply use salt and pepper.

1 Remove Backbone

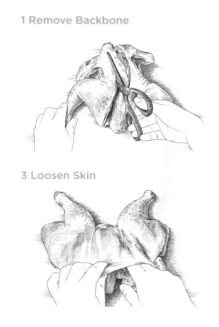

2 Flatten Chicken

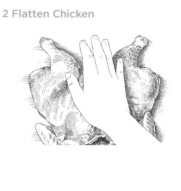

3 Loosen Skin

HOW TO MAKE CHICKEN CUTLETS

Store-bought chicken cutlets are often ragged and they vary widely in size and thickness. Instead, buy boneless, skinless chicken breasts and make the cutlets yourself. You'll not only guarantee your cutlets are of equal size but you'll also save a little money in the process.

Remove tenderloin from 6- to 8-ounce boneless, skinless chicken breast. Also trim any excess fat, gristle, or pieces of bone that might remain where wing and ribs were attached. Lay chicken breast flat on cutting board, smooth side facing up. Rest your hand on top of chicken and, using chef's knife, slice chicken in half horizontally. If you have time, you can freeze breasts for 15 minutes first to make slicing easier. Each cutlet should weigh 3 to 4 ounces and be about ½ inch thick. Place cutlets, smooth side down, on large sheet of plastic wrap. Cover with second sheet of plastic and pound gently to even thickness.

1 Remove Tenderloin

2 Slice Breasts in Half Crosswise

3 Separate Cutlets

4 Pound Cutlets to Even Thickness

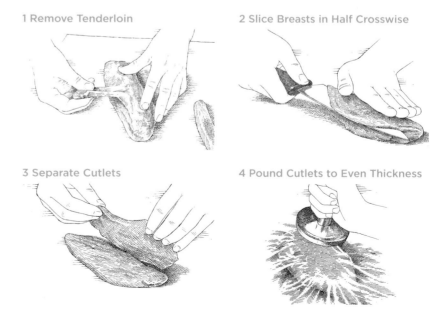

HOW TO TRIM BEEF TENDERLOIN

Trimmed beef tenderloins have the outer layer of fat and silverskin already removed. Trimmed tenderloins are convenient and can save you about 20 minutes of trimming time, but they are expensive— roughly $25 per pound. An untrimmed roast costs about $14 per pound (and often sells for as little as $9 per pound at warehouse clubs); given the huge savings in cost, we prefer to do the work ourselves.

Pull away outer layer of fat to expose fatty chain of meat. Pull chain of fat away from roast, cut it off, and discard chain. Scrape silverskin at creases in thick end to expose lobes, then trim by slicing under it and cutting upward. Remove remaining silverskin in creases at thick end. Turn tenderloin over and remove fat from underside.

1 Strip Outer Fat

2 Remove Fatty Chain

3 Peel Away and Trim Silverskin

4 Remove Fat from Underside

HOW TO TIE A ROAST

Most roasts are unevenly shaped, which leads to uneven cooking. For cylindrical cuts, such as beef tenderloin, we even out the thickness with a series of ties down the length. You can also fold the thin end under the roast and tie it in place. For squat roasts such as the eye round, we wrap longer pieces of kitchen twine around the perimeter to cinch in the sides and give the roast a neater shape.

For long roasts, fold thin end, if needed, under roast. Wrap piece of kitchen twine around roast and fasten with double knot, repeating along length of roast, spacing ties about 1½ inches apart. For squat roasts, wrap piece of kitchen twine around roast about 1 inch from bottom and tie with double knot. Repeat with second piece of twine, wrapping it about 1 inch from top.

1A For Long Roasts

1B For Squat Roasts

HOW TO PREPARE FISH

How you prepare fish for cooking depends on the recipe, the type of fish, and the cooking method. While we recommend buying thicker center-cut fillets when shopping for meaty fish like salmon, that's not really possible when shopping for thinner fish like flounder or sole. In that case, you can even out the cooking time by tucking the tails under. Sometimes we like to keep the skin on the fish and crisp it to add texture to the final dish, but in other cases we remove the skin prior to cooking.

A Tuck Tail Under

Fold thinner portion of fish under before cooking to ensure even cooking.

B Remove Pinbones (Fillet)

For fillet, run your fingers over surface to locate pinbones. Remove and discard.

C Remove Pinbones (Side of Salmon)

For large side of salmon, drape fish skin side down over inverted bowl to make pinbones easier to see. Grasp protruding pinbones with needle-nose pliers or tweezers and pull to remove.

D Cut Your Own Fillets

To ensure servings of equal size that will cook evenly, buy whole center-cut fillet and cut it yourself into smaller fillets.

E1 Skin Fillets

Using tip of boning knife or sharp chef's knife, cut skin away from fish at corner of fillet.

E2 Skin Fillets

When sufficient skin is exposed, grasp skin firmly with paper towel, hold it taut, and slice remaining skin off flesh.

HOW TO PREPARE SCALLOPS, MUSSELS, AND CLAMS

Shellfish you buy at the grocery store or fish market today require very little in the way of prep before cooking. If you are harvesting clams and mussels yourself, they may require a little more attention than those you buy at the market, but with several rinses of cold water and a little scrubbing (and debearding in the case of mussels) they will be ready to cook.

A Remove Muscle from Scallops

B Debeard Mussels

Use your fingers to peel crescent-shaped muscle that is often attached to side of scallop. Holding mussel in your hand, tug beard (weedy piece protruding from between shells) after placing it between flat side of paring knife and your thumb. Place mussels or clams in colander and scrub briefly with vegetable brush under cold running water. Discard any mussels that are cracked or open. Submerge clams in large bowl of cold water, then drain; repeat several times before cooking. If cooking soft-shell clams (such as razor clams and steamers), you must also strain cooking liquid (paper coffee filter works best). You may want to rinse cooked clams, too.

C Scrub Mussels, Hard-Shell Clams

D Soak Soft-Shell Clams

HOW TO PREPARE SHRIMP

Once shrimp is thawed, it is easy to both peel and devein. For most recipes, you will want to do both of those things. Whether or not you take the peel off the tail end of the shrimp depends on the recipe; sometimes the tail is left on for presentation purposes, and other times it needs to be removed. See our Pan-Seared Shrimp (page 280).

1 Defrost

2 Peel Shells

Thaw shrimp either overnight in refrigerator in covered bowl or in colander under cool running water for about 10 minutes. Break shell under swimming legs; legs will come off as shell is removed. Leave tail end intact if desired, or tug tail end to remove shell. If buying shrimp labeled "EZ-peel" (in which shell has been already split), simply pull shell around and off shrimp, leaving tail end intact if desired. Use paring knife to make shallow cut along back of shrimp to expose vein. Use tip of knife to lift vein out. Discard vein by wiping blade against paper towel. Dry thoroughly before cooking.

3 Devein with Knife

4 Discard Vein

HOW TO CARVE A WHOLE BIRD

While carving isn't difficult, there is definitely a correct way to approach it. Before you start, make sure that you've let the bird rest so the juices can redistribute. While you might think a carving knife is the proper tool for this task given its name, a chef's knife is, in fact, the better choice because of the maneuvering carving requires. The technique for carving a whole turkey is laid out here; you can also use the same steps to carve a whole roast chicken. See our Weeknight Roast Chicken (page 254) and Classic Roast Turkey (page 262).

1 Start with Leg Quarters

Remove any kitchen twine. Start by slicing turkey through skin between leg and breast to expose hip joint.

2 Remove Leg Quarters

Pull leg quarters away from carcass. Separate joint by gently pressing leg out to side and pushing up on joint. Carefully cut through joint.

3 Separate Drumsticks from Thighs

Cut through joint that connects drumstick to thigh. Repeat on second side. Slice meat off drumsticks and thighs, leaving some skin attached to each slice.

4 Remove Wings

Pull wings away from carcass and carefully cut through joint between wing and breast to remove wings. Cut wings in half for easier eating.

5 Remove Breast Meat

Cut down along 1 side following breastbone, pulling meat away from bone as you cut. Continue until breast has been removed.

6 Slice Breast Meat

Cut breast meat crosswise into slices for serving.

HOW TO CARVE A SPIRAL-SLICED HAM

Spiral-sliced bone-in half ham is our favorite wet-cured ham because the meat is not pumped up with water (the label should read "ham with natural juices") and because it is so easy to carve.

Using tip of paring or carving knife, cut around bone to loosen attached slices. Using long carving knife, slice horizontally above bone and through spiral-cut slices, toward back of ham. Pull cut portion away from bone and cut between slices to separate fully. Beginning at tapered end, slice above bone to remove remaining chunk of meat. Flip ham over and repeat procedure for other side.

1 Loosen Slices

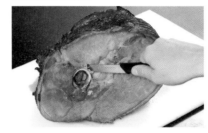

2 Slice Horizontally

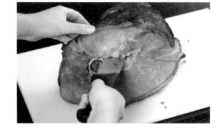

3 Remove from Bone

4 Remove Remaining Meat

HOW TO CARVE PRIME RIB

Prime rib is a hefty, expensive, and extraordinarily flavorful cut. If you shell out the extra money for this premium roast, make sure you carve it the right way. Don't be impatient and slice into the roast too soon. The meat needs time for the muscle fibers to relax. If you cut into the roast too soon, the muscle fibers won't be able to hold onto their juices, which will flood onto the carving board and result in a drier roast. Use these tips for our Best Prime Rib (page 272).

Using carving fork to hold roast in place, cut along rib bones to sever meat from bones. Set roast cut side down; carve meat across grain into thick slices.

1 Cut Meat off Ribs

2 Carve Meat

HOW TO CARVE A T-BONE STEAK

T-bone steak is named for the T-shaped bone that runs through the meat. This bone separates the flavorful strip, or shell (left) and the buttery tenderloin (right). The carving directions here will also work for a porterhouse steak, which is really just a huge T-bone steak with a larger tenderloin section. Like T-bone steak, porterhouse has well-balanced flavor and texture.

Cut along bone to remove large top loin, or strip, section. Cut smaller tenderloin section off bone. Cut each large piece crosswise into ½-inch-thick slices for serving.

1 Remove Strip

2 Remove Tenderloin

3 Slice Meat

HOW TO BONE A WHOLE FISH

If properly cooked, a whole fish should need just a few strategic cuts in order to cleanly, easily remove the meat from the bones in a single piece. A large, flat spatula is key for lifting the meat neatly off the bones.

Using sharp knife, make vertical cut just behind head from top of fish to belly. Make another cut along top of fish from head to tail. Use spatula to lift meat from bones, starting at head and lifting out fillet. Repeat on other side of fish. Discard head and skeleton.

1 Cut Top to Belly

2 Cut Head to Tail

3 Remove One Fillet

4 Remove Second Fillet

HOW TO FLAMBÉ

A flambé is the ignition of alcohol vapor above a pan, a reaction that generates significant amounts of heat, which in turn causes flavor-boosting chemical reactions in the food. Reactions involving sugar, such as caramelization and browning, occur at temperatures higher than 300 degrees. When flamed, the surface of the alcohol can reach above 500 degrees, which allows for this type of flavor development. A simmered alcohol, in contrast, maintains a steady temperature of about 180 degrees at its surface.

1 Be Prepared

Turn off exhaust fan, tie back long hair, and have lid ready to smother dangerous flare-ups.

2 Use Proper Equipment

Pans with flared sides allow more oxygen to mingle with alcohol vapors. If possible, use long chimney matches and light alcohol with your arm extended to full length.

3 Warm Alcohol

Heating alcohol to 100 degrees Fahrenheit (best achieved by adding alcohol to pan off heat, then letting it heat for 5 to 10 seconds) produces moderate, yet long-burning flames.

4 Light Alcohol Off Heat

If using gas burner, be sure to turn off flame to eliminate accidental ignitions near side of pan. Removing pan from heat also gives you more control over alcohol's temperature.

5 Prepare for Dangerous Flare-Ups

If flare-up occurs, slide lid over top of skillet (come in from side of, rather than over, flames). Let alcohol cool and start again.

6 If Alcohol Won't Light

Ignite alcohol in separate small skillet or saucepan; once flame has burned off, add reduced alcohol to remaining ingredients.

HOW TO SET UP A CHARCOAL GRILL

A charcoal grill offers some advantages over gas, including more options for custom fires and a better ability to impart smoke flavor. Make sure to position the grill on a flat surface, well away from the house or other structures. Never grill indoors or in the garage. Locate the grill away from the usual foot traffic, especially areas where kids or pets play. Also see How to Create Custom Grill Fires, page 224.

Remove cooking grate from grill and open bottom grill vent. Fill bottom of chimney starter with crumpled newspaper, set starter on charcoal rack, and fill with charcoal briquettes. Ignite newspaper and burn charcoal until briquettes on top are partly covered with layer of gray ash. Distribute briquettes onto grill as indicated in recipe. Set cooking grate in place, cover, and heat for about 5 minutes. Use grill brush to scrape grate clean. Using tongs, dip wad of paper towels in vegetable oil and wipe cooking grate several times. This seasoning must be reapplied every time you grill.

1 Get Coals Hot

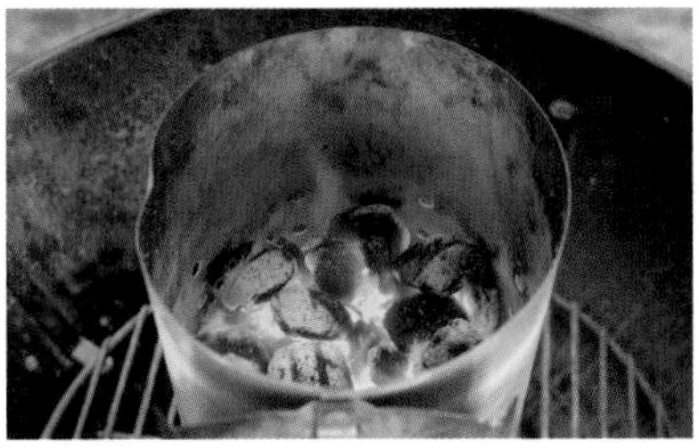

2 Get Grate Hot

3 Scrub Grate Clean

4 Oil Grate

HOW TO SET UP A GAS GRILL

Read your owner's manual thoroughly for directions regarding the order in which the burners must be lit. Make sure to position the grill on a flat surface, well away from the house or other structures. Never grill indoors or in the garage. Locate the grill away from the usual foot traffic, especially areas where kids or pets play. Also see How to Create Custom Grill Fires, page 224.

If grill is equipped with gas gauge or tank scale, check to make sure you have enough fuel. If grill doesn't have gauge, bring about 1 cup water to boil in teakettle or saucepan, then pour boiling water over side of tank. Place your hand on tank. Where water succeeds in warming tank, tank is empty; where tank remains cool to touch, there is fuel inside. Light with lid up, then cover grill and let it heat for about 15 minutes. Once grill is hot, scrape grate clean with grill brush. Using tongs, dip wad of paper towels in vegetable oil and wipe grate several times to prevent sticking. Adjust burners as directed in recipe to create custom grill fire.

1 Check Propane Level

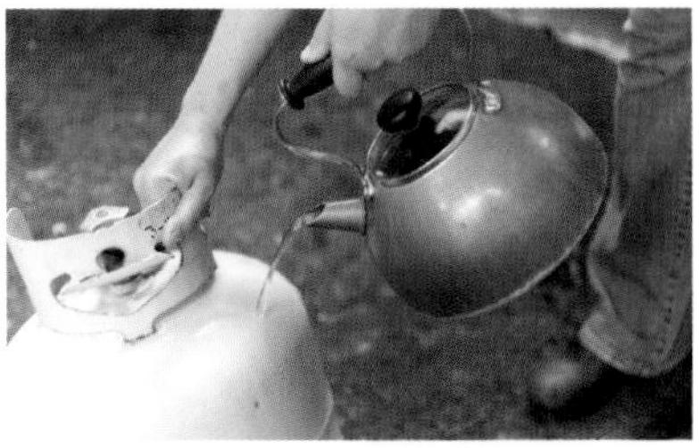

2 Light with Lid Up

3 Cover Grill and Get Grate Hot

4 Clean and Oil Grate

HOW TO CREATE CUSTOM GRILL FIRES

Different types of foods require different types of fires. For instance, a single-level fire is often used for small, quick-cooking foods like sausages and fish. Two-level fires and banked fires create several different heat zones, which allow for a variety of cooking applications including searing, gentle indirect cooking, and high-heat cooking over concentrated heat, depending on the setup. A gas grill's primary burner is the one that must be left on; see your owner's manual if in doubt.

A Single-Level Fire

CHARCOAL Distribute lit coals in even layer across bottom of grill. **GAS** After preheating, turn all burners to heat setting as directed in recipe.

B Two-Level Fire

CHARCOAL Distribute two-thirds lit coals over half of grill and remainder over other half. **GAS** After preheating, leave primary burner on high and turn other(s) to medium.

C Half-Grill Fire

CHARCOAL Distribute lit coals over half of grill in even layer. Leave other half of grill free of coals. **GAS** After preheating, adjust primary burner if directed in recipe and turn off other burner(s).

D Banked Fire

CHARCOAL Bank all lit coals steeply against one side of grill, leaving rest of grill free of coals. **GAS** After preheating, adjust primary burner as directed in recipe and turn off other burner(s).

E Double-Banked Fire

CHARCOAL Split lit coals between opposite sides of grill. Leave center empty. **GAS** After preheating, turn off all burners but primary burner and burner at opposite end of grill.

HOW TO USE WOOD ON A GRILL

Wood chips or chunks are essential for deep smoky flavor in barbecuing. Wood chips will work on either a charcoal or a gas grill, but chunks are suited only to charcoal fires since they must rest in a pile of lit coals. Soaked wood chunks can be added directly to lit charcoal, but wood chips require a little more prep before putting them on the fire. One medium chunk is equivalent to 1 cup of chips.

Place amount of chips or chunks specified in recipe in bowl and cover with water. Soak chips for 15 minutes; soak chunks for 1 hour. Drain. Using large piece of heavy-duty aluminum foil, wrap soaked chips in 8 by 4½-inch foil packet. (Make sure chips do not poke holes in packet.) Cut 2 evenly spaced 2-inch slits in top of packet. Packet can hold up to 2 cups of chips; if recipe calls for more, divide chips between multiple packets. For gas grill, place soaked and drained chips in disposable aluminum pan and add water to pan. Set pan on primary burner before lighting grill. For charcoal grill, place packet on coals as directed in recipe.

1 Soak Thoroughly

2A Wrap Chips in Foil

2B Use Disposable Pan for Gas Grill

3 Place Chips on Grill

HOW TO KNEAD DOUGH IN A MIXER

The goal of kneading is to create a strong network of cross-linked proteins that will allow the bread to expand without bursting, resulting in a bubbly, chewy crumb. We generally prefer using a stand mixer for this task. Many home bakers add excessive flour when trying to knead dough by hand, which compromises the texture of the baked loaf.

After kneading several minutes, evaluate consistency of dough. It should be starting to pull away from sides of bowl. If it is not, add flour, 1 or 2 tablespoons at a time, with mixer running, allowing 30 to 60 seconds between additions. It's not unusual to add as much as ¼ cup flour at this stage. Continue kneading as directed in recipe until dough has pulled away from sides of bowl and forms compact mass. Do not overknead.

1 Evaluate Dough Consistency

2 Add More Flour If Needed

3 Continue Kneading

4 Do Not Overknead

HOW TO KNEAD DOUGH BY HAND

If you don't own a mixer, you can still make great bread using just your hands. The trick is to use a rhythmic, gentle motion that stretches and massages the dough. Most dough will require 15 to 25 minutes of hand kneading to form a smooth, round ball. These instructions will work with all but the very wettest doughs, such as ciabatta, which really do require a stand mixer.

Whisk liquid ingredients together in medium mixing bowl. Whisk dry ingredients together in large mixing bowl. Mix liquid mixture into dry ingredients until dough comes together and looks shaggy. Turn dough onto lightly floured counter and shape into rough ball. Start each stroke by gently pressing dough down and forward using heel of your hand. Lift edge of dough farthest away from you and fold dough in half toward you. Press dough forward again using heel of your hand. When dough is finally smooth and elastic (after 15 to 25 minutes of hand kneading), transfer to greased bowl and let rise as directed in recipe.

1 Mix Dough

2 Press Down and Forward

3 Lift and Fold

4 Press Dough Forward

HOW TO SHAPE LOAF BREADS

It is important to work bread dough gently during the shaping process to preserve the air from the first rise. Don't use a rolling pin; your hands are a better bet. Make sure to flour them, as well as the counter. Note that loaf pan sizes vary, and even small differences will affect the loaf. Use the exact size specified in each recipe.

Scrape dough out of bowl and onto lightly floured counter. Using your hands, press dough into square. For 9 by 5-inch loaf pan, press dough into 9-inch square. For 8½ by 4½-inch loaf pan, press dough into 8½-inch square. Starting at side closest to you, roll dough into tight cylinder. Start by folding over edge of dough closest to you, then roll dough, tucking it under as you go. Once dough has been rolled into cylinder, pinch seam together to secure. This will help dough hold its shape as it proofs in loaf pan. Place dough seam side down in prepared loaf pan to help ensure that seam doesn't split open as loaf rises.

1 Shape Dough into Square

2 Roll Dough into Cylinder

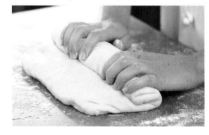

3 Pinch Seam

4 Transfer to Pan

HOW TO BROWN BUTTER

Browned butter, or *beurre noisette* (hazelnut butter) as it is called in French, is a key ingredient in many recipes. The French call it hazelnut butter because the butter takes on the flavor and aroma of toasted nuts as it browns. Browned butter is used in both baked goods and savory preparations; brightened with lemon juice, it can also serve as a simple sauce for fish or vegetables.

Cut butter into chunks and place in heavy-bottomed skillet or saucepan with light-colored interior. Turn heat to medium-high and cook, swirling pan occasionally, until butter melts and begins to foam. Continue to cook, swirling pan constantly, until butter is dark golden brown and has nutty aroma, 1 to 3 minutes. Immediately transfer browned butter to large heatproof bowl to avoid overcooking from residual heat.

1 Let It Foam

2 Swirl and Watch

3 Cool Quickly

HOW TO TOAST AND CHOP NUTS

You have two options for toasting nuts—a skillet or a rimmed baking sheet. We prefer to buy whole nuts or nut halves and then chop after toasting. If you have prechopped nuts, simply skip chopping. If you're storing nuts in the freezer, toasting times might be slightly longer than indicated.

For small batches, place nuts in empty skillet and heat to medium. Toast nuts, stirring occasionally, until fragrant and lightly browned, 2 to 5 minutes. For large batches, spread nuts in single layer over rimmed baking sheet. Toast in 350-degree oven, shaking sheet every few minutes, until nuts are fragrant and lightly browned, 5 to 10 minutes. Transfer toasted nuts to cutting board to cool. To chop with apple cutter, gather nuts into pile and press straight down with cutter. For knife method, shape damp dish towel into ring on cutting board, leaving enough room for nuts and knife blade. Chop nuts. This is especially helpful for rounded nuts.

1A Toast Small Batches on Stovetop

1B Toast Large Batches in Oven

2A Chop with Apple Cutter

2B Chop with Knife and Towel

HOW TO CHOP AND MELT CHOCOLATE

Most recipes that call for chocolate also call for chopping and melting that chocolate. If left in large chunks, the chocolate will melt unevenly and you increase the risk of scorching it. Small pieces melt faster and more evenly. Once the chocolate is chopped, you can use the old-fashioned stovetop method to melt it or you can streamline the operation in the microwave.

Hold chef's knife at 45-degree angle to 1 corner of chocolate block and bear down evenly. After cutting about 1 inch from corner, repeat with other corners. Or use 2-tined carving fork to split into smaller pieces. To melt on stovetop, place chopped chocolate in heatproof bowl set over saucepan of simmering water (water should not touch bowl). Adjust heat as necessary to maintain simmer, and stir until chocolate melts. To melt in microwave, place chopped chocolate in microwave-safe bowl and heat in microwave at 50 percent power for 1 minute. Stir chocolate and continue heating until melted, stirring every 30 seconds.

1A Chop with Knife

1B Break Up with Carving Fork

2A Melt on Stovetop

2B Melt in Microwave

HOW TO MAKE A FOIL SLING

Lining a pan with a foil sling (you can use parchment, if you prefer) prevents any casualties with brownies or bar cookies. Once cooled, the treats can be lifted easily from the pan and transferred to a cutting board in one piece. You should be able to slide the foil out from under the block and then cut it into tidy squares or rectangles. See our Cream Cheese Brownies (page 322).

Fold 2 long sheets of aluminum foil to be same width as baking pan. (If dish is rectangular, sheets will be of different widths.) Lay sheets of foil in pan, perpendicular to one another, with extra foil hanging over edges of pan. Push foil into corners and up sides of pan. Try to iron out wrinkles in foil, smoothing it flush with pan. Coat foil sling with vegetable oil spray, making sure to cover bottom and all four sides. After baking, use foil overhang to cleanly lift food from pan.

1 Fold and Line

2 Smooth Out Wrinkles

3 Grease Well

4 Use Overhang to Lift

HOW TO CREAM BUTTER

Many cake recipes require that you cream butter and sugar together until pale and fluffy. This makes the butter malleable and helps incorporate air into the batter, giving the cake lift. Starting this process with softened butter is a must, but don't let the butter get too warm; if the butter is soft and greasy it won't hold air when creamed. We prefer to use a stand mixer, but a handheld mixer will also work.

Let butter warm on counter until its temperature reaches 65 to 67 degrees. Softened butter should give slightly when pressed but still hold its shape. Using stand mixer fitted with paddle, beat softened butter with sugar until incorporated. Start with mixer at medium-low and gradually increase speed to medium-high. Stop mixer and scrape down sides of bowl as necessary with rubber spatula. Continue to beat butter and sugar until mixture is pale in color and fluffy in texture, about 3 minutes. Don't overbeat butter; if mixture begins to appear greasy or dense, stop mixer immediately.

1 Soften Butter

2 Beat Butter with Sugar

3 Continue Beating until Fluffy

4 Do Not Overbeat

HOW TO REVERSE-CREAM

For many cakes, we prefer a method known as "reverse creaming" rather than regular creaming. In reverse creaming, softened butter is beaten into the dry ingredients, coating the proteins in the flour with fat and thus minimizing gluten development. The result is a tender cake with a delicate crumb. We prefer to use a stand mixer, but a handheld mixer will also work.

Whisk dry ingredients together in bowl of stand mixer. Combine wet ingredients in large liquid measuring cup. Fit stand mixer with paddle and with mixer on low speed, add softened butter, one 1-inch piece at a time. Mix until only pea-size pieces remain, about 1 minute. Adding butter gradually ensures that proteins in flour are evenly coated with fat. Add half of liquid mixture, increase speed to medium-high, and beat until fluffy. Reduce speed to medium-low, add remaining liquid mixture, and beat until incorporated, about 30 seconds. Give batter final stir with rubber spatula.

1 Whisk Together Dry Ingredients

2 Combine Liquids

3 Beat in Softened Butter

4 Add Liquid in Stages

HOW TO PREPARE CAKE PANS

To ensure a dependable release every time, cake pans should be greased and floured and lined with parchment paper. The steps below show how to prepare a round cake pan; however, the same method can be used to prepare square or 13 by 9-inch cake pans. Don't skip this crucial step. See our Yellow Layer Cake (page 326).

Place cake pan on sheet of parchment paper and trace around bottom of pan with pencil or pen. Cut on inside of line so that round fits snugly inside pan. Evenly spray bottom and sides of cake pan with vegetable oil spray. Fit trimmed piece of parchment into pan. Paper prevents formation of tough outer crust and helps cake hold together when it is removed from pan. Spray parchment with oil spray, then sprinkle several tablespoons of flour into pan. Shake and rotate pan to coat evenly with flour. Once pan is coated, shake out excess flour.

1 Trace Circle

2 Grease Pan

3 Line Pan with Parchment Paper

4 Grease Parchment and Flour Pan

HOW TO USE A PASTRY BAG

A large pastry bag (roughly 18 inches long) will give you enough length to grip and twist the top. While canvas is traditional, we like materials such as plastic and coated canvas that are easier to clean. We recommend a round tip for writing, a star tip for decorating, and a large round tip for piping cookies. If you plan on decorating cakes often, you will want to invest in a more extensive set.

Holding bag in one hand, fold top down about halfway. Insert selected tip into point of bag and press it securely in place. Scrape frosting into bag until bag is half full. Don't overfill or you will end up squeezing frosting out of top and onto your hands. Pull up sides of bag, push down frosting, and twist tightly. Push down on bag to squeeze air out and move frosting into tip. Grab base of bag, twist, and squeeze to pipe out frosting. Practice briefly on sheet of parchment paper before decorating cake.

1 Fit Tip Inside Bag

2 Fill Bag

3 Squeeze Out Air

4 Practice First

HOW TO BAKE CAKE LAYERS

Consistency is key in producing a perfect layer cake. Weighing the pans is the simplest and easiest way to make sure the layers are even. Note that while a sheet cake cools in the pan for several hours, these cakes should only cool in the pan for 10 minutes. Also see How to Prepare Cake Pans, page 230, and How to Frost a Layer Cake, page 232. Use these tips on our recipe for Yellow Layer Cake (page 326).

Divide batter evenly between prepared pans. Gently tap pans on counter to release air bubbles; if left in batter these bubbles can cause tunnels in baked cake. Bake cake layers side by side on middle oven rack until toothpick inserted in center comes out clean, rotating position of cake pans at halfway mark in baking time. Transfer pans to wire racks and let cool for 10 minutes. Working with 1 pan at a time, set wire rack on top of pan. Flip cake out of pan onto wire rack. Flip cake onto second wire rack so that cake layer is right side up. Always cool cake layers completely before wrapping in plastic or frosting.

1 Divide Evenly, Then Tap On Counter

2 Test for Doneness

3 Cool Briefly in Pan

4 Turn Out to Finish Cooling

HOW TO CUT CAKE LAYERS

Some recipes call for cutting a baked cake layer into two thinner layers before frosting. For instance, most four-layer cakes actually require baking two cake layers, which are each halved. If the layers are cut unevenly, the thinner portion will be extremely delicate and can fall apart as you attempt to fill and frost the cake. Also see How to Frost a Layer Cake, page 232.

Measure height of cake. Use paring knife to mark midpoint at several places around sides of cake. If cake is seriously domed, trim domed top first. Using marks as guide, score entire circumference of cake with long serrated knife. Following score lines, run knife around cake several times, slowly cutting inward. Once knife is inside cake, use back-and-forth motion. Keep your hand on top of cake and make sure knife remains aligned with scoring around sides. Once knife cuts through cake, separate layers, gently inserting your fingers between them. Lift top layer and place it on counter.

1 Measure and Mark

2 Score Sides

3 Saw Slowly

4 Lift and Separate

HOW TO FROST A LAYER CAKE

A polished cake is easy if you have the right tools and techniques. Starting with flat, fully cooled layers is absolutely essential. If the layers are still warm, the frosting will start to melt. Regularly dipping the spatula into a glass of warm water will keep extra frosting from piling up and make sure the frosting is smooth. While not essential, a turntable-style cake stand elevates the cake, giving the baker a better view and making it possible to hold the spatula steady while rotating the stand. Also see How to Bake Cake Layers, page 231. Use these tips to frost our Yellow Layer Cake (page 326).

1 Remove Dome if Necessary

Using serrated knife, gently slice back and forth with sawing motion to remove domed portion from each cake layer. Brush crumbs off cake since they can mar frosting.

2 Prepare Platter and Anchor Cake

Cover edges of cake stand or platter with strips of parchment and anchor bottom layer with small dollop of frosting. Once cake is frosted, you can discard parchment.

3 Frost First Layer

Dollop large portion of frosting in center of cake layer. Spread frosting into even layer right to edge of cake.

4 Align Second Layer

Place second layer on top, making sure it is aligned with first layer. Don't push down on it or you risk squeezing frosting out sides of cake.

5 Frost Top, Then Sides

Frost top layer, pushing frosting slightly over edge of cake. Gently smear several tablespoons of frosting onto side of cake. Repeat until side is covered.

6 Smooth Out Rough Spots

Gently run edge of spatula around sides to smooth frosting. Remove strips of parchment. (If decorating frosted cake, leave parchment in place.)

HOW TO MAKE A CRUMB CRUST

A crumb crust is a classic choice in many single-crust pies. It's more durable than pie dough, making it the right choice for moist custard-based fillings. Graham crackers are the most common choice. For chocolate cookie crusts, we prefer Oreos. If using sandwich cookies instead of graham crackers, use only 4 tablespoons of melted, cooled butter and omit the sugar; the sweeter cookies don't need it.

Break 8 whole graham crackers (or 16 sandwich cookies) into rough pieces and place in food processor. Process to fine crumbs. Sprinkle 3 tablespoons sugar (if using) and 5 tablespoons melted, cooled butter over crumbs and pulse to incorporate. Sprinkle mixture into pie plate and use bottom of dry measuring cup to press evenly across bottom of plate. Then tightly pack crumbs against side of pie plate using side of measuring cup. Adjust oven rack to middle position and heat oven to 325 degrees. Bake until crust is fragrant and beginning to brown, 13 to 18 minutes. Use crust immediately or cool as directed in pie recipe.

1 Grind Crumbs

2 Add Butter

3 Shape into Crust

4 Bake until Just Browning

HOW TO ROLL OUT AND FIT PIE DOUGH

We recommend using a dowel-style rolling pin without handles and baking the pie in a tempered glass pie plate, such as Pyrex. Also see How to Make and Bake a Single-Crust Pie Shell, page 234; How to Make a Double-Crust Pie, page 235; and How to Make a Lattice Top, page 236. Use these tips to make our Lemon Meringue Pie (page 332) and Deep-Dish Apple Pie (page 334).

Flour counter. Roll dough outward from center into 12-inch circle, giving dough quarter turn after every few rolls. If making double-crust pie, leave second piece of dough in refrigerator while you roll out and fit bottom crust. Toss additional flour underneath dough as needed to keep dough from sticking. Loosely roll dough around rolling pin. Gently unroll dough over 9-inch pie plate, then lift dough and gently press into pie plate, letting excess hang over pie plate's edge. For double-crust pie, cover crust fitted in pie plate lightly with plastic wrap and refrigerate for at least 30 minutes before filling and topping with second crust.

1 Roll and Turn

2 Flour Generously

3 Roll Dough Around Pin

4 Fit Dough into Pie Plate

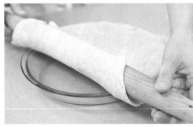

HOW TO MAKE AND BAKE A SINGLE-CRUST PIE SHELL

Although on rare occasions we might fill a single-crust pie shell raw, we typically partially or fully bake the crust before adding the filling. This ensures that the pie crust is perfectly brown, crisp, and flaky—not soggy—once the filling has been added and the pie has been finished. Read each recipe carefully and have the filling ready when the pie shell comes out of the oven if so directed. Also see How to Roll Out and Fit Pie Dough, page 233. Use these tips to make our Lemon Meringue Pie (page 332).

1 Make Thick Edge

Trim pie dough to hang ½ inch over lip of pie plate, then tuck overhang underneath itself to form tidy, even edge. From here, you have 2 options for finishing edge.

2A Finish with Fluted Edge

FOR FLUTED EDGE Using index finger of 1 hand and thumb and index finger of other hand, create fluted ridges perpendicular to edge of pie plate.

2B Finish with Ridged Edge

FOR RIDGED EDGE Press tines of fork into dough to flatten it against rim of pie plate.

3 Chill Pie Crust

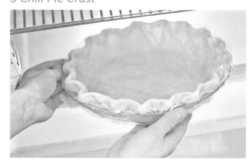

Wrap dough-lined pie plate loosely in plastic wrap. Place in freezer until dough is fully chilled and firm, about 30 minutes.

4 Line Crust with Foil, Weight, and Bake

Line chilled crust with double layer of aluminum foil, covering edges. Fill with pie weights. Bake in 375-degree oven until set and lightly colored, 25 to 30 minutes.

5 Remove Foil and Weights

Remove foil and weights. For partially baked crust, transfer to wire rack. For fully baked crust, return crust to oven and bake 10 to 12 more minutes. Transfer to wire rack.

HOW TO MAKE A DOUBLE-CRUST PIE

Double-crust pies do not require prebaking the crust. Instead the raw bottom crust is filled and the top crust is rolled out and used to seal the pie prior to baking. Once the bottom crust has been fit into the pie plate and chilled for 30 minutes (see How to Roll Out and Fit Pie Dough, page 233), you can fill the pie and add the second crust. Start the steps below after the bottom crust has been fitted into the pie plate. Use these tips to make our Deep-Dish Apple Pie (page 334).

1 Roll and Chill Top Crust

Remove dough from refrigerator. Roll into 12-inch circle on floured counter. Transfer to parchment-lined baking sheet and cover with plastic wrap. Refrigerate 30 minutes.

2 Unroll Top Crust over Filling

Loosely roll chilled top crust around rolling pin, then gently unroll over filled bottom crust. Trim overhanging dough ½ inch beyond lip of pie plate.

3 Create a Sturdy Edge

Pinch edges of top and bottom crusts firmly together. Tuck overhand under itself. Tucking sealed edges of top and bottom crusts down into pie plate ensures that seam won't split open in oven.

4 Crimp Edges

Use index finger of 1 hand and thumb and index finger of other hand to create fluted ridges perpendicular to edge of pie plate.

5 Cut Steam Vents

Use paring knife to cut at least 4 slits in top crust. (Very juicy pies might need more.) If you don't cut vents in top crust, steam will tear holes in crust.

6 Bake on Foil-Lined Baking Sheet

Place pie on rimmed baking sheet that has been lined with foil and bake on lowest oven rack.

HOW TO MAKE A LATTICE TOP

A lattice top is an attractive way to finish a double-crust pie. Although making a lattice top does require a bit more work than a regular double-crust pie, it serves a vital function in pies made with juicy summer fruits by allowing for maximum evaporation. Thus a lattice top is traditional with peach, cherry, and berry pies, but it is not recommended with drier fruits, such as apples, because all that evaporation can cause the fruit to become leathery. See How to Roll Out and Fit Pie Dough, page 233; start these steps after the bottom crust has been fitted into the pie plate.

1 Cut and Freeze Dough

Roll dough into 13 by 10-inch rectangle, then slice lengthwise into eight 13 by 1¼-inch strips. Cover with plastic and freeze until very firm, 30 minutes.

2 Start Weaving

Lay 4 strips of chilled dough parallel and evenly over filled bottom crust. Weave fifth strip in opposite direction, lifting every other strip to facilitate weaving.

3 Finish Weaving

Continue to weave remaining 3 strips of dough, one at a time, to create evenly spaced lattice, rotating pie as needed. Adjacent strips follow opposite patterns.

4 Trim Strips

Let dough thaw and soften for 5 to 10 minutes, then use kitchen shears to trim overhanging edges of each strip to leave about ½ inch hanging over edge of pie.

5 Tuck Ends Under

Press edges of bottom crust and ends of lattice strips together, then fold pressed edge under, tucking it inside pie plate.

6 Crimp Edge

Crimp dough evenly around edge of pie plate, using index finger of 1 hand and thumb and index finger of other hand.

HOW TO MAKE A CLASSIC TART SHELL

Rolling out tart dough is pretty much the same as rolling out pie dough, although because the dough can be sticky due to the heavy cream and egg yolk in the dough, it's best to roll out tart dough between two pieces of parchment paper. Otherwise, the rolling out process is quite similar. However, fitting tart dough into its pan is a bit different from fitting pie dough into a pie plate, plus tarts require you to blind-bake the tart shell. Use these tips to make our Rustic Walnut Tart (page 336).

1 Gently Unroll Dough

Roll refrigerated 11-inch circle of dough loosely around rolling pin, then unroll over 9-inch tart pan with removable bottom.

2 Fit Dough

Lifting edge of dough, ease it into pan. Press dough into fluted sides of pan and into corners. Don't try to place and fit dough simultaneously.

3 Trim Excess Dough and Patch as Needed

Run rolling pin over top of tart pan to remove any excess dough and make clean edge. If parts of edge are too thin, reinforce using excess dough.

4 Freeze Before Baking

Wrap dough-lined tart pan loosely in plastic and freeze until fully chilled, about 30 minutes. (Wrapped dough-lined tart pan can be frozen for up to 1 month.)

5 Weight

Set frozen pan on rimmed baking sheet. Line pan with double layer of aluminum foil. Press foil over dough and up over edges of pan. Fill with pie weights.

6 Bake

Bake on middle rack in 375-degree oven. Timing for baking and for removing foil and weights will depend on type of tart and whether it needs further baking after filling.

PUTTING IT ALL TOGETHER

CLASSIC DEVILED EGGS

Serves 4 to 6
Total Time 1 hour

Be sure to use large eggs that have no cracks and are cold from the refrigerator. If you don't have a steamer basket, use a spoon or tongs to gently place the eggs in the water. It does not matter if the eggs are above the water or partially submerged. For filling the eggs, a spoon works fine, but for best results use a pastry bag fitted with a star tip, or make your own pastry bag by pressing the filling into the corner of a zipper-lock bag and snipping off the corner with scissors. We like the flavor of cider vinegar here, but any type will work. Dust the filled eggs with paprika for a traditional look. See How to Hard-Cook Eggs, page 208.

---

6 **large eggs, chilled**
3 **tablespoons mayonnaise**
1½ **teaspoons cider vinegar**
¾ **teaspoon whole-grain mustard**
¼ **teaspoon Worcestershire sauce**
 Salt and pepper

1   Bring 1 inch water to rolling boil in medium saucepan over high heat. Place eggs in steamer basket. Transfer basket to saucepan. Cover, reduce heat to medium-low, and cook eggs for 13 minutes. When eggs are almost finished cooking, combine 2 cups ice cubes and 2 cups cold water in medium bowl. Using tongs or spoon, transfer eggs to ice bath; let sit for 15 minutes.

2   Peel eggs and slice each in half lengthwise with paring knife. Transfer yolks to small bowl. Arrange whites on serving platter. Mash yolks with fork until no large lumps remain. Add mayonnaise, vinegar, mustard, and Worcestershire and season with salt and pepper to taste. Mix with rubber spatula, mashing mixture against side of bowl until smooth. (Egg whites and yolk filling can be refrigerated, separately, for up to 2 days.)

3   Fit pastry bag with large open-star tip. Fill bag with yolk mixture, twisting top of pastry bag to help push mixture toward tip of bag. Pipe yolk mixture into egg white halves, mounding filling about ½ inch above flat surface of whites. Serve at room temperature.

VARIATIONS
Deviled Eggs with Anchovy and Basil
Add 8 anchovy fillets, rinsed, patted dry, and finely chopped, and 2 teaspoons chopped fresh basil to filling. Sprinkle eggs with 4 teaspoons shredded basil before serving.

Deviled Eggs with Tuna, Capers, and Chives
Omit Worcestershire. Add ½ cup drained and finely chopped canned tuna, 1 tablespoon rinsed and chopped capers, and 1 tablespoon minced fresh chives to filling. Sprinkle eggs with 1 teaspoon minced fresh chives before serving.

1 **Boil a Small Amount of Water**
Bring 1 inch of water to a rolling boil in a medium saucepan over high heat. Place the eggs in a steamer basket. WHY? The eggs will cook in the steam instead of directly in the water.

2 **Steam the Eggs**
Put the steamer basket in the pan. Cover, reduce the heat, and cook the eggs for 13 minutes. WHY? This method makes the egg-white proteins shrink away from the shell membrane for easier peeling.

3 **Make an Ice Bath**
Combine 2 cups of ice cubes and 2 cups of cold water. Using tongs or a spoon, transfer the eggs to the ice bath for 15 minutes. WHY? The ice bath stops the eggs from cooking further.

4 **Peel the Eggs and Separate the Whites and Yolks**
Peel the eggs and slice each one in half lengthwise. Transfer the yolks to a bowl. Arrange the whites on a platter. WHY? The shells slip right off since the white has shrunk away from the membrane.

5 **Make a Smooth Filling Using the Yolks**
Mash the yolks with a fork until no large lumps remain. Mix in the other filling ingredients and mash with a rubber spatula until smooth. WHY? This helps avoid pockets of hard, powdery yolk.

6 **Pipe the Filling Attractively into the Egg Whites**
Fit a pastry bag with an open-star tip and fill it with the yolk mixture. Gently pipe the mixture into the egg whites. WHY? Using a pastry bag (or zipper-lock bag) makes filling the egg whites easy.

ALL-AMERICAN POTATO SALAD

Serves 4 to 6
Total Time 2 hours (includes 1 hour for chilling)

Note that this recipe calls for celery seeds (which add complexity of flavor), not celery salt; if only celery salt is available, use the same amount but omit the salt in the dressing. When testing the potatoes for doneness, simply taste a piece; do not overcook the potatoes or they will become mealy and will break apart. The potatoes must be just warm, or even fully cooled, when you add the dressing. If the potato salad seems a little dry, add up to 2 tablespoons more mayonnaise. See How to Hard-Cook Eggs, page 208.

2 pounds russet potatoes, peeled and cut into ¾-inch cubes

Salt

2 tablespoons distilled white vinegar

½ cup mayonnaise

3 tablespoons sweet pickle relish

1 celery rib, chopped fine

2 tablespoons finely chopped red onion

2 tablespoons minced fresh parsley

¾ teaspoon dry mustard

¾ teaspoon celery seeds

¼ teaspoon pepper

2 large hard-cooked eggs, peeled and cut into ¼-inch cubes (optional)

1 Place potatoes in large saucepan and add water to cover by 1 inch. Bring to boil over medium-high heat. Add 1 tablespoon salt, reduce heat to medium, and simmer, stirring occasionally, until potatoes are tender, about 8 minutes.

2 Drain potatoes and transfer to large bowl. Add vinegar and toss gently to combine, using rubber spatula. Let stand until potatoes are just warm, about 20 minutes.

3 Meanwhile, combine mayonnaise, relish, celery, onion, parsley, mustard, celery seeds, pepper, and ½ teaspoon salt in small bowl. Using rubber spatula, gently fold mayonnaise mixture and eggs, if using, into potatoes. Refrigerate until chilled, about 1 hour. Serve. (Salad can be refrigerated for up to 24 hours.)

Learn How All-American Potato Salad

1 Use Russet Potatoes
Peel 2 pounds of russet potatoes. WHY? Russets have a strong, earthy flavor that shines through the mayonnaise dressing. Their starchy texture makes for a pleasant, crumbly salad when mixed.

2 Cut the Potatoes into Uniform Pieces
Once the potatoes are peeled, cut them into ¾-inch cubes. WHY? Uniform cubes cook through evenly and at the same rate.

3 Start the Potatoes in Cold Water
Add the cut potatoes to a large saucepan with cold water. Bring to a boil, reduce the heat, and simmer until tender. WHY? Starting in cold water helps the potatoes hold their shape.

4 Test Doneness by Tasting
To test the potatoes for doneness, remove a piece from the pot, let it cool slightly, and taste it. WHY? If you try to stab them with a knife or fork, the pieces of potato will simply break apart.

5 Toss the Warm Potatoes with Vinegar
After draining the cooked potatoes, toss them gently with vinegar and let them stand for about 20 minutes. WHY? Seasoning the potatoes while they're hot maximizes their flavor.

6 Gently Fold the Dressing into the Potatoes
Once the potatoes have cooled, gently fold in the mayonnaise dressing to coat. WHY? It is important to handle the potatoes gently at this point, as their texture will be quite delicate.

BUTTERMILK COLESLAW

½ medium head red or green cabbage, cored,
    quartered, and shredded (6 cups)
    Salt and pepper
1 carrot, peeled and shredded
½ cup buttermilk
2 tablespoons mayonnaise
2 tablespoons sour cream
1 small shallot, minced
2 tablespoons minced fresh parsley
½ teaspoon cider vinegar
½ teaspoon sugar
¼ teaspoon Dijon mustard

1 Toss shredded cabbage and 1 teaspoon salt in
   colander set over large bowl and let sit until wilted,
   at least 1 hour or up to 4 hours. Rinse cabbage
   under cold running water. Press, but do not squeeze,
   to drain, and blot dry with paper towels.

2 Combine wilted cabbage and carrot in large bowl.
   In separate bowl, whisk buttermilk, mayonnaise,
   sour cream, shallot, parsley, vinegar, sugar, mustard,
   ¼ teaspoon salt, and ⅛ teaspoon pepper together.
   Pour dressing over cabbage-carrot mixture and toss
   to combine. Refrigerate until chilled, about
   30 minutes. Serve. (Coleslaw can be refrigerated
   for up to 3 days.)

VARIATIONS

Buttermilk Coleslaw with Scallions and Cilantro

Omit mustard. Substitute 1 tablespoon minced
fresh cilantro for parsley and 1 teaspoon lime
juice for cider vinegar. Add 2 thinly sliced scallions
to dressing.

Lemony Buttermilk Coleslaw

Substitute 1 teaspoon lemon juice for vinegar.
Add 1 teaspoon minced fresh thyme and
1 tablespoon minced fresh chives to dressing.

Serves 4
**Total Time 1 hour 45 minutes
(includes 30 minutes for chilling)**

If you are planning to serve the coleslaw
immediately, rinse the salted cabbage in a large
bowl of ice water, drain it in a colander, pick
out any ice cubes, and pat the cabbage dry
before dressing.

1 Core and Shred the Cabbage
Separate the cored cabbage quarters into stacks of leaves and cut each stack into long, thin pieces. WHY? Pressing the leaves flat helps create uniform shreds for the coleslaw.

2 Salt the Cabbage
Toss the shredded cabbage with salt in a colander set over a large bowl and let stand until the cabbage wilts. WHY? The salt draws excess moisture out of the cabbage.

3 Rinse the Salted Cabbage Well
Rinse the cabbage thoroughly under cold running water. WHY? Salting leaves the cabbage too salty, so it needs to be thoroughly rinsed.

4 Drain and Dry the Wilted Cabbage
Press, but don't squeeze, the cabbage in the colander to drain it and blot it dry with paper towels. WHY? The cabbage must be dry so the dressing will cling and won't get diluted.

5 Dress and Season the Coleslaw
Transfer the cabbage and carrot to a large bowl. Whisk the dressing and pour it over the vegetables. WHY? Dressing the vegetables together ensures that they get evenly coated.

6 Chill the Coleslaw
Cover the coleslaw and refrigerate until chilled, about 30 minutes, before serving. WHY? Chilling makes the coleslaw very crisp and allows the flavors to develop even more.

CHICKEN STOCK

1 tablespoon vegetable oil

3 pounds whole chicken legs, backs, and/or wings, hacked into 2-inch pieces

1 onion, chopped

8 cups water

2 teaspoons salt

2 bay leaves

1   Heat oil in Dutch oven or stockpot over medium-high heat until just smoking. Brown half of chicken lightly on all sides, about 5 minutes; transfer to large bowl. Repeat with remaining chicken using fat left in pot, and transfer to bowl.

2   Add onion to fat left in pot and cook until softened, about 3 minutes. Return browned chicken and any accumulated juices to pot, cover, and reduce heat to low. Cook, stirring occasionally, until chicken has released its juices, about 20 minutes.

3   Add water, salt, and bay leaves and bring to boil. Cover, reduce heat to gentle simmer, and cook, skimming as needed, until stock tastes rich and flavorful, about 20 minutes longer.

4   Remove large bones from pot, then strain stock through fine-mesh strainer. Let stock settle for 5 to 10 minutes, then defat using wide, shallow spoon or fat separator. (Stock can be refrigerated for up to 4 days or frozen for up to 1 month.)

Makes 8 cups
Total Time 1 hour 30 minutes

Use a meat cleaver or the heel of a chef's knife to cut the chicken into smaller pieces. Any chicken meat left over after straining the stock will be very dry and flavorless; it should not be eaten. Chicken thighs can be substituted for the legs, backs, and wings in a pinch. Make sure to use a 7-quart or larger Dutch oven for this recipe. See How to Cut Up a Whole Chicken, page 214.

1 Cut Up the Chicken
Use a meat cleaver or the heel of a chef's knife to hack the chicken parts into 2-inch pieces. WHY? This exposes more surface area and bone marrow, which are key for both rich flavor and full body.

2 Sauté the Chicken to Build Flavor
Heat the oil in a Dutch oven until it's just smoking. Lightly brown the chicken on all sides in two batches. WHY? Browning the chicken helps fond to form on the bottom of the pot and builds flavor.

3 Use a Minimum of Flavor Enhancers
Add the chopped onion to the fat left in the pot and cook until the onion is softened. WHY? Since the chicken flavor is strong, you don't need much else to enhance the stock.

4 Sweat the Chicken to Extract Its Juices
Return the chicken and accumulated juices to the pot, cover, and reduce heat to low. Cook, stirring occasionally. WHY? Low heat helps to release the chicken's rich, flavorful juices.

5 Simmer Gently, Covered
Add the water, salt, and bay leaves and bring to a boil. Cover, reduce to a gentle simmer, and cook, skimming as needed. WHY? Covering the pot prevents evaporation and accelerates cooking.

6 Strain the Stock and Remove the Fat
Pour the stock through a fine-mesh strainer. After 5 to 10 minutes, use a spoon to remove the fat that rises to the surface. WHY? Removing the excess fat keeps the stock from being greasy.

BEST GROUND BEEF CHILI

Serves 8 to 10
Total Time 2 hours 30 minutes to 3 hours

Diced avocado, sour cream, and shredded cheddar cheese are good options for garnishing. For a spicier chili, use the larger amount of chipotle. This chili is intensely flavored and should be served with tortilla chips and/or steamed white rice.

2	pounds 85 percent lean ground beef
2	tablespoons plus 2 cups water
	Salt and pepper
¾	teaspoon baking soda
6	dried ancho chiles, stemmed, seeded, and torn into 1-inch pieces
1	ounce tortilla chips, crushed (¼ cup)
2	tablespoons ground cumin
1	tablespoon paprika
1	tablespoon garlic powder
1	tablespoon ground coriander
2	teaspoons dried oregano
½	teaspoon dried thyme
1	(14.5-ounce) can whole peeled tomatoes
1	tablespoon vegetable oil
1	onion, chopped fine
3	garlic cloves, minced
1–2	teaspoons minced canned chipotle chile in adobo sauce
1	(15-ounce) can pinto beans
2	teaspoons sugar
2	tablespoons cider vinegar
	Lime wedges
	Coarsely chopped cilantro
	Chopped red onion

1 Adjust oven rack to lower-middle position and heat oven to 275 degrees. Toss beef with 2 tablespoons water, 1½ teaspoons salt, and baking soda in bowl until thoroughly combined. Set aside for 20 minutes.

2 Meanwhile, place anchos in Dutch oven set over medium-high heat; toast, stirring frequently, until fragrant, 4 to 6 minutes, reducing heat if anchos begin to smoke. Transfer to food processor and let cool.

3 Add tortilla chips, cumin, paprika, garlic powder, coriander, oregano, thyme, and 2 teaspoons pepper to food processor with anchos and process until finely ground, about 2 minutes. Transfer mixture to bowl. Process tomatoes and their juice in now-empty workbowl until smooth, about 30 seconds.

4 Heat oil in now-empty pot over medium-high heat until shimmering. Add onion and cook, stirring occasionally, until softened, 4 to 6 minutes. Add garlic and cook until fragrant, about 1 minute. Add beef and cook, stirring with wooden spoon to break meat up into ¼-inch pieces, until beef is browned and fond begins to form on pot bottom, 12 to 14 minutes. Add ancho mixture and chipotle; cook, stirring frequently, until fragrant, 1 to 2 minutes.

5 Add beans and their liquid, sugar, tomato puree, and remaining 2 cups water. Bring to boil, scraping up any browned bits. Cover, transfer to oven, and cook until meat is tender and chili is slightly thickened, 1½ to 2 hours, stirring occasionally to prevent sticking.

6 Remove chili from oven and let stand, uncovered, for 10 minutes. Stir in any fat that has risen to top of chili, then add vinegar and season with salt to taste. Serve, passing lime wedges, cilantro, and chopped onion separately. (Chili can be made up to 3 days in advance.)

Learn How Best Ground Beef Chili

1 Treat the Beef with Salt and Baking Soda
Toss the beef with water, salt, and baking soda and set it aside for 20 minutes. WHY? The baking soda and salt help the meat hold on to moisture, while the water helps them dissolve evenly.

2 Toast the Chiles
Place the dried ancho chiles in a Dutch oven over medium-high heat and toast until fragrant. WHY? The toasted chiles make a powerful flavor base for our homemade chili powder.

3 Make Homemade Chili Powder; Add Tortilla Chips
Process tortilla chips into the spice mixture for the chili. WHY? The ground tortilla chips thicken the chili slightly. Homemade chili powder is an easy way to amp up the flavor of your dish.

4 Brown the Meat in One Batch
Add the beef and cook until it is browned, then add the ancho mixture and chipotle. WHY? The treated meat browns much more quickly and can be cooked in just one batch.

5 Cook the Chili Gently in the Oven
Add the remaining ingredients. Bring the chili to a boil, cover, and transfer to the oven. WHY? The ambient heat of a 275-degree oven cooks the chili gently to allow the flavors to meld.

6 Stir in the Fat and Season
After cooking, stir back in any fat that has risen to the top of the chili, then add vinegar and season with salt to taste. WHY? If you discard the fat, you rob the chili of tons of long-cooked flavor.

BEST BEEF STEW

Serves 6 to 8
Total Time 3 hours 30 minutes

Use a good-quality, medium-bodied wine, such as a Côtes du Rhône or Pinot Noir. Try to use well-marbled beef. You can use 4 pounds of blade steaks, trimmed, instead of the chuck-eye roast.

---

2   garlic cloves, minced
4   anchovy fillets, rinsed and minced
1   tablespoon tomato paste
1   (4-pound) boneless beef chuck-eye roast, pulled apart at seams, trimmed, and cut into 1½-inch pieces
2   tablespoons vegetable oil
1   large onion, halved and sliced ⅛ inch thick
4   carrots, peeled and cut into 1-inch pieces
¼   cup all-purpose flour
2   cups red wine
2   cups chicken broth
4   ounces salt pork, rinsed
2   bay leaves
4   sprigs fresh thyme

1   pound Yukon Gold potatoes, unpeeled, cut into 1-inch pieces
1½ cups frozen pearl onions, thawed
2   teaspoons unflavored gelatin
½   cup water
1   cup frozen peas, thawed
    Salt and pepper

1   Adjust oven rack to lower-middle position and heat oven to 300 degrees. Combine garlic and anchovies in small bowl; press with back of fork to form paste. Stir in tomato paste and set aside.

2   Pat meat dry with paper towels. Do not season. Heat 1 tablespoon oil in Dutch oven over high heat until just smoking. Add half of beef and cook until well browned on all sides, about 8 minutes. Transfer beef to large plate. Repeat with remaining 1 tablespoon oil and remaining beef, leaving second batch of meat in pot after browning.

3   Reduce heat to medium and return first batch of beef to pot. Stir in onion and carrots and cook, scraping up any browned bits, until onion is softened, 1 to 2 minutes. Add garlic mixture and cook, stirring constantly, until fragrant, about 30 seconds. Add flour and cook, stirring constantly, until no dry flour remains, about 30 seconds.

4   Slowly add wine, scraping up any browned bits. Increase heat to high and simmer until wine is thickened and slightly reduced, about 2 minutes. Stir in broth, salt pork, bay leaves, and thyme sprigs. Bring to simmer, cover, transfer to oven, and cook for 1½ hours.

5   Remove pot from oven; discard bay leaves and salt pork. Stir in potatoes, cover, return to oven, and cook until potatoes are almost tender, about 45 minutes.

6   Using large spoon, skim excess fat from surface of stew. Stir in pearl onions; cook over medium heat until potatoes and onions are cooked through and fork slips easily in and out of beef (meat should not be falling apart), about 15 minutes. Meanwhile, sprinkle gelatin over water in small bowl and allow to soften for 5 minutes.

7   Increase heat to high, stir in softened gelatin mixture and peas; simmer until gelatin is fully dissolved and stew is thickened, about 3 minutes. Season with salt and pepper to taste; serve. (Stew can be refrigerated for up to 2 days.)

1 Create a Savory Base
Make a paste from the garlic and anchovies, stir in the tomato paste, and set aside. WHY? These glutamate-rich ingredients contribute huge savory flavor to the traditional stew base.

2 Brown the Beef in Batches
Heat 1 tablespoon oil in a Dutch oven over high heat. Brown half the beef, transfer to a plate, and repeat with the remaining beef and oil. WHY? Browning helps develop great flavor and fond.

3 Add the Aromatics
Cook the beef, onion, and carrots until the onion is softened. Add the garlic mixture and cook, stirring constantly, until fragrant. WHY? These ingredients build a strong flavor base.

4 Add Wine and Broth; Transfer to Oven
Add the wine, scraping the pan to loosen the fond. Simmer, then stir in broth, salt pork, and herbs. Simmer, cover, and transfer to the oven. WHY? The even heat of the oven cooks the stew perfectly.

5 Add the Potatoes and Pearl Onions
Stir in the potatoes and cook until almost tender. Add the pearl onions and cook until potatoes and onions are cooked through. WHY? Adding these ingredients late keeps them from overcooking.

6 Incorporate the Gelatin Mixture
Combine the gelatin and water. Add this mixture and the peas to the stew; simmer until thickened. WHY? Gelatin mimics the luxurious texture of stew made with homemade beef stock.

PAN-ROASTED CHICKEN BREASTS WITH SHALLOT-THYME SAUCE

Serves 4
Total Time 55 minutes

We prefer to split whole chicken breasts ourselves because store-bought split chicken breasts are often sloppily butchered. However, if you prefer to purchase split chicken breasts, try to choose 10- to 12-ounce pieces with the skin intact. You will need a 12-inch ovensafe skillet for this recipe. If using kosher chicken, do not brine. If brining the chicken, do not season with salt in step 1.

Chicken
4 (10- to 12-ounce) bone-in split chicken breasts, trimmed, brined if desired (see page 351)
Salt and pepper
1 tablespoon vegetable oil

Shallot-Thyme Sauce
1 large shallot, minced
¾ cup chicken broth
½ cup dry vermouth or white wine
2 sprigs fresh thyme
3 tablespoons unsalted butter, cut into 3 pieces and chilled
Salt and pepper

1 **For the Chicken**
Adjust oven rack to middle position and heat oven to 450 degrees. Pat chicken dry with paper towels and season with salt and pepper.

2 Heat oil in 12-inch ovensafe skillet over medium-high heat until just smoking. Cook chicken, skin side down, until well browned, 6 to 8 minutes, reducing heat if pan begins to scorch. Flip chicken and brown lightly on second side, about 3 minutes. Flip chicken skin side down, transfer skillet to oven, and roast until chicken registers 160 degrees, 15 to 18 minutes.

3 Using potholder (skillet handle will be hot), remove skillet from oven. Transfer chicken to serving platter and let rest while making sauce.

4 **For the Shallot-Thyme Sauce**
Being careful of hot skillet handle, pour off all but 1 teaspoon fat left in skillet. Add shallot and cook over medium-high heat until softened, about 2 minutes. Stir in broth, vermouth, and thyme sprigs, scraping up any browned bits, and simmer until thickened and measures ⅔ cup, about 6 minutes.

5 Stir in any accumulated chicken juices; return to simmer and cook for 30 seconds. Off heat, discard thyme sprigs and whisk in butter, 1 piece at a time. Season with salt and pepper to taste. Spoon sauce over chicken and serve.

1 Trim the Chicken Breasts
Using kitchen shears, trim off the rib section from each bone-in split chicken breast. WHY? Removing the ribs allows for more even cooking since the breasts can lay flat in the skillet.

2 Get the Skillet Hot
Heat the vegetable oil in a 12-inch ovensafe skillet over medium-high heat until just smoking. WHY? If the oil isn't hot enough, the chicken won't brown properly and will stick to the pan.

3 Brown the Chicken
Cook the chicken breasts skin side down until they are well browned on the first side, then flip and brown lightly on the second side. WHY? Browning the chicken renders the fat and crisps the skin.

4 Transfer the Skillet to the Oven
Flip the chicken skin side down and transfer to a 450-degree oven. Roast until the breasts register 160 degrees. WHY? This allows the skin to crisp while the meat cooks through relatively quickly.

5 Remove the Chicken and Let it Rest
Remove the skillet from the oven and transfer the chicken to a serving platter to rest while making the sauce. WHY? Allowing the chicken to rest lets it reabsorb its natural juices.

6 Make the Pan Sauce
Pour off all but 1 teaspoon of fat. Make the sauce, scraping up the browned bits, and simmer; add the cold butter last, off the heat. WHY? Finishing with cold butter thickens the sauce.

WEEKNIGHT ROAST CHICKEN

Serves 3 to 4
Total Time 1 hour 25 minutes

We prefer to use a 3½- to 4-pound chicken for this recipe. If roasting a larger bird, increase the time when the oven is on in step 2 to 35 to 40 minutes. You will need a 12-inch ovensafe skillet for this recipe. If making a pan sauce, be sure to save 1 tablespoon of the pan drippings. See How to Carve a Whole Bird, page 219.

1 (3½- to 4-pound) whole chicken, giblets discarded
1 tablespoon vegetable oil
  Salt and pepper

1 Adjust oven rack to middle position, place 12-inch ovensafe skillet on rack, and heat oven to 450 degrees. Pat chicken dry with paper towels. Rub entire surface with oil, season with salt and pepper, and rub in with your hands to coat evenly. Tie legs together with twine and tuck wingtips behind back.

2 Transfer chicken, breast side up, to hot skillet in oven. Roast chicken until breast registers 120 degrees and thighs register 135 degrees, 25 to 35 minutes. Turn oven off and leave chicken in oven until breast registers 160 degrees and thighs register 175 degrees, 25 to 35 minutes.

3 Transfer chicken to carving board, tent loosely with aluminum foil, and let rest for 20 minutes. Carve and serve.

SHERRY-ROSEMARY PAN SAUCE

Makes about ¾ cup
Total Time 20 minutes

Pour off pan drippings from skillet, reserving 1 tablespoon. Add 1 tablespoon vegetable oil to now-empty skillet and heat over medium-high heat until shimmering. Add 1 minced shallot and cook until softened, about 2 minutes. Stir in ¾ cup chicken broth, ½ cup dry sherry, and 2 sprigs fresh rosemary, scraping up any browned bits. Bring to simmer and cook until thickened and measures ⅔ cup, about 6 minutes. Stir in reserved pan drippings. Off heat, discard rosemary and whisk in 3 tablespoons unsalted butter, cut into 3 pieces and chilled, 1 piece at a time. Season with salt and pepper to taste.

MUSTARD AND CIDER PAN SAUCE

Makes about ¾ cup
Total Time 20 minutes

Pour off pan drippings from skillet, reserving 1 tablespoon. Add 1 tablespoon vegetable oil to now-empty skillet and heat over medium-high heat until shimmering. Add 1 minced shallot and ¼ teaspoon salt and cook until softened, about 2 minutes. Stir in 1¼ cups apple cider and 2 tablespoons cider vinegar, scraping up any browned bits, and simmer until reduced and slightly syrupy, about 8 minutes. Stir in reserved pan drippings. Off heat, whisk in 3 tablespoons unsalted butter, cut into 3 pieces and chilled, 1 piece at a time, and stir in 2 teaspoons minced fresh parsley and 2 teaspoons whole-grain mustard. Season with salt and pepper to taste.

1 Heat a Skillet in the Oven
Place a 12-inch ovensafe skillet on the middle oven rack and heat the oven to 450 degrees. WHY? Less of the chicken's juices evaporate in a skillet than a roasting pan, which leaves more for a pan sauce.

2 Rub the Skin with Oil
Rub the chicken's skin with oil and season with salt and pepper. WHY? Rubbing oil onto the skin of the chicken helps the skin crisp.

3 Tie the Legs and Tuck the Wings
Tie the chicken's legs together and tuck the wingtips behind the back. WHY? Tucking prevents the delicate wingtips from burning.

4 Roast Breast Side Up and Don't Flip
Cook the chicken in the preheated skillet breast side up. WHY? Putting the thighs in direct contact with the hot skillet ensures that they will finish cooking at the same time as the breast meat.

5 Turn Off the Oven
When the breast registers 120 degrees and thighs are 135 degrees, turn off the oven and cook the chicken for 25 to 35 minutes more. WHY? Using the residual oven heat creates moist, tender meat.

6 Temp the Chicken to Gauge Doneness
Cook until the breast registers 160 degrees and the thighs register 175 degrees. WHY? Using an instant-read thermometer is the most accurate way to know when your chicken is done.

CRISP ROAST BUTTERFLIED CHICKEN WITH ROSEMARY AND GARLIC

2 tablespoons extra-virgin olive oil

1 teaspoon minced fresh rosemary

1 garlic clove, minced

1 (3½- to 4-pound) whole chicken, giblets discarded

Salt and pepper

1 Adjust oven rack to lowest position, place 12-inch cast-iron skillet on rack, and heat oven to 500 degrees. Meanwhile, combine 1 tablespoon oil, rosemary, and garlic in bowl; set aside.

2 With chicken breast side down, use kitchen shears to cut through bones on either side of backbone; discard backbone. Flip chicken over, tuck wingtips behind back, and press firmly on breastbone to flatten. Pat chicken dry with paper towels, then rub with remaining 1 tablespoon oil and season with salt and pepper.

3 When oven reaches 500 degrees, place chicken breast side down in hot skillet. Reduce oven temperature to 450 degrees and roast chicken until well browned, about 30 minutes.

4 Using potholders, remove skillet from oven. Being careful of hot skillet handle, gently flip chicken skin side up. Brush chicken with oil mixture, return skillet to oven, and continue to roast chicken until breast registers 160 degrees and thighs register 175 degrees, about 10 minutes. Transfer chicken to carving board, tent loosely with aluminum foil, and let rest for 15 minutes. Carve chicken and serve.

Serves 4
Total Time 1 hour 10 minutes

Be aware that the chicken may slightly overhang the skillet at first, but once browned it will shrink to fit; do not use a chicken larger than 4 pounds. Serve with lemon wedges. See How to Butterfly a Whole Chicken, page 215.

1 Preheat the Skillet and Make a Flavorful Oil
Place a 12-inch cast-iron skillet on the lowest oven rack and heat the oven to 500 degrees. Combine olive oil, garlic, and rosemary. WHY? The preheated skillet is a superhot cooking surface.

2 Butterfly the Chicken
Cut out the backbone. Flip the chicken over, tuck the wingtips behind the back, and press on the breastbone to flatten. WHY? Butterflying the chicken encourages even cooking and crisp skin.

3 Start the Chicken Breast Side Down
Place the chicken breast side down in the hot skillet. Reduce the oven to 450 degrees and roast the chicken until well browned. WHY? Starting the chicken breast side down helps the skin crisp up.

4 Flip the Chicken
Being careful of the hot skillet handle, gently flip the chicken skin side up. WHY? This keeps the crisp skin from getting soggy as the chicken cooks in its own juices.

5 Brush with the Oil
Brush the chicken with the oil mixture and roast until the breast registers 160 degrees and the thighs register 175 degrees. WHY? Adding the oil toward the end keeps the flavors bright and fresh.

6 Rest the Meat Before Carving the Chicken
Transfer the chicken to a carving board, tent it loosely with aluminum foil, and let it rest for 15 minutes. WHY? Tenting with foil keeps heat and moisture in without compromising the crisp skin.

EXTRA-CRUNCHY FRIED CHICKEN

2 tablespoons salt

2 cups plus 6 tablespoons buttermilk

3½ pounds bone-in chicken pieces (2 split breasts cut in half crosswise, 2 drumsticks, and 2 thighs), trimmed

3 cups all-purpose flour

2 teaspoons baking powder

¾ teaspoon dried thyme

½ teaspoon pepper

¼ teaspoon garlic powder

4–5 cups peanut oil

1 Dissolve salt in 2 cups buttermilk in large bowl or container. Add chicken, cover, and refrigerate for 1 hour. Remove chicken from brine and pat dry with paper towels.

2 Whisk flour, baking powder, thyme, pepper, and garlic powder together in large bowl. Add remaining 6 tablespoons buttermilk and rub into flour mixture using your hands until evenly incorporated and flour mixture resembles coarse, wet sand.

3 Set wire rack in rimmed baking sheet. Coat chicken thoroughly with flour mixture, pressing gently to adhere. Gently shake off excess flour and transfer chicken to prepared wire rack.

4 Line platter with triple layer of paper towels. Add oil to large Dutch oven to measure ¾ inch deep and heat over medium-high heat to 375 degrees. Place chicken pieces skin side down in oil, cover, and fry for 4 minutes. Remove lid and lift chicken pieces to check for even browning; rearrange if browning is uneven. Adjust burner, if necessary, to maintain oil temperature of about 315 degrees. Cover and continue frying until deep golden brown on first side, 4 to 6 minutes.

5 Turn chicken pieces over using tongs. Continue to fry, uncovered, until chicken pieces are deep golden brown on second side, 6 to 8 minutes longer. Using tongs, transfer chicken to prepared platter; let sit for 5 minutes. Serve. (Fried chicken can be refrigerated for up to 24 hours; reheat on wire rack in 400-degree oven for 10 to 15 minutes.)

Serves 4
Total Time 1 hour 45 minutes
(includes 1 hour for brining)

Don't let the chicken soak in the buttermilk brine much longer than 1 hour or it will be too salty. You will need at least a 6-quart Dutch oven for this recipe. If you want to produce a slightly lighter version of this recipe, you can remove the skin from the chicken before soaking it in the buttermilk. The chicken will be slightly less crunchy.

1 Brine the Chicken in Salted Buttermilk
Dissolve 2 tablespoons of salt in 2 cups of butter-milk. Add the chicken and soak for 1 hour before cooking. WHY? Brining the chicken in salted buttermilk helps it to retain its moisture.

2 Make the Flour Coating
Whisk together the dry ingredients. Add the remaining buttermilk and rub with your fingers until the mixture resembles coarse, wet sand. WHY? This creates a thick, crunchy coating.

3 Thoroughly Coat the Chicken
Remove the chicken from the brine and pat it dry. Coat the chicken evenly with the flour mixture, pressing on the flour. WHY? Gently pressing on the flour mixture helps it to adhere to the chicken.

4 Use Peanut Oil for Frying
Add peanut oil to a Dutch oven until it measures ¾ inch deep. Heat the oil to 375 degrees and use a thermometer to check the temperature. WHY? We prefer the neutral flavor of peanut oil for frying.

5 Add the Chicken and Fry Covered
Place the pieces skin side down in the hot oil. Cover and fry until the chicken is golden brown on the first side. WHY? Covering the pot helps the chicken cook through faster and keeps the oil hot.

6 Turn the Chicken Pieces and Fry Uncovered
Carefully turn the pieces using tongs. Finish frying, uncovered, until the pieces are deep golden brown on the second side. WHY? Finishing the chicken uncovered keeps the crust crisp.

CLASSIC BARBECUED CHICKEN

Serves 4 to 6
Total Time 1 hour 30 minutes

Don't try to grill more than 10 pieces of chicken at a time; you won't be able to line them up as directed in step 4.

1 teaspoon salt

1 teaspoon pepper

¼ teaspoon cayenne pepper

3 pounds bone-in chicken pieces (split breasts cut in half, drumsticks, and/or thighs), trimmed

1 (13 by 9-inch) disposable aluminum pan (if using charcoal)

1 recipe Kansas City Barbecue Sauce for Chicken

1 Combine salt, pepper, and cayenne in bowl. Pat chicken dry with paper towels and rub with spices. Measure out 2 cups barbecue sauce for cooking; set aside remaining sauce for serving.

2A For a Charcoal Grill
Open bottom vent completely and place disposable pan on 1 side of grill. Light large chimney starter filled with charcoal briquettes (6 quarts). When top coals are partially covered with ash, pour evenly over other half of grill (opposite disposable pan). Set cooking grate in place, cover, and open lid vent completely. Heat grill until hot, about 5 minutes.

2B For a Gas Grill
Turn all burners to high, cover, and heat grill until hot, about 15 minutes. Leave primary burner on high and turn other burner(s) off. (Adjust primary burner as needed to maintain grill temperature around 350 degrees.)

3 Clean and oil cooking grate. Place chicken, skin side down, on cooler side of grill. Cover and cook until chicken begins to brown, 30 to 35 minutes.

4 Slide chicken into single line between hotter and cooler sides of grill. Cook uncovered, flipping chicken and brushing every 5 minutes with some of sauce for cooking, until sticky, about 20 minutes.

5 Slide chicken to hotter side of grill and cook, uncovered, flipping and brushing with remaining sauce for cooking, until well glazed, breasts register 160 degrees, and/or thighs/drumsticks register 175 degrees, about 5 minutes. Transfer to platter, tent loosely with aluminum foil, and let rest for 5 to 10 minutes. Serve with reserved sauce.

KANSAS CITY BARBECUE SAUCE FOR CHICKEN
Makes about 4 cups
Total Time 1 hour 10 minutes
Heat 1 tablespoon vegetable oil in large saucepan over medium heat until shimmering. Add 1 onion, chopped fine, and pinch salt and cook until softened, 5 to 7 minutes. Whisk in 4 cups chicken broth, 1 cup brewed coffee, 1¼ cups cider vinegar, ¾ cup molasses, ½ cup tomato paste, ½ cup ketchup, 2 tablespoons brown mustard, 1 tablespoon hot sauce, and ½ teaspoon garlic powder. Bring sauce to simmer and cook, stirring occasionally, until thickened and measures 4 cups, about 1 hour. Off heat, stir in ¼ teaspoon liquid smoke. Let sauce cool to room temperature. Season with salt and pepper to taste.

1 Make the Sauce

Whisk the sauce ingredients together in a saucepan and bring them to a simmer; cook until thickened. WHY? Homemade barbecue sauce is easy to make and tastes the best.

2 Build a Half-Grill Fire

For both charcoal and gas grills, concentrate all of the heat on just one side of the grill. WHY? A half-grill fire creates two cooking zones with dramatically different heat levels.

3 Start the Chicken on the Cooler Side

Place the chicken skin side down on the cooler side of the grill. Cover and cook until the chicken begins to brown. WHY? Starting over lower heat slowly renders the fat and prevents flare-ups.

4 Move the Chicken and Baste

Slide the chicken to the middle of the grill. Cook, flipping the pieces and brushing them with sauce every 5 minutes for about 20 minutes. WHY? This helps build up a thick, multilayered coat of sauce.

5 Move the Chicken to the Hotter Side and Glaze

Slide the chicken to the hotter side of the grill and cook, flipping pieces and brushing with sauce, until they are cooked through. WHY? The high-heat finish gives the chicken a robust, crusty char.

6 Let the Chicken Rest

Transfer the chicken to a platter, tent it loosely with aluminum foil, and let it rest for 5 to 10 minutes before serving. WHY? Resting allows the chicken's juices to redistribute.

CLASSIC ROAST TURKEY

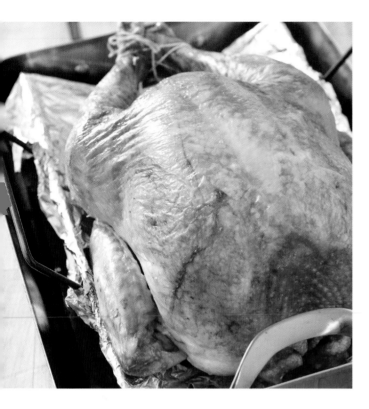

Serves 10 to 22
Total Time 3 hours to 4 hours 30 minutes, plus brining time

If you have time and can plan ahead, we recommend brining the turkey, as this further enhances the flavor and texture (see page 351 for instructions on brining). If using a disposable roasting pan, support it underneath with a rimmed baking sheet. Depending on the size of the turkey, total roasting time will vary from 2 to 3½ hours. If using a self-basting turkey (such as a frozen Butterball) or a kosher turkey, do not brine. If brining the turkey, do not season with salt in step 3. Serve with Classic Turkey Gravy (page 264). See How to Carve a Whole Bird, page 219.

1 (12- to 22-pound) turkey, brined if desired, neck, giblets, and tailpiece removed and reserved for gravy (optional)
2 onions, chopped coarse
2 carrots, peeled and chopped coarse
2 celery ribs, chopped coarse
2 tablespoons minced fresh thyme or 2 teaspoons dried
4 tablespoons unsalted butter, melted
   Salt and pepper
1 cup chicken broth, as needed

1   Adjust oven rack to lowest position and heat oven to 425 degrees. Pat turkey dry with paper towels. Trim tailpiece, tie legs together, and tuck wings under bird. Chop neck and giblets into 1-inch pieces if using them for gravy.

2   Spread onions, carrots, celery, and thyme in large roasting pan. Line V-rack with heavy-duty aluminum foil and poke several holes in foil. Set rack inside roasting pan and spray foil with vegetable oil spray.

3   Brush breast side of turkey with half of butter and season with salt and pepper. Lay turkey in rack breast side down. Brush back of turkey with remaining butter and season with salt and pepper. Roast turkey for 1 hour.

4   Remove turkey from oven. Lower oven temperature to 325 degrees. Tip juice from cavity of turkey into pan. Flip turkey breast side up using clean dish towels or wads of paper towels. Continue to roast turkey until thickest portion of breast registers 160 degrees and thighs register 175 degrees, 1 to 2½ hours longer. (Add broth as needed to prevent drippings from burning.)

5   Tip turkey so that juice from cavity runs into roasting pan. Transfer turkey to carving board and let rest, uncovered, for 30 minutes. (Meanwhile, use roasted vegetables and drippings in pan to make gravy, if desired.) Carve and serve.

1 Prepare the Turkey

If possible, brine the turkey, then remove it from the brine and pat it dry. Trim the tailpiece, tie the legs together, and tuck the wings. WHY? Brining adds moisture and flavor to the meat.

2 Line the V-Rack and Poke Holes in Foil

Add the vegetables to the pan. Line the V-rack and poke several holes in the foil. WHY? The V-rack elevates the bird for even cooking. Holes in the foil let the juices drip down onto the vegetables.

3 Start the Turkey Breast Side Down

Place the turkey breast side down on the V-rack. WHY? Starting the turkey breast side down promotes browning and allows the dark meat to get a head start.

4 Roast, Then Turn the Turkey Over

After 1 hour, turn the turkey breast side up and lower the oven temperature to 325 degrees. WHY? Turning the bird gets the legs to cook faster and protects the breast meat from overcooking.

5 Continue Roasting

Continue to roast the turkey breast side up until the breast registers 160 degrees and thighs register 175 degrees. WHY? The lower oven temperature let the turkey gently finish cooking.

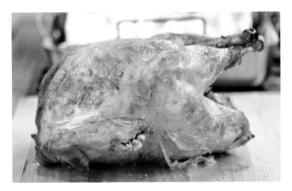

6 Let the Turkey Rest Before Carving

Transfer the turkey to a carving board and let it rest, uncovered, for 30 minutes before carving. WHY? Letting the turkey rest allows the juices to redistribute.

CLASSIC TURKEY GRAVY

Serves 12 to 15
Total Time 2 hours 30 minutes

The giblets can be omitted, if desired.

1 tablespoon vegetable oil
  Reserved turkey neck, giblets, and tailpiece (from Classic Roast Turkey, page 262)
1 onion, chopped
4 cups chicken broth
2 cups water
2 sprigs fresh thyme
8 sprigs fresh parsley
3 tablespoons unsalted butter
¼ cup all-purpose flour
1 cup dry white wine
  Salt and pepper

1 Heat oil in Dutch oven over medium heat until shimmering. Add neck, giblets, and tailpiece and cook until golden, about 5 minutes. Stir in onion and cook until softened, about 5 minutes. Reduce heat to low, cover, and cook until turkey parts and onion release their juices, about 15 minutes. Increase heat to high, stir in broth, water, thyme sprigs, and parsley sprigs and bring to boil. Reduce heat to low and simmer, skimming as needed, until broth is rich and flavorful, about 30 minutes.

2 Pour broth through fine-mesh strainer into large container. Discard solids. If desired, reserve giblets; let cool slightly and chop fine. Refrigerate broth and giblets, separately, until needed, or for up to 24 hours.

3 While turkey is roasting, bring broth to simmer in large saucepan over medium-high heat. In separate large saucepan, melt butter over medium-low heat. Add flour and cook, whisking constantly, until nutty brown and fragrant, 10 to 15 minutes. Vigorously whisk in all but 1 cup of hot broth. Increase heat to high, bring to boil, then reduce to simmer and cook, stirring often, until gravy is lightly thickened and very flavorful, about 30 minutes; cover and set aside.

4 While roasted turkey rests on carving board, spoon out and discard as much fat as possible from roasting pan, leaving caramelized herbs and vegetables. Place pan over 2 burners set on medium-high heat. Add wine, scraping up any browned bits, and boil until reduced by half, about 5 minutes. Add remaining 1 cup broth and simmer for 15 minutes. Strain juices through fine-mesh strainer into saucepan of gravy, pressing to extract as much liquid as possible out of vegetables. Discard solids. Stir in reserved giblets, if using, and return to boil. Season with salt and pepper to taste, and serve.

VARIATION
Classic Turkey Gravy for a Crowd
Serves 16 to 24
Using large Dutch oven to make gravy, increase chicken broth to 6 cups, water to 3 cups, butter to 5 tablespoons, flour to 6 tablespoons, and wine to 1½ cups.

1 **Make the Turkey Broth**
Brown the turkey parts and sauté the onion. Add chicken broth, water, and herbs and simmer for 30 minutes. WHY? This rich homemade turkey broth provides the base for the gravy.

2 **Strain the Turkey Broth**
Strain the broth into a large container and reserve the giblets. WHY? Straining the broth separates out the solids, allowing you to remove and discard the turkey neck and tailpiece.

3 **Make a Dark Roux and Simmer the Gravy**
Make a dark roux. Whisk all but 1 cup of the hot broth into the roux. Bring the gravy to a boil, then simmer until gravy is lightly thickened. WHY? The roux provides flavor and functions as a thickener.

4 **Place the Roasting Pan on the Stovetop**
Once the turkey is resting, discard the fat left in the pan, keeping the herbs and vegetables. Place the pan on the stove. WHY? The fond left behind in the pan adds important flavor to the gravy.

5 **Add the Wine, Reduce, and Add Remaining Broth**
Add wine to the pan of caramelized vegetables, scraping up any browned bits. Bring to a boil and reduce by half. Add the remaining broth and simmer. WHY? The liquids help loosen the fond.

6 **Strain the Pan Juices into the Gravy**
Strain the pan juices into the gravy, pressing on the vegetables. Add the reserved giblets, if desired, and season to taste. WHY? Pressing on the vegetables extracts every last bit of flavor.

JUICY GRILLED HAMBURGERS

Serves 4
Total Time 1 hour 45 minutes (includes 1 hour 5 minutes for freezing)

This recipe requires freezing the meat twice, for a total of 1 hour 5 minutes to 1 hour 20 minutes, before grilling. When stirring the salt and pepper into the ground meat and shaping the patties, take care not to overwork the meat or the burgers will become dense. Sirloin steak tips are also sold as flap meat. Serve the burgers with your favorite toppings. You can toast the buns on the grill while the burgers rest.

1½ pounds sirloin steak tips, trimmed and cut into ½-inch chunks
4 tablespoons unsalted butter, cut into ¼-inch pieces
Kosher salt and pepper
1 (13 by 9-inch) disposable aluminum pan (if using charcoal)
4 hamburger buns

1 Place beef chunks and butter on large plate in single layer. Freeze until meat is very firm and starting to harden around edges but still pliable, about 35 minutes.

2 Place one-quarter of meat and one-quarter of butter cubes in food processor and pulse until finely ground into pieces size of rice grains (about ⅟₃₂ inch), 15 to 20 pulses, stopping and redistributing meat around bowl as necessary to ensure beef is evenly ground. Transfer meat to baking sheet. Repeat grinding in 3 batches with remaining meat and butter. Spread mixture over sheet and inspect carefully, discarding any long strands of gristle or large chunks of hard meat, fat, or butter.

3 Sprinkle 1 teaspoon pepper and ¾ teaspoon salt over meat and gently toss with fork to combine. Divide meat into 4 portions. Working with 1 portion at a time, lightly toss from hand to hand to form ball, then gently flatten into ¾-inch-thick patty. Press center of patties down with your fingertips to create ¼-inch-deep depression. Transfer patties to platter and freeze for 30 to 45 minutes.

4A For a Charcoal Grill
Using skewer, poke 12 holes in bottom of disposable pan. Open bottom vent completely and place disposable pan in center of grill. Light large chimney starter two-thirds filled with charcoal briquettes (4 quarts). When top coals are partially covered with ash, pour into disposable pan. Set cooking grate in place, cover, and open lid vent completely. Heat grill until hot, about 5 minutes.

4B For a Gas Grill
Turn all burners to high, cover, and heat grill until hot, about 15 minutes. Leave all burners on high.

5 Clean and oil cooking grate. Season 1 side of patties liberally with salt and pepper. Using spatula, flip patties and season other side. Place burgers on grill (directly over coals if using charcoal) and cook, without pressing on them, until browned and meat easily releases from grill, 4 to 7 minutes. Flip burgers and continue to grill until browned on second side and meat registers 125 to 130 degrees (for medium-rare) or 135 to 145 degrees (for medium), 4 to 7 minutes longer.

6 Transfer burgers to plate and let rest for 5 minutes. Serve on buns.

1 Freeze the Meat and the Butter
Freeze the beef chunks and butter until the meat is very firm but still pliable. WHY? It's easier to process the meat and butter into a uniform mixture if they are frozen first.

2 Process the Meat with the Butter
Process the meat and butter in batches until finely ground. Discard any gristle or large chunks of hard meat, fat, or butter. WHY? The butter adds flavor and moisture and encourages browning.

3 Shape the Patties and Make a Dimple
Form the meat into four ¾-inch-thick patties. Make a ¼-inch deep depression in each, then freeze for 30 to 45 minutes. WHY? Dimpling prevents the patties from bulging when they cook.

4 Prepare the Grill
For a charcoal grill, use a disposable pan filled with 4 quarts of prepared charcoal. For a gas grill, simply turn all burners to high. WHY? These setups create a superhot fire for a great char.

5 Grill the Burgers over High Heat
Place the burgers on the grill and cook, without pressing, until they are browned and easily release from the grill. WHY? High heat guarantees an excellent charred crust without overcooking.

6 Let the Burgers Rest Before Serving
Transfer the burgers to a plate and let them rest for 5 minutes. WHY? Letting the meat rest after grilling guarantees juicy burgers by allowing the juices to redistribute as the proteins relax.

GRILLED BONELESS STEAKS

Serves 4
Total Time 1 hour 45 minutes
(includes 1 hour for salting)

We prefer these steaks cooked to medium-rare, but if you prefer them more or less done, see the chart on page 352. This recipe works best with strip steaks, rib-eye steaks, filets mignons, sirloin steak, and flank steak; try to buy steaks of even thickness so they cook at the same rate. If cooking filet mignon, look for steaks that are on the thicker side, about 2 inches.

2–2½ **pounds boneless beef steaks, 1 to 2 inches thick, trimmed**
Kosher salt and pepper
Vegetable oil

1 Season steaks thoroughly with 1 teaspoon salt and let sit at room temperature for 1 hour. Pat steaks dry with paper towels, brush lightly with oil, and season with pepper.

2A **For a Charcoal Grill**
Open bottom vent completely. Light large chimney starter filled with charcoal briquettes (6 quarts). When top coals are partially covered with ash, pour two-thirds evenly over half of grill, then pour remaining coals over other half of grill. Set cooking grate in place, cover, and open lid vent completely. Heat grill until hot, about 5 minutes.

2B **For a Gas Grill**
Turn all burners to high, cover, and heat grill until hot, about 15 minutes. Leave primary burner on high and turn other burner(s) to medium.

3 Clean and oil cooking grate. Place steaks on hotter side of grill. Cook (covered if using gas), turning as needed, until nicely charred on both sides, 4 to 6 minutes. Slide steaks to cooler side of grill and continue to cook until they register 120 to 125 degrees (for medium-rare), 4 to 8 minutes.

4 Transfer steaks to platter, tent with aluminum foil, and let rest for 5 to 10 minutes before serving.

Learn How Grilled Boneless Steaks

1 Salt the Steaks
Season the steaks thoroughly with kosher salt and let them sit at room temperature for 1 hour. WHY? Salt (and time) improves the texture of many cuts. Salting the meat also brings out its flavor.

2 Brush the Steaks with Oil
Brush the steaks lightly with oil and season with pepper. WHY? Brushing the meat with oil promotes a good sear. The oil also helps protect thin or lean steaks like flank and filet mignon.

3 Build the Right Fire
Build a two-level charcoal fire (see page 224) or leave the primary burner of a gas grill on high and turn the other burner(s) to medium. WHY? These setups provide a fire with two cooking zones.

4 Sear the Steaks
Cook the steaks on the hotter side of the grill until charred on both sides, 4 to 6 minutes. WHY? The hotter side of the grill is used to sear the exterior of the steaks to develop color and flavor.

5 Cook the Steaks Through
Move the steaks to the cooler side of the grill. Cook until they register 120 to 125 degrees for medium-rare. WHY? The slightly lower heat allows the steaks to finish cooking through more gently.

6 Let the Steaks Rest
Tent the steaks with aluminum foil and let them rest for 5 to 10 minutes before serving. WHY? A short rest gives the muscle fibers in the meat time to relax and reabsorb their natural juices.

PAN-SEARED STEAKS WITH RED WINE PAN SAUCE

Serves 4
Total Time 30 minutes

Use a 12-inch traditional skillet to ensure the steaks have enough room to sear and to develop the fond, which is the key to a flavorful sauce. Strip steaks and rib-eye steaks are our favorites to use in this recipe, but a boneless top sirloin will also work well. We prefer these steaks cooked to medium-rare, but if you prefer them more or less done, see our guidelines on page 352.

Steaks

4 (8-ounce) boneless beef steaks, 1 to 1¼ inches thick, trimmed

Kosher salt and pepper

1 tablespoon vegetable oil

Red Wine Pan Sauce

2 shallots, minced

2 teaspoons packed brown sugar

½ cup dry red wine

½ cup chicken broth

1 bay leaf

1 tablespoon balsamic vinegar

1 teaspoon Dijon mustard

3 tablespoons unsalted butter, cut into 6 pieces

1 teaspoon minced fresh thyme

Salt and pepper

1 For the Steaks
Pat steaks dry with paper towels and season with salt and pepper. Heat oil in 12-inch skillet over medium-high heat until just smoking. Brown steaks on first side, about 4 minutes.

2 Flip steaks and continue to cook until meat registers 120 to 125 degrees (for medium-rare), 4 to 6 minutes. Transfer steaks to plate, tent loosely with aluminum foil, and let rest while making sauce (do not clean skillet or discard accumulated fat).

3 For the Red Wine Pan Sauce
Add shallots and sugar to skillet off heat; using pan's residual heat, cook, stirring frequently, until shallots are softened and browned and sugar is melted, about 45 seconds. Return skillet to high heat, add wine, broth, and bay leaf; bring to boil, scraping up any browned bits. Boil until liquid is reduced to ⅓ cup, about 4 minutes. Stir in vinegar and mustard; cook over medium heat to blend flavors, about 1 minute longer.

4 Off heat, whisk in butter, one piece at a time. Add thyme and season with salt and pepper to taste. Discard bay leaf, spoon sauce over steaks and serve.

Learn How Pan-Seared Steaks with Red Wine Pan Sauce

1 Trim the Fat
Use a sharp paring or chef's knife to trim the hard, white fat from the perimeter of the steak so it is no more than ⅛ inch thick. WHY? Trimming the excess fat keeps splattering to a minimum.

2 Pat the Steaks Dry
Blot the steaks dry with paper towels. WHY? Browning equals flavor, and browning occurs only once all the surface moisture has evaporated.

3 Season the Steaks Liberally with Kosher Salt
Sprinkle both sides of the steaks with kosher salt and freshly ground black pepper. WHY? We prefer the large crystals of kosher salt because they are easier to distribute evenly.

4 Get the Pan Very Hot
Heat 1 tablespoon vegetable oil in a large skillet. Wait until the oil just begins to smoke. WHY? When the oil begins to smoke, the pan is about 450 degrees, perfect for searing.

5 Judge Doneness by Temperature
Once the steaks are well browned on both sides, check them with an instant-read thermometer. WHY? Inserting the thermometer through the side of the steak gives the most accurate results.

6 Rest the Steaks Before Serving
Transfer the steaks to a plate, loosely cover with aluminum foil, and let rest 5 to 10 minutes. WHY? A short rest allows meat to reabsorb its juices and gives you time to make a quick pan sauce.

BEST PRIME RIB

Serves 6 to 8
Total Time 5 to 6 hours, plus 24 hours for salting

Look for a roast with an untrimmed fat cap (ideally ½ inch thick). We prefer the flavor and texture of prime-grade beef, but choice grade will work as well. Monitoring the roast with a meat-probe thermometer is best. If you use an instant-read thermometer, open the oven door as little as possible and remove the roast from the oven while taking its temperature. If the roast has not reached the correct temperature in the time range specified in step 4, reheat the oven to 200 degrees for 5 minutes and then shut it off and continue to cook the roast until it reaches the desired temperature. See How to Carve Prime Rib, page 220.

1 (7-pound) first-cut beef standing rib roast (3 bones)
  Kosher salt and pepper
2 teaspoons vegetable oil

1 Using sharp knife, cut roast from bones. Cut slits 1 inch apart in crosshatch pattern in fat cap of roast, being careful not to cut into meat. Rub 2 tablespoons salt thoroughly over roast and into slits. Place meat back on bones (to save space in refrigerator), transfer to large plate, and refrigerate, uncovered, for at least 24 hours or up to 4 days.

2 Adjust oven rack to middle position and heat oven to 200 degrees. Heat oil in 12-inch skillet over high heat until just smoking. Remove roast from bones. Sear top and sides of roast until browned, 6 to 8 minutes; do not sear side of roast that was cut from bones.

3 Fit roast back onto bones, let cool for 10 minutes, then tie together with kitchen twine between ribs. Transfer roast, fat side up, to wire rack set in rimmed baking sheet and season with pepper. Roast until meat registers 110 degrees, 3 to 4 hours.

4 Turn oven off and leave roast in oven, without opening door, until meat registers 115 to 120 degrees (for rare) or 120 to 125 degrees (for medium-rare), 30 minutes to 1¼ hours.

5 Remove roast from oven (leave roast on baking sheet), tent with aluminum foil, and let rest for at least 30 minutes or up to 1¼ hours.

6 Adjust oven rack 8 inches from broiler element and heat broiler. Remove foil from roast, form into 3-inch ball, and place under ribs to elevate fat cap. Broil until top of roast is well browned and crisp, 2 to 8 minutes. Transfer roast to carving board, remove twine, and remove roast from ribs. Slice meat into ¾-inch-thick pieces, season with salt, and serve.

1 Remove the Roast from the Bones
Using a sharp knife, cut the meat from the bones in a single piece. WHY? This facilitates browning the meat in a skillet before the roast (tied back onto the bones) goes into a low-temperature oven.

2 Crosshatch the Fat Cap, then Salt and Refrigerate
Cut a crosshatch pattern in the fat cap of the roast. Rub with kosher salt. Place the meat back on the bones and refrigerate for 1 to 4 days. WHY? The crosshatches speed up rendering in the oven.

3 Sear the Roast
Remove the roast from the bones and sear it in a hot skillet until browned. Do not sear the backside. WHY? The roast won't brown sufficiently unless it first spends some time in a skillet.

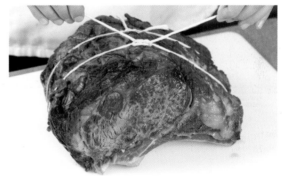

4 Tie the Meat Back onto the Bones
Fit the browned roast back onto the bones, let cool for 10 minutes, and tie them together with kitchen twine. WHY? The bones provide insulation in the oven and ensure more even cooking.

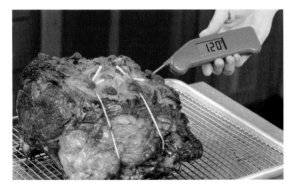

5 Roast Slowly
Roast in a 200-degree oven until the meat registers 110 degrees. Turn the oven off and leave the roast in the oven until the meat is done. WHY? A low-temperature oven ensures even cooking.

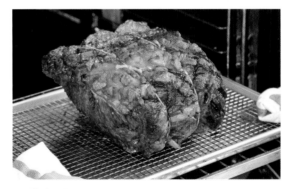

6 Broil the Top
Let the roast rest for 30 minutes to 1¼ hours and then broil until the top is well browned and crisp, 2 to 8 minutes. WHY? A quick stint under the broiler ensures a crisp, browned exterior.

TUSCAN PORK LOIN WITH GARLIC AND ROSEMARY

Serves 6 to 8
Total Time 5 hours 45 minutes (includes 1 hour 30 minutes to 2 hours for brining)

The shape of the roast determines the cooking time.

Pork and Brine

1 (4-pound) bone-in center-cut pork rib roast, trimmed
2⅓ cups packed dark brown sugar
1 cup salt
10 large garlic cloves, lightly crushed and peeled
5 sprigs fresh rosemary
1 tablespoon olive oil
1 cup dry white wine
1 teaspoon pepper

Garlic-Rosemary Paste

8 garlic cloves, minced
1½ tablespoons minced fresh rosemary
1 tablespoon extra-virgin olive oil
1 teaspoon pepper
Pinch salt

Jus

1 shallot, minced
1½ teaspoons minced fresh rosemary
1¾ cups chicken broth
2 tablespoons unsalted butter, cut into 4 pieces and softened

1 For the Pork and Brine
Cut meat away from bones. Dissolve sugar and salt in 2 quarts cold water in large container. Stir in garlic and rosemary. Submerge pork and bones in brine, cover, and refrigerate for 1½ to 2 hours.

2 For the Garlic-Rosemary Paste
While pork brines, mix all ingredients in bowl to form paste; set aside.

3 Remove meat and ribs from brine and pat dry with paper towels. Adjust oven rack to middle position and heat oven to 325 degrees. Heat oil in 12-inch skillet over medium heat until just smoking. Place roast fat side down in skillet and cook until well browned on 1 side, about 8 minutes. Transfer roast browned side up to carving board; set aside to cool. Pour off fat from skillet and add wine; increase heat to high and bring to boil, scraping up any browned bits. Set aside off heat.

4 Turn roast fat side down. Slice through center of entire length of meat, stopping 1 inch shy of edge, and open like book. Rub with one-third of garlic paste. Rub remaining garlic paste on cut side of ribs. Fold meat back together and tie back on ribs. Sprinkle browned side with pepper. Set roast rib side down in roasting pan. Pour reserved wine and browned bits from skillet into pan. Roast, basting with pan drippings every 20 minutes, until meat registers 140 degrees, 1 hour 5 minutes to 1 hour 20 minutes. (If wine evaporates, add ½ cup water to pan.) Transfer roast to carving board and tent loosely with aluminum foil; let rest for 15 minutes.

5 For the Jus
While roast rests, spoon off fat from pan and place over 2 burners at high heat. Add shallot and rosemary and scrape up any browned bits; boil until drippings are reduced by half and shallot has softened, about 2 minutes. Add broth and cook, stirring occasionally, until reduced by half, about 8 minutes. Add any accumulated pork juices and continue to cook 1 minute longer. Off heat, whisk in butter; strain jus into serving bowl. Cut twine from roast and remove meat from bones. Cut into ¼-inch-thick slices. Serve, passing jus separately.

Learn How Tuscan Pork Loin with Garlic and Rosemary

1 Remove the Meat from the Bones and Brine It
Carefully cut the meat from the bones. Submerge both in brine. Refrigerate for 1½ to 2 hours. WHY? Brining produces a succulent, well-seasoned roast.

2 Brown the Roast
Dry the meat and cook it fat side down in a skillet over medium heat for about 8 minutes. WHY? Searing the roast before transferring it to the oven helps develop good browning and adds flavor.

3 Butterfly the Roast and Rub It with an Herb Paste
Slice through the length of the meat and open it like a book. Rub it with a garlic-rosemary paste. WHY? Butterflying increases the surface area, making it easier to infuse the meat with flavor.

4 Tie the Meat Back onto the Bones
Fold the meat back together and tie it back on the rib bones. WHY? The ribs serve as a sort of roasting rack that insulates the meat and protects it from direct contact with the roasting pan.

5 Cook the Roast
Roast the meat in a 325-degree oven, basting with pan drippings every 20 minutes, until the meat registers 140 degrees. WHY? A relatively low oven temperature helps keep lean roasts moist.

6 Make the Jus
While the meat is resting, spoon the fat off the roasting pan and make jus with the drippings. WHY? Making a jus takes advantage of the resting time and all the flavorful pan drippings.

POACHED SALMON WITH HERB AND CAPER VINAIGRETTE

Serves 4
Total Time 45 minutes

To ensure uniform pieces of fish that cook at the same rate, we prefer to buy a whole center-cut fillet and cut it into four pieces ourselves.

---

2 lemons (1 cut into ¼-inch-thick slices, 1 cut into wedges)

2 tablespoons minced fresh parsley, stems reserved

2 tablespoons minced fresh tarragon, stems reserved

1 large shallot, minced

½ cup dry white wine

½ cup water

1 (1¾- to 2-pound) skinless salmon fillet, about 1½ inches thick

2 tablespoons capers, rinsed and minced

2 tablespoons extra-virgin olive oil

1 tablespoon honey

Salt and pepper

1 Arrange lemon slices in single layer in 12-inch skillet. Top with parsley and tarragon stems and 2 tablespoons shallot. Add wine and water. Cut salmon crosswise into 4 fillets and lay, skinned side down, on lemon slices.

2 Set pan over high heat and bring liquid to simmer. Reduce heat to low, cover, and cook until center of salmon is still translucent when checked with tip of paring knife and registers 125 degrees (for medium-rare), 11 to 16 minutes.

3 Remove pan from heat. Using spatula, carefully transfer salmon and lemon slices to paper towel–lined plate. Tent salmon with aluminum foil.

4 Return pan with poaching liquid to high heat and simmer until liquid has reduced to 2 tablespoons, 4 to 5 minutes. Strain liquid through fine-mesh strainer into bowl. Whisk in minced parsley, minced tarragon, remaining shallot, capers, oil, and honey. Season with salt and pepper to taste.

5 Season salmon with salt and pepper. Using spatula, carefully transfer salmon, without lemon slices, to plates. Serve with sauce and lemon wedges.

VARIATION
Poached Salmon with Dill and Sour Cream Sauce

Substitute 2 tablespoons minced fresh dill plus 8 to 12 dill stems for parsley and tarragon. Omit capers, olive oil, and honey. After straining reduced poaching liquid, return it to skillet and whisk in remaining shallot and 1 tablespoon Dijon mustard; simmer until slightly thickened, about 4 minutes. Whisk in 2 tablespoons sour cream, season with lemon juice to taste, and simmer until thickened, about 1 minute. Off heat, whisk in 2 tablespoons unsalted butter and minced dill.

1 Line the Pan with Lemon Slices
Arrange lemon slices in a skillet and top with the herb stems and shallots. WHY? The lemons keep the fillets elevated for even poaching. The shallots and stems contribute flavor to the cooking liquid.

2 Add Water and Wine
Add ½ cup each of white wine and water to the skillet. WHY? Using less liquid actually helps the fish cook more gently because the fish is steamed rather than simmered.

3 Lay the Salmon Fillets in the Skillet
Lay the fillets, skinned side down, on top of the lemons. WHY? This leaves the nonskinned side above the liquid, preserving the fillets' appearance and making them more presentable.

4 Bring to a Simmer, Reduce the Heat, and Cover
Once the poaching liquid is simmering, turn down the heat and cover the pan. WHY? This allows the salmon to cook gently and provides a gentle steaming environment, protecting the delicate fish.

5 Let the Salmon Drain
Transfer the cooked fish and lemon slices to a paper towel–lined plate, cover with foil, and let drain. WHY? If you skip this step, the fish will leak liquid onto the plate and water down the sauce.

6 Reduce, Then Strain the Poaching Liquid
Return the pan with the poaching liquid to high heat and reduce. Strain the reduced liquid and use it to create a vinaigrette. WHY? This acidic liquid is used as the "vinegar" in the sauce.

PAN-ROASTED FISH FILLETS

**4 (6- to 8-ounce) skinless white fish fillets,
1 to 1½ inches thick**

Salt and pepper

½ teaspoon sugar

1 tablespoon vegetable oil

1 Adjust oven rack to middle position and heat oven to 425 degrees. Pat fish dry with paper towels, season with salt and pepper, and sprinkle sugar lightly over 1 side of each fillet.

2 Heat oil in 12-inch ovensafe nonstick skillet over high heat until just smoking. Lay fillets, sugared side down, in skillet and press lightly to ensure even contact with pan. Cook until browned, 1 to 1½ minutes.

3 Turn fish over using 2 spatulas and transfer skillet to oven. Roast fish until centers are just opaque and register 140 degrees, 7 to 10 minutes.

4 Using potholders (skillet handle will be hot), remove skillet from oven. Transfer fish to plates and serve.

Serves 4
Total Time 30 minutes

Thick white fish fillets with a meaty texture, like halibut, cod, sea bass, or red snapper, work best in this recipe. Because most fish fillets differ in thickness, some pieces may finish cooking before others—be sure to immediately remove any fillet that reaches 140 degrees. You will need an ovensafe 12-inch nonstick skillet for this recipe. Serve with lemon wedges, a compound butter, or a relish.

Learn How Pan-Roasted Fish Fillets

1 Pat the Fish Dry
Pat the fish fillets dry with paper towels and season them with salt and pepper. WHY? For a good sear, the fish must be dry. Damp fish will just steam, not brown.

2 Sprinkle the Fish with Sugar
Sprinkle a very light dusting of sugar (about ⅛ teaspoon) evenly over one side of each fillet. WHY? A bit of sugar helps caramelize the exterior of the fish for a perfectly browned crust.

3 Sear the Fish in a Hot Pan
Heat the oil until just smoking. Place the fillets sugared side down and press lightly to ensure even contact with the pan. WHY? The stovetop jump-starts the browning process.

4 Flip the Fish Carefully
Cook until the fillets are just browned, 1 to 1½ minutes. Using two spatulas, flip the fillets. WHY? Using two spatulas makes flipping the delicate fish much easier.

5 Transfer the Skillet to a Hot Oven
Transfer the skillet to the middle rack in a 425-degree oven. WHY? A short cooking time in a very hot oven ensures the fillets are properly and evenly cooked through.

6 Roast the Fish
Roast the fillets until their centers are just opaque and register 140 degrees. WHY? White fish will be very dry if it is overcooked. Remove the fish from the hot pan or it will continue to cook.

PAN-SEARED SHRIMP

1 Pat shrimp dry with paper towels and sprinkle with ¼ teaspoon salt, ¼ teaspoon pepper, and sugar. Heat 1 tablespoon oil in 12-inch nonstick skillet over high heat until just smoking. Add half of shrimp to skillet in single layer and cook, without stirring, until spotty brown and edges turn pink, about 1 minute.

2 Remove skillet from heat, flip shrimp, and let sit until opaque in very center, about 30 seconds; transfer to bowl. Repeat with remaining 1 tablespoon oil and remaining shrimp; transfer to bowl.

3 Off heat, return all shrimp and any accumulated juices to skillet. Add butter, lemon juice, and parsley and toss to coat until butter melts. Cover and let sit until shrimp are cooked through, 1 to 2 minutes. Season with salt and pepper to taste. Serve with lemon wedges.

VARIATIONS

Pan-Seared Shrimp with Chipotle-Lime Glaze

Combine 2 tablespoons lime juice, 2 tablespoons chopped fresh cilantro, 4 teaspoons packed brown sugar, and 1 teaspoon minced canned chipotle chile in adobo sauce plus 2 teaspoons adobo sauce. Substitute mixture for butter, lemon juice, and parsley in step 3.

Pan-Seared Shrimp with Ginger-Hoisin Glaze

Add ¼ teaspoon red pepper flakes with salt, pepper, and sugar in step 1. Combine 2 tablespoons hoisin sauce, 1 tablespoon rice vinegar, 2 teaspoons grated fresh ginger, 2 teaspoons water, 1½ teaspoons soy sauce, and 2 thinly sliced scallions in small bowl. Substitute mixture for butter, lemon juice, and parsley in step 3.

Pan-Seared Shrimp with Garlic-Lemon Butter

Beat 3 tablespoons softened unsalted butter with fork in small bowl until light and fluffy. Stir in 2 tablespoons chopped fresh parsley, 1 tablespoon lemon juice, 1 minced garlic clove, and ⅛ teaspoon salt. Substitute mixture for butter, lemon juice, and parsley in step 3.

Serves 4
Total Time 30 minutes

The cooking time is for extra-large shrimp (21 to 25 shrimp per pound). If using smaller or larger shrimp, be sure to adjust the cooking time as needed. Serve with rice. See How to Prepare Shrimp, page 218.

1½ **pounds extra-large shrimp (21 to 25 per pound), peeled and deveined**

 Salt and pepper

⅛ **teaspoon sugar**

2 **tablespoons vegetable oil**

2 **tablespoons unsalted butter**

1 **tablespoon lemon juice, plus lemon wedges for serving**

1 **tablespoon minced fresh parsley**

Learn How Pan-Seared Shrimp

1 Peel and Devein the Shrimp
Peel off the shrimp shells. Cut along the back and use the tip of a paring knife to lift out the vein. WHY? Don't buy prepeeled and deveined shrimp—it's easy to perform this prep yourself.

2 Dry Season Instead of Brining
Pat the shrimp dry and season it with sugar, salt, and pepper. WHY? Skip brining, which inhibits browning, and instead use salt, pepper, and sugar to bring out the shrimp's natural sweetness.

3 Brown Half the Shrimp
Heat oil over high heat until just smoking and then add half the shrimp. WHY? Cooking half the shrimp at a time prevents overcrowding in the pan to ensure the shrimp brown, rather than steam.

4 Flip the Shrimp
Take the pan off the heat, flip the shrimp, and let them sit until they are opaque. Repeat with the rest of the shrimp. WHY? This gentle treatment keeps the delicate shrimp from overcooking.

5 Create a Flavorful Sauce
Return all the shrimp to the pan and add butter, lemon juice, and parsley. WHY? This simple sauce has acidity and richness to counter the sweetness of the shrimp.

6 Finish Cooking in the Sauce
Toss until the shrimp are completely coated. Cover the pan and let it stand until shrimp are cooked through. WHY? Finishing off the heat in the sauce helps amp up the flavors and avoids overcooking.

SIMPLE CHEESE LASAGNA

Serves 6 to 8
Total Time 1 hour 10 minutes

Do not use nonfat ricotta or fat-free mozzarella. You can substitute 4 cups jarred tomato sauce combined with one 28-ounce can diced tomatoes, drained, for the Chunky Tomato Sauce, if desired.

- 1 pound (2 cups) whole-milk ricotta cheese
- 2½ ounces Parmesan cheese, grated (1¼ cups)
- ½ cup chopped fresh basil
- 1 large egg, lightly beaten
- ½ teaspoon salt
- ½ teaspoon pepper
- 1 recipe Chunky Tomato Sauce
- 12 no-boil lasagna noodles
- 1 pound whole-milk mozzarella cheese, shredded (4 cups)

1 Adjust oven rack to middle position and heat oven to 375 degrees. Mix ricotta, 1 cup Parmesan, basil, egg, salt, and pepper together in bowl.

2 Spread ¼ cup tomato sauce over bottom of 13 by 9-inch baking dish. Lay 3 noodles in dish, spread generous 3 tablespoons ricotta mixture over each noodle, then top with 1 cup mozzarella and 1½ cups sauce (in that order). Repeat layering process 2 more times. Top with remaining 3 noodles, remaining sauce, remaining mozzarella, and remaining Parmesan.

3 Cover dish tightly with greased aluminum foil and bake for 15 minutes. Uncover and continue to bake until cheese is browned and sauce is bubbling, about 25 minutes. Let casserole cool for 10 minutes. Serve.

CHUNKY TOMATO SAUCE
Makes 6 cups
Total Time 25 minutes
Although this sauce was created specifically for lasagna and other pasta casseroles, it also tastes great over regular pasta.

Cook 1 tablespoon extra-virgin olive oil, 1 finely chopped onion, and 1 teaspoon salt in large saucepan over medium heat until onion is softened, 5 to 7 minutes. Stir in 6 minced garlic cloves, ¼ teaspoon dried oregano, and ⅛ teaspoon red pepper flakes and cook until fragrant, about 30 seconds. Stir in one 28-oz can crushed tomatoes and one 28-oz can diced tomatoes with their juice and simmer until sauce is slightly thickened and measures 6 cups, about 15 minutes. Season with salt and pepper to taste.

Learn How Simple Cheese Lasagna

1 Add Some Sauce to the Baking Dish
Spread ¼ cup tomato sauce over the bottom of a 13 by 9-inch baking dish. WHY? Adding a little sauce to the bottom of the pan keeps the noodles from sticking.

2 Add Noodles and Ricotta Mixture
Arrange three lasagna noodles on the sauce, leaving space between them. Spoon 3 tablespoons of filling onto each noodle. WHY? The noodles will expand during baking and fill the space.

3 Add Mozzarella and Sauce and Repeat
Sprinkle the first layer evenly with mozzarella, then pour tomato sauce over the cheese. Repeat the layering process two more times WHY? Careful layering ensures a well-constructed lasagna.

4 Top with Two Types of Cheese
Place three noodles on top. Spread the remaining sauce over the noodles. Sprinkle with mozzarella and Parmesan. WHY? Finishing with two types of cheese makes for an appealingly browned dish.

5 Cover the Dish and Start Baking
Spray a sheet of aluminum foil with vegetable oil spray and cover the lasagna. Bake for 15 minutes. WHY? Covering the lasagna helps it cook through without drying out.

6 Finish Baking Uncovered
Remove the foil and continue to bake until the cheese is browned and the sauce is bubbling. WHY? Baking uncovered for the last 25 minutes gives the top of the lasagna a chance to brown.

EGGPLANT PARMESAN

Serves 6 to 8
Total Time 1 hour 40 minutes

Use kosher salt when salting the eggplant; the coarse grains don't dissolve as readily as regular table salt, so any excess can be easily wiped away.

2 pounds eggplant, sliced into ¼-inch-thick rounds
  Kosher salt and pepper
8 slices hearty white sandwich bread,
  torn into quarters
3 ounces Parmesan cheese, grated (1½ cups)
1 cup all-purpose flour
4 large eggs
6 tablespoons vegetable oil
1 recipe Small-Batch Chunky Tomato Sauce
8 ounces whole-milk or part-skim mozzarella
  cheese, shredded (2 cups)
10 fresh basil leaves, roughly torn

1 Toss eggplant with 1½ teaspoons salt and let drain in colander until it releases about 2 tablespoons liquid, 30 to 45 minutes; wipe excess salt from eggplant. Line baking sheet with triple layer of paper towels, spread eggplant over top, and cover with more paper towels. Press firmly on eggplant to remove as much liquid as possible.

2 Meanwhile, pulse bread in food processor to fine, even crumbs, about 15 pulses. Transfer crumbs to large, shallow dish and stir in 1 cup Parmesan, ¼ teaspoon salt, and ½ teaspoon pepper. Combine flour and 1 teaspoon pepper in 1-gallon zipper-lock bag. Whisk eggs together in separate shallow dish.

3 Adjust oven racks to upper-middle and lower-middle positions, place rimmed baking sheet on each rack, and heat oven to 425 degrees. Working with 8 to 10 eggplant slices at a time, toss eggplant with flour mixture in bag to coat, dip in egg, then coat with bread-crumb mixture, pressing gently to adhere; set breaded slices on wire rack set in rimmed baking sheet. Repeat with remaining eggplant.

4 Carefully remove preheated baking sheets from oven, brush each with 3 tablespoons oil, then lay eggplant on sheets in single layer. Bake until eggplant is well browned and crisp, about 30 minutes, flipping eggplant and switching and rotating baking sheets halfway through cooking.

5 Spread 1 cup tomato sauce over bottom of 13 by 9-inch baking dish. Lay half of baked eggplant slices in dish, overlapping them as needed to fit. Spoon 1 cup sauce over top and sprinkle with 1 cup mozzarella. Lay remaining eggplant in dish, dot with 1 cup sauce (leaving most of eggplant exposed so it will remain crisp), and sprinkle with remaining Parmesan and remaining 1 cup mozzarella. Bake until cheese is browned, 13 to 15 minutes. Let casserole cool for 10 minutes. Sprinkle with basil leaves and serve with remaining sauce.

SMALL-BATCH CHUNKY TOMATO SAUCE
Makes 4 cups
Total Time 25 minutes
Cook 1 tablespoon extra-virgin olive oil, 1 finely chopped onion, and 1 teaspoon salt in large saucepan over medium heat until onion is softened, 5 to 7 minutes. Stir in 3 minced garlic cloves, ¼ teaspoon dried oregano, and ⅛ teaspoon red pepper flakes and cook until fragrant, about 30 seconds. Stir in one 28-oz can crushed tomatoes and one 14.5-oz can diced tomatoes with their juice and simmer until sauce is slightly thickened and measures 4 cups, about 15 minutes. Season with salt and pepper to taste.

Learn How Eggplant Parmesan

1 Salt and Dry the Eggplant
Toss the eggplant with kosher salt and let the slices drain in a colander for 30 to 45 minutes. Wipe off the excess salt, then pat dry thoroughly. WHY? Salting draws moisture from the eggplant.

2 Make Fresh Bread Crumbs
Pulse sandwich bread in a food processor to fine, even crumbs. Transfer to a shallow dish and stir in Parmesan, salt, and pepper. WHY? Fresh bread crumbs have superior flavor and crunch.

3 Prepare a Simple Tomato Sauce
Sauté the aromatics, then add the crushed and diced tomatoes and simmer until thickened. WHY? This easy-to-make homemade sauce tastes fresher than store-bought.

4 Bread the Eggplant
Flour eggplant, dip into egg, then coat with bread crumbs, pressing gently to adhere. WHY? Dipping the eggplant in flour, then egg, then bread crumbs creates a substantial coating that crisps up nicely.

5 Bake the Eggplant
Bake the eggplant in a single layer on preheated and well-oiled baking sheets. WHY? This technique creates crisp, golden-brown results. It's also easier and less messy than frying.

6 Assemble the Layers
Layer the dish with tomato sauce, eggplant, more sauce, mozzarella, more eggplant, more sauce, Parmesan, and more mozzarella. WHY? Precise portioning ensures even layers.

PASTA WITH CLASSIC BOLOGNESE SAUCE

Serves 4 to 6
Total Time 4 hours

If you would like to double this recipe, increase the simmering times for the milk and the wine to 30 minutes each, and the simmering time to 4 hours once the tomatoes are added. Just about any pasta shape complements this meaty sauce, but fettuccine and linguine are the test kitchen favorites. If you can't find meatloaf mix, use 6 ounces of 85 percent lean ground beef and 6 ounces of ground pork. See How to Cook Dried Pasta, page 213.

5 tablespoons unsalted butter
2 tablespoons finely chopped onion
2 tablespoons minced carrot
2 tablespoons minced celery
12 ounces meatloaf mix
Salt and pepper
1 cup whole milk
1 cup dry white wine
1 (28-ounce) can whole peeled tomatoes, drained with juice reserved, tomatoes chopped fine
1 pound fettuccine or linguine
Grated Parmesan cheese

1 Melt 3 tablespoons butter in Dutch oven over medium heat. Add onion, carrot, and celery and cook until softened, 5 to 7 minutes. Stir in meatloaf mix and ½ teaspoon salt and cook, breaking up meat with wooden spoon, until no longer pink, about 3 minutes.

2 Stir in milk, bring to simmer, and cook until milk evaporates and only rendered fat remains, 10 to 15 minutes. Stir in wine, bring to simmer, and cook until wine evaporates, 10 to 15 minutes.

3 Stir in tomatoes and reserved tomato juice and bring to simmer. Reduce heat to low so that sauce continues to simmer just barely, with occasional bubble or two at surface, until liquid has evaporated, about 3 hours. Season with salt to taste. (Sauce can be refrigerated for up to 2 days or frozen for up to 1 month.)

4 Meanwhile, bring 4 quarts water to boil in large pot. Add pasta and 1 tablespoon salt and cook, stirring often, until al dente. Reserve ½ cup cooking water, then drain pasta and return it to pot. Add sauce and remaining 2 tablespoons butter and toss to combine. Season with salt and pepper to taste, and add reserved cooking water as needed to adjust consistency. Serve with Parmesan.

VARIATION
Pasta with Beef Bolognese Sauce
Substitute 12 ounces 85 percent lean ground beef for meatloaf mix.

1 Sauté the Aromatics in Butter
Melt the butter in a Dutch oven and cook the onion, carrot, and celery until softened. WHY? Sautéing the aromatics in butter rather than oil adds rich flavor to the base of the sauce.

2 Add the Meatloaf Mix
Stir in the meatloaf mix and salt and cook, breaking up the meat, until it is no longer pink. WHY? A combination of ground beef, veal, and pork makes this sauce especially complex.

3 Stir in the Milk and Simmer
Add the whole milk and simmer until it evaporates and only the rendered fat remains. WHY? Adding whole milk provides just enough dairy flavor to complement the meat.

4 Stir in the Wine and Simmer
Add dry white wine and simmer until it evaporates. WHY? The acidity of the wine balances the richness of the meat and adds further depth to the sauce.

5 Add the Tomatoes and Cook for 3 Hours
Add the drained and chopped whole tomatoes and their juices. Simmer until the liquid has evaporated, about 3 hours. WHY? The long simmer time tenderizes the meat and builds flavor.

6 Finish with Butter and Pasta Cooking Water
Add the remaining butter to the cooked pasta along with the sauce. Add pasta cooking water as needed to adjust the consistency. WHY? The butter contributes richness to the sauce.

MEATBALLS AND MARINARA

8 ounces sweet Italian sausage, casings removed

2 ounces Parmesan cheese, grated (1 cup)

½ cup minced fresh parsley

2 large eggs

2 garlic cloves, minced

1½ teaspoons salt

2½ pounds 80 percent lean ground chuck

2 pounds spaghetti

1 **For the Sauce**
Heat oil in Dutch oven over medium-high heat until shimmering. Add onions and cook until golden, 10 to 15 minutes. Stir in garlic, oregano, and pepper flakes and cook until fragrant, about 30 seconds. Transfer half of onion mixture to bowl; set aside for meatballs.

2 Stir tomato paste into onion mixture left in pot and cook over medium-high heat until fragrant, about 1 minute. Stir in wine and cook until slightly thickened, about 2 minutes. Stir in water and tomatoes and simmer over low heat until sauce is no longer watery, 45 minutes to 1 hour. Stir in Parmesan and basil and season with salt and pepper to taste.

3 **For the Meatballs and Pasta**
Meanwhile, line 2 rimmed baking sheets with aluminum foil and spray with vegetable oil spray. Adjust oven racks to lower-middle and upper-middle positions and heat oven to 475 degrees. Mash bread and milk in large bowl until smooth. Mix in reserved onion mixture, sausage, Parmesan, parsley, eggs, garlic, and salt. Add beef and gently knead with your hands until well combined.

4 Shape meat mixture into 30 meatballs (about ¼ cup each) and place on prepared sheets, spaced evenly apart. Roast meatballs until well browned, about 20 minutes. Transfer meatballs to pot with sauce and simmer for 15 minutes. (Meatballs and marinara can be refrigerated for up to 3 days or frozen for up to 1 month.)

5 Meanwhile, bring 8 quarts water to boil in 12-quart pot. Add pasta and 2 tablespoons salt and cook, stirring often, until al dente. Reserve 1 cup cooking water, then drain pasta and return it to pot. Add several spoonfuls of sauce (without meatballs) and toss to combine. Add reserved cooking water as needed to adjust consistency. Serve pasta with remaining sauce and meatballs.

Serves 8 to 10
Total Time 2 hours

The meatballs and sauce both use the same onion mixture. See How to Cook Dried Pasta, page 213.

Sauce

¼ cup extra-virgin olive oil

3 onions, chopped fine

8 garlic cloves, minced

1 tablespoon dried oregano

½ teaspoon red pepper flakes

1 (6-ounce) can tomato paste

1 cup dry red wine

1 cup water

4 (28-ounce) cans crushed tomatoes

1 ounce Parmesan cheese, grated (½ cup)

¼ cup chopped fresh basil

Salt and pepper

Meatballs and Pasta

4 slices hearty white sandwich bread, torn into pieces

¾ cup milk

Learn How Meatballs and Marinara

1 Cook the Onions and the Aromatics
Cook the onions. Add the garlic, oregano, and red pepper flakes and cook until fragrant. Reserve half of the mixture for the meatballs. WHY? It saves time to cook one large batch of aromatics.

2 Make the Sauce
Add the tomato paste to the onion mixture and cook, then add the red wine and cook. Add the tomatoes and water and simmer. WHY? Some of the alcohol will cook off as the wine reduces.

3 Make a Panade
Mash the sandwich bread and milk together until smooth, then add the remaining meatball ingredients. WHY? The panade binds the meatballs and adds moisture and richness.

4 Add the Ground Chuck Last
Using your hands, gently work 2½ pounds of 80 percent lean ground chuck into the sausage and panade mixture. WHY? Overworked ground beef makes for dense, rubbery meatballs.

5 Form into Balls and Brown in the Oven
Gently roll the mixture into meatballs and bake them in a 475-degree oven until well browned. WHY? This gives the meatballs a tasty seared crust and is easier than browning on the stovetop.

6 Finish the Meatballs in the Sauce
Transfer the browned meatballs to the pot with the marinara and simmer for 15 minutes. WHY? The meatballs will finish cooking evenly in the sauce (and will flavor the sauce in the process).

BAKED MACARONI AND CHEESE

8 tablespoons unsalted butter

1 cup panko bread crumbs

Salt and pepper

1 pound elbow macaroni or small shells

1 garlic clove, minced

1 teaspoon dry mustard

¼ teaspoon cayenne pepper

6 tablespoons all-purpose flour

3½ cups whole milk

2¼ cups chicken broth

1 pound Colby cheese, shredded (4 cups)

8 ounces extra-sharp cheddar cheese, shredded (2 cups)

1 Adjust oven rack to middle position and heat oven to 350 degrees. Melt 2 tablespoons butter, then toss with panko in bowl and season with salt and pepper. Spread panko onto rimmed baking sheet and bake until golden, about 10 minutes. Increase oven temperature to 400 degrees.

2 Meanwhile, bring 4 quarts water to boil in large pot. Add macaroni and 1 tablespoon salt and cook, stirring often, until nearly al dente. Drain pasta and set aside.

3 Dry now-empty pot, add remaining 6 tablespoons butter, and melt over medium heat. Stir in garlic, mustard, and cayenne and cook until fragrant, about 30 seconds. Stir in flour and cook for 1 minute. Slowly whisk in milk and broth until smooth. Simmer, whisking often, until thickened, about 15 minutes.

4 Off heat, gradually whisk in Colby and cheddar until melted. Season with salt and pepper to taste. Stir in cooked pasta, breaking up any clumps. Pour into 13 by 9-inch baking dish and sprinkle with toasted bread-crumb mixture. Bake until golden and bubbling around edges, 25 to 35 minutes. Let casserole cool for 10 minutes. Serve.

To Make Ahead

Assembled, unbaked casserole can be refrigerated for up to 24 hours. To serve, cover with greased aluminum foil and bake in 400-degree oven until hot throughout, 20 to 25 minutes. Uncover and continue to bake until crumbs are crisp, 10 to 20 minutes.

Serves 6
Total Time 1 hour 35 minutes

The macaroni will still be firm after cooking according to the directions in step 2 (it will finish cooking in the oven).

1 Combine the Bread Crumbs and Butter
Toss the panko bread crumbs with melted butter,
spread them on a rimmed baking sheet, and bake
until golden. WHY? Coating the crumbs in butter
before baking gives them even more crunch.

2 Undercook the Pasta
Bring 4 quarts of water to a boil. Add the macaroni
and cook until nearly al dente. Drain the pasta.
WHY? Undercooking the pasta ensures that it
won't overcook during the baking stage.

3 Make the Sauce
Melt the butter and stir in the garlic, mustard
powder, and cayenne. Add flour, whole milk, and
chicken broth and simmer until thickened. WHY?
Broth keeps this sauce from becoming too rich.

4 Use Two Kinds of Cheese
Take the pot off the heat and gradually whisk
in the Colby and cheddar cheeses until melted.
WHY? Using a combination of cheeses creates
ultracheesy flavor and a creamy texture.

5 Add the Pasta
Stir in the cooked pasta, breaking up any clumps.
WHY? Adding the pasta to the finished sauce
helps ensure an even coating.

6 Top with Bread Crumbs and Bake Uncovered
Pour the pasta into a baking dish and sprinkle with
the toasted bread crumbs. Bake until the pasta
is golden and bubbling around the edges. WHY?
Finishing in the oven creates a crunchy top layer.

SCALLOPED POTATOES

1 cup chicken broth
1 cup heavy cream
2 bay leaves
4 ounces cheddar cheese, shredded (1 cup)

1 Adjust oven rack to middle position and heat oven to 425 degrees. Melt butter in Dutch oven over medium-high heat. Add onion and cook until softened, 5 to 7 minutes. Stir in thyme, garlic, salt, and pepper and cook until fragrant, about 30 seconds. Add potatoes, broth, cream, and bay leaves and bring to simmer.

2 Cover, reduce heat to medium-low, and simmer until potatoes are almost tender (paring knife can be slipped in and out of potato slice with some resistance), about 10 minutes.

3 Discard bay leaves. Transfer mixture to 8-inch square baking dish and press into even layer. Sprinkle evenly with cheddar. Bake until bubbling around edges and top is golden brown, about 15 minutes. Let casserole cool for 10 minutes before serving.

To Make Ahead
Do not top casserole with cheddar; casserole can be refrigerated for up to 24 hours. To serve, cover dish tightly with greased aluminum foil and bake in 400-degree oven until hot throughout, about 45 minutes. Uncover, top with cheddar, and continue to bake until cheddar is lightly browned, about 30 minutes. Let casserole cool for 10 minutes before serving.

VARIATIONS

Scalloped Potatoes with Chipotle Chile and Smoked Cheddar Cheese
Add 2 teaspoons minced canned chipotle chile in adobo sauce to pot with potatoes. Substitute smoked cheddar for cheddar.

Scalloped Potatoes with Wild Mushrooms
Add 8 ounces cremini mushrooms, trimmed and sliced ¼ inch thick, and 4 ounces shiitake mushrooms, stemmed and sliced ¼ inch thick, to pot with onion; cook as directed.

Serves 4 to 6
Total Time 1 hour 10 minutes

Prep and assemble all of the other ingredients before slicing the potatoes or they will begin to brown. If the potato slices do start to discolor, put them in a bowl and cover with the cream and chicken broth. Slicing the potatoes ⅛ inch thick is crucial for the success of this dish; use a mandoline, a V-slicer, or a food processor fitted with a ⅛-inch-thick slicing blade. You can substitute Parmesan for the cheddar if desired.

2 tablespoons unsalted butter
1 onion, chopped fine
1 tablespoon minced fresh thyme or 1 teaspoon dried
2 garlic cloves, minced
1¼ teaspoons salt
¼ teaspoon pepper
2½ pounds russet potatoes, peeled and sliced ⅛ inch thick

Learn How Scalloped Potatoes

1 Thinly Slice Russet Potatoes
Peel and slice the potatoes ⅛ inch thick using a mandoline, V-slicer, or food processor. WHY? If cut thicker, the potatoes won't hold together. If too thin, the potatoes will melt together entirely.

2 Sauté the Aromatics
Cook the onion until softened. Stir in the thyme, garlic, salt, and pepper. WHY? Sautéing the onion and garlic helps build the base for the sauce. Thyme complements the earthy potatoes.

3 Simmer the Potatoes in Broth and Cream
Add the potatoes, chicken broth, cream, and bay leaves and simmer until the potatoes are almost tender. WHY? Parcooking the potatoes in broth and cream infuses them with flavor.

4 Transfer the Potatoes to a Baking Dish
Transfer the potatoes to a baking dish and press them into an even layer. WHY? Cooking the potatoes on the stovetop creates the sauce, so there is no need for fussy layering, saving time.

5 Top with Shredded Cheese and Bake
Sprinkle the casserole with cheddar cheese. Bake until the cream is bubbling and the top is golden brown. WHY? The precooked potatoes need only a short time in the oven to finish cooking.

6 Let the Casserole Cool for 10 Minutes
Remove the casserole from the oven and let it cool for 10 minutes before serving. WHY? Cooling the casserole gives it time to set up, ensuring you get attractive portions.

ALMOST HANDS-FREE RISOTTO WITH CHICKEN AND HERBS

Serves 6
Total Time 1 hour 30 minutes

We recommend that you use a timer when simmering the rice to ensure that the rice does not wind up soft and overcooked. If you prefer a brothy risotto, add the extra broth in step 6. Homemade Chicken Stock (page 246) will yield the best-tasting risotto, but store-bought broth will work. For best results, make sure to use genuine Italian Parmigiano-Reggiano, not domestically made Parmesan cheese.

5 cups chicken broth

2 cups water

1 tablespoon olive oil

2 (12-ounce) bone-in split chicken breasts, trimmed and halved crosswise

4 tablespoons unsalted butter

1 large onion, chopped fine

   Salt and pepper

1 large garlic clove, minced

2 cups Arborio rice

1 cup dry white wine

2 ounces Parmesan cheese, grated (1 cup)

2 tablespoons chopped fresh parsley

2 tablespoons chopped fresh chives

1 teaspoon lemon juice

1 Bring broth and water to boil in large saucepan over high heat. Reduce heat to medium-low to maintain gentle simmer.

2 Pat chicken dry with paper towels. Heat oil in Dutch oven over medium heat until just smoking. Add chicken, skin side down, and cook without moving until golden brown, 4 to 6 minutes. Flip chicken and cook on second side until lightly browned, about 2 minutes. Transfer chicken to saucepan of simmering broth and cook until thickest part registers 160 degrees, 10 to 15 minutes. Transfer to large plate.

3 Melt 2 tablespoons butter in now-empty pot over medium heat. Add onion and ¾ teaspoon salt; cook, stirring frequently, until onion is softened but not browned, 4 to 5 minutes. Add garlic and cook until fragrant, about 30 seconds. Add rice and cook, stirring frequently, until grains are translucent around edges, about 3 minutes.

4 Add wine and cook, stirring constantly, until fully absorbed, 2 to 3 minutes. Stir 5 cups warm broth mixture into rice; reduce heat to medium-low, cover, and simmer until almost all liquid has been absorbed and rice is just al dente, 16 to 18 minutes, stirring twice during cooking.

5 Add ¾ cup warm broth mixture to risotto and stir gently and constantly until risotto becomes creamy, about 3 minutes. Stir in Parmesan. Remove pot from heat, cover, and let stand for 5 minutes.

6 Meanwhile, discard skin and bones from chicken and shred meat into bite-size pieces. Gently stir shredded chicken, parsley, chives, lemon juice, and remaining 2 tablespoons butter into risotto. Season with salt and pepper to taste. If desired, add up to ½ cup additional broth mixture to loosen texture of risotto. Serve.

1 Sear and Then Simmer the Chicken
Sear the chicken breasts and then transfer to a saucepan of simmering broth-water mixture to cook through. WHY? This technique adds great flavor to the broth.

2 Sauté the Aromatics
Add butter to the now-empty Dutch oven. Once it has melted, cook the onion and garlic. WHY? This builds a flavorful base for the risotto.

3 Toast the Rice
Add the rice and cook, stirring frequently, until the grains are translucent around the edges, about 3 minutes. WHY? Toasting the rice briefly before adding the liquid gives it a pleasant, nutty taste.

4 Add Most of the Liquid
Add the wine and 5 cups of the warm broth-water mixture. Reduce the heat, cover, and simmer until the rice is just al dente. WHY? This method eliminates the need for constant stirring.

5 Add a Bit More Liquid
Add ¾ cup of the warm broth mixture. Stir gently and constantly until the risotto becomes creamy. WHY? This short stint of last-minute stirring and final addition of liquid helps loosen the risotto.

6 Add Parmesan and Remove the Pot from the Heat
Stir in the Parmesan. Remove the pot from the heat, cover, and let it stand for 5 minutes. Add the remaining ingredients. WHY? This ensures that the rice won't burn and creates a creamy sauce.

CUBAN BLACK BEANS AND RICE

Serves 6 to 8
Total Time 9 hours 45 minutes
(includes 8 hours for soaking the beans)

It is important to use lean—not fatty—salt pork. If you can't find it, substitute six slices of bacon. If using bacon, decrease the cooking time in step 3 to 8 minutes. You will need a Dutch oven with a tight-fitting lid for this recipe.

Salt
1 cup dried black beans, picked over and rinsed
2 cups chicken broth
2 cups water
2 large green bell peppers, halved, stemmed, and seeded
1 large onion, halved crosswise
1 garlic head (5 cloves minced, rest of head halved crosswise with skin left intact)
2 bay leaves
6 ounces lean salt pork, rind removed, cut into ¼-inch pieces
2 tablespoons vegetable oil
4 teaspoons ground cumin

1 tablespoon minced fresh oregano
1½ cups long-grain white rice, rinsed
2 tablespoons red wine vinegar
2 scallions, sliced thin
Lime wedges

1 Dissolve 1½ tablespoons salt in 2 quarts cold water in large container. Add beans and soak at room temperature for at least 8 hours or up to 24 hours. Drain and rinse well.

2 Combine drained beans, broth, water, 1 bell pepper half, root end of onion half, garlic head halves, bay leaves, and 1 teaspoon salt in Dutch oven. Bring to simmer over medium-high heat. Cover, reduce heat to low, and cook until beans are just soft, 30 to 40 minutes. Discard bell pepper, onion, garlic, and bay leaves, then drain beans in colander set over bowl; reserve 2½ cups bean cooking liquid.

3 Meanwhile, adjust oven rack to middle position and heat oven to 350 degrees. Cook salt pork and 1 tablespoon oil in now-empty pot over medium-low heat, stirring often, until lightly browned and fat is rendered, 15 to 20 minutes. Coarsely chop remaining bell pepper halves and onion half, then pulse in food processor into ¼-inch pieces, about 8 pulses; set aside.

4 Add remaining 1 tablespoon oil, processed vegetables, cumin, and oregano to salt pork. Increase heat to medium and cook, stirring often, until vegetables begin to brown, 10 to 15 minutes. Stir in minced garlic and cook until fragrant, about 30 seconds. Stir in rice until evenly combined.

5 Stir in drained beans, reserved cooking liquid, vinegar, and ½ teaspoon salt. Increase heat to medium-high and bring to simmer. Cover pot and transfer to oven. Bake until liquid is absorbed and rice is tender, about 30 minutes.

6 Fluff rice and beans with fork. Let rest, uncovered, for 5 minutes. Serve with scallions and lime wedges.

VARIATION
Vegetarian Cuban Black Beans and Rice
Substitute water for chicken broth, and omit salt pork. Add 1 tablespoon tomato paste to pot with processed vegetables in step 4. Increase salt to 1½ teaspoons in step 5.

1 Salt-Soak the Beans
Dissolve salt in cold water. Add the beans and soak at room temperature for at least 8 hours. Drain and rinse well. WHY? Salt-soaking shortens the cooking time and results in a creamier texture.

2 Simmer the Beans
Simmer the beans with the aromatics, then discard the aromatics and drain the beans, reserving 2½ cups of the cooking liquid. WHY? Aromatic vegetables infuse the beans with extra flavor.

3 Process the Pepper and Onion
Process the remaining bell pepper and onion into ¼-inch pieces. WHY? The processed vegetables are small enough to blend into the texture of the dish.

4 Sauté Salt Pork, Then Cook Peppers and Onion
Cook the salt pork with oil until the pork fat is rendered, then add the processed vegetables, cumin, and oregano. WHY? Browning the vegetables in the pork fat creates great flavor.

5 Cover the Pot and Move to the Oven
Add the rice, beans, and reserved liquid. Cook in the oven until the liquid is absorbed and the rice is tender. WHY? The indirect heat of the oven ooks the rice gently and evenly.

6 Fluff the Rice and Beans and Let Them Rest
Fluff the rice and beans with a fork and let them rest, uncovered, for 5 minutes. WHY? Letting the dish rest uncovered allows the rice and beans to absorb any excess moisture.

INDIAN-STYLE CURRY WITH POTATOES, CAULIFLOWER, PEAS, AND CHICKPEAS

Serves 4 to 6
Total Time 1 hour

This curry is moderately spicy; for more heat, reserve, mince, and add the ribs and seeds from the chile. Serve with rice.

2 tablespoons sweet or mild curry powder

1½ teaspoons garam masala

¼ cup vegetable oil

3 garlic cloves, minced

1 tablespoon grated fresh ginger

1 serrano chile, stemmed, seeded, and minced

1 tablespoon tomato paste

1 (14.5-ounce) can diced tomatoes

2 onions, chopped fine

12 ounces red potatoes, unpeeled, cut into ½-inch pieces

½ head cauliflower (1 pound), cored and cut into 1-inch florets

1¼ cups water

1 (15-ounce) can chickpeas, rinsed

Salt

1½ cups frozen peas

¼ cup heavy cream or canned coconut milk

1 Toast curry powder and garam masala in 8-inch skillet over medium-high heat, stirring constantly, until spices darken slightly and become fragrant, about 1 minute. Transfer spices to small bowl and set aside. In separate small bowl, stir 1 tablespoon oil, garlic, ginger, serrano, and tomato paste together. Pulse tomatoes with their juice in food processor until coarsely chopped, 3 to 4 pulses.

2 Heat remaining 3 tablespoons oil in Dutch oven over medium-high heat until shimmering. Add onions and potatoes and cook, stirring occasionally, until onions are caramelized and potatoes are golden brown around edges, about 10 minutes. (Reduce heat to medium if onions darken too quickly.)

3 Reduce heat to medium. Clear center of pot, add garlic mixture, and cook, mashing mixture into pan, until fragrant, 15 to 20 seconds. Stir garlic mixture into vegetables. Add toasted spices and cook, stirring constantly, for 1 minute longer. Add cauliflower and cook, stirring constantly, until spices coat florets, about 2 minutes longer.

4 Add tomatoes, water, chickpeas, and 1 teaspoon salt, scraping up any browned bits. Bring to boil over medium-high heat. Cover, reduce heat to medium, and cook, stirring occasionally, until vegetables are tender, 10 to 15 minutes. Stir in peas and cream and continue to cook until heated through, about 2 minutes longer. Season with salt to taste, and serve.

VARIATION

Indian-Style Curry with Sweet Potatoes, Eggplant, Green Beans, and Chickpeas

Substitute 12 ounces sweet potato, peeled and cut into ½-inch pieces, for red potatoes. Substitute 8 ounces green beans, trimmed and cut into 1-inch pieces, and 1 pound eggplant, cut into ½-inch pieces, for cauliflower. Omit peas.

Learn How Indian-Style Curry with Potatoes, Cauliflower, Peas, and Chickpeas

1 Toast the Spices
Toast the spices until they become fragrant, then set them aside. WHY? Toasting store-bought curry powder in a skillet turns it into a flavor powerhouse.

2 Cook the Potatoes and Onions
Cook the onions and potatoes over medium-high heat until the onions are caramelized and the potatoes are golden brown around the edges. WHY? This gives the potatoes a jump start.

3 Incorporate the Aromatics
Clear the center of the pot, add the aromatics, and cook, mashing into the pan, until fragrant. Stir the mixture into the vegetables. WHY? This technique adds deep flavor to the vegetables.

4 Add the Cauliflower, Chickpeas, and Tomatoes
Add the cauliflower and cook, stirring constantly, until it's coated in spices, then add the tomatoes, water, chickpeas, and salt. WHY? This ensures that all the different vegetables cook through properly.

5 Simmer the Curry
Simmer the dish over medium heat until the vegetables are tender. WHY? The simmering sauce infuses all the vegetables with deep flavor.

6 Add the Cream and Peas at the End
Stir in the peas and cream and continue to cook until heated through, about 2 minutes longer. WHY? These delicate ingredients require very little cooking so we reserve them until the end.

STIR-FRIED TOFU AND BOK CHOY

Serves 4
Total Time 45 minutes

One pound of baby bok choy may be used in place of regular bok choy if available; simply quarter it lengthwise. It is important to use extra-firm tofu in this recipe. Serve with rice.

Sauce
½ cup vegetable broth
¼ cup soy sauce
2 tablespoons Chinese rice wine or dry sherry
1 tablespoon sugar
2 teaspoons cornstarch
1 teaspoon toasted sesame oil

Stir-Fry
14 ounces extra-firm tofu, cut into 1-inch cubes
⅓ cup cornstarch
3 scallions, minced
3 garlic cloves, minced
1 tablespoon grated fresh ginger
3 tablespoons vegetable oil
1 pound bok choy, stalks and greens separated, stalks sliced thin, and greens cut into 1-inch pieces
2 carrots, peeled and cut into matchsticks

1 **For the Sauce**
Whisk all ingredients together in bowl.

2 **For the Stir-Fry**
Spread tofu out over paper towel–lined baking sheet and let drain for 20 minutes. Gently pat tofu dry with paper towels, then toss with cornstarch in bowl. Transfer coated tofu to fine-mesh strainer and shake gently over bowl to remove excess cornstarch.

3 Combine scallions, garlic, ginger, and 1 teaspoon oil in bowl; set aside. Heat 2 tablespoons oil in 12-inch nonstick skillet over high heat until just smoking. Add tofu and cook until crisp and well browned on all sides, 10 to 15 minutes; transfer to bowl.

4 Add remaining 2 teaspoons oil to skillet and return to high heat until shimmering. Add bok choy stalks and carrots and cook until vegetables are crisp-tender, about 4 minutes. Clear center of skillet, add garlic mixture, and cook, mashing mixture into skillet, until fragrant, about 30 seconds. Stir garlic mixture into vegetables.

5 Return tofu to skillet. Stir in bok choy greens. Whisk sauce to recombine, then add to skillet. Cook, stirring constantly, until sauce is thickened, 1 to 2 minutes. Serve.

1 Slice and Drain the Tofu
Cut the tofu into 1-inch cubes. Spread over a paper towel–lined baking sheet. Let sit for 20 minutes and then pat dry with paper towels. WHY? Removing excess water ensures crispy tofu.

2 Coat the Tofu with Cornstarch
Toss the tofu in batches with ⅓ cup cornstarch. Place the coated tofu in a fine-mesh strainer and shake off any excess cornstarch. WHY? A cornstarch coating makes the tofu extra-crispy.

3 Get the Skillet Hot and Stir-Fry the Tofu
Heat the oil over high heat until just smoking. Add the tofu and cook until it's well browned on all sides. WHY? It's crucial to heat the oil until just smoking or the tofu won't brown properly.

4 Stagger Cooking the Vegetables
Cook the bok choy stalks and carrots until the vegetables are crisp-tender. WHY? Starting with the thicker bok choy stalks and carrots ensures they cook through completely.

5 Add the Aromatics
Clear the center of the skillet, add the garlic-ginger mixture and cook until fragrant. Stir the mixture into the vegetables. WHY? This ensures the aromatics soften and flavor the vegetables.

6 Return the Tofu to the Pan and Add the Sauce
Add the tofu and the bok choy greens. Whisk the sauce to recombine and add it to the skillet. Cook until the sauce has thickened. WHY? This marries the sauce with all the other ingredients.

FLUFFY DINER-STYLE CHEESE OMELET

3 tablespoons heavy cream, chilled

5 large eggs, room temperature

¼ teaspoon salt

2 tablespoons unsalted butter

2 ounces sharp cheddar cheese, shredded (½ cup)

1 Adjust oven rack to middle position and heat oven to 400 degrees. Using handheld mixer, whip cream on medium-low speed in bowl until foamy, about 1 minute. Increase speed to high and whip until soft peaks form, 1 to 3 minutes. Set whipped cream aside.

2 Using dry, clean whisk attachment, whip eggs and salt in large bowl on high speed until frothy and eggs have at least doubled in volume, about 2 minutes. Using rubber spatula, gently fold whipped cream into eggs.

3 Melt butter in 10-inch ovensafe nonstick skillet over medium-low heat, swirling to coat pan. Add egg mixture and cook until edges are nearly set, 2 to 3 minutes. Sprinkle with ¼ cup cheddar and transfer to oven. Bake until eggs are set and edges are beginning to brown, 6 to 8 minutes.

4 Carefully remove skillet from oven (handle will be hot), then sprinkle eggs with remaining ¼ cup cheddar. Let sit, covered, until cheese melts, about 1 minute. Tilt skillet and, using rubber spatula, push half of omelet onto cutting board, then fold omelet over itself on cutting board to form half-moon shape. Cut omelet in half and serve.

VARIATION

Fluffy Diner-Style Cheese Omelet with Sausage and Bell Pepper

Before cooking eggs, cook 4 ounces crumbled sweet Italian sausage in 10-inch nonstick skillet over medium heat until browned, about 6 minutes; transfer to paper towel–lined plate. Add 1 tablespoon unsalted butter, 1 finely chopped small onion, and ½ finely chopped red bell pepper to now-empty skillet and cook over medium heat until softened, about 10 minutes; transfer to plate with sausage. Clean skillet and cook omelet as directed, sprinkling half of sausage mixture over omelet with cheese in step 3 and remaining filling with remaining cheese in step 4.

Serves 2
Total Time 25 minutes

A handheld mixer makes quick work of whipping such a small amount of cream, but you can also use a stand mixer fitted with the whisk attachment. To make two omelets, double this recipe and cook the omelets simultaneously in two skillets, or set half of the ingredients aside to make the second omelet; be sure to wipe out the skillet before making the second omelet. You will need a 10-inch ovensafe nonstick skillet with a tight-fitting lid for this recipe.

1 Whip the Cream and the Eggs
Whip the chilled cream until soft peaks form. Whip the eggs and salt until they double in volume. WHY? Whipping the eggs makes for an extra-fluffy omelet. The whipped cream adds richness.

2 Fold the Cream into the Eggs
Gently fold the whipped cream into the whipped eggs. WHY? Gently folding the cream into the eggs ensures that everything stays light and airy.

3 Melt the Butter, Then Add the Egg Mixture
Melt the butter in an ovensafe nonstick skillet. Add the egg mixture and cook until the edges are nearly set. WHY? A nonstick skillet ensures that the omelet will be easy to remove.

4 Add Half of the Cheese and Transfer to the Oven
Sprinkle half of the cheese (and filling, if using) over the eggs. Bake until the eggs are set and the edges begin to brown. WHY? The oven is the best way to set the omelet's top and cook the interior.

5 Remove from the Oven, Add Cheese, and Cover
Remove the pan from the oven. Sprinkle with remaining cheese (and filling, if using). Cover and let sit, off the heat, until the cheese melts. WHY? The lid traps just enough heat to finish the omelet.

6 Slide, Then Fold the Omelet onto a Cutting Board
Tilt the skillet and, with a spatula, push half of the omelet onto a cutting board. Then tilt the skillet so that the omelet folds over itself. WHY? This technique prevents the omelet from tearing.

LIGHT AND FLUFFY BUTTERMILK BISCUITS

Makes 12 biscuits
Total Time 45 minutes

When cutting the biscuits, be sure to press down with firm, even pressure and avoid twisting the cutter.

3 cups (15 ounces) all-purpose flour
1 tablespoon sugar
1 tablespoon baking powder
½ teaspoon baking soda
1 teaspoon salt
8 tablespoons unsalted butter, cut into ½-inch pieces and chilled
4 tablespoons vegetable shortening, cut into ½-inch pieces and chilled
1¼ cups buttermilk

1 Adjust oven rack to middle position and heat oven to 450 degrees. Line rimmed baking sheet with parchment paper. Pulse flour, sugar, baking powder, baking soda, and salt in food processor until combined, about 5 pulses. Sprinkle chilled butter and shortening over top and pulse until mixture resembles coarse meal, about 15 pulses.

2 Transfer flour mixture to large bowl. Stir in buttermilk until combined. Turn dough out onto lightly floured counter and knead briefly, 8 to 10 times, to form smooth, cohesive ball. Roll dough into 9-inch circle, about ¾ inch thick.

3 Cut biscuits into rounds using 2½-inch biscuit cutter, dipping cutter in flour as needed. Gather dough scraps together, pat gently into ¾-inch-thick circle, and cut out additional rounds. Place biscuits upside down on prepared baking sheet. (Raw biscuits can be refrigerated for up to 24 hours; bake as directed.)

4 Bake until biscuits begin to rise, about 5 minutes. Rotate sheet, reduce oven temperature to 400 degrees, and continue to bake until golden brown, 10 to 12 minutes. Transfer biscuits to wire rack, let cool for 5 minutes, and serve.

VARIATIONS

Light and Fluffy Buttermilk Biscuits with Cheddar and Scallions
Stir ½ cup shredded cheddar cheese and 2 thinly sliced scallions into flour mixture before adding buttermilk.

Light and Fluffy Buttermilk Biscuits with Parmesan and Black Pepper
Stir ¾ cup grated Parmesan cheese and 1 teaspoon coarsely ground black pepper into flour mixture before adding buttermilk.

Light and Fluffy Buttermilk Biscuits with Fontina and Rosemary
Stir ½ cup shredded fontina cheese and ½ teaspoon minced fresh rosemary into flour mixture before adding buttermilk.

1 Chill the Fat
Cut 8 tablespoons of unsalted butter and 4 tablespoons of vegetable shortening into ½-inch pieces and refrigerate until chilled. WHY? The cold fat is easier to cut into the dry ingredients.

2 Cut the Fat Into the Flour
Scatter the chilled fat over the dry ingredients in a food processor. Pulse until the mixture resembles coarse meal. WHY? This cuts the fat into the dry ingredients quickly without warming the butter.

3 Add the Buttermilk by Hand
Transfer the flour mixture to a large bowl. Gently stir in the buttermilk until the dough forms. WHY? Stirring in the buttermilk by hand ensures that the dough is uniformly combined without overmixing.

4 Knead the Dough and Then Roll It Out
Knead the dough briefly to form a cohesive ball and then roll it into a 9-inch circle, about ¾ inch thick. WHY? Kneading develops gluten, which helps to produce tall biscuits.

5 Stamp, Don't Twist
Stamp out the biscuits by pushing straight down with a floured biscuit cutter. WHY? If you twist the cutter as you stamp out the biscuits, the edges will fuse together and the biscuits won't rise as high.

6 Flip the Biscuits and Then Bake Them
Place the biscuits upside down on a lined baking sheet and bake. Rotate the sheet and lower the oven temperature 5 minutes into baking. WHY? Starting at a higher temperature jump-starts rising.

BAKERY-STYLE MUFFINS

Makes 12 muffins
Total Time 50 minutes

This recipe is a simple muffin base into which flavorings can be added; see the variations for our favorite combinations.

3 cups (15 ounces) all-purpose flour
1 cup (7 ounces) sugar
1 tablespoon baking powder
½ teaspoon baking soda
½ teaspoon salt
1½ cups plain whole-milk or low-fat yogurt
2 large eggs
8 tablespoons unsalted butter, melted and cooled

1 Adjust oven rack to middle position and heat oven to 375 degrees. Grease 12-cup muffin tin.

2 Whisk flour, sugar, baking powder, baking soda, and salt together in large bowl. In separate bowl, whisk yogurt and eggs until smooth. Gently fold yogurt mixture into flour mixture until just combined. Fold in melted butter; do not overmix.

3 Divide batter evenly among prepared muffin cups. Bake until golden brown and toothpick inserted in center comes out clean, 20 to 25 minutes, rotating muffin tin halfway through baking.

4 Let muffins cool in muffin tin for 5 minutes, then transfer to wire rack and let cool for 10 minutes before serving.

VARIATIONS

Lemon-Blueberry Muffins
Frozen blueberries can be substituted for the fresh blueberries; rinse and dry the frozen berries (do not thaw) before tossing with the flour.

Add 1 teaspoon grated lemon zest to yogurt mixture. Add 1½ cups fresh blueberries to flour mixture and toss gently before combining with yogurt mixture.

Lemon–Poppy Seed Muffins
Add 3 tablespoons poppy seeds to flour mixture and 1 tablespoon grated lemon zest to yogurt mixture. While muffins bake, simmer ¼ cup sugar and ¼ cup lemon juice together in small saucepan over medium heat until it turns into light syrup, 3 to 5 minutes. Brush warm syrup over warm baked muffins before serving.

Mocha Chip Muffins
Add 3 tablespoons instant espresso powder to yogurt mixture, and gently fold 1 cup semisweet chocolate chips into batter.

Apricot-Almond Muffins
Add ½ teaspoon almond extract to yogurt mixture. Gently fold 1 cup finely chopped dried apricots into batter. Sprinkle with ¼ cup sliced almonds before baking.

Learn How Bakery-Style Muffins

1 Grease the Muffin Tin Well
Grease a 12-cup nonstick muffin tin. WHY? Greasing the pan with vegetable oil spray rather than using paper liners enables the muffins to brown, adding flavor and textural interest.

2 Gently Mix the Muffin Batter
Use a rubber spatula to fold the wet ingredients into the dry ingredients and then fold in the melted butter. WHY? This technique prevents overmixing, which can make for tough muffins.

3 Portion the Batter Carefully
Using either a greased ⅓-cup measure or a spring-loaded portion scoop, portion the batter into each muffin cup. WHY? Careful portioning is critical to ensure that your muffins bake at the same rate.

4 Bake the Muffins and Test for Doneness
Bake the muffins until a toothpick inserted in the center of one comes out clean, rotating the tin halfway through baking. WHY? Rotating the tin ensures that all the muffins are evenly baked.

5 Let the Muffins Cool Briefly in the Tin
Transfer the muffin tin to a wire cooling rack and let cool for 10 minutes. WHY? Cooling the muffins in the tin will give them time to set and make them easier to remove.

6 Flip the Muffins Out of the Tin
Turn the muffin tin over so the muffins fall out onto the wire rack. Use the edge of a knife to loosen any that stick. WHY? If you have properly greased the tin, the muffins should pop out easily.

MONKEY BREAD

Serves 6 to 8
Total Time 5 hours 30 minutes

Do not leave the bread in the pan for more than 5 minutes after baking, or it will stick. See How to Knead Dough by Hand, page 226.

Dough
3¼   cups (16¼ ounces) all-purpose flour
2¼   teaspoons instant or rapid-rise yeast
 2   teaspoons salt
 1   cup whole milk, room temperature
 ⅓   cup water, room temperature
 ¼   cup (1¾ ounces) granulated sugar
 2   tablespoons unsalted butter, melted

Brown Sugar Coating
 1   cup packed (7 ounces) light brown sugar
 2   teaspoons ground cinnamon
 8   tablespoons unsalted butter, melted and cooled

Glaze
 1   cup (4 ounces) confectioners' sugar
 2   tablespoons whole milk

1 **For the Dough**
Whisk flour, yeast, and salt together in bowl of stand mixer. Whisk milk, water, sugar, and melted butter in 4-cup liquid measuring cup until sugar dissolves. Using dough hook on low speed, slowly add milk mixture to flour mixture and mix until cohesive dough starts to form and no dry flour remains, about 2 minutes, scraping down bowl as needed. Increase speed to medium-low and knead until dough is smooth and elastic and clears sides of bowl but sticks to bottom, 8 to 10 minutes.

2 Transfer dough to lightly floured counter and knead by hand to form smooth, round ball, about 30 seconds. Place dough seam side down in lightly greased large bowl, cover tightly with plastic wrap, and let rise until doubled in size, 1½ to 2 hours. (Unrisen dough can be refrigerated for at least 8 hours or up to 16 hours; let sit at room temperature for 1 hour before shaping in step 4.)

3 **For the Brown Sugar Coating**
Thoroughly grease 12-cup nonstick Bundt pan. Combine sugar and cinnamon in medium bowl. Place melted butter in second bowl.

4 Transfer dough to lightly floured counter and press into 8-inch square. Cut into 8 even strips, then cut each strip into 8 pieces (64 pieces total). Cover dough pieces loosely with greased plastic.

5 Working with a few pieces of dough at a time (keep remaining pieces covered), place on clean counter and, using your cupped hand, drag in small circles until dough feels taut and round. Dip balls in melted butter, then roll in sugar mixture to coat. Place balls in prepared pan, staggering seams where dough balls meet as you build layers.

6 Cover pan tightly with plastic and let rise until balls reach 1 to 2 inches below lip of pan, 1½ to 2 hours.

7 Adjust oven rack to middle position and heat oven to 350 degrees. Bake until top is deep golden brown and caramel begins to bubble around edges, 30 to 35 minutes. Let bread cool in pan for 5 minutes, then invert onto serving platter and let cool for 10 minutes.

8 **For the Glaze**
Meanwhile, whisk sugar and milk in bowl until smooth. Drizzle glaze over cooled bread, letting it run down sides. Serve warm.

1 Use Butter and Milk in the Dough
Add milk, water, sugar, and melted butter mixture to the flour mixture and mix until a cohesive dough starts to form. WHY? Butter and milk keep the dough tender.

2 Knead by Hand
Transfer the dough to a lightly floured counter and knead by hand for about 30 seconds. WHY? Only a brief period of hand kneading is required to bring the dough together.

3 Cut the Dough into Even Pieces
Cut the dough into eight even strips and cut each strip into eight even pieces (64 pieces total). WHY? Cutting the dough into even pieces ensures that each piece will bake at the same rate.

4 Roll the Pieces in Cinnamon Sugar
Dip the dough balls in melted butter and then roll them in a mixture of cinnamon and light brown sugar. WHY? This simple coating adds warm spice and molasses notes to the bread.

5 Let the Dough Rise in the Pan
Place the balls in the prepared pan, cover the pan with plastic wrap, and let rise for 1½ to 2 hours. WHY? This second rise helps pack the dough balls into the pan as closely as possible.

6 Let the Bread Cool in the Pan for 5 Minutes
After baking, let the bread cool in the pan for just 5 minutes, invert onto a serving platter, and let cool for 10 minutes more. WHY? Cooling briefly in the pan helps the monkey bread cohere.

SOUTHERN-STYLE SKILLET CORNBREAD

Serves 12
Total Time 1 hour

We prefer a cast-iron skillet here, but any ovensafe 10-inch skillet will work fine. You can substitute any type of fine- or medium-ground cornmeal here; do not use coarse-ground cornmeal.

2¼ cups (11¼ ounces) stone-ground cornmeal
2 cups buttermilk
¼ cup vegetable oil
4 tablespoons unsalted butter, cut into 4 pieces
1 teaspoon baking powder
1 teaspoon baking soda
¾ teaspoon salt
2 large eggs

1 Adjust oven racks to middle and lower-middle positions and heat oven to 450 degrees. Heat 10-inch cast-iron skillet on upper rack for 10 minutes. Spread cornmeal over rimmed baking sheet and bake on lower rack until fragrant and color begins to deepen, about 5 minutes. Transfer hot cornmeal to large bowl, whisk in buttermilk, and set aside.

2 Carefully add oil to hot skillet and continue to heat in oven until oil is just smoking, about 5 minutes. Remove skillet from oven, add butter, and carefully swirl pan until butter is melted. Pour all but 1 tablespoon hot oil mixture into cornmeal mixture. Whisk baking powder, baking soda, and salt into cornmeal mixture until combined, then whisk in eggs.

3 Quickly pour cornmeal mixture into hot skillet with remaining fat. Bake on upper rack until top begins to crack and sides are golden brown, 12 to 16 minutes, rotating skillet halfway through baking. Let cornbread cool in pan for 5 minutes before serving.

Learn How Southern-Style Skillet Cornbread

1 Preheat the Skillet
Heat the oven to 450 degrees. Heat a 10-inch cast-iron skillet on the middle rack until hot. WHY? Preheating the cast-iron skillet ensures that the cornbread will have a crunchy brown crust.

2 Toast the Cornmeal
While the pan preheats, spread the cornmeal on a rimmed baking sheet and toast it in the oven until it's fragrant and lightly golden. WHY? Toasting the cornmeal for a few minutes deepens its flavor.

3 Soften the Cornmeal with Buttermilk
Transfer the toasted cornmeal to a bowl, whisk in the buttermilk, and let it soften for several minutes before making the batter. WHY? The softened cornmeal leads to a tender, moist crumb.

4 Use Oil and Butter
Add the oil to the hot skillet. Swirl in the butter until melted. Mix all but 1 tablespoon of the hot fat into the cornmeal mixture. WHY? Vegetable oil is good for high heat while butter adds flavor.

5 Add the Batter to the Hot Skillet
Quickly pour the batter into the hot skillet and bake until the top begins to crack, rotating halfway through baking. WHY? The hot skillet is what gives this bread its crunchy crust.

6 Cool the Cornbread in the Skillet, Then Flip It Out
Carefully remove the skillet from the oven. Let the cornbread cool for 5 minutes, then flip it out onto a wire rack. WHY? Cooling briefly in the pan keeps the cornbread from crumbling apart.

ULTIMATE NEW YORK–STYLE PIZZA

Makes two 13-inch pizzas
Total Time 26 hours 25 minutes (includes 24 hours for refrigerating dough)

You will need a pizza peel for this recipe. Shape the second dough ball while the first pizza bakes, but don't top the pizza until right before you bake it. It is important to use ice water in the dough to prevent it from overheating in the food processor. Use our Easy Pizza Sauce or substitute store-bought. See How to Knead Dough by Hand, page 226.

Dough

- 3 cups (16½ ounces) bread flour
- 2 teaspoons sugar
- ½ teaspoon instant or rapid-rise yeast
- 1⅓ cups ice water
- 1 tablespoon vegetable oil
- 1½ teaspoons salt

Pizza

- 1 cup pizza sauce
- 1 ounce Parmesan cheese, grated (½ cup)
- 8 ounces whole-milk mozzarella cheese, shredded (2 cups)

1 For the Dough
Pulse flour, sugar, and yeast in food processor to combine, about 5 pulses. With processor running, slowly add ice water and process until dough is just combined and no dry flour remains, about 10 seconds. Let dough rest for 10 minutes.

2 Add oil and salt to dough and process until it forms sticky ball that clears sides of workbowl, 30 to 60 seconds. Transfer to lightly oiled counter and knead until smooth, about 1 minute. Shape dough into tight ball and place in lightly greased large bowl. Cover bowl tightly with plastic wrap and refrigerate for at least 24 hours or up to 3 days.

3 For the Pizza
One hour before baking pizza, adjust oven rack 4½ inches from broiler element, set baking stone on rack, and heat oven to 500 degrees. Remove dough from refrigerator and divide in half. Shape each half into smooth, tight ball. Put on lightly oiled baking sheet, at least 3 inches apart, cover loosely with greased plastic wrap, and let stand for 1 hour.

4 Heat broiler for 10 minutes. Meanwhile, coat 1 ball of dough generously with flour and place on well-floured counter. Gently flatten dough into 8-inch disk with your fingertips, leaving 1 inch of outer edge slightly thicker than center. Using your hands, gently stretch dough into 12-inch round, giving dough quarter-turns as you stretch. Transfer dough to well-floured peel and stretch into 13-inch round. Using back of spoon, spread ½ cup sauce evenly over dough, leaving ¼-inch border. Sprinkle ¼ cup Parmesan and 1 cup mozzarella evenly over sauce.

5 Slide pizza onto stone. Return oven to 500 degrees. Bake until crust is browned and cheese is bubbly and partially browned, 8 to 10 minutes, rotating pizza halfway through baking. Transfer pizza to wire rack, and cool for 5 minutes. Slice and serve.

6 Heat broiler for 10 minutes. Repeat steps 4 and 5 with remaining ingredients to make second pizza. Return oven to 500 degrees when pizza is placed on stone.

EASY PIZZA SAUCE
Makes 2 cups
Total Time 5 minutes
Process one 28-ounce can whole peeled tomatoes, drained with juice reserved; 1 tablespoon extra-virgin olive oil; 1 teaspoon red wine vinegar; 2 minced garlic cloves; 1 teaspoon dried oregano; ½ teaspoon salt; and ¼ teaspoon pepper in food processor until smooth, about 30 seconds. Transfer to liquid measuring cup and add reserved tomato juice until sauce measures 2 cups.

1 Make the Dough and Refrigerate Overnight

Make the dough in a food processor. Knead briefly before refrigerating for at least 24 hours. WHY? Refrigerating the dough overnight allows a slow fermentation, which builds flavor.

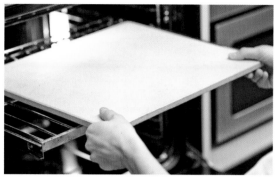

2 Preheat the Baking Stone

Heat the oven to 500 degrees for 1 hour with a baking stone 4½ inches from the broiler element, then heat the broiler for 10 minutes. WHY? This superhot setup mimics a traditional pizza oven.

3 Bring the Dough to Room Temperature

Meanwhile, remove the dough from the refrigerator and divide into two smooth, tight balls. Let stand for 1 hour. WHY? This make the dough easier to stretch and roll out.

4 Shape the Pizza

Coat the first dough ball with flour. Gently flatten into an 8-inch disk and stretch into a 12-inch round. WHY? The dough is very easy to work with and is easily shaped using your hands.

5 Top the Pizza with Sauce and Cheese

Transfer the dough to a floured pizza peel and stretch into a 13-inch round. Add sauce, Parmesan, and mozzarella. WHY? We keep toppings to a minimum as an overloaded pizza bakes up soggy.

6 Bake the Pizza

Slide the pizza carefully onto the hot baking stone. Bake until the crust is well browned and the cheese is bubbly. WHY? The preheated baking stone quickly bakes the pizza and crisps the crust.

EASY SANDWICH BREAD

Makes 1 loaf
Total Time 2 hours, plus 3 hours for cooling

The test kitchen's preferred loaf pan measures 8½ by 4½ inches; if you use a 9 by 5-inch loaf pan, start checking for doneness 5 minutes earlier than advised in the recipe. To prevent the loaf from deflating as it rises, do not let the batter come in contact with the plastic wrap. We do not recommend mixing this dough by hand.

  2 cups (11 ounces) bread flour
  6 tablespoons (2 ounces) whole-wheat flour
2¼ teaspoons instant or rapid-rise yeast
1¼ cups plus 2 tablespoons (11 ounces) warm water (120 degrees)
  3 tablespoons unsalted butter, melted
  1 tablespoon honey
  ¾ teaspoon salt
  1 large egg, lightly beaten with 1 tablespoon water and pinch salt

1 Whisk bread flour, whole-wheat flour, and yeast together in bowl of stand mixer. Whisk 1¼ cups warm water, 2 tablespoons melted butter, and honey in 4-cup liquid measuring cup until honey has dissolved.

2 Using paddle on low speed, slowly add water mixture to flour mixture and mix until batter comes together, about 1 minute. Increase speed to medium and mix for 4 minutes, scraping down bowl and paddle as needed. Cover bowl tightly with plastic wrap and let batter rise until doubled in size, about 20 minutes.

3 Adjust oven rack to lower-middle position and heat oven to 375 degrees. Grease 8½ by 4½-inch loaf pan. Dissolve salt in remaining 2 tablespoons warm water, then add to batter and mix on low speed until water mixture is mostly incorporated, about 40 seconds. Increase speed to medium and mix until thoroughly combined, about 1 minute.

4 Transfer batter to prepared pan and smooth top. Cover tightly with plastic and let rise until batter reaches ½ inch below lip of pan, 15 to 20 minutes. Uncover and continue to let rise until center of batter is level with lip of pan, 5 to 10 minutes.

5 Gently brush loaf with egg mixture and bake until deep golden brown and loaf registers 205 to 210 degrees, 40 to 45 minutes, rotating pan halfway through baking.

6 Let loaf cool in pan for 15 minutes. Remove loaf from pan and transfer to wire rack. Brush top and sides with remaining melted butter. Let cool completely, about 3 hours, before serving.

1 Use Bread Flour
Combine the bread flour, whole-wheat flour, and yeast in the bowl of the mixer. WHY? Higher-protein bread flour helps create maximum gluten development in a short amount of time.

2 Make a Wet Dough
Whisk 1¼ cups warm water, 2 tablespoons melted butter, and 1 tablespoon honey together. WHY? A high amount of water enhances the bread's gluten structure without requiring prolonged kneading.

3 Use the Paddle
Using the paddle on low speed, add the water mixture to the flour mixture until the batter comes together. WHY? Using the paddle instead of the dough hook shortens the mixing time.

4 Add the Salt Later
Dissolve the salt in 2 tablespoons of warm water, then add it to the batter. WHY? Withholding the salt until the second mix gives our bread more spring and lift.

5 Brush the Crust with Egg Wash and Butter
Make an egg wash with water and salt and brush it on the loaf before baking. After baking, brush the top and sides of the loaf with melted butter. WHY? These additions help create a golden-brown crust.

6 Bake the Loaf and Check for Doneness
Bake the bread until it is golden brown and registers 205 to 210 degrees, rotating it halfway through baking. WHY? Using both a thermometer and visual cues ensures a perfectly baked loaf.

ALMOST NO-KNEAD BREAD

Makes 1 loaf
Total Time 11 hours 30 minutes (includes 8 hours for resting), plus 2 hours for cooling

Use a Dutch oven that holds 6 quarts or more. An enameled cast-iron Dutch oven with a tight-fitting lid works best. Make sure the knob on the pot lid is ovensafe at 425 degrees. Use a mild-flavored lager, such as Budweiser (mild nonalcoholic lager also works). In step 3, start the 30-minute timer as soon as you put the bread in the cold oven; do not wait until the oven has preheated or the bread will burn. The bread is best eaten the day it is baked, but it can be wrapped in aluminum foil and stored in a cool, dry place for up to two days.

  3 **cups (15 ounces) all-purpose flour**
1½ **teaspoons salt**
 ¼ **teaspoon instant or rapid-rise yeast**
 ¾ **cup plus 2 tablespoons water, room temperature**
  6 **tablespoons mild-flavored lager,**
     room temperature
  1 **tablespoon distilled white vinegar**
     Vegetable oil spray

1 Whisk flour, salt, and yeast together in large bowl. Add water, lager, and vinegar. Using rubber spatula, fold mixture, scraping up dry flour from bottom of bowl, until shaggy ball forms. Cover bowl with plastic wrap and let dough sit at room temperature for at least 8 hours or up to 18 hours.

2 Lay 18 by 12-inch sheet of parchment paper on counter and spray with oil spray. Transfer dough to lightly floured counter and knead 10 to 15 times. Shape dough into ball by pulling edges into middle. Transfer dough, seam side down, to center of parchment and spray surface of dough with oil spray. Pick up dough by lifting parchment overhang and lower into large Dutch oven (let any excess parchment hang over pot edge). Cover loosely with plastic and let rise at room temperature until dough has doubled in size and does not readily spring back when poked with your finger, about 2 hours.

3 Adjust oven rack to middle position. Remove plastic from pot. Lightly flour top of dough and, using razor blade or sharp knife, make one 6-inch-long, ½-inch-deep slit along top of dough. Cover pot and place in oven. Heat oven to 425 degrees. Bake bread for 30 minutes.

4 Remove lid and continue to bake until loaf is deep golden brown and registers 210 degrees, 20 to 30 minutes longer. Carefully remove bread from pot; transfer to wire rack and let cool completely, about 2 hours, before serving.

VARIATIONS
Almost No-Knead Seeded Rye Bread
Reduce all-purpose flour to 1½ cups plus 1 tablespoon. Add 1 cup plus 2 tablespoons rye flour and 2 tablespoons caraway seeds to flour mixture.

Almost No-Knead Whole-Wheat Bread
Substitute 1 cup whole-wheat flour for 1 cup all-purpose flour. Stir 2 tablespoons honey into water before adding to dry ingredients in step 1.

Almost No-Knead Cranberry-Pecan Bread
This bread makes especially good toast.

Add ½ cup dried cranberries and ½ cup toasted pecan halves to flour mixture.

1 Mix the Dough and Let It Rest
Make the dough and let it sit at room temperature
for at least 8 hours. WHY? Letting the dough sit for
a long time actually develops the gluten, much like
kneading—this is the trick to this bread.

2 Knead the Dough Just 10 to 15 Times by Hand
Turn the dough out onto a lightly floured counter.
Knead by hand to form a smooth, round ball,
10 to 15 times. WHY? Just a few turns by hand
make a big difference to the texture of the final loaf.

3 Shape the Loaf
After kneading the loaf, shape the dough into a
ball by pulling the edges into the middle. WHY?
Pulling up the sides of the dough ball helps avoid
an overly wide, flat loaf.

4 Let the Dough Rise in a Dutch Oven
Transfer the loaf to a Dutch oven using a piece of
greased parchment paper. Let it rise until doubled
in size, about 2 hours. WHY? It's convenient to let
the bread rise in the baking vessel.

5 Start the Dough In a Cold Oven
Put the dough in the oven in a covered pot and
then turn the oven to 425 degrees. WHY?
Starting the dough in a cold oven prevents the
bottom of the loaf from burning.

6 Bake Covered, Then Uncovered
Bake the bread covered for 30 minutes. Remove
the lid and bake until the crust is deep golden
brown. WHY? Baking both covered and uncovered
creates a chewy interior and a thick crust.

MOLASSES SPICE COOKIES

⅓ cup (2⅓ ounces) granulated sugar, plus ½ cup for rolling
2¼ cups (11¼ ounces) all-purpose flour
1½ teaspoons ground cinnamon
1½ teaspoons ground ginger
1 teaspoon baking soda
½ teaspoon ground cloves
¼ teaspoon ground allspice
¼ teaspoon pepper
¼ teaspoon salt
12 tablespoons unsalted butter, softened
⅓ cup packed (2⅓ ounces) dark brown sugar
1 large egg yolk
1 teaspoon vanilla extract
½ cup mild or robust molasses

1 Adjust oven rack to middle position and heat oven to 375 degrees. Line 2 baking sheets with parchment paper. Spread ½ cup granulated sugar in shallow dish; set aside. Whisk flour, cinnamon, ginger, baking soda, cloves, allspice, pepper, and salt together in medium bowl; set aside.

2 Using stand mixer fitted with paddle, beat butter, brown sugar, and remaining ⅓ cup granulated sugar on medium-high speed until light and fluffy, about 3 minutes. Reduce speed to medium-low and add egg yolk and vanilla; increase speed to medium and beat until incorporated, about 20 seconds. Reduce speed to medium-low and add molasses; beat until fully incorporated, about 20 seconds, scraping down bowl as needed. Reduce speed to low and add flour mixture; beat until just incorporated, about 30 seconds, scraping down bowl as needed. Give dough final stir by hand to ensure that no flour pockets remain. (Dough will be soft.)

3 Working with 1 heaping tablespoon dough at a time, roll into balls with your dampened hands, then roll in granulated sugar and toss to coat. Space balls 2 inches apart on prepared sheets. Bake, 1 sheet at a time, until browned but still puffy, and edges have begun to set but centers are still soft (cookies will look raw in cracks and seem underdone), about 11 minutes, rotating sheet halfway through baking. Do not overbake.

4 Let cookies cool on sheet for 5 minutes, then transfer to wire rack. Let cookies cool completely before serving.

Makes 22 cookies
Total Time 50 minutes

When rolling the balls of dough, we found that dipping our hands in water prevented the dough from sticking to our hands while also helping the granulated sugar stick to the dough. For the best texture and appearance, be sure to bake the cookies one sheet at a time and pull them from the oven when they look substantially underdone. They will continue to bake and harden as they cool, with the insides remaining soft and moist. Mild or light molasses gives the cookies a milder flavor; for a stronger flavor, use robust molasses. See How to Cream Butter, page 229.

Learn How Molasses Spice Cookies

1 Add Lift with Baking Soda
Whisk baking soda in with the dry ingredients. WHY? Molasses is a mildly acidic ingredient, so it reacts with an alkali like baking soda to provide lift. A full teaspoon gives the cookies nice height.

2 Spice Up the Dough
Use black pepper as well as cinnamon, ginger, cloves, allspice, and salt. WHY? In combination with common baking spices, black pepper adds complexity.

3 Combine White and Brown Sugars
Beat the butter, dark brown sugar, and granulated sugar together until light and fluffy. WHY? Using equal amounts of granulated and brown sugars is ideal for rich flavor.

4 Pick the Right Molasses
Make the dough using mild or robust molasses. WHY? Blackstrap molasses is overpowering and bitter here but cookies made with robust molasses have bold flavor and rich color.

5 Toss the Dough in Granulated Sugar
Roll the dough into balls 1 tablespoon at a time, then roll the balls in granulated sugar and toss to coat. WHY? Rolling the dough in granulated sugar before baking gives the cookies a great crunch.

6 Underbake the Cookies
Bake the cookies until they are browned but still puffy and the edges have begun to set but the centers are still soft. WHY? This ensures great chewy texture even after the cookies cool fully.

CHOCOLATE CRINKLE COOKIES

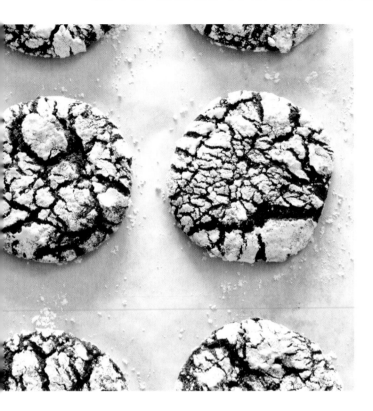

1 cup (5 ounces) all-purpose flour
½ cup (1½ ounces) unsweetened cocoa powder
1 teaspoon baking powder
¼ teaspoon baking soda
½ teaspoon salt
1½ cups packed (10½ ounces) brown sugar
3 large eggs
4 teaspoons instant espresso powder (optional)
1 teaspoon vanilla extract
4 ounces unsweetened chocolate, chopped
4 tablespoons unsalted butter
½ cup granulated sugar, for rolling
½ cup confectioners' sugar, for rolling

1 Adjust oven rack to middle position and heat oven to 325 degrees. Line 2 baking sheets with parchment paper. Whisk flour, cocoa, baking powder, baking soda, and salt together in bowl.

2 Whisk brown sugar; eggs; espresso powder, if using; and vanilla together in large bowl. Combine chocolate and butter in bowl and microwave at 50 percent power, stirring often, until melted, 2 to 3 minutes.

3 Whisk chocolate mixture into brown sugar mixture until combined. Fold in flour mixture until no dry streaks remain. Let dough sit at room temperature for 10 minutes.

4 Spread granulated sugar and confectioners' sugar in separate shallow dishes. Working with 2 table-spoons dough at a time, roll into balls (or use #30 scoop). Drop dough balls into granulated sugar and roll to coat. Transfer dough balls to confectioners' sugar and roll to coat evenly. Evenly space dough balls on prepared sheets, 11 per sheet.

5 Bake cookies, 1 sheet at a time, until puffed and cracked and edges have begun to set but centers are still soft (cookies will look raw between cracks and seem underdone), about 12 minutes, rotating sheet halfway through baking. Do not overbake. Let cool completely on sheet on wire rack before serving.

Makes 22 cookies
Total Time 40 minutes

Both natural and Dutch-processed cocoa will work in this recipe. See How to Chop and Melt Chocolate, page 228.

Learn How Chocolate Crinkle Cookies

1 Use Baking Powder and Baking Soda
Whisk the flour, cocoa, baking powder, baking soda, and salt together in a bowl. WHY? The two leaveners combined help create a more crackly, fissured surface on the cookies.

2 Keep Things Not-Too-Sweet
Melt the chopped unsweetened chocolate and butter. WHY? Along with unsweetened cocoa, the unsweetened chocolate gives these cookies deep chocolate flavor and tempered sweetness.

3 Let the Dough Sit
Let the dough sit for 10 minutes at room temperature after mixing. WHY? This brief rest allows the dough to firm up enough to roll and bake the cookies.

4 Roll the Dough in Two Types of Sugar
Roll the dough balls in the granulated sugar and then in the confectioner's sugar. WHY? The double sugar coating keeps the confectioners' sugar from dissolving into the dough and disappearing.

5 Underbake the Cookies
Bake the cookies until the edges have begun to set but the centers are still soft. WHY? Overbaking will cause the cracks to open too wide, drying out the cookies' interiors.

6 Cool the Cookies Completely
Let the cookies cool completely on a baking sheet on a wire rack before serving. WHY? Because the cookies are underbaked, they will crumble if you serve them before they've fully cooled.

CREAM CHEESE BROWNIES

Makes 16 brownies
Total Time 1 hour, plus 2 hours for cooling

To accurately test the doneness of the brownies, be sure to stick the toothpick through part of the brownie and not the cream cheese. See How to Chop and Melt Chocolate, page 228, and How to Make a Foil Sling, page 228.

Cream Cheese Filling

- 4 ounces cream cheese, cut into 8 pieces
- ½ cup sour cream
- 2 tablespoons sugar
- 1 tablespoon all-purpose flour

Brownies

- ⅔ cup (3⅓ ounces) all-purpose flour
- ½ teaspoon baking powder
- ½ teaspoon salt
- 4 ounces unsweetened chocolate, chopped fine
- 8 tablespoons unsalted butter
- 1¼ cups (8¾ ounces) sugar
- 2 large eggs
- 1 teaspoon vanilla extract

1 Adjust oven rack to middle position and heat oven to 325 degrees. Make foil sling for 8-inch square baking pan by folding 2 long sheets of aluminum foil so each is 8 inches wide. Lay sheets of foil in pan perpendicular to each other, with extra foil hanging over edges of pan. Push foil into corners and up sides of pan, smoothing foil flush to pan, and grease foil.

2 **For the Cream Cheese Filling**
Microwave cream cheese in bowl until soft, 20 to 30 seconds. Whisk in sour cream, sugar, and flour.

3 **For the Brownies**
Whisk flour, baking powder, and salt together in bowl. Microwave chocolate and butter together in separate bowl at 50 percent power, stirring often, until melted, 1 to 2 minutes. In medium bowl, whisk sugar, eggs, and vanilla together. Whisk in melted chocolate mixture until incorporated. Fold in flour mixture with rubber spatula.

4 Spread all but ½ cup of brownie batter in prepared pan. Spread cream cheese mixture evenly over top. Microwave remaining brownie batter until warm and pourable, 10 to 20 seconds. Using spoon, dollop softened batter over cream cheese filling (6 to 8 dollops). Using knife, swirl brownie batter through cream cheese topping, making marbled pattern, leaving ½-inch border around edges.

5 Bake brownies until toothpick inserted in center comes out with few moist crumbs attached, 35 to 40 minutes, rotating pan halfway through baking. Let brownies cool in pan for 1 hour.

6 Using foil overhang, lift brownies from pan. Transfer to wire rack and let cool completely, about 1 hour. Cut into squares and serve.

1 Make a Foil Sling
Make a sling from two long sheets of aluminum foil. Push the foil into the corners and up the sides of the pan. WHY? A foil sling makes lifting out the baked brownies (and cleaning up the pan) a cinch.

2 Add Sour Cream to the Cream Cheese Filling
Add sour cream, sugar, and flour to the softened cream cheese for the filling. WHY? The tang of the sour cream keeps the swirls of filling from getting overly sweet.

3 Keep the Brownies on the Cakey Side
Use ⅔ cup of flour and two eggs in the brownie batter. WHY? If the brownies are cakey they won't get too soggy or dense when you add the wet cream cheese filling.

4 Reserve Some Brownie Batter
Transfer ½ cup of the batter to the bowl used to melt the chocolate for the brownies. WHY? The reserved batter will be used to create the swirls on the top layer of the brownies.

5 Spread the Cream Cheese Filling in an Even Layer
Spread the brownie batter in the prepared pan and then spread cream cheese filling evenly over the batter. WHY? This method ensures cream cheese filling in every bite of brownie.

6 Dollop Reserved Batter over the Filling and Swirl
Microwave the reserved batter until it's pourable and dollop it over the filling. Use a knife to make swirls. WHY? This keeps the components from getting muddled and creates attractive swirls.

EASY POUND CAKE

Serves 8
Total Time 1 hour 30 minutes, plus 2 hours for cooling

The test kitchen's preferred loaf pan measures 8½ by 4½ inches; if you use a 9 by 5-inch loaf pan, start checking for doneness 5 minutes early.

1½	cups (6 ounces) cake flour
1	teaspoon baking powder
½	teaspoon salt
1¼	cups (8¾ ounces) sugar
4	large eggs, room temperature
1½	teaspoons vanilla extract
16	tablespoons unsalted butter, melted and hot

1 Adjust oven rack to middle position and heat oven to 350 degrees. Grease and flour 8½ by 4½-inch loaf pan. Whisk flour, baking powder, and salt together in bowl.

2 Process sugar, eggs, and vanilla in food processor until combined, about 10 seconds. With processor running, add hot melted butter in steady stream until incorporated. Pour mixture into large bowl.

3 Sift flour mixture over egg mixture in 3 additions, whisking to combine after each addition until few streaks of flour remain. Continue to whisk batter gently until almost no lumps remain (do not overmix).

4 Scrape batter into prepared pan, smooth top, and gently tap pan on counter to settle batter. Bake cake until toothpick inserted in center comes out with few crumbs attached, 50 minutes to 1 hour, rotating pan halfway through baking.

5 Let cake cool in pan for 10 minutes. Run paring knife around edge of cake to loosen. Gently turn cake out onto wire rack and let cool completely, about 2 hours. Serve.

VARIATIONS

Easy Lemon Pound Cake
Add 2 tablespoons grated lemon zest (2 lemons) and 2 teaspoons lemon juice to food processor with sugar, eggs, and vanilla.

Easy Orange Pound Cake
Add 1 tablespoon grated orange zest and 1 tablespoon orange juice to food processor with sugar, eggs, and vanilla.

Easy Almond Pound Cake
Add 1 teaspoon almond extract and ¼ cup slivered almonds to food processor with sugar, eggs, and vanilla. Sprinkle 2 tablespoons slivered almonds over cake before baking.

Easy Ginger Pound Cake
Add 3 tablespoons minced crystallized ginger, 1½ teaspoons ground ginger, and ½ teaspoon ground mace to food processor with sugar, eggs, and vanilla.

1 Grease and Flour the Loaf Pan
Grease an 8½ by 4½-inch loaf pan with butter and dust it with flour. WHY? The flour helps the pound cake batter climb the sides of the pan and prevents the edges from forming a hard, crusty lip.

2 Start the Batter in a Food Processor
Process the sugar, eggs, and vanilla in a food processor until combined, about 10 seconds. WHY? The food processor ensures that the ingredients are evenly combined.

3 Add Hot Melted Butter
With the processor running, add the hot melted butter in a steady stream until incorporated. WHY? The blade of the food processor ensures perfect emulsification of the eggs and butter.

4 Transfer to a Bowl and Sift in the Dry Ingredients
Sift the flour mixture over the egg mixture in three stages, whisking after each. Whisk gently until almost no lumps remain. WHY? This helps prevent overmixing, which can lead to a dense cake.

5 Tap the Pan on the Counter
Scrape the batter into the prepared pan, smooth the top, and gently tap the pan on the counter. WHY? Tapping the pan releases large air bubbles that could cause holes in the finished cake.

6 Cool Briefly in the Pan
After baking, let the cake cool in the pan for 10 minutes. WHY? Cooling the cake briefly in the pan allows it to firm up so that it won't break apart when removed from the pan.

YELLOW LAYER CAKE

Serves 10 to 12
Total Time 3 hours 20 minutes (includes 2 hours for cooling cake layers)

Be sure to use cake pans with at least 2-inch-tall sides. See page 356 for information on buttermilk substitutes. See How to Whip Egg Whites, page 207; How to Prepare Cake Pans, page 230; and How to Bake Cake Layers, page 231.

2½ cups (10 ounces) cake flour

1¾ cups (12¼ ounces) sugar

1¼ teaspoons baking powder

¼ teaspoon baking soda

¾ teaspoon salt

1 cup buttermilk, room temperature

3 large eggs, separated, plus 3 large yolks, room temperature

10 tablespoons unsalted butter, melted and cooled

3 tablespoons vegetable oil

2 teaspoons vanilla extract

Pinch cream of tartar

1 recipe Chocolate Frosting (page 328)

1 Adjust oven rack to middle position and heat oven to 350 degrees. Grease two 9-inch round cake pans, line with parchment paper, grease parchment, and flour pans. Whisk flour, 1½ cups sugar, baking powder, baking soda, and salt together in bowl. In separate bowl, whisk buttermilk, egg yolks, melted butter, oil, and vanilla together.

2 Using stand mixer fitted with whisk, whip egg whites and cream of tartar on medium-low speed until foamy, about 1 minute. Increase speed to medium-high and whip whites to soft billowy mounds, about 1 minute. Gradually add remaining ¼ cup sugar and whip until glossy, stiff peaks form, 2 to 3 minutes; transfer to third bowl.

3 Add flour mixture to now-empty mixer bowl. With mixer on low speed, gradually add buttermilk mixture and mix until almost incorporated (a few streaks of dry flour will remain), about 15 seconds. Scrape down bowl, then beat on medium-low speed until smooth and fully incorporated, 10 to 15 seconds.

4 Using rubber spatula, stir one-third of whites into batter. Gently fold remaining whites into batter until no white streaks remain. Divide batter evenly between prepared pans, smooth tops, and gently tap pans on counter to settle batter. Bake cakes until toothpick inserted in centers comes out clean, 20 to 22 minutes, rotating pans halfway through baking.

5 Let cakes cool in pans for 10 minutes. Remove cakes from pans, discard parchment, and let cool completely on wire rack, about 2 hours. (Cakes can be stored at room temperature for up to 24 hours or frozen for up to 1 month; defrost cakes at room temperature.)

6 Line edges of cake platter with 4 strips of parchment paper to keep platter clean, and place small dab of frosting in center of platter to anchor cake. Place 1 cake layer on platter. Spread 1½ cups frosting evenly over top, right to edge of cake. Top with second cake layer, press lightly to adhere, then spread remaining 2½ cups frosting evenly over top and sides of cake. To smooth frosting, run edge of offset spatula around cake sides and over top. Carefully remove parchment strips before serving. (Frosted cake can be refrigerated for up to 24 hours; bring to room temperature before serving.)

CONTINUED

1 Use Melted Butter and Oil
Melt the butter, let it cool to room temperature, and whisk it into the buttermilk with the egg yolks, oil, and vanilla. WHY? The mix of oil and melted butter gives the cake a moist texture.

2 Whip the Egg Whites
Whip the egg whites and cream of tartar. Gradually add ¼ cup sugar and whip until glossy, stiff peaks form. WHY? Cream of tartar helps produce a stable, voluminous foam.

3 Combine Flour Mixture and Buttermilk Mixture
Mix the flour mixture and buttermilk mixture on low speed until almost incorporated and then beat on medium-low speed until smooth. WHY? The low mixer speed prevents lumps from forming.

4 Fold in the Whipped Whites
Stir in one-third of the egg whites and gently fold in the remaining whites. WHY? The first addition of egg whites loosens the batter. Gently folding in the remaining whites preserves their fluffy texture.

5 Portion the Batter
Divide the batter between the two prepared cake pans, smooth the tops, and tap the pans on the counter. WHY? Tapping the pans releases any air bubbles trapped in the batter.

6 Bake and Test for Doneness
Bake the cakes (rotating the pans halfway through baking) until a toothpick inserted in the cakes comes out clean. WHY? We've found the toothpick test to be the most foolproof.

CHOCOLATE FROSTING

Makes about 4 cups
Total Time 10 minutes

Bittersweet, semisweet, or milk chocolate can be used in this recipe. See How to Frost a Layer Cake, page 232.

26 tablespoons (3¼ sticks) unsalted butter, softened
1⅓ cups (5⅓ ounces) confectioners' sugar
 1 cup (3 ounces) Dutch-processed cocoa powder
   Pinch salt
 1 cup light corn syrup
1½ teaspoons vanilla extract
10 ounces chocolate, melted and cooled

Process butter, sugar, cocoa, and salt in food processor until smooth, about 30 seconds, scraping down bowl as needed. Add corn syrup and vanilla and process until just combined, 5 to 10 seconds. Scrape down bowl, then add chocolate and process until smooth and creamy, 10 to 15 seconds. (Frosting can be kept at room temperature for up to 3 hours or refrigerated for up to 3 days; if refrigerated, let stand at room temperature for 1 hour before using.)

MAKING SMALLER OR LARGER BATCHES OF CHOCOLATE FROSTING

3 Cups (24 Cupcakes or Top Of Sheet Cake)

Butter	2½ sticks
Confectioners' Sugar	1 cup
Dutch-Processed Cocoa	¾ cup
Salt	pinch
Light Corn Syrup	¾ cup
Vanilla Extract	1 teaspoon
Chocolate	8 ounces

5 Cups (3-Layer Cake)

Butter	3¾ sticks
Confectioners' Sugar	1½ cups
Dutch-Processed Cocoa	1 cup
Salt	⅛ teaspoon
Light Corn Syrup	1 cup
Vanilla Extract	1½ teaspoons
Chocolate	12 ounces

FOOLPROOF SINGLE-CRUST PIE DOUGH

Makes enough for one 9-inch pie
Total Time 2 hours 30 minutes (includes 1 hour 30 minutes for chilling)

Vodka is essential to the tender texture of this crust and imparts no flavor—do not substitute water. This dough is moister than most standard pie doughs and will require lots of flour to roll out (up to ¼ cup). A food processor is essential to making this dough—we don't recommend making it by hand. See How to Roll Out and Fit Pie Dough, page 233, and How to Make and Bake a Single-Crust Pie Shell, page 234.

1¼ cups (6¼ ounces) all-purpose flour
1 tablespoon sugar
½ teaspoon salt
6 tablespoons unsalted butter, cut into ¼-inch pieces and chilled
4 tablespoons vegetable shortening, cut into 2 pieces and chilled
2 tablespoons vodka, chilled
2 tablespoons ice water

1 Process ¾ cup flour, sugar, and salt in food processor until combined, about 5 seconds. Scatter butter and shortening pieces over top and process until incorporated and mixture begins to form uneven clumps with no remaining floury bits, about 10 seconds.

2 Scrape down sides of bowl and redistribute dough evenly around processor blade. Sprinkle remaining ½ cup flour over dough and pulse until mixture has broken up into pieces and is evenly distributed around bowl, 4 to 6 pulses.

3 Transfer mixture to large bowl. Sprinkle vodka and ice water over mixture. Stir and press dough together, using stiff rubber spatula, until dough sticks together.

4 Turn dough onto sheet of plastic wrap and flatten into 4-inch disk. Wrap tightly and refrigerate for 1 hour. Before rolling dough out, let it sit on counter to soften slightly, about 10 minutes. (Dough can be refrigerated for up to 2 days or frozen for up to 1 month. If frozen, let dough thaw completely on counter before rolling it out.)

5 Lay dough on generously floured counter and roll dough outward from its center into 12-inch circle, giving dough quarter turn after every few rolls. Loosely roll dough around rolling pin and gently unroll it over 9-inch pie plate. Lift dough and gently press it into pie plate, letting excess hang over plate's edge.

6 Trim all but ½ inch of dough overhanging edge of pie plate. Tuck dough underneath itself to form tidy, even edge that sits on lip of pie plate. Crimp dough evenly around edge of pie using your fingers. Wrap dough-lined pie plate loosely in plastic and freeze until dough is firm, about 30 minutes.

7 Adjust oven rack to middle position and heat oven to 375 degrees. Line chilled pie crust with double layer of aluminum foil, covering edges to prevent burning, and fill with pie weights or pennies.

8A **For a Partially Baked Crust**
Bake until pie dough looks dry and is pale in color, 25 to 30 minutes. Transfer pie plate to wire rack and remove weights and foil. Following particular pie recipe, use crust while it is still warm or let it cool completely.

CONTINUED

8B For a Fully Baked Crust

Bake until pie dough looks dry and is pale in color, 25 to 30 minutes. Remove weights and foil and continue to bake crust until deep golden brown, 10 to 12 minutes. Transfer pie plate to wire rack. Following particular pie recipe, use crust while it is still warm or let it cool completely.

VARIATION
Foolproof Double-Crust Pie Dough
Makes enough for one 9-inch pie
See How to Roll Out and Fit Pie Dough, page 233; How to Make a Double-Crust Pie, page 235; and/or How to Make a Lattice Top, page 236.

2½ cups (12½ ounces) all-purpose flour
2 tablespoons sugar
1 teaspoon salt
12 tablespoons unsalted butter, cut into ¼-inch pieces and chilled
8 tablespoons vegetable shortening, cut into 4 pieces and chilled
¼ cup vodka, chilled
¼ cup ice water

1 Process 1½ cups flour, sugar, and salt in food processor until combined, about 5 seconds. Scatter butter and shortening pieces over top and process until incorporated and mixture begins to form uneven clumps with no remaining floury bits, about 15 seconds.

2 Scrape down sides of bowl and redistribute dough evenly around processor blade. Sprinkle remaining 1 cup flour over dough and pulse until mixture has broken up into pieces and is evenly distributed around bowl, 4 to 6 pulses.

3 Transfer mixture to large bowl. Sprinkle vodka and ice water over mixture. Stir and press dough together, using stiff rubber spatula, until dough sticks together.

4 Divide dough into 2 even pieces. Turn each piece of dough onto sheet of plastic wrap and flatten each into 4-inch disk. Wrap each piece tightly and refrigerate for 1 hour. Before rolling dough out, let it sit on counter to soften slightly, about 10 minutes. (Dough can be refrigerated for up to 2 days or frozen for up to 1 month. If frozen, let dough thaw completely on counter before rolling it out.)

5 Lay 1 piece of dough on generously floured counter and roll dough outward from its center into 12-inch circle. Loosely roll dough around rolling pin and gently unroll it over 9-inch pie plate. Lift dough and gently press it into pie plate, letting excess hang over plate's edge. Wrap loosely in plastic and refrigerate until dough is firm, about 30 minutes.

6A For a Traditional Top Crust

Roll second piece of dough into 12-inch circle on generously floured counter, transfer to parchment paper–lined baking sheet, cover with plastic, and refrigerate for 30 minutes.

6B For a Lattice Top Crust

Roll second piece of dough into 13½ by 10½-inch rectangle on generously floured counter, then transfer to parchment paper–lined baking sheet. Trim dough to 13 by 10-inch rectangle and slice lengthwise into eight 13-inch-long strips. Separate strips slightly, cover with plastic, and freeze until very firm, about 30 minutes.

1 Cut and Chill the Butter and Shortening
Cut the butter and shortening into pieces and chill
in the freezer. WHY? Shortening adds tenderness,
while butter provides flavor. Chilling allows the fats
to be cut into the dough without softening.

2 Process the Flour with the Chilled Fat
Process the butter, shortening, and a portion of
the dry ingredients to uneven clumps. Add the
remaining flour and pulse until evenly distributed.
WHY? This method helps the dough hold together.

3 Use Two Liquids
Add water and vodka to the flour. WHY? Gluten
forms in water, making dough tough, but it
doesn't form in alcohol, so swapping in some vodka
makes for a more tender, easy-to-roll-out dough.

4 Chill the Dough
Turn the dough onto a sheet of plastic wrap and
flatten into a 4-inch disk (two disks for double
crust). Refrigerate for at least 1 hour. WHY? Gluten
relaxes as the dough chills, ensuring a tender crust.

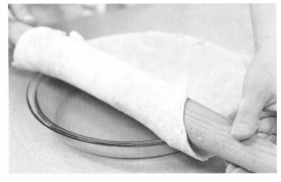

5 Warm Up the Dough and Roll It Out
Let the dough soften before rolling it out on a
well-floured counter. WHY? Warming up the dough
before rolling it out means less risk of overworking
the dough.

6 Fit the Dough into the Pie Plate
Loosely roll the flattened dough around the rolling
pin and gently unroll it over the pie plate. Lift the
dough and gently press it into the pie plate. WHY?
Gently fitting the dough ensures it doesn't tear.

LEMON MERINGUE PIE

Serves 8
Total Time 1 hour, plus 2 hours for cooling

Make the pie crust, let it cool, and then begin work on the filling. As soon as the filling is made, press a piece of lightly greased parchment paper against the surface and then start working on the meringue topping. You want to add warm filling to the cooled pie crust and then apply the meringue topping and quickly get the pie into the oven. You can use our Foolproof Single-Crust Pie Dough (page 329) or store-bought pie dough in this recipe. See How to Whip Egg Whites, page 207.

Filling

1½ **cups water**
1 **cup (7 ounces) sugar**
¼ **cup (1 ounce) cornstarch**
⅛ **teaspoon salt**
6 **large egg yolks**
1 **tablespoon grated lemon zest plus ½ cup juice (3 lemons)**
2 **tablespoons unsalted butter, cut into 2 pieces**

Meringue

⅓ **cup water**
1 **tablespoon cornstarch**
4 **large egg whites**
½ **teaspoon vanilla extract**
¼ **teaspoon cream of tartar**
½ **cup (3½ ounces) sugar**

1 **recipe single-crust pie dough, fully baked and cooled**

1 For the Filling
Adjust oven rack to middle position and heat oven to 325 degrees. Bring water, sugar, cornstarch, and salt to simmer in large saucepan over medium heat, whisking constantly. When mixture starts to turn translucent, whisk in egg yolks, two at a time. Whisk in lemon zest and juice and butter. Return mixture to brief simmer, then remove from heat. Lay sheet of lightly greased parchment paper directly on surface of filling to keep warm and prevent skin from forming.

2 For the Meringue
Bring water and cornstarch to simmer in small saucepan over medium-high heat and cook, whisking occasionally, until thickened and translucent, 1 to 2 minutes. Remove from heat and let cool slightly.

3 Using stand mixer fitted with whisk, whip egg whites, vanilla, and cream of tartar on medium-low speed until foamy, about 1 minute. Increase speed to medium-high and beat in sugar, 1 tablespoon at a time, until incorporated and mixture forms soft, billowy mounds. Add cornstarch mixture, 1 tablespoon at a time, and continue to beat to glossy, stiff peaks, 2 to 3 minutes.

4 Meanwhile, remove plastic from filling and return to very low heat during last minute or so of beating meringue (to ensure filling is warm).

5 Pour warm filling into cooled prebaked pie crust. Using rubber spatula, immediately distribute meringue evenly around edge and then center of pie, attaching meringue to pie crust to prevent shrinking. Using back of spoon, create attractive swirls and peaks in meringue. Bake until meringue is light golden brown, about 20 minutes. Let pie cool on wire rack until filling has set, about 2 hours. Serve.

1 Make the Filling
Simmer the water, sugar, cornstarch, and salt.
When it starts to turn translucent, combine it with
the egg yolks, lemon zest and juice, and butter.
WHY? Cornstarch helps create a rich, firm filling.

2 Whip the Egg Whites to Billowy Peaks
Whip the sugar into the egg whites, vanilla, and
cream of tartar until the mixture forms soft, billowy
mounds. WHY? This gives the meringue the
necessary volume.

3 Stabilize the Meringue
Combine ⅓ cup of water and 1 tablespoon
of cornstarch and cook until thickened. Beat
into the meringue 1 tablespoon at a time. WHY?
The cornstarch helps stabilize the meringue.

4 Add the Filling While Warm
Pour the warm filling into the cooled prebaked pie
crust and immediately add meringue. WHY?
The warm filling helps ensure that the bottom of the
meringue will be fully baked.

5 Attach the Meringue to the Crust
Use a rubber spatula to distribute the meringue on
top of the warm filling, attaching it to the edges of
the pie crust. WHY? This keeps the meringue from
shrinking away from the edge as the pie bakes.

6 Bake in a Gentle Oven
Bake the pie for about 20 minutes in a 325-degree
oven. WHY? Keeping the oven temperature
relatively low ensures that the top of the meringue
won't overcook.

DEEP-DISH APPLE PIE

Serves 8
Total Time 2 hours 20 minutes, plus 2 hours for cooling

You can substitute Empire or Cortland apples for the Granny Smith apples, and Jonagold, Fuji, or Braeburn for the Golden Delicious apples. You can use our Foolproof Double-Crust Pie Dough (page 330) or store-bought pie dough in this recipe.

2½ pounds Granny Smith apples, peeled, cored, and sliced ¼ inch thick

2½ pounds Golden Delicious apples, peeled, cored, and sliced ¼ inch thick

½ cup (3½ ounces) plus 1 tablespoon granulated sugar

¼ cup packed (1¾ ounces) light brown sugar

½ teaspoon grated lemon zest plus 1 tablespoon juice

¼ teaspoon salt

⅛ teaspoon ground cinnamon

1 recipe double-crust pie dough, bottom crust fitted into 9-inch pie plate and top crust rolled out into 12-inch round

1 large egg white, lightly beaten

1 Toss apples, ½ cup granulated sugar, brown sugar, lemon zest, salt, and cinnamon together in Dutch oven. Cover and cook over medium heat, stirring often, until apples are tender when poked with fork but still hold their shape, 15 to 20 minutes. Transfer apples and their juices to rimmed baking sheet and let cool to room temperature, about 30 minutes.

2 Adjust oven rack to lowest position and heat oven to 425 degrees. Line clean rimmed baking sheet with aluminum foil. Drain cooled apples thoroughly in colander set over bowl, reserving ¼ cup of juice. Stir lemon juice into reserved apple juice.

3 Spread apples into dough-lined pie plate, mounding them slightly in middle, and drizzle with apple juice mixture. Loosely roll top crust around rolling pin, then gently unroll it over filling.

4 Trim overhanging dough ½ inch beyond lip of pie plate. Pinch edges of top and bottom crusts firmly together. Tuck overhang under itself; folded edge should be flush with edge of pie plate. Use index finger of 1 hand and thumb and index finger of other hand to crimp dough evenly around edge of pie. Cut four 2-inch slits in top of dough. Brush surface with beaten egg white and sprinkle evenly with remaining 1 tablespoon granulated sugar.

5 Place pie on prepared sheet and bake until crust is light golden brown, about 25 minutes. Reduce oven temperature to 375 degrees, rotate baking sheet, and continue to bake until juices are bubbling and crust is deep golden brown, 30 to 40 minutes longer. Let pie cool on wire rack until filling has set, about 2 hours. Serve slightly warm or at room temperature.

1 Use Two Types of Apples

Peel, core, and cut 2½ pounds each of Granny Smith and Golden Delicious apples into ¼-inch-thick slices. WHY? A mix of tart and sweet apples provides the right flavor.

2 Cook the Apples

Cover and cook the apples, sugars, and seasonings until the apples are tender but still hold their shape. WHY? Precooking the fruit helps keep the pie from getting soggy by cooking off the juices.

3 Cool and Drain the Apples

Cool the cooked apples then drain them. Reserve ¼ cup of the drained juice and mix it with the lemon juice. WHY? Adding back some of the apple juices helps control the moisture in the pie.

4 Assemble Double-Crust Pie

Spread the apples into a dough-lined pie plate. Drizzle the apple juice mixture over them and then add the top crust. WHY? Since the apples are slightly softened, you can pack them in firmly.

5 Crimp the Crusts and Cut Vent Holes

Crimp the dough around the edge of the pie, then cut four 2-inch vent holes in the top crust. WHY? A properly crimped crust helps prevent leaks during baking while vents allow steam to escape.

6 Bake at Two Temperatures

Start the pie at 425 degrees, lower the heat to 375 degrees, and bake until the crust is deep golden brown. WHY? The lower temperature enables the pie to bake through without burning.

RUSTIC WALNUT TART

Serves 8 to 10
Total Time 5 hours 50 minutes (includes 2 hours for cooling crust), plus 2 hours for cooling tart

Pecans can be substituted for the walnuts. See How to Make a Classic Tart Shell (page 237).

Tart Shell
1 large egg yolk
1 tablespoon heavy cream
½ teaspoon vanilla extract
1¼ cups (6¼ ounces) all-purpose flour
⅔ cup (2⅔ ounces) confectioners' sugar
¼ teaspoon salt
8 tablespoons unsalted butter, cut into ¼-inch pieces and chilled

Filling
½ cup packed (3½ ounces) light brown sugar
⅓ cup light corn syrup
4 tablespoons unsalted butter, melted and cooled
1 tablespoon bourbon or dark rum
2 teaspoons vanilla extract

½ teaspoon salt
1 large egg
1¾ cups walnuts, chopped coarse

1 **For the Tart Shell**
Whisk egg yolk, cream, and vanilla together in bowl. Process flour, sugar, and salt in food processor until combined, about 5 seconds. Scatter butter pieces over top and pulse until mixture resembles coarse cornmeal, about 15 pulses. With machine running, add yolk mixture and continue to process until dough just comes together, about 12 seconds. Turn dough onto sheet of plastic wrap and flatten into 6-inch disk. Wrap tightly and refrigerate for 1 hour. Before rolling dough out, let it sit on counter to soften slightly, about 10 minutes.

2 Roll dough into 11-inch circle on lightly floured counter. Place dough round on baking sheet, cover with plastic, and refrigerate for 30 minutes.

3 Loosely roll dough around rolling pin and gently unroll it onto 9-inch tart pan with removable bottom, letting excess dough hang over edge. Lift dough and gently press it into corners and fluted sides of pan. Run rolling pin over top of pan to remove any excess dough. Wrap loosely in plastic, place on large plate, and freeze until dough is fully chilled and firm, about 30 minutes.

4 Meanwhile, adjust oven rack to middle position and heat oven to 375 degrees. Set dough-lined tart pan on rimmed baking sheet, line with double layer of aluminum foil, and fill with pie weights. Bake until shell is golden and set, about 30 minutes, rotating sheet halfway through baking. Carefully remove weights and foil and continue to bake until shell is golden brown, 5 to 10 minutes. Transfer tart shell with baking sheet to wire rack. Let shell cool completely, about 2 hours.

5 **For the Filling**
Adjust oven rack to middle position and heat oven to 375 degrees. Whisk sugar, corn syrup, butter, bourbon, vanilla, and salt in large bowl until sugar dissolves. Whisk in egg until combined. Pour filling into cooled shell and sprinkle with walnuts. Bake until filling is set and walnuts begin to brown, 30 to 40 minutes, rotating sheet halfway through baking. Let tart cool completely, about 2 hours.

6 To serve, remove outer ring from tart pan, slide thin metal spatula between tart and tart pan bottom, and carefully slide tart onto serving platter or cutting board. Slice tart into pieces and serve.

Learn How Rustic Walnut Tart

1 Use Confectioners' Sugar in the Tart Dough
Process the flour, confectioners' sugar, and salt in a food processor until combined. Add the butter and pulse, then add the egg mixture. WHY? Pastry made with confectioners' sugar has a crisp texture.

2 Chill, Roll Out, and Fit the Dough
Refrigerate the dough for 1 hour, then roll it out and chill it again before fitting it into the tart pan. WHY? Chilled dough is easier to lift and press into the tart pan.

3 Freeze the Tart Shell Before Baking
Wrap the dough-lined tart pan in plastic and freeze until the dough is fully chilled and firm. WHY? Freezing gives the gluten in the dough time to relax, reducing the risk of shrinkage during baking.

4 Fully Bake the Tart Shell
Blind bake the shell for about 30 minutes, then remove the weights and foil and bake until golden brown. WHY? Prebaking ensures that the finished filled shell won't end up doughy or underbaked.

5 Use Bourbon in the Tart Filling
Whisk the sugar, corn syrup, butter, bourbon, vanilla, and salt together for the filling. WHY? The liquor cuts through the sweetness of the filling and accentuates the flavor of the nuts.

6 Add the Nuts on Top of the Tart
Sprinkle the walnuts evenly over the filling. WHY? Sprinkling the walnuts over the top rather than mixing them in with the filling allows them to form a distinct layer that browns evenly in the oven.

BLUEBERRY COBBLER WITH BISCUIT TOPPING

Serves 8
Total Time 1 hour 25 minutes

Before preparing the filling, taste the fruit, adding a smaller amount of sugar if the fruit is on sweet side, more if the fruit is tart. Do not let the biscuit batter sit for longer than 5 minutes before baking. If you don't have a deep-dish glass pie plate, use a round baking dish of similar size. For information on buttermilk substitutions, see page 356.

Fruit Filling

⅓–⅔ cup (2⅓ to 4⅔ ounces) sugar
4 teaspoons cornstarch
30 ounces (6 cups) blueberries
1 tablespoon lemon juice
½ teaspoon ground cinnamon

Biscuit Topping

1½ cups (7½ ounces) all-purpose flour
¼ cup (1¾ ounces) plus 2 teaspoons sugar
1½ teaspoons baking powder
¼ teaspoon baking soda

¼ teaspoon salt
¾ cup buttermilk, chilled
6 tablespoons unsalted butter, melted and hot
⅛ teaspoon ground cinnamon

1 **For The Fruit Filling**
Adjust oven rack to middle position and heat oven to 400 degrees. Whisk sugar and cornstarch together in large bowl. Add blueberries, lemon juice, and cinnamon and toss gently to combine. Transfer fruit mixture to 9-inch deep-dish glass pie plate, cover with aluminum foil, and set on foil-lined rimmed baking sheet. (Fruit filling can be held at room temperature for up to 4 hours.)

2 **For The Biscuit Topping**
Line rimmed baking sheet with parchment paper. Whisk flour, ¼ cup sugar, baking powder, baking soda, and salt together in large bowl. In separate bowl, stir buttermilk and melted butter together until butter forms small clumps. Using rubber spatula, stir buttermilk mixture into flour mixture until just incorporated and dough pulls away from sides of bowl.

3 Using greased ¼-cup measure, scoop out and drop 8 mounds of dough onto prepared baking sheet, spaced about 1½ inches apart. Combine remaining 2 teaspoons sugar with cinnamon in bowl, then sprinkle over biscuits. Bake biscuits until puffed and lightly browned on bottom, about 10 minutes. Remove biscuits from oven and set aside. (Parbaked biscuits can be held at room temperature for up to 4 hours.)

4 Place fruit in oven and bake until fruit is hot and has released its juices, 20 to 25 minutes. Remove fruit from oven, uncover, and stir gently. Arrange parbaked biscuits over top, squeezing them slightly as needed to fit into dish. Bake cobbler until biscuits are golden brown and fruit is bubbling, about 15 minutes, rotating dish halfway through baking. Transfer to wire rack and let cool for 15 minutes. Serve warm.

VARIATION

Peach or Nectarine Cobbler with Biscuit Topping

Substitute 3 pounds peaches or nectarines, peeled, halved, pitted, and cut into ½-inch-thick wedges, for blueberries. Omit cinnamon. Reduce cornstarch to 1 tablespoon and lemon juice to 1 teaspoon. Add 1 teaspoon vanilla extract to bowl with fruit.

1 Make the Drop Biscuits
Using a greased ¼-cup measure, drop 8 mounds of dough onto the prepared baking sheet. WHY? The measuring cup makes portioning out evenly sized biscuits very easy.

2 Parbake the Biscuits
Bake the biscuits until they're lightly browned on the bottom. (They will not be fully baked.) WHY? Parbaking prevents the biscuits from getting soggy when they're placed on the fruit filling.

3 Parbake the Fruit Filling
Parbake the fruit filling in a covered dish until the fruit has released its juices. WHY? This ensures that when the cobbler is assembled the biscuits and filling will finish cooking at same time.

4 Put the Fruit and Biscuits Together
Remove the fruit from the oven and stir it gently. Arrange the parbaked biscuits over the top. WHY? Stirring the filling ensures its temperature is uniform before adding the biscuits.

5 Bake Until the Filling Is Bubbling
Bake the cobbler until the biscuits are golden brown and the fruit is bubbling, rotating the dish halfway through baking. WHY? This final baking step makes the dish more cohesive.

6 Cool the Cobbler
Transfer the cobbler to a wire rack and let it cool for 15 minutes. Serve the cobbler warm. WHY? Letting the cobbler cool a bit gives the fruit juices time to cool and thicken into a glossy sauce.

CHOCOLATE MOUSSE

Serves 6 to 8
Total Time 2 hours 30 minutes (includes 2 hours for chilling)

When developing this recipe, we used Ghirardelli Bittersweet Chocolate Baking Bar, which contains about 60 percent cacao. If you want to use a chocolate with a higher percentage of cacao, see our variation, Premium Dark Chocolate Mousse. If you choose to make the mousse a day in advance, let it sit at room temperature for 10 minutes before serving. Serve with whipped cream if desired. See How to Whip Egg Whites, page 207.

8 ounces bittersweet chocolate, chopped fine

5 tablespoons water

2 tablespoons Dutch-processed cocoa powder

1 tablespoon brandy

1 teaspoon instant espresso powder

2 large eggs, separated

1 tablespoon sugar

⅛ teaspoon salt

1 cup plus 2 tablespoons heavy cream, chilled

1 Place chocolate, water, cocoa, brandy, and espresso powder in medium heatproof bowl set over saucepan filled with 1 inch barely simmering water, making sure that water does not touch bottom of bowl and stirring frequently until chocolate is melted, cocoa is dissolved, and mixture is smooth. Remove from heat.

2 Whisk egg yolks, 1½ teaspoons sugar, and salt in medium bowl until mixture lightens in color and thickens slightly, about 30 seconds. Whisk in melted chocolate mixture until combined. Let cool until just warmer than room temperature, 3 to 5 minutes.

3 Using stand mixer fitted with whisk, whip egg whites on medium-low speed until foamy, about 1 minute. Add remaining 1½ teaspoons sugar, increase speed to medium-high, and whip until soft peaks form, about 1 minute. Using whisk, stir about one-quarter of whipped egg whites into chocolate mixture to lighten it. Gently fold in remaining egg whites with rubber spatula until few white streaks remain.

4 In now-empty mixer bowl, whip cream on medium-low speed until foamy, about 30 seconds. Increase speed to high and whip until soft peaks form, 1 to 3 minutes. Using rubber spatula, fold whipped cream into mousse until no white streaks remain. Spoon mousse into 6 to 8 individual serving dishes. Cover with plastic wrap and refrigerate until set and firm, at least 2 hours or up to 24 hours. Serve.

VARIATIONS

Premium Dark Chocolate Mousse
This recipe is designed to work with a boutique chocolate that contains a higher percentage of cacao than that in our master recipe.

Use 62 percent to 70 percent cacao bittersweet chocolate, increase water to 7 tablespoons, and increase eggs to 3. Increase sugar to 3 tablespoons, adding extra 2 tablespoons to chocolate mixture in step 1.

Chocolate-Raspberry Mousse
Chambord is our preferred brand of raspberry-flavored liqueur for this recipe. Serve the mousse with fresh raspberries, if desired.

Reduce water to 4 tablespoons, omit brandy, and add 2 tablespoons raspberry-flavored liqueur to melted chocolate mixture in step 1.

Learn How Chocolate Mousse

1 Melt the Chocolate
Heat the chocolate, water, cocoa, brandy, and espresso over a saucepan of barely simmering water, stirring frequently until smooth. WHY? A double boiler ensures the chocolate won't scorch.

2 Add the Chocolate to the Egg Yolks
Whisk the yolks, sugar, and salt together. Whisk in the chocolate until combined. WHY? This helps loosen up the chocolate so that it's easier to fold in the whipped egg whites and whipped cream.

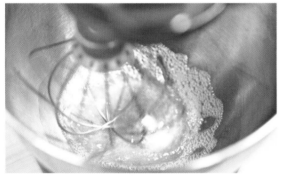

3 Whip the Egg Whites
Using a stand mixer fitted with a whisk, whip the egg whites until foamy, then add sugar and whip to soft peaks. WHY? The whipped egg whites are crucial to the light texture of the mousse.

4 Add the Egg Whites to the Chocolate Mixture
Whisk one-quarter of the egg whites into the chocolate. Fold in the remaining egg whites with a rubber spatula. WHY? This helps preserve the egg whites' airy texture.

5 Whip the Cream
Whip the cream until soft peaks form. WHY? The richness of the whipped cream rounds out the chocolate flavor, and its soft, whipped texture makes the mousse smooth and silky.

6 Fold in the Whipped Cream and Chill
Using a rubber spatula, fold the whipped cream into the mousse until no white streaks remain. WHY? A stiff rubber spatula lets you fold in the whipped cream completely but gently.

APPENDICES

THE COOK'S VOCABULARY: TERMS EVERY COOK SHOULD KNOW

The first step to the successful completion of a recipe is understanding what the recipe is telling you to do. Unfamiliar language and terminology can be a real problem. The following are some common culinary terms you should know.

Al Dente A doneness instruction usually used with pasta, rice, and other grains. From the Italian for "to the tooth," this phrase indicates food that is fully cooked but still firm when bitten into.

Barbecue To cook large, tough cuts of meat using indirect, gentle heat from an outdoor fire. Barbecued foods derive their "barbecued" flavor from wood chips or chunks.

Baste To moisten food regularly with a liquid (usually butter or pan drippings) during cooking.

Beat To stir into a froth or foam, usually with a whisk, fork, or electric mixer. See also **Whip**.

Blanch To briefly submerge fruits or vegetables in boiling water to set their color, flavor, and texture. Often followed by immediately transferring the food to an ice bath to halt cooking.

Blind-Bake To prebake a component of a dish, usually the crust of a pie or tart, under a layer of weighted parchment paper or aluminum foil in order to ensure that it turns out fully cooked.

Bloom To cook ground spices or dried herbs in fat to intensify their flavor.

Boil To heat liquid until large bubbles break the surface at a rapid and constant rate.

Braise To cook food by gently simmering it in a flavorful liquid in a covered pot.

Brine To soak food in a water and salt solution to season and tenderize it before cooking. See also **Marinate**.

Butterfly To remove the backbone from a whole chicken, turkey, or other poultry, in order to flatten the bird for fast, even cooking. Also known as spatchcocking.

Carryover Cooking The term used to describe the fact that meat continues to cook even after it has been removed from a heat source.

Chiffonade A style of preparing herbs that entails stacking several leaves, rolling them tightly, and slicing them into thin strips. Often used for basil.

Chop To cut into small pieces. Recipes will frequently call for foods to be chopped fine, medium, or coarse. Fine corresponds to food cut into ⅛- to ¼-inch pieces, medium to ¼- to ½-inch pieces, and coarse to ½- to ¾-inch pieces.

Cream To combine sugar and a fat into a homogeneous mixture.

Crimp To seal and embellish the edge of a pie crust or other pastry. See also **Flute**.

Deep-Fry To cook in hot oil deep enough to fully surround the food.

Deglaze To use liquid (usually wine or broth) to loosen the brown fond that develops and sticks to a pan during the sautéing or searing process.

Dice To cut into uniform cubes (the size of the dice depends on the recipe).

Emulsion A mixture of two liquids—such as oil and water—that would not ordinarily stay combined. To create an emulsion, one liquid (often the fat) is broken into very small droplets that are suspended in the other liquid (often water).

En Papillote A cooking method characterized by enclosing the food in a parchment paper packet. The food steams in its own juices so that the flavors are pure and clean. Although parchment is the traditional choice in this classic French technique, aluminum foil can be used.

Flambé To ignite the alcohol vapor above a pan of food in order to create a set of high-temperature reactions for flavor development.

Flute To create a scalloped pattern around the edge of a pie crust or other pastry. See also **Crimp**.

Fold To mix delicate batters and incorporate fragile ingredients using a gentle under-and-over motion that minimizes deflation.

Fond The caramelized browned bits that remain on the bottom of the pan after food has been sautéed or pan-seared.

Glaze To coat food with a glossy syrup or paste (frequently sugar-based).

Grate To shred a food into small, uniform pieces using a tool like a box grater or rasp grater.

Grill To cook relatively small, individually sized, and quick-cooking foods such as steaks, chops, and skewers directly over an outdoor fire.

Grill-Roast To cook large, tender cuts of meat using indirect, moderate heat from an outdoor fire.

Julienne To cut into matchstick-size pieces, usually about 2 inches long and ⅛ inch thick.

Knead To manipulate bread dough to develop gluten and create a strong network of cross-linked proteins.

Macerate To toss an ingredient (often fruit) with sugar and leave it to sit to draw out moisture.

Maillard Reaction The chemical reaction that occurs when proteins and sugars are subjected to a high temperature, leading to browning and the creation of new flavor compounds; named for French chemist Louis Camille Maillard, who first described the phenomenon in the early 1900s.

Marinate To let food sit in a seasoned mixture of oil, liquid, herbs, spices, and other flavorings before cooking to increase flavor and improve texture. See also **Brine**.

Mince To cut food into ⅛-inch pieces or smaller.

Mise en Place Preparing and measuring the ingredients for a dish before you begin to cook; from the French for "putting in place."

Panade A paste of milk and bread that is typically used to help foods like meatballs and meatloaf hold their shape and moisture.

Peel To remove the outer skin, rind, or layer from a food, usually a piece of fruit or vegetable.

Poach To cook food in hot water or other liquid that is held below the simmering point.

Proof A stage in the rising of dough when a shaped loaf is set out for its final rise and fermentation before baking. The word "proof" can also be used to refer to the process of testing yeast to confirm that it is active.

Puree To grind ingredients to a fine, uniform consistency, often in a food processor or blender.

Reduce To partially evaporate liquids to concentrate flavors and thicken consistency.

Roast To cook food in a pan in a hot oven.

Sauté To cook food in a small amount of fat over moderately high heat, usually with the goal of browning the food. Traditionally, sautéed food is tossed about by jerking the pan back and forth. Stirring food accomplishes the same thing.

Scald To bring a liquid to the verge of a boil.

Score To make shallow cuts on the surface of a food in order to maximize surface area, increase marinade penetration, or create a rough texture.

Sear To cook food over high heat, usually with the goal of creating a deeply browned crust. While sautéing involves frequent stirring, seared foods are best left alone so that a crust can develop.

Shallow-Fry To cook in hot oil deep enough to partially surround the food. Also called pan-frying.

Sift To move a powdered ingredient such as flour through a fine mesh to aerate and break up clumps.

Simmer To heat liquid until small bubbles gently break the surface at a variable and infrequent rate.

Skim To remove the fat that floats to the surface of pan drippings or braising liquids after roasting or braising fatty cuts of beef, pork, or poultry.

Slice To cut into pieces with two flat edges (the thickness of the slices will depend on the recipe).

Steam To cook foods using the steam released from boiling liquid.

Stir-Fry To quickly cook thinly cut food in oil over high heat.

Sweat To cook over gentle heat in a small amount of fat in a covered pot.

Temper To gradually increase the temperature of a sensitive ingredient such as dairy or eggs to prevent it from breaking or curdling once added to a hot soup or sauce.

Toast To cook or brown food by dry heat, and without adding fat, using an oven or skillet.

Truss To tie up a chicken, turkey, or other bird with twine in order to keep the wings and legs close to the body and encourage even cooking.

Whip To quickly stir an ingredient such as egg whites or cream with a whisk or electric mixer in order to aerate and stabilize the ingredient and add volume. See also **Beat**.

Zest The outer layer of peel on a citrus fruit, which is often removed and used as a flavoring. Does not include the white pith layer under the peel.

HANDY CHARTS

No matter how experienced you are in the kitchen, there will be times when you need a quick reminder about some of the basics.

COOKING VEGETABLES
Follow the directions in this chart to cook vegetables in the simplest (and quickest) way possible.

Type of Vegetable	Amount/ Yield	Preparation	Boiling Time (Amount of Water and Salt)	Steaming Time	Microwaving Time (Amount of Water)
Asparagus	1 bunch (1 pound)/ serves 3	tough ends trimmed	2 to 4 minutes (4 quarts water plus 1 tablespoon salt)	3 to 5 minutes	3 to 6 minutes (3 tablespoons water)
Beets	1½ pounds (6 medium)/ serves 4	greens discarded and beets scrubbed well	X	35 to 55 minutes	18 to 24 minutes (¾ cup water)
Broccoli	1 bunch (1½ pounds)/ serves 4	florets cut into 1- to 1½-inch pieces, stalks peeled and cut into ¼-inch-thick pieces	2 to 4 minutes (4 quarts water plus 1 tablespoon salt)	4 to 6 minutes	4 to 6 minutes (3 tablespoons water)
Brussels Sprouts	1 pound/ serves 4	stem ends trimmed, discolored leaves removed, and halved through stem	6 to 8 minutes (4 quarts water plus 1 tablespoon salt)	7 to 9 minutes	X
Carrots	1 pound/ serves 4	peeled and sliced ¼ inch thick on bias	3 to 4 minutes (4 quarts water plus 1 tablespoon salt)	5 to 6 minutes	4 to 7 minutes (2 tablespoons water)
Cauliflower	1 head (2 pounds)/ serves 4 to 6	cored and florets cut into 1-inch pieces	5 to 7 minutes (4 quarts water plus 1 tablespoon salt)	7 to 9 minutes	4 to 7 minutes (¼ cup water)
Green Beans	1 pound/ serves 4	stem ends trimmed	3 to 5 minutes (4 quarts water plus 1 tablespoon salt)	6 to 8 minutes	4 to 6 minutes (3 tablespoons water)
Red Potatoes	2 pounds (6 medium)/ serves 4	scrubbed and poked several times with fork	16 to 22 minutes (4 quarts water plus 1 tablespoon salt)	18 to 24 minutes	6 to 10 minutes (no water and uncovered)
Russet Potatoes	2 pounds (4 medium)/ serves 4	scrubbed and poked several times with fork	X	X	8 to 12 minutes (3 tablespoons water)
Snap Peas	1 pound/ serves 4	stems trimmed and strings removed	2 to 4 minutes (4 quarts water plus 1 tablespoon salt)	4 to 6 minutes	3 to 6 minutes (3 tablespoons water)
Snow Peas	1 pound/ serves 4	stems trimmed and strings removed	2 to 3 minutes (4 quarts water plus 1 tablespoon salt)	4 to 6 minutes	3 to 6 minutes (3 tablespoons water)
Squash (Winter)	2 pounds/ serves 4	peeled, seeded, and cut into 1-inch chunks	X	12 to 14 minutes	8 to 11 minutes (¼ cup water)
Sweet Potatoes	2 pounds (3 medium)/ serves 4	peeled and cut into 1-inch chunks	X	12 to 14 minutes	8 to 10 minutes (¼ cup water)

X = Not recommended

COOKING RICE

Here are three simple methods for basic rice cooking: boiling, pilaf-style (which we think yields the best results), and microwaving. If you want to make rice for a crowd, use the boiling method and double the amount of rice (there's no need to add more water or salt). We don't recommend cooking more than 1 cup of rice in the microwave.

Pilaf-Style Directions

Rinse rice. Heat 1 tablespoon vegetable or olive oil in medium saucepan (preferably nonstick) over medium-high heat until shimmering. Stir in rice and cook until edges of grains begin to turn translucent, about 3 minutes. Stir in water and ¼ teaspoon salt. Bring mixture to simmer, then reduce heat to low, cover, and continue to simmer until rice is tender and has absorbed all of the water, following cooking times given in chart below. Off heat, place clean folded dish towel under lid and let rice sit for 10 minutes. Fluff rice with fork.

Microwave Directions

Rinse rice. Combine water, rice, 1 tablespoon vegetable or olive oil, and ¼ teaspoon salt in bowl. Cover and microwave on high (full power) until water begins to boil, 5 to 10 minutes. Reduce microwave heat to medium (50 percent power) and continue to cook until rice is just tender, following cooking times given in chart below. Remove from microwave and fluff with fork. Cover bowl with plastic wrap, poke several vent holes in plastic with tip of knife, and let sit until completely tender, about 5 minutes.

Boiling Directions

Bring water to boil in large saucepan. Stir in rice and 2½ teaspoons salt. Return to boil, then reduce to simmer and cook until rice is tender, following cooking times given in chart below. Drain.

Type of Rice	Cooking Method	Amount of Rice	Amount of Water	Cooking Time
Short- or Medium-Grain White Rice	Pilaf-Style	1 cup	1¾ cups	10 to 15 minutes
	Boiled	1 cup	4 quarts	10 to 15 minutes
	Microwave	X	X	X
Long-Grain White Rice	Pilaf-Style	1 cup	1¾ cups	16 to 18 minutes
	Boiled	1 cup	4 quarts	12 to 17 minutes
	Microwave	1 cup	2 cups	10 to 15 minutes
Short- or Medium-Grain Brown Rice	Pilaf-Style	1 cup	1¾ cups	40 to 50 minutes
	Boiled	1 cup	4 quarts	22 to 27 minutes
	Microwave	1 cup	2 cups	25 to 30 minutes
Long-Grain Brown Rice	Pilaf-Style	1 cup	1¾ cups	40 to 50 minutes
	Boiled	1 cup	4 quarts	25 to 30 minutes
	Microwave	1 cup	2 cups	25 to 30 minutes
Wild Rice	Pilaf-Style	X	X	X
	Boiled	1 cup	4 quarts	35 to 40 minutes
	Microwave	X	X	X
Basmati, Jasmine, or Texmati Rice	Pilaf-Style	1 cup	1¾ cups	16 to 18 minutes
	Boiled	1 cup	4 quarts	12 to 17 minutes
	Microwave	1 cup	2 cups	10 to 15 minutes

X = Not recommended

COOKING GRAINS

Pilaf-style is our favorite method because it produces fluffy grains with a slightly toasted flavor.

Pilaf-Style Directions

Rinse and then dry grains on towel. Heat 1 tablespoon vegetable or olive oil in medium saucepan (preferably nonstick) over medium-high heat until shimmering. Stir in grain and toast until lightly golden and fragrant, 2 to 3 minutes. Stir in water and ¼ teaspoon salt. Bring mixture to simmer, then reduce heat to low, cover, and continue to simmer until grain is tender and has absorbed all of the water, following times given below. Off heat, let grain stand for 10 minutes, then fluff with fork.

Boiling Directions

Bring water to boil in large saucepan. Add grain and ½ teaspoon salt. Return to boil, reduce to simmer and cook until tender, using times in chart. Drain.

Microwave Directions

Rinse grain. Combine water, grain, 1 tablespoon vegetable or olive oil, and ¼ teaspoon salt in bowl. Cover and cook using times and temperatures below. Remove from microwave and fluff with fork. Cover bowl with plastic wrap, poke several holes, and let sit until completely tender, about 5 minutes.

Type of Grain	Cooking Method	Amount of Grain	Amount of Water	Cooking Time
Amaranth*	Pilaf-Style	1 cup	1½ cups	20 to 25 minutes
	Boiled	X	X	X
	Microwave	1 cup	2 cups	5 to 10 minutes on high, then 15 to 20 minutes on medium
Pearl Barley	Pilaf-Style	X	X	X
	Boiled	1 cup	4 quarts	20 to 25 minutes
	Microwave	X	X	X
Buckwheat (Kasha)	Pilaf-Style	1 cup	2 cups	10 to 15 minutes
	Boiled	1 cup	2 quarts	10 to 12 minutes
	Microwave	X	X	X
Bulgur (Medium- to Coarse-Grind)	Pilaf-Style**	1 cup	1 cup	16 to 18 minutes
	Boiled	1 cup	4 quarts	5 minutes
	Microwave	1 cup	1 cup	5 to 10 minutes on high
Farro	Pilaf-Style	X	X	X
	Boiled	1 cup	4 quarts	15 to 20 minutes
	Microwave	X	X	X
Millet	Pilaf-Style***	1 cup	2 cups	15 to 20 minutes
	Boiled	X	X	X
	Microwave	X	X	X
Oat Berries	Pilaf-Style	1 cup	1 ⅓ cups	30 to 40 minutes
	Boiled	1 cup	4 quarts	30 to 40 minutes
	Microwave	X	X	X
Quinoa (any color)	Pilaf-Style	1 cup	1 cup + 3 tablespoons	18 to 20 minutes
	Boiled	X	X	X
	Microwave	1 cup	2 cups	5 minutes on medium, then 5 minutes on high
Wheat Berries	Pilaf-Style	X	X	X
	Boiled	1 cup	4 cups	1 hour
	Microwave	X	X	X

* Do not rinse.

X = Not recommended

** For pilaf, do not rinse. Skip toasting step and add grain to pot with liquid.

*** For pilaf, toast until grains begin to pop, about 12 minutes.

SCALING BASIC EGG RECIPES

Our basic techniques for frying, scrambling, and poaching eggs can be found on page 209, 210, and 211 in Chapter 3. If you want to scale those dishes, use the ratios outlined here.

Fried Eggs

The trick to frying eggs is using two bowls to add the eggs to the skillet. (Put two eggs in each bowl if cooking four eggs.) Make sure to use a nonstick skillet.

Eggs	Vegetable Oil	Unsalted Butter	Seasonings	Skillet Size
2	1 teaspoon	1 teaspoon, cut into 2 pieces and chilled	pinch salt, pinch pepper	8- or 9-inch
4	2 teaspoons	2 teaspoons, cut into 4 pieces and chilled	pinch salt, pinch pepper	12- or 14-inch

Scrambled Eggs

Half-and-half adds liquid that turns to steam when eggs are cooked, thus helping them cook into soft, fluffy mounds. You need 1 tablespoon of half-and-half for each serving of eggs.

Servings	Eggs	Half-And-Half	Seasonings	Butter	Skillet Size	Cooking Time
1	2 large, plus 1 yolk	1 tablespoon	pinch salt, pinch pepper	¼ tablespoon	8 inches	30 to 60 seconds over medium-high, 30 to 60 seconds over low
2	4 large, plus 1 yolk	2 tablespoons	⅛ teaspoon salt, ⅛ teaspoon pepper	½ tablespoon	8 inches	45 to 75 seconds over medium-high, 30 to 60 seconds over low
3	6 large, plus 1 yolk	3 tablespoons	¼ teaspoon salt, ⅛ teaspoon pepper	¾ tablespoon	10 inches	1 to 2 minutes over medium-high, 30 to 60 seconds over low
4	8 large, plus 2 yolks	¼ cup	¼ teaspoon salt, ¼ teaspoon pepper	1 tablespoon	10 inches	1½ to 2½ minutes over medium-high, 30 to 60 seconds over low

Poached Eggs

The timing is the only thing that will change if you scale this recipe up; the amounts of salt, vinegar, and water used stay the same.

Number of Eggs	Cooking Time
2 large	3½ minutes
4 large	4 minutes
8 large	5 minutes
12 large	6 minutes

SALTING MEAT AND POULTRY

Over the years, we have found that salting improves the texture and flavor of nearly every type of meat. Salting helps proteins retain their own natural juices and is the best choice for meats that are already relatively juicy and/or well marbled. When salt is applied to raw meat, juices inside the meat are drawn to the surface. The salt then dissolves in the exuded liquid, forming a brine that is eventually reabsorbed by the meat. Unlike brining, salting does not require fitting a large container of salt water in the fridge, and it won't thwart the goal of crispy skin on poultry or well-browned crust on steaks, chops, or roasts since no moisture is added to their exteriors. We prefer to use kosher salt because it's easier to distribute the salt evenly. We use Diamond Crystal Kosher Salt; if using Morton Kosher Salt, reduce the amounts listed by 25 percent (e.g. use ¾ teaspoon Morton Kosher Salt in place of 1 teaspoon Diamond Crystal).

Salting Meat

Cuts	Time	Kosher Salt	Method
Steaks, Lamb Chops, Pork Chops	1 hour	¾ teaspoon per 8-ounce chop or steak	Apply salt evenly over surface and let rest at room temperature, uncovered, on wire rack set in rimmed baking sheet.
Beef, Lamb, and Pork Roasts	At least 6 hours and up to 24 hours	1 teaspoon per pound	Apply salt evenly over surface, wrap tightly with plastic wrap, and let rest in refrigerator.

Salting Poultry

Cuts	Time	Kosher Salt	Method
Whole Chicken	At least 6 hours and up to 24 hours	1 teaspoon per pound	Apply salt evenly inside cavity and under skin of breast and legs and let rest in refrigerator on wire rack set in rimmed baking sheet. (Wrap with plastic wrap if salting for longer than 12 hours.)
Bone-In Chicken Pieces, Boneless or Bone-In Turkey Breast	At least 6 hours and up to 24 hours	¾ teaspoon per pound	If poultry is skin-on, apply salt evenly between skin and meat, leaving skin attached, and let rest in the refrigerator on wire rack set in rimmed baking sheet. (Wrap with plastic wrap if salting for longer than 12 hours.)
Whole Turkey	At least 24 hours and up to 2 days	1 teaspoon per pound	Apply salt evenly inside cavity and under skin of breast and legs, wrap tightly with plastic wrap, and let rest in refrigerator.

BRINING PORK AND POULTRY

Brining works pretty much the same way as salting. Salt in the brine seasons the meat and promotes a change in its protein structure, reducing its overall toughness and creating gaps that fill up with water and keep the meat juicy and flavorful. Brining works faster than salting and can also result in juicier lean cuts since it adds, rather than merely retains, moisture—which is why we prefer brining to salting in poultry and lean cuts of pork. Note that brining does inhibit browning, however, and it entails fitting a brining container in the fridge. We prefer to use table salt for brining since it dissolves quickly in the water. Do not brine kosher birds or enhanced pork.

Brining Directions

Dissolve salt in water in container large enough to hold brine and meat, following amounts in chart. Submerge meat completely in brine. Cover and refrigerate, following times in chart (do not brine for longer or meat will be overly salty). Remove meat from brine and pat dry with paper towels.

Meat	Cold Water	Table Salt	Time
Chicken			
1 (3- to 8-pound) whole chicken	2 quarts	½ cup	1 hour
2 (3- to 8-pound) whole chickens	3 quarts	¾ cup	1 hour
4 pounds bone-in chicken pieces (whole breasts, split breasts, whole legs, thighs, and/or drumsticks)	2 quarts	½ cup	½ to 1 hour
Boneless, skinless chicken breasts (up to 6 breasts)	1½ quarts	3 tablespoons	½ to 1 hour
Turkey			
1 (12- to 17-pound) whole turkey	2 gallons	1 cup	6 to 12 hours
1 (18- to 24-pound) whole turkey	3 gallons	1½ cups	6 to 12 hours
Bone-in turkey breast	1 gallon	½ cup	3 to 6 hours
Pork			
Bone-in pork chops (up to 6)	1½ quarts	3 tablespoons	½ to 1 hour
Boneless pork chops (up to 6)	1½ quarts	3 tablespoons	½ to 1 hour
1 (2½- to 6-pound) pork roast	2 quarts	¼ cup	1½ to 2 hours

DONENESS TEMPERATURES FOR MEAT, POULTRY, AND FISH

Since the temperature of cooked beef and pork will continue to rise as they rest, they should be removed from the oven, grill, or pan when they are 5 to 10 degrees below the desired serving temperature. Carryover cooking doesn't apply to poultry and fish, so they should be cooked to the desired serving temperatures. The following temperatures should be used to determine when to stop the cooking process. A thin steak or chop should then rest for 5 to 10 minutes, a thicker roast for 15 to 20 minutes. And when cooking a huge turkey (18 pounds or more), the bird should rest for 30 minutes before it is carved. To keep meat warm while it rests, tent it loosely with foil. The chart below is geared toward maximum juiciness and flavor. For optimum safety, follow USDA guidelines: Cook whole cuts of meat to an internal temperature of at least 145 degrees and let rest for at least 3 minutes. Cook ground meat to an internal temperature of at least 160 degrees. Cook all poultry, including ground poultry, to an internal temperature of at least 165 degrees. For more information on determining the internal temperature of foods, see pages 180–181.

For This Ingredient...	Cook to This Temperature
Beef/Lamb/Veal	
Chops, Cutlets, Steaks, and Roasts	
Rare	115 to 120 degrees (120 to 125 degrees after resting)
Medium-Rare	120 to 125 degrees (125 to 130 degrees after resting)
Medium	130 to 135 degrees (135 to 140 degrees after resting)
Medium-Well	140 to 145 degrees (145 to 150 degrees after resting)
Well-Done	150 to 155 degrees (155 to 160 degrees after resting)
Ground Beef, Lamb, or Veal	
Medium-Rare	125 to 130 degrees
Medium	135 to 145 degrees
Medium-Well	145 to 160 degrees
Well-Done	160 degrees and up
Pork	
Chops and Tenderloin	
Medium-Well	145 degrees (150 degrees after resting)
Well-Done	160 degrees
Loin Roasts	
Medium-Well	140 degrees (145 degrees after resting)
Well-Done	160 degrees
Ground Pork	160 degrees
Poultry	
White Meat	160 degrees
Dark Meat	175 degrees
Fish	
Rare	110 degrees (for tuna only)
Medium-Rare	125 degrees (for tuna or salmon)
Medium	140 degrees (for white-fleshed fish)

DONENESS TEMPERATURES FOR VARIOUS OTHER FOODS

We rely on temperature to gauge when many foods are done cooking, not just meat, poultry, and seafood. Here's a partial list, including temperatures for frying oil and for water for bread baking.

Food	Doneness Temperature
Oil, for frying	325 to 375 degrees
Sugar, for caramel	350 degrees
Yeast bread, rustic and lean	195 to 210 degrees
Yeast bread, sweet and rich	190 to 200 degrees
Custard, for ice cream	180 degrees
Custard, for crème anglaise or lemon curd	170 to 180 degrees
Custard, baked (such as crème brûlée or crème caramel)	170 to 175 degrees
Water, for bread baking	105 to 115 degrees (dependent on recipe)

WEIGHTS AND MEASURES FOR COMMON BAKING INGREDIENTS

Baking is an exacting science. Because measuring by weight is far more accurate than measuring by volume, and thus more likely to produce reliable results, in our recipes we provide ounce measures in addition to cup measures for many ingredients. Refer to the chart below to convert these measures into grams.

Ingredient	Ounces	Grams
1 cup all-purpose flour*	5	142
1 cup cake flour	4	113
1 cup whole-wheat flour	5½	156
1 cup granulated (white) sugar	7	198
1 cup packed brown sugar (light or dark)	7	198
1 cup confectioners' sugar	4	113
1 cup cocoa powder	3	85
4 tablespoons butter† (½ stick, or ¼ cup)	2	57
8 tablespoons butter† (1 stick, or ½ cup)	4	113
16 tablespoons butter† (2 sticks, or 1 cup)	8	227

* U.S. all-purpose flour, the most frequently used flour in this book, does not contain leaveners as some European flours do. These leavened flours are called self-rising or self-raising. If you are using self-rising flour, take this into consideration before adding leavening to a recipe.

† In the United States, butter is sold both salted and unsalted. We generally recommend unsalted butter. If you are using salted butter, take this into consideration before adding salt to a recipe.

CONVERSIONS AND EQUIVALENTS

Some say cooking is a science and an art. We would say that geography has a hand in it, too. Flours and sugars manufactured in the United Kingdom and elsewhere will feel and taste different from those manufactured in the United States. So we cannot promise that the pie crust you bake in Canada or England will taste the same as a pie crust baked in the States, but we can offer guidelines for converting weights and measures. We also recommend that you rely on your instincts when making our recipes. Refer to the visual cues provided. If the pie dough hasn't "come together," as described, you may need to add more water—even if the recipe doesn't tell you to. You be the judge.

The recipes in this book were developed using standard U.S. measures following U.S. government guidelines. The charts below offer equivalents for U.S. and metric measures. All conversions are approximate and have been rounded up or down to the nearest whole number.

Example:
1 teaspoon = 4.9292 milliliters, rounded up to 5 milliliters
1 ounce = 28.3495 grams, rounded down to 28 grams

Volume Conversions

U.S.	Metric
1 teaspoon	5 milliliters
2 teaspoons	10 milliliters
1 tablespoon	15 milliliters
2 tablespoons	30 milliliters
¼ cup	59 milliliters
⅓ cup	79 milliliters
½ cup	118 milliliters
¾ cup	177 milliliters
1 cup	237 milliliters
1¼ cups	296 milliliters
1½ cups	355 milliliters
2 cups (1 pint)	473 milliliters
2½ cups	591 milliliters
3 cups	710 milliliters
4 cups (1 quart)	0.946 liter
1.06 quarts	1 liter
4 quarts (1 gallon)	3.8 liters

Weight Conversions

Ounces	Grams
½	14
¾	21
1	28
1½	43
2	57
2½	71
3	85
3½	99
4	113
4½	128
5	142
6	170
7	198
8	227
9	255
10	283
12	340
16 (1 pound)	454

Converting Oven Temperatures

Fahrenheit	Celsius	Gas Mark (U.K.)
225	105	¼
250	120	½
275	135	1
300	150	2
325	165	3
350	180	4
375	190	5
400	200	6
425	220	7
450	230	8
475	245	9

Converting Fahrenheit To Celsius

We include doneness temperatures in many of the recipes in this book. We recommend an instant-read thermometer for the job. Refer to the chart to convert Fahrenheit degrees to Celsius. Or, for temperatures not represented in the chart, use this simple formula:

Subtract 32 degrees from the Fahrenheit reading, then divide the result by 1.8 to find the Celsius reading.

EXAMPLE:
"Roast chicken until thighs register 175 degrees."

To convert:

175 °F–32 = 143 °
143 ° ÷ 1.8 = 79.44 °C, rounded down to 79 °C

Equivalent Measures

Chefs know how to calculate ingredient amounts and measurements almost instinctively, but for the home cook those kinds of calculations are not always so easy. They can also be worrisome because a misstep in measuring can be costly. Whether your tablespoon measure has disappeared for the moment or you want to halve or double a recipe, this chart will help. Ounce measurements are for liquids only.

3 teaspoons = 1 tablespoon
4 tablespoons = ¼ cup
5 tablespoons + 1 teaspoon = ⅓ cup
8 tablespoons = ½ cup
10 tablespoons + 2 teaspoons = ⅔ cup
12 tablespoons = ¾ cup
16 tablespoons = 1 cup = 8 fluid ounces
2 cups = 1 pint = 16 fluid ounces
2 pints = 1 quart = 32 fluid ounces
2 quarts = ½ gallon = 64 fluid ounces
4 quarts = 1 gallon = 128 fluid ounces

EMERGENCY SUBSTITUTIONS

We tested scores of widely published ingredient substitutions to figure out which ones work under what circumstances and which ones simply don't work.

To Replace	Amount	Substitute			
Whole Milk	1 cup	⅝ cup skim milk + ⅜ cup half-and-half ⅔ cup 1 percent low-fat milk + ⅓ cup half-and-half ¾ cup 2 percent low-fat milk + ¼ cup half-and-half ⅞ cup skim milk + ⅛ cup heavy cream			
Half-and-Half	1 cup	¾ cup whole milk + ¼ cup heavy cream ⅔ cup skim or low-fat milk + ⅓ cup heavy cream			
Heavy Cream	1 cup	1 cup evaporated milk (Not suitable for whipping or baking.)			
Eggs	Large	Jumbo	Extra-Large	Medium	For half of an egg, whisk the yolk and white together and use half of the liquid.
	1	1	1	1	
	2	1½	2	2	
	3	2½	2½	3½	
	4	3	3½	4½	
	5	4	4	6	
	6	5	5	7	
Buttermilk	1 cup	¾ cup plain whole-milk or low-fat yogurt + ¼ cup whole milk 1 cup whole milk + 1 tablespoon lemon juice or distilled white vinegar (Not suitable for raw applications, such as a buttermilk dressing.)			
Sour Cream	1 cup	1 cup plain whole-milk yogurt (Nonfat and low-fat yogurts are too lean.)			
Plain Yogurt	1 cup	1 cup sour cream			
Cake Flour	1 cup	⅞ cup all-purpose flour + 2 tablespoons cornstarch			
Bread Flour	1 cup	1 cup all-purpose flour (Recipes may bake up with slightly less chew.)			
Baking Powder	1 teaspoon	¼ teaspoon baking soda + ½ teaspoon cream of tartar (Use right away.)			
Light Brown Sugar	1 cup	1 cup granulated sugar + 1 tablespoon molasses	Pulse the molasses in a food processor along with the sugar or simply add it along with the other wet ingredients.		
Dark Brown Sugar	1 cup	1 cup granulated sugar + 2 tablespoons molasses			
Confectioners' Sugar	1 cup	1 cup granulated sugar + 1 teaspoon cornstarch, ground in a blender, not a food processor (Works well for dusting over cakes, less so in frostings and glazes.)			
Table Salt	1 teaspoon	1½ teaspoons Morton Kosher Salt or fleur de sel 2 teaspoons Diamond Crystal Kosher Salt or Maldon Sea Salt (Not recommended for use in baking recipes.)			
Fresh Herbs	1 tablespoon	1 teaspoon dried herbs			
Wine	½ cup	½ cup broth + 1 teaspoon wine vinegar (added just before serving) ½ cup broth + 1 teaspoon lemon juice (added just before serving) (Vermouth also makes an acceptable substitute for wine.)			
Unsweetened Chocolate	1 ounce	3 tablespoons cocoa powder + 1 tablespoon vegetable oil 1½ ounces bittersweet or semisweet chocolate (remove 1 tablespoon sugar from the recipe)			
Bittersweet or Semisweet Chocolate	1 ounce	⅔ ounce unsweetened chocolate + 2 teaspoons sugar (Works well with fudgy brownies. Do not use in a custard or cake.)			

THE AMERICA'S TEST KITCHEN SHOPPING GUIDE

EQUIPMENT

Chapter 1 of this book highlighted some of the equipment we believe to be essential for a working home kitchen, but there are many other tools and gadgets you may want or need to add to your personal collection based on the kind of cooking you are interested in doing. This chart collects information about the wide variety of equipment we have tested over the years, from the basics to highly specialized items, and offers information to help you when you're shopping for a new tool. Prices in this chart are based on shopping at online retailers and will vary. See AmericasTestKitchen.com for updates to these testings.

Knives and More	Item	What to Look For	Test Kitchen Favorites
MUST-HAVE ITEMS	**Chef's Knife**	• High-carbon stainless-steel knife • Thin, curved 8-inch blade • Lightweight • Comfortable grip and nonslip handle	Victorinox Swiss Army Fibrox Pro 8-Inch Chef's Knife $39.95
	Serrated Knife	• 10-inch blade • Fewer broader, deeper, pointed serrations • Thinner blade angle • Comfortable, grippy handle • Medium weight	Mercer Culinary Millennia 10" Wide Bread Knife $22.10
	Slicing Knife	• Tapered 12-inch blade for slicing large cuts of meat • Oval scallops (called a granton edge) carved into blade • Fairly rigid blade with rounded tip	Victorinox Swiss Army Fibrox Pro 12-Inch Granton Edge Slicing/Carving Knife $54.65
	Paring Knife	• 3- to 3½-inch blade • Thin, slightly curved blade with pointed tip • Comfortable grip	Wüsthof Classic with PEtec, 3½-Inch $39.95 Best Buy: Victorinox Swiss Army Fibrox Pro 3¼-Inch Paring Knife $4.95
	Serrated Paring Knife	• Thin blade with razor-sharp serrations for safe, precise slicing • Hefty but nimble	Wüsthof Classic 3.5-Inch Fully Serrated Paring Knife $59.95 Best Buy: Victorinox Serrated Paring Knife $5.95

See AmericasTestKitchen.com for updates to these testings.

Knives and More	Item	What to Look For	Test Kitchen Favorites
	Steak Knives	• Super-sharp, straight-edged blade • Sturdy—not wobbly—blade	**Victorinox Swiss Army 6-Piece Rosewood Steak Set, Spear Point, Straight Edge** $170.74 for a set of six Best Buy: **Chicago Cutlery Walnut Tradition 4-Piece Steak Knife Set** $17.95 for a set of four
	Santoku Knife	• 6½-inch blade • Narrow, curved, and short blade • Comfortable grip	**MAC Superior Santoku Knife** $74.95
	Boning Knife	• 6-inch blade • Narrow, highly maneuverable, and razor-sharp blade • Comfortable grip and nonslip handle	**Victorinox 6-Inch Fibrox Pro Flexible Boning Knife** $27.20
	Meat Cleaver	• Razor-sharp blade • Balanced weight between handle and blade • Comfortable grip	**Global 6-Inch Meat Cleaver** $144.95 Best Buy: **LamsonSharp 7-Inch Meat Cleaver** $48.00
	Vegetable Cleaver	• Slim blade for slicing through thick, hard vegetables • Lightweight	**MAC Japanese Series 6½-Inch Japanese Vegetable Cleaver** $95.00
	Hybrid Chef's Knife	• High-carbon stainless-steel knife • Lightweight • Thin blade that tapers from spine to cutting edge and from handle to tip	**Masamoto VG-10 Gyutou, 8.2"** $136.50
	Carbon-Steel Knife	• 8-inch blade • Sloping ergonomic handle • Narrow, razor-sharp blade	**Bob Kramer 8" Carbon Steel Chef's Knife by Zwilling J.A. Henckels** $299.95 Best Buy: **Togiharu Virgin Carbon Steel Gyutou, 8.2"** $98.50
	Mandoline	• Razor-sharp blade(s) • Hand guard to shield your fingers • Gripper tongs to grasp food • Measurement-marked dial for precision cuts • Storage for extra blades	**Swissmar Börner Original V-Slicer Plus Mandoline** $29.99

See AmericasTestKitchen.com for updates to these testings.

Knives and More	Item	What to Look For	Test Kitchen Favorites
	Carving Board	• Trenches can contain ½ cup of liquid • Large and stable enough to hold large roasts • Midweight for easy carrying, carving, and cleaning	J.K. Adams Maple Reversible Carving Board $69.95
	Cutting Board Wooden	• Roomy work surface of at least 20 by 15 inches • Teak board for minimal maintenance • Durable edge-grain construction (wood grain runs parallel to surface of board)	Proteak Edge Grain Teak Cutting Board $84.99
	Plastic	• Rubber strips on both sides keep board anchored to counter • Dishwasher-safe	OXO Good Grips Carving & Cutting Board $21.99
	Knife Sharpener	• Reliable notch removal and diamond sharpening material in electric sharpeners • Clear, precise user instructions • Easy and comfortable to use	Electric: Chef'sChoice Trizor XV Knife Sharpener, Model #15 $149.99 Electric, Best Buy: Chef'sChoice Diamond Sharpener for Asian Knives, Model #316 $79.99 Manual: Chef'sChoice Pronto Manual Diamond Hone Asian Knife Sharpener, Model #463 $49.99
	Universal Knife Block	• Holds up to nine knives • Narrow base for easy storage • Removable dishwasher-safe lining	Bodum Bistro Universal Knife Block $44.95
	Magnetic Knife Strip	• 16½-inch strip that holds five knives, plus kitchen shears • Easy to install and clean • Bamboo surface that is gentle on blades	Messermeister Bamboo Knife Magnet $50.00
	Cut-Resistant Glove	• Tightly woven fabric for durability • Stretchy fabric for comfortable fit • Fits either your right or left hand	Microplane Specialty Series Cut Resistant Glove $14.95

MUST-HAVE ITEMS

See AmericasTestKitchen.com for updates to these testings.

Pots and Pans	Item	What to Look For	Test Kitchen Favorites
	**Traditional Skillet**	• Stainless-steel interior and fully clad for even heat distribution • 12-inch diameter and flared sides • Comfortable, ovensafe handle • Cooking surface of at least 9 inches • Good to have smaller (8- or 10-inch) skillets too	All-Clad 12-Inch Stainless Fry Pan $154.95
	**Nonstick Skillet**	• Dark, nonstick surface • 12- or 12½-inch diameter, thick bottom • Comfortable, ovensafe handle • Cooking surface of at least 9 inches • Good to have smaller (8- or 10-inch) skillets too	OXO Good Grips Non-Stick 12-inch Open Frypan $39.99
	**Cast-Iron Skillet** Traditional	• Thick bottom and straight sides • Roomy interior (cooking surface of at least 9¼ inches) • Preseasoned	Lodge Classic 12-Inch Cast Iron Skillet $33.31
	Enameled	• Balanced weight, wide pour spouts, and oversized helper handle for comfortable use • Durable, satiny surface that does not require preseasoning • Easy to clean	Le Creuset Signature 11¾" Iron Handle Skillet $179.95 Best Buy: Mario Batali by Dansk 12" Open Sauté Pan $59.95
	**Eco-Friendly Skillet**	• PFOA-free (perfluorooctanoic acid) surfaces are nonstick and more durable than silicone coatings • Roomy interior (cooking surface of at least 9 inches) NOTE: We prefer our favorite nonstick skillet for its superior performance.	Scanpan Professional 12.50" Fry Pan $129.95
	**Dutch Oven**	• Enameled cast iron or stainless steel • Capacity of at least 6 quarts • Diameter of at least 9 inches • Tight-fitting lid • Wide, sturdy handles	Heavier Choice: Le Creuset 7¼-Quart Round French Oven $349.95 Lighter Choice: All-Clad Stainless 8-Quart Stockpot $279.95 Best Buy: Lodge Color Enamel 6-Quart Dutch Oven $76.82

MUST-HAVE ITEMS

MUST-HAVE ITEM

See AmericasTestKitchen.com for updates to these testings.

Pots and Pans	Item	What to Look For	Test Kitchen Favorites
	Dutch Oven, Innovative	• Large capacity • Sturdy, thick base • Silicone oil chamber in base spreads heat slowly and evenly • Good heat retention	Pauli Cookware Never Burn Sauce Pot, 10 Quart $229.99
	Saucepan	• Large saucepan with 3- to 4-quart capacity and small nonstick saucepan with 2- to 2½-quart capacity • Tight-fitting lids • Rounded corners that a whisk can reach into • Long, comfortable handles that are angled for even weight distribution	Large: All-Clad Stainless 4-Quart Saucepan with Lid and Loop $224.95 Best Buy: Cuisinart MultiClad Unlimited 4-Quart Saucepan $69.99 Small: Calphalon Contemporary Nonstick 2½ Quart Shallow Saucepan with Cover $39.95
	Rimmed Baking Sheet	• Light-colored surface (heats and browns evenly) • Sturdy but lightweight pan • Dimensions of 18 by 13 inches • Good to have at least two	Nordic Ware Bakers Half Sheet $14.97
	Sauté Pan	• Aluminum core surrounded by layers of stainless steel • Relatively lightweight • 9¾-inch diameter • Stay-cool helper handle	All-Clad Stainless 3-Quart Tri-Ply Sauté Pan $224.95 Best Buy: Cuisinart MultiClad Pro Stainless 3½-Quart Sauté Pan with Helper and Cover $78.13
	Omelet Pan	• Gently sloped sides for easy turning and rolling of omelets • Nonstick finish • Heavy construction for durability and even heat distribution • 8-inch size for French omelets	Original French Chef Omelette Pan $139.95
	Grill Pan	• Cast-iron pan with enamel coating for heat retention and easy cleanup • Tall ridges (4 to 5.5 mm high) to keep food above rendered fat • Generous cooking area	Staub 12-Inch American Square Grill Pan and Press $219.95, including press Best Buy: Lodge Square Grill Pan and Lodge Ribbed Panini Press $18.97, grill pan $14.58, panini press
	Stovetop Griddle	• Anodized aluminum for even heating • Nonstick coating • Lightweight (about 4 pounds) • Heat-resistant loop handles • At least 17 by 9 inches • Pour spout for draining grease	Anolon Advanced Double Burner Griddle $68.99

See AmericasTestKitchen.com for updates to these testings.

Pots and Pans	Item	What to Look For	Test Kitchen Favorites
MUST-HAVE ITEMS 	**Stockpot**	• 12-quart capacity • Thick bottom to prevent scorching • Wide body for easy cleaning and storage • Flat or round handles that extend at least 1¾ inches	All-Clad Stainless 12-Quart Stock Pot $389.95 Best Buy: Cuisinart Chef's Classic Stainless 12-Quart Stock Pot $69.99
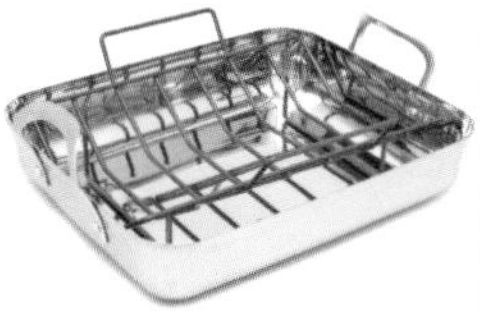	**Roasting Pan**	• At least 15 by 11 inches • Stainless-steel interior with aluminum core for even heat distribution • Upright handles for easy gripping • Light interior for better food monitoring	Calphalon Contemporary Stainless Roasting Pan with Rack $99.99 Best Buy: Calphalon Commercial Hard-Anodized Roasting Pan with Nonstick Rack $59.99
	**V-Rack**	• Fixed, not adjustable, to provide sturdiness • Tall, vertical handles positioned on long side of rack	All-Clad Nonstick Large Rack $24.95
	**Cookware Set**	• Fully clad stainless steel with aluminum core for even heat distribution • Moderately heavy, durable construction • Lids included • Ideal mix of pans includes 12-inch skillet, 10-inch skillet, 2-quart saucepan, 4-quart saucepan, and 8-quart stockpot	All-Clad Stainless Steel Cookware Set, 10-piece $799.95 Best Buy: Tramontina 18/10 Stainless Steel TriPly-Clad Cookware Set, 8-piece $144.97

Handy Tools	Item	What to Look For	Test Kitchen Favorites
MUST-HAVE ITEMS 	**Kitchen Shears**	• Take-apart scissors (for easy cleaning) • Super-sharp blades • Sturdy construction • Works for both right- and left-handed users	Kershaw Taskmaster Shears/Shun Multi-Purpose Shears $49.95 Best Buy: J.A. Henckels International Kitchen Shears—Take Apart $14.95
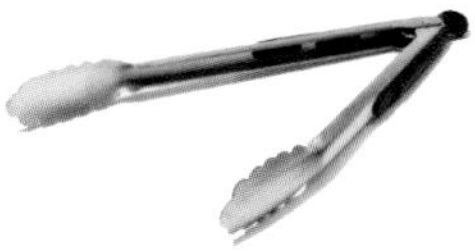	**Tongs**	• Scalloped edges • Slightly concave pincers • Length of 12 inches (to keep your hand far from the heat) • Open and close easily	OXO Good Grips 12-Inch Locking Tongs $12.09

See AmericasTestKitchen.com for updates to these testings.

Handy Tools	Item	What to Look For	Test Kitchen Favorites
MUST-HAVE ITEMS	**Wooden Spoon**	• Slim yet broad bowl • Stain-resistant bamboo • Comfortable handle	SCI Bamboo Wood Cooking Spoon $2.40
	Slotted Spoon	• Lightweight • Wide, shallow bowl • Thin-edged bowl • Long, comfortable handle	Cuisinart Stainless Steel Slotted Spoon $9.12
	Basting Spoon	• Thin, shallow bowl • Handle at least 9 inches in length • Slight dip from handle to bowl	Rösle Basting Spoon with Hook Handle $28.95
MUST-HAVE ITEMS	**All-Around Spatula**	• Head about 3 inches wide and 5½ inches long • 11 inches in length (tip to handle) • Long, vertical slots • Useful to have a metal spatula to use with traditional cookware and plastic for nonstick cookware	Metal: Wüsthof Gourmet Turner/Fish Spatula $44.95 Best Buy: OXO Good Grips Flexible Turner Steel $7.99 Plastic: Matfer Bourgeat Pelton Spatula $8.23
	Rubber/Silicone Spatula	• Wide, stiff blade with a thin edge that's flexible enough to conform to the curve of a mixing bowl • Heatproof	Rubbermaid Professional 13½-Inch High-Heat Scraper $18.99 Best Buy: Tovolo Silicone Spatula $8.99
	Offset Spatula	• Flexible blade offset to a roughly 30-degree angle • Enough usable surface area to frost the radius of a 9-inch cake • Comfortable handle	OXO Good Grips Bent Icing Knife $9.99
	Jar Spatula	• Slim, flexible head maneuvers tight corners and edges • Strong enough to lift heavy food • Seamless silicone for easy cleaning and comfortable feel	GIR Skinny Spatula $12.95 Best Buy: OXO Good Grips Silicone Jar Spatula $5.95
MUST-HAVE ITEM	**All-Purpose Whisk**	• At least 10 wires • Wires of moderate thickness • Comfortable rubber handle • Balanced, lightweight feel	OXO Good Grips 11″ Balloon Whisk $9.99

See AmericasTestKitchen.com for updates to these testings.

Handy Tools	Item	What to Look For	Test Kitchen Favorites
MUST-HAVE ITEMS	**Pepper Mill**	• Easy-to-adjust, clearly marked grind settings • Efficient, comfortable grinding mechanism • Generous capacity	Cole & Mason Derwent Gourmet Precision Pepper Mill $40.00
	Ladle	• Stainless steel • Hook handle • Pouring rim to prevent dripping • Handle 9 to 10 inches in length	Rösle Hook Ladle with Pouring Rim $34.00 Best Buy: OXO Good Grips Brushed Stainless Steel Ladle $9.99
	Can Opener	• Easy to attach • Smooth and comfortable turning motions • Pulls off removed lid for safe and easy disposal	Fissler Magic Smooth-Edge Can Opener $29.00
	Jar Opener	• Strong, sturdy clamp grip • Adjusts quickly to any size jar	Amco Swing-A-Way Jar Opener $5.99
MUST-HAVE ITEM	**Garlic Press**	• Large capacity that holds multiple garlic cloves • Curved handles • Long handle and short distance between pivot point and plunger	Kuhn Rikon Stainless Steel Epicurean Garlic Press $39.95
MUST-HAVE ITEMS	**Serrated Fruit Peeler**	• Comfortable grip and nonslip handle • Sharp blade	Messermeister Serrated Swivel Peeler $5.50
	Vegetable Peeler	• Sharp carbon steel blade • 1-inch space between blade and peeler to prevent jamming • Lightweight and comfortable	Kuhn Rikon Original Swiss Peeler $3.50
	Rasp Grater	• Sharp teeth (requires little effort or pressure when grating) • Maneuverable over round shapes • Comfortable handle	Microplane Classic Zester Grater $12.35

See AmericasTestKitchen.com for updates to these testings.

Handy Tools	Item	What to Look For	Test Kitchen Favorites
MUST-HAVE ITEM	**Grater**	• Sharp, large holes and broad grating plane • Solid, rigid frame and grippy rubber feet • Easy to use at any angle, including flat over medium or large bowls	Rösle Coarse Grater $35.95
	Rotary Grater	• Barrel at least 2 inches in diameter • Classic turn-crank design • Comfortable handle • Simple to disassemble for easy cleanup	Zyliss All Cheese Grater $19.95
	Manual Citrus Juicer	• Handheld squeezer with comfortable handle • Durable exterior • Large, slat-like holes for efficient draining	Chef'n FreshForce Citrus Juicer $23.04
	Ice Cream Scoop	• Comfortable handle • Gently curved bowl for easy releasing • Scoop warms on contact with your hand to slightly melt ice cream	Zeroll Original Ice Cream Scoop $18.44
	Meat Pounder	• At least 1½ pounds in weight • Vertical handle for better leverage and control	Norpro GRIP-EZ Meat Pounder $17.50
	Bench Scraper	• Sturdy blade • Ruler marks (for easy measuring) • Comfortable handle with plastic, rubber, or nylon grip	Dexter-Russell 6″ Dough Cutter/Scraper—Sani-Safe Series $7.01
	Bowl Scraper	• Curved shape with comfortable grip • Rigid enough to move dough but flexible enough to scrape up batter • Thin, straight edge doubles as dough cutter or bench scraper	iSi Basics Silicone Scraper Spatula $5.99
MUST-HAVE ITEM	**Rolling Pin**	• Moderate weight (1 to 1½ pounds) • 19-inch straight barrel • Slightly textured wooden surface to grip dough for easy rolling	J.K. Adams Plain Maple Rolling Dowel $13.95

See AmericasTestKitchen.com for updates to these testings.

Handy Tools	Item	What to Look For	Test Kitchen Favorites
MUST-HAVE ITEMS	**Mixing Bowls** Stainless Steel	• Lightweight and easy to handle • Durable • Conducts heat well for double boiler	Vollrath Economy Stainless Steel Mixing Bowls $2.90, 1½ quart $4.50, 3 quart $6.90, 5 quart
	Glass	• Tempered to increase impact and thermal resistance • Can be used in microwave • Durable	Pyrex Smart Essentials Mixing Bowl Set with Colored Lids $27.98 for a 4-bowl set
	Mini Prep Bowls	• Variety of useful sizes that nest for compact storage • Wide, shallow bowls • Glass to resist stains and not absorb odors • Oven- and microwave-safe	Anchor Hocking 6-Piece Nesting Prep Bowl Set $11.00
	Bowl Stabilizer	• Firmly attaches bowls to every work surface in the kitchen • Accommodates bowls from 6 to 21 inches in diameter • Forms a tight seal in double boilers	Staybowlizer $19.95
MUST-HAVE ITEM	Oven Mitt	• Form-fitting and not overly bulky for easy maneuvering • Machine washable • Flexible, heat-resistant material	Kool-Tek 15-Inch Oven Mitt by KatchAll $44.95 each
	Cookie Cutters	• Metal cutters • Thin, sharp cutting edge and round or rubber-grip top • Depth of at least 1 inch	Little difference among various brands
	Cookie Press	• Plunger creates a tight seal, clearing the barrel of all dough • Nonslip base to hold press steady • Easy to use	Wilton Cookie Pro Ultra II $24.99
	Pastry Brush	• Silicone bristles (heat-resistant, durable, and easy to clean) • Perforated flaps (to trap liquid) • Angled head to reach tight spots • Comfortable handle	OXO Good Grips Silicone Pastry Brush $6.99

See AmericasTestKitchen.com for updates to these testings.

Handy Tools	Item	What to Look For	Test Kitchen Favorites
	**Splatter Screen**	• Diameter of at least 13 inches • Lollipop-shaped design • Tightly woven mesh face	Progressive Prepworks Splatter Screen $11.67
	**Bouillon Strainer/Chinois**	• Conical shape • Depth of 7 to 8 inches • At least one hook on rim for stability	Winco Reinforced Extra Fine Mesh Bouillon Strainer $33.78
	**Colander**	• 4- to 7-quart capacity • Metal ring attached to bottom for stability • Many holes for quick draining • Small holes so pasta doesn't slip through	RSVP International Endurance Precision Pierced 5 Qt. Colander $25.99
	**Fine-Mesh Strainer**	• At least 6 inches in diameter (measured from inside edge to inside edge) • Sturdy construction	CIA Masters Collection Fine-Mesh Strainer $27.49
	**Collapsible Mini Colander**	• Compact yet sturdy • Folds down to height of 1 inch for easy storage • Removable plastic base to seal drainage holes and catch drips	Progressive International Collapsible Mini Colander $13.70
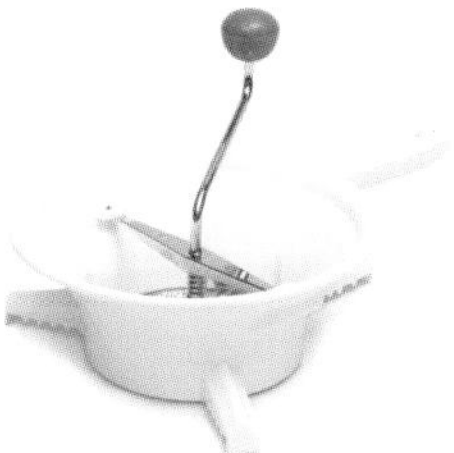	**Food Mill**	• Sturdy but lightweight plastic construction • Easy to turn	RSVP Classic Rotary Food Mill $24.95
	**Fat Separator**	• Bottom-draining model • Detachable bowl for easy cleaning • Strainer for catching solids	Cuisipro Fat Separator $33.95
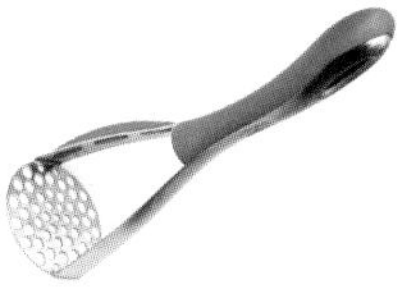	**Potato Masher**	• Solid mashing disk with many small holes • Comfortable grip • Long handle	Zyliss Stainless Steel Potato Masher $12.99

MUST-HAVE ITEMS

MUST-HAVE ITEM

See AmericasTestKitchen.com for updates to these testings.

Handy Tools	Item	What to Look For	Test Kitchen Favorites
MUST-HAVE ITEM	**Salad Spinner**	• Ergonomic and easy-to-operate hand pump • Wide base for stability • Flat lid for easy cleaning and storage	OXO Good Grips Salad Spinner $29.99
	Steamer Basket	• Collapsible stainless-steel basket with feet • Adjustable and removable center rod for easy removal from pot and easy storage	OXO Good Grips Pop-Up Steamer $16.99
	Mortar and Pestle	• Heavy, stable base with tall, narrow walls • Rough interior to help grip and grind ingredients • Comfortable, heavy pestle	Frieling "Goliath" Mortar and Pestle Set $49.95
	Innovative Mortar and Pestle	• Heavy ceramic ball quickly crushes spices and garlic • Dishwasher-safe	Jamie Oliver Flavour Shaker $29.95

Measuring Equipment	Item	What to Look For	Test Kitchen Favorites
MUST-HAVE ITEMS	**Dry Measuring Cups**	• Accurate measurements • Easy-to-read measurement markings • Durable measurement markings • Stable when empty and filled • Strong and durable design • Handles perfectly flush with cups • Stacks and stores neatly	OXO Good Grips Stainless Steel Measuring Cups $19.99
	Liquid Measuring Cup	• Crisp, unambiguous markings that include ¼- and ⅓-cup measurements • Heatproof, sturdy cup with handle • Good to have in a variety of sizes (1, 2, and 4 cups)	Pyrex 2-Cup Measuring Cup $5.99
	Adjustable Measuring Cup	• Plunger-like bottom (with a tight seal between plunger and tube) that you can set to correct measurement, then push up to cleanly extract sticky ingredients (such as shortening or peanut butter) • 1- or 2-cup capacity • Dishwasher-safe	KitchenArt Adjust-A-Cup Professional Series, 2-Cup $12.95

See AmericasTestKitchen.com for updates to these testings.

Measuring Equipment	Item	What to Look For	Test Kitchen Favorites
MUST-HAVE ITEMS	Measuring Spoons	• Long, comfortable handles • Rim of bowl flush with handle (makes it easy to "dip" into a dry ingredient and "sweep" across the top for accurate measuring) • Slim design	Cuisipro Stainless Steel Measuring Spoons Set $11.95
	Kitchen Ruler	• Stainless steel and easy to clean • 18 inches in length • Large, easy-to-read markings	Empire 18-Inch Stainless Steel Ruler $8.49
	Digital Scale	• Easy-to-read display not blocked by weighing platform • At least 7-pound capacity • Accessible buttons • Gram-to-ounce conversion feature • Roomy platform	OXO Good Grips 11 lb. Food Scale with Pull Out Display $49.99 Best Buy: Ozeri Pronto Digital Multifunction Kitchen and Food Scale $11.79

Thermometers and Timers	Item	What to Look For	Test Kitchen Favorites
MUST-HAVE ITEMS	Instant-Read Thermometer	• Digital model with automatic shut-off • Quick-response readings in 10 seconds or fewer • Wide temperature range (-40 to 450 degrees) • Long stem that can reach interior of large cuts of meat • Water-resistant	ThermoWorks Thermapen Mk4 $99.00 Best Buy: ThermoWorks Thermopop $29.00
	Oven Thermometer	• Clearly marked numbers for easy readability • Large, sturdy base • Large temperature range (up to 600 degrees)	CDN Pro Accurate Oven Thermometer $8.70
	Meat Probe/ Candy/Deep-Fry Thermometer	• Digital model • Easy-to-read console • Mounting clip (to attach probe to the pan)	Thermoworks ChefAlarm $59.00 Best Buy: Polder Classic Digital Thermometer/Timer $24.99
	Refrigerator/ Freezer Thermometer	• Clear digital display • Wire probe for monitoring refrigerator and freezer simultaneously	Maverick Cold-Chek Digital Refrigerator/Freezer Thermometer $19.99

See AmericasTestKitchen.com for updates to these testings.

Thermometers and Timers	Item	What to Look For	Test Kitchen Favorites
	Remote Thermometer	• Easy to set up • Reports accurate readings from up to 100 feet from its base	iDevices Kitchen Thermometer $78.00
	Kitchen Timer	• Lengthy time range (1 second to at least 10 hours) • Able to count up after alarm goes off • Easy to use and read • Able to track multiple events	OXO Good Grips Triple Timer $19.99

MUST-HAVE ITEM

Bakeware	Item	What to Look For	Test Kitchen Favorites
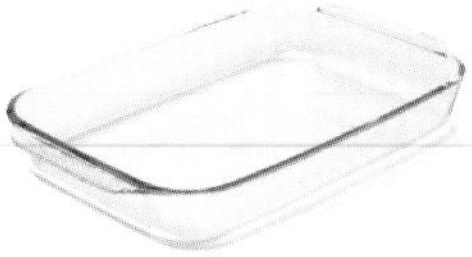	Glass Baking Dish	• Dimensions of 13 by 9 inches • Large enough to hold casseroles and large crisps and cobblers • Handles	Pyrex Bakeware 9 x 13-Inch Baking Dish $9.09
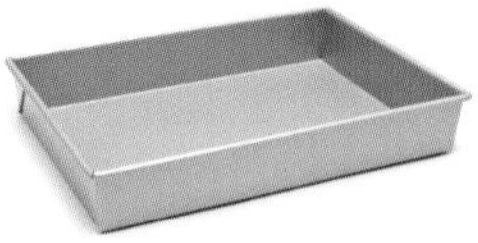	Metal Baking Pan	• Dimensions of 13 by 9 inches • Straight sides • Nonstick coating for even browning and easy release of cakes and bar cookies	Williams-Sonoma Goldtouch Nonstick Rectangular Cake Pan, 9" x 13" $32.95
	Square Baking Pan	• Straight sides • Light gold or dark nonstick surface for even browning and easy release of cakes • Good to have both 9-inch and 8-inch square pans	Williams-Sonoma Goldtouch Nonstick Square Cake Pan, 8" $21.00
	Round Cake Pan Best All-Around	• Best for cake • Straight sides • Light finish for tall, evenly baked cakes • Nonstick surface for easy release	Nordic Ware Naturals Nonstick 9-Inch Round Cake Pan $14.32
	Best for Browning	• Dark finish is ideal for pizza and cinnamon buns • Nonstick	Chicago Metallic Non-Stick 9" Round Cake Pan $10.97
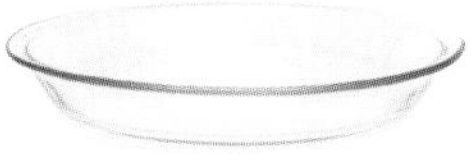	Pie Plate	• Glass promotes even browning and allows progress to be monitored • ½-inch rim (makes it easy to shape decorative crusts) • Shallow angled sides prevent crusts from slumping • Good to have two	Pyrex Bakeware 9 Inch Pie Plate $8.16

MUST-HAVE ITEMS

See AmericasTestKitchen.com for updates to these testings.

Bakeware	Item	What to Look For	Test Kitchen Favorites
MUST-HAVE ITEM	**Loaf Pan**	• Light gold or dark nonstick surface for even browning and easy release • Good to have both 8½ by 4½-inch and 9 by 5-inch pans	Williams-Sonoma Goldtouch Nonstick Loaf Pan $21.00
MUST-HAVE ITEMS	**Springform Pan**	• Tight seal between band and bottom of pan prevents leakage • Raised base makes cutting and removing slices easy • Light finish for controlled, even browning	Williams-Sonoma Goldtouch Springform Pan, 9″ $49.95 Best Buy: Nordic Ware 9″ Leakproof Springform Pan $16.22
	Muffin Tin	• Nonstick surface for even browning and easy release • Wide, extended rims and raised lip for easy handling • Cup capacity of ½ cup	Anolon Advanced Bakeware 12-Cup Muffin Pan $24.99
	Cooling Rack	• Grid-style rack with tightly woven, heavy-gauge bars • Should fit inside a standard 18 by 13-inch rimmed baking sheet • Dishwasher-safe	CIA Bakeware 12-Inch x 17-Inch Cooling Rack $15.95
	Baker's Cooling Rack	• Sturdy rack • Four collapsible shelves • Unit folds down for easy storage	Linden Sweden Baker's Cooling Rack $17.99
	Biscuit Cutters	• Sharp edges • A set with a variety of sizes	Ateco 5357 11-Piece Plain Round Cutter Set $14.95
	Bundt Pan	• Heavyweight cast aluminum • Silver platinum nonstick surface for even browning and easy release • Clearly defined ridges • 15-cup capacity	Nordic Ware Platinum Collection Anniversary Bundt Pan $26.95
	Tart Pan	• Tinned steel for even browning and easy release • Removable bottom • If you bake a lot, it's good to have multiple sizes, though 9 inches is standard	Kaiser Tinplate 9.5-Inch Quiche Pan with Removable Bottom $9.00

See AmericasTestKitchen.com for updates to these testings.

Bakeware	Item	What to Look For	Test Kitchen Favorites
	Tube Pan	• Heavy pan (at least 1 pound) • Heavy bottom for leak-free seal • Dark nonstick surface for even browning and easy release • 16-cup capacity • Feet on the rim	Chicago Metallic Professional Nonstick Angel Food Cake Pan with Feet $19.95
	Pullman Loaf Pan	• Squared-off pan (4 by 4 inches) • Nonstick aluminized steel for easy cleanup • Light surface for even browning	USA Pan 13 by 4-Inch Pullman Loaf Pan & Cover $33.95
	Soufflé Dish	• Round dish with straight sides • Not-too-thick side walls	HIC 64 Ounce Soufflé $15.12
	Baking Stone	• Substantial but not too heavy to handle • Dimensions of 16 by 14 inches • Clay, not cement, for evenly browned crusts • Tough and durable	Old Stone Oven Pizza Baking Stone $59.95

Small Appliances	Item	What to Look For	Test Kitchen Favorites
MUST-HAVE ITEM	Food Processor	• 14-cup capacity • Sharp and sturdy blades • Wide feed tube • Should come with basic blades and disks: steel blade, dough blade, shredding/slicing disk	Cuisinart Custom 14-Cup Food Processor $199.99
	Stand Mixer	• Planetary action (stationary bowl and single mixing arm) • Powerful motor • Bowl size of at least 4½ quarts • Slightly squat bowl to keep ingredients in beater's range • Comes with basic attachments: paddle, dough hook, metal whisk	KitchenAid Pro Line Series 7-Qt Bowl Lift Stand Mixer $549.95 Best Buy: KitchenAid Classic Plus Series 4.5-Quart Tilt-Head Stand Mixer $199.99
MUST-HAVE ITEM	Handheld Mixer	• Lightweight model • Slim wire beaters without central post • Variety of speeds	KitchenAid 5-Speed Ultra Power Hand Mixer $69.99 Best Buy: Cuisinart PowerSelect 3-Speed Hand Mixer $26.77

See AmericasTestKitchen.com for updates to these testings.

Small Appliances	Item	What to Look For	Test Kitchen Favorites
MUST-HAVE ITEM	**Blender**	• Mix of straight and serrated blades at different angles • Jar with curved base • At least 44-ounce capacity • Heavy base for stability	Vitamix 5200 $449.00 Best Buy: Breville The Hemisphere Control $199.99
	Immersion Blender	• Lightweight and easy to operate • Detachable shaft for easy cleaning • Wide blade cage so food can circulate	KitchenAid 3-Speed Hand Blender $59.99
	Electric Egg Cooker	• Boiling capacity of seven eggs • Well-fitting lid, not too tight, for safety • Audible timer • Easy to use	West Bend Automatic Egg Cooker $24.99
	Electric Griddle	• Large cooking area (about 21 by 12 inches) • Attached pull-out grease trap (won't tip over) • Nonstick surface for easy cleanup	BroilKing Professional Griddle $99.99
	Electric Juicer	• Ideal for making a large amount of fruit or vegetable juice • Centrifugal, not masticating, model for fresher-tasting juice • 3-inch-wide feed tube • Easy to assemble and clean	Breville Juice Fountain Plus $149.99
	Adjustable Electric Kettle	• Heats water to a range of different temperatures • Automatic shutoff • Separate base for cordless pouring • Visible water level	Zojirushi Micom Water Boiler & Warmer $114.95

See AmericasTestKitchen.com for updates to these testings.

Small Appliances	Item	What to Look For	Test Kitchen Favorites
	Coffee Maker	• Thermal carafe that keeps coffee hot and fresh with capacity of at least 10 cups • Short brewing time (6 minutes is ideal) • Copper, not aluminum, heating element • Easy-to-fill water tank • Clear, intuitive controls	Technivorm Moccamaster 10-Cup Coffee Maker with Thermal Carafe $299.00 Best Buy: Bonavita 8-Cup Coffee Maker with Thermal Carafe $189.99
	Meat Grinder	• All-metal machine • Motorized grinder with reverse mode for unclogging stuck pieces • Easy to assemble	Waring Pro Professional Meat Grinder $199.99
	Deep-Fryer	• Rotating basket that submerges food, reducing amount of oil needed • Window in lid to monitor cooking NOTE: We prefer to deep-fry in a Dutch oven for superior temperature control and larger capacity.	Waring Pro Professional Digital Deep Fryer $139.95
	Portable Induction Burner	• Large cooking surface for even heating of pans • Basic push buttons and dial controls for ease of use	Max Burton Induction Cooktop $124.25
	Warming Tray	• Features a range of heat settings to keep food at a safe serving temperature • Keeps food hot for 4 hours • Stay-cool handles for easy maneuvering • Easily wiped clean and cool after use in 20 minutes' time	BroilKing Professional Stainless Warming Tray $126.06 Best Buy: Oster Stainless Steel Warming Tray $38.15
	Ice Cream Maker	• Compact size for easy storage • Simple to use and clean • Produces dense, smooth ice cream	Cuisinart Automatic Frozen Yogurt, Ice Cream & Sorbet Maker $49.95
	Pressure Cooker	• Solidly built • Stovetop model with low sides and wide base for easy access and better browning and heat retention • Easy-to-read pressure indicator	Fissler Vitaquick 8½-Quart Pressure Cooker $279.95 Best Buy: Fagor Duo 8-Quart Stainless Steel Pressure Cooker $109.95

See AmericasTestKitchen.com for updates to these testings.

Small Appliances	Item	What to Look For	Test Kitchen Favorites
	Slow Cooker	• At least 6-quart capacity • Insert handles • Clear lid to see progress of food • Dishwasher-safe insert • Intuitive control panel with programmable timer and warming mode	KitchenAid 6-Quart Slow Cooker with Solid Glass Lid $99.99
	Rice Cooker	• Produces tender-chewy white, brown, and sushi rice • Digital timer with clear audio alert and a delayed-start function • Removable lid for hassle-free cleanup • Small countertop footprint	Aroma 8-Cup Digital Rice Cooker and Food Steamer $29.92
	Toaster Oven	• Quartz heating elements for steady, controlled heat • Roomy but compact interior • Simple to use	The Smart Oven by Breville $249.95 Best Buy: Hamilton Beach Set & Forget Toaster Oven with Convection Cooking $99.99
	Waffle Iron	• Indicator lights and audible alert • Makes two waffles at a time • Six-point dial for customizing waffle doneness	Waring Pro Double Belgian Waffle Maker $89.99

Grilling Equipment	Item	What to Look For	Test Kitchen Favorites
	Gas Grill	• Large main grate • Built-in thermometer • Two burners for varying heat levels (three is even better) • Made of thick, heat-retaining materials such as cast aluminum and enameled steel	Weber Spirit E-310 Gas Grill $499.00
	Charcoal Grill	• Sturdy construction for maintaining heat • Well-designed cooking grate, handles, lid, and wheels • Generous cooking and charcoal capacity • Well-positioned vents to control air flow • Gas ignition instantly and easily lights coals • Ash catcher for easy cleanup	Weber Performer Deluxe Charcoal Grill $399.00 Best Buy: Weber Original Kettle Premium Charcoal Grill, 22-Inch $149.00

See AmericasTestKitchen.com for updates to these testings.

Grilling Equipment	Item	What to Look For	Test Kitchen Favorites
	Smoker	• Large cooking area • Water pan • Multiple vents for precise temperature control	Weber Smokey Mountain Cooker Smoker 18" $298.95
	Chimney Starter	• 6-quart capacity • Holes in the canister so air can circulate around the coals • Sturdy construction • Heat-resistant handle • Dual handle for easy control	Weber Rapidfire Chimney Starter $14.99
	Grill Tongs	• 16 inches in length • Scalloped, not sharp and serrated, edges • Opens and closes easily • Lightweight • Moderate amount of springy tension	OXO Good Grips 16-Inch Locking Tongs $14.99
	Grill Brush	• Long handle (about 14 inches) • Large woven-mesh detachable stainless-steel scrubbing pads	Grill Wizard 18-Inch China Grill Brush $31.50
	Grill Grate Cleaning Block	• Use for once-per-season grill reconditioning • Pumice scrubber to strip all accumulated gunk even from cold grates	GrillStone Value Pack Cleaning Kit by Earthstone International $9.99
	Grill Spatula	• Long handle to keep your hands away from flames • Head about 4 inches wide • Plastic grips	Weber Original Stainless Steel Spatula $14.99
	Basting Brush	• Silicone bristles • Angled brush head • Handle 8 to 13 inches in length • Heat-resistant	Elizabeth Karmel's Super Silicone Angled Barbecue Brush $9.16
	Skewers	• Flat and metal • $3/16$ inch thick	Norpro 12-Inch Stainless Steel Skewers $6.85 for a set of 6
	Grill Gloves	• Excellent heat protection • Gloves, rather than mitts, for dexterity • Long sleeves to protect your forearms	Steven Raichlen Ultimate Suede Grilling Gloves $29.99 per pair

See AmericasTestKitchen.com for updates to these testings.

Grilling Equipment	Item	What to Look For	Test Kitchen Favorites
	Rib Rack	• Sturdily supports six racks of ribs • Doubles as roasting rack (when flipped upside down) • Nonstick coating for easy cleanup	Charcoal Companion Reversible Rib Rack $14.95
	Grill Lighter	• Flexible neck • Refillable chamber with large, easy-to-read fuel window • Comfortable grip	Zippo Flexible Neck Utility Lighter $18.35
	Disposable Grill	• Kit includes aluminum pan, metal grate, and charcoal • Large grilling area (about 12 by 10 inches) • After use, can be thrown away or recycled	EZGrill Disposable Instant Grill, party size $10.99
	Outdoor Grill Pan	• Narrow slits and raised sides so food can't fall through or off • Sturdy construction with handles	Weber Professional-Grade Grill Pan $19.99
	Grill Grate Set	• Stainless-steel grate for 22½-inch charcoal grill • Removable inner circle of grate can be replaced with crosshatched sear grate (shown), griddle, or wok (sold separately)	Weber 7420 Gourmet BBQ System, Sear Grate Set $54.99
	Pizza Grilling Kit	• Metal collar that elevates the grill's lid • Brings grill heat to over 700 degrees • Cutout that lets you insert pizzas without losing heat	KettlePizza Pro 22 Kit $299.95
	Stovetop Smoker	• Sliding snug, flat metal lid • Large drip tray • Rack with parallel wires • Stay-cool handles	Camerons Stovetop Smoker $54.95
	Smoker Box	• Cast iron for slow heating and steady smoke • Easy to fill, empty, and clean	GrillPro Cast Iron Smoker Box by Onward Manufacturing Company $12.79
	Grilling Basket for Whole Fish	• Two-piece metal cage with nonstick coating to keep fish from sticking • Wires less than 2 inches apart to secure both large and small fish • Removable handle for easy cleanup	Charcoal Companion Ultimate Nonstick Fish-Grilling Basket $24.99

See AmericasTestKitchen.com for updates to these testings.

Grilling Equipment	Item	What to Look For	Test Kitchen Favorites
	Vertical Roaster	• Helps poultry cook evenly • 8-inch shaft keeps chicken above fat and drippings in pan • Attached basin catches drippings for pan sauce • Sturdy construction	Vertical Roaster with Infuser by Norpro $22.11 Best Buy: Elizabeth Karmel's Grill Friends Porcelain Chicken Sitter $11.99

Specialty Pieces	Item	What to Look For	Test Kitchen Favorites
	Apple Corer	• Sharp, serrated barrel edges • Blade diameter measuring ¾ to 1 inch	Cuisipro Apple Corer $9.95
	Apple Slicer	• Sharp, serrated corer with 1-inch diameter • Ability to cut eight or 16 slices • Comfortable handle	Williams-Sonoma Dial-A-Slice/Adjustable Apple Divider $19.95
	Grapefruit Knife	• Sturdy, lightweight handle • Gently angled blade for precise cutting	Messermeister Pro-Touch 4-Inch Grapefruit Knife $15.39
	Strawberry Huller	• Huller with four spring-loaded metal prongs that slice out leaves, stem, and core • Easy and safe to use • Compact for easy storage	StemGem Strawberry Hull Remover by Chef'n $7.95
	Pineapple Cutter	• Corkscrew design • Easy to use • Narrow slicing base for easy storage	OXO Good Grips Stainless Steel Ratcheting Pineapple Slicer $19.99
	Corn Stripper	• Safer than using chef's knife • Attached cup to catch kernels • Comfortable grip and sharp blade	OXO Good Grips Corn Stripper $11.99
	Manual Nut Chopper	• Sharp, sturdy stainless-steel chopping tines • Dishwasher-safe	Prepworks from Progressive Nut Chopper with Non-Skid Base $11.70

See AmericasTestKitchen.com for updates to these testings.

Specialty Pieces	Item	What to Look For	Test Kitchen Favorites
	Nutcracker	• Lever-style model • Solidly built • Extra-long handle for good leverage and easy cracking	Get Crackin' Heavy Duty Steel Lever Nutcracker $35.99
	Spiral Slicer (Spiralizer)	• Includes three blades that are stored in the base • Stabilizing suction cups make for safer slicing • Pronged to hold fruit and vegetables against blade for optimal spiralizing • Large rectangular chamber accommodates vegetables up to 10 inches long or 7 inches thick	Paderno World Cuisine Tri-Blade Plastic Spiral Vegetable Slicer $33.24
	Milk Frother	• Easy to use and clean • Immersion blender–style wand • Battery operated	Aerolatte Milk Frother $19.99
	Oyster Knife	• Sturdy, flat blade with slightly curved tip for easy penetration • Slim, nonstick handle for secure, comfortable grip	R. Murphy New Haven Oyster Knife with Stainless Steel Blade $16.65
	Seafood Scissors	• Thin, curved blades to fit into shells • Strong and sturdy	RSVP International Endurance Seafood Scissors $14.99
	Silicone Microwave Lid	• Thin, silicone round to cover splatter-prone food during microwave heating • Easy to clean • Doubles as jar opener	Piggy Steamer $18.00
	Recipe Holder	• Holds pages at perfect angle for viewing • Compact yet sturdy • Strong magnet	Recipe Rock by Architec $9.99
	Oil Mister	• Clear plastic makes it easy to monitor oil level • Consistent, fine spray • Easy to refill • Dishwasher-safe	Orka Flavor and Oil Mister with Filter $6.94

See AmericasTestKitchen.com for updates to these testings.

Specialty Pieces	Item	What to Look For	Test Kitchen Favorites
	Microwave Rice Cooker	• Sturdy and compact • 6-cup capacity • Easy to clean	Progressive International Microwave Rice Cooker Set $8.99
	Tortilla Press	• Wood or heavy cast iron • Large pressing surface of 8 inches • Easy to operate	La Mexicana Tortilladora de Madera Barnizada/Mesquite Tortilla Press $64.95 Best Buy: Imusa Cast Iron Tortilla Press $23.99
	Pastry Bag	• Plastic-coated canvas pastry bag (for durability and easy cleanup) or disposable bags • Large bag (about 18 inches in length) for easier gripping and twisting • Accommodates standard-size tips	Ateco 18-Inch Plastic-Coated Pastry Bag $4.45
	Cheese Wire	• Comfortable plastic handles • Narrow wire	Fante's Handled Cheese Wire $2.99
	Pizza Cutter	• Comfortable, soft-grip handle • Thumb guard to protect your fingers	OXO Good Grips 4" Pizza Wheel $12.99
	Baking Peel	• Wood board • Pastry cloth threaded through board makes it essentially nonstick when well floured • Gentle touch for bread loaves	Super Peel by EXO Products, Inc. $55.00
	Potato Ricer	• Hopper with many holes so more food can travel through • Comfortable handles • Easy to assemble and clean	RSVP International Potato Ricer $13.95

See AmericasTestKitchen.com for updates to these testings.

Specialty Pieces	Item	What to Look For	Test Kitchen Favorites
	Pancake Batter Dispenser	• Tall plastic cylinder • Easy to use • Heat-resistant silicone tip	Tovolo Pancake Pen $9.95
	Insulated Ice Cream Keeper	• Foam-core insulated base and gel pack–lined lid • Can hold 1 pint of ice cream • Keeps ice cream frozen for 90 minutes	Zak! Designs Ice Cream Tubbie $10.12
	Quick Popsicle Maker	• Nonstick cast-aluminum mold with proprietary solution inside base to ensure quick freezing • Slots for three popsicles • Reusable plastic popsicle sticks	Zoku Quick Pop Maker $49.95
	Cupcake and Cake Carrier	• Fits both round and square cakes and cupcakes • Snap locks • Nonskid base • Collapses for easy storage	Progressive Collapsible Cupcake and Cake Carrier $29.95
	Cake Stand	• Elevated rotating stand so you can hold the spatula steady for easy frosting • Solid, light construction	Winco Revolving Cake Decorating Stand $29.98
	Cream Whipper	• Slim canister for one-handed squeezing • Slender metal tip to make rosettes and mounds	Liss Polished Stainless Steel Cream Whipper, 1 Pint $149.95
	Spice/Coffee Grinder	• Electric, not manual, grinders • Deep bowl to hold ample amount of coffee beans • Easy-to-control texture of grind • Good to have two, one each for coffee grinding and spice grinding	Krups Fast-Touch Coffee Mill, Model 203 $19.99

See AmericasTestKitchen.com for updates to these testings.

Specialty Pieces	Item	What to Look For	Test Kitchen Favorites
	Moka Pot	• Classic design that uses steam pressure to force hot water from bottom chamber up through coffee grounds • Stovetop, not electric, model • Easy to use	Bialetti Moka Express, 3 cups $24.95
	French Press	• Fine-mesh filter to eliminate sediment • Insulated pot to keep coffee hot • Smooth, simple, dishwasher-safe parts for easy cleanup	Bodum Columbia French Press Coffee Maker, Double Wall, 8 Cup $79.95
	Cold Brew Coffee Maker	• Easy to use • Produces smooth, rich-tasting cold brew concentrate • Enough concentrate to make sixty-four 4-ounce cups of coffee	Toddy Cold Brew System $34.95
	Manual Espresso Maker	• Includes milk foamer, measuring scoop, and adapter for making two shots simultaneously • Easy and intuitive to use	ROK Manual Espresso Maker $150.00
	Innovative Teapot	• Contained ultrafine-mesh strainer keeps tea leaf dregs separate • One-piece design for easy cleaning	ingenuiTEA by Adagio Teas $14.95
	Tea Machine	• Perforated tea basket for thorough infusion • Programmable temperature and steep times • Fully automated brewing • Dishwasher-safe accessories	Breville Tea Maker $249.99 Best Buy: Cuisinart PerfecTemp Programmable Tea Steeper & Kettle $99.00

See AmericasTestKitchen.com for updates to these testings.

Specialty Pieces	Item	What to Look For	Test Kitchen Favorites
MUST-HAVE ITEM	**Wine Opener**	• Durable design • Teflon-coated worm • Ergonomically curved body and hinged fulcrum	Pulltap's Classic Evolution Corkscrew by Pulltex $39.95 Best Buy: Trudeau Double Lever Corkscrew $12.99
	Electric Wine Opener	• Sturdy, quiet corkscrew • Broad base that rests firmly on bottle	Waring Pro Professional Cordless Wine Opener $39.99
	Wine Aerator	• Long, tube-like design that exposes wine to air as it is being poured • Neat, hands-free aerating	Nuance Wine Finer $19.95
	Wine Saver	• Minimizes amount of contact wine has with air • Easy, reliable mechanism • Keeps wine drinkable for at least one month	Air Cork The Wine Preserver $24.95
	Cocktail Shaker	• Double-walled canister to prevent condensation for slip-free gripping • Convenient pop-up spout • Tight-sealing lid	Metrokane Fliptop Cocktail Shaker $29.95
	Silicone Ice Cube Tray	• Sturdy silicone construction • Large cubes that keep drinks from tasting watered-down	Tovolo King Cube Silicone Ice Cube Tray $7.95
	Cooler	• Insulating layer of plastic lining • Lightweight, durable, sturdy, and easy to move, even when full • Easy to clean	California Cooler Bags T-Rex Large Collapsible Rolling Cooler $75.00

See AmericasTestKitchen.com for updates to these testings.

Specialty Pieces	Item	What to Look For	Test Kitchen Favorites
	Insulated Food Carrier	• Designed to carry two 13 by 9-inch baking dishes • Sturdy, expandable frame • Insulation keeps food above 140 degrees for more than 3 hours	Rachael Ray Expandable Lasagna Lugger $26.95
	Insulated Shopping Tote	• Shoulder straps for easy toting • Insulation keeps groceries at a food-safe temperature for 2 hours in a 90-degree room	Rachael Ray ChillOut Thermal Tote $17.99
	Seltzer Maker	• Easy to use and easy-to-control level of fizz • Cartridges carbonate up to 60 liter-size bottles	SodaStream Source Starter Kit $99.95
	Sous Vide Machine	• Slowly cooks vacuum-sealed food in water bath at precise temperatures • Easy to set up and use • Quiet	Anova One $199.00
	Vacuum Robot	• Easy to use and program • Recharging dock • Efficient, grid-pattern cleaning program • Unique shape fits into corners and along walls	Neato Botvac D80 $499.99
	Compost Bucket	• Plastic pail to collect food scraps for composter • Carbon filter prevents odors from escaping and allows oxygen to enter so decomposition can occur • Easy-to-open lid that latches securely in place • 2.4-gallon capacity	Exaco Trading Kitchen Compost Waste Collector $19.98

See AmericasTestKitchen.com for updates to these testings.

Kitchen Supplies	Item	What to Look For	Test Kitchen Favorites
	Fire Extinguisher	• Easy to operate • Powerful, controlled spray	Kidde Kitchen Fire Extinguisher $18.97
	Plastic Wrap	• Clings tightly and resticks well • Packaging with sharp teeth that aren't exposed (to avoid snags on clothing and skin) • Adhesive pad to hold cut end of wrap	Glad Cling Wrap Clear Plastic $1.20 per 100 square feet
	Food Storage Bags	• Low-porosity plastic to keep moisture in • Airtight seal (zippers are better than sliders)	Ziploc Brand Double Zipper Gallon Freezer Bags with the Smart Zip Seal $3.99 for 30 bags
	Parchment Cooking Bags	• Easy to fill and fold	PaperChef Culinary Parchment Cooking Bags $7.98 for 10 bags
	Cheese Storage Wraps	• Two-ply wax-coated paper • Bags are easy to fill and fold	Formaticum Cheese Bags and Cheese Paper $9 for 15 bags $9 for 15 sheets with stickers
	Plastic Food Storage Container	• Snap-style seal with ridge on underside to ensure tight seal • Low, flat rectangle for easy storage and more efficient heating and chilling • Made of plastic free of BPA (bisphenol-A)	Snapware Airtight $7.99 for 8-cup rectangle
	Kitchen Twine	• Look for "kitchen" or "food-safe" label • 100% cotton	Librett Cotton Butcher's Twine $8.29 for 370 feet
	Soap-Filled Dish Brush	• Handle for easy gripping and to keep your hands dry • Tight seal to prevent soap from leaking	OXO Steel Soap Squirting Dish Brush $11.99

MUST-HAVE ITEMS

See AmericasTestKitchen.com for updates to these testings.

Kitchen Supplies	Item	What to Look For	Test Kitchen Favorites
MUST-HAVE ITEM	All-Purpose Spray Cleaner	• Natural, green product • Cuts through grease and food splatters quickly and efficiently • Pleasant, not overpowering, scent	Method All-Purpose Natural Surface Cleaner, French Lavender $3.79 for 28 ounces
	Cast-Iron Pot Scrubber	• 4-inch square of chain mail made of 16-gauge stainless steel • Ideal for cleaning cast-iron cookware and all other cookware surfaces except nonstick	CM Scrubber $19.98
	Heavy-Duty Handled Scrub Brush	• Short, stiff bristles • Built-in scraper • Compact size • Thick nonslip handle	Caldrea Dishwashing Brush $5.00
MUST-HAVE ITEM	Dish Towels	• Thin cotton for absorbency and flexibility • Dries glassware without steaks • Washes clean without shrinking	Williams-Sonoma Striped Towels $19.95 for a set of four
	Apron	• Adjustable neck strap and long strings • Full coverage; chest area reinforced with extra layer of fabric • Stains wash out completely	Bragard Travail Bib Apron $27.95
MUST-HAVE ITEM	Liquid Dish Soap	• High concentration of surfactants to wash away oil • Clean scent	Mrs. Meyer's Clean Day Liquid Dish Soap, Lavender $3.99 for 16 ounces
	Laundry Stain Remover	• Clear instructions • Contains enzymes and surfactants to eliminate old and new stains from fabric • Stained fabrics emerged bright as new	OxiClean Versatile Stain Remover $8.59 for 3-pound tub

See AmericasTestKitchen.com for updates to these testings.

INGREDIENTS

You can read general tips for buying and storing ingredients of all kinds (plus specific brand recommendations for some of the ingredients we use the most) in Chapter 2 of this book. This chart presents those winning brands as well as dozens more for the supermarket products you buy every day. See AmericasTestKitchen.com for updates to these tastings.

	Item	Why We Like It	Test Kitchen Favorites
	Almond Butter	• Homogeneous, creamy texture • Clean and distinct almond flavor • Well seasoned with salt and sugar • Made with almonds that are blanched and roasted	Jif Creamy Almond Butter
	Anchovies	• Right amount of salt • Savory without being fishy • Firm, meaty texture • Minimal bones • Aged 4 to 6 months	King Oscar Anchovies — Flat Fillets in Olive Oil
	Applesauce	• An unusual ingredient, sucralose, sweetens this applesauce without overpowering its fresh, bright apple flavor • Pinch of salt boosts flavor above weak, bland, and too-sweet competitors • Coarse, almost chunky texture, not slimy like applesauces sweetened with corn syrup	Musselman's Lite Apple Sauce
	Bacon, Supermarket	• Good balance of saltiness and sweetness • Smoky and full flavored • Very meaty, not too fatty • Crisp and hearty texture	Farmland Thick Sliced Bacon and Plumrose Premium Thick Sliced Bacon
	Baking Powder	• Double-acting formulation helps baked goods rise higher • Makes chewy cookies, fluffy biscuits, and moist but airy cakes	Argo Double Acting Baking Powder
	Barbecue Sauce, Supermarket	• Spicy, fresh tomato taste • Good balance of tanginess, smokiness, and sweetness • Robust flavor from molasses • Sweetened with sugar and molasses, not high-fructose corn syrup, which caramelizes and burns quickly	Bull's-Eye Original Barbecue Sauce
	Barbecue Sauce, High-End	• Generous amounts of vinegar, salt, chili paste, and liquid smoke for bold spicy flavor • Tangy kick • Good body	Pork Barrel Original BBQ Sauce

See AmericasTestKitchen.com for updates to these tastings.

	Item	Why We Like It	Test Kitchen Favorites
	Beans, Canned Baked	• Firm and pleasant texture with some bite • Sweetened with molasses for complexity and depth	B&M Vegetarian Baked Beans
	Beans, Canned Black	• Clean, mild, and slightly earthy flavor • Firm, almost al dente texture, not mushy or pasty • Good amount of salt	Bush's Best Black Beans
	Beans, Canned Chickpeas	• Firm yet tender texture bests pasty and dry competitors • Clean chickpea flavor • Enough salt to enhance but not overwhelm the flavor	Pastene Chick Peas
	Beans, Canned White	• Well seasoned, with both sweet and savory flavor • Ultracreamy and smooth texture with a nice firm bite • Big and meaty beans	Goya Cannellini
	Beans, Dried White	• Creamy and smooth texture • Fresh taste • Nutty and sweet flavors	Rancho Gordo Classic Cassoulet Bean
	Beans, Refried	• Well-seasoned mixture • Supersmooth texture, not overly thick, pasty, or gluey	Taco Bell Home Originals Refried Beans
	Bread, Gluten-Free Multigrain Sandwich	• Great flavor from plenty of fat and salt • Light, fluffy texture from baking soda and yeast • Made with brown rice flower plus sunflower and flax seeds	Glutino Gluten Free Multigrain Bread
	Bread, White Sandwich	• Subtle sweetness, not tasteless or sour • Perfect structure, not too dry or too soft	Arnold Country Classics White Bread
	Bread, Whole-Wheat Sandwich	• Whole-grain, nutty, earthy flavor • Dense, chewy texture, not gummy or too soft • Not too sweet, contains no corn syrup and has low sugar level (unlike competitors) NOTE: Available only east of the Mississippi River.	Pepperidge Farm 100% Natural Whole Wheat Bread

See AmericasTestKitchen.com for updates to these tastings.

	Item	Why We Like It	Test Kitchen Favorites
	Bread Crumbs	• Crisp, with a substantial crunch • Not too delicate, stale, sandy, or gritty • Oil-free and without seasonings or undesirable artificial flavors	Ian's Panko Breadcrumbs, Original Style
	Broth, Beef	• Deep savory profile with rich notes • Contains flavor-enhancing ingredients such as yeast extract	Better Than Bouillon Beef Base
	Broth, Chicken	• Rich chicken flavor • Clean, savory taste • Not too salty when reduced	Swanson Chicken Stock Best Buy: Better Than Bouillon Chicken Base
	Broth, Vegetarian	• Good robust, savory flavor without bitter or cloying off-flavors • Contains flavor boosters like salt and yeast extract	Orrington Farms Vegan Chicken Flavored Broth Base & Seasoning
	Broth, Vegetable, Low-Sodium	• Mild, chicken-y flavor • Unctuous, meaty body • Lends a clean, fresh flavor to risottos and vegetable soups	Edward & Sons Low Sodium Not-Chick'n Natural Bouillon Cubes
	Brownie Mix	• Rich, balanced chocolate flavor from both natural and Dutch-processed cocoa • Moist, chewy, and fudgy with perfect texture	Ghirardelli Chocolate Supreme Brownie Mix and Barefoot Contessa Outrageous Brownie Mix
	Butter, Salted	• Premium brand perfect for toast or use as a condiment • Extra-salty, savory flavor • Foil wrapping helps protect butter from off-flavors	Lurpak Slightly Salted Butter Best Buy: Kate's Homemade Butter
	Butter, Unsalted	• Sweet and creamy • Complex tang and grassy flavor • Moderate amount of butterfat so that it's decadent and glossy but not so rich that baked goods are greasy	Plugrá European-Style Unsalted Butter Best Buy: Land O'Lakes Unsalted Sweet Butter

See AmericasTestKitchen.com for updates to these tastings.

Item	Why We Like It	Test Kitchen Favorites
Cheese, American	• Nutty, sharp, tangy flavor • Superthin slices for perfect melting • Tender, slightly soft texture	Boar's Head American Cheese
Cheese, Asiago	• Sharp, tangy, and complex flavor, not mild • Firm and not too dry • Melts, shreds, and grates well	BelGioioso Asiago Cheese
Cheese, Blue	• Milder cheese is better for dressings • Crumbly texture • Nicely balanced flavor with mild sweetness	Stella Blue Runner-Up: Danish Blue
Cheese, Brie	• Buttery, earthy flavor with gooey, silky texture • Soft, pillowy rind	Fromager d'Affinois
Cheese, Cheddar, Extra-Sharp	• Balance of salty, creamy, and sweet flavors • Considerable but well-rounded sharpness, not overwhelming • Firm, crumbly texture, not moist, rubbery, or springy • Aged at least 12 months for complex flavor	Cabot Private Stock Cheddar Cheese Runner-Up: Cabot Extra-Sharp Cheddar Cheese
Cheese, Cheddar, Artisanal	• Earthy complexity with nutty, buttery, and fruity flavors • Dry and crumbly with crystalline crunch, not rubbery or overly moist • Aged no more than 12 months to prevent overly sharp flavor	Milton Creamery Prairie Breeze Runner-Up: Cabot Cellars at Jasper Hill Clothbound Cheddar
Cheese, Cheddar, Presliced	• Slightly crumbly, not rubbery or processed, texture characteristic of block cheddar • Strong, tangy, and salty flavor, not bland or too mild	Tillamook Presliced Sharp Cheddar
Cheese, Cheddar, Low-Fat	• Ample creaminess • Strong cheesy flavor • Good for cooking	Cracker Barrel Reduced Fat Sharp Cheddar Cheese
Cheese, Cheddar, Sharp	• Sharp, clean, and tangy flavor • Firm, crumbly texture, not moist, rubbery, or springy • Aged a minimum of 12 months for complex flavor	Cabot Vermont Sharp Cheddar

See AmericasTestKitchen.com for updates to these tastings.

	Item	Why We Like It	Test Kitchen Favorites
	Cheese, Cottage	• Rich, well-seasoned, and buttery flavor • Velvety, creamy texture • Pillowy curds	Hood Country Style Cottage Cheese
	Cheese, Cream, Supermarket	• Rich, tangy, and milky flavor • Thick, creamy texture, not pasty, waxy, or chalky	Philadelphia Brand Cream Cheese
	Cheese, Cream, Artisanal	• Supercreamy and smooth texture • Impressive depth of flavor	Zingerman's Creamery Fresh Cream Cheese
	Cheese, Feta	• Strong tangy, salty flavor • Creamy, dense texture • Pleasing crumbly texture	Mt. Vikos Traditional Feta
	Cheese, Fontina For Cheese Plate	• Strong, earthy aroma • Somewhat elastic texture with small irregular holes • Grassy, nutty flavor—but can be overpowering in cooked dishes	Fontina Val d'Aosta
	For Cooking	• Semisoft, supercreamy texture • Mildly tangy, nutty flavor • Melts well	Italian Fontina
	Cheese, Goat	• Rich-tasting, grassy, tangy flavor • Salt content enhances flavor and texture • Smooth and creamy both unheated and baked	Laura Chenel's Chèvre Fresh Chèvre Log
	Cheese, Gruyère	• Grassy, salty flavor, not bland or pedestrian • Creamy yet dry texture, not plasticky like some competitors • Aged a minimum of 10 months for strong and complex flavor • Melts especially well	Gruyère Reserve Wheel
	Cheese, Mozzarella	• Creamy and buttery with clean dairy flavor • Soft, not rubbery, chew	Sorrento Galbani Whole Milk Mozzarella (formerly Sorrento)
	Cheese, Parmesan, Supermarket	• Rich and complex flavor balances tanginess and nuttiness • Dry, crumbly texture, yet creamy with a crystalline crunch, not rubbery or dense • Aged a minimum of 12 months for better flavor and texture	Boar's Head Parmigiano-Reggiano Best Buy: BelGioioso Parmesan

See AmericasTestKitchen.com for updates to these tastings.

	Item	Why We Like It	Test Kitchen Favorites
	Cheese, Pepper Jack	• Buttery, tangy cheese • Clean, balanced flavor with assertive spice	Boar's Head Monterey Jack Cheese with Jalapeño
	Cheese, Provolone	• Bold, nutty, and tangy flavor, not plasticky or bland • Firm, dry texture	Provolone Vernengo
	Cheese, Ricotta	• Clean, fresh flavor, not rancid or sour from addition of gums or stabilizers • Creamy texture with perfect curds, unlike chalky, grainy, and soggy competitors	Calabro Part Skim Ricotta Cheese
	Cheese, Swiss For Cheese Plate	• Subtle flavor with sweet, buttery, nutty, and fruity notes • Firm yet gently giving texture, not rubbery • Aged longer for better flavor, resulting in larger eyes • Mildly pungent yet balanced	Edelweiss Creamery Emmentaler Switzerland Swiss Cheese Runner-Up: Emmi Kaltbach Cave-Aged Emmentaler Switzerland AOC
	For Cooking	• Mild nutty flavor • Smooth texture when melted	Boar's Head Gold Label Switzerland Swiss Cheese
	For Cheese Plate or Cooking	• Creamy texture • Salty mildness preferable for grilled cheese sandwiches	Emmi Emmentaler Cheese AOC
	Chicken, Breasts, Boneless Skinless	• Juicy and tender with clean chicken flavor • Not salted or brined • Air-chilled • Aged on bone for at least 6 hours after slaughter for significantly more tender meat	Bell & Evans Air Chilled Boneless, Skinless Chicken Breasts
	Chicken, Whole	• Great, savory chicken flavor • Very tender • Air-chilled for minimum water retention and cleaner flavor	Mary's Free Range Air Chilled Chicken (also sold as Pitman's) Runner-Up: Bell & Evans Air Chilled Premium Fresh Chicken
	Chili Powder	• Blend of chile peppers with added seasonings, not assertively hot, overly smoky, or one-dimensional • Balance of sweet and smoky flavors • Potent but not overwhelming	Morton & Bassett Chili Powder

See AmericasTestKitchen.com for updates to these tastings.

Item	Why We Like It	Test Kitchen Favorites
Chocolate, Dark	• Creamy texture, not grainy or chalky • Dark, bold flavor with notes of cherries, wine, and smoke • Balance of sweetness and bitterness	Ghirardelli 60% Cacao Bittersweet Chocolate Premium Baking Bar Runner-Up: Callebaut Intense Dark Chocolate, L-60-40NV
Chocolate, Dark Chips	• Intense, complex flavor beats one-dimensional flavor of competitors • Low sugar content highlights chocolate flavor • High amount of cocoa butter ensures creamy, smooth texture, not gritty and grainy • Wider, flatter shape and high percentage of fat help chips melt better in cookies	Ghirardelli 60% Cacao Bittersweet Chocolate Chips
Chocolate, Milk	• Intense, full, rich chocolate flavor • Supercreamy texture from abundant milk fat and cocoa butter • Not overwhelmingly sweet	Dove Silky Smooth Milk Chocolate
Chocolate, Milk Chips	• Bold chocolate flavor outshines too-sweet, weak chocolate flavor of other chips • Complex with caramel and nutty notes • Higher fat content makes texture creamier than grainy, artificial competitors	Hershey's Milk Chocolate Chips
Chocolate, Unsweetened	• Well-rounded, complex flavor • Assertive chocolate flavor and deep notes of cocoa	Hershey's Unsweetened Baking Bar
Chocolate, White Chips	• Creamy texture, not waxy or crunchy • Silky smooth meltability from high fat content • Complex flavor like high-quality real chocolate, no artificial or off-flavors	Guittard Choc-Au-Lait White Chips
Cinnamon	• Warm, fragrant aroma with clove, fruity, and slightly smoky flavors • Mellow start with spicy finish • Strong yet not overpowering • Not harsh, bitter, dusty, or gritty NOTE: Available only through mail order, Penzeys (800-741-7787, Penzeys.com).	Penzeys Extra Fancy Vietnamese Cassia Cinnamon
Cocoa Powder, Supermarket	• Full, strong chocolate flavor • Complex flavor with notes of coffee, cinnamon, orange, and spice	Hershey's Cocoa Natural Unsweetened

See AmericasTestKitchen.com for updates to these tastings.

Item	Why We Like It	Test Kitchen Favorites
Coconut Milk For Savory Recipes	• Strong coconut flavor • Smooth and creamy texture superior to competitors • Not very sweet, ideal for savory recipes like soups and stir-fries	Chaokoh Coconut Milk
For Sweet Recipes	• Rich, velvety texture, not too thin or watery • Fruity and complex flavor, not mild or bland • Ideal sweetness for desserts	Ka-Me Coconut Milk
Coffee, Whole-Bean, Supermarket Dark Roast	• Deep, complex, and balanced flavor without metallic, overly acidic, or otherwise unpleasant notes • Smoky and chocolaty with a bitter, not burnt, finish	Millstone Colombian Supremo
Medium Roast	• Extremely smooth but bold-tasting with a strong finish • Rich chocolate and toast flavors • Few defective beans and low acidity	Peet's Coffee Café Domingo and Millstone Breakfast Blend
Coffee, Decaf	• Smooth, mellow flavor without being acidic or harsh • Complex, with a slightly nutty aftertaste • Made with only flavorful Arabica beans	Maxwell House Decaf Original Roast
Cornish Game Hens, Whole	• Juicy meat and crisp skin when cooked • Clean, pure flavors	Bell and Evans Cornish Game Hens
Cornmeal	• Clean, pure corn flavor comes from using whole-grain kernels • Ideal texture resembling slightly damp, fine sand, not too fine or too coarse	Arrowhead Mills Organic Yellow Cornmeal
Couscous, Israeli	• Large pearls with a firm, springy texture • Sweet, toasty flavor • Sold in an airtight jar	Roland Israeli Couscous
Crabmeat	• Moist, plump, meaty chunks • Taste comparable to freshly picked crabmeat	Phillips Premium Crab Jumbo

See AmericasTestKitchen.com for updates to these tastings.

	Item	Why We Like It	Test Kitchen Favorites
	Curry Powder	• Balanced, neither too sweet nor too hot • Complex and vivid earthy flavor, not thin, bland, or one-dimensional NOTE: Available only through mail order, Penzeys (800-741-7787, Penzeys.com).	Penzeys Sweet Curry Powder
	Dinner Rolls, Frozen	• Pleasantly wheaty and yeasty flavor • Chewy, tender insides and crispy crust • Tastes closest to fresh homemade	Pepperidge Farm Stone Baked Artisan French Dinner Rolls
	Five-Spice Powder	• Woodsy, sweet, and aromatic taste • Harmonious flavor with a nice spice kick	Frontier Natural Products Co-op Five Spice Powder
	Flour, All-Purpose	• Fresh, toasty flavor • No metallic taste or other off-flavors • Consistent results across recipes • Makes tender, flaky pie crust, hearty biscuits, crisp cookies, and chewy, sturdy bread	King Arthur Unbleached Enriched All-Purpose Flour
		• Clean, toasty, and hearty flavor • No metallic taste or other off-flavors • Consistent results across recipes • Makes flaky pie crust, chewy cookies, and tender biscuits, muffins, and cakes	Pillsbury Unbleached Enriched All Purpose Flour
	Flour, Whole-Wheat	• Finely ground for hearty but not overly coarse texture in bread and pancakes • Sweet, nutty flavor	King Arthur Premium 100% Whole Wheat Flour
	Garam Masala	• Blend contains traditional spices: black pepper, dried chiles, cinnamon, cardamom, and coriander • Mellow, well-balanced flavor profile	McCormick Gourmet Collection Garam Masala
	Garlic Powder	• Adds subtle garlic flavor in spice rubs • Clean, pungent flavor • No dusty or stale off-flavors	Spice Islands Garlic Powder

See AmericasTestKitchen.com for updates to these tastings.

Item	Why We Like It	Test Kitchen Favorites
Ginger, Ground	• Spicy but not overpowering • Toasty, fragrant flavor profile	Spice Islands Ground Ginger
Grapefruit Juice	• Clean, refreshing taste • Closest to fresh-squeezed • Balanced sweet-sour flavor	Natalie's 100% Florida Grapefruit Juice Runner-Up: Florida's Natural Ruby Red Grapefruit Juice
Gnocchi, Supermarket	• Tender, pillow-like texture • Nice potato flavor • Slightly sour taste that disappears when paired with tomato sauce	Gia Russa Gnocchi with Potato
Ham, Black Forest Deli	• Good texture • Nice ham flavor	Dietz & Watson Black Forest Smoked Ham with Natural Juices
Ham, Prosciutto	• Tender and buttery flavor • Silky and supple texture • Very thin slices	Volpi Traditional Prosciutto Best Buy: Del Duca Prosciutto
Ham, Spiral-Sliced, Honey-Cured	• Good balance of smokiness, saltiness, and sweetness • Moist, tender yet firm texture, not dry or too wet • Clean, meaty ham flavor	Cook's Spiral Sliced Hickory Smoked Bone-In Honey Ham
Hoisin Sauce	• Balances sweet, salty, pungent, and spicy flavors • Initial burn mellows into harmonious and aromatic blend without bitterness	Kikkoman Hoisin Sauce
Honey, Supermarket	• Raw, unfiltered product • Complex flavor with mild sweetness and slight acidity • Good both plain and in recipes	Nature Nate's 100% Pure Raw and Unfiltered Honey

See AmericasTestKitchen.com for updates to these tastings.

	Item	Why We Like It	Test Kitchen Favorites
	Horseradish	• No preservatives, just horseradish, vinegar, and salt (found in the refrigerated section) • Natural flavor and hot without being overpowering	Boar's Head Pure Horseradish
	Hot Dogs	• Meaty, robust, and hearty flavor, not sweet, sour, or too salty • Juicy but not greasy • Firm, craggy texture, not rubbery, mushy, or chewy	Nathan's Famous Skinless Beef Franks
	Hot Fudge Sauce	• True fudge flavor, not weak or overly sweet • Thick, smooth, and buttery texture	Hershey's Hot Fudge
	Hot Sauce	• Right combination of punchy heat, saltiness, sweetness, and garlic • Full, rich flavor • Mild heat that's not too hot	Huy Fong Sriracha Hot Chili Sauce Runner-Up: Frank's RedHot Original Cayenne Pepper Sauce
	Hummus, Supermarket	• Nutty, earthy flavor • Thick, creamy texture • Clean flavor of tahini	Sabra Classic Hummus
	Ice Cream, Chocolate	• Deep, concentrated chocolate flavor, not too light or sweet • Dense and creamy texture	Ben & Jerry's Chocolate Ice Cream
	Ice Cream, Vanilla	• Complex yet balanced vanilla flavor from real vanilla extract • Sweetness solely from sugar, rather than corn syrup • Creamy richness from both egg yolks and a small amount of stabilizers	Ben & Jerry's Vanilla Ice Cream
	Iced Tea Loose Leaf	• Distinctive flavor with herbal notes • Balanced level of strength and astringency	Tazo Iced Black Tea
	Bottled, with Lemon	• Bright, balanced, and natural tea and lemon flavors • Uses concentrated tea leaves to extract flavor	Lipton PureLeaf Black Tea with Lemon

See AmericasTestKitchen.com for updates to these tastings.

	Item	Why We Like It	Test Kitchen Favorites
	Ketchup	• Clean, pure sweetness from sugar, not high-fructose corn syrup • Bold, harmonious punch of saltiness, sweetness, tang, and tomato flavor	Heinz Organic Tomato Ketchup Best Buy: Hunt's Tomato Ketchup
	Lemonade	• Natural-tasting lemon flavor, without artificial flavors or off-notes • Perfect balance of tartness and sweetness, unlike many overly sweet competitors • Contains 20% lemon juice	Natalie's Natural Lemonade
	Liquid Egg Whites	• Organic product • Functions similarly to fresh egg whites in cooked applications	Eggology 100% Egg Whites
	Macaroni & Cheese	• Reinforces flavor with blue and cheddar cheeses • Uses creamy, clingy liquid cheese sauce • Dry noodles, rather than frozen, for substantial texture and bite • Crunchy, buttery bread-crumb topping	Kraft Homestyle Macaroni & Cheese Dinner Classic Cheddar Cheese Sauce
	Maple Syrup	• Rich caramel flavor and deep molasses-like hue NOTE: We found that all Grade A Dark Amber maple syrups at supermarkets taste similar, so our advice is to buy the cheapest all-maple product available.	Grade A Dark Amber Maple Syrup
	Mayonnaise	• Great balance of taste and texture • Richer, deeper flavor from using egg yolks alone (no egg whites) • Short ingredient list that's close to homemade	Blue Plate Real Mayonnaise
	Mayonnaise, Light	• Bright, balanced flavor close to full-fat counterpart, not overly sweet like other light mayos • Not as creamy as full-fat but passable texture NOTE: Hellmann's is known as Best Foods west of the Rocky Mountains.	Hellmann's Light Mayonnaise
	Mirin (Japanese Rice Wine)	• Good straight up or in teriyaki sauce • Balanced flavors with woodsy overtones and smoky aftertaste	Mitoku Organic Mikawa Mirin Sweet Rice Seasoning Best Buy: Eden Mirin Rice Cooking Wine

See AmericasTestKitchen.com for updates to these tastings.

Item	Why We Like It	Test Kitchen Favorites
Molasses	• Acidic yet balanced • Strong and straightforward raisin-y taste • Pleasantly bitter bite	Brer Rabbit All Natural Unsulphured Molasses Mild Flavor
Mustard, Brown	• Complex and balanced flavor • Not too spicy • Smooth texture	Gulden's Spicy Brown Mustard
Mustard, Coarse-Grain	• Spicy, tangy burst of mustard flavor • High salt content amplifies flavor • Contains no superfluous ingredients that mask mustard flavor • Big, round seeds add pleasant crunch • Just enough vinegar, not too sour or thin	Grey Poupon Harvest Coarse Ground Mustard and Grey Poupon Country Dijon Mustard
Mustard, Dijon	• Potent, bold, and very hot, not weak or mild • Good balance of sweetness, tanginess, and sharpness • High ratio of mustard seeds for balanced but impactful heat	Trois Petits Cochons Moutarde de Dijon
Mustard, Yellow	• Lists mustard seeds second in the ingredients for rich mustard flavor • Good balance of heat and tang • Relatively low salt content	Annie's Naturals Organic Yellow Mustard
Oats, Rolled	• Rich oat flavor with nutty, barley, and toasty notes • Creamy, cohesive texture • Plump grains with decent chew	Bob's Red Mill Organic Extra Thick Rolled Oats
Oats, Steel-Cut	• Rich and complex oat flavor with buttery, earthy, nutty, and whole-grain notes • Creamy yet firm texture • Moist but not sticky NOTE: Not recommended for baking.	Bob's Red Mill Organic Steel-Cut Oats
Olive Oil, Extra-Virgin, Supermarket	• Complex finish with fresh flavors • Aromatic and fruity, not bland or bitter • Clean taste, comparable to a fresh-squeezed olive, outshines bland, greasy competitors	California Olive Ranch Everyday Extra Virgin Olive Oil

See AmericasTestKitchen.com for updates to these tastings.

Item	Why We Like It	Test Kitchen Favorites
Olives, Pimento-Stuffed Green	• Meaty and juicy • Bright taste when cooked • Calcium chloride helps to firm flesh	Mezzetta Super Colossal Spanish Queen Pimiento Stuffed Olives
Orange Juice	• Squeezed within 24 hours of shipping • Superfresh taste with no flavor manipulation • Gentler pasteurization helps retain fresh-squeezed flavor • Pleasantly variable flavor with notes of guava and mango	Natalie's 100% Florida Orange Juice, Gourmet Pasteurized
Oyster Sauce	• Intense, fishy flavor • Balanced saltiness and sweet caramel undertones	Lee Kum Kee's Premium Oyster Flavored Sauce
Pancake Mix	• Flavorful balance of sweetness and tang well-seasoned with sugar and salt • Light, extra-fluffy texture • Requires vegetable oil (along with milk and egg) to reconstitute the batter	Hungry Jack Buttermilk Pancake and Waffle Mix
Paprika, Smoked	• Deep, rich smoky taste • Balanced flavor • Made in Spain according to traditional methods	Simply Organic Smoked Paprika
Paprika, Sweet	• Complex flavor with earthy, fruity notes • Bright and bold, not bland and boring • Rich, toasty aroma NOTE: Available only through mail order, The Spice House (312-274-0378, TheSpiceHouse.com).	The Spice House Hungarian Sweet Paprika
Pasta, Cheese Ravioli, Supermarket	• Creamy, plush, and rich blend of ricotta, Romano, and Parmesan cheeses • Pasta with nice, springy bite • Perfect dough-to-filling ratio	Rosetto Cheese Ravioli
Pasta, Cheese Tortellini, Supermarket	• Robustly flavored filling from a combination of ricotta, Emmentaler, and Grana Padano cheeses • Tender pasta that's sturdy enough to withstand boiling but not so thick that it becomes doughy	Barilla Three Cheese Tortellini

See AmericasTestKitchen.com for updates to these tastings.

Item	Why We Like It	Test Kitchen Favorites
Pasta, Egg Noodles	• Balanced, buttery flavor with no off-flavors • Light and fluffy texture, not gummy or starchy	Pennsylvania Dutch Wide Egg Noodles
Pasta, Elbow Macaroni	• Rich, wheaty taste with no off-flavors • Pleasantly hearty texture, not mushy or chewy • Ridged surface and slight twist in shape hold sauce especially well	Barilla Elbows
Pasta, Fresh	• Firm but yielding, slightly chewy texture, not too delicate, gummy, or heavy • Faint but discernible egg flavor with no chemical, plasticky, or otherwise unpleasant flavors • Rough, porous surface absorbs sauce better than dried pasta	Contadina Buitoni Fettuccine
Pasta, Lasagna Noodles No-Boil	• Taste and texture of fresh pasta • Delicate, flat noodles	Barilla No Boil Lasagna
Whole-Wheat	• Complex nutty, rich wheat flavor • Substantial chewy texture without any grittiness	Bionaturae Organic 100% Whole Wheat Lasagne
Pasta, Penne	• Hearty texture, not insubstantial or gummy • Wheaty, slightly sweet flavor, not bland	Mueller's Penne Rigate
Pasta, Spaghetti	• Rich, nutty, wheaty flavor • Firm, ropy strands with good chew, not mushy, gummy, or mealy • Semolina flour for resilient texture • Dried at a moderately low temperature for 18 hours to preserve flavor	De Cecco Spaghetti No. 12
Pasta, Spaghetti, Gluten-Free	• Springy texture • Clean-tasting flavor • No off-flavors or gumminess	Jovial Organic Gluten Free Brown Rice Spaghetti
Pasta, Spaghetti, Whole-Wheat	• Chewy and firm, not mushy or rubbery • Full and nutty wheat flavor	Bionaturae Organic 100% Whole Wheat Spaghetti

See AmericasTestKitchen.com for updates to these tastings.

	Item	Why We Like It	Test Kitchen Favorites
	Jarred Pasta Sauce	• Fresh-cooked, balanced tomato flavor, not overly sweet • Pleasantly chunky, not too smooth or pasty • Not overseasoned with dry herbs like competitors	Bertolli Tomato and Basil Sauce
	Pasta Sauce, Premium	• Nice, bright acidity that speaks of real tomatoes • Robust flavor comparable to homemade	Victoria Marinara Sauce
	Peanut Butter, Creamy	• Smooth, creamy, and spreadable • Good balance of sweet and salty flavors	Skippy Peanut Butter
	Peanut Butter, Crunchy	• Nice roasted-peanut flavor • Well-balanced sweetness • Good crunch	Jif Natural Crunchy Peanut Butter Spread
	Peppercorns, Black Artisanal	• Enticing and fragrant, not musty, aroma with flavor to back it up and moderate heat • Fresh, complex flavor at once sweet and spicy, earthy and smoky, fruity and floral NOTE: Available only by mail order, Kalustyan's (800-352-3451, Kalustyans.com).	Kalustyan's Indian Tellicherry Black Peppercorns
	Supermarket	• Spicy but not too hot • Sharp, fresh, classic pepper flavor	Morton & Bassett Organic Whole Black Peppercorns
	Peppercorns, Sichuan	• Fresh, potent aroma with floral, citrus, herbal, and black tea notes • Sharp, zippy tingling effect	Dean & DeLuca Szechuan Peppercorns Best Buy: Savory Spice Shop Peppercorns, Szechwan
	Peppers, Roasted Red	• Balance of smokiness and sweetness • Mild, sweet, and earthy red pepper flavor • Firm texture, not slimy or mushy • Packed in a simple yet strong brine of salt and water without the distraction of other strongly flavored ingredients	Dunbars Sweet Roasted Peppers
	Pepperoni, Supermarket	• Nice balance of meatiness and spice • Tangy, fresh flavor with hints of fruity licorice and peppery fennel • Thin slices with the right amount of chew	Margherita Italian Style Pepperoni

See AmericasTestKitchen.com for updates to these tastings.

Item	Why We Like It	Test Kitchen Favorites
Pickles, Bread-and-Butter	• Subtle, briny tang • All-natural solution that uses real sugar, not high-fructose corn syrup	Bubbies Bread & Butter Chips
Pickles, Whole Kosher Dill	• Authentic, garlicky flavor and firm, snappy crunch • Balanced salty, sour, and garlic flavors • Fresh and refrigerated, not processed and shelf-stable	Boar's Head Kosher Dill Pickles
Pork, Premium	• Deep pink tint, which indicates higher pH level and more flavorful meat • Tender texture and juicy, intensely porky flavor	Snake River Farms American Kurobuta Berkshire Pork Runner-Up: D'Artagnan Berkshire Pork Chops, Milanese-Style Cut
Potato Chips	• Big potato flavor, no offensive off-flavors • Perfectly salted • Slightly thick chips that aren't too delicate or brittle • Not too greasy	Lay's Kettle Cooked Original Potato Chips
Potato Chips, Reduced Fat	• Real potato flavor with excellent crunch and texture • Contain only potatoes, canola oil, and salt • With less sodium than many competitors, they have just the right balance of salt	Cape Cod 40% Reduced Fat Potato Chips
Preserves, Apricot	• Deep, authentic apricot taste • Visible fruit suspended in spreadable jam • Sweetened with sugar and syrup rather than with flavor-muting fruits	Smucker's Apricot Preserves
Preserves, Raspberry	• Clean, strong raspberry flavor, not too tart or sweet • Not overly seedy • Ideal, spreadable texture, not too thick, artificial, or overprocessed	Smucker's Red Raspberry Preserves
Preserves, Strawberry	• Big, distinct strawberry flavor • Natural-tasting and not overwhelmingly sweet • Thick and spreadable texture, not runny, slimy, or too smooth	Welch's Strawberry Preserves

See AmericasTestKitchen.com for updates to these tastings.

	Item	Why We Like It	Test Kitchen Favorites
	Relish, Sweet Pickle	• Piquant, sweet flavor, lacks out-of-place flavors such as cinnamon and clove present in competitors • Fresh and natural taste, free of yellow dye #5 and high-fructose corn syrup • Good texture, not mushy like competitors	Cascadian Farm Sweet Relish
	Rice, Arborio	• Creamier than competitors • Smooth grains • Characteristic good bite of Arborio rice in risotto where al dente is ideal	RiceSelect Arborio Rice Runner-Up: Riso Baricella Superfino Arborio Rice
	Rice, Basmati	• Very long grains expand greatly with cooking, a result of being aged for a minimum of one year, as required in India • Ideal, fluffy texture, not dry, gummy, or mushy • Nutty taste with no off-flavors • Sweet aroma	Tilda Pure Basmati Rice
	Rice, Brown	• Firm yet tender grains • Bold, toasty, nutty flavor	Lundberg Organic Brown Long Grain Rice
	Rice, Jasmine	• Floral fragrance • Separate, firm grains	Dynasty Jasmine Rice
	Rice, Long-Grain White	• Nutty, buttery, and toasty flavor • Distinct, smooth grains that offer some chew without being overly chewy	Lundberg Organic Long Grain White Rice
	Rice, Ready Brown	• Fully cooked, ready in 60 seconds • Lightly oiled and salted • Firm, bouncy grains	Minute Ready to Serve Brown Rice
	Rice, Ready White	• Parboiled long-grain white rice that is ready in less than 2 minutes • Toasted, buttery flavor • Firm grains with al dente bite	Minute Ready to Serve White Rice
	Rice, Wild	• Plump grains • Firm texture • Woodsy flavor	Goose Valley Wild Rice

See AmericasTestKitchen.com for updates to these tastings.

Item	Why We Like It	Test Kitchen Favorites
Salsa, Hot	• Good balance of bright tomato, chile, and vegetal flavors • Chunky, almost crunchy texture, not mushy or thin • Spicy and fiery but not overpowering	Pace Hot Chunky Salsa
Salt	• Light and airy texture • Delicately crunchy flakes • Not so coarse as to be overly crunchy or gritty nor so fine as to disappear	Maldon Sea Salt
Sausage, Breakfast	• Nice and plump with crisp, golden crust • Good balance of sweetness and spiciness with hints of maple • Tender, superjuicy meat, not rubbery, spongy, or greasy	Jimmy Dean Fully Cooked Original Pork Sausage Links
Smoked Salmon	• Subtle smoky flavor balanced with clean, fresh salmon taste • Thinly sliced for easy eating • Firm and flaky, even when cooked • Uniformly silky and buttery, thanks to manufacturer's trimming of pellicle	Spence & Co. Traditional Scottish Style Smoked Salmon
Soup, Canned Chicken Noodle	• Organic chicken and vegetables and plenty of seasonings give it a fresh taste and spicy kick • Firm, not mushy, vegetables and noodles • No off-flavors	Muir Glen Organic Chicken Noodle Soup
Soup, Canned Tomato	• Includes fresh, unprocessed tomatoes, not just tomato puree like some competitors • Tangy, slightly herbaceous flavor • Balanced seasoning and natural sweetness • Medium body and slightly chunky texture	Progresso Vegetable Classics Hearty Tomato Soup
Soy Sauce	• Good salty-sweet balance • Long fermentation (6 to 8 months) • Simple ingredient list (wheat, soybeans, water, and salt) with no added sugar or flavor enhancers	Kikkoman Soy Sauce
Sweetened Condensed Milk	• Made with whole milk • Creamier in desserts and balances more assertive notes from other ingredients	Borden Eagle Brand Sweetened Condensed Milk and Nestlé Carnation Sweetened Condensed Milk

See AmericasTestKitchen.com for updates to these tastings.

Item		Why We Like It	Test Kitchen Favorites
Tartar Sauce		• Creamy, nicely balanced sweet/tart base • Lots of vegetable chunks	Legal Sea Foods Tartar Sauce
Tea, Black For Plain Tea		• Bright, bold, and flavorful yet not too strong • Fruity, floral, and fragrant • Smooth, slightly astringent profile preferred for tea without milk	Twinings English Breakfast Tea
For Tea with Milk and Sugar		• Clean, strong taste • Caramel notes and pleasant bitterness • Full, deep, smoky flavors • Good balance of flavor and intensity • More astringent profile stands up to milk	Tetley British Blend
Teriyaki Sauce		• Distinct teriyaki flavor without offensive or dominant flavors, unlike competitors • Smooth, rich texture, not too watery or gluey	Annie Chun's All Natural Teriyaki Sauce
Tomatoes, Canned **Crushed**		• Chunky texture, not pasty, mushy, or watery • Bright, fresh tomato taste • Balance of saltiness, sweetness, and acidity NOTE: Available only in New England, the Mid-Atlantic, and Florida.	Tuttorosso Crushed Tomatoes in Thick Puree with Basil
Tomatoes, Canned **Diced**		• Bright, fresh tomato flavor that balances sweet and tart • Firm yet tender texture	Hunt's Diced Tomatoes
Tomatoes, Canned **Fire-Roasted**		• Intense smoky flavor • Natural tomato texture	DeLallo Fire-Roasted Diced Tomatoes in Juice with Seasonings
Tomatoes, Canned **Puree**		• Full tomato flavor without any bitter, sour, or tinny notes • Pleasantly thick, even consistency, not watery or thin	Muir Glen Organic Tomato Puree
Tomatoes, Canned **Whole**		• Pleasing balance of bold acidity and fruity sweetness • Firm yet tender texture, even after hours of simmering	Muir Glen Organic Whole Peeled Tomatoes

See AmericasTestKitchen.com for updates to these tastings.

406 WHAT GOOD COOKS KNOW

Item	Why We Like It	Test Kitchen Favorites
Tomato Paste	• Bright, robust tomato flavors • Balance of sweet and tart flavors	Goya Tomato Paste
Tortilla Chips	• Buttery, sweet corn flavor, not bland, artificial, or rancid • Sturdy yet crunchy and crisp texture, not brittle, stale, or cardboardlike	On the Border Café Style Tortilla Chips
Tortillas, Flour	• Thin and flaky texture, not doughy or stale • Slightly rich and buttery	Old El Paso 6-Inch Flour Tortillas
Tostadas, Corn	• Crisp, crunchy texture • Good corn flavor • Flavor and texture that are substantial enough to stand up to hearty toppings	Mission Tostadas Estilo Casero
Tuna, Canned	• Rich, fresh-tasting, and flavorful, but not fishy • Hearty, substantial chunks of tuna	Wild Planet Wild Albacore Tuna
Tuna, Canned Premium	• Creamy, delicate meat and tender yet firm fillets • Full, rich tuna flavor	Nardin Bonito Del Norte Ventresca Fillets Best Buy: Tonnino Tuna Ventresca Yellowfin in Olive Oil
Turkey, Heritage	• Distinct layer of fat below the skin for moist, flavorful meat • Long-legged with an angular breast and almost bluish-purple dark meat (the sign of a well-exercised bird)	Mary's Free-Range Heritage Turkey Best Buy: Heritage Turkey Farm Heritage Turkey

See AmericasTestKitchen.com for updates to these tastings.

	Item	Why We Like It	Test Kitchen Favorites
	Turkey, Whole	• Moist and dense texture without being watery, chewy, or squishy • Meaty, full turkey flavor • Buttery white meat • Koshering process renders brining unnecessary	Empire Kosher Turkey
	Vanilla Beans	• Moist, seed-filled pods • Complex, robust flavor with caramel notes	McCormick Madagascar Vanilla Beans
	Vanilla Extract	• Strong, rich vanilla flavor where others are weak and sharp • Complex flavor with spicy, caramel notes and a sweet undertone	McCormick Pure Vanilla Extract
	Vegetable Oil, All-Purpose	• Unobtrusive, mild flavor for stir-frying and sautéing and for use in baked goods and in uncooked applications such as mayonnaise and vinaigrette • Neutral taste and absence of fishy or metallic flavors when used for frying	Crisco Blends
	Vinegar, Apple Cider	• Good balance of sweet and tart • Distinct apple flavor with a floral aroma and assertive, tangy qualities	Heinz Filtered Apple Cider Vinegar
	Vinegar, Balsamic, High-End	• Aged for 25 years • Smoky, caramel flavor • Coats the tongue • Ideal for drizzling over fish or fresh berries	Cavalli Gold Seal Extra Vecchio Aceto Balsamico Tradizionale de Reggio Emilia Best Buy: Oliviers & Co. Premium Balsamic Vinegar of Modena
	Vinegar, Balsamic, Supermarket	• Syrupy texture when used in a vinaigrette • Notes of apple, molasses, and dried fruit when served plain	Bertolli Balsamic Vinegar of Modena

See AmericasTestKitchen.com for updates to these tastings.

Item	Why We Like It	Test Kitchen Favorites
Vinegar, Red Wine	• Crisp red wine flavor balanced by stronger than average acidity and subtle sweetness • Complex yet pleasing taste from multiple varieties of grapes	Laurent Du Clos Red Wine Vinegar
Vinegar, White Wine For Cooking	• Balance of tanginess and subtle sweetness, not overly acidic or weak • Fruity, bright, and perfumed	Colavita Aged White Wine Vinegar
For Vinaigrettes	• Rich, dark flavor tastes fermented and malty, not artificial or harsh • Fruity flavor with caramel, earthy, and nutty notes	Spectrum Naturals Organic White Wine Vinegar
Yogurt, Frozen, Supermarket	• Balanced sweetness • Straightforward vanilla flavor • Smooth texture	TCBY Classic Vanilla Bean Frozen Yogurt
Yogurt, Whole-Milk Greek	• Rich taste and satiny texture, not thin, watery, or soupy • Buttery, tangy flavor	Fage Total Classic Greek Yogurt
Yogurt, Nonfat Greek	• Smooth, creamy consistency, not watery or puddinglike, with no added thickeners like pectin or gelatin • Pleasantly tangy, well-balanced flavor, not sour or metallic	Fage Total 0% Nonfat Greek Yogurt
Yogurt, Whole-Milk	• Rich, well-rounded flavor, not sour or bland • Especially creamy, smooth texture, not thin or watery • Higher fat content contributes to flavor and texture	Brown Cow Cream Top Plain Yogurt

See AmericasTestKitchen.com for updates to these tastings.

INDEX

Note: Page references in *italics* indicate recipe photographs.

G

P

Panade, defined, 345
Pancake batter dispensers, buying, 381
Pancake mix, buying, 400
Panko bread crumbs, buying, 156, 389
Pan-Roasted Chicken Breasts with Shallot-Thyme
    Sauce, *252,* 252–253
Pan-Roasted Fish Fillets, *278,* 278–279
Pan-Seared Shrimp, *280,* 280–281
    with Chipotle-Lime Glaze, 280
    with Garlic-Lemon Butter, 280
    with Ginger-Hoisin Glaze, 280
Pan-Seared Steaks with Red Wine Pan Sauce, *270,*
    270–271
Papayas, about, 85
Paprika, buying, 92, 400
Parchment cooking bags, buying, 385
Paring knives, buying, 15, 357
Parmesan
    about, 103
    Almost Hands-Free Risotto with Chicken and
        Herbs, *294,* 294–295
    and Black Pepper, Light and Fluffy Buttermilk
        Biscuits with, 304
    buying, 103, 391
    Eggplant, *284,* 284–285
    Simple Cheese Lasagna, *282,* 282–283
    Ultimate New York–Style Pizza, *312,* 312–313
Parsley, about, 89
Parsnips, about, 80
Passion fruit, about, 85
Pasta
    Baked Macaroni and Cheese, *290,* 290–291
    with Beef Bolognese Sauce, 286
    cheese ravioli, buying, 132, 400
    cheese tortellini, buying, 132, 400
    with Classic Bolognese Sauce, *286,* 286–287
    couscous, buying, 134
    dried, about, 132
    dried, cooking and saucing, 213
    egg noodles, buying, 401
    fresh, buying, 132, 401
    gnocchi, buying, 396
    lasagna noodles, buying, 132, 401
    macaroni, buying, 401
    macaroni and cheese mix, buying, 398
    matching shapes and sauces, 133
    Meatballs and Marinara, *288,* 288–289
    penne, buying, 401

Pasta (cont.)
    Simple Cheese Lasagna, *282,* 282–283
    spaghetti
        gluten-free, buying, 132, 401
        gluten-free, inside the tasting, 136
        semolina, buying, 132, 401
        whole-wheat, buying, 132, 401
Pasta sauce, buying, 402
Pastries, browning, 186
Pastry bags
    buying, 380
    how to use, 230
Pastry brushes, buying, 366
Pastry flour, about, 154
Peach(es)
    about, 83
    Cobbler with Biscuit Topping, 338
Peanut butter
    about, 161
    alternatives to, 161
    creamy, buying, 161, 402
    creamy, inside the tasting, 164–165
    crunchy, buying, 161, 402
    keeping it creamy, 165
Peanut oil, about, 144
Pearl barley
    about, 135
    cooking chart, 348
Pears, about, 80
Peas
    Best Beef Stew, *250,* 250–251
    frozen, buying, 69
    Potatoes, Cauliflower, and Chickpeas, Indian-Style
        Curry with, *298,* 298–299
    shelling, about, 80
    snap
        about, 80
        cooking chart, 346
        frozen, avoiding, 69
        trimming, 204
    snow
        about, 80
        cooking chart, 346
        frozen, avoiding, 69
        trimming, 204
Pecan-Cranberry Bread, Almost No-Knead, 316
Pecorino Romano cheese, about, 103
Peel, defined, 345
Penne pasta, buying, 401

R

Radishes, about, 82

Raisins, about, 81

Ramen noodles, about, 133

Raspberry(ies)

  -Chocolate Mousse, 340

  preserves, buying, 403

  volume and weight for, 70

Ravioli, buying, 132, 400

Recipe holders, buying, 379

Recipes

  cooking times, notes about, 179, 189

  creating *mis en place,* 179

  following the directions, 179

  learning from mistakes, 179

  reading carefully, 179

  tasting dishes before serving, 179

  Test Kitchen baking ingredient rules, 156

  tips to make you a better cook, 179

Red snapper, about, 125

Reduce, defined, 345

Refrigerator/freezer thermometers

  buying, 9, 369

  using, 174, 177

Refrigerators

  crisper or humidity compartments, 177

  defrosting foods in, 176

  organizing food in, 178

  placing hot foods in, note about, 176

  recommended food storage temperatures, 174

  temperature basics, 177

  tips and guidelines, 177–178

Reheating foods, 176

Relish, sweet pickle, buying, 404

Residual cooking, science of, 192

Reverse creaming, method for, 229

Rhubarb, about, 83

Rib racks, buying, 377

Rice

  Almost Hands-Free Risotto with Chicken and Herbs, *294,* 294–295

  Arborio, buying, 134, 404

  basmati, buying, 134, 404

  basmati, cooking chart, 347

  boiling directions, 347

  brown, buying, 134, 404

Rice (cont.)

  brown, cooking chart, 347

  cooking methods, 347

  Cuban Black Beans and, *296,* 296–297

  Cuban Black Beans and, Vegetarian, 296

  jasmine, buying, 134, 404

  jasmine, cooking chart, 347

  microwave directions, 347

  pilaf, preparing, 212

  pilaf-style directions, 347

  ready brown, buying, 134, 404

  ready white, buying, 134, 404

  types of, 134

  white, cooking chart, 347

  white long-grain, buying, 134, 404

  wild, buying, 134, 404

  wild, cooking chart, 347

Rice cookers, buying, 375

Rice cookers, microwave, buying, 380

Rice noodles, about, 133

Ricotta cheese

  about, 103

  buying, 103, 392

  Simple Cheese Lasagna, *282,* 282–283

Rimmed baking sheets, buying, 22, 361

Risotto, Almost Hands-Free, with Chicken and Herbs, *294,* 294–295

Roast, defined, 345

Roasting pans, buying, 22, 362

Rolling pins, buying, 34, 365

Rolls, frozen dinner, buying, 395

Rosemary

  about, 89

  and Fontina, Light and Fluffy Buttermilk Biscuits with, 304

  and Garlic, Crisp Roast Butterflied Chicken with, *256,* 256–257

  and Garlic, Tuscan Pork Loin with, *274,* 274–275

  -Sherry Pan Sauce, 254

Round cake pans, buying, 32, 370

Rustic Walnut Tart, *336,* 336–337

Rutabagas, about, 83

Rye Bread, Almost No-Knead Seeded, 316